The Masculine Self

Fifth Edition

Christopher Kilmartin
University of Mary Washington

Andrew P. Smiler
Private Practice

Sloan Publishing
220 Maple Road
Cornwall on Hudson, NY 12520

Library of Congress Cataloging-in-Publication Data

Kilmartin, Christopher.
The masculine self / Christopher Kilmartin, Andrew M. Smiler. -- Fifth edition.
pages cm
Includes bibliographical references and index.
ISBN 978-1-59738-053-9
1. Masculinity. 2. Men--Psychology. 3. Men. I. Smiler, Andrew M. II. Title.
BF692.5.K55 2015
155.3'32--dc23
2014042635

Cover photo by oliveromg on Shutterstock.com
Cover design by K&M Design

© 2015 by Sloan Publishing, LLC

Sloan Publishing, LLC
220 Maple Road
Cornwall-on-Hudson, NY 12520

Printed in the United States of America

10 9 8 7 6 5 4 3 2 1

ISBN-13: 978-1-59738-053-9
ISBN-10: 1-59738-053-9

For Jim and Larry, who raised us well.

Contents

Preface

TO THE STUDENT

You may never have heard about Men's Studies before picking up this text and taking the course that goes with it, but it is a legitimate area of study. Every time people uses phrases like "be a man," "man up," "grow a pair," or "stop being such a sissy," they are invoking masculine gender roles. In this book, we take a close and critical look the effects of these social demands on the lives of boys and men. As you will learn, cultural stereotypes about masculinity have the potential to do real harm to everyone. You will also see that most boys and men are only masculine some of the time and in some ways, and you will discover that their lives are more complicated than we tend to think. Men and boys are not simple, even though people may believe that they are. Ultimately, we hope that you begin to think more complexly and critically about the lives of boys and men. We also hope that this book challenges and changes some of the ways you think about, interact with, and behave around them.

TO THE INSTRUCTOR

This fifth edition marks a substantial change in *The Masculine Self*, most notably the addition of Andrew P. Smiler as co-author, and of guest author Matthew Yeazel of Anne Arundel Community College (Maryland) on Chapter 15, Masculinity and Sport, a topic which is certainly central to the lives of many boys and men. At the same time, we sought to maintain as much of the structure of the fourth edition as possible. Thus, the text continues to have three major sections. In the first section (Chapters One and Two), we introduce readers to contemporary concepts of gender and masculinity. In the second (Three through Seven), we apply these concepts to perspectives on masculine development from a variety of theoretical perspectives, as well as the effects of intersectionality (or "masculinities") on men's lives. The last section is an exploration of themes and issues common to many men, such as work, relationships, mental health, and violence. We reviewed the available scholarship in each area—a body of literature that is constantly changing and growing. This book is a snapshot in time—a map of a territory that continues to evolve.

This edition includes several substantive changes. Chapters Two (measurement), Three (Biologically-Based Theories), Four (Socially-Based Theories), Eleven (Sexuality), and Thirteen (Relationships) have been substantially edited and re-written. Dr. Smiler's training as a developmental psychologist becomes apparent with his attention to some age-related issues regarding sexuality and relationships. We believe these changes will strengthen the book and students' understanding of the field.

The fifth edition of *The Masculine Self* is another attempt to cover the territory of men's studies as comprehensively as possible. We have summarized and synthesized the latest research, and we have integrated it with the classic work that remains relevant to the topics under discussion. At the same time, we have not forgotten that we are telling stories about human beings. In fact, Chris Kilmartin's work as a playwright (of solo performance works, *Crimes Against Nature* and *Guy Fi: The Fictions that Rule Men's Lives*) and Dr. Smiler's work as a blogger have taught us both the importance of storytelling as a mode of understanding. Therefore, we have tried to give research data a human face without sacrificing a full explanation of its complexity.

DR. KILMARTIN'S THOUGHTS

I have been interested in Men's Studies for nearly my entire professional career. It has been gratifying to see a burgeoning literature in this area produced over the last quarter century. The field has come of age and attracted impressive scholars from a wide variety of disciplines. It seems to me that it has become more and more important to introduce students to gender concepts, similarly to, I would argue, teaching students computer skills, as they are only going to become more important as time goes on and the gendered world changes at a fast pace.

I have been writing the fifth edition of *The Masculine Self* ever since I finished the manuscript for the fourth in 2010. As new data and ideas emerged, I found myself sometimes rethinking and even disagreeing with aspects of my own work from the first four editions, found many things that would further enhance the text, and continued to think critically about the book. In short, I wished for yet another chance to correct mistakes, change emphases, and incorporate current events and new findings that relate to the topic at hand. With this fifth edition of *The Masculine Self*, I get my wish, and it is exciting to have the opportunity to add what I have learned in these past few years to the information from the first editions, and to bring it to the reader. And I am very grateful to add Andrew Smiler as co-author, as our areas of expertise are quite complementary, making this fifth edition the strongest so far.

DR. SMILER'S THOUGHTS

It's quite an honor to have become Dr. Kilmartin's co-author of *The Masculine Self*. I was flattered and a little surprised when he invited me to join him; I actually turned him down. But he persisted and I eventually agreed. Our collaboration also marks an important milestone: Dr. Kilmartin's interest and experience with Men's Studies dates back the early days of the field when there were nearly no textbooks, no journals, and very little scholarship on the topic. My own training relied on perspectives, texts, and journals that his generation produced. I am pleased to join the franchise known as *The Masculine Self* and honored to play a role in shaping the next generation.

Editing and authoring a textbook has forced me to expand my knowledge of masculinity in ways I never anticipated. For me, this has been a thrilling, and occasionally daunting, journey through topics and literatures I don't usually address. I hope you learn as much—or more—than I did.

ACKNOWLEDGEMENTS

We are grateful to a number of people who have helped in the formulation and realization of this work. Bill Webber did a wonderful job of overseeing the entire process of editing and production for Sloan. Colleagues such as Michael Addis, Fred Rabinowitz, Jim O'Neil, members of the Society for the Psychological Study of Men and Masculinity, members of the American Men's Studies Association, and many others have helped us sort out difficult theoretical and conceptual issues. We are also especially indebted to our partners, Allyson Poska, Ph.D. and Kate Irwin-Smiler, J.D., for hours of conversation and insights, as well as their support when we spent so much time writing this book. It is wonderful for both of us to have partners who make us smarter.

Chapter One

Introduction

The biological categorization of sex is perhaps the most basic division among human beings and often the first characteristic we notice about others. There is evidence to suggest that even very young children are able to make this distinction (Maccoby, 1998), and a profound distinction it is. Every culture in the world prescribes norms for behavior that are assigned on the basis of sex. Obviously, reproductive roles (childbirth, impregnation, and lactation) are bound in biology, but the socially perceived division of behavior based on sex goes far beyond reproduction into areas of work, child care, and social convention. Cultures even ascribe personality characteristics such as aggressiveness or nurturance disproportionately to one sex or the other. Many people believe that males and females should and do wear different colors, drink different drinks, enjoy different activities, and desire different things in relationships.

Developmental psychology literature abounds with comparisons in the socialization of males and females as well as speculations about the effects of these social practices on the personalities of adult men and women (Lytton & Romney, 1991). Biological psychologists compare brain structure and hormone levels of males and females and attempt to describe these influences on behavior. Social psychologists seek to specify the interpersonal conditions that give rise to gendered actions. And, of course, other social scientists, including sociologists, historians, anthropologists, linguists, economists, and philosophers, have long been interested in the study of male and female.

Beginning around the 1960's, modern feminist writers began to make strong critiques of mainstream social science theory and research methods. New ideas about female development and functioning gave rise to a new field, Women's Studies. Theorists and researchers in this area urged people to take seriously the idea that a person's sex and gender have important effects on his or her behavior and on the ways that others react to him or her. If we want to understand human behavior in all of its complexity, we would do well to take these effects into consideration when we construct our theories and research designs. Thus, Women's Studies created a stronger awareness of people as *gendered beings*.

In the early 1970's, scholars expanded this awareness into a new area, Men's Studies. They began to ask the question, "If the experience of being female has a profound effect on a woman's behavior and on others' reactions to her, does the experience of being male have similarly powerful implications for men?" The answer would seem to be an emphatic "yes."

The idea that men need their own area of intellectual inquiry was (and sometimes still is) greeted with skepticism. As psychologists, we have frequently heard the argument that *all* Psychology is the Psychology of Men because mainstream psychological theory was constructed largely by males. In fact, many research studies in the early days of Psychology were undertaken using only male participants, as if male behaviors generalized to the entire human race. It was said that, in psychology experiments, "even the rat was male." Therefore, the argument against the existence of such a field is that, since scholars have studied males as the *normative referent* for behavior, we do not need to identify a new area of inquiry to investigate male behavior and experience.

Joseph Pleck (1988) made a compelling counterargument in favor of distinguishing the study of men as a normative referent from the study of men from a *gender aware perspective*. The literature is replete with models of men as "generic human beings," but (prior to the emergence of Men's Studies) it was difficult to find reference to men as *gendered beings*. Men are powerfully affected by the experiences of growing up male, having people respond to them as males, expecting and having others expect certain behaviors based on "masculine gender roles," subscribing to beliefs about the natures of males and females, and having feelings about their masculinities.

Harry Brod (1987a) pointed out that traditional scholarship is "about men only by virtue of not being about women" (p. 264). Men's Studies move masculinity from the periphery of inquiry into its center. The subject of investigation is not, as in most traditional scholarship, about men as historical, political, and cultural actors, but rather about men *as men*.

There exists a good deal of confusion about Men's Studies. When I tell people that I am a psychologist specializing in the study of "Men's Issues," the typical reactions are:

1. "Why do we need to look at men's issues? Men have all the power and get to do whatever they want."
2. "Men are becoming a bunch of complainers who can't deal with women being strong."
3. "It's surprising that a psychologist would be 'anti-woman' or antifeminist."
4. "What are 'men's issues'? I didn't know men had any issues."

These reactions come from both men and women, and they reveal misunderstandings about, and biases against, the study of men from a gender aware perspective. We would respond to these reactions with the following:

1. While it is true that men-as-a-group have enormous social power, and that many men often get to do what they want, there are also many men who feel quite

powerless and have been damaged by harsh masculine socialization. By virtue of their greater social power, men are also in a unique position to help shift this power into better balance. Men need an understanding of the effects of masculine privilege to do so, and only a gender aware perspective can bring this understanding. (We use the hyphenated construction "men-as-a-group" in several places in this book to emphasize that we are talking about men in the aggregate, as there are great variations among men.)

2. It is true that many men have trouble dealing with strong women, having been socialized to believe that men should be powerful and dominant. As a result, they may experience strong women as threats to masculinity. This is an issue that men must address, because women *are* powerful, and men must learn to accept and deal with them in constructive ways. Men's Studies can enlighten us to various aspects of relationships between the sexes and contribute to agendas for alliances between the sexes.

3. Although there are some Men's Studies scholars and "Men's Movement" leaders who might be considered anti-women or antifeminist, there are others who can be characterized as just the opposite. The purpose of studying men from a gender aware perspective is not to further oppress women, but to address quality of life issues for men and women. Men's issues are often very compatible with women's issues. For instance, if we can understand the causes of gender-based violence, most of which is perpetrated by men against women, we can take steps to decrease that violence, which would improve the quality of life for both women and men.

4. What are "men's issues?" Consider the following:

   • Most males are encouraged from an early age to suppress their feelings. Emotional constriction may lead to a variety of psychological, physical, and relational problems (Wong, Pituch, & Rochlen, 2006).

   • Men's conformity to traditional masculine ideologies is associated with poorer relationship satisfaction (Burn & Ward, 2005). Many experts regard intimacy as a basic human need.

   • Men have significant psychological difficulties adjusting to divorce and separation (Buser & Sternes, 2009), and wives initiate about 75 percent of divorces (Marguiles, 2004). It is doubtful that men are as emotionally independent as the social image of masculinity would have us believe.

   • Men commit most acts of violence (U.S. Department of Justice, 2008).

   • Males comprise the vast majority of incarcerated (Webb, 2009) and homeless (Gugliotta, 1994) people.

   • The average lifespan of a man is significantly shorter than a woman's average lifespan (CDC, 2013).

   • Fathers' focus on building traditional masculine ideologies in their sons may put sons at risk for a number of negative outcomes (Levant and Wimer, 2010).

- The general quality of men's relationships with others is often impoverished (Bergman, 1995).
- Definitions of masculinity change over time (Kimmel, 2006).

This is a partial list. As you read on, you will come across many more men's issues. It should be clear from this list that all is not well with men. Although there are many positive facets to traditional masculinity, there are also many destructive ones, both for individual men and for others around them.

DESCRIBING MASCULINITIES

"Snips and snails and puppy dog tails." This is the first description of masculinity we remember hearing as children, the answer to the question, "What are little boys made of?" And what are little girls made of? "Sugar and spice and everything nice." These sayings purport to describe personality differences between the sexes. It is not too difficult to interpret the statement about girls. Sugar and spice are pleasant and palatable. A "sweet" person is someone who can evoke positive responses from others, someone who cares about people. The statement about boys is a little more cryptic, but it seems to evoke images of being dirty, scattered, and hyperactive (puppy dog tails don't remain still for very long).

From the earliest days of childhood, cultures bombard males with messages about what it means to be masculine. These messages serve to communicate expectations for their behavior. Some messages, like the one described above, are verbal. Others are more subtle, such as a parent's communication of silent approval for behaviors like refusing to cry when one is sad or hurt, or selecting toys that they consider appropriate for boys. Because a good deal of behavior is learned through imitation, boys receive many of these messages through merely observing the behaviors of men in their families, neighborhoods, and in the media.

These messages have powerful effects on boys, who often learn to act in culturally-defined "masculine" ways and to avoid behaviors that are considered "feminine." The social settings in which adult men find themselves tend to reinforce these standards. For example, a man who displays aggression at a business meeting might gain the approval of his colleagues, whereas a woman might experience disapproval for exactly the same behavior.

What is masculinity? How does one define it? We see romanticized views of masculinity in Boxes 1.1 and 1.2. The stereotypical man can be described as having certain personality traits:

strong	tough
independent	aggressive
achieving	unemotional
hard working	physical
dominant	competitive
heterosexual	forceful

We could also describe him in terms of activities or behaviors, i.e., what a man *does*:
      earns money
      initiates sex
      solves problems
      gets the job done
      takes control
      takes action
      enjoys "masculine" activities (e.g., hunting, sports, drinking)
      takes physical risks
      supports his family financially
      protects women and children from physical threats

We can describe him in terms of proscribed activities, i.e., what a man *does not do* (see box 1.1):
      cry
      express feelings other than anger
      perform "women's work" (e.g., wash dishes, change diapers)
      back down from a confrontation
      get emotionally close to other men
      ask for help
      behave in "feminine" ways

We can describe him in terms of stereotypical *roles*:
      athlete
      professional
      working man
      father
      husband
      buddy
      playboy
      leader

What do these varying definitions have in common? Robert Brannon's classic (1985) essay described four major themes of traditional masculinity in the United States:

1. *Antifemininity*: Males are encouraged from an early age to avoid behaviors, interests, and personality traits that are considered "feminine." Among these are expression of feeling, emotional vulnerability, sexual feelings for other men, and feminine professions (e.g., elementary school teacher, nurse, secretary). Brannon labeled this masculine norm *"No Sissy Stuff."*

2. *Status and Achievement*: Men gain status by being successful in all that they do, especially in sports, work, and heterosexual "conquest." Powerful men earn the respect and admiration of others. Brannon called this dimension *"The Big Wheel."*

Box 1.1   A Negative Description of Masculinity

The following is a definition of "gentleman" from an old version of the handbook of the Virginia Military Institute:

Without a strict observance of the fundamental code of honor, no man, no matter how 'polished' can be considered a gentleman. The honor of a gentleman demands the inviolability of his word and the incorruptibility of his principles. He is the descendant of the knight, the crusader, he is the defender of the defenseless and the champion of justice—or he is not a gentleman.

A gentleman *does not* discuss his family affairs in public or with acquaintances.

Does not speak more than casually about his wife or girlfriend.

Does not go to a lady's house if he is affected by alcohol. He is temperate in the use of alcohol.

Does not lose his temper nor exhibit anger, fear, hate, embarrassment, ardor, or hilarity in public.

Does not hail a lady from a club window.

Never discusses the merits or demerits of a lady.

Does not borrow money from a friend, except in dire need. Money borrowed is a debt of honor and must be repaid as promptly as possible. Debts incurred by a deceased parent, brother, sister, or grown child are assumed by honorable men as a debt of honor.

Does not display his wealth, money, or possessions.

Does not put his manners on and off, whether in the club or in a ballroom. He treats people with courtesy, no matter what their social positions may be.

Does not slap strangers on the back nor so much as lay a finger on a lady.

Does not 'lick the boots of those above him' nor 'kick the face of those below him on the social ladder.'

Does not take advantage of another's helplessness or ignorance and assumes that no gentleman will take advantage of him.

A gentleman respects the reserves of others but demands that others respect those which are his.

A gentleman *can* become what he wills to be...

Notice that the positive parts of the description (what gentlemen *are* and what they *do*) are rather vague: defender of the defenseless, champion of justice, etc. These are high ideals that do not necessarily transfer easily into a prescription for any specific behavior. When the description turns to negative guidelines (what gentlemen *do not do*), however, there are very specific behaviors stated. You might notice the prohibitions against acknowledging a connection to another person ("never speaks more than casually about his wife or girlfriend"), expressing emotion ("does not exhibit fear, hate, ardor..."), and being vulnerable or in need of help ("does not borrow money from a friend..."). The last line reflects the masculine value on self-determination.

3. *Inexpressiveness and Independence*: Men are expected to maintain emotional composure and self control even in the most difficult of situations, to solve problems without help, to keep their feelings to themselves, and to disdain any display of weakness. This dimension is *"The Sturdy Oak"* or *"The Male Machine."*

4. *Adventurousness and Aggressiveness*: Masculinity is characterized by a willingness to take physical risks and become violent if necessary. Brannon called this masculine norm "Give 'Em Hell."

Many theorists (Chodorow, 1978; O'Neil, 1981a; Brannon, 1985; Hartley, 1959) consider *antifemininity* to be the central organizing principle from which all other masculine social demands derive. In other words, social expectations devalue and punish the open display of vulnerable emotions, orientations toward relationships, and self-protection for men because these characteristics are culturally defined as feminine. There is ample evidence that, beginning early in childhood, adults and peers punish males for acting in feminine ways (termed *cross-gender* or *out-role* behavior) more harshly than females who violate social gender expectations (Lytton & Romney, 1991; McCreary, 1994). Thus, antifemininity acts as a powerful enforcer of masculine gender behavior. For example, in mainstream U.S. culture, perhaps the worst insult for a boy is to suggest that he throws, looks, or acts like a girl.

Homophobia, the hostility, fear, and intolerance of sexual attraction or behavior between persons of the same sex, is a construct closely related to antifemininity (We often refer to homophobia as "antifemininity's vicious little brother."). For males, acting like a stereotypical female is likely to result in social disapproval, and few things are socially defined as more feminine than loving or being sexually attracted to a man. Males who act in socially-defined feminine ways are often suspected of being gay (McCreary, 1994; Blumenfeld, 1992). The term "sissy" can refer to either femininity or homosexuality, which are closely linked in many people's minds. The threats of being considered homosexual or feminine also act as a powerful enforcer of gender norms for males, who are much more likely than females to hold negative attitudes toward gay men and lesbians (Herek, 1991, 1994). Male peer groups use antifemininity and homophobia to police the boundaries of acceptable behavior (Plummer, 2001). If a boy or man behaves in ways associated with women or gay men, others may ridicule, shame, or even physically attack him. Not surprisingly, homophobic attitudes are strongly related to traditional gender role ideologies (Korobov, 2004). If attitudes toward same-sex marriage are any indication, homophobia is in sharp descent in the United States (see the final chapter).

There are variations in the cultural definitions and stereotypes of masculinity (see Chapter Six), which lead many theorists to describe masculine role expectations using the plural *masculinities* (Brod, 1987b; Connell, 2005; Kahn, 2009, and others). For example, African-American men are considered more emotionally expressive than White American men (Basow, 1992). Jewish men are encouraged to incorporate a love of knowledge into their conception of masculinity, in contrast with some other groups of men (Brod, 1987b). Tahitian men do not tend to display aggressiveness or other traits that people from most other cultures would consider masculine; in fact they are hard to differentiate from Tahitian women in their everyday behavior (Gilmore, 1990).

Box 1.2   Thinking about Masculinity

Below is Rudyard Kipling's (1940) classic poem, "If-," which reflects a romanticized view of masculinity. As you read the poem, try to answer the following questions:

1. What kinds of masculine traits is Kipling describing?
2. Which of these traits are positive, negative, or neutral? Why?
3. Are there differences in what is judged to be positive or negative for the *individual* compared with *society*?
4. In what ways is modern masculinity different or similar to Kipling's description, which Gilmore (1990) refers to as "iffy" masculinity)?

If-
If you can keep your head when all about you
Are losing theirs and blaming it on you,
If you can trust yourself when all men doubt you,
But make allowance for their doubting too;
If you can wait and not be tired by waiting,
Or being lied about, don't deal in lies,
Or being hated, don't give way to hating,
And yet don't look too good, nor talk too wise:
If you can dream—and not make dreams your master;
If you can think and not make thoughts your aim;
If you can meet with Triumph and Disaster
And treat those two imposters just the same;
If you can bear to hear the truth you've spoken
Twisted by knaves to make a trap for fools,
Or watch the things you gave your life to, broken,
And stoop and build 'em up with worn-out tools;
If you can make one heap of all your winnings
And risk it on one turn of pitch-and-toss,
And lose, and start again at your beginnings
And never breathe a word about your loss;
If you can force your heart and nerve and sinew
To serve your turn long after they are gone,
And so hold on when there is nothing in you
Except the Will which says to them: "Hold on!"
If you can talk with crowds and keep your virtue,
Or walk with Kings—nor lose the common touch
If neither foes nor loving friends can hurt you,
If all men count with you, but none too much;
If you can fill the unforgiving minute
With sixty seconds' worth of distance run,
Yours is the Earth and everything that's in it,
And—which is more—you'll be a Man, my son!

Source: *Rudyard Kipling's Verse: Definitive Edition*. Garden City, NY: Doubleday.

At the same time, there is a good deal of cross-cultural similarity in gender roles. Williams and Best (1990a) found that men were described as forceful, active, and strong across a variety of cultures.

Most cultures encourage men to be unemotional, task and achievement oriented, aggressive, fearless, and status seeking. Male gender roles are powerful influences on behavior partly because men who are seen as "masculine" receive many social rewards. For instance, financially successful men gain the admiration of others and are seen as more sexually desirable than other men. As actress Zsa Zsa Gabor (quoted in James, 1984) said, "No rich man is ugly." Competitive and inexpressive men are seen as good candidates for promotion in many work environments. The man who shows a willingness to be "one of the boys" may enjoy the approval of others and have a large circle of supportive acquaintances.

On the other hand, men who are seen as "unmasculine" may experience a good deal of social and even physical punishment. Gay men are subject to abusive comments, stigmatization and sometimes unprovoked violence. Men who display vulnerable emotions are judged to be unhealthy (Lutz, 2001). Males who ask for help may garner negative reactions from others (Addis & Mahalik, 2003).

In general, men who overemphasize the negative aspects of traditional masculinity risk losing their self-esteem, health, freedom, connectedness with others, and even their lives. Men commit suicide four times more often than women (CDC, 2013). There are nearly nine times more men in U.S. prisons than women (West, 2010), and males comprise close to 80 percent of the United States homeless population (Gugliotta, 1994).

STEREOTYPES AND REALITY

It is important to note that the above descriptions are stereotypes, and that there is a great deal of variation in the actual behaviors of individual men. We define gender as *a social pressure to behave and experience the self in ways that the culture considers appropriate for one's sex.* And so gender is, in a critical sense, "in the air." It is important to keep in mind that individual responses to gender pressure are highly variable. In defiance of masculine norms, some men are emotional, gentle, and interpersonally connected, just as some women fit masculine stereotypes. Many people possess characteristics of both masculine and feminine stereotypes (such people are termed *androgynous*). Thus, it is possible to be both gentle and strong, both independent and connected, and in parenting, both strict and nurturing.

All men do not display or even aspire to stereotypical masculinity. In fact, there is a great deal of variation in men's endorsements of masculine ideologies (Thompson & Pleck, 1995). Therefore, the description above does not apply to some unchangeable essence that all individual men share, but rather to the social influence that nearly all males experience. Although some men make masculine striving a major goal in their lives (these men are often referred to as *macho*), others reject masculine expectations, and most men find some middle ground between masculine conformity and individual personality expression. And, the level of stereotypical masculinity often varies even within an individual as a function of changes in his age, relationships, and social settings. For example, we might ask heterosexual women, "Are there ways in which your husband or boyfriend behaves *when he is just with you* that might surprise some of his buddies?" Many respond with a resounding "yes," citing among other things, laughter, dancing, emotional tenderness, and playfulness. Thus, gender is not a once-and-forever, static entity, even for an individual person.

BEWARE THE "TURKEY THEORY"

When I (C. K.) was a graduate student at Virginia Commonwealth University, one of the members of the faculty was Dr. John P. Hill, a remarkable scholar and researcher who had a profound effect on my thinking about gender. At that time, I mainly concentrated on the gender *socialization* of males, i.e., the ways in which boys are raised that lead to certain characteristics and behaviors when they become adult men. Dr. Hill pointed out to me that, although childhood socialization undoubtedly has a powerful effect on adults' behavior, an exclusive emphasis on these forces reflects an acceptance of the "turkey theory."

The "turkey theory" is the belief that the adult behavioral process is parallel to the preparation of a Thanksgiving turkey. As Dr. Hill explained, the socialization emphasis assumes that we get "stuffed" with characteristics when we are young, and then, as adults, we come out of the "oven"—a completed "turkey," tasting (behaving) on the basis of what we have been "stuffed" with.

His point was that, although the childhood "stuffing" undoubtedly shapes people's habits and senses of self, people respond to much more than what they learned as children. They are also strongly influenced by social forces that occur in the moment. Robert Brannon (1985) makes this point powerfully when he asks what the typical reaction would be if one man were to say to another, "Mike, I've been so upset since we had that argument. I could hardly sleep last night. Are you *sure* you're really not mad at me?" (p. 307). As defined by mainstream contemporary United States culture, this language is decidedly "feminine," and men who use engage in this kind of behavior are often ostracized, attacked, ridiculed, or neglected by others. Therefore they tend to avoid such behaviors, not necessarily because their boyhood experiences have led them to be unconnected to others, but because the social pressure of the moment threatens these behaviors with negative social consequences. If you are a young, stereotypically heterosexual man, what would happen if, in a group of your friends, you initiated a conversation about how much you love your girlfriend and how close you feel to her. That conversation might meet with uncomfortable silence. At worst, it would meet with ridicule and shame.

Shawn Meghan Burn (1996) reviews a number of studies indicating that people behave more gender-stereotypically in public than in private, suggesting that they are, at least partially, responding to the perceived gender pressure of the social setting of that particular moment and not merely to internal forces. To carry the above examples further, we might ask, "Is it possible that I *was* so upset about my conversation with Mike that I couldn't sleep?" "Is it possible that many men *do* love their girlfriends and feel close to them?" Nearly everyone acknowledges that these are quite possible, perhaps even likely. There is a significant component of *social performance* in masculinity. As Addis & Mahalik (2003) said, "Gender is a verb rather than a noun" (p. 3).

Because social contexts are so influential, we should be careful not to take behaviors, even stereotypical ones, at face value. Seeing a group of men behaving in similar ways, we are tempted to think that all men are alike. But within the group, there might be enormous variations in internal experiences such as the level of comfort with the behavior. To add a non-gendered example, have you ever laughed at a joke you didn't think was funny? Nearly everyone acknowledges that he or she has. If someone else watched you laugh at the joke, the other person would think that you considered it funny unless you told him or her that your internal reaction was different from your external behavior. It is not only childhood socialization that keeps many boys and men behaving within narrow gender roles, it is also *ongoing* forces within their social environments. See Box 1.3.

Avoiding the "turkey theory" is important because, although we cannot change the events that adult men experienced as boys, we can change the social environments that support the stereotypical masculine behaviors that are destructive. A solid understanding of the interactions between masculine socialization and interpersonal pressure can lead to changes in the negative aspects of masculinity.

CONSEQUENCES OF MASCULINE GENDER ROLES

Cultural norms of masculinity are enforced and maintained through expectations, rewards, and social sanctions. Adhering to traditional masculine gender roles has positive and negative, long and short term effects on individual men and on societies.

Benefits

The man who is able to live up to gender role demands has the opportunity to reap many rewards. Chief among these are money, status, and privilege. Men who are "winners" are often able to live in the lap of luxury, enjoy the admiration of others, and do basically what they want to do. The traditional man bases his self-esteem in work, wealth, and achievement. Men who acquire large amounts of these things may feel quite good about themselves, and they are often viewed as desirable lovers, friends, and associates.

Work, wealth, and achievement are often very quantifiable. It is much easier for one to evaluate success by how much money one has made rather than, for example, by how good a parent one has been. The latter (which has been traditionally defined as "women's work") is a more difficult judgment because it is more qualitative. Thus, a traditional man can operate in somewhat of a closed system, with his worth as a person measured by a convenient and relatively unambiguous "yardstick." Such a man can be singular in his purpose and rarely has to deal with mixed feelings.

The traditional man is a "breadwinner," supporting his family financially by working hard. Whether or not he is a "big wheel," a man can take a great deal of pride in fulfilling this role. Working hard every day so that your family can have food, shelter, and other resources is a very loving thing to do. The contribution of the provider role

Box 1.3   The Power of the Social Context

Masculinity can be conceptualized as a set of "rules" that many men follow to avoid unpleasant outcomes like social ostracizing or emotional discomfort. But these rules are suspended in certain contexts. For instance, "big boys don't cry" is a social rule, but in old soldiers' reunions, funerals, and even sporting events, male crying can be seen as normative. Homophobic prohibitions often dictate that men should not touch, but it is permissible to slap your football teammate on his rear end or to hug him when he makes a good play, or to put your arm around your buddy as you walk down the street after a night of drinking.

Hebl, King, McGuire, and Turchin (2008) demonstrated how alternate definitions of the social context could change men's behavior. They asked all-male and all-female teams of college students to participate in a "grapefruit race." The first teammate wedges a grapefruit between his or her chin and chest and passes it to the second person, who must do the same, without using his or her hands. The grapefruit passes to each subsequent teammate until all have accomplished the task.

When the experimenters told the participants that the grapefruit passing was "an exercise," the women's teams finished the task at faster times (an average of 18 seconds) than the men's (an average of 145 seconds). But when the task was framed as "a competition," men's and women's times were nearly identical. Men who participated in the task when it was framed as an exercise showed more signs of discomfort than when it was framed as a competition. This experiment is an excellent demonstration of how "rules" about same-sex physical intimacy are relaxed when sports are involved and perhaps clues us into the meaning of the almost religious nature of sports in some men's lives.

Richard Eisler and his colleagues have explored the effect of contextual framing on men's physiological responses. In the first study (Lash, Gillespie, Eisler, & Southard, 1991), the researchers measured men's cardiovascular reactions to pain using the *cold pressor test*, in which the person immerses the arm in a vat of ice water and leaves it there as long as he/she can stand it. In the "gender relevant" condition, the task was presented to participants as a test of their perseverence and will power, thus it was perceived as a masculine challenge. Control group participants (the gender-neutral condition) were told that the task was to monitor physiological responses to cold. Men who were given the masculine instructions showed significantly higher blood pressure changes and heart rate reactivity compared with women and with control group men.

In a more recent study (Cosenzo, Franchina, Eisler, & Krebs, 2008), men were asked to do a time-pressured serial subtraction task: to count backwards from a specified number by fours to the beat of a metronome that clicked every 0.3 seconds. Men in the gender relevant condition were told that men do better than women on mathematical tasks, and that the task at hand requires precision and focused attention, which are necessary to succeed in science and business. Control group men were told that researchers were interested in measuring changes in heart rate and blood pressure that occur during cognitive tasks. Again, the men in the gender relevant condition showed greater cardiovascular reactivity than the control group men. Moreover, they made more mistakes on the subtraction task.

Taken together, the two physiological experiments demonstrated that men's hearts react when their masculinity is experienced as being "on the line." All three experiments show us how a perceived social context affects behavior and gives us hope that men may behave in different ways if we can provide them with healthier ways of framing these contexts.

to family is one of the most positive aspects of traditional masculinity. Men have also usually participated in other aspects of family life like physical work in and around the house, money management, protecting others, and everyday problem solving. Certain aspects of masculinity are well suited to these important activities.

The masculine achievement and problem solving orientation has resulted in a great many positive contributions to society and the world. Men's achievements in engineering, literature, and the sciences, for example, should not be overlooked, nor should the contributions of working men who produce goods, build houses, and otherwise labor for the greater good. This is not to deny that women have made significant contributions (a fact which has historically been downplayed), but only to note that the traditional masculine ethic of "getting the job done" has had enormous positive implications for the quality of life and is one aspect of gender that deserves to be celebrated. Importantly, however, if we value these attributes of human activities, they should be available to everyone, not just to men, and therefore they can be redefined as human rather than masculine.

Costs

It is clear that there has also been a price to pay for some aspects of traditional masculinity, both for society and for individual men. Living up to masculine gender demands is largely an impossible task that often exacts a heavy toll.

The expectations that men compete, achieve, be "on top," and always want more have left many men feeling driven, empty, disillusioned, and angry. No matter how talented and hard working one is, winning every time is impossible. There is always another man who has more money, higher status, a more attractive partner, or a bigger house. The traditional man can never get enough, and thus he can never really enjoy what he has. He must constantly work harder and faster. Such a lifestyle sometimes results in stress-related physical and psychological symptoms. Families in which the male is sole wage earner are now a very small minority (Levant & Wimer, 2010), and so new models of work and family are emerging. Clinging to the old models of past generations will result in many men being left behind.

To strip a man of his emotional life is to take away one of the most basic aspects of human existence. The experience of positive emotion would seem to be profoundly important. When a man is made into a machine, he loses his humanity and is rendered less capable of having empathic, caring, intimate relationships with other people. Emotional intimacy requires one to share power, be vulnerable, and disclose oneself. Traditional masculine socialization is antithetical to these behaviors (Jourard, 1971). The damage that destructive masculinity does to the quality of connectedness to other people and to feelings about the self can hardly be overestimated. Many men feel alienated from their partners, children, and other men, and these feelings are often mutual.

The most serious result of being interpersonally unconnected to others is its influence on men's willingness to do physical and psychological harm to others. It is easier to hurt people when one can not identify or empathize with them. Many men are socialized away from understanding their own feelings or those of others, and this enables them to be cruel toward anyone who gets in their way. The disproportionate participation of men in war, violence, damage to the Earth, the oppression of marginalized social groups, and psychological cruelty must (at least partly) be laid at the doorstep of traditional masculinity.

CONTEXTS FOR THE STUDY OF MASCULINITY

Gender roles are embedded within several important historical, social, political, economic, and ideological contexts. Therefore, one can only achieve a thorough understanding of men and masculinity by learning about these various frames of reference. By way of introduction to these important issues, the following are brief sketches of some of the themes that will run throughout this book.

Definitions of Sex and Gender

Many people use the terms *sex* and *gender* interchangeably, and this linguistic convention can contribute to misunderstandings of the relative contributions of biology and social forces (a subject of heated debate which we will take up later). Rhoda Unger (1979) suggested that we reserve the term *sex* for referral to biological entities, i.e., genes, hormones, genitalia, etc., and that we use the term *gender* when speaking of social forces such as socialization, stereotyping, social role behavior, and self-presentation. Thus, we use the terms *male* and *female* when referring to sex and the terms *masculine* and *feminine* when referring to gender. Although biological forces may have effects on social behaviors, the use of biological terms (e.g., *male aggression*, *maternal instinct*) to describe behaviors communicates the assumption that biological forces have been demonstrated to be the singular causes of those behaviors. The connection between biology and behavior is an empirical matter, i.e., one that researchers investigate through scientific methods. *Gender* is a broader and more inclusive term than *sex*, as it refers to behaviors, mental, and social processes that are determined by biology and/or social forces (Lips, 2008).

Patriarchy and Power

Patriarchy is a system in which a society confers greater levels of economic power, influence, and prestige on males-as-a-group than on females-as-a-group (albeit with significant variations among individuals within each group). According to historian Gerda Lerner (1986), patriarchy has existed in most parts of the world for more than 5000 years. It is expressed in the typical behaviors that people believe are appropriate for males and females, in the dominant values of the culture, in social customs and economic arrangements, and in what Lerner terms "leading metaphors, which become part of the cultural construct and explanatory system" (p. 212). For example, many theologies are constructed around male gods and female subservience, which, by extension, privileges male experience over female experience in the collective consciousness of the culture. In many places (including the United States well into the twenty-first century), male-centered ideologies have been used to justify the exclusion of women from educational opportunities, owning property, voting, or having legal recourse if their husbands rape them. Although laws in many parts of the world prohibit discrimination against women, the persistence of patriarchal ideologies and traditions continues to bestow on men a disproportionate amount of social power and privilege. Sexist language (see Box 1.4) and marked vs. unmarked status (see Box 1.5) are two manifestations of patriarchal ideology.

Because of the long tradition of men's dominance of women, *power*, the influence and access to resources that are provided by authority, force, strength, and control, is a word that occupies a central place in the world of gender studies. As Michael Kaufman (1994) stated, "In a world dominated by men, the world of men is, by definition, a world of power. That power is a structured part of the economies and systems of political and social organization; it forms part of the core of religion, family, forms of play, and intellectual life" (p. 142). Collectively, men have the vast majority of power in the forms of money, social influence, and control of the world. For instance, in the United States, White men hold 65 percent of elected offices (Henderson, 2014), a collective power that has them far overrepresented compared to their proportion of the population.

And yet, as Kaufman points out, many individual men do not feel powerful. Poor men often feel little sense of control over their lives. Men of color and gay men are often systematically oppressed by a White- and heterosexually-dominated society. Even a man whom one might consider powerful, for example, a man of relative wealth, may feel powerless because others are more wealthy or because he is alienated and disliked by his friends and family.

Johnson (1997) provides an important perspective on the contrast between *feeling* powerful and *being* powerful:

> Men's misery *does* deserve sympathy, but not if it means we ignore where it comes from and what men get in exchange for it. It's all too easy to go from sympathy for men to forgetting that patriarchy and male privilege even exist. Part of what makes it so easy is misunderstanding what privilege is, where it comes from, and how it is distributed. Many men argue, for example that men *are* privileged only to the degree that they *feel* privileged. A key aspect of privilege, however, is to be unaware of it *as* privilege. In addition, even though men as a group are privileged in society, factors such as race and class affect how much gender each man gets to enjoy and how he experiences it. (p. 175, emphasis original)

One example of the invisibility of privilege is flying first class on an airplane. You have a great deal more room than people in the coach class in the rear of the aircraft and are served better food, but you do not know that others are cramped and hungry unless you turn around and look at them, and then try to imagine how they feel. Owning a private plane takes the invisibility of privilege one step further. Michael Kimmel (2013a) compared privilege to having the breeze at one's back. Peggy McIntosh

Box 1.4   The Power of Language

Language can communicate gender expectations in subtle ways, and linguistic distinctions between the sexes have received a good deal of attention in recent years. Sexist terms like *chairman, mankind* and the use of the generic masculine pronoun he (instead of *chairperson, humankind,* and constructions like *he/she*) communicate that males are the standard and females the exceptions. People frequently complain that using newer, nonsexist terms is awkward and overly "p.c." ("politically correct"). However, many researchers have discovered that the use of masculine-biased language results in readers and listeners predominantly perceiving males (Gastil, 1990; Hamilton, 1991). Therefore, the use of generic masculine language is poor communication when a speaker or writer intends to refer to people of both sexes.

The opposite sex and the *battle of the sexes* are two frequently used and pernicious terms. Both communicate the belief that males and females have little common ground. *Battle of the sexes* implies that men and women are natural enemies, yet the vast majority of heterosexual people are loving and having children with these enemies—a curious "battle" indeed!

The opposite sex communicates that male and female are not only different, they are contrary and antithetical to each other. This view of the sexes is analagous to acids and bases—adding acid to a base makes the substance more acidic, and vice versa. A more modern view would conceptualize the sexes as different but not opposite, like salt and pepper (adding salt to a food does not make it less peppery) or IBM-type and MacIntosh personal computers. In this view, we would be more accurate to use the term *the other sex*. Humans have 46 chromosomes; only

one is different between the sexes. In fact, males and females share 99.8 percent of their genetic material (Eliot, 2009). Even reproductive roles are not opposite; they are complementary. We would not describe impregnation as the opposite of gestation, or, to use a basic parallel to genitalia, a bolt as the opposite of a nut or an arm the opposite of a sleeve.

Richardson (2009) describes a variety of ways in which the common use of the English language disparages women. For instance, it is quite common to refer to adult females as *girls,* implying that, like children, they are immature and relatively powerless. An adult man is rarely referred to as a *boy* except in a conscious attempt to disparage him. Richardson also notes the variant gender meanings of linguistically equivalent terms such as *master* (someone with power) and *mistress* (a sexual partner), governor (official) and governess (nanny), *lord* and *lady.* "*Sir* and *mister* [are] titles of courtesy, but at some time, *madam, miss,* and *mistress* have come to designate, respectively, a brothelkeeper, a prostitute, and an unmarried sexual partner of a male." (p. 120, emphases original).

Martin (1991) provides an interesting perspective on the use of language to smuggle (albeit perhaps in a nonconscious way) gender stereotypes into scientific language. She notes that most human sexuality books describe conception as a set of events that involve active (male) sperm swimming to and penetrating passive (female) eggs. In reality, female reproductive anatomy is anything but passive. Within women's bodies, cilia direct sperm along the path to the egg, and the egg changes chemically to favor some sperm but not others. Zuk (2005) observed that several scholarly articles refer to young birds as "illegitimate" when they had been fathered by males that were not pair-bonded with the mother "as if their parents had tiny avian marriage licenses and chirped their vows." (p. 14). Another paper refers to "wife-sharing" among male birds. Cases in which more than one female are associated with a male are never referred to as "husband sharing." Zuk points out that this language casts the males as the active parties—"they 'share' the female, as if she were a six-pack of beer." (p. 14). The subtext of subjective gender stereotypes finds its way into language even in fields many people consider "objective."

(2009) describes it as "an invisible weightless knapsack of special provisions, assurances, tools, maps, guides, codebooks, passports, visas, clothes, compass, emergency gear, and blank checks" (p. 12). Ted Bunch (Bunch & Porter, 2003) likened privilege to having an "E-Z Pass" that allows one to bypass lines of cars at toll booths. Bunch, an African American man, said that the first time he used his E-Z Pass, he thought, "this is what it's like to be a White man in America!"

This seeming contradiction between collective power and individual senses of powerlessness comprises a core issue in Men's Studies. Some theorists go so far as to describe women as more powerful than men (see Chapter Sixteen), a proposition that many people find preposterous, arrogant, and offensive.

Many men find it very difficult to appreciate the relative privilege they have by virtue of being male. For example, White males can:

- expect that people will take them seriously.
- go out in public feeling rather certain that they will not be followed or harassed.
- have people of their sex disproportionately represented at the highest positions in government, business, education and other institutional structures.
- see people who look like them widely and positively portrayed in media.
- take college courses that give attention to members of their sex as important historical actors.
- be paid better than most women for the same work.
- have successes or failures attributed to efforts and abilities.
- and go to work in a female-dominated profession and expect not to be harassed or paid a lower salary than others.

This is a partial list; you may be able to think of other social privileges for men-as-a-group. Because men have always lived in a world where their ways of being are privileged over those of most others, and because men are not encouraged to identify with women, it is easy for male privilege to be invisible in their experiences. As Kimmel (1994) puts it, "Men's experience of powerlessness is *real*—the men actually feel it and certainly act on it—but it is not *true*, that is, it does not actually describe their condition" (p. 137). He later added that to deny privilege is to engage in "'windchill' psychology: it doesn't really matter what the actual temperature is; what matters is

Box 1.5 On Entitlement and Being "Marked"

Karen Rosenblum and Toni-Michelle Travis (2003) frame race, sex, class, and sexual orientation as having "master statuses." In mainstream U. S. culture, these statuses are White, male, wealthy, and heterosexual. They point out that "Two privileges in particular appear common among non-stigmatized statuses: the sense of entitlement and the privilege of being 'unmarked.'" (p. 182).

My former student, Laura Ramsey (2005), provided an example of entitlement in an interview with a young heterosexual man, who said:

Everybody on TV as far as I'm concerned is a homosexual nowadays. That's why I don't like to watch television, you know what I mean? It's like, you turn it on and you got *Queer Eye for the Straight Guy* and *Will and Grace*. It's like the media is almost trying to breed homosexuals as far as I'm concerned. Not that I have a problem with gays. It's just like, you turn it on and it's like gay gay gay gay gay, you know? I guess that's what they're pushing right now.

In fact, this person would have great difficulty citing other television programs that are dominated by gay characters. He has extrapolated to all of television from these two shows for several possible reasons. First, he has probably failed to notice the preponderance of heterosexual characters on television. Second, he may have strong feelings of revulsion to gay characters. Third, he has likely not engaged in much critical reflection on his reactions. His sexuality is displayed as the norm nearly everywhere but he does not notice it. Therefore, when heterosexuality is not the norm, he raises his hand and says that he feels excluded. Ettinger

(quoted in Rosenblum & Travis, 2003) notes that, if, as a marginalized person, "I wanted to raise my hand every time I felt excluded, I would have to glue my wrist to the top of my head." (p. 182).

With regard to gender, the unmarked status (e.g., "judge") presents men as the taken-for-granted norm and the marked status ("woman judge") presents women as the stigmatized exception. Bonvillain (2001) notes that many female names are derived from male names by adding endings like -a, -ette, and -ine (e.g., Alexandra, Bernadette, Josephine) as markers, and that the ending -ette is also used as a diminutive, which denotes smallness ("kitchenette," "booklet," "kittenette"). Women who advocated voting rights in the early twentieth century were termed "suffragettes." Modern feminist scholars now refer to them as "suffragists" to erase the diminutive implication.

One can see a good deal of marked and unmarked statuses in athletic teams. The men's team is the "Eagles," and the woman's team is the "*Lady* Eagles." In remarkable oxymoronic fashion, the Fairfield University (CT) women's teams are the "Lady Stags" and a number of teams (Johnson C. Smith College, NC; University of South Florida; Hereford High School, MD; an Arizona AAU team) are the "Lady Bulls." These titles convey a secondary status for girls' and women's athletics.

Rosenblum and Travis note that "those in marked statuses appear to be operating from an 'agenda' or 'special interest,' while those in unmarked statuses can appear to be agenda-free" (p. 182). Criticisms of people in unmarked statuses are more likely to refer to the individual ("He was a lousy mechanic"), conveying the assumption that the rest of the group are competent until proven othewise. Conversely, criticism of people from marked statuses may include the assumption that the entire group is flawed ("I shouldn't have let a woman mechanic work on my car").

what it feels like." (Kimmel, 2013a, p. 16). True gender awareness for men involves not only their understanding of the pressures of traditional masculinity role, but also the appreciation of their advantaged social positions.

As Alan Johnson (2001) explains, "Privilege generally allows people to assume a certain level of acceptance, inclusion, and respect in the world, to operate within a relatively wide comfort zone" (p. 33), but it does not necessarily make one happy or fulfilled. Male privilege also puts men into a position of feeling that they have to compete and prove themselves repeatedly.

Race and Class

The privilege of masculinity does not extend to all males in equal shares. Goffman (1963) explains that, in the United States, there is only one "complete, unblushing male... a young, married, white, urban, northern heterosexual, Protestant father of college education, fully employed, of good complexion, weight and height, and a recent record in sports.... Any male who fails to qualify in any one of these ways is likely to view himself... as unworthy, incomplete, and inferior" (p. 128). Therefore, masculinity is somewhat of a "deficit model." The opportunity to reap all of the social benefits of being a so-called "real man" are available to relatively few men even though many (perhaps most) men accrue some of these benefits. Social conceptions of masculinity exert somewhat similar pressures on nearly all men to experience themselves and the world, and to behave in prescribed ways, but these demands interact in important ways with the oppression of racism, classism, and heterosexism.

Essentialism vs. Social Constructionism

One major debate in gender studies is the distinction between essentialist and social constructionist models. *Essentialists* argue that the collections of attitudes, behaviors, and social conditions that we call masculinities are "hard-wired" into males through biology (see Thornhill & Palmer, 2000) and/or the heritability of human psyche (see Jung, 1959/1989; Bly, 1990). They view masculinity as static, transhistorical, cross-cultural, and cross-situational. From this perspective, gender change is either impossible, or it involves the use of powerful force to constrain what is seen as "naturally" male.

The opposing view of *social constructionism* is summarized by Michael Kimmel (1994), who views masculinity as "a constantly changing collection of meanings that we construct through our relationships with ourselves, with each other, and with our world. Manhood is neither static nor timeless; it is historical. Manhood is not the manifestation of an inner essence; it is socially constructed. Manhood does not bubble up to consciousness from our biological makeup; it is created in culture. Manhood means different things at different times to different people" (p. 120). From this perspective, social definitions of masculinity are quite malleable and thus have the potential to shift in response to changes in ideologies, values, social conditions, economic factors, and historical events.

Even the most extreme essentialists do not deny the influence of social forces on behavior, just as even the most extreme social constructionists do not deny the effect of biology. However, scholars show a strong tendency to position themselves within one camp or the other. Essentialist E.O. Wilson (1979) once remarked that biology holds behavior on a "leash," but Steven J. Gould (1987) adds that the important debate is about the length and tightness of that leash. Essentialists like Wilson see it as very short and tight; but Gould (1987) sees the leash as "long and nonconstraining, though well worth our continued examination" (p. 115).

In a study of college students, Andrew Smiler and Susan Gelman (2008) found that men tend to think in essentialist terms more than women, and to conceptualize masculinity as essentialist more than femininity. Moreover, men who subscribe to traditional gender norms tended to see masculinity as more "hard-wired" than men who did not.

Essentialism and social constructionism provide very different sets of assumptions about gender as backdrops for very different views on what exists, why it exists, whether it can change, whether it should change, and how it can change. It is important to think critically about these assumptions to fully evaluate each of the many perspectives of Men's Studies scholars.

GOALS FOR STUDENTS

Gender is an area of intellectual inquiry, but it is also a very personal topic, because we all experience the social pressure to conform to cultural conventions based on whether we are (perceived as) male or female. One of the most rewarding aspects of taking on the study of gender is to integrate the intellectual and the personal. To that end, we suggest the following goals for students:

- *To see the self as a gendered being.* You will be better able to understand the gender pressures in your own lives.

- *To explore the range of possibilities in response to gender pressure.* Everyone has choices about how they respond to these forces. As you make progress toward the first goal of identifying gendered influences in your own life, you will be in a better position to resist these influences when doing so is in concert with your values and life choices. People who cannot identify gender effects have a great deal of difficulty resisting them, as it is quite difficult to resist a pressure that one cannot name (see Box 1.6). Gender education moves gendered behavior from non-conscious into conscious ideologies and put the person into a better position to make informed choices rather than just "going along with the program."

- *To build intellectual skills by investigating the histories, cultures, psychologies, images, and mechanisms of gender.* Taking on this area of inquiry contributes to the more general skills of critical thinking.

Box 1.6 Resetting the "Default Options": The Importance of Men's Studies

Sandra Bem (1993) defined gender roles as the "default options" that a culture "programs" into its natives. The most common modern use of the term "default options" is in describing computer functions that are set at the factory and remain in place unless the computer user changes them. If we carry the computer analogy forward in examining gender roles, we find that changing a default option requires at least three conditions:

1. *Awareness*: the person must *know that the* option *exists*.

On a standard personal computer, you can change the size of the icons that appear on the screen when you first boot the computer. If you do not know that you can, you surely will not change them, except by accident. By the same token, many people consciously and unconsciously accept gender arrangements as "the way things are" because they have no awareness that things could be different. Men's studies, with its examinations of cultural, individual, and social-environmental variations in men's behaviors, can illuminate these options. Gender studies are developing the language that we need to undertake an in-depth examination of the use of gender as a cultural organizing principle.

2. *Motivation:* The person must *be motivated to change* from the default option.

Maybe you know that you can change the size of the icons on your screen, but you don't want to do so. However, if your eyesight is not good, you might want them to be larger; if you have many icons you want to display, you might want them to be smaller. Or you may merely want your computer screen to look different from others; it's a fash-

ion choice. You need a motivation to change—otherwise it is easiest to allow things to remain as they are.

So it is with gender roles. Even if men know that they could behave otherwise, they may feel no particular urge to do so. Men's Studies can point out the important quality-of-life issues involved in adhering to rigid gender beliefs for both the individual and the society. People who see the disadvantages of rigid gendering through a process of formal and informal education may become more motivated to change individually and to work for social change.

3. *Ability and Skill:* The person must *know how to change* from the default option.

Perhaps you want to change the size of your computer icons, but you do not know the procedure for doing so. Obviously, you would need to find out to make that change. Men's studies can inform in the service of investigating methods for individual and social change of the destructive aspects of traditional masculinity. Men's Studies experts are investigating aspects of gender in individuals, social groups, public policy, and culture.

Judith Lorber (1986) articulated the direction of gender studies from a feminist perspective: "The long term goal of feminism must be no less than the eradication of gender as an organizing principle of postindustrial society (p. 568). Coltrane (1998) adds: "Paradoxically, one of the ways to work toward this long-term political goal of reducing the importance of gender is for scholars to call attention to it… ultimately to reduce its importance in everyday life." (p. 78).

> Gender is a set of social pressures, and it is quite difficult to resist a pressure that one cannot name. One goal of Men's Studies is to help men to articulate this pressure and make informed choices about their lives rather than merely conforming to the "default options."

- *To facilitate empathy for men and women.* Understanding gendered forces allows the person to take the perspectives of others better.

- *To explore the possibilities for social justice work.* Much of gendering involves social inequality, and an awareness of it may encourage the student to make efforts toward making the world a better place.

- *To understand the risks involved in uncritically accepting the dominant forms of masculinity, both for individuals and for groups.* Some aspects of masculinity, such as the valuing of aggression, emotional constriction, and sexism toward women, have dire negative consequences for men and others around them. Men who wholly conform to gender pressures are at risk for reducing their quality of life as well as that of others.

- *To gain an awareness of how gender affects one's daily life and experiences.* In teaching Men's Studies, many instructors ask students to keep journals in which they observe gendered arrangements in their everyday lives. Within a few weeks, they often state, "It's everywhere!"

- *To join with the other sex in respectful ways to work toward common goals.* Contrary to what some people believe, men and women are not enemies, and gender study can lead to an appreciation of our commonalities.

THE ORGANIZATION OF THIS BOOK

The Masculine Self is oriented toward understanding masculinity in the contexts of social scientific theory. This first chapter is a description of masculine gender roles and the multiple contexts in which they are embedded. Chapter Two will provide the necessary background for conceptualizing the many different facets of gender roles as well as reviewing the attempts to measure the varied components of gendered behaviors and beliefs.

Part II (Chapters Three through Seven) provides some theoretical viewpoints on men and masculinity as seen by scholars in major schools of social scientific thought (sociobiological, psychoanalytic, historical, anthropological, sociological, cross-cultural, and psychological). These chapters contain a wide variety of sometimes overlapping, sometimes competing perspectives.

Part III (Chapters Eight through Fifteen) examines research findings and other scholarship related to various themes that have been identified as "Men's Issues": emotion, physical health, work, sexuality, violence, relationships, mental health, and sport. The final chapter is a description of contemporary topics related to Men's Studies.

SUMMARY

1. The distinction between the sexes is learned very early in life, and gender roles are culturally assigned based on this distinction. Only recently have researchers and theorists begun a serious investigation of the effect of gender on boys and men. This study has met with a good deal of resistance due to misunderstanding and mistrust. Nevertheless, there is a growing body of literature which suggests that masculinity is an important cultural construct highly worthy of investigation.

2. From very early in life, males receive messages about what it means to be a man. These messages are communicated through interpersonal relationships and the culture, and they are later reinforced in adult social settings. There is considerable similarity in gender role definitions across cultures but also great variation in the ways that individual males respond to gender pressures.

3. Traditional gender roles provide expectations that men be unemotional, independent, aggressive, competitive, achieving, and unfeminine. Living in these roles can have positive results, such as financial rewards, social status, and contribution to family and society. However, there can also be negative effects, including overattention to work, impoverished emotional life, poor relationships, and violence.

4. The terms *sex*, *male*, and *female* refer to biological essences such as hormones, genes, instincts, and anatomical structures. The terms *gender*, *masculine*, and *feminine* refer to behavioral aspects of social roles.

5. Masculinity is embedded in the historical context of patriarchy, a 5,000-year-old system by which men-as-a-group retain the vast majority of power in a society. However, there is a contradictory experience of men's aggregate power and individual men's feelings of powerlessness. Many men do not have an appreciation of male privilege and therefore fail to appreciate their social power.

6. Masculine demands interact strongly with race, class, sexual orientation, and other forms of social identity and status.

7. Essentialism is the belief that gender resides in a biological or psychical substrate that is unchangeable and/or very slow and difficult to change. Social constructionism is the view that gender is a product of highly malleable social forces. These two opposing perspectives form the assumptive background of most gender theorists.

8. Undertaking the study of gender entails a personal journey in addition to an intellectual pursuit.

Chapter Two

Models for Understanding and Measuring Masculinity

Masculinity is complicated. Like any complex psychological phenomenon, researchers have developed a variety of ways of studying and measuring it. In this chapter, we examine some big-picture, or meta-theoretical, conceptualizations of masculinity and how each of these affects how masculinity is measured. We address broad conceptions and measurement together because the manner in which researchers measure masculinity is determined by how they understand it (Morawski, 1985; Smiler, 2004).

Before we talk about researchers' definitions of masculinity, take a moment to consider your own. You might ask yourself "what does it mean to be a real man?" If you ask the Internet that question, you might learn that "real men do it [move things] in one trip" or "real men don't buy girls/women." You might also remember commercials about Man Laws and Real Men of Genius.

You can also try one of the activities listed in Box 2.1: Masculinity Violations or imagine what it would be like to see a man doing one of these things.

How did it feel for you to perform these behaviors? How did others react to you? Was there a difference in the reactions of men and women? Of older and younger adults? Of people who know you well and people who do not? What does your experience of gender role violation tell you about masculinity, yourself, and the culture?

As you consider, try, or witness these activities, you might think that some are more acceptable or tolerable than others. At times, researchers focus on thoughts or attitudes, labeling them cognitions. You might also consider some of these behaviors more comfortable than others. At the emotional or affective level, you might have a range of emotional reactions, seeing these activities as funny, disgusting, or courageous. The *ABC model* (Affect, Behavior, and Cognition), describes reactions as not only being what you think (cognition) but also how you feel (affect) and what you do (behavior). The ABC model is important because it helps delineate the ways in which people can have multiple and inconsistent responses to the same event (Myers, 2008).

Imagine, for example, that you arrive in biology and sit next to Dave in your usual spot. The two of you usually talk sports and are lab partners, but you don't "hang out" as close friends do. As you sit down, you realize that Dave is wearing a dress. Your

---

Box 2.1   Masculine Gender Role Violation Exercises

Choose a behavior from the list below. Evaluate your thoughts and feelings as well as the reactions of those around you as you perform the behavior.

1. Wear colored nail polish to class or some other public place.

2. If you are in a satisfying relationship with a woman, talk at length with some male friends about how much you love your girlfriend and how good she makes you feel (without talking about sex).

3. Tell a male friend how much you value his friendship (without being drunk).

4. Spend a half hour in a conversation with a group of people without interrupting or telling a story.

5. Walk to class carrying your books at your chest instead of at your side.

6. Share an umbrella with another man.

7. Make a comment about the physical attractiveness of some man.

How did it feel for you to perform these behaviors? How did others react to you? Was there a difference in the reactions of men and women? Of older and younger adults? Of people who know you well and people who do not? What does your experience of gender role violation tell you about masculinity, yourself, and the culture?

---

affect may include anxiety because you're not sure how to respond, fear or desire that Dave will hit on you, fear that bigoted people will assault Dave, and pride in Dave for being so courageous to flaunt a powerful social norm. At the behavioral level, you have to decide whether or not you're going to say anything about his fashion choice (because speech is a form of behavior). If you choose to say something, you then have to decide if it will be supportive or not. At the cognitive level, and linked to your behavior, are your thoughts about men wearing dresses. You may find yourself wondering if this is Dave sending a message about his sexual orientation, if he lost a bet, or thinking that he has a nice butt. The ABC model is quite popular in some areas of psychology and some of these distinctions appear in the theories and measures we'll discuss in this chapter.

THE GENDER BINARY: MASCULINITY OR FEMININITY

You're undoubtedly familiar with the rather widely-held belief that men and women are opposites with different but complementary strengths. The areas of difference most often cited include: aggressiveness, nurturance, mathematical ability, verbal ability, visual-spatial ability, achievement motivation, competitiveness, dominance, morality, conformity, and communication styles. Many television programs and popular books have capitalized on people's tendency to think in gender dualisms by displaying "experts" who make sweeping generalizations about purported sex differences.

This dualistic, either-or notion is called the *gender binary* because it is made up of only two options, male and female (or masculine and feminine). This binary is at the root of common insults against boys and men such as "you throw like a girl" or "don't be such a sissy" (because sissy was a term of endearment for one's sister) (Smiler, Kay, & Harris, 2008). The gender binary leads to a simple classification of people: they're either masculine or feminine; there is no in-between.

Male-Female Comparison, also known as "Sex Differences"

Are males and females really different? More accurately, we might ask: *how different* are males and females? or *how similar* are the sexes? These questions are empirical ones—we cannot know the answers without careful scientific investigations.

Researchers have made comparisons between males and females on a variety of dimensions. Historically, this area of research has been referred to as the study of "sex differences" rather than "sex similarities" or "sex comparisons." The use of this term indicates that many researchers believed that important sex differences exist (Deaux, 1985), and that the scientific task is to discover and describe these differences. Research on sex differences is among the older areas of psychological study, with papers on the topic dating back as far as 1908 (Hare-Mustin & Marecek, 1990b). The focus on difference has been called an *alpha bias* by some theorists, who express concern about the lack of studies examining similarity or *beta bias* (Hare-Mustin & Marecek, 1990a). Measurement of sex differences relies on a simple question: are you female or male?

The Measurement of Characteristics. If one measures enough people in a population on any psychological characteristic and then graphs the results, the picture that emerges nearly always approximates a normal curve (Figure 2.1). Most people's scores on the dimension of study cluster around the middle (average) of the distribution, and relatively few people's scores are found at the extremes. For example, if we were to give an intelligence test to 10,000 people, most would score around the average of 100 IQ points, approximately 2.5 percent of people would have very high scores that qualify them as gifted, and a similar number of people would have very low scores that might qualify them as developmentally delayed (although a diagnosis of developmentally delayed requires more than just a low IQ). The majority of people would score somewhere between these two extremes.

Sex comparison research tends to treat males and females as two different populations and describes average differences between the population of females and that of males with reference to the characteristic of interest. Within each group, the distribution of scores usually approximates a normal curve. The sex comparison question is, "to what extent do the curves diverge and overlap?" A large sex difference would look like Figure 2.2. A small difference would look like Figure 2.3.

Differences are nearly always a matter of *degree* because there are so few behaviors that are seen exclusively in one sex and not the other. Men may be more aggressive, but obviously women also display aggressive behaviors. Women may be nurturing more often, but men can also nurture. In fact, the only behaviors which are seen exclu-

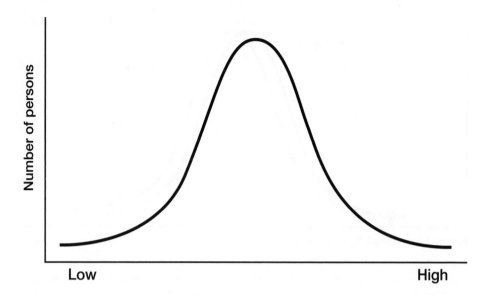

Figure 2.1   The Normal Curve

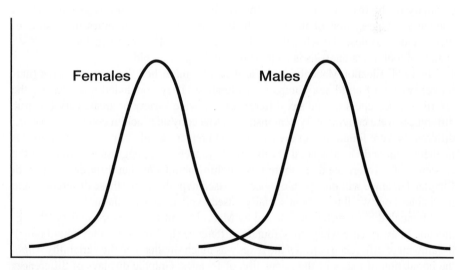

Figure 2.2   A Large Sex Difference

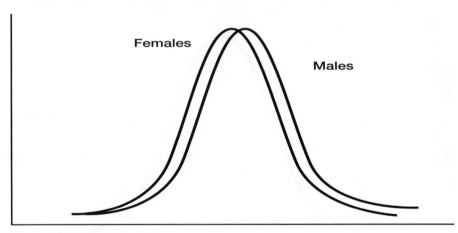

Females

Males

Figure 2.3   A Small Sex Difference

sively in one sex or the other are those associated with reproductive roles: women can menstruate, give birth, and lactate; men can impregnate (Money, 1987).

Research in Sex Comparison.   An in-depth review of the voluminous sex comparison literature is well beyond the scope of this book. What follows is the barest summary of some studies in which scholars have organized large amounts of research. Reviews of the literature come in two forms. A *narrative review* provides a text-based summary of the research, much like this textbook does. A *meta-analysis* provides a mathematic aggregation of the research. In other words, it combines the results of many studies to describe what the body of research, taken together, indicates. As a statistical tool, meta-analysis is approximately thirty years old.

In 1974, Eleanor Maccoby and Carol Jacklin published the first extensive (narrative) review of child sex comparison literature. They concluded that, despite the efforts of researchers to find sex differences in a wide variety of areas, very few true differences were convincingly demonstrated. Maccoby and Jacklin concluded that sex differences were found in four areas: girls had greater verbal ability, boys had greater mathematical and visual-spatial ability, and boys were more aggressive. Note that the existence of a difference does not tell us anything about *why* that difference exists. In Chapter Three we will discuss biologically-based hypotheses for these differences and in Chapter Four we'll talk about socially-based explanations for them.

Although the sex differences found by Maccoby and Jacklin were statistically significant, in every case where they found a difference (in most areas they found none), the amount of difference *between* the sexes was much smaller than the variability *within* the population of males or the population of females. Graphic displays of differences resembled Figure 2.3, not Figure 2.2. Figure 2.4 illustrates the relative sizes of between-sex and within-sex differences. For instance, although boys-as-a-group outperformed girls-as-a-group in mathematics, girls who did very well still outperformed the vast majority of boys; boys who did very poorly were still outperformed by the vast majority of girls. See Box 2.2 for a discussion of sex comparison in various performances.

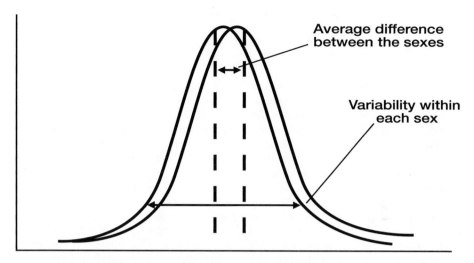

Figure 2.4   Within-Group and Between-Group Variance

As evidence that even these average differences are not necessarily biologically based, subsequent studies of mathematics performance on the Scholastic Aptitude Test (SAT) and other one-time tests indicate that girls virtually caught up with boys within 20 years following Maccoby and Jacklin's 1974 work (Hedges & Nowell, 1995; Lindberg, Hyde, Petersen, & Linn, 2010). At the same time, results from a meta-analysis of school grades indicates that females outperform males overall, and in every core subject area (language, math, science, social studies, etc.), from elementary through graduate school. Although the difference in academic grades is small as in Figure 2.3 and represents the difference between a B and a B+, it is consistent, pervasive, and widespread (Voyer & Voyer, 2014). Regardless of whether the review relies on a narrative or meta-analytic process, researchers often find that the differences are not as widesread as expected. (Deaux, 1985; Hyde, 2005; Hyde & Plant, 1995; Leaper & Tenenbaum, 2002; Lytton & Romney, 1991; Voyer & Voyer, 2014). In her meta-analysis Janet Hyde (2005) found that 75 percent of psychological gender differences are in either the small or "close to zero" range.

What are the meanings of these similarities and differences? On the one hand, it is clear that predicting an individual's behavior based on his or her biological sex is not a very fruitful enterprise, and that people should only make generalizations about the sexes with extreme caution, if at all. On the other hand, as Deaux (1985) points out, a small difference at the *midpoint* of a distribution is accompanied by a relatively large difference at the *extremes* of the distribution. For example, although there is a very small difference between normal (average) men and women on physical aggression, there are many more highly aggressive men than there are highly aggressive women. In fact, men commit more than eight times more violent crimes than women (U. S. Department of Justice, 2008). Thus, small sex differences have important implications when extremes of the behavior have major consequences (as is the case with violent behaviors). Clearly, however, saying that *all* men are aggressive is a gross inaccuracy since most are not.

Box 2.2   Sex Comparisons in Performance

In 1964, the world record for the women's marathon (a 26.2 mile footrace) was around 3 hours and 30 minutes. The men's record at that time was around 2 hours and 10 minutes. Most people at the time probably believed that this rather large difference was due to biological differences between the sexes, but if we fast forward to 2009, the women's record had improved by one hour and 15 minutes (2:15:25) and the men's record, around six minutes (2:03:59). What appeared in 1964 to be a robust sex difference turns out to be rather small by comparison, and who is to say that some talented woman might not someday eclipse the men's record?

In 2005, Harvard University President Lawrence Summers caused uproar by suggesting that the lack of women in the sciences at Harvard might be due to biologically-based differences in intellectual abilities between the sexes. His assumptions appeared to be that the world is a fair place with equal opportunities for all and that Harvard has no sex bias in hiring. Apparently he was not aware of 35 years of research comparing the sexes on a wide variety of dimensions, including a mathematics performance discrepancy that has shrunk in similar proportions to the marathon record.

Small sex differences do not tell us anything about individual men and women. Paula Radcliffe, the current women's marathon world record holder, can outperform 99 percent of male marathoners. At 13 years of age, Mo'ne Davis was one of two girls to play in the 2014 Little League World Series (LLWS), and the 18th girl to play in LLWS history. She was the first girl to throw a scoreless game ("shutout') in LLWS history and pitched the entire game (Axson, 2014; Hampl, 2014). Japan's Takuma Takahashi was the only other pitcher to throw a complete game shutout in the 2014 LLWS, doing so twice (LLWS, 2014). Davis is probably better than 99 percent of 13-year-old male pitchers.

98–pound Sonya Thomas has won many competitive eating contests, beating some very large men. She has eaten seven 12–ounce hamburgers in 10 minutes, 43 tacos in 11 minutes, 23 barbecue sandwiches in 12 minutes, nearly 5 pounds of fruitcake in 10 minutes, and, in the buffalo chicken wing eating contest, she beat a 415-pound man by eating 167 wings (Carlson, 2004). In 2005, she won bratwurst and grilled cheese sandwich eating contests in addition to consuming 44 lobsters in 12 minutes, easily outdistancing her competition ("Eating Champ Downs 44 Lobsters in Win," 2005).

Women also hold the record for the fastest swimming of the English Channel in both directions, and for the number of times that feat was accomplished (Allison Streeter, 32 times). In 1998, Paula Newby Fraser's Ironman Triathlon time was faster than all but 10 of the male contestants. Ann Trason twice completed the 100–mile Western States Endurance run ahead of all but one male, and Susan Butcher won the Iditarod dog sledding race four times (Lips, 2008). Race car driver Danica Patrick has been a Top 10 finisher in both Nascar and IndyCar Series races, outperforming many other drivers who do not qualify for racing's top tiers as well as many who do qualify.

At age 64, Diana Nyad became the first person to swim from Cuba to Florida without the use of a protective shark cage (Sloane, Hanna, & Ford, 2013).

> These performances tell us that it is possible for the sex of the participant to become a secondary or even irrel- evant consideration compared with other dimensions.

When differences exist, even when they are small, they give us clues to the strengths and weaknesses of each gender role and the characteristic struggles of men and women. These clues contribute to the awareness of the psychological importance of gender.

The Gender Identity Model

The oldest psychological model of gender roles carried with it the assumption that it was important for boys and men to display "appropriately masculine" behavior and for girls and women to be appropriately "feminine." These *Gender Identity Models* included the conceptualization of femininity and masculinity as opposites, relying on the gender binary we described earlier, illustrated in figure 2.4. Although this model allows the identification of feminine men and masculine women, there are no options for someone being "neither masculine nor feminine" or "both masculine and feminine."

Within the gender identity perspective, sex differences are understood to be based in biology and/or some sort of "natural order." The assumption here is that men are and should be different from women because of differences between the sexes in natural social roles, a position characteristic of the *essentialist* approach to gender. Gender differences were assumed to pervade virtually every aspect of human experience, including affect, behavior, and cognition.

Another assumption of the Gender Identity Model is that the healthiest and most productive men are those who are the most masculine. Thus, a fundamental developmental task for every boy is to establish an appropriate *gender role identity*, or a solid and appropriate sense of himself as masculine. This notion remains with us today and can be heard when people talk about boys' need for a father or "father figure" who will show him how to "be a man."

Because masculinity and femininity were seen as opposites, boys and men who displayed feminine traits were seen as having problems and considered to be unhealthy. To some thinkers, including Freud, gay men were seen as *gender inverted;* they were biological males but displayed all the characteristics of femininity. We'll discuss Freud's theory in more detail in Chapter Three. For now, it is important to say that Freud did not consider homosexuality an illness. Rather, he viewed it as a variation, much like left-handedness, which is seen in a minority of the population but is not a pathology.

Historically, some theorists (Toby, 1966; Adorno, Frenkel-Brunswick, Levinson, & Sanford, 1950) have proposed that insecure masculine gender identity leads men into exaggerated behaviors that are attempts to prove their masculinity to others as well as to the self. These behaviors have been labeled *hypermasculine* and include violence, physical risk taking, and hostility directed toward women and gays. The picture that emerges is of a man who is not really masculine, but is more of a caricature of masculinity used to cover up insecurity.

Gender Role Identity Measures. Terman and Miles (1936) published the first measure of masculinity and femininity in 1936. Called the Attitude Interest Analysis Test to disguise its purpose to test takers, it is often referred to as the MF test today and consisted of approximately 450 multiple choice questions. Each question had four possible responses, including one to three masculine responses, one to three feminine responses, and zero to two neutral responses (only one category had two responses for any particular question). A masculine response received a score of +1, a neutral one a score of 0, and a feminine one a score of −1. The total was then computed; a positive score indicated the person was masculine and a negative score indicated femininity. For example, test takers were asked to read the word on the left (in all capitals). Next, read across the line and circle the word that you think is the best match for the word on the left.

| POLE: | Barber | Cat | North | Telephone |
| DATE: | Appointment | Dance | Fruit | History |

The masculine answers for Pole are cat and telephone; for Date they are dance, fruit, and history. Feminine answers for Pole are North and for Date are appointment.

In her review of Terman and Miles' MF test, Jill Morawski (1985) described how to get a highly masculine or highly feminine score: "Masculinity scores are gained by replying that you dislike foreigners, religious men, women cleverer than you are, dancing, guessing games, being alone, and thin women. Femininity points are accrued by indicating dislike for sideshow freaks, bashful men, riding bicycles, giving advice, bald-headed men, and very cautious people" (p. 206).

This scale became a prototype for other early attempts at gender measurement. The Minnesota Multiphasic Personality Inventory (MMPI) (Hathaway & McKinley, 1951) and the updated MMPI-2 (Butcher, Dahlstrom, Graham, Tellegen, & Kaemmer, 1989) are used to diagnose a broad variety of mental illnesses including thought, anxiety, and personality disorders. The questionnaires contain more than 500 statements to which the person answers "true" or "false" in relation to the self, such as "I have often wished I were a girl," (or if you are a girl) "I have never been sorry that I am a girl."

The original MMPI contained an "Mf" scale that was originally designed to differentiate male heterosexuals from homosexuals (Groth-Marnat, 2003). The MMPI-2 maintained the Mf scale, which can produce GM and GF subscales that measure stereotypicality (Graham, 1992).

A few other scales based on a similar conception of gender roles followed. Among these were the California Psychological Inventory (CPI) "Fe" scale (Gough, 1957), the Strong Vocational Interest Inventory (Strong, 1943), and the Feminine Gender Identity Scale (Freund, Nagger, Langevin, Zajac, & Steiner, 1974).

Limitations and Criticisms of the Gender Binary

The gender binary allows only two options: male and female, or masculine and feminine. Yet we know today that there are other options, including transgender, genderqueer, and a-gender (i.e., not gendered). We have also learned that sexual orientation is separate from gender. Football player Michael Sam, Welsh national rugby team captain Gareth Thomas, and heavy metal rocker Rob Halford of Judas Priest have all publicly acknowledged their homosexuality and yet they all seem to fit American cultural conceptions of what it means to be highly masculine.

One of the major criticisms of the MMPI and the CPI was that they used relatively insignificant aspects of the personality (e.g., liking mechanics magazines) to make inferences about characteristics of central importance like erotic orientation, level of aggressiveness, and gender identity (Pleck, 1975), thus confusing gender with sex and sexual orientation. Reporting traditionally feminine interests such as cooking resulted in interpretations of poor adjustment and lack of masculinity.

For its original purpose, the MMPI's "Mf" scale was a total failure, probably because of the flaws in theory described above. Currently, this scale is considered to be a measure of breadth and stereotypy of interest. College-educated men tend to score more "feminine" on this scale compared with the general population of men (Groth-Marnat, 2003). Under the original intent of the scale, this finding would mean that college men tend to be disturbed with gender identity problems. The reality is that these men tend to be broader and less stereotypical than the general population of men in their preferences for activities, perhaps as the consequences of higher than average intelligence and socioeconomic level, and more experiences of being exposed to a rich variety of ideas.

BEYOND THE BINARY: THEORIES COMBINING MASCULINITY AND FEMININITY

As you already know, gender is about more than your genitalia. Theories of androgyny and sexism came out of the Feminist movement of the 1970s. Both approaches address masculinity and femininity together, but instead of positioning them as opposites, they're seen as independent entities—a key assumption differentiating them from gender identity models. They also include the assumption that gender is *constructed* or defined by society rather than being innate and natural.

The Androgyny Model

Gender theorists and researchers began to question the gender identity model's assumption that masculinity and femininity were opposites as depicted in Figure 2.4. Theorists like Sandra Bem, Janet Spence, and Robert Helmreich argued that masculinity and femininity are not opposite. For example, traditionally masculine realms like work and reason are not antithetical to traditionally feminine realms like home and emotion, as work and home are not opposites. These theorists believed that it was possible and desirable for people to have *both* masculine and feminine traits. Thus, a person could be effective both at work and at home, and could be both rational and emotional.

They proposed *the androgyny model*, which assumes that femininity and masculinity can be measured separately. Each person displays some amount of femininity and also displays some amount of masculinity, as indicated by the axes in figure 2.5.

Masculinity   **Femininity**

Figure 2.5   A Bipolar View of Gender Role Identity

Simplifying this into low and high scores, each individual can then be categorized in one of four ways:

Androgynous: high in both femininity and masculinity
Masculine: high in masculinity and low in femininity
Feminine: high in femininity and low in masculinity
Undifferentiated: low in both femininity and masculinity

It is important to note that any person, regardless of his or her biological sex, can be placed in any one of these four categories. When a man is classified as masculine and a woman is classified as feminine, they are considered to be *gender-typed* or *gender-conforming.* When a man is classified as feminine or a woman is classified as masculine, that person is considered to be *cross-gender-typed* (Bem, 1974; Spence & Helmreich, 1978).

Androgyny theorists think of traditional femininity and masculinity as strategies for adaptation. Sometimes it is adaptive to express one's feelings (feminine); sometimes it is better to shut down one's emotions and get the job done (masculine). In stereotypical personality development, each sex acquires about half of the attitudes, skills, and behaviors necessary for coping in the world. Theoretically, the person who can incorporate both masculine and feminine characteristics into the personality will have a wide repertoire of coping strategies at his or her disposal, and this gender flexibility renders the person more adaptive than a traditionally gender-typed person. Thus, for some theorists, androgyny is seen as a mental health ideal. We'll review this proposition in Chapter Fourteen.

Androgyny Measures

The most popular of the androgyny measures was the Bem Sex Role Inventory (BSRI) (Bem, 1974), a list of 60 adjectives, 20 of which are descriptive of traditional masculinity (e.g., "self-reliant," "analytical"), 20 of traditional femininity (e.g., "warm," "gentle"), and 20 gender neutral (e.g., "conscientious," "likable"). The person rates himself or herself on each adjective using a seven-point scale ranging from "never or almost never true" to "always or almost always true." All adjectives reflect the socially desirable aspects of each gender role due to the theory that the combination of positive traits of both roles is the ideal.

The Personality Attributes Questionnaire (PAQ), published by Janet Spence and Robert Helmreich (1978) has also been very popular. It consists of 8 masculine- and 8 feminine-typed adjectives. Using a 5-point scale from "not at all" to "very," participants indicate how aggressive or emotional they are (e.g., "not at all aggressive" to "very aggressive").

The BSRI and PAQ yield separate scores for Masculinity and Femininity. To determine what category an individual fits into, the researcher begins by computing the group averages for masculinity and femininity. Then each individual's masculinity score is compared to the average masculinity score to determine if the person has a low or high score, then the process is repeated with femininity scores. Finally, the person is classified into one of the four groups (androgynous, feminine, masculine, undifferentiated) based on the combination of high or low scores.

SEXISM

Psychologists define *sexism* as differential attitudes and behaviors directed toward people based on their biological statuses as male or female. We include it in this section because it requires conceptions of both masculinity and femininity. For example, one might comfort a female friend when she exhibits vulnerability, but avoid a male friend who exhibits the same behavior. Or the assertive behavior of a man might be described as "forceful" while the identical behavior, performed by a woman, might be labeled "bitchy."

Because some beliefs about gender can be subtle, because we have a natural propensity toward categorizing and stereotyping, because there are emotional and unconscious aspects to gender roles, and because we have all been socialized in a gender schematic and sexist society, we are probably all sexist in some measure.

Because we live in a patriarchal society in which males wield the vast majority of institutional power, the most serious forms of sexism involve the disrespect of women. A woman who makes less money than a man in the same job is a victim of *institutional sexism*. An adult woman who is called a "girl" or addressed as "honey" (two disempowering terms in most social contexts) is a victim of *interpersonal sexism*. And a woman who limits her own potential because she has received repeated messages that she is incompetent (and she incorporates these messages into her sense of self) is a victim of *internalized sexism*. Although these forms of sexism are presented here as distinct categories, they are interrelated. Sexist culture perpetuates all forms of sexism.

Two Forms of Sexism

The initial discussion and measures of sexism focused on beliefs that seem obviously sexist today, such as that "swearing is worse for a girl than a guy." Not surprisingly, both male and female college students have become less and less likely to agree with statements like this since the 1970s (Twenge, 1997a). *Mad Men's* Don Draper may have been typical for his time, but it's hard to imagine that kind of attitude and behavior is typical of today's men.

One result of this generational change has been an effort to examine more subtle forms of sexism. In an impressive program of research undertaken with more than 15,000 people in 19 countries, Peter Glick and Susan Fiske (2001) demonstrated that sexism takes two different but related forms. *Hostile sexism*, the hatred of women, is the kind of sexism that springs to mind when one thinks of prejudicial attitudes toward women. However, overall attitudes toward women within a population are usually quite positive. Women are believed to be nice, caring, and nurturing (Glick, 2005). At the same time these qualities are ascribed, women are also perceived as being incompetent and thus in need of men's protection, help, and financial support. *Benevolent sexism*, which Glick and Fiske (2001) dubbed the "women are wonderful effect," serves to reward women for cooperating in a system that denies them significant resources and reduces their resistance to this inequality. It allows men to "maintain a positive self-image as protectors and providers who are willing to sacrifice their own needs to care for the women in their lives... [and] promises that men's power will be used to women's advantage, if only they can secure a high-status male protector" (p. 111).

Hostile sexism can be reserved for women who challenge the status quo: powerful women, lesbians, and outspoken feminists. To illustrate: contrast the cultural attitudes between Secretaries of State Condoleeza Rice (2005–2009) and Hillary Clinton (2009–2012), both of whom followed in the steps of the first woman U.S. Secretary of State Madeleine Albright (1997–2001). Rice had been on the Board of Directors for Chevron Oil company, Provost at Stanford University, and National Security Advisor prior to her nomination; Clinton had been a lawyer, "First Lady" (a title that some find offensive), and a United States Senator. Both received their share of criticism for their policies and politics, but Clinton's outspoken style and refusal to back down have earned her a level of vitriol that Rice, with her quieter and more stereotypical style, and who was endorsed by a politically and socially conservative president, did not face.

Across 19 nations, Glick, Fiske, and their colleagues (Glick et al., 2000) found that hostile sexism scores tended to be lower than benevolent sexism scores. They also found remarkably high correlations between hostile and benevolent sexism within all of the cultures they studied. In countries where there was strong endorsement of hostile sexism, people also showed a strong tendency to endorse benevolent sexism. In the opinion of these researchers, these two forms of sexism act in complementary fashion as justifications of gender inequality (Glick & Fiske, 2001). Box 2.3 lists some ways to reduce sexism against women.

Prejudices also extend towards men, who are often seen as arrogant, emotionally cold, aggressive, and exploitive. In fact, men report liking and trusting women more than they do other men, a positive out-group bias that is not seen in other forms of prejudice such as racism. This attitude is disrespectful of men, at least in some ways, yet it also supports the characterization of men as being oriented towards dominance and power (Glick, et. al., 2004).

Chivalry

Chivalry is a term derived from the French *Chevalier*, a heavily armed horseman in the French military (Keen, 1984). It is a set of attitudes and behaviors directed toward women by men of privilege (in medieval times, horsemen were knights and/or nobles; most common men could not afford horses). Chivalry is a form of benevolent sexism that manifests itself in a set of "gentlemanly" helpful behaviors such as holding a door open for a woman, helping her get seated at a dining table, standing when she enters or leaves a room, and filling her wine glass at social occasions. Glick (2005) points out that these are "trivial niceties" that send the message that women are special, but

---

Box 2.3   Reducing Sexism (Against Women)

Although it may be difficult to change sexist *behaviors*, it is often even more difficult to change sexist *reactions* that may be emotional and unconscious. Prejudiced and non-prejudiced people do not differ in *stereotype activation* (Fazio & Olson, 2003). However, the non-prejudiced person has made a commitment to be aware of and resistant to the tendency to stereotype. Over time, the stereotype activation itself decreases (Kawakami, Dovidio, Moll, Hermsen, & Russin, 2000). To reduce sexism, a person must expend efforts to understand socialization and gender role attitudes, recognize when he or she is engaging in stereotypical thinking, and resist inclinations to behave in sexist ways. Over time, this "self-training" should lead to nonsexist responses that are somewhat automatic.

The concept of chivalry could potentially be replaced with values of courtesy, civility, helping those in need, and thoughtfulness. We often tell men that if they are treating women differently than they treat other men, they ought to have a good reason for doing so. For instance, one might help a short woman to put her baggage into an overhead bin on a plane, given men's average advantage in height and upper body strength. On the other hand, should a man help a tall, female bodybuilder to store her luggage? Should an old man in poor health offer his seat to a young, fit woman on a crowded bus? Should a young, fit woman offer her seat to a father carrying a newborn baby?

Several women have described this same scenario to us. The woman is walking toward a public building with a set of doors that opens into a small foyer, where there is a second set of doors that open into the place of business. A man opens the outer door for her, which is courteous. Because she enters the foyer first, she reaches the inner set of doors and opens it for the man, who then refuses to walk through first. She is being equally courteous, but he does not accept her courtesy because he has learned that men do not accept help from women. Does his behavior reflect a respectful attitude?

---

that they are also incompetent and in need of men's assistance. The function of such customs is to reinforce male dominance and undermine women's resistance to it. Chivalric men believe that they are being helpful to women, but most do not help with things that really matter such as gendered pay inequity, child care, or men's violence against women.

Chivalry is believed to communicate respect for women, but true respect involves listening to the other person's desires and negotiating relationship behaviors. In contrast to true respect, chivalry is a rigid set of rules based on the faulty assumption that all women are alike and all men must treat them the same way. Many of the men whom our students have interviewed express disappointment and anger that many women seem not to appreciate their chivalric behavior, an indication that these gestures are undertaken not for the woman's sake, but to bolster the man's self-image.

As a form of benevolent sexism, chivalry secures women's cooperation with male dominance. A parallel would be an employer who underpays an employee by thousands of dollars all year but gives him/her a holiday bonus of a few hundred dollars.

This gesture allows the employer to believe that he/she is generous and may influence the employee to remain loyal to the company.

Chivalric behaviors may not have the intent of reinforcing inequality and the belief that women are more special but less competent than men, but these behaviors may have the impact of doing so. A letter writer in Carolyn Hax's (2009) syndicated advice column described her frustration with her boyfriend. When they attend a party and he wants to go home, he feels uncomfortable leaving without her because he "was raised" to never let a "lady" go unescorted to a social event. Therefore, her options are to leave when he wants to go, feel badly for "making" him stay, and not go to parties that he does not want to attend. He is impervious to the fact she "was raised" with the idea that a woman can be comfortable and behave appropriately when attending a social gathering alone. This situation is a good illustration of how chivalry can be an agent of men's dominance and how it can communicate that women are helpless without men.

Limitations and Criticisms of Theories Combining Masculinity and Femininity

Results from studies relying on androgyny theory haven't entirely supported the theory, as we'll see in Chapter Fourteen. The BSRI and PAQ have both been criticized for relying strictly on positive characteristics, which lead Spence and Helmreich to develop the Extended PAQ that adds eight negative characteristics of masculinity and eight negative characteristics of femininity (Spence, Helmreich, & Holahan, 1979). The focus on positive traits may be one reason why mean scores for both male and female undergraduates have increased for both the femininity and masculinity scales of both measures over last few decades (Twenge, 1997b). Between the rising means and the older age of these scales, Andrew Smiler and Marina Epstein (2010) recommended limited use of the PAQ. They further suggested the BSRI only be used for replications of earlier studies because it has poor psychometric properties.

Research on sexism has been affected by a trend toward more egalitarian responses over the years, at least among adolescents and undergraduates (Twenge, 1997a). It has been limited by a focus on attitudes that privilege men over women, with minimal discussion of the reverse: attitudes that privilege women over men. Discussion of, and especially the practice of, benevolent sexism has also met criticism. Young men whom we have spoken with have complained that they were taught to hold the door open for everyone, but they are asked about, and sometimes criticized, when they do this for women.

BYE, BYE BINARY: MASCULINITY ALONE AND COMPLICATED

The third set of models, focused solely on masculinity, also relied heavily on the feminist critique of psychology in the 1970s. As with other measures of that era, they carry with them the assumptions that masculinity is constructed rather than essential, that masculinity and femininity are distinct entities, not polar opposites and that masculinity is multidimensional or multifaceted. If you took an Introductory Psychology course, you probably learned that there is a debate regarding intelligence, with some authors arguing for a single intelligence that can be measured by IQ and others that there are a number of distinct intelligences (Davis, Christodoulou, Seider, & Gardner, 2011; Sternberg, 1999). The approaches and measures described in this section all favor models that sound like multiple intelligences, called facets or dimensions of masculinity but not multiple masculinities.

Masculine Roles, Scripts, Norms, and Ideologies

In practice, the following theories all rely on our cognitive abilities. We'll define each of the models briefly, then discuss the gender role approach in more detail to illustrate its strengths and weaknesses.

Role Theory is an appeal to behavior akin to that of an actor on screen or stage. Gender roles, however, are not limited to one particular venue (or TV show), but rather extend across all aspects of an individual's life. The focus here is very much on the individual with minimal attention to the context in which they find themselves.

Script Theory appeals to a computer script (or program), where a script is defined as a set of instructions for what to do in a given situation (Bem, 1993). Scripts may be context specific, so there is some balance and interplay between the individual and the content. Schema-based approaches are similar and the two terms (script, schema) are sometimes used interchangeably, although they should not be. For our purposes, you might also think of scripts as recipes or formulas.

Norm-based approaches are descriptions of commonly held standards of behavior to which people attempt to adhere (Mahalik et al., 2003). Norms may be broad and cultural, like the expectation that American men rarely (or never) wear skirts in their day-to-day lives (Pleck, 1981a, 1995). Norms can also be much more localized and micro-contextualized. For example, you might have one professor who insists on being called "doctor" or "professor" and another who insists that you use his or her first name. Like script theory, the focus is on the interplay between the individual and the context.

Ideological approaches position masculinity as a belief system (Levant, 1996). In this way, they are comparable to an individual's system of values, political beliefs, or religious beliefs in that they provide an overarching set of ideals about how people should behave. Similar to role theory, the focus here is on the individual with little attention to the context.

Below, we discuss role theory in detail to provide a sense of how gender roles work and some of the problems of this approach. We focus on role theory because many of the subsequent approaches were in the service of adopting the strengths of role theory while attempting to address its weaknesses.

Social roles define a set of expected behaviors for a person in any given social position. For example, the social role of *student* includes the expectations that one will attend classes, take tests, and complete assignments. Note that the role comprises expectations but not necessarily performance. Some students do not fulfill their assigned role while others vary in how well they fulfill that role (David and Brannon, 1976).

A *gender role* is a generalized social role, one that cuts across many situations and is comprised of a set of expectations for affect, behavior, and cognition that is based on a person's (perceived) biological sex. If you were to obtain a part in a stage play, you would have a script that told you what to say and how to behave while acting. On occasion, actors will improvise, saying or doing things that are not in the script. If you decided to do so, the director of the play might or might not tolerate it, depending on his or her rigidity and on whether or not your improvisation was consistent with the role. However, if you were to improvise too extensively or in a way that was inconsistent with the role, the director would probably discipline you or throw you out of the play. If you feel strongly enough about changing the role, you might be willing to risk this outcome.

Actors (we use this term to refer to both males and females, as is increasingly the convention) know that they have to stick to their roles to keep their jobs. Social roles are a little less well defined than stage roles; nobody gives a boy an explicit script telling him how to act in masculine ways (although beer commercials with descriptions of "man laws" come close). But social roles and gender roles are every bit as powerful. One may incur severe punishment for stepping outside of one's prescribed role and great social approval for staying within it. In the gender role arena, for instance, a boy who cries or plays with girls may be ostracized by his male peers. The power of gender roles is most evident when the prescriptions of the role are violated, as we alluded to when discussing violations of masculinity at the beginning of the chapter (Box 2.1).

Who are the "directors" of the "plays" when it comes to gender roles? They are everyone who can reward the individual for staying within gender role boundaries and everyone who can punish the person for stepping outside of them. They are real-life and media models who display stereotypical behavior or talk in ways that reinforce stereotypical beliefs about men and women. Families, friends, employers, romantic partners, media figures, and others all have the power to enforce gender role norms. Sometimes their sanctions are subtle, such as a mildly disapproving look. At other times they are more overt, through insults like "you throw like a girl" or a refusal to befriend a man who is too effeminate.

Because men (and women) are socialized in a gender-typed society, they often internalize gender roles and become their own "directors" to some extent. A great many men incorporate masculine stereotypes and norms into their ideal self-concepts and attempt to live up to these norms. If one accepts such standards uncritically, then the content of masculine gender role norms becomes the yardstick by which the man judges his worth. Pleck (1981b) described such men as "prisoners of manliness" who compulsively conform their behavior to masculine role norms and lose sight of their individuality in the process. Instead of prioritizing gender as a way to organize and understand the people around us, we could adopt a different frame of reference. Box 2.4 lists several alternatives.

Regardless of the exact theoretical approach, all measures of this type are often labeled as measures of *masculinity ideology* (Smiler, 2004; Thompson & Pleck, 1995). Participants are given a series of questions and asked to use a scale from one to four (or six or seven) to indicate the strength of their agreement (from "completely disagree" to "completely agree") or the extent to which a statement describes them (from "does

Box 2.4   Reducing Gender Schematic Processing

Sandra Bem (1998) notes that there are many ways to think about people without reference to their gender. The first three of these are Bem's suggestions, the remainder are ours.

Individual differences schema: people vary widely in their habits, attitudes, and temperament. A person may act aggressively, not because he is a man, but because he has an aggressive personality and/or finds himself in a situation in which aggression is adaptive.

Cultural relativism schema: "different people believe different things" (p. 271). Roman Catholics do not allow women to be priests, but some Episcopalians do.

Sexism schema: although beliefs differ, some beliefs about gender are wrong. Women should be allowed to be Roman Catholic priests.

Situational pressure schema: people tend to behave in certain ways when situations exert different pressures. A man may keep his feelings to himself while with his male friends, not because men are unemotional, but because other men might not give him a compassionate response. He may be very emotionally expressive as a client in psychotherapy or when he is in the company of women who are his friends.

External variability schema: people do not always behave in concert with how they feel; two people can vary to a great extent in their external reactions to exactly the same internal thoughts and feelings. Two men may hold equally sexist attitudes, but one decides not to display them because he wants the approval of women.

not describe me at all" to "describes me very much"). For example, the *Male Role Attitudes Scale* (Pleck, Sonenstein, & Ku, 1993) asks participants to indicate how much they agree or disagree with statements like "It is essential for a guy to get respect from others" using a four-point scale.

Most scales provide separate scores for each component of masculinity, although some of the shortest scales, such as the 8–item *Male Role Attitudes Scale* (Pleck et al., 1993) provide only a total score. The longest scale published to date is the *Conformity to Masculine Norms Inventory* (CMNI; Mahalik et al., 2003) which consists of 94 items that assess eleven distinct components of masculinity. The use of subscales allows researchers to pinpoint which aspect(s) of masculinity have the strongest connection to the outcomes (or dependent variables) being examined.

Strain and Stress Models

Other related models include the emphasis that not only is masculinity complex, but also that the effort of living up to its standards of behavior is inherently stressful. In introducing his *Gender Role Strain* theory, James O'Neil (1981a) pointed out that compulsive dominance, passivity, and emotional constriction, are downright maladaptive. He also argued, as did Josph Pleck (O'Neil, 1982; Pleck, 1981a, 1981b), that trying to become androgynous presented a different—but still potentially stressful—set of standards that may be even greater than the expectation to live up to traditional masculinity.

For men, traditional gender roles included demands for competitiveness, aggression, and task orientation. Androgyny demands emotional expression, relationship orientation, and gentleness *in addition to* the role requirements of traditional masculinity.

The key assumptions of strain and stress models include the hypothesis that trying to be masculine is inherently stressful, that masculinity and masculine role stress have several distinct components that can be measured individually, that masculinity and femininity are partial opposites, and that masculinity is constructed.

Gender Role Strain is a psychological situation in which gender role demands have negative consequences for the individual or others (O'Neil, 1981a). The negative effects of masculine gender role strain can be described in terms of stress, conflict, health, and mental health problems for the individual. Violence and poor relationships are potential negative consequences for others who come into contact with the individual.

A person experiences this strain when gender role demands conflict with his or her *naturally occurring tendencies*. For example, males in most Western cultures are socialized to be unemotional. For a naturally emotional man, the demand created by this socialization may cause him to feel a good deal of pressure to conform his behavior to the cultural norm. As a result, he may experience negative consequences, such as depression or high blood pressure. The net effect of gender role strain is the restriction of the person's ability to reach his or her full human potential (O'Neil, 1981a). In the above example, the man's depression or high blood pressure may restrict his potential by lowering his functioning in his work, affecting his relationship with his partner, or even shortening his life.

Strain and Stress Measures.   There are two measures of strain and stress. James O'Neil's *Gender Role Conflict Scale* (GRCS) has been much more popular than Richard Eisler and Jay Skidmore's (1987) *Masculine Gender Role Stress Scale* (MGRSS). These measures were developed for use with only male subjects and are designed to assess the degree to which a man endorses attitudes, behaviors, and values that have been associated with negative psychological effects.

On each scale, participants respond to a set of statements using a scale anchored by "strongly agree" to "strongly disagree." The MGRSS, for example, asks participants to indicate how stressful "having a female boss" is (or would be) using a seven-point scale anchored at the extremes by "not at all stressful" and "very stressful." The GRCS is the most frequently used of any masculinity-only measure (Whorley & Addis, 2006) and we will refer to its findings throughout the latter half of this text. It examines four categories of conflict:

1. *Success, Power, and Competition*: the pressure to gain wealth, obtain authority, and be a winner.

2. *Restrictive Emotionality*: difficulty in expressing one's feelings or allowing others to do so.

3. *Restrictive Affectionate Behavior between Men*: limiting the expression of warm feelings for other men.

4. *Conflict between Work and Family Relations*: difficulty balancing these sometimes conflicting demands.

Limitations and Criticisms of Masculinity Alone

The approaches described above—roles, scripts, norms, and ideologies—highlight conceptually different aspects of people's beliefs about masculinity. One criticism is that they often do not reconcile differences but simply provide different points of emphasis. For example, the *Conformity to Masculine Norms Inventory* emphasizes conformity and thus provides participants with "I" statements such as "In general, I will do anything to win." However, the *Male Role Norms Inventory, Revised* (MRNI-R, Levant et al. 2007) focuses on participants' normative beliefs and thus asks about "men" with questions such as "A man should always be the boss." Yet researchers have discovered differences between young men's self-descriptions ("I") and their descriptions of "most men" (Street, Kimmel, & Kromrey, 1995). Perhaps this finding is not surprising, as most people see themselves as significantly gender nonconforming, and most men (and probably most women as well) overestimate the gender conformity of same-sex peers (Kilmartin, Smith, Green, Heinzen, Kuchler, & Kolar, 2008).

It is not clear how important these differences are. In one meta-analysis that included both types of measures, as well as the BSRI's masculinity scale, researchers found the same pattern of results for all measures of masculinity reviewed: men with higher masculinity scores were more supportive of attitudes that facilitate sexual assault against women (Murnen, Wright, & Kaluzny, 2002). A separate correlational study that included the different types of measures found that men with higher masculinity scores expressed greater desire for higher numbers of sexual partners (Walker, Tokar, & Fischer, 2000).

As you can see, theorists and researchers have approached the study of masculinity in a variety of ways. Comedian and author Erin Judge proposes the approach illustrated in Figure 2.6 to describe a person using the frequent label "real man." Table 2.1 lists several of the key assumptions that delineate psychological approaches.

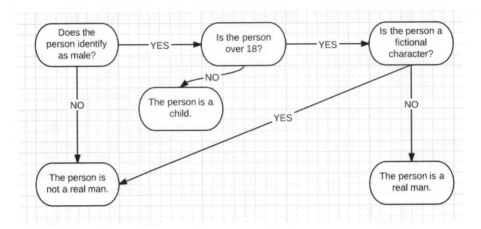

Figure 2.6

Table 2.1   Summary of Measurement Approaches

	Essential or Constructed?	*Relationship Between Masculinity and Femininity*	*Number of Scores*	*Focus*
Gender Binary				
Gender Identity	Essential	Opposites	1	
Sex Comparison	Essential	Opposites	1	
Beyond Binary				
Androgeny	Constructed	Separate	2 (Masc., Fem.)	
Sexism	Constructed	Related	1	Cognition
Bye Bye Binary				
Masculinity Alone	Constructed	Partial opposites	Multiple	Cognition
Strain & Stress	Constructed	Partial opposties	Multiple	Cognition

SUMMARY

1. Measures include and reflect the assumptions of the theory under which they are developed.
2. Measures and approaches to the measurement of gender and masculinity have changed over time.
3. Binary models of gender emphasize male or female, or masculine vs. feminine.
4. Reviews of the research on sex differences indicate that (group) average differences tend to be small.

5. Gender identity models rely on the assumption that men need to be masculine to have healthy development.

6. In effect, gender identity measures tend to measure conformity to gender stereotypes.

7. *Androgyny models* position masculinity and femininity as separate constructs.

8. *Androgyny models* include the assumption that the ability to draw from both masculinity and femininity leads to healthy development.

9. *Sexism* focuses on power relations between males and females.

10. *Sexism* takes many forms, including institutional sexism, internalized sexism, benevolent sexism, and hostile sexism.

11. *Masculinity ideology* approaches position masculinity as a multifaceted construct that is partially opposed to femininity.

12. *Stress and strain* approaches include the assumption that efforts to adhere to cultural expectations of masculinity are inherently problematic.

Chapter Three

It's In My Genes: Biologically-Based Theoretical Perspectives on Males and Gender

One obvious place to begin a study of male behavior and experience is with biological theory. In this chapter, we explore three approaches that take biology as the starting point for explanations of gender. Strictly biological approaches highlight differences based explicitly on genetic allotment and the so-called "sex hormones." Evolutionary psychology attempts to apply the theory of evolution to social behaviors. Psychoanalysis is a narrative of how basic biological survival mechanisms interact with human relationships to form the personality, part of which is gendered.

Parents of large families often say that their children have differing personalities, and that these differences were evident even in the first few days after they were born. Such differences could be due to misperception or memory distortion on the part of the parents, or from prenatal events such as difficult pregnancies. But it is also possible that what these parents perceive are some real differences that are based in biology.

Developmental psychologists have long known that infants differ in *psychological temperament*. Some babies are relatively quiet and content. Others have higher activity levels or are more disposed toward crankiness. Temperamental differences are thought to be determined largely by infants' genes, hormones, and other biological forces, which continue to affect their behavior throughout their lives (Thomas & Chess, 1977; Sigelman & Rider, 2009).

It is clear that males and females have differing biologies in some ways, although we should keep in mind that in *most* ways, they do not. There are differences in genetic and hormonal composition that lead to average male/female differences in height, weight, muscularity, genitalia, and secondary sex characteristics such as breasts and facial hair. There is little dispute that biological sex differences produce these usual physical differences, most of which are *average* differences as discussed in Chapter Two. But, to what extent do they produce *behavioral* sex differences as well? The central question concerns to what extent "boys will be boys" because of their biological compositions, and to what extent "boys will be boys" because we socialize them to act in certain ways. In this chapter, we focus on biological explanations to that question. In the next chapter, we'll address answers focused on the socialization process.

A rather complex sequence of biological events is necessary to ensure that most healthy men and women will have the physiological wherewithal to reproduce (Fausto-Sterling, 2000). Of course, the development of these basic structures is not enough to ensure the survival of the species. Sexual behaviors are also necessary. There is little doubt that hormonal events affect brain structures and pathways, which then have strong influences over these behaviors. But what is the difference in the biological basis of *sexual* behaviors (those necessary for reproduction) on the one hand, and *gender role* behaviors (social behaviors attributed strongly to either males or females) on the other?

CHROMOSOMAL AND HORMONAL APPROACHES

The twenty-third pair of human chromosomes are called the *sex chromosomes*. Individuals who have two X chromosomes, XX, are female and those with an XY combination are male. Many people are unaware that approximately 1 or 2 of every 1,000 live births does not follow this pattern (Fausto-Sterling, 2000). Individuals who are neither XX nor XY are often referred to as "intersexual" or "intersexed;" officially, they have a *disorder of sexual development* (DSD; Vilain et al., 2007). Table 3.1 lists several of these disorders and the frequency with which a child is born with that disorder.

This list includes a pair of disorders that focus on the "sex hormones," estrogen and testosterone, and not chromosomal issues per se. When all such disorders—chromosomal, hormonal, and others, are included, we may be talking about as many as 1 or 2 of every 100 births (Fausto-Sterling, 2000). Here, we focus on two disorders regarding testosterone. Keep in mind that all humans, regardless of their chromosomal allotment, produce testosterone, and that prior to puberty, boys and girls have similar amounts of testosterone. Testosterone's functions include bone growth (size, density) and muscle mass. There are two developmental periods when testosterone interacts with the Y-chromosome in ways that are particularly male-oriented. The first is approximately 8 weeks after conception. If the fetus has a Y-chromosome, it triggers the release of testosterone so that male genitalia, as well as the related musculature and

Table 3.1   Frequency of Selected Disorders of Sexual Development

Disorder	Frequency (among live births)
Klinefelter's Syndrome (XXY)	1 in 1,000
Other non-XX or non-XY	1 in 1,666
Androgen Insensitivity Syndrome (complete)	1 in 13,000
Androgen Insensitivity Syndrome (partial)	1 in 130,000
Congenital Adrenal Hyperplasia ("Classic" CAH)	1 in 13,000
Total number of people whose bodies differ from standard male or female	1 in 100

Values from the Intersex Society of North America (ISNA, undated)

vasculature, are formed. Without testosterone at this point in time, children develop female genitalia. The second time is puberty.

Androgen Insensitivity Syndrome (AIS), which can be either complete (CAIS) or partial (PAIS), describes individuals whose bodies are unable to break down and process *androgens*, a class of hormones that includes testosterone and adrenaline, both of which are produced by the adrenal gland. XY Males who have AIS are unable to process testosterone, in much the same way that an individual who is lactose intolerant can't process lactose (and thus becomes ill if he or she ingests milk products). One result is that XY males with AIS do not develop normally-sized male genitalia. At birth, they may have a vagina, a micropenis, or another structure that is neither vagina nor penis. Those who appear to have a vagina at birth are often assumed to be girls; their disorder is not typically discovered until puberty. For children whose condition is evident at birth, the parents face a series of difficult decisions described in Box 3.1.

Box 3.1 Decisions for Parents Whose Children Have Ambiguous Genitalia

The American Association of Pediatrics once described the birth of such child as a "social emergency" (AAP, 2000) but has subsequently changed its stance. Nonetheless, many parents and medical personnel still react to this unexpected phenomenon as though it is a major problem. Parents face a series of difficult questions, including:

What will we tell family and friends?

Do we choose a gender, and possibly plastic surgery, now, or do we wait? If we wait, how long?

What happens if we choose the "wrong" gender?

There are no easy answers to these questions, and professional guidelines continue to be rewritten and evolve as we learn more. Parents who choose plastic surgery for their children aren't choosing a one-time surgery; they are committing themselves and their child to a series of surgeries throughout childhood and adolescence.

In general, research tends to show that CAH girls are more masculine and less feminine than non-CAH girls. Similarly, AIS boys tend to be more feminine and less masculine than non-AIS boys. CAH boys and AIS girls do not differ from their same-sex peers (Cohen-Bendahan, van de Beek, & Berenbaum, 2005).

However, findings tend to be specific to some aspects of masculinity (or femininity) and some sex hormones, but not others, and some findings are more consistent than others. Evidence that male-typed spatial abilities such as the ability to mentally rotate an object ("spatial rotation") are linked to androgens is fairly robust, for example, while evidence for female-typed abilities such as verbal fluency are less consistent. One extensive review concluded that "it seems likely that androgens are responsible for some of the differences between the sexes in these traits, although it is not as clear how much they contribute to variations within males and within females" (Cohen-Bandahan et al., 2005, p. 377). The picture is further complicated by the fact that testosterone levels vary naturally during the day and that specific situations, such as being challenged or becoming sexually aroused, further increase testosterone (Archer, 2006).

Another disorder is *Congenital Adrenal Hyperplasia* (CAH), in which the developing fetus is exposed to a large dose of androgens in utero at just the right (wrong?) moment and the fetus subsequently becomes "masculinized" and develops a penis. This exposure causes no problems if it's an XY fetus, but it does alter the development of an XX fetus. One such result is a change in genital development that may lead to a penis, a micropenis, or some other structure. Although individuals with CAH are not particularly common in the general population, their ongoing connection to the medical system has allowed researchers to study them in some detail. Most of the research has relied on children's and parent's reports of their children's behavior, although some observational studies have been conducted.

Criticism of Chromosomal and Hormonal Approaches

This approach to the study of gender has received some criticism. One concern is the lack of detail in exactly how a chromosome or a hormone produces a behavior. This is particularly troubling given evidence that hormones contribute to male vs. female differences, but androgens, for example, do not explain differences among males (Cohen-Bandahan et al., 2005). The reliance on a gender binary is another concern (Smiler & Epstein, 2010).

EVOLUTIONARY PSYCHOLOGY

Evolutionary psychology (EP) is an approach to the study of human behavior that focuses on the adaptive value of behavior. A behavior is considered adaptive if it would have allowed ancestral humans to survive in a life-threatening environment or would have provided an individual with an advantage that would have increased the likelihood that they would produce offspring and thus pass their genes on to the next generation (Tooby & Cosmides, 2005). As you might guess, this work finds its roots in Charles Darwin's (1871) evolutionary theory and the idea of "survival of the fittest."

EP posits that our brain is comprised of different modules, each of which has a particular function. Over time, modules may come to be used in a situation other than the situation which shaped their evolution. When this happens, a behavior is said to have been *ex-apted* (Tooby & Cosmides, 2005). Aspects of the visual system that help us quickly identify motion, which developed in the wild and allowed proto-humans to recognize prey and other hunters, are currently being ex-apted to help people obtain high scores in video games like Halo. Whether or not this will ultimately lead to a reproductive advantage for the player is an open question.

At its best, EP draws together knowledge from many segments of study, including emotion, cognition, developmental, and biological psychology. It also draws from other fields such as computer science (because some aspects of cognition are computer-like), history (because biological change is a slow process), sociology and demography (because evolutionary change should be apparent throughout the species), and anthropology (because different types of cultures, such as hunter-gatherer tribes, tell us something about how widespread a phenomenon is and give us models for much earlier forms of civilization). Some of EP's basic tenets were established by an earlier approach known as sociobiology, although EP has attempted to address some of the problems associated with sociobiology (Tooby & Cosmides, 2005).

Evolutionary psychologists conduct work on a broad variety of topics, but we will highlight two areas because they are the root of several important male-female comparisons and align with issues of masculinity: sex and violence. Both of these topics will be the focus of later chapters, but we address them here briefly. Evolutionary psychology positions sex differences in behavior as the result of differences in males' and females' *reproductive investments*, which in turn affect the *reproductive strategies* of each sex. Reproductive investment refers to the amount of time and resources that are expended in producing offspring. Reproductive strategy is the behavioral pattern employed to ensure that one's genes will be passed on to the succeeding generation (Buss & Schmitt, 1993; Schmitt, 2005).

According to EP, reproductive investment differs dramatically for women and men and creates different reproductive strategies. Physiologically, males need only a few seconds to make their genetic contribution to the reproductive process. Millions of sperm can be deposited in this period of time, and a healthy young male can ejaculate several times a day. Males are capable of impregnating females for almost all of their adult lives, making sperm an abundant and renewable resource.

In contrast, females usually only produce one ovum per month and have a more limited number of reproductive years. Therefore, females have a greater investment in the reproductive process than males. In humans, females carry and nourish the fetus for nine months, during which time they cannot begin another pregnancy. Following birth, they must feed and protect children during the period of helpless infancy if the young are to survive. Whereas sperm are an abundant resource, eggs are a relatively scarce one.

Sexuality

These differences in reproductive investment have led to sex-differentiated reproductive strategies, according to EP theorists. The female must be selective in her choice of sexual partner and should choose a high-status male who can provide for and protect her and the child. The male, on the other hand, has two options. He might adopt a short-term mating strategy in which he tries to impregnate as many females as possible while also preventing other males from copulating with his partners by using aggression and other forms of dominance. Alternately, he might adopt a long-term mating strategy in which he mates with a single partner repeatedly over a long period of time, producing multiple offspring with her. In theory, women might also adopt the short-term strategy, although EP has paid little research attention to this possibility.

Within EP, research focused on sexual behavior typically follows this logic, which is known as *Sexual Strategies Theory* (SST) (Buss & Schmitt, 1993; Schmitt, 2005). Whereas sociobiology suggested that all women adopted the long-term mating strategy and all men adopted the short-term mating strategy (Daly & Wilson, 1983), SST posits that both males and females may choose either strategy but that men are more likely to choose the short-term strategy (Buss & Schmitt, 1993; Schmitt, 2005). Reviews conducted outside the SST framework, one examining the role of testosterone (Archer,

2006) and the other examining reported number of sexual partners (Smiler, 2013), indicate that a small number of men routinely engage in short-term mating while the majority choose longer-term partners. Males who choose to have a series of short-term partners tend to have higher levels of testosterone (Archer, 2006).

SST's proponents, like sociobiology's advocates, rely on and point to several male-female differences in sexual behavior (Buss & Schmitt, 1993; Schmitt, 2005; Symons, 1987), many of which have long been known:

- Many more societies allow polygyny (men having more than one wife or partner) than allow polyandry (women having multiple partners) (Murdock, 1967).
- Men report more desired sexual partners than do women, a finding that SST's authors have demonstrated to be applicable worldwide (Schmitt et al., 2003)
- Boys and men report more actual sexual partners than girls and women, a finding that has long been documented (Oliver & Hyde, 1993).
- Men agree to sex with a hypothetical partner more quickly than women (Buss & Schmitt, 1993).

Violence

Following sociobiologists, evolutionary psychologists have also offered explanations for male aggressiveness, competition, risk taking, and dominance (Barash & Lipton 1997). Just as rams butt horns to win the right to reproduce with ewes, so do men fight with one another in the competition to inseminate women. According to these theories, a male has to take a chance on being hurt or killed in competition to gain a mate directly or to gain the status which will subsequently give him access to mates. In either case, the benefit of aggressive behavior is an opportunity to pass on his genes. Sociobiologists Daly and Wilson (1983) described the process using an animal example:

> Imagine a bull elephant seal that has no stomach for the dominance battles of the breeding beach. Very well. He can opt out: remain at sea, never endure the debilitating months of fast and battle, outlive his brothers. But mere survival is no criterion of success. Eventually he will die, and his genes will die with him. The bull seals of the future will be the sons of males that found the ordeal of the beach to be worth the price (p. 92).

Researchers Daniel Kruger and Randy Nesse (2004, 2006a, 2006b) have completed a series of compelling studies that suggest men have long been more violent than women and that this is a worldwide phenomenon. Using mortality data from more than 20 countries, they documented that men age 15 to 34 are approximately three times more likely to die than women of their same age among samples from the U. S., Russia, Norway, and Croatia, among others. Where data are available, they suggest this 3:1 ratio has been stable through most of the 20th century. This is the time in life when males reach the apex of physical development, are most sexually virile, and are attempting to "make their mark" on the world. These researchers and their colleagues find a similar male-female ratio among "teen" and "young adult" chimpanzees. Among humans, homicide and suicide rates drive these disparities. Kruger and Nesse argue that homicide represents an extreme version of male vs. male competition for mates and status, while suicide represents self-identified failure in that same competition. They argue that the historical, cross-national, and cross-species data give credence to the argument that this violence is at least partially the result of evolutionary forces. However, we should remember that the apparent universality of a behavior does not guarantee that it is necessarily "hard-wired" (see Chapter Five for an alternate explanation).

General Critique of Evolutionary Psychology

Darwin himself expressed serious doubts that sexual selection processes are paramount in human behavior, particularly in modern societies (Eagly & Wood, 1999). Evolutionary psychology, like sociobiology before it, has faced serious criticism regarding its underlying propositions as well as some of its research claims.

Many people may find sociobiological theory to be compelling because it provides a simple explanation for a complex phenomenon or because it allows them to maintain the sexual status quo. This theory may be especially appealing for traditional men who may be motivated to dominate, disrespect, and overpower women, and to engage in competitions for dominance with other men. In bookstores, one usually finds sociobiological works in the biology section rather than the social science section despite the fact that these books are almost wholly focused on explaining social behavioral phenomena. It seems that many people view biology as "real" science and view the social sciences with a greater level of skepticism. The relative statuses of the sciences can be used to validate the unequal social statuses of men and women. Although sociobiological propositions based on the theory of evolution are subject to serious criticism, the theory of evolution itself is well accepted, and it may be difficult for an uncritical observer to separate the two. Sociobiologists look for biological correlates of behavior in a quest to prove that sex differences are of "real" nature, not "trivial" nurture (Money, 1987a).

Goldfoot and Neff (1987) argued that sociobiological methods were too simplistic. The typical approach is to hold constant, or to eliminate, social variables that are known to affect the behavior being studied. For example, researchers might study sexual behavior in primates by raising a male and a female primate in a cage together and observing some behavior of interest. Such research ignores the effects of known social influences such as dominance hierarchies and coalition formation within primate troops.

Other critics have pointed to circular or faulty logic. There is often an assumption in biopsychological research that animals (humans included) behave from the "inside out." If there is hormonal variation and change in behavior at the same time, the bias is to see the hormonal change as the cause of the behavioral change. There is evidence to suggest that a hormonal change may sometimes be an effect, rather than a cause, of behavioral change. For instance, although testosterone may be a partial cause of aggression, the attainment of dominance (sometimes through aggressive behavior) results in testosterone surges, both for humans (male and female) and animals, and therefore testosterone can also be seen as an effect of aggression (Archer, 2006; Sapolsky, 1997). This makes it difficult to determine when increases in testosterone cause aggression and when aggression causes an increase in testosterone. We review the link between testosterone and aggression in Chapter Twelve.

Most people can find a good demonstration of the influence of an environmental event on physiology in their experience. Consider the following scenario: you are very attracted to someone. You begin dating this person and become even more attracted to him or her. At some point, you kiss this person for the first time. You can feel some strong emotional changes (excitement, sexual arousal, happiness), and we could measure concomitant physiological changes in heart rate, respiration, sexual response, and brain waves. Although hormonal and neural fluctuations "caused" your emotional experience, is it not also true that the kiss "caused" the hormonal and neural changes? So, although the brain affects experience, experience also affects the brain. As Lise Eliot (2009) points out, the more that boys and girls engage in similar activities, the more similar their brains become.

Another logical error is the assumption that a widespread behavior must be genetically based. Anne Fausto-Sterling (1992) cites an example of a primate troop that learned a behavior and passed it down to its next generation. Someone who observed the behavior (which had become universal in the troop) in the second generation, might wrongly assume that this learned behavior was instinctual and genetically-based. In the laboratory, Frans de Waal (2005) has demonstrated several instances of cultural behavior transmission among primates. Fausto-Sterling's criticism is that sociobiologists assume that universal behaviors must be genetic and that genetic behaviors must be universal, a circular logic. Hubbard (1998) makes an eloquent counterargument:

> If a society puts half its children into short skirts and warns them not to move in ways that reveal their panties, while putting the other half into jeans and overalls, and encouraging them to climb trees, play ball, and participate in other vigorous outdoor games; if later, during adolescence, the children who have been wearing trousers are urged to 'eat like growing boys,' while the children in skirts are warned to watch their weight and not get fat; if the half in jeans runs around in sneakers or boots, while the half in skirts totters about on spike heels, then these two groups of people will be biologically as well as socially different. (p. 150)

The largest body of critical attacks on sociobiology comes from counterexamples of human and animal behavior that do not support the theory of differential reproductive strategies, some of which suggest a pattern of selective but "cherry-picked" examples. One challenge is to question the hypothesis that it is natural for all males to lack parental involvement. In some bird species, such as penguins, the male takes the major responsibility for incubating the eggs, and many birds mate for life. Male primates will protect or adopt orphaned infants, and in the pair-bonding marmoset, the father carries the young more often than the mother after the first few weeks of life (Rosenblum, 1987). Frans de Waal (1997) describes the behavior of the bonobo, a primate that is a close genetic relative of humans. Female bonobos occupy prominent positions in the primate society, which is cooperative and rarely aggressive. On both sides of the argument, the tendency is to choose specie-level examples with little attention to biological families or orders.

de Waal (2005) also notes that, contrary to the stereotype that they are aggressive bullies, most primate "alpha males" (those at the top of the troops' dominance hierarchies) are more accurately described as peacemakers or "populists" that break up fights and ensure that food is shared within the troop. He also noted that the Darwinian fitness tends to be interpreted as an ability to eliminate the unfit, but that there are many more ways to be fit than to be aggressive, such as having the ability to find food or de-escalate conflicts within the troop (de Waal, 2007).

Critics have pointed out that these types of evolutionary arguments are often used to justify double standards and the status quo. In humans, the greater involvement of females in the care of children can be accounted for largely by cultural factors. In most cultures, girls are encouraged to partake in nurturing behavior from an early age (Whiting & Edwards, 1988). In cultures that encourage boys to take part in caring for children, no sex differences are found in adult parental involvement (Basow, 1992).

Hubbard (1998) notes that some nineteenth-century physicians warned girls that developing their brains through education would sap energy from their reproductive organs and render them unable to bear children. Kimmel & Mosmiller (1992) note how purported biological explanations of women's "fragile" nature were used to argue against allowing women to vote or go to college in the United States. The assumptions about male promiscuity, violence, and competition for mates can be interpreted as justifying destructive masculine behaviors such as rape, violence, and indifference to children.

One could also construct a list of behaviors that are difficult to explain from a sociobiological perspective. Homosexuality and sexual behaviors other than genital intercourse are good examples. So are the large numbers of men who are faithful husbands and good fathers, and men who have never had a physical fight in their lives. Bleier (1984) lists a number of theoretically sound sociobiological hypotheses that are not supported by available data.

Critics have also noted that sociobiologists and evolutionary psychologists often ignore or explain away behaviors that do not fit their models. In the search for the universality of sex-dimorphic behavior across different animal species, one may find that animal behavior is much more diverse than it appears to be at first glance. Human behavior is even more diverse, as almost any social scientist will attest.

Despite many serious criticisms of this theory we should be careful not to "throw the baby out with the bath water." Many researchers who are not identified with sociobiology (e.g., Money, 1987a; Maccoby, 1987) agree that biology probably produces different sensitivities to behavioral influences in males and females. Social influence can exaggerate or modify these sensitivities, and possibly not in a simple, straightforward way. The quest to discover the relative strengths of biological vs. social influences and the nature of the interactions between them is ongoing. It seems certain, however, that biology does not constitute a "whole program" (Money, 1987a, p. 15) for behavior. A man is not "destined" to become violent or promiscuous any more than a tall person is "destined" to become a basketball player.

Gender-Based Critique of Evolutionary Claims.   Sociobiologists and evolution-ary psychologists temper their claims with the warnings that cultural influences are also important, that no predictions for individuals are possible, and that describing biological influences is different from prescribing how people should act (Barash and Lipton 1997). Nevertheless, a proposed description of a gender-typed "human nature" emerges, and the picture of "male nature" (as well as men's treatment of women) is not a pretty one. Although sociobiologists often propose that learning about sex dif-ferences in behavior will allow us to design social interventions that will result in a more gender-egalitarian and less violent world (Thornhill & Palmer, 2000), they rarely say specifically what these interventions should be, and their seeming lack of interest in modifying these destructive behaviors that they see as natural makes their motives suspect in the eyes of many of their critics.

The male is characterized as an aggressive, driven, immoral, impulsive, uncaring, unfaithful, distrustful, jealous, promiscuous, and cruel animal whose core motivation is to fight off other men and impregnate as many women as possible, at almost any cost, even risking his life in the pursuit of his evolutionary goals. This view serves to normalize and excuse many of the most destructive aspects of the masculine gender role: over-competitiveness, attention to task and not relationship, the unimportance of emotions other than sexual and aggressive feelings, and the risking of the body in the compulsive attempt to prove one's masculinity. However, a man can never prove his sociobiological masculinity once and for all, as there are always more men to fight off and more women to impregnate. He can never be sure of his own paternity, so he must be on guard against other men at all times. Eventually he will grow old and be sup-planted by younger and stronger men. The picture that emerges is one of a roaming, violent, restless creature who can never be satisfied.

From this perspectrive, the only hope for a civilized society is to tame the barbaric nature of masculinity. Sociobiologists see male nature as antisocial and valueless, and female nature more civilized, positive, and morally superior. They view the two sexes as inherently competitive with each other (Clatterbaugh, 1997). Gilder (1986) argues that a socialized order can only be maintained if male sexual impulses and antisocial tendencies are subordinated to female nature. He assigns the task of civilizing the world to women, who must use their erotic power to keep men in line by demanding monogamy and commitment from them in exchange for sexual access. The idea is that men have no control and that it is women's job to control them (as if women did not have enough to do!). This view would seem disrespectful towards men and downright exhausting for women.

Gilder's ideal society seems to be one with traditional morals, where women refuse to have sex before marriage, and where monogamy is strictly enforced. Many sociobiologists do not believe that this arrangement will work because of the primacy of biological forces over social ones (Barash, 1982). For these theorists, "boys will be boys" forever, and therefore war, rape, and the adversarial "battle of the sexes" is unavoidable.

This ideal normalizes the sexual double standard, male sexual irresponsibility, vio-lence, noninvolvement with children, and a lack of a human connection with women. If we see these attributes as biologically ordained, then there is little hope in changing the standard of male dominance. Several authors (Fausto-Sterling, 1992; Kimmel & Mosmiller, 1992; Tavris, 1992) have noted that, historically, arguments that appeal to science have been used to justify the exclusion of women from public status equal to that of men and to defend gender inequality as the natural and unchangeable order of things. Gould (1981) noted that the same kind of process has been used to exclude people of color from equal participation in the public sphere. Sociobiologists downplay the effects of social forces, specifically a historical imbalance of power between the sexes (see Chapter Four), that provide plausible alternative explanations to their claims.

Specific Critiques of Evolutionary Claims. Criticism has also focused on the choice to position promiscuous sexuality and acts of violence as the basis for human sex differences because these are relatively infrequent behaviors. Public health studies reveal that no more than 5 percent of men report having three or more sexual partners for each of three consecutive years (Dariotis et al., 2008; Humblet et al., 2003) and other studies indicate that no more than 15 percent to 20 percent have more than three partners in any given year (Smiler, 2013). Violence, especially at the level of criminal assault or homicide, is committed by a very small percentage of men (Kilmartin, 2010).

Natalie Angier (1999a), challenges the argument of differential reproductive investment, arguing that male promiscuity is not a sound evolutionary strategy:

> Just how good a reproductive strategy is this chronic, random shooting of the gun? A woman is fertile only two or three days a month. Her ovulation is concealed. The man doesn't know when she's fertile. She might be in the early stages of pregnancy when he gets to her; she might still be lactating and thus not ovulating. Moreover, even if our hypothetical Don Juan hits a day on which a woman is ovulating, his sperm only has a 20 percent chance of fertilizing her egg; human reproduction is complicated, and most eggs and sperm are not up to the demands of proper fusion. Even if conception occurs, the resulting embryo has a 25 to 30 percent chance of miscarrying at some point in gestation. In sum, each episode of fleeting sex has a remarkably small probability of yielding a baby…the probability is less than one percent. And because the man is beating and running, he isn't able to prevent any of his one-night stands from turning around and mating with other men…[If he were] to spend a bit more time with one woman…the odds of his getting the woman during her fertile time would increase and he'd be monopolizing her energy and keeping her from the advances of other sperm-bearers. It takes the average couple four months, or 120 days, of regular sexual intercourse to become pregnant. That number of days is approximately equal to the number of partners our hypothetical libertine needs to sleep with to have one of them result in a 'fertility unit,' that is, a baby. (pp. 336–337)

SST's methods and findings have been critiqued directly. One of the most persistent, and perhaps most concerning, challenge comes from the fact that studies examining the desired number of sexual partners rely almost exclusively on the use of undergraduate students and that the modal, or most common, answer is one partner in the next 30 days. This response is typically produced by more than half of the young men who complete surveys. Keep in mind that these are anonymous surveys and the vast majority of survey participants are unmarried 18- to 22-year-old men who live on college campuses alongside thousands of 18- to 22-year-old women. If there were ever a group of young men who could "get away with" saying they wanted to have a lot of partners in a short time period, this would be the group. Yet the common finding is that approximately 25 percent of men say they want 2 or more partners in the next 30 days (Hazan & Diamond, 2000; Smiler, 2011). There is a large male-female difference because approximately 6 percent of women express a desire for multiple partners in that time frame (e.g., Schmitt et al., 2003).

Critics have also pointed out that:

- Regardless of whether a society allows polygyny or polygamy, only a small percentage of the population actually has multiple long term partners (Murdock, 1967).

- Persistent evidence of a male-female difference in number of actual sexual partners or willingness to have sex with a stranger does not tell us anything about cause. Sexual double standards are also a logical cause.

THE CHILD INSIDE THE MAN: PSYCHOANALYTIC PERSPECTIVES

It is fitting that a discussion of psychoanalysis follows one of biology; the two are somewhat related. Psychoanalysis is based on the interaction of childhood psychological history with purported biological and psychological instincts. The biological perspective is that prenatal events set up propensities for behavior; the analytic perspective attempts to specify the interplay of these propensities and the important events of early childhood.

Psychoanalysis is a psychology of *meaning*. In the area of gender, it addresses questions about the deep, underlying sense of the masculine self in the adult man's life, as understood in the context of the impact of childhood psychological dramas. Many analytic writers view masculine gender behaviors as the result of the typical early experience of being a boy, one that differs markedly from that of being a girl.

There are several different versions of psychoanalytic theories, and so a good starting point is to address the question, "What makes a theory psychoanalytic?" May (1986) suggests that there are four broad commonalities among these theories. First, analytic theories emphasize the importance of *unconscious processes*. These are the areas of an individual's mind which are outside of awareness, but that nevertheless have effects on behavior and identity. Analytic theorists believe that these deeper regions of the psyche are more important in understanding behavior than the conscious sense of self or the person's thought processes. Psychoanalytic theory is often referred to as an "iceberg theory." Just as most of an iceberg lies beneath the surface of the water, most psychological functioning lies beneath the surface of consciousness. From this perspective, masculinity is a deep process that goes to the core of a man's being and affects a great deal of his behavior, often without his awareness.

Second, analytic theories emphasize a *developmental and historical approach* to understanding behavior. They consider the relevance of early childhood experience to be profound, and they view the adult's behavior as reflecting and reworking childhood psychological issues. The psychoanalytic view of behavior in the gender role arena is that it is mostly a result of the boy's early relationship with his parents.

Third, analytic theories emphasize the importance of *biology and body.* When we combine this emphasis with the relevance of early childhood, we see the importance of the child's awareness of self as separate from mother, the awareness of physical sex differences, and the emergence of sexual feelings in the construction of masculinity.

Finally, analytic theories emphasize the inescapability of *internal conflict.* The person is seen as inevitably caught in the middle of at least two great and irresolvable forces. A man finds himself struggling with the demands of instinct vs. social demands, desire for women vs. fear of women, dependency needs vs. desire for independence, feminine vs. masculine feelings, and the desire for something that he cannot possess. These conflicts are seen as having a never-ending quality; nobody can ever resolve them completely. The best the person can hope for is to develop a workable compromise, such as finding a comfortable way to deal with the need to be connected and the need to be on one's own at the same time.

The Freudian Legacy

Few thinkers have had as much impact on the world as Sigmund Freud (1856–1939). His prolific works, along with those of analytic theorists who followed him, provide interesting and controversial frameworks for the understanding of men and masculinity. Freud's perspective on gender can best be understood in the context of his personality theory. Therefore, we now provide a thumbnail sketch of the parts of this theory that are relevant to men's issues.

A major tenet of Freud's biological orientation is the importance of instinct in shaping personality. Instincts are innate bodily conditions which give direction to psychological processes (Hall, Lindzey, & Campbell, 1998). They include hunger, thirst, need for oxygen, body temperature regulation, aggression, and the reproductive instinct. Freud believed that, in contrast to more basic instincts like hunger and thirst, the complex sexual and aggressive instincts (broadly, love and hate) can be expressed through a wide variety of behaviors, attitudes, and emotions. For instance, one can love a person, or love learning, conversation, money, or creative pursuits. Likewise, one can express animosity toward a person, or an idea, or the self. For Freud, the personality is largely a result of the person's pattern of expressing the sexual and aggressive instincts. And, as mentioned earlier, most of this psychic functioning occurs in the unconscious.

If instinctual gratification were the only problem we ever faced, life might not be easy, but it would be rather uncomplicated. However, because we live with other people, instinctual needs inevitably come into conflict with the social world. One cannot merely act out an aggressive instinct because he or she might hurt someone else and be punished for it. The person must learn how to gratify needs in a socially acceptable way. The process of maturing is one in which primitive, impulse-driven people become transformed into civilized people who are able to delay gratification until the appropriate time and place. A good deal of what we teach children in kindergarten and elementary school is in the service of learning impulse control and social rules: wait your turn, share, consider others' feelings, and so on.

From the Freudian perspective, newborns are nothing more than instinctually driven bundles of biology with storehouses of psychic energy. Infants are helpless, and parents or caretakers work hard at fulfilling children's instincts. They feed babies, keep them warm enough, and remove irritants from their bodies when they change their diapers. Babies are incapable of doing these things for themselves; they need help to manage their instincts. The part of the personality that is primitive, instinctual, and present at birth is called the *id*. It is a collection of biological needs and undirected psychic energy.

Slowly, children begin to develop another part of personality. They become less and less helpless as they grow. Early in life, people have to feed them, but after a while they begin to grab the food themselves and put it into their mouths. Around age two or three, a new part of personality, the *ego*, begins to form. The ego is more organized than the id and can deal with the real world. In the healthy person, the ego gains more and more strength as the person matures. The ego can plan, and it mediates between the id and the outside world until a suitable object can be found. It becomes the center of the personality, the person's identity. (Note that the Freudian term ego is different from the common social use of the term, which implies self-absorption).

Eventually, parents begin to make social demands on children, and because children are attached to parents, they begin to internalize these demands. In other words, we all carry our parents around with us, for better or worse. The first important imposition of social demand is toilet training, when, for the first time, the child is required to exert physical control over an instinctual process (Hall, Lindzey, & Campbell, 1998).

Robert Bly (1988) is fond of saying, "You came into this world with all kinds of energy, but your parents wanted a 'nice boy' [or a 'nice girl']." In some ways, parents care less about instinctual gratification than they care about your being socialized. They want you to be able to handle your instincts and live in the social world. Freud called the internalized parent the *superego*, which starts to develop around age five or six and has two parts. The *ego ideal* contains our parents' aspirations for us. It is this part of the superego that makes us feel good when we do something our parents value, like achieving in school. The other part, the *conscience*, causes us to feel guilty or ashamed when we go against parental wishes.

After the formation of the superego, the ego finds itself in a clash between id, which is always pulling for pleasure, and superego, which is always pushing for perfection. Thus, it mediates between these two internal forces as well as the outside world. The healthy person has *ego strength*, which allows him or her to balance these conflicting demands. If the id dominates the personality, the person will be impulsive and antisocial. If the superego dominates, he or she will be tense and uncomfortable due to the unrelieved tension of the instincts (Hall, Lindzey, & Campbell, 1998).

What do id, ego, and superego have to do with masculinity? We can make a number of important connections of both the positive and the negative aspects of masculine gender roles. The analytic ideal is a paragon of positive masculinity: the person who can love and work. Such a man can achieve a satisfactory balance between his biological and his social sides. He is able to be responsible both in his work and his dedication to his partner and family.

Note here that the analytic ideal is quite the social conformist, but note also that there are many men who fit this description: dedicated, principled, hard-working, caring individuals who enjoy life and contribute to the greater good. In psychoanalytic terms, the man described above has high ego strength, which was built by his having learned to deal with problems and assert his will. He is also a person with a strong ego ideal and a reasonable conscience. He can be goal directed and achieving. Socially, society encourages the development of these structures in men. Some men are not so fortunate, however. Destructive masculinity can be conceptualized as being the result of poor superego development, rigid, harsh, or destructive content of the superego, or poor ego strength.

Theoretically, the id is constant. It is biological and innate, so it exerts about the same amount of influence on everybody. Differences among people reflect differences in the way the id is handled and directed. In the case of poor ego and superego development, the id is the most powerful part of the personality, and so it is allowed to run amok. The result is a person who is antisocial and destructive, giving vent to sexual and aggressive impulses without restraint. Sometimes, parents and the society at large teach girls to worry about everyone else except themselves and boys to only worry about themselves. Both of these lessons are problematic because they both lead to a poor balance of id and superego.

We can conceptualize violent criminals as people with poor ego and superego development. Most of these people are men. In fact, males commit more than four of every five violent crimes in the United States (FBI, 2011). The major inhibitor of destructive id impulses is the superego, which makes the boy feel guilty when he is destructive and good when he is prosocial. According to Freud, male superego development depends critically on a boy's identification with his father or "father figure." If the father is absent, emotionally distant, or overly punitive, the identification is weakened. Unfortunately, a lot of fathers fit this description. According to psychoanalytic theory, a lack of ego ideal in the boy leaves him aimless and unable to reward or restrain himself appropriately.

It is also possible for id and superego to be strong but the ego to be weak. In this case, the result is a pattern of behavior in which the person does things which are harmful to someone else, feels guilty about it and expresses regret, but then repeats the same bad behavior later. Baseball great Babe Ruth fit this pattern. He was well known for his public misbehavior. Occasionally, he felt guilty about his negative effects on people, especially on children who looked up to him as a hero and role model, and he would make heartfelt public apologies for his misdeeds. Nevertheless, he would continue to engage in embarrassing incidents, not because he was insincere in his apologies, but because, if one applies Freudian theory, he lacked the ego strength to restrain the id in a society that fails to hold elite athletes accountable for their behavior.

In other cases, the content of the superego may be especially harsh, rigid, and/or destructive. This may happen if the parents' demands on the child are extreme. If the parent inculcates the demands of destructive masculinity into the boy, he will have a punitive superego that can make him feel chronically unworthy and unmasculine. This is the case for many men, for whom the superego demands that he be competitive, wealthy, in control at all times, and dominant over women.

The Oedipus Conflict

We can see another important perspective on masculinity in Freud's model of psychosexual development. Freud believed that instinctual energy (called *libido*) courses through stages of psychosexual development that are defined in relation to certain parts of the body (called *erogenous zones*). Each stage entails a crisis which the child must resolve to achieve healthy psychosexual development.

Following the oral and anal stages, in which boys and girls go through similar developmental challenges, children enter the phallic stage, and Freud proposed that sex differences emerge at that time. The phallic period (roughly, between age three and six) is the first primitive manifestation of what will later become adult sexuality. Children at this age become very aware of and concerned about sex differences. Masturbatory activity and some forms of sexual play among children at this age are not unusual.

Freud believed that, for both boys and girls, sexual interest at this stage centers around the penis (hence the term phallic, which refers to the penis, rather than a term that refers to the genitalia of either sex). The child also begins to experience unconscious sexual feelings toward the other-sex parent. It is not unusual for the girl to say she is going to marry her father or a boy, his mother. As a result of the desire for the other-sex parent, the child unconsciously perceives the same-sex parent as a rival for the affection of the other parent. This is a psychologically dangerous and uncomfortable love triangle, and the child must resolve this difficulty. Freud called this crisis the *Oedipus conflict*, after the king of Thebes in Greek mythology who kills his father and marries his mother.

A boy feels desire for his mother, who is affectionate and caring. Strong sexual feelings are centered in his genitals, and he betrays this fact by touching his penis often. Parents often punish this masturbatory activity, and the boy gets the message that he might get punished by having his penis removed. This *castration anxiety* is also fueled by the rivalry with his big, powerful father, who might punish him for having these feelings toward his mother. When the boy first sees female genitalia, he perceives the female as a castrated male and unconsciously perceives that this fate could befall him (Freud, 1924/1989).

At the height of the Oedipal conflict, the boy senses that gratifying his desire for his mother would mean losing his penis, and it's just not worth it. In the normal resolution of this psychic conflict, he gives up these sexual feelings for his mother and displaces them on to a more appropriate object, such as the girl next door. Part of this solution involves the boy's development of a psychological identification with his father. Identification allows the son to feel less threatened by his father and also to experience romantic feelings with the mother vicariously through the father. This is an important step in superego development, as the boy begins to internalize the father's values and characteristics. The sexual love for the mother is converted into feelings of tender affection.

Box 3.2   Freud, Women, and Femininity

Freud believed that girls experience themselves as castrated males, and that therefore when they desire their fathers and see their mothers as rivals, their love is mixed with bitter feelings because they want a protruding sex organ like their father's. Thus, according to Freud, girls suffer from *penis envy*. The resolution to girls' conflict is to give up her desire for her father and displace it onto another male. Freud thought that penis envy was converted into the desire to bear a child. He also thought that, because girls do not experience the powerful motivator of castration threat, they do not give up their father desire as easily and they do not identify with their mothers as fully. As a result, they have less well developed superegos. Freud once stated that women are morally inferior to men for this reason (Freud, 1915/1989).

Many theorists have roundly criticized Freud for this view of women. The great feminist analyst Karen Horney (1932) countered that women envy men's privileged social positions, not their penises. In support of this hypothesis, Nathan (1981) demonstrated through cross-cultural research that penis envy dreams among women are more common in cultures where women have low social status. Horney's view is that a girl's psychosexual development centers around her own genitalia, and not the male's. Hare-Mustin and Maracek (1990a) noted Freud's sexism in his characterization of "women's bodies as *not having* a penis rather than as *having* the female external genitalia." (p. 32, emphasis original). Freud himself felt unsatisfied with this part of his theory, as he knew many women whose moral development equaled or surpassed that of men. At one point, Freud stated that it was the task of

women analysts to describe the female psyche (Freud, 1915/1989).

Freud's theoretical construction of the Oedipus conflict was partly based on the famous case of "Dora" (Freud, 1905/1963), an 18–year-old patient whom Freud saw for eleven weeks of psychoanalysis in 1900 to treat a number of psychological and psychophysiological symptoms (e.g. migraine headaches and depression) (Gay, 1989). Dora reported to Freud that, when she was 14 years old, Herr K., a close friend of her father, had embraced and kissed her against her will. Dora was quite disgusted and unnerved by Herr K.'s behavior. She told her parents about it and requested that they break off their friendship with Herr K. and his wife. Dora's father confronted Herr K., who emphatically denied that he had made sexual advances toward Dora, and Dora's father believed his friend rather than his daughter.

Eventually, Freud came to believe that Dora was really in love with Herr K., and he insisted that Dora's disgust was a disguise for her real feelings of sexual arousal. In historical perspective, we now know that it is not unusual for adult men to make such advances upon young girls nor for girls to respond as Dora did. Hare-Mustin and Maracek (1990a) point to the importance of Freud's reframing of Dora's experience in the patriarchal context of privileging men's perspectives over women's. In effect, Freud blamed the victim for her emotional reaction and relegated her perspective to a secondary position to his own, implying that he (and men) knew Dora (and women) better than she knew herself. As psychoanalysis became scientific orthodoxy, its antifeminine character further justified the marginalization of women.

Oedipus and Masculinity

Theoretically, the childhood Oedipal crisis colors the adult man's approach to relationships with women (originally represented by mother) and authority figures (originally represented by father). Fine's (1987) view of the Oedipal situation is that confusion results when parents or other adults punish the boy's sexual expression. He loves his mother, but he cannot approach her sexually, and an early split between sex and affection can result. These are the roots of the so called "Madonna/Whore complex." The man feels that virtuous women, those whom he respects, are not sexual (the Madonna was conceived without original sin—absolutely pure), and that sexual women ("whores") are not worthy of respect. Thus, he has a tendency to degrade a woman if she is sexual with him. This sexuality/love contradiction causes extreme problems in the man's relationships with women and perhaps in his sexual functioning. The boy who successfully resolves the Oedipal conflict becomes a man who can love and be sexual with the same woman. The boy who does not may grow up to be misogynist, promiscuous, or sexually dysfunctional as he plays out the unresolved Oedipal drama again and again. As Freud (1924/1989) said, "the finding of an object [Freud's term for the thing or person that fulfills the instinct] is in fact a refinding of it" (p. 288).

Fathering may have an important effect on the Oedipal situation. If the father is caring and attentive to the boy, he will facilitate his son's positive identification with him and mitigate the son's castration anxiety. If, however, the father is harsh, punitive, and demanding with his son, the identification process will cause the boy to become intropunitive, and castration anxiety may be exaggerated. The boy grows up fearful and without a strong sense of himself as masculine. He may act "macho" to cover up his insecurity. He may be aggressive to defend against the unconscious threat of castration (Tyson, 1986), or he may derogate women to feel better about his masculinity. Lisak (1991) noted that sexual assault perpetrators have feelings of bitterness toward their fathers, who caused them to feel inadequate and unmasculine.

Critique of Freudian Theory

Many criticisms of Freud are leveled at his assumption that sexual instinct is the primary determinant of personality. Even some of his closest followers abandoned the sexual theory, although most maintained their belief in the importance of the unconscious and early childhood events. If we look at the parent-child attachment as one that is not primarily sexual, very different conclusions about male functioning become possible. And, even if one accepts the premise that sexuality is the basis of human personality, some of Freud's conclusions are open to debate. The description of castration anxiety as being fairly resolvable is highly contested.

Freud's position is that the Oedipal crisis in the boy is touched off by his realization that he could lose something valuable. In the girl, it is stimulated by her imagining that she has already lost it. If you have lost something valuable, it is greatly disappointing at first. After a while, you usually accept that it is gone and move on. If, however, you have a deep-seated fear of losing something, you are obligated to anxiously protect it all of your life. The penis is also in somewhat of a vulnerable place, being outside of the body. It seems that castration anxiety would follow many more men into adulthood than penis envy (if it exists at all) would follow women.

In 1932, Karen Horney published a classic essay on male psychology entitled *The Dread of Women* in which she argues that the process of psychosexual development produces in the boy a profound yet unconscious fear of the feminine, and that much stereotypical masculine behavior in adulthood is a reflection of this dread. Horney argued that the vagina, with its ability to engulf, is a psychic threat to the male. The threat of castration by the father does not approach the threat of engulfment from the mother. Horney illustrated this in metaphor: "Sampson, whom no man could conquer, is robbed of his strength by Delilah" (Horney, 1932/1966, p. 84).

If, as Freud believed, the other-sex parent is the love object in this stage, then the size difference between parent and child leads to a difference in how boys and girls experience themselves. Girls, Horney believed, begin to have unconscious desires to take in the penis. If the father is the love object, then her vagina is too small for him, and so she fears that he could hurt her. The boy, with his mother as love object, senses that his penis is much too small for her, and reacts with feelings of inadequacy. He anticipates that his mother (and later other love objects) will ridicule and deride him.

The implications of Horney's theory for masculine psychology are far reaching. Horney proposed that every man has a deep sense of apprehension that a woman can destroy his self-respect, and that his penis (and thus his manhood) is not large enough nor good enough. Masculinity, then, is never on very solid ground. Rather it is fraught with dread, and the man must make extreme efforts to manage his anxiety around his masculine adequacy. He has basically two options: he can withdraw from women or compensate for these uncomfortable feelings.

Withdrawal solutions include staying away from women either physically or emotionally. Compensation solutions involve going to extremes to prove one's manhood over and over again. Part of this strategy may involve debasing and controlling women. By doing so, the man can deny the that women have the power to hurt him. At the extreme of masculine inadequacy, we see desperate behaviors like rape and domestic violence, which can be seen as aggressive reactions to the extreme dread of the feminine. Horney goes so far as to suggest that patriarchy, men's institutional oppression of women, is a reaction to this inadequacy in the collective male psyche. Horney's theory also provides a possible explanation of the core attitude of antifemininity that characterizes traditional masculinity.

IDENTIFYING WITH MOM: EGO PSYCHOLOGY AND MASCULINITY

Many of the theorists who followed Freud disagreed with him on one major point. They believed that some aspects of ego functioning were independent of the id. For these theorists, the ego is not something that merely serves to direct and control the instincts, but also drives the person to deal with basic psychological tasks like developing a sense of self, relating to others, learning to work, and developing values. Many of these "neo-analytic" theories center around the person's motivation to develop a sense of identity.

People's behavior varies across different situations and roles, but identity is the part of the person that ties all of this varying behavior together. The formation of this sense of self begins in infancy with the child's realization that he or she is separate from the mother. As the individual progresses through adolescence and adulthood, the expression of identity can be seen through a variety of decisions around relationships, work, sexuality, values, and preferences.

Gender identity is the part of overall identity that defines for the person what it means to be male or female. After children learn that they are not a part of their mothers, boys learn that they are similar to their fathers and different from their mothers in a basic way, and girls learn the converse. Children as young as two to four years of age become very upset if someone says to them "What a nice girl (or boy) you are," using the incorrect sex label, evidence that gender identity is learned very early and that it has a strong emotional component (Lewis, 1987). The strength of the emotion associated with gender identity attests to its central place in overall identity, although the origin of that centrality (biological, social, and/or cultural) is open to question.

Because of sex-differentiated child rearing, the formation of gender identity is thought to proceed very differently for males and females, with important implications for the personalities of adult men and women. Gender identity is formed mainly through the child's interactions with his or her parents, and women are the primary caretakers of infants in most cultures. The amount of time a typical mother spends with the infant far outweighs the typical father's time (Cohen, 1998). Thus, the most striking sex difference in early parent-child interactions is that girls are usually raised mainly by the same-sex parent, boys by the other-sex parent.

Ruth Hartley (1959) first proposed that the impact of this sex difference in early experience is considerable. Before they perceive sex differences in early childhood, children of both sexes feel continuous with their mothers and thus identify with her. In the formation of gender identity, girls learn "I am what mom is." They experience themselves as continuous with their mothers and define themselves through the process of attachment. This process continues in the same direction throughout childhood, since girls are the same sex as their mothers.

Boys, on the other hand, learn "I am what mom is not" more than they learn "I am what dad is." The boy experiences himself as different from the mother and defines himself through the process of separation. "I am what mom is not" defines the content of gender identity in a negative way. Rather that starting out with some sense of masculinity, the boy starts out with a sense of antifemininity.

Boys' gender identity development critically depends on switching tracks. From this view, boys must put rigid boundaries between themselves and their mothers to define themselves as masculine. If we believe that some identification with the mother has already taken place by the time a boy knows that he is different from her, then the separation process entails a repression of the mother identification.

Freud (1910/1989) believed that homosexuality was one possible result, and it would not be difficult to find people who agree. Assuming a gender binary, the logic says that if a boy does too many feminine things, he might end up identifying with women. He would then end up being like a woman in every way, including a sexuality that is oriented toward men (and adherents to this position usually see homosexuality as a decidedly negative developmental outcome, although Freud did not). However, Kurdek (1988) reported that gay men and lesbians are more likely to exhibit a mixture of masculine and feminine characteristics as opposed to a set of characteristics usually seen in the other sex. In other words, they tend to be relatively androgynous in their gender expression, not *inverted*, as Freud thought. It is also worth noting that there is a great deal of variation in gender role behavior within the populations of gays and lesbians, just as there is within the population of heterosexuals.

These dramas get played out again and again, according to analytic theory. The result of this separation process is that the boy's gender identity rests on his putting rigid psychological barriers not just between himself and mother, but between himself and anything feminine. Included are "feminine activities" and, of course, girls and women themselves. Having already identified with the mother, the boy must also repress the feminine parts of himself, usually represented by his emotional experiences and feelings of relatedness to others. Girls are under no such pressure. They do not have to deny the masculine to define themselves as feminine (Chodorow, 1978). This is one possible explanation for the tolerance of "tomboys" but not "sissies." Martin (1995) reported that stereotypes of tomboys resembled stereotypes of traditional boys. However, the stereotype of the sissy did not resemble that of a traditional girl. Instead, it was defined narrowly and related to many negative characteristics.

Alan Johnson (2001), notes that there are derogatory terms for men who are dominated by their wives (e.g., henpecked or "whipped") but no corresponding terms for women who are dominated by their husbands. A psychoanalytic thinker—and Johnson is not one—might theorize that female domination in a relationship is seen as a threat to masculine identity.

The mother-identified parts of the boy are relegated to the unconscious because they pose a threat to the ego. When "feminine" experiences like sentimental feelings or a desire for attachment surface from the unconscious, they generate anxiety, which the boy must then defend against. In a typical scenario, a man may go to a sentimental movie, begin to identify with a character and feel some strong and vulnerable emotions. He may sense that this experience is a threat to his masculinity and detach himself from his feelings by putting his mind on something else. Eventually, he may begin to avoid these types of movies. Traditionally masculine men in mainstream United States culture often avoid movies that have feminine themes, calling them "chick flicks" that hold no interest for them.

The early childhood gender-typed mix of separation and attachment is considered by some to result in an enduring approach to the world. Nancy Chodorow (1978) described women as "selves in communion," meaning that they tend to experience themselves in the context of relationships, and men as "selves in separation," oriented toward independence and task completion.

From this standpoint, a straightforward solution to male antifeminine anxiety is an increase in fathers' involvement in child care. Coltrane (1998) provides some anthropological evidence in support of the hypothesis that antifemininity results from boys' lack of meaningful contact with their fathers. He notes that in cultures in which men participate in child rearing (and in which women have the power to control property), there are "significantly fewer displays of manliness, less wifely deference, less husband dominance, and less ideological female inferiority..." (p. 81). One psychoanalytic interpretation is that, because fathers are more psychologically available to sons, there is less need for compulsive separation from the mother, thus less fear of women and femininity, and thus less of a need to compensate for this fear through hypermasculine posturing and mistreatment of women.

SUMMARY

1. There is little doubt among developmental psychologists that biology affects personality and behavior, although there is little consensus about the extent of these effects. Because there are some differences in male and female biology, there is a good deal of speculation and research about the behavioral implications of these differences.

2. Chromosomal and hormonal differences appear to cause differences, at least at the level of comparisons between males and females.

3. The exact mechanisms linking chromosomes and hormones to demonstrated behavior remain unclear, and hormone levels do not appear to reliably predict differences within sex-based groups.

4. Evolutionary psychology assumes that biology profoundly affects behavior by establishing predispositions toward certain activities. These predispositions have survival value for the organism and its genes, and thus they were established through the process of evolution.

5. Evolutionary psychology argues that major behavioral sex differences are thought to reflect different male and female reproductive strategies. Males who impregnate a large number of females are "successful" from an evolutionary standpoint because they insure maximum and varied reproduction of their genes. In contrast to females, males can participate in the reproductive process with a minimum investment of time and resources. Differences in reproductive strategies are thought to underlie important differences in male and female "nature."

6. Social scientists have leveled a number of theoretical and methodological criticisms against evolutionary psychology and its predecessor, sociobiology. Criticism includes concerns about oversimplification, logical errors, highly selected examples, and a failure to consider other explanations. Some critics charge these approaches with being patriarchal ideology disguised as science.

7. Psychoanalytic approaches to the understanding of masculinity emphasize biological, unconscious, and early childhood determinants of behavior.

8. Freud emphasized the role of sexual instinct and its conflict with social forces. If the young boy does not develop a strong social structure (superego), he will become impulsive, destructive, self-absorbed, and antisocial.

9. According to Freudian theory, the most important period for the development of masculine gender identity is the phallic stage (ages 3 to 6), in which the boy

experiences strong sexual feelings for his mother and views his father as a rival. He fears that he will be castrated for these desires, and so he transfers his sexual feelings onto a more appropriate object. If the Oedipal crisis is resolved poorly, the boy may later have sexual problems and/or problems relating to women.

10. Karen Horney viewed the Oedipal period as a time when males developed deep-seated feelings of insecurity associated with the feminine. She believed that misogyny and even violence toward women are attempts to compensate for masculine inadequacy.

11. Ego psychology theories emphasize the processes of attachment and separation in early childhood. Because boys are usually raised mainly by their mothers, they must put rigid boundaries between themselves and the feminine to attain a strong sense of masculinity. Males tend to avoid "feminine" behaviors because they are accompanied by anxiety, causing difficulty when situations call for such behavior.

Chapter Four

"It's the Way I was Raised":
Socially-Based Theoretical Perspectives
on Males and Gender

Boys and girls are treated differently from each other in nearly all cultures (Gilmore, 1990; Whiting & Edwards, 1988). In this chapter, we explore several approaches that take the social setting as the starting point for explanations of gender. Social approaches position gender-typed behavior as the result of how children are raised, so they focus on the child's experiences and understanding of gender, as well as cultural messages they receive during their formative years and beyond.

In a study conducted by Katherine Karraker, Dena Vogel, and Margaret Lake (1995), fathers and mothers were asked to describe their infants in a series of open-ended comments at two days of age and then a week later. Parents were equally likely to use gender-typed terms, such as "big" or "strong" to describe their sons and "pretty" or "beautiful" to describe their daughters at two days of age. A week later, fathers maintained their gender-typed language but mothers had scaled it back. Parents were also asked to rate their children on a variety of characteristics using a 1- to 9-point scale. They rated boys as stronger, hardier, more masculine, and less fine-featured than girls. For the record, baby boys and baby girls have the same average size. We don't know if you've spent any time with newborns, but we can assure you they don't do much more than eat, sleep, and poop at that age. And it's not as though the uterus includes weightlifting or Pilates classes.

Or imagine that you are visiting the house of some friends who are the parents of an eight-year-old boy, as John Lynch and Christopher Kilmartin (2013) suggested. The boy tells you that he wants to show you his room and you agree. When he opens the bedroom door, what do you expect to see? When you offer to play with him, do you expect to "horse around," play catch, or have a tea party? When you ask him about being a grown up, do you focus on career or his plans to become a parent?

If you were to look at most middle class children's bedrooms, you would probably have little difficulty guessing the sex of the child. Girls' bedrooms often contain dolls

(Snow, Jacklin, & Maccoby, 1981) and are often decorated with flowers, lace, or other stereotypically feminine designs. Boys' bedrooms often contain sports equipment and transportation toys (Pomerleau, Bolduc, Malcuit, & Cossette, 1990).

In the first half of this chapter, we'll describe some research examining children's early experience with gender, the importance of the environments that children are placed in, and some key milestones in gender development. In the second half, we'll review some theories that help us understand how these factors shape children into gender-typed beings.

THE GENDERED CHILD: EARLY EXPERIENCE

Developmental psychologists often describe parents as children's first teachers, and that is certainly the case for learning gender. Even before birth, many parents (and their families and friends) often choose gender-based colors, clothing, and toys for the newborn. Can you imagine gifting a baby boy with a pink outfit? (Do boys get "outfits?") Buying him Princess movies at age two or three?

It doesn't stop there. Parents tend to communicate gender stereotypes in children's play and household chores (Lytton & Romney, 1991). Parents in Western cultures, especially fathers, play with boys more roughly, perhaps as a result of the perception that boys are stronger and tougher, although this pattern is not universal (Hewlett, 2005). Children who choose gender-typed toys tend to get more positive responses from their parents than those who do not (Caldera, Huston, & O'Brien, 1989). Recall from Chapter One, Carver and Vaccaro's (2007) research demonstrating that children are very sensitive to parents' expressions of disgust even before they learn how to talk. An uncomfortable parent does not have to say anything or even intend to communicate to the child that he or she is choosing a "gender inappropriate" toy or activity; children nevertheless are influenced by parents' facial expressions of disapproval.

Developmental psychologists often view play and family activity as a rehearsal for later social roles. For instance, putting puzzles together is rehearsal for task completion and problem solving. "Playing house" is a rehearsal for relationships and domestic work. Here again, parents tend to be gender-typed in their treatment of children. Boys are taught to develop structures, to experiment with new approaches to solving problems, to attend to task and performance, and to master the situation. Girls are encouraged to be cooperative and compliant (Block, 1984). In household chores, parents often assign boys activities that take them away from the residence, such as yard work, animal care, or taking out the garbage, whereas girls are assigned more domestic chores such as baby sitting, cooking, or doing dishes (Ferrar, Olds, & Waters, 2012; Rowlands, Pilgrim, & Eston, 2008). Although parents' choices may reflect differences in activity levels (Pellegrini, 2004), this pattern of chores keeps girls physically closer to adults both at home and at school, while boys are given more distance. Reflecting on this longstanding pattern (Inchley, Currie, Todd, Akhtar, & Currie, 2005; Lytton & Romney, 1991), developmental psychologist Jeanne Block (1984) described these practices as giving boys "wings" and girls "roots."

Comparisons of fathers' and mothers' gender typing of children reveal that fathers tend to be more stereotypic in their definitions of gender appropriate activities, especially with their sons (Lytton & Romney, 1991). That finding was also true for descriptions of newborns; stereotypical descriptions and ratings were strongest when fathers described sons (Karraker et al., 1995). Perhaps as a consequence of their less frequent contact with children, fathers embellish a lack of information by the use of stereotypes (Basow, 1992). Overall, the level of a son's gender stereotyping is strongly related to the father's level (Tennenbaum & Leaper, 2002). In some ways, father presence (vs. absence) may be the cause; boys raised by a heterosexual couple are more stereotypically masculine than boys raised by their single mothers (Stevenson & Black, 1988).

Another consistent research finding is that boys are punished for cross-gender behavior earlier in life and more harshly than girls (Carver, Egan, & Perry, 2003; Wood et al., 2013). Saying to a boy, "you run like a girl," is a frequent insult. A girl can associate with a male group without fearing a loss of status, yet boys who play with girls or prefer stereotypically feminine activities are often ridiculed by and ostracized from male social groups (Carver et al., 2003; Maccoby, 1998). Because of punishment for "feminine" behaviors, boys may begin to view femininity and females with contempt. The inclusion of antifemininity as part of our cultural definition of masculinity has its developmental origins in this devaluing of attributes and behaviors that are thought to be reserved for females.

The typical family, as well as other cultural forces, encourages boys to control their feelings and conform their behavior to external standards like performance in sports. In sharp contrast, these same forces often encourage girls to "look inside" and think about their feelings (Pollack, 1998; Shields, 2013). Adams, Kuebli, Boyle, and Fivush (1995) found that parents refer to most emotions much more frequently when talking with daughters than they do with sons. At 40 months of age, the researchers found no male vs. female differences in children's use of words that describe emotions, but by 70 months, girls' language contained more emotional terms than boys'.

Behavioral differences are observable as early as 24 months. In a laboratory setting where children played while their mothers sat quietly in a chair in the same room, researchers provoked fear responses by having an unfamiliar member of the research team enter the room (i.e., a stranger) and provoked frustration by encouraging children to play with toys in a clear box that the child could not open (although the researchers "realized" their error after two minutes, apologized to the child, and opened the box). Although boys and girls showed fear and anger (when frustrated), girls were more fearful and boys more angry (Buss, Brooker, & Leuty, 2008). We discuss anger and other emotions in more detail in Chapter Eight.

The net result of these differences in childrearing is that parents tend to teach girls about the salience of feelings in the early stages of language acquisition, and they teach boys to focus on doing instead of feeling. It is little wonder that boys' and men's emotional worlds—and their emotional vocabularies—are smaller than girls' and women's. Collectively, this lack of emphasis on (internal) feelings, coupled with encouragement to focus on chores and other activities outside the house may contribute to social definitions of masculinity that emphasize the external: job status, money, material possessions, athletic performance, power over others, and even the attractiveness of one's partner. It is important to note that this external focus is not only a remnant of childhood rewards; the encouragement is ongoing. In adolescence and adulthood, many social and other rewards come to males whose behavior conforms to masculine cultural images.

At the same time, these aspects of male socialization may also be responsible for some of the most adaptive aspects of masculinity (Hammer & Good, 2010). Boys are rewarded from an early age for going out into the world, solving problems, achieving, and competing. Although competition and ambition can get out of hand, this orientation to the world is associated with good occupational functioning and enhanced self-esteem, especially when it is balanced with socioemotional orientations. However, if this socialization is adaptive, it ought not to be limited to males.

Parents' punishment practices are also important to understanding boys' development. Parents punish boys more often than girls, but they also praise boys more often (Lytton & Romney, 1991). One reason is that parents, as well as other family members, peers, and other actors, often punish boys for being insufficiently masculine and thus hope to encourage more masculine gender role behaviors. At the extreme, parents are much more likely to seek psychological treatment for gender-nonconforming boys than girls. Boys age 11 and younger are brought to treatment for Gender Identity Disorder approximately four times more frequently than girls (and 33 times more frequently among only three-year-old children); among those age 12 to 20, boys and young men are brought for or seek out treatment approximately 2.5 times more frequently (Wood et al., 2013). According to the fourth edition of the *Diagnostic and Statistical Manual* (DSM-IV-TR; American Psychiatric Association, 2007), boys were approximately four times more likely to be diagnosed with a Gender Identity Disorder. The diagnosis was removed from the fifth edition and replaced with Gender Dysphoria, which covers a broader range of conditions (American Psychiatric Association, 2013).

Another reason to examine punishment is that boys are more likely to be punished physically, while girls are more likely to be punished with social disapproval (Lytton & Romney, 1991). Physical punishment has the effect of actually *increasing* aggression in children over the long run (Patterson, Reid, & Dishion, 1992). There may be somewhat of a vicious cycle for the acting-out boy. He is active and undercontrolled as a result of temperament and socialization. He is physically punished for his behaviors, and these punishments are likely to result in further aggression.

Third, fathers tend to do more punishing than mothers (Block, 1984). The boy's experience of physical pain in the presence of the father may inhibit positive feelings and identification, especially if the father is not around much and/or there is a dearth of positive father-son interactions (Lynch & Kilmartin, 2013). In the worst-case scenario, the mother spends much more time with the son, but the punishment duties are relegated to the father. The son who is told, "Wait until your father gets home," does not learn that he gets punished when he does something inappropriate. Rather, he learns that he gets punished when his father gets home, and he may well develop feelings of fear, anger, and resentment toward his father.

Early Experience at School

This differential socialization can cause problems for boys in elementary school settings that emphasize behaviors like cooperating, sitting still, and listening, which are contradictory to these gendered expectations. Concerns that school is a "girl's world" that rewards feminine-type behavior such as self-control and conformity date back to the creation of mandatory schooling in the early 1900s (Hantover, 1977) and have been voiced throughout the last hundred years (Kagan, 1964; Sax, 2009). These contradictory demands for boys may contribute to their higher incidences of behavior and academic problems (Sax, 2009). (We discuss schooling in detail in the final chapter.)

At the same time, we should be careful not to think of schools as favoring girls. There is ample evidence that there is an interaction between sex and race, with teachers tending to give White boys the strong message that they are more important than girls. However, Black males receive less support in the academic environment and from their peers than any other group (Basow, 1992; Majors & Billson, 1992). Some have argued that it would be good to adapt schools to be more "boy friendly" (e.g., Gurian & Stevens, 2005; Neu & Weinfeld, 2007). Alternately, perhaps we need to socialize boys so they are better equipped to adapt to school, or to find some middle ground between these two extremes.

Gender typing of children is greatly accelerated by typical early educational experiences, which Luria and Herzog (cited in Maccoby, 1987) refer to as "gender school." Readers and book- and story-series' designed to help children learn grammar and vocabulary become more stereotyped as children move from first to fifth grade (Evans & Davies, 2000). And despite teachers' efforts to treat boys and girls the same, there is ample evidence that they often do not. Boys receive both more positive and more negative attention in the classroom than girls (Sadker & Sadker, 1985). Boys' behavior is more likely to be taken seriously than that of girls, and boys learn that what they do has tangible consequences. One of the reasons for greater frequencies of punishment is that boys get into more mischief than girls, perhaps as a result of a relatively higher average activity level (Pellegrini, 2004).

But it's not just about teachers; during the elementary school years, children often segregate themselves into same-sex play groups. They will mix when adults reward them for doing so or punish them for not doing so, but they frequently re-segregate when adult sanctions are removed (Maccoby, 1998). Social scientists have observed sex segregation in many different cultures (Whiting & Edwards, 1988). In boys' play groups, we see a great deal of reward for aggression, beginning at an early age (Fagot & Hagan, 1985). Boys' groups tend to demand rigid conformity to masculine behavior by harshly punishing cross-gender behavior, or anything they perceive as "girly" or feminine (Pascoe, 2007). In fact, there is a "social dosage effect"—the more time that children spend with same-sex peers, the more stereotypical their behavior is (Martin & Fabes, 2001). Thus, parents, teachers, and same-sex peers all "conspire" to promote gender-typical behavior.

Situational Influence

So far, we have talked about who influences boys, including how and when they encourage or punish gender-typical behavior. We now turn to the effect of the settings, or immediate environments, where boys often spend their time.

A person often finds himself or herself in the company of others, and there is powerful pressure to behave in certain ways in these situations. For example, when you go to a restaurant, you are highly likely to wait to be seated, be polite, ask for the food that you want, and pay the bill when you are finished. You are highly unlikely to push people aside because they are sitting where you want to sit, get your own food from the kitchen, put it on the floor and stir it up with your feet, and leave without paying for your meal. Except for very unusual people, restaurant behavior falls within a rather narrow and predictable range. Children in restaurants often behave in ways that are considered inappropriate for adults, partly because they have not learned the normative adult perception of the situation. Under most circumstances, most (teens and) adults act in ways that situations dictate.

Men (and women) often experience pressure to behave in gender-typical ways that they perceive as appropriate to the social setting. For example, it is not unusual for men to describe women in denigrating terms in some all-male groups. There is tremendous pressure in these situations for individual men to laugh, or at least remain silent in reaction to these comments. In a survey of college males, Kilmartin and his colleagues (2008) discovered that most young men reported feeling uncomfortable with these kinds of comments, yet only a very small minority of men express their discomfort or confront the man who makes the offensive comment. Doing so would require a man to resist the group pressure to go along with the attitude being expressed, and this study attests to the considerable power of this group pressure. In the typical male peer group situation where a misogynist (anti-woman) attitude is displayed, it is not necessarily the attitudes of individual men that allow this behavior to go unchallenged, it is the influence of a social context that carries its own momentum.

Of course, groups are made up of individuals who can affect the social atmosphere and its influences. In the above example, it is quite possible for an individual man to recognize his discomfort and confront the man who made the misogynist comment. In doing so, he might be successful in changing the social pressure of the group in the direction of disapproval of these kinds of comments. As we shall see, it is likely that he will find support for his view from others in the group who hold attitudes that are similar to his. Education and training to help college men break out of the passive bystander role in these kinds of situations are a promising development in efforts to decrease violence against women (see Chapter Twelve).

In the 1950s and 1960s, social psychologists began to describe and measure the considerable influence of interpersonal situations, often in quite dramatic fashion. Three landmark studies, all conducted by male researchers using male assistants and mostly male participants, demonstrated how the social context could dominate an individual's personality or preferences.

Solomon Asch (1965) demonstrated that group pressure can cause a person to report incorrect perceptual judgments. Experimenters presented a series of three lines and asked research participants in groups of eight to say which of the lines was closest to the length of a (fourth) standard line. The people in the group consistently gave answers that were obviously wrong, because they were actually accomplices of the experimenter who were hired to pose as volunteers. The study was designed to investigate the frequency with which the actual research participant will go along with the group. Only 20 percent remained independent of the group opinion on every trial, even though one line was unquestionably more similar to the standard than the others. By contrast, when people were asked to make the same judgment without influence from others, they gave the correct answer nearly every time. Asch's experiments demonstrated the power of *conformity*—change in behavior in response to implicit and unspoken social pressure.

There are other important considerations with regard to Asch's findings. First, if the conformity is unspoken, it may be inferred. Christopher Kilmartin and his students demonstrated that college men overestimate their male peers' acceptance of sexist and rape supportive attitudes (Kilmartin, Smith, Green, Kuchler, Heinzen, & Kolar, 2008). Said differently, young men believed their peers were moderately to highly sexist and held attitudes that generally supported rape but the reality was that the men in the group weren't sexist and didn't support ideologies that are commonly used to justify rape. Second, the presence of a single ally in the group significantly reduces conformity. Having just one person who voices a dissenting opinion emboldens others. In other words, it is much easier to be one of two against eight than it is to be alone against nine. Therefore, if men speak up when they are offended by sexism, they may well find that there is more support among other men than they might have predicted.

The next key study was conducted by Stanley Milgram, who had studied with Asch. He performed a series of studies in which a "teacher" was asked to help a "learner" learn a series of word pairs by administering an electric shock for every wrong answer. (In reality, the learner was one of Milgram's assistants and was never shocked). The teacher's control panel started at 15 volts and worked up to 450 volts in steps of 15 volts. It was labeled with "mild" to "severe" and finally "xxx." The learner was in a separate room but his scripted reaction to the shocks could easily be heard by the teacher (Milgram, 1963).

More than 50 percent of research volunteers were willing to inflict 450–volt shocks to the victim in response to pressure from an authority figure in a white lab coat, even though they expressed concern for the learner's health and well-being. Milgram's experiments demonstrated the power of *compliance*—change in behavior as the result of direct and explicit social pressure. Recently, Jerry Burger (2009) performed a partial replication of this study. Although the teachers had the same 15 to 450 volt range, the researchers stopped them at the 150–volt level because very few of Milgram's participants stopped between 150 and 450 volts. Burger's results were essentially the same as Milgram's. There were no sex differences in compliance, indicating that the power of the situation may have overwhelmed any gendered socializations to behave differently.

The final study that we'll highlight was conducted by Phillip Zimbardo and his colleagues (Haney, Banks, & Zimbardo, 1973), who set up a mock prison in the basement of the Stanford University psychology building. Male students volunteered to be randomly assigned to the roles of prisoners and guards. The prisoners were "arrested," given numbers, dressed in prison garb, and put behind bars. Within a short time, a significant number of guards became abusive toward the prisoners, who responded with a variety of symptoms: panic, physical illness, depression, and apathy. The experiment was terminated earlier than originally scheduled because of the danger to prisoners. Zimbardo's experiment demonstrated the power of social roles—people assigned to social statuses (or roles) are motivated to act in accordance with these statuses.

(We note here that Zimbardo's prison experiment was unethical because researchers placed volunteers in dangerous psychological and physical situations and did not allow them to stop participating. The same concerns have been raised about Milgram's study. Modern safeguards have since been enacted to prevent experiments like these from taking place today, as was the case in Burger's 2009 replication of Milgram.)

These studies, as well as many others, tell us that people do not always behave from the "inside out." It would be foolish to characterize all of Asch's judges as blind, Milgram's teachers as sadistic, or Zimbardo's guards as cruel. Yet the vast majority of these otherwise normal people responded to the direct or indirect social pressure of the immediate environment.

We discuss these studies here because these social settings influence people's decisions to conform to gender stereotypes. When coupled with consideration of direct consequences such as praise or mocking, as well as implicit consequences such as maintenance or loss of a friendship, understanding the environmental context furthers our understanding of the power of gender norms.

Milestones

When it comes to gender, there are a few things that all children do. They learn about their culture's stereotypical beliefs about gender, they learn that they have a gender identity, and they develop gender constancy. Research on gender stereotypes or gender roles with very young children is difficult due to their limited language and researchers' desire not to ask leading questions. Yet children as young as two years of age can often tell researchers if a toy, piece of clothing, or anything that can be easily illustrated is appropriate for a girl, a boy, both a boy and a girl, or neither a boy nor a girl (Martin & Ruble, 2010).

In a classic experiment, Sandra Bem (1989) presented three- and four-year-old children with pictures of a boy dressed as a boy, a girl, and fully nude, as well as a girl dressed as a boy, as a girl, and fully nude; the "clothed" pictures were partial nudes that showed the children's genitalia. Although the vast majority of children could accurately list the content of gender stereotypes, slightly fewer than half were able to correctly identify the sex of the child in all the photos they saw. And only about half knew that their own sex would remain unchanged, called *gender constancy.*

This study was inspired by an experience Bem had. Or rather, her four-year-old son Jeremy had. Sandra and Daryl Bem were trying to raise him without gender schemas and, at his request, allowed him to wear a barrette to nursery school. A schoolmate told him that he must be a girl because he was wearing a barrette. Four-year-old Jeremy informed his classmate that being male only means "having a penis and testicles" and, somewhat exasperatedly, "finally pulled down his pants as a way of making his point more convincingly" (Bem, 1985, p. 216). The other child remained unconvinced of Jeremy's maleness.

Although we may find Jeremy's experience amusing, it comes from our greater knowledge. As adults, we know that gender differences are related, at least conceptually, to the sexual binary; they're about being XX or XY, having a penis or a vagina. Most children don't know that these biological differences are the basis for our categories of male and female, nor are those differences readily visible. Instead, children rely heavily on superficial cues like clothing and hairstyle to determine the sex of other children (Bem, 1993). By contrast, preschool children use body shape to determine the sex of adults (Johnson, Lurye, & Tassinary, 2010). These age-differentiated patterns are also true for adults. If you saw a five year old child while in the mall, how would you decide if it was a girl or boy?

Bem's findings are important because she helped demonstrate that children's acquisition of gender stereotypes is separate from their development of their own gender identity or the concept of gender constancy. *Gender identity* refers to a child's knowledge that they are male or female (or, theoretically, intersex) and *gender constancy* refers to the knowledge that one's sex is constant or permanent. Approximately half of 6-year-olds understand that gender is constant (Zhentao & Fuxi, 2006). In the psychoanalytic theories discussed in Chapter Three, a child first learns his or her gender identity and then makes an effort to conform to that gender's stereotypes.

THEORETICAL EXPLANATIONS

Theories help us understand research by telling us how different findings fit together. We next review three theories in detail. The first, *social cognitive theory*, emphasizes the individual and his or her immediate environment. The second, *social structural theory*, emphasizes the cultural setting. The third, *gender script theory*, combines both the individual and the culture. Although there are other theories, we focus on these three because they illustrate the breadth of factors that can be included in social explanations.

Experience: Social Cognitive Theory

Albert Bandura developed social cognitive theory (SCT) to explain how humans and other organisms learn from their environment (Bussey & Bandura, 1999). The emphasis is on the role of experience, including both personal experience and learning vicariously by watching others.

Bandura recognized that we engage in *vicarious learning* by watching both the actions others perform and the consequences they experience, pleasant or unpleasant. Bandura's initial experiment involved children who were in a play room that included a "Bobo doll," a blow up toy with a weighted bottom that stands back up after it is knocked over. You hit Bobo, it falls over, then "stands" back up. The play room had a monitor that showed an (undergraduate) model in the same room who either punched the Bobo doll or ignored it. Almost all children who witnessed the model punching Bobo were themselves aggressive toward Bobo; less than half of children who saw the video in which the model ignored Bobo were violent toward the doll (Bandura, Ross, & Ross, 1961). In follow up studies, the violent video was changed so that the model either got in trouble for attacking Bobo or was joined in the attack by a second (undergraduate) model. Children who saw the model get in trouble had moderate rates of attacking Bobo, whereas nearly all children who saw both models attack Bobo were aggressive towards the doll (Bandura, Ross, & Ross, 1963b). From these results, Bandura demonstrated how children learn by watching others.

Subsequently, researchers have examined the issue further and have revealed that some models are more likely to be imitated than others. One factor is contact: the more time a person spends with the model, the more likely he or she is to imitate this person's behavior (Bandura et al., 1961). This factor may help explain why boys raised with a mother and a father display more gender-typed behavior than boys raised by a single mother (Stevenson & Black, 1988).

Another factor is the child's perception of having characteristics similar to the model. In other words, you are more likely to imitate someone if you think you are like them in important ways. As sex is a basic division among human beings and is often highlighted as important by cultural forces, it is not surprising to find that children imitate same sex models more readily than models of the other sex, and this process begins to occur as early as three years of age (Bandura, Ross, & Ross, 1963a). Boys imitate females less often than girls imitate males (Bussey & Bandura, 1992). This difference may be due to a number of factors, including differential punishment for cross-gender behavior, the antifemininity bias in masculine gender roles, and the higher social status of males in most cultures (which disempowers males who act in feminine ways and empowers females who act in masculine ways).

Drawing from cognitive psychology, Bandura (1989) argued that we develop *scripts*: sequences of behaviors to be enacted in particular settings. For a stereotypical heterosexual family, the "take out the trash" script might specify that the adult male gathers trash from all rooms in the house, takes it out to the trash can, and brings the trash can to the street in front of the house on Tuesday night. Note that this script specifies who does what, as well as the setting or context which triggers that script (Tuesday night). If a child has enough scripts that are male-specific, he or she may then develop an abstract, unarticulated concept of masculine behavior (Perry & Bussey, 1979). If the child is male, he is more likely to imitate these behaviors.

From a social cognitive perspective, "gender identity" is formed through the abstraction of masculine and feminine categories of behavior together with the understanding of physical sex differences and the imitation of same-sex models (Bussey & Bandura, 1999). As the boy increasingly behaves like his father and other males, his identification as masculine becomes more and more stable (Lips, 2008). Because of this abstraction, however, he is less likely to imitate a male whom he perceives as behaving in a feminine way (Eisenstock, 1984). Within Social Cognitive Theory, behaving in a gender-stereotypical way helps the child develop an identity that includes his or her gender group, male or female.

David Lynn (1959; 1966; 1969) was one of the first modern writers to theorize about the implications of the historical inaccessibility of fathers as role models. When they are young, children tend to spend much more time with mothers than with fathers. This arrangement continues when children move into child care and elementary school; women comprise more than 80 percent of those fields (Bureau of Labor Statistics, undated). Therefore, girls get a good deal of exposure to same-sex models. In constructing ideas about how women act and femininity, they have a lot of information on which to base their imitation.

In sharp contrast, boys do not get nearly as much of an opportunity to observe their fathers and other adult males. Therefore, they must extrapolate a good deal in constructing a sense of what masculinity is. Boys must fill in large gaps of information, and they tend to do so by using other, more available male models such as peers, older boys, and males in the media. Goldberg (1977) concluded that girls identify with a real person, whereas boys identify largely with a fantasy.

These other models are sometimes not good sources of realistic, secure, positively defined masculinity. This fantasy may be heavily laden with unrealistic, hypertrophied aspects of stereotypical masculine gender roles. In television and movies, for example, male characters are often rewarded for using violence to solve problems, and the viewing of this "justified" violence may be even more damaging than viewing villainous violence, as boys learn that physical aggression is a part of being one of the "good guys" (see Chapter Twelve). This phenomenon may explain why children who spend large amounts of time watching television tend to be more gender-typed than others (Ward & Friedman, 2006). Sociologist Michael Kimmel (2008) argued that many of today's young men live in an unrealistic "Guyland" that minimizes responsibility while emphasizing promiscuous sexuality, getting drunk and using other drugs, and looking for a relatively quick financial "score." Because their image of adult men is based in fantasy, the transition from boyhood to adult roles may be somewhat discontinuous for many males (Archer, 1984). Perhaps this is one reason why many adult men place such importance on professional sports or "macho" media figures who provide an avenue for vicarious fulfillment of hypermasculine fantasy.

A sense of emotional invulnerability is an important aspect of many of these unrealistic masculine fantasies. Consider action movies, for example. How often do we see male characters express sadness at the death of a friend or buddy, a romantic or sexual partner? Does that sadness last more than a moment or two? Does the male hero display other common characteristics of grief, such as difficulty focusing, loss of energy, or spontaneous sadness and crying over the next several days? If the boy identifies with a fantasy—or fantastic—version of his father, as many sons do, and if his father does not express vulnerable feelings such as fear or anxiety, then it is easy for the boy to believe his father does not even experience any type of vulnerability.

And this understanding would become his basis for understanding all men. Consider how often you've heard a man say "I'm worried about X" in comparison to how often you've heard a woman say that. Of course, a father experiences fear and anxiety like any other human being, but he may hide his reactions. The son is likely to deduce that worry and fearful feelings do not exist in "real men." Inevitably, the boy experiences fear, as everyone does from time to time, and he may feel unmasculine and inadequate at these times because he compares his inner experience with this appearance of his father and other men (Lynch & Kilmartin, 2013).

Criticism of Social Cognitive Theory. Behavioral models emphasize that humans (and other organisms) are very attentive to the environment (Skinner, 1974). But when applied to the world around us, it is very hard to predict behavior because we can't say exactly what stimulus, or set of stimuli, a person is responding to. Young men tell us they behave differently in all-male groups than in mixed-sex groups (Wight, 1994), but we do not know if this is a function of the physical setting (because all-male groups also choose different activities), one specific member of the group, the group as a whole, or some combination of these reasons.

Another criticism focuses on models. We do not know how they are selected, if men invoke different models in different settings, or if men create an amalgamated model that blends multiple inputs (Wade, 1998). Imagine the iconic angel and devil on your shoulders. Which one do you listen to and in what settings? Do you have multiple angels and devils?

Society: Social Structural Theory (aka Social Role Theory)

In contrast to Social Cognitive Theory's focus on the individual, Alice Eagly's social structural theory attempts to explain why the behavior of males differs from that of females (Eagly, 1987; Eagly, Wood, & Diekman, 2000). The theory focuses on large-scale and cultural factors that create gender-differentiated behavior. It is sometimes also called social role theory (Eagly, 1987).

Social structural theory begins with the recognition that women have long been the primary caretakers of young children. This arrangement is due to the fact that women were (and often still are) young children's primary food source, and thus having multiple children who were relatively close in age required women to "stay home with the children" for multiple years. And taking care of children full-time prevented women from doing (paid) activities that required sustained attention or concentration or uninterrupted time. Men rarely experienced these constraints. Several relevant changes are historically recent: mandatory schooling, women's right to own property, and the marketing of baby formula are approximately 100 years old; modern contraceptives like the birth control pill are about 75 years old. Without these resources, most women had few options but to stay home and raise the kids after they had their first child.

The result, according to Eagly, is that adult women were forced to adopt a caretaking role that kept them with their children, required "common" household skills such as cooking and washing, and prevented them from obtaining or using high wage skills. Men, by contrast, were not limited to the home after having children and so could engage in any trade or profession and fill almost any societal role. They have greater upper-body strength than women (on average), a fact that makes them better suited to a broad variety of roles and jobs in both agricultural and industrial cultures and settings. Eagly argues that we have effectively blended (or confused) "women" with the caretaking role they have typically and historically filled. Similarly, we have confused men with their roles: producing goods or selling their labor, filling a broad variety of occupations, and able to use their physical strength for pay. Thus, we have come to believe that women's primary focus is on the home and children, that their primary personality attributes are being loving, kind, and caring, and that they are of somewhat limited intelligence. We have come to believe that men are primarily focused on their work, that their primary personality attributes are being active (or doing), solving problems, having a facility for using tools and technology, and capable of learning any skill or knowledge area from medicine to masonry (Eagly et al., 2000).

According to social structural theory, children do not choose gender-typical behavior because they have chosen same sex models as social cognitive theory suggests, but rather they conform to their culture's gender stereotypes because the culture pushes them—and perhaps even requires them—to adhere to the stereotypes. This approach allows societies to vary from highly to minimally gender-typed (Hofstede, 1998; Williams & Best, 1990b) and explains why children come to reflect and possess the gender roles their society endorses (e.g., Gilmore, 1990).

Given its focus on differences between the sexes, social role theory is often positioned as being in opposition with Buss and Schmitt's (1993) sexual strategies theory (described in Chapter Three). Eagly and Wood (1999) have argued that social structural theory is compatible with the broader evolutionary psychology framework; the challenge is strictly about the explanation of gender differences as biologically—or culturally—based. After David Buss (Buss., 1989) demonstrated sex differences in the desired number of sexual partners in 37 cultures, Eagly and Wood (1999) reanalyzed the data and added measures of gender equality developed by the United Nations. Those equality measures explained much of the difference between men and women. Said differently, the more equal a society was, the smaller the difference in the number of partners desired by men and women. Other researchers have demonstrated that these kinds of global measures, as well as women's representation in elected government positions and research jobs, can explain part of the difference in boys' better math performance on international tests (Else-Quest, Hyde, & Linn, 2010). By identifying the factors that cause group differences and statistically demonstrating that they explain some of the difference, social structural theory appears to be a better explanation than sexual strategies theory.

Criticism of Social Structural Theory

The primary criticism of social structural theory is that it does not explain differences among males or among females; it only explains differences between the two groups. (This is also a criticism of sexual strategies theory.) As we discussed in Chapter Two, there is often more variability within these groups than differences between the two groups.

Experience & Society: Gendered Scripts (a.k.a. Gender Schema Theory)

Sandra Bem (1981; 1985; 1987; 1993) developed her theory of gendered scripts by combining perspectives on children's cognitive development with cultural factors that emphasize gender. Bem argued that cognitive development and gender role development are parallel in some regards. She also believed that gender-typed information processing is taught to children by a culture that emphasizes sex differences for virtually every domain of behavior. If our culture were not so gender-typed, children would learn to use other categories to organize their experiences.

According to Bem, children categorize events according to gender only because we live in a culture that communicates to people that sex is important in occupation, clothing, hobbies, children's toys, and other areas where it need not be viewed as important. For instance, a high school graduation ceremony made the news when a female graduate was not allowed to participate because she ordered blue graduation robes in defiance of the school tradition in which girls wear white robes and boys blue robes. The excluded graduate stated that a senior class sponsor told her that the school makes this distinction because "white represents purity, while darker colors signify strength" (Krishnamurthy, 1998, p. C1). Bem would say that drawing a distinction between the sexes in such a non-gender dependent activity as graduating from high school encourages children to use sex as a cognitive guide for understanding the world. We wouldn't ask graduating seniors to wear different colors to indicate different races or socioeconomic groups, so why is it appropriate to do so for sex-based groups?

Barrie Thorne (2009) described several elementary school situations in which teachers and other adults needlessly called attention to students' sexes. These included statements like "the girls are ready and the boys aren't" (p. 178), or classroom contests in which a teacher-chosen team of all boys competes against a team of all girls. In these situations, adults highlighted gender and made it more likely that children would emphasize gender and gender-based differences. Although these examples seem unconsequential, they may be more powerful than we think. In a novel experiment, Lacey Hilliard and Lynn Liben (2010) worked with two otherwise similar preschools. In both settings, the teachers tended to be gender neutral; they rarely compared the girls to the boys or otherwise segregated the students based on sex. The research team observed whom each child played with during unstructured times such as "free play"

Many seem comfortable with calling attention to gender in an educational ceremony where the male and female graduates' achievements are identical. Few would support this practice with regard to racial, religious, or other identities.

Photo: Mark Gail/The Washington Post

and "playground." At the beginning of the study, students at the two schools were similar in how often they played with familiar same- or other-sex peers and how willing they were to play with an unfamiliar same- or other-sex such as a child from another class. On assessments of their knowledge of gender stereotypes, the students from the two schools were similar.

In one school, the teachers were asked to maintain their gender-neutral behavior. In the other, Hilliard and Liben asked the teachers of three- to five-year-old children to emphasize gender for two weeks by having separate bulletin boards for boys' and girls' work, making the kinds of spontaneous comments Thorne observed, and saying things like "I need a boy [or girl] to do X" instead of "I need a volunteer to do X." Children in both schools were observed and tested at the end of the two week period. In the preschool where teachers didn't do anything differently, the students hadn't changed either. But at the end of two weeks, children in the "gender-salient" preschool showed less interest in playing with familiar other-sex peers, less willingness to play with an unfamiliar child of the other sex, and lower frequency of playing with other-sex peers during observation. The effects were limited to avoidance of other-sex peers; children's preference for same-sex peers did not change in any area assessed by the researchers. And remember, these are the effects for teachers who had been emphasizing gender for less than two weeks.

We see many examples of sex-differentiated terms in the English language. For instance, there are work titles that differ depending on the sex of the person who occupies the role. The linguistic distinctions between waiters and waitresses, policewomen and policemen, actors and actresses, and comedians and comediennes may lead people to believe that the sex of the role occupant is an important distinction for human beings at work. The increased use of nonsexist terms such as firefighter, chairperson, and letter carrier should encourage people to use different, nongendered ways to categorize. Box 4.1 further explores the issue of sexism in language.

This cultural emphasis on sex distinctions interacts with children's cognitive development. Because humans take in so much information, we must categorize and organize it to avoid a sensory overload (Gelman, 2003). To do so, we develop *schemata* (the plural of *schema*), cognitive structures that allow us to anticipate and understand events. As a child observes males and females in a gender-typed environment, he or she gathers information about gender. The child makes associations among different aspects of masculinity and femininity and uses these resulting associations to organize new information.

Proponents of both gender schema theory and social cognitive theory propose that children learn sequences of behavior (schemata, scripts) and eventually extrapolate larger constructs known as femininity and masculinity. Because social cognitive theory is rooted in behaviorism, the focus is primarily on behavior and memory. Gender schema theory focuses on cognition and adds the ability to anticipate and draw meaning from (or interpret) behavior, reflecting other aspects of thought.

Children are quite good at organizing information, even if they can't always remember it or we adults can't quite understand their organizational system. We have seen that they organize behavior into patterns (schemata, scripts) and ultimately use these patterns to generate concepts such as masculine and feminine. Young children's

Box 4.1
Sexist Language, Non-Sexist Language, and "Political Correctness"

Consider the many sex-specific terms contained in the English language. To cite only a very few: mailman, chairman, mankind, newspaper boy, fireman, hostess, freshman, coed. English also has a tradition of using the generic masculine. When writing or talking about people in general, people often use masculine pronouns. Thus, the sentence "Every person needs to plan for his retirement" may be intended to refer to both men and women.

Many proponents of gender egalitarianism have leveled strong criticisms against the uses of sexist role terms and the generic masculine. They suggest gender neutral terms like: police officer, humankind, fire fighter, and server and a change in the linguistic convention of the generic "he" to constructions such as she/he or s/he. Some have even suggested the adoption of a new set of pronouns that are gender neutral such as "hir" or "tir." Social conservatives have often been critical of these proposed changes, citing the following arguments:

1. Everybody is used to the old way of doing things and knows what the communicator is referring to. Therefore, there is no reason to change. To change a pronoun is to change standard English, which nobody should do.

2. Using terms like "he or she" rather than "he" is bulky and interrupts the flow of writing and speaking.

3. The movement toward nonsexist language is just another example of political correctness ("P.C."), a movement designed to make people feel guilty for not being a member of an oppressed minority group.

Are these arguments compelling enough to justify maintaining the status quo? Proponents of nonsexist language offer the following:

1. Language is not a static entity. It changes in response to the needs of the culture. If I were to tell you a story, you would naturally envision the events in your mind's eye. There is evidence that, when readers or listeners apprehend the generic masculine, they imagine males (Lips, 2008). Most children are not aware that masculine pronouns can potentially refer to females (Hyde, 1984). Therefore, the use of this construction constitutes poor communication when one is trying to refer to people of either sex.

2. It is true that these terms are sometimes bulky and awkward, but people should be willing to tolerate this mild discomfort rather than passively communicating that males' experience constitutes a standard and females' experience a variation. As Basow (1992) stated, "Use of the generic 'he' is not just an arbitrary custom, but a continuing statement about the social roles of men and women" (p. 142).

3. "Political correctness" is a pejorative term used by people who are in power and seek to maintain it. Calling someone "P.C." is an attempt to shame them for their sensitivity and respectfulness. The demonization of the term is a political strategy to influence people to refuse adoption of the principle to maintain the status quo of male dominance.

ability to accurately learn language may provide a useful parallel. They learn to speak reasonably clearly before starting school, and they do so despite the complexity of language and simply by being exposed to adults who use the language (Chomsky, 1957). If you asked a very young child about the rule for past tense, he or she would probably not be able to explain it to you (even if you went to great lengths to explain the question in the child's language). However, you would hear many examples in the child's everyday language, proof that he or she has learned the rule without conscious effort. When children have learned a rule but not the exceptions, such as when they say "we go-ed to the store" instead of "we went to the store," researchers call it *over-regularization*. A rigid gender schema would seem to represent the same kind of over-regularization. Parents (and others) often correct a child's language errors; they may or may not correct their child's gender "errors."

According to gender schema theory, once children developed gender constancy, they begin to mold their behavior to fit their understanding of gender. Not only do children learn that certain behaviors are gender-specific and make efforts to conform to their conceptions of gender, they also learn that the same behavior may mean different things for each sex. If you walked into a coffee shop and saw a woman sitting alone, crying quietly, and staring in disbelief at her cell phone, what would you think? If you saw a man doing the same thing, would you think something different? This interpretive step defines what Bem called "the lenses of gender."

Bem describes the gendered lens as a "nonconscious ideology" (1987) and a set of "default options" (1993) for behavior. Most people are not aware that they organize their perceptions on the basis of gender, nor are they aware that alternative conceptualizations are possible. As she eloquently stated, "Look through the lens of gender and you perceive the world as falling into the masculine and feminine categories. Put on a different pair of lenses, however, and you perceive the world as falling into different categories." (Bem, 1987, p. 309).

In Bem's view, the only time when it makes sense to be gender schematic is in the realm of biology, and yet the gender schema is extrapolated into many other domains. She suggests that some of the destructive aspects of gender stereotyping could be transformed by providing people with alternative ways of thinking about the world and the self, such as with an "individual difference" schema (that people within any group vary widely), or a "cultural relativism" schema (that different people believe different things). (See Box 4.2.) In this way, sex can be understood as a biological category that is not important in every setting. Bem (1993) clearly emphasizes the role of education in social change, and her theory can be applied to the social change agenda of men's studies.

Criticism of Gender Schema Theory. Gender schema theory has been criticized on several fronts. One such criticism is the claim that young children consistently use schemata to direct their behavior. Bem's description implies a level of conscious control of behavior and activities that likely overestimates children's reality. The theory has also been criticized heavily for its inability to specify the content of scripts, when they are employed, or why two children with similar experiences may develop very different scripts (Martin, Ruble, & Szkyrbalo, 2002).

Box 4.2
Reducing Gender Schematic Processing

Sandra Bem (1998) observed that there are many ways to think about people without reference to their gender. The first three of these are Bem's suggestions; the remainder are ours.

1. *Individual differences schema*: People vary widely in their habits, attitudes, and temperament. A person may act aggressively, not because he is a man, but because he has an aggressive personality and/or finds himself in a situation in which aggression is adaptive.

2. *Cultural relativism schema*: "Different people believe different things" (p. 271). Roman Catholics do not allow women to be priests, but some Episcopalians do.

3. *Sexism schema*: Although beliefs differ, some beliefs about gender are wrong. Women should be allowed to be Roman Catholic priests.

4. *Situational pressure schema*: People tend to behave in certain ways when situations exert different pressures. A man may keep his feelings to himself while with his male friends, not because men are unemotional, but because other men might not give him a compassionate response. He may be very emotionally expressive as a client in psychotherapy or when he is in the company of female friends.

5. *External variability schema*: People do not always behave in concert with how they feel; two people can vary to a great extent in their external reactions to exactly the same internal thoughts and feelings. Two men may hold equally sexist attitudes, but one decides not to display them because he wants the approval of women.

6. *Internal variability schema*: Two people can act the same way even though their thoughts and feelings differ. One man may laugh at a sexist joke because it reflects how he feels about women; another may also laugh even though he finds the joke offensive, to avoid being ostracized from a social group.

FINAL COMMENTS

There are too many socially-based theories for us to review all of them effectively. Kay Deaux's discussion of how the immediate environment influences gender-typed behavior gives more precedence to the situation than the approaches we've described here (Deaux & LaFrance, 1998). Diane Ruble and Carol Martin's (1998) *cognitive developmental theory* is more detailed and nuanced than gender schema theory, and these authors have recently developed an approach rooted in dynamic systems theory (formerly known as "chaos theory") that more effectively blends children's cognitive abilities, environmental influences, and biological factors (Martin & Ruble, 2010).

Janet Shibley Hyde (2005) recently put forth her *gender similarities hypothesis*. As the name suggests, this is not a theory that explains how boys and girls come to behave differently, but rather a reminder that females and males are more similar than different. Hyde argues that these similarities also need to be explained within a gender-based model. In other words, the gender similarities hypothesis is a reminder to theorists and researchers to avoid the alpha bias.

Socially-based theories identify ways in which gender roles, or at least our understanding of them, develop and can be changed. It is often said that "the fish is unaware of the water" because it has never experienced anything else. Because many aspects of culture have long considered masculinity as a normative referent for experience, many men have not noticed the gender-schematic nature of their approach to the world. Men have often remained unaware of the culture of patriarchy because it benefits them, just as fish benefit from water. Women and other marginalized groups of people are usually more aware of sexism, racism, classism, and other forms of unequal resource allocation because they usually suffer the adverse effects of these arrangements, often on a daily basis. A fish has the luxury to remain unaware of the water. A drowning mammal does not.

To become conscious of one's ideologies would seem to require psychological-mindedness, nondefensiveness, introspection, and a willingness to listen to others' points of view. Males have been socialized away from every one of these activities. As femininity has long been associated with loss of power and status for men, there has been a good deal of reward for men's attending to the world in gender schematic fashion. Men who begin to break out of this stereotyped information processing are finding that they can evaluate themselves with standards that are less punitive and more reasonable. If Bem is correct that gender schematic processing is destructive and unessential to human development, then we ought to support countervailing educational and therapeutic activities such as consciousness raising, gender awareness curricula, women's studies, and men's studies.

SUMMARY

1. Parents treat children differently based on the child's sex, starting at birth.

2. Fathers tend to be more stereotypical than mothers, at least with sons. Boys are punished more harshly than girls for violating gender norms.

3. Schools appear to favor feminine-typed behaviors, and teachers respond to boys of different ethnicities in very different manners. Schools continue gender lessons taught at home, both through teachers and through access to peers, which often separate into sex-based groups.

4. Social settings can have substantial and dramatic influence on behavior, including gender-typed behaviors.

5. Gender milestones include the achievement of gender identity (self as male or female) and gender constancy (male and female as permanent and unchanging).

6. *Social cognitive theory* emphasizes experience—direct and observed—as well as the influence of the environment. Models are particularly important in this theory and boys have direct access to fewer adult male models than girls have to adult female models.

7. *Social structural theory* emphasizes the power of culture and hypothesizes that our beliefs about men and women have been derived from the social roles they typically inhabit.

8. *Gendered script theory* emphasizes the interaction between being raised in a culture that highlights gender as a central organizing principle and children's cognitive development.

Chapter Five

Masculinities I:
Ethnic Identities and Men's Ways of Being

Consider the following:

- Unlike peoples in most parts of the world, Tahitian (south Pacific) and Semai (central Malaysian) people have very little differentiation of social roles based on sex (Gilmore, 1990).

- In much of the Middle East and South America, men express their emotions as freely as women. There is a great deal of cultural variation in the gendered expression of emotion, with some cultures considering women to be the "emotional sex," some allowing wide latitude for expression in both sexes, and some expecting both men and women to control their emotions (Wade & Tavris, 2008).

- As societies become more industrialized and urban, gender arrangements tend to become less traditional (Best & Williams, 1993).

- During World War II, U.S. women took over most traditionally masculine factory work. After the war, they were encouraged to quit their jobs to make room for returning male soldiers in need of work (French & Poska, 2006).

- Gender arrangements tend to be more egalitarian at higher levels of education and social class (see Adler, 1993).

- A man with long hair or an earring would likely have been socially condemned in the United States in the 1950s.

- In combat situations, an estimated 85 percent of soldiers have tried not to kill, instead firing their weapons into the air or running away (Grossman, 1995).

- The kinds of employment that are considered "women's work" and "men's work" vary to a significant degree from culture to culture (Wade & Tavris, 2008).

As we can see from these examples, gender roles vary according to social settings; they are not transhistorical, cross-cultural, or cross-situational. Social conceptions of gender are influenced by a variety of factors, including ethnic patterns, economic conditions, religion, language, family socialization, cultural expectations, and the spirit of the times.

In this chapter and the next, we describe the features of masculinities within specific subgroups as a product of critical factors that affect men's ways of being: culture, race, age, ethnicity, sexuality, socioeconomic class, and historical era. We will not provide an exhaustive review of all of the ways in which masculinity is defined across time and place—to do so would require several volumes. Our goal is to give you a sampling of the variations in masculinities and a sense of theorists' speculations about the sources of these variations. Keep in mind that these cultural forces exert pressure on men to behave and experience themselves in certain ways, but that the reactions of individual men to this pressure are widely variable. For example, mainstream U.S. masculinity exerts pressure on men to deny emotional vulnerability, value athletics, and strive for economic success, but there are certainly men who are emotionally expressive, do not like sports, and/or are not oriented toward making a lot of money.

CULTURE AND MASCULINITY

Questions of cultural variations in gender and their development are not particularly new ones. More than sixty years ago, anthropologist Margaret Mead (1949) wrote:

> How are men and women to think about their maleness and their femaleness in this twentieth century, in which so many of our old ideas must be made new? Have we over-domesticated men, denied their natural adventurousness, tied them down to machines that are after all only glorified spindles and looms, mortars and pestles and digging sticks, all of which were once women's work? Have we cut women off from their natural closeness to their children, taught them to look for a job instead of the touch of a child's hand, for status in a competitive world rather than a unique place by a glowing hearth? In educating women like men, have we done something disastrous to both men and women alike, or have we only taken one further step in the recurrent task of building more and better on our original human nature?... These are questions which are being asked in a hundred different ways in contemporary America. (p. 13)

Mead's words could easily have been written today. As we have already seen, people continue to debate these same questions in the twenty first century. We may never answer them completely and for all time, but social scientists have begun to provide clues to their answers through careful research.

There is no question that cultures vary greatly in the ways that they exert pressure on people to think, feel, and act in certain ways. For instance, in mainstream United States culture, it is common for people to make eye contact during conversations, but in many Asian and Native American cultures, eye contact is a sign of aggression and disrespect. The standard vacation for a U.S. worker is two weeks per year, but many western Europeans take three times that amount or more. Industrialized societies tend to be strictly organized around time; being more than a few minutes late is a violation of standards of acceptable conduct. But in polychronic cultures (most rural, agriculturally-based economies), being a day or even a week "late" is quite acceptable (Wade & Tavris, 2008).

Cultural rules regarding sex, gender, and sexuality are no exception to the phenomenon of cultural variation. Sandra Bem (1993) noted,

> The analysis of how conventionally gendered women and men are made is... a special case of how cultural natives are made.... Preprogramming an individual's daily experience into the default options of a particular culture is apparent in the most superficial analysis of how children have been made into unmistakably different kinds of social beings in different cultures and different historical epochs. (p. 139)

Cultural gender arrangements constitute a set of the "default options" to which Bem refers. Through its customs, language, and power interrelationships, cultures transmit expectations about how men and women should process their experiences, think of themselves, and behave. Becoming a gender non-conformist requires a person to resist a considerable amount of cultural momentum. Bem points out that doing so is made more difficult by the fact that the process of enculturation tends to transfer values, beliefs and attitudes to its natives in nonconscious ways as a *subliminal pedagogy*—a set of meanings that are so embedded in social practices that they are virtually invisible to most people. She states that children learn about "their culture's way of construing reality without yet being aware that other construals are possible" (p. 140) through this process of cultural transfer, which "is initiated every time the active, pattern-seeking child is exposed to a culturally significant social practice" (p. 141). It is quite difficult to resist a cultural pressure that you cannot even name—to answer a question when you cannot even articulate the question. One of the goals of gender studies is to articulate the context of gendered default options so that people can more freely choose between these options and alternatives, including those that they otherwise would not have known were available to them.

Cultural Variation in Gender Roles

Anthropologist Margaret Mead (1935, 1949) is generally credited with popularizing the interest in cross-cultural gender variations. In *Sex and Temperament in Three Primitive Societies* (1935), she described widely variant cultural ideals among different tribes in New Guinea for the often gender-typed behavior of aggression. According to Mead, the Mundugumor tribe is characterized by aggressive behavior in both men and women. The Arapesh tribe values non-aggression for both sexes. The Tchambuli expect females to be aggressive and males to be passive, the complete opposite of most Western cultures.

Joseph Pleck (1987) emphasizes that Mead did not intend to describe *actual* sex differences within each culture, even though many writers have interpreted her work in this way. Instead, she sought to describe cultural differences in gender *ideologies*, or *ideal types* from the perspective of each dominant cultural climate. In fact, she included chapters describing the ways that each culture deals with people who deviate from the ideal. Do not be misled into thinking that *all* Arapesh men or *all* Mundugumor women behave in the same ways. As Pleck points out, "Mead's real point was that a man or woman perfectly adapted to the [gender]-role norms of one culture could be a misfit (a term Mead used repeatedly) in another" (p. 27).

One commonality across cultures is that misfits tend not to be treated very well by the rest of the society. (If you want to experience the social disapproval that befalls a gender misfit, try some of the gender role violations that we suggested in Chapter One.) Mead's great contribution was to challenge the essentialist notions of male and female by proposing that the *content* of the gender ideal and, by extension, the content of the gender role violator's or misfit's behavior and sense of self, vary among different cultures. Thus, she sparked a new awareness of cultural relativism in gender.

In the time since Mead's work, anthropologists, cross-cultural psychologists, sociologists, and other social scientists have sought to specify the content of gender ideologies among various groups, and to describe similarities and differences in the ways in which cultures address the distinction (or lack of it) between male and female. Again, keep in mind as you read each description that researchers are describing cultural gender ideologies, and that individuals within every culture vary in their actual behavior.

Many people assume that there are only two sexes (male and female), two gender roles (masculine and feminine), and three sexual orientations (homosexual, bisexual, and heterosexual). However, researchers have pointed out that there are more than two sexes (Fausto-Sterling, 1996, 2000; Lorber, 1994). In addition to unambiguous males and unambiguous females, there are hermaphrodites, male pseudohermaphrodites ("merms"), female pseudohermaphrodites ("ferms"), male-to-female transsexuals, and female-to-male transsexuals. Although much of Western culture has virtually ignored intersexed individuals, some cultures have extensive norms for dealing with them. Anne Fausto-Sterling (1996) suggests that, if cultures were to acknowledge intersexuality, then the apparent male-female dichotomy, from which gender and sexual orientation arrangements proceed, would have to fall away and be replaced by other ways of categorizing people.

If the biological category of sex is not as unambiguous as is generally believed, then the psychological and behavioral categories of sexual orientation and gender are even murkier. There are wide variations in sexual behaviors, attractions, relationships, and fantasies. The categories of homosexual, bisexual, and heterosexual do not capture the richness and intricacy of sexual orientation.

There are also several cultural exceptions to the two-gender standard. One frequently cited example is the North American Indian *berdache*, an anatomical male who behaves much like most of the females of the tribe. These people are not considered to be deviant males; they are not scorned or shamed for their behaviors. Thus, we cannot consider them gender misfits. Instead, berdache is a third gender within the tribe (Williams, 1996). Several other cultures also have third genders, such as the *nadle*, *alyha*, and *hwame* of the Mohave Indians, the *hijiras* of northern India, and the *xaniths* of Oman, all of whom fulfill culturally approved social and sexual roles apart from the usual masculine and feminine genders (Doyle & Paludi, 1998). Cultures with more than two genders are more the exception than the rule, but they provide an expanded view of the possibilities.

Within two-gender cultures, there are many commonalities among conceptions of male and female. In most cases, men are more aggressive than women, handle the large-game hunting, and avoid activities considered to be feminine (Gilmore, 1990; Adler, 1993; Tavris & Wade, 2001). Women tend to do a majority of household work and child care, are considered to be more emotional, and have lower social statuses than men, although their status is not uniformly low across classes or cultures (Glick & Fiske, 2001).

Perhaps the most important and ambitious anthropological work on men and gender in relatively recent times is David Gilmore's (1990) *Manhood in the Making*. Gilmore studied many cultures around the world and described important commonalities and differences in social conceptions of masculinity. He found a "family resemblance" in masculinities for most (but not all) of the world. In the majority of the cultures Gilmore studied, masculinity was characterized by strength, risk taking, avoidance of femininity, aggression, and sexual initiative. These findings mirror those of Williams' and Best's (1990a) study of 14 countries and Adler's (1993) collection of gender descriptions in 31 countries. Gilmore also noted that, in most of the world, masculinity is regarded as an achievement—something that the culture must build into males through various socialization processes (hence the title of his book). The dominant conception is that men do not become masculine simply by growing into adulthood. Instead, they must endure some sort of ordeal, often involving considerable physical pain. In recent research, U.S. investigators have documented widely held beliefs that manhood is defined by social proof more than it is by biological markers (Vandello, Bosson, Cohen, Burnaford, & Weaver, 2008).

The ubiquity of rites of passage into manhood may tell us that many cultures have evolved social processes that dissuade men from their natural inclinations to avoid pain and express their feelings. The existence of these processes is evidence that men fulfill specific functions within social groups and that emotional or physical vulnerability are often viewed as being incompatible with these functions.

There are many variations within the basic masculine themes that Gilmore described. For instance, there seems to be more of an emphasis in fathering children as an expression of masculinity in circum-Mediterranean cultures than in most others. The culture of Truk Island (in the south Pacific) is marked by heavy drinking and brawling among men, and the Trukese consider fighting to be sexy. The Samburu (East Africa) stress the element of generosity in masculinity. Several cultures, such as the Mehinaku of Brazil and the Sambians of Papua New Guinea, view the willingness to engage in dangerous hunting or fishing as a sign of manliness.

One of the most striking aspects of Gilmore's work is his description of two cultures, Tahiti (in Polynesia) and Semai (in central Malaysia) in which gender ideologies are very different from most of the world. He describes Semai as a gentle, noncompetitive culture with little or no sexual jealousy or overt aggression. According to Gilmore, visitors to Tahiti are often struck by the "bizarre [by Western standards] lack of sexual differentiation on the island…. Tahitian women had a remarkably high status and were permitted to do almost everything that the men did…. Men are no more aggressive than women; women do not seem 'softer' or 'more maternal' than the men… there is no stress on proving manhood, no pressure on men to appear in any significant way different from women or children. Men have no fear of acting in ways Westerners would consider effeminate. During dances, for instance, adult men will dance together in close bodily contact, rubbing against each other without any anxiety" (p. 202–203).

Williams and Best (1990a) note a degree of difference in gender ideologies on a continuum ranging from traditional (male-dominated) to modern (egalitarian) (see Box 5.1). Together with Gilmore's descriptions, we can conclude that, although most of the world holds similar cultural views of the roles of men and women, there are variations in the degree to which particular cultures subscribe to traditional ideologies, and in some cases, there are radical departures from what is commonly expected of men and women in most societies.

Box 5.1   Male Initiation Rituals

Gilbert Herdt (1982) stated that "Femininity unfolds naturally, whereas masculinity must be achieved, and here is where the male ritual cult steps in" (p. 55). Many cultural rites of passage for males involve undergoing painful and frightening experiences in the service of making them into warriors who will face danger by surpressing vulnerable emotion. Following are some rites of passage described by Gilmore (1990):

Samburu (East Africa): Adolescent boys are subjected to "bloody circumcision rites" to which they "must submit without so much as flinching under the agony of the knife. If a boy cries out while his flesh is being cut, if he so much as blinks an eye or turns his head, he is shamed for life as unworthy of manhood, and his entire lineage is shamed as a nursery of weaklings" (p. 13). The cutting may last four minutes or more.

The New Guinea highlands: Boys must endure "whipping, flailing, beating, and other forms of terrorization by older men" (p. 14).

Tewa (indigenous peoples of New Mexico): Boys are taken away from their homes, undergo ritual purification, and are beaten by Kachina spirits (their fathers in disguise). The stiff yucca whip causes bleeding and leaves permanent scars.

Sambia (New Guinea): In addition to physical beating, boys undergo a bloodletting ritual in which "stiff, sharp grasses are thrust up the nostrils until the blood flows copiously" (p. 156).

There are also some nonviolent rites of passage, like the Jewish bar mitzvah, which is centered around ordeals of learning and reciting tenets of faith, and rites that involve physical discomfort but not violence, such as the African Ju/'hoansi, where young men go into the bush and experience extremes of hunger, thirst, cold, and extreme fatigue. Raphael (1988) provides another description:

Thonga (South Africa): "… youths are continually beaten during their three-month initiation ritual. They are also denied water and forced to eat unsavory foods, such as the half-digested grass found in the bowels of an antelope. They are made to lie naked on the cold winter nights, sleeping only on their backs while being bitten incessantly by bugs in the ground." (p. 5)

Many cultures have less formal rites of passage, such as challenges around enduring humiliation and taking risks in all-male groups. Some fraternity, lodge, military, and street gang initiations are a few examples.

Rites of passage may be important indicators of cultures' masculine ideologies. Whether they are violent or not, most involve separation from the mother and other women of the group, a strong message that masculinity is formed in the context of homosocial experiences and relationships. There is also a pervasive sense that childhood is left behind. In fact, many rituals involve the symbolic death of the boy as a part of the birth of the man (Gilmore, 1990; Raphael, 1988). In part, this "death" may involve the turning away from feeling, experience, and connection toward the world of independence and task-orientation. Some authors (e.g. Horne, Jolliff, & Roth, 1996; Bly, 1990; Raphael, 1988) have mainly positive views of male initiation rites, seeing them as necessary, and, in some cases, biologically-based. There is a sense of boys coming to power as they are accepted into the world of men. But would males need to have this separating experience of power if women were just as powerful as men?

Social psychologists often view initiation rites in the context of *cognitive dissonance*, the tendency to have one's behavior match one's values and attitudes (Aronson, 2012). When a person conforms his or her behavior to extreme demands, he or she is then motivated to endorse the values and attitudes that are connected with these demands. In other words, if I endure a hardship, it is vital to my sense of self to believe that the outcome was worth the pain; otherwise I am a fool. Cognitive dissonance explains the intense loyalty to a group that many people exhibit when they have gone to great lengths to become a part of that group and also the willingness to do harmful acts to justify one's beliefs (Tavris & Aronson, 2008).

EXPLANATIONS OF CULTURAL SIMILARITIES AND DIFFERENCES IN GENDER IDEOLOGIES

The finding that gender ideologies often bear some resemblance to one another tempts us to embrace gender essentialism. Some evolutionary theorists such as Barash & Lipton (1997) use the finding of cross-cultural similarity as an argument for the pre-eminence of biological bases for gendered behavior. We are inclined to say that, if people are so similar on gender dimensions worldwide, then there must be something in genes, hormones, brain structure and function, and/or some other biological essence that make them so. On the other hand, the findings of cross-cultural differences, especially the striking exceptions of Tahiti and Semai, and the various "third genders" tempt us to embrace social constructionism, as we are inclined to say that, if some places are so different, then gender must be very malleable (not only at the individual level, where it undoubtedly is, but also at the cultural level). An essentialist argument must include an explanation of differences; a social constructionist argument must include an explanation of similarities.

Very few essentialists would deny that culture has a powerful effect on human behavior, and so their explanations of difference are constructed around a culture's ability to dissuade its natives from whatever the theorist considers to be human nature. In our view, most essentialists spend very little time dealing with exceptions to their predictions, preferring to chalk up these differences as a reflection of expected variation in behavior and unspecified sociocultural forces.

Social constructionists seem to fare much better in explaining the similarities in gender ideologies across cultures. The basic argument is this: cultural similarity is no guarantee of a hard-wired biological basis for behavior. Instead, these similarities may well reflect *cultural redundancies*—sociocultural forces that have affected many cultures in similar ways. Various theorists have proposed specific kinds of these forces, mainly historical and economic ones. Theoretically, exceptional cases such as Tahiti and Semai are marked by either the absence of the usual cultural forces or the presence of unusual ones.

As we mentioned in Chapter One, an important historical view of gender considers the centrality of patriarchy, a 5,000 year-old system by which men have dominated women in public and private life. Many historians and anthropologists believe that this system evolved in reaction to societies' economic needs. As Nancy Bonvillain (2001) proposes, "Gender is a basic criterion for the assignment of economic work in most cultures and is therefore deeply entwined in a society's mode of production" (p. 1).

In her landmark book, *The Creation of Patriarchy*, Gerda Lerner (1986) argues that male domination of women is largely embedded in the development of agriculture. Prior to the Neolithic period, humans lived in hunter/gatherer societies that were largely nomadic. In these foraging societies, children were not the economic resource that they later became. Their existence meant that there were more mouths to feed on a daily basis, and children only became valuable if they could develop to a point where they could produce more food than they consumed. Because it was difficult for people in these societies to accumulate surpluses of food or to stay in one place, children stretched resources and inhibited mobility.

The character of work and survival changed radically with the development of the ability to cultivate crops and maintain food surpluses. At that point, children became a labor resource, and having lots of them meant that a family or social group could till more land and thus have a much better chance of accumulating wealth. The relative burden of moving the children to more plentiful sources of food fell away, as groups could stay in the same places for generations. Land also became a valuable resource to be defended.

According to Lerner, hunter/gatherer societies were relatively gender-egalitarian, as women, who often did more gathering than men, produced more than their share of the wealth (food). With the advent of agriculture, however, women became most valuable for producing children, and similarly to land, they became a resource to acquire. The society then had an interest in controlling women's reproductive capacities, and, by extension, their sexuality. The means of *production* for women became the means of *reproduction*. Lerner describes the process by which women

> were exchanged or bought in marriages for the benefit of their families; later, they were conquered or bought in slavery, where their sexual services were part of their labor and where their children were the property of their masters. In every known society it was women of conquered tribes who were first enslaved, whereas men were killed. It was only after men had learned how to enslave the women of groups who could be defined as strangers, that they learned how to enslave men of these groups and, later, subordinates from within their own societies. (pp. 212–213)

Gender ideologies, including laws, customs, and religions based on the "counterfactual metaphor of male procreativity" (p. 220) flowed from these fundamental changes in the character of work. Over the course of 2,500 years, cultures established

Former President George W. Bush walks hand in hand through the flower garden at his ranch in Crawford, Texas with Crown Prince Abdullah of Saudi Arabia. Although Bush is conventionally gendered and handholding between men is proscribed in mainstream U.S. culture, the same behavior is a commonplace gesture of friendship in Saudi Arabia.

Photo © AP Images.

systems by which the male came to be valued over the female in virtually every sphere of public life. Lerner makes it clear that the oppression of patriarchy for women and the privilege for men have never applied equally to all people, but rather that it interacts with social class to have profound effects on people's lives and resulted in women-as-a-group living in a "relatively greater state of un-freedom than men" (p. 214) from that point to the present day.

Nancy Bonvillain (2001) provides some anthropological evidence in support of Lerner's theory. Bonvillain describes two cultures in which social gender arrangements changed in concert with economic developments. The Ju/'hoansi (ju-TWAN-si, also known as the !Kung in anthropological literature) of the Kalahari Desert in Africa were mainly a foraging people with egalitarian gender roles, an arrangement that Bonvillain ties to men's and women's relatively equal contribution to the band's subsistence (actually, women provided more of the total caloric intake for the group than men). One marker of this gender equality is the lack of a sexual double standard—females are as free to express their sexuality as males. (Recall Lerner's contention that the sexual double standard is an expression of the patriarchal control of women's lives. Gilmore, 1990, also noted a lack of sexual double standard in Tahiti.) For the Ju/'hoansi, the social and interpersonal costs of having extramarital affairs are equal for men and women. Two other important features of this culture reflect the absence of patriarchal arrangements; wife-beating and rape were very rare—perhaps non-existent—and fathers' participation in child care was considerable. Coltrane

(1998) notes that the level of fathers'child care involvement is inversely related to the level of masculine aggressiveness in the culture. One could argue that this connection is both cause and effect of gender equality and promoting male caregiving is a central feature of the gendered violence reduction efforts by the international organization *Promundo* (2014). If violence and inequality are born of disconnection, then building human connections would seem to be an important part of the solution.

In the early twentieth century, Ju/'hoansi economic arrangements began to change as European Boers came to the area, appropriated land, established agriculture, and hired natives as farm laborers. At the same time, the British established schools and various missionaries came to the area. Both wielded considerable influence over the ideologies of the natives. By the 1960s, most Ju/'hoansi were involved in farming and herding, which are mostly carried out by men. A division of labor developed, with women relegated mainly to domestic chores. Men became the owners of the herds and fields, and women's work became regarded as subsidiary. The sexes experienced a greater degree of separation than ever before, with men becoming more mobile and women more homebound. As a result, work roles came to be defined more rigidly along gender lines, men-as-a-group came to higher status compared with women-as-a-group, and gender arrangements moved toward models found in much of the world. The antifeminine ethic evolved, with men increasingly refusing to do "women's work."

The Arctic Inuit provide another example of change from what was an unusual cultural gender arrangement. Inuit society was marked by a limited male dominance, i.e., there were some features of patriarchal tradition (e.g. violence against women, physical and social segregation of the sexes) and some indicators of women's power in the culture (i.e., no sexual double standard, considerable child care participation by fathers, low division of labor, and *uxorilocal* residence—a couple initially lived near the wife's family following marriage). Bonvillain ties the male dominance aspect to men's provision of most meat and fish and the egalitarian aspects to the considerable contribution of women's labor to the group's subsistence in the harsh environment of the Arctic—women do some hunting and fishing, and they do the majority of sewing, a critical survival function because clothing that protects people from the elements must be expertly made and replaced often.

Inuit economies underwent a transformation in the early twentieth century, when trapping animals for fur replaced whaling as the main source of income. As the Inuit moved from a subsistence hunting society to one in which wealth could be accumulated, men spent increasing amounts of time away from home, checking traps and trading furs for food and other commodities. Male dominance increased and gender roles moved toward the arrangements we have described as "traditional" throughout this book, although they are anything but traditional for the Inuit.

Bonvillain tracks concomitant economic and gender changes in several other societies, such as the indigenous North Americans of the Great Plains, the Igbo of Nigeria, and the Jivaro of Peru. She concludes that gender equality depends on women and men sharing control over the acquisition and use of resources, and post-marital residence rules favoring women. These conditions have been relatively absent in much of the world for centuries.

The history of masculinity is also a history of warfare and other danger. When the survival of the society depends on dangerous hunting, intertribal competition for food, or fighting off intruders, those tasks have always fallen to men (until very recently) for three major reasons. First, men have relatively greater upper-body strength than women and are thus better suited to many aspects of these tasks, especially prior to the development of modern weapons and labor saving devices. Second, men's physical role in the reproductive process is minimal. They do not become pregnant or nurse children, and so their time can be invested in other tasks. Third, men are, in a sense, expendable. The survival of a society, in terms of producing children, requires many fewer men than women.

But facing danger is not natural. The self-preservation instinct provides a strong motivation to run away from it. Therefore, a society has to offer men great incentives for risking death, and the rewards for men who survive generally take the forms of power, status, and sexual access. Women must cooperate by being subservient for this arrangement to function. Men must be stripped of their vulnerable emotions to perform this work, which involves going against their natural inclinations. Thus, they have to be "made" into masculine men by some "unnatural" process. Gilbert Herdt (1982) believes that harsh male initiation rites serve this purpose of making men into machines. The rewards for succeeding as a man are great; so are the costs of failing.

Therefore, a social constructionist explanation of cross-cultural similarities in masculinity is that many cultures have found it necessary to defend land and compete for scarce resources to survive, and that the gender ideology of men as risk-taking, aggressive, powerful, and dominant provided a cultural context for men as hunters and warriors. Gilmore (1990) explains it thus: "Manhood is the social barrier that societies must erect against entropy, human enemies, the forces of nature, time, and all the human weaknesses that endanger group life" (p. 226).

We return to the exceptional cultures of Tahiti and Semai as evidence in support of this argument. Although most cultures have historically been served by male dominance and aggression, these two cultures have not. Gilmore (1990) notes that the economic and social conditions that have existed in most of the world were never present in these cultures. Tahiti is an island paradise where there is no dangerous or strenuous work. The food sources are fish and agriculture. Unlike the situation for the Mehinaku of Brazil, fishing in Tahiti is not dangerous, nor is hunting. There is always a plentiful supply of food. There is no shortage of arable land or domesticated animals. As Tahiti is an island remote from the rest of the world, there has been no need to defend its borders and therefore no culture of warriors. Thus, the social and economic forces that promote competition, aggression, and a gendered division of labor are noticeably absent.

The Semai have plentiful land and no private ownership. Although only men hunt, this activity is not dangerous or strenuous—small wild pigs are the largest game pursued. Trapping and fishing provide a much larger amount of the food supply, and, again, the fishing is not difficult or dangerous; children often fish by hand. There has been no warfare. Gilmore summarizes the striking differences between most of the world and these two cultures, describing Tahiti and Semai as places where:

> There is no want of natural resources and thus no economic incentive to strive or to compete, no agonistic ethos, no open market for skills. Because the economy is cooperative, ambition is devalued. There are no serious hazards in the external world that the men are expected to defend against.... Neither society feels threatened by invaders; neither engages in warfare. There is little pressure for worldly success. There is no concept of a secluded private sphere of women and children that men must protect. Men have no interest in defining themselves as different from or superior to women, or as their defenders. In short, there is little basis for an ideology of manhood that motivates men to perform under pressure or to defend boundaries. (pp. 217–218)

From this perspective, it seems that the "default options" of traditional gender that Bem (1993) describes are constructed from social, historical and economic conditions, that traditional masculinity is constructed as a psychological and social response to perceived and/or actual threat, and that the natural human default options are cooperation and gender-egalitarianism.

If social and economic conditions are responsible for producing traditional gender roles and ideologies, will these arrangements change if and when the conditions that produced them change? There is evidence that this is indeed the case. Best's and Williams' (1993) study of 14 countries demonstrated that gender ideologies are strongly related to the social and economic development of the culture. The modern conditions of urbanization and industrialization are accompanied by more modern gender arrangements. Many of the authors in Adler's (1993) edited volume, *The International Handbook of Gender Roles*, noted that this phenomenon seemed to hold within a culture, i.e., that urban people and people with non-traditional occupations tended to be more gender-egalitarian than their rural and traditional counterparts within the same countries.

The finding that two things go together (modern work roles and modern gender roles) does not necessarily mean that one causes the other, but we can make a strong argument for this relationship as a causal one with the use of a functional analysis. Industrialization greatly diminishes the need for a sexual division of labor. The skills required by most modern work do not require physical strength or risk-taking. We have also seen profound changes in reproduction. Reliable contraception is increasingly allowing people to control when and if they will have children (Tavris & Wade, 2001), and children are not the economic resource they were in agricultural societies. Thus, it is possible for people to have children for reasons other than economic ones, and people tend to have many fewer children as a result. Women or men are capable of performing all child care duties, as demonstrated by a small but growing number of stay-at-home fathers in the United States. Overall, modern societies can offer many more options in the world of work than traditional societies could, and changes in gender ideologies occur as a result. For example, there have been significant increases in the proportion of women in the U.S. military over the last several decades. Social constructionists view traditional gender arrangements in the modern world as historical artifacts that will continue to evolve into modern arrangements over time, just as patriarchy began to evolve in response to social and economic changes some 5,000 years ago. The recent interest in studying gender is but one indication that social changes are taking place. We may be coming full circle, as the economic bases of urbanization and industrialization recapitulate the resource control that women had in foraging societies.

DIVERSITY AMONG AMERICAN MEN: THE IMPACT OF ETHNICITY AND SOCIAL CLASS

We have seen the impact of various cultural forces on the social construction of masculinity, and we have noted both continuity and change in gender ideologies across cultures. We now turn to a more detailed description of some of these social factors within various groups in the United States.

Historical Considerations

The content of masculine gender ideology in mainstream U.S. culture is not a static entity. It has evolved in response to changes in the spirit of the times across history. Two comprehensive descriptions of historical changes in masculinity as culturally constructed in the United States are Anthony Rotundo's (1993) *American Manhood: Transformations in Masculinity from the Revolution to the Modern Era* and Michael Kimmel's (2006) *Manhood in America: a Cultural History*.

Rotundo conceptualizes changes in social conceptions of masculinity in three phases. The first, *communal masculinity*, characterized colonial times. It emphasized a man's usefulness to the community more than his economic success. The major expression of masculinity was in meeting the needs and expectations of one's family and neighbors. There was a fundamental value of male superiority that was based in the belief of men's supposedly greater ability to reason and to control emotions. These beliefs were the bases of laws and other social arrangements that gave men and women unequal status. For example, women were not allowed to vote in the United States until well into the twentieth century.

In the late eighteenth century, the service orientation of communal masculinity gave way to the economic orientation of *self-made manhood*, with its emphasis on business and professional success and the accumulation of wealth. Rotundo believes that this change came about as an effect of an increased political and economic climate that emphasized individuality over the collective. People believed that unfettered competition would reward the most deserving men. The ethic of controlling one's passions gave way to an emphasis on channeling them into expressions of dominance and independence. Although men were seen as the more virtuous of the sexes under communal masculinity, they came to be seen as selfish and aggressive under self-made manhood, and people came to regard women as virtuous people whose social role was to civilize and control the animal passions of men.

During this period, there was an increasing emphasis on what both Rotundo and Kimmel refer to as the *doctrine of separate spheres*. The cultural assumption that men and women are fundamentally different led to the belief that the sexes function best in settings (spheres) that conform to their supposedly natural proclivities. Women's domain was defined as the home, men's as the world-at-large. People considered the world to be an evil and dangerous place from which "fragile" women must be protected. A man came home from work to renew himself for the next day's battle. As Rotundo so eloquently puts it, "the social fabric was torn every day in the world and mended every night at home. Men's sphere depleted virtue; women's sphere renewed it.... While men of the colonial era had struggled to reconcile ideals of public virtue and personal interest, those ideals realigned themselves along a male-female axis in the nineteenth century" (pp. 23–24).

Kimmel (2006) describes the self-made man as a restless person who had to prove himself every day, but who could never demonstrate his worth once and for all. Therefore, he had to compete with other men both at work and in the other "homosocial preserves" (all-male environments) such as men's clubs and sporting events. These settings became a very important proving ground for masculinity in the nineteenth century, and they continue to hold this function in the present day. Because the doctrine of separate spheres sharply distinguished the domains of men and women, too much influence from women's sphere, the home, was believed to feminize and thus emasculate men. They experienced an increasing need to prove themselves to other men in places away from the home—in sports, at clubs, and for children, in an aggressive "boy culture" (Rotundo, 1993). The colonial emphasis on connection to home evolved into an ethic of somewhat of a disconnection, increasingly emphasizing the social definition of masculinity as antifemininity.

The nineteenth century also saw the rise of homophobia as a consequence of the rise of masculine competition and antifemininity. Kimmel writes that, "Homophobia is more than an irrational fear of homosexuals.... Homophobia is the fear of other men—that other men will unmask us, emasculate us, reveal to us and the world that we do not measure up" (p. 8). Homosocial preserves were at once de-pressurizing and re-pressurizing; they were an escape from the pressures of the working world and women's sphere, the home, but they were also an immersion in highly competitive, rough, and aggressive all-male environments. A boy wants to go off with his male friends to escape from the feminizing influence of his mother, but there he must conform his behavior to masculine standards or risk being ostracized as a "sissy."

The late nineteenth and early twentieth centuries saw the rise of *passionate manhood*, which Rotundo describes as, "...in some respects an elaboration of self-made manhood, but it stretched those beliefs in directions that would have shocked the old individualists of the early 1800s" (p. 5). The major change was the view that being competitive and aggressive moved beyond the world of work to become regarded as ends in themselves. Rotundo describes this social change:

> Where nineteenth-century views had regarded the self and its passions suspiciously as objects of manipulation (self-control, self-denial), twentieth-century opinion exalted them as a source of identity and personal worth (self-expression, self-enjoyment). Play and leisured entertainment—once considered marks of effeminacy—became approved activities for men as the nineteenth century ended ... A man defined his identity not just in the workplace but through modes of enjoyment and self-fulfillment outside of it. In a world where the passions formed a vital part of the self, older forms of virtue—self-restraint, self-denial, became suspect. (p. 6).

We see common threads of more modern conceptions of masculinity in all of these historical phases: independence, antifemininity, toughness, competition, homophobia, and aggression. Yet the relative emphases of these masculine ethics changed from era to era. Social constructionists view all of these changes as reflections of the economic and social needs of a society, a connection we will explore further in the descriptions of masculinity and work in Chapter Eight.

There are important interactions between the social demands that come with gendered status and those that come with memberships in other socially defined groups. Following are brief descriptions of masculinities in the contexts of several ways in which society perceives people as different in important ways. In this chapter we explore the connections between masculinity and ethnicity. In the next we examine three other forms of identity: sexual orientation, socioeconomic class, and age.

Ethnicities and Masculinity

Ethnic identity is a strong identification with one's cultural group. The United States is a collection of many peoples, and each group has cultural modes of language, customs, food, religion, and dress that make it distinctive. Ethnic identities also include psychological characteristics like world view, moral values, and rules about appropriate behavior. These cultural characteristics are passed from one generation to the next within family systems, and there is evidence of the effects of ethnicities even many generations after immigration (Tavris & Wade, 2001). *Acculturation* is an identification with the dominant culture, which in the United States could be described as white, heterosexual, middle-class, Christian, and western European in origin.

The ways of being of ethnic and acculturated values sometimes come into conflict, but researchers have demonstrated that ethnic identity and acculturation are not opposite ends of a single continuum. In other words, an individual does not necessarily become less ethnically identified as he or she becomes more acculturated. Rather, these two processes are relatively independent. A person with a strong ethnic identity and weak acculturation is termed *ethnic separatist.* A person with a strong ethnic identity and strong acculturation is termed *bicultural.* An immigrant who conforms to the "melting pot" ethic, the value on rapid acculturation and abandonment of ethnic identity, is termed *assimilated.* And, some *marginal* people have weak identification with both the dominant group and their culture of origin. Individuals vary with regard to degree of ethnic identity and acculturation (Tavris & Wade, 2001).

Gender roles are obviously important components of ethnicities. As we have already seen, societies have many different ways of handling perceived divisions of labor, sexuality, and personality characteristics between the sexes. For example, German American fathers are known for their interpersonal distance, low emotionality, and strong discipline, often including the use of physical punishment. The traditional German man was the unquestioned head of the family, and his main role was that of economic provider. Wives were expected to do domestic chores and maintain order within the home. They are considered to be more emotionally available to children than their husbands (Winawer & Wetzel, 2005). Many German American families continue to follow this model of male dominance, even though the German culture from which they descended has evolved into one of the more gender-egalitarian cultures in the modern world (Williams & Best, 1990a).

Italian American men resemble German American men in most respects, but the cultural standards for emotional expression are a distinct exception. Italian Americans tend to have close-knit nuclear and extended family ties, and families are viewed as a source of help for problems and central to an individual's decision making. Going outside of the family for help with personal difficulties is strongly discouraged (Giordano, McGoldrick, & Guarino Klages, 2005). Thus, we see significant variations, even within two well-established European American cultures, but there is also a high degree of similarity between these two groups in cultural concepts of masculinity.

One way to observe cultural differences in the conceptions of "men's work" and "women's work" is to visit traditional ethnic restaurants. In Greek or Indian restaurants, seating customers and waiting on tables are considered men's work. In Polish and Ethiopian eateries, women perform these functions (Rybarczyk, 1994). And these arrangements change over time. The first time I (C. K.) visited Spain in the early 1990s, waiters were nearly exclusively males. On my most recent trip there in 2010, women were as visible as men in these jobs.

To illustrate the effects of ethnicity on masculinity, we will briefly describe some of the research on the three largest groups of ethnic men in the United States, Latino, African American, and Asian men, all of whom have prominent ethnic identities.

Latino Men

The term *Hispanic* is used by the United States government to refer to all Spanish-speaking ethnic groups. This term can refer to people of any race from as many as 20 distinct cultures, including Cuban, Puerto Rican, Spain, the Dominican Republic, and Mexico (Garcia-Preto, 2005). The histories and ethnic identities of these groups are often very different from one another. For example, many Salvadorans and Nicaraguans emigrated to the United States during civil wars in their home countries. Compared with some other Latinos, they were more likely to come from low socioeconomic backgrounds and had relatively little preparation for moving to the United States. In contrast, many Chilean and Cuban immigrants have more educational advantage, higher socioeconomic status, and many had made arrangements and established local support before emigrating. Central Americans are much more likely than most other groups to have experienced war and to have been forcibly displaced from their homes (Comas-Díaz, 1993).

By far, the largest group of Hispanic peoples in the United States are Latinos/Latinas, people whose ethnic backgrounds are in the Spanish-speaking countries of the Americas. Compared with the dominant Anglo culture, which tends to be centered in the nuclear family, Latino culture places more emphasis on extended families. The value of *familismo* (familism) emphasizes these kinship relationships in the context of values like interdependence, cooperation, and affiliation (Falicov, 2005).

Latino/Latina cultures largely endorse hierarchical family arrangements whereby fathers are expected to be authoritarian and mothers submissive. There are strong traditions of gender-differentiated ideologies, with men thought to be strong, brave, independent, and rational. Women are thought to be intuitive, gentle, submissive, and dependent (Comas-Díaz, 1993). However, there is considerable variation among individual families. Many are egalitarian, and women dominate in others (Falicov, 2005). Comas-Díaz (1993) also notes that traditional gender roles among Latino/Latina immigrants are undergoing change in reaction to exposure to mainstream United States culture, and also because wives tend to have an easier time finding employment than their husbands. Again, we see the influence of economic power on gender relations.

The stereotype of the Latino centers on *machismo*, the display of strong and aggressive masculinity. In mainstream U.S. society, this term is usually used to describe the negative qualities of physical aggression, sexual promiscuity, dominance of women, and excessive use of alcohol (Gutierrez, 1990). Some authors have argued that machismo is little more than a negative stereotype of Latinos that the mainstream culture uses to rationalize prejudice and discrimination (Lips, 2008), and that the cultural definition of machismo more accurately describes not just negative qualities, but also the positive qualities of courage, generosity, dignity, respect for others, and love for family (Arciniega, Anderson, Tovar-Blank, & Tracey, 2008).

Machismo may be more of a public display than a common personality trait. Baca Zinn (1995) has noted that a number of nontraditional gender traits are quite common in Mexican American men, such as shared decision-making, nurturing fatherhood, and participation in family-oriented social and recreational activities. At the same time, patriarchal ideologies remain fairly strong in Latino culture, reflected largely in the continued tradition of father as undisputed head of the household. Latino masculinity is an illustration of many common themes of continuity and change, cultural diversity within a group often perceived as unitary, individual behavior within the context of group ideology, and the interactions among race, class, and gender.

African American Men

Because racial characteristics such as skin color are visible, race often plays a prominent role in social relations. In contrast, ethnicity is usually more fluid, sometimes changing in response to acculturation, selectively expressed (e.g., at family functions and religious ceremonies, but perhaps not at work), or concealed (e.g., by changing one's surname) (Rybarczyk, 1994).

In many cases, dominant cultures consider people of minority races to be different from others in important ways. *Racism* is a set of behaviors, values, and attitudes that reflect a belief in the innate superiority of one race over another. This belief need not be conscious to have profound effects. Institutional racism in the United States has resulted in segregation, discrimination, stigmatization, and alienation for minority peoples. All of these maltreatments have profound influences on people's behavior and senses of self.

Any description of African American men must be imbedded in the contexts of slavery as well as racism, which is both historical and ongoing, both personal and institutional. African American men's gender identities and their expressions of masculinities have been shaped in response to racism and its social consequences such as isolation from mainstream culture, underemployment, poverty, and unequal treatment in legal systems. Racism often results in predictable psychological responses such as low self-esteem, suspiciousness of people from the dominant culture, and anger (Aronson, 2012).

African American men have struggled for many generations in response to a mainstream culture that has denied them personhood and dignity. Prior to the late 1960s, adult African American men were often referred to as *boys*, a label that denies their status as adults (Franklin, 1984). (Note here that many people persist in referring to adult women as *girls*, a sexist parallel to this racist practice). Many people have described the situation of African American men as a national crisis, as this population is beset by high rates of unemployment, drug and alcohol abuse, premature death by violence and preventable diseases, crime victimization, and incarceration (Gibbs, 1992). Nearly one out of every three (29 percent) African American males is incarcerated in state or federal prison at some time during his life, compared with about one in six Hispanic males and one in 25 White males (*The Sentencing Project*, 2013).

Lemann (1991) proposed that the lack of employment opportunity has created a cycle of poverty and powerlessness for African Americans. Although they achieved emancipation from slavery in the nineteenth century, economic opportunities have been slow to arrive. In the late 1800s, many people found subsistence living in the exploitive system of share cropping. Even these jobs became untenable following the dramatic improvement of farm technology in the 1940s. As a result, many African Americans migrated from the rural South to Northern cities to seek work in industry. This was the largest migration in United States history, and 81 percent of African Americans continue to live in large urban areas (Hines & Boyd-Franklin, 2005). The availability of industrial work decreased as the U.S. moved to post-industrial economies, creating high unemployment and underemployment among African Americans within a context of race-driven discrimination in education, housing and employment (Wilson, 1987). Individualistic explanations of problems in these communities (i.e., that African Americans are not as bright, hard working, or ambitious as everyone else) are victim-blaming rationalizations that ignore the centuries-long history of racism in the United States.

The development of a masculine gender identity among African American males tends to take a different path from that of their European American counterparts, who often grow up with the social message that "power and control are their birthright" (Lee, 1990, p. 126). Lacking much of an opportunity to achieve socially defined masculinity, but with this goal nonetheless important, African American men have often constructed alternative masculinities.

In a classic work, Majors and Billson (1992) described a frequent approach, the cultural signature of *cool pose*, a social style that many African American males adopt to survive psychologically. Cool pose involves a set of ritualized behaviors that involve toughness, detachment, control, and a stylish, sometimes flamboyant presentation. Filmmaker Byron Hurt (2006) explored the influence of this cultural demand in hip-hop culture. Majors and Billson describe it thus:

> The purpose of posing and posturing—being cool—is to enhance social competence, pride, dignity, self-esteem, and respect. Cool enhances masculinity. Being cool also expresses bitterness, anger, and distrust toward the dominant society

> for many years of hostile mistreatment and discrimination. Cool pose helps keep
> the dominant society off balance and puzzled and accentuates the expressive self.
> (p. 105)

This kind of psychological response is a show of pride and strength and a refusal to display vulnerability. However, it may come at some cost to close relationships, which require attachment and emotional expression. Cool pose is also used to teach men to restrain their anger, because expressing it directly to someone more powerful can lead to negative consequences. Social training for doing so takes the form of "playing the dozens"—a ritualized game of insulting one another. An older African American man traces the survival value of being able to do so back to the days of slavery:

> It was a game slaves used to play, only they wasn't just playing for fun. They was
> playing to teach themselves and their sons how to stay alive. The whole idea was
> to learn to take whatever the master said to you without answering back or hitting
> him 'cause that was the way a slave had to be, so's he could go on living (Guffy,
> 1971, in Majors and Billson, 1992, p. 101).

The social stress on African American men is also reflected in the high rates of physical ailments such as hypertension, heart disease, stroke, and cirrhosis of the liver, all of which have psychosocial and behavioral components (see Chapter Nine). The suicide rate for young African American males has tripled in the last 30 years (although it remains considerably lower than that of White males), and deaths from high-risk behaviors like smoking, drug abuse, and reckless driving affect this population disproportionately (Gibbs, 1994).

Some would have us believe that racism is a thing of the past. However, evidence clearly indicates that African Americans as a group continue to struggle in a dominant culture that marginalizes them, and that the cumulative effects of segregation, economic inequality, and the reality of centuries of slavery has been to maintain a hostile and unpredictable environment for African American males. An understanding of contemporary social constructions of African American masculinity is achieved largely through an analysis of a systematic inequality that pervades the educational, economic, criminal justice, health care, and virtually every other institution of mainstream United States society (Gibbs, 1994).

Asian American Men

In the same way that the categories of Hispanic and Latino encompass a wide variety of cultures, Asian men are a diverse group of people. Despite mainstream Americans' seeming view of Asians as indistinguishable from one another (Chan, 2004), Asian Americans' origins are in a wide variety of places such as China, Japan, Korea, Vietnam, Laos, Malaysia, and India, to name only a few, each culture with its unique history and gendered traditions (Liu, 2002).

As with all ethnicities, the conditions of immigration strongly shape the consciousness of the culture. For example, in the late nineteenth and early twentieth century, the United States immigration policy allowed for an influx of Chinese men but very few

Chinese women (Many of these men were married and left their wives and children behind out of necessity). As a result, the sex ratio in this ethnic group in 1890 was an astounding 27 males for every woman, and there were similar, although not as pronounced, patterns for Japanese, Korean, and Filipino people. Because Asians were not permitted to date or marry outside of their race, heterosexual Asian men were effectively desexualized and "bachelor societies" developed in a re-definition of the family. Immigration policies were not made gender egalitarian until years later, and many Asian wives and (then adult) children emigrated to join their husbands and fathers after decades apart. During World War II, the United States government incarcerated ("interned") more than 100,000 Japanese and Japanese Americans, undermining their dignity and effectively erasing the economic gains of a generation and creating a pervasive sense of hopelessness. Later, many Asian men served in the war and helped to reduce prejudice against Asian peoples (Espiritu, 2008).

Yen Le Espirtu (2007) notes that there are now two "distinct chains of emigration from Asia: one comprising the relatives of working-class Asians... the other of highly trained immigrants. In other words, today's Asian American men both join Whites in the well-paid, educated white collar sector of the workforce *and* join Latino immigrants in lower-paying secondary sector jobs" (p. 37). Whites' inability to distinguish Asian peoples may lead to a perception of Asians as relatively privileged. This may be true for many Chinese and Japanese whose well-educated grandparents and great grandparents immigrated into the country, but it is not true for the vast majority of, for example, first generation Hmong, many of whom struggle merely to survive.

In summary, we see some of the same issues in Asian American men as in other ethnicities: diversity within a group considered by the mainstream to be homogenous, a tension between ethnically defined masculinity and that of the dominant culture, and the intersection of racism and prejudice with gendered strivings.

SUMMARY

1. Social conceptions of gender are influenced by a variety of factors, including ethnic patterns, economic conditions, religion, language, family socialization, cultural expectations, and the spirit of the times. Mainstream gender roles constitute the "default options" of a culture. Becoming a gender non-conformist requires a person to resist a considerable amount of cultural momentum, a task made more difficult by the nonconscious quality of gender ideology. Gender roles contain a set of meanings that are so embedded in social practices that they are virtually invisible to many.

2. There is a "family resemblance" in masculinities for most (but not all) of the world, often characterized by strength, risk taking, avoidance of femininity, aggression, and sexual initiative. In most of the world, masculinity is regarded as an essence that males achieve, not merely grow into.

3. In a minority of cultures, gender ideologies are strikingly different from most of the world. These cultures are marked by unusual social, historic, and economic circumstances.

4. Patriarchy, the male domination of women, largely originated in the development of agriculture. Changes in economic conditions have fostered changes in gender ideology, with more modern societies exhibiting correspondingly modern (egalitarian) gender arrangements.

5. The dominant ideology of masculinity in the United States has undergone significant changes during the past two centuries, from an emphasis on service to one on individualism to an emphasis on competition for its own sake. The colonial emphasis on connection to home evolved into an ethic of somewhat of a disconnection, increasingly emphasizing the social definition of masculinity as antifemininity.

6. The United States is a collection of many groups of ethnic peoples, and each group has cultural modes of being that are passed from one generation to the next within family systems, and that have effects on behavior for many generations after immigration. Gender roles are important components of ethnicities.

7. Latino/Latina cultures place a strong emphasis on extended families and largely endorse heirarchical family arrangements and gender-differentiated ideologies. *Machismo*, the display of strong and aggressive masculinity, carries both negative and positive connotations. Machismo may be more of a public display rather than a common personality trait. A number of nontraditional gender traits are quite common in Latinos.

8. Race also has an important impact on the expression of masculinity. African-American men, who are subject to widespread and longstanding racial oppression, experience a variety of unique problems, including high rates of unemployment, premature death, and incarceration. "Cool pose" is one reaction to being denied masculine power and privilege. The majority of working class African American men, who are well adjusted in spite of social circumstances, have been ignored by social scientists and the media.

9. As a group, Asian American men struggle with some of the same issues as other minorities: a mainstream view of a diverse group as homogenous, some disconnection between definitions of masculinity in the dominant culture and the ethnic culture, and a need to negotiate the boundaries of gender and identity within a context of racial and ethnic prejudice.

Chapter Six

Masculinities II: Intersections of Masculinity with Other Forms of Identities

Masculinities become more complicated and interesting when they combine with other forms of identity such as socioeconomic status, age, physical ability, and sexualities. In this chapter, we explore some of these intersections. As with Chapter Five, our aim is not to undertake an exhaustive review, but to give a sense of the effects of cultural masculinity as it relates to some of the most common social statuses that interact with gender.

SOCIAL CLASS

Gender stereotypes are somewhat variant at different levels of education, occupation, and income. For instance, Barbara Ehrenreich (1983) has noted that working-class masculinity in mainstream United States culture is more overtly aggressive and angry than professional-class masculinity. Power is central to social definitions of masculinity, and many see economic power as the best kind to have. Lacking this essence, low-income men may turn to other sources of power: the physically and the interpersonally dominant. R. W. Connell (1995) describes the difficulty in achieving standard masculine "success":

> in the marginal class situation, where the claim to power that is central to hegemonic [dominant] masculinity is constantly negated by economic and cultural weakness... these men have lost most of the patriarchal dividend... One way to resolve this contradiction is a spectacular display, embracing the marginality and stigma and turning them to account. At the personal level, this translates as a constant concern with front or credibility. (p. 116)

Therefore, masculine posturing, misogyny, and violence are ways of counterbalancing a deep-seated, perhaps unconscious sense of weakness. Connell once again echoes the theme of negative masculinity as a defense against powerlessness and the need for marginalized men to construct alternative models to a masculinity that includes the high social status that comes with wealth. Many of the authors in editor Lenore Adler's (1993) collection of international gender role descriptions noted that men and women tended to have more egalitarian statuses in the more educated and higher socioeconomic classes.

However, we should not paint too rosy a picture of economically successful men. Because masculinity is defined as being "number one," many of these men may view their levels of success as not good enough. As a result, they may see themselves as deprived, as their relative privilege is often invisible to them. One marker of masculine insecurity is family violence. A common view is that child abusers and wife batterers commit violent acts to defend against chronic low self-esteem by dominating less powerful others. Richard Gelles (1997) notes that there is a connection between low socioeconomic class and family violence. Unemployed and underemployed men beat their wives at double the rate of fully employed men, a testament to the centrality of earning to the masculine self-concept. However, the fact that poorer men are more likely to be violent should not obscure the fact that family violence is present in all social strata nor the fact that most poor men are not violent. Economic conditions interact with individual psychology and other social forces to encourage or inhibit family violence and other toxic masculine behavior.

Because of centuries of institutionalized inequality, socioeconomic class is often intertwined with race and sex. United States median income levels show sharp disparities by race. In 2006, Hispanic and Black households had median incomes sharply lower than those of non-Hispanic Whites and Asians. Among full-time, year-round workers, women earn an average of 76 percent of what men earn (median for males: $42,261; for females: $32,515) (DeNavas-Walt, Proctor, & Smith, 2007). Negative stereotypes of women and people of color are both cause and effect of these imbalances, as people other than White men are often disadvantaged in hiring and promotion practices. Their lack of visibility in high-status occupations then fuels negative gender and race ideologies.

SEXUAL ORIENTATION

The dominant definition of United States masculinity includes heterosexuality as one of its central characteristics. Therefore, gay, bisexual, transgendered, and transsexual men, like men of color and economically disadvantaged men, tend to construct their identities in ways that are different from mainstream masculine ideologies. These orientations entail much more than just the sexual behavior of the person. They also involve considerations of personal identity, culture, and lifestyle.

Cultures vary widely in their attitudes toward non-heterosexual behavior, from severe negative sanction to tolerance to acceptance to encouragement. For example, ritual homosexual behaviors between older men and younger boys is obligatory in Sambia (Herdt, 1982; Gilmore, 1990) and other societies in eastern Melanesia. However, most Western cultures have long traditions of repressing and discouraging sexual behavior between same-sex persons. In many cases, these attitudes were codified into laws prohibiting such contact. Historically, many states prohibited most common same-sex sexual behaviors, even though it was legal for heterosexual couples to engage in these same behaviors. These "sodomy laws" were ruled unconstitutional by the United States Supreme Court in the landmark Lawrence vs. Texas case in 2003 (sodomylaws.org, 2009).

The right to same-sex marriage is another recent legal controversy in the United States. A variety of rights and privileges available to married heterosexual people are not available to couples of the same sex, such as spousal health insurance, social security benefits, family and medical leave, and emergency health care decisions. The U.S. General Accounting Office (2004) has identified more than 1,000 federal protections and rights in which marital status in part determines eligibility. In 2003, Massachusetts became the first state to allow same sex marriage, and by 2014, 18 other states had joined it. The remaining 31 states had laws and/or constitutional amendments banning same-sex marriage (gaymarriage.procon.org, 2014). It is curious that so many believe it necessary to enact a law refusing a right that a group of people did not have in the first place. In 2014, the U.S. Supreme court refused to review a case in which Virginia's same-sex marriage ban was overturned, effectively expanding the right to marry from 19 to 30 states and making it unlikely that any state will be able to sustain a same-sex marriage ban for very long. In fact, same-sex couples began to marry in Virginia the day of that decision (Associated Press, 2014).

The label *homosexual*, as a description of a person (not merely a behavior) emerged in the United States in the 1880s (Rotundo, 1993). Barbara Sherman Heyl (1996) describes the effect of this new term:

> Until that time the moral and legal debates on homosexual behavior centered on just that—behavior. The shift in focus defined homosexuality as a 'state of being' that could exist prior to and without any overt homosexual act and, from somewhere inside the person, compelled a lifelong habitual preference for same-sex partners. Homosexuals became a highly stigmatized category of persons. (p. 121)

Anthony Rotundo (1993) traces the late eighteenth-century shift from a linguistic tendency of describing the behavior (e.g., "sodomy," "unnatural acts") to the use of a variety of new and pejorative words that label the person—"degenerate," "pervert," "fairy." As a result of the social polarization of homosexuals and heterosexuals, people whose sexual desires were oriented toward their same sex began to think of themselves as distinct social groups. They formed communities in large cities to find support in a mainstream environment that persecuted them, and to develop relationships with people who would nurture their social and sexual identities.

Anti-gay sentiments are centered in antifeminine ones. Masculinity is socially defined as antifemininity, and what could be more socially feminine than loving a man? Rotundo puts the emergent notion of homosexual identity into the context of masculine ideology:

> The image of the male homosexual played an especially important role in the redefinition of middle-class manhood that was taking place at the turn of the [twentieth] century. The effeminate homosexual provided a negative referent for the new masculinity, with its heavy emphasis on the physical marks of manliness. The emergent homosexual image soon acquired an awesome power to stigmatize.

> By the turn of the century, men were using the same terms of scorn for homosexual
> males that they used for artistic, tender-minded, or reformist men. (p. 278)

Thus, "homosexual" and "feminine" became parallel and negative concepts in reference to masculine character. Prior to that time, males engaged in romantic nonsexual friendships with one another, writing passionate letters to one another and often sleeping in the same bed. But romantic friendships disappeared with the new homophobia of the late nineteenth century, as it dramatically increased men's motivation to distinguish themselves from the feminine. Close male-male friendships developed into "buddyships" in which men bonded around sports, work, and antifemininity rather than sharing their emotional lives more directly. Thus, homophobia had, and continues to have, negative effects on both gay and heterosexual men.

It is important to note that identifying as a non-heterosexual man is not wholly dependent on sexual behavior per se. The term "men who have sex with men" (sometimes abbreviated MSM) is being increasingly used to acknowledge that some heterosexually identified men engage in homosexual sex. In the African-American community, men who do this, usually in secret, are described as being "on the Down Low" (King & Hunter, 2004). When U.S. Senator Larry Craig was arrested in 2007 for soliciting sex with a man in a Minneapolis airport rest room (he later pled guilty to a lesser charge of disorderly conduct), he said in a subsequent news conference, "I am not gay" (Minnesota Public Radio, 2007). Assuming that he engaged in sexual behavior with a man or even if he does so regularly, he is nevertheless, in an important sense, not gay, as this term implies a cultural identification that goes beyond sexual behavior. Because this chapter is focused on identity, we will save the discussion of MSM for the chapter on sexuality (Chapter 11).

Non-heterosexually identified men are not immune to the social pressures of mainstream cultural masculinity, and they must find solutions to the contradictions of these pressures and their sexualities (Szymanski, Kashubeck-West, & Meyer, 2008). The strategies they use in dealing with these two considerable forces are many and varied. John Loughery (1998) points out that, contrary to stereotype, there has never been any set of personality and lifestyle attributes that we could describe as characteristic of *the* gay man.

Although some non-heterosexual men have traditionally masculine characteristics, they are more likely than heterosexual men to consider and adopt a broader range of gendered behavior (Heyl, 1996). It is possible that an awareness of being different frees an individual to consider more than the usual options, and to develop a sense of identity by clarifying and affirming what he is not, i.e., a masculine man as defined by the society (Herek, 1985). As heterosexual men may affirm their in-group identities by contrasting themselves with the out-group of men of other sexualities, a parallel process may take place with regard to the gendered behaviors of members of the out-group. In other words, the statement of what one *is* often begins with a statement of what one *is not*.

Within gay communities, *gay identity* is not an exclusively sexual one. It also includes emotional, lifestyle, and political aspects of living (Levine & Evans, 1996). These lifestyles range from the stereotypical "camp" and "drag" (flamboyantly feminine performances) to the embracing of traditional masculine features (except heterosexuality) that Martin Levine (1998) referred to as *gay macho*.

Ruth Fassinger (1998) proposed a stage model of lesbian/gay identity development which describes typical paths of individual and group identity changes that many gays and lesbians experience as they learn more about themselves and deal with both the mainstream and gay cultures. In the first stage, the individual becomes aware that he or she feels different sexual feelings than most others seem to feel. Around the same time, he or she also comes to a heightened awareness of the existence of a variety in sexual orientations in others. In the second stage, the person explores erotic desires for same-sex others and the possibilities for being a part of an identified group of gay or lesbian people. This stage involves self-acknowledgment of these desires and may or may not include actual sexual behavior. At the group level, the person thinks about fitting in to a social group of like-minded others.

The third stage involves deepening commitment to one's sexual orientation and the choices that grow out of it. At the group level, the person becomes more personally involved with the social reference group and often painfully aware of the societal oppression of non-heterosexuals. He or she begins to understand both the positive and negative consequences of embracing a lifestyle that is condemned by many.

Fassinger labels the fourth stage Internalization/Synthesis. In this final stage, the person is able to integrate his or her sexual attraction and attachment to same-sex people into the overall identity as an individual and as a member of a social group. Fassinger believes that the individual and group aspects of identity are "mutually catalytic," meaning that consideration of one's personal identity tends to highlight group issues, and vice versa.

Coming out, the process of revealing one's sexual orientation to others, is an important event in the psychological and social life of gay men. The opposite of being *out* is being *closeted* (keeping one's sexual orientation secret). The pervasive mainstream cultural assumption of heterosexuality makes being closeted the default option, and it also means that coming out is not an event that takes place one day and leaves the person "out" once and for all, perhaps with the exception of those in the public eye. There are many decisions about whom to come out to, how, and when, and there are different degrees of being out. Some people are out to virtually everyone they know. Others may be out to nearly everyone except their families of origin, to one parent but not the other, in a community but not at work, and all the endless variations in between.

The Stonewall Riot is the community parallel to the individual's coming out. The Stonewall was a popular gay bar in the Greenwich Village area of New York City. On June 28, 1969, police cleared the bar of patrons and shut it down, ostensibly for liquor law violations. As the police emerged from the bar, a crowd of angry gay men threw objects at them and a riot ensued. Herdt and Boxer (1991) describe Stonewall as a watershed historical event in gay political activism, one that crystallized a gay liberation movement that had begun quietly in the 1950s. In other words, it was the gay community's coming out, and it moved the focus of the gay world "from the secretive bar to the far more elaborate gay and lesbian communities of major cities around the world" (p.1). Herdt and Boxer describe individual coming out and community pride as emblematic of the transition from *homosexual* (secret) to *gay* (public and affirmative).

The last several decades have seen a new level of cultural identity for gay, lesbian, and bisexual people. Gay cultures have become more elaborated and, in many cases, more accepted. The American Psychiatric Association removed homosexuality from its official list of mental disorders in 1973 (The World Health Organization followed suit, but not until 1993) (van Hertum, 1992), and the American Psychological Association (APA) has taken many gay-affirmative public positions in the last 30 years, for instance an affirmation of full legal rights for gay and lesbian people (American Psychological Association, 2005). Some municipalities have passed ordinances prohibiting housing and employment discrimination on the basis of sexual orientation, and by the end of 2004, 216 of Fortune 500 corporations had extended spousal benefits to include same-sex partners, a tenfold increase since 1995. 410 of these corporations included sexual orientation in their non-discrimination policies (Joyce, 2005). At the same time, there is a visible social conservative backlash against gay rights. Gay, lesbian, bisexual, and transgendered people's struggle for recognition and equality is ongoing.

Herdt and Boxer (1991) described the differing experiences of four age cohorts of gay men in the United States. The first extends from 1900 to 1940. These were men who nearly all grew into adulthood without ever coming out. Now in their seventies and beyond, many of those who survive remain closeted.

The second cohort spanned the time period from World War II to the 1969 Stonewall riot. According to the authors, many of these men came to awareness and fulfillment of their same-sex erotic desires for the first time while serving in the armed forces. The Mattachine Society (an underground network of gay men) was founded in the 1950s and provided a new level of community, as did the emergence of gay bars in the 1960s. Still, gay communities largely remained secretive, and partly as a result, many men experienced their sexualities in negative terms (Levine, 1991). The hiding of such an important part of the self is often associated with feelings of shame.

Gay Pride Day marks the June anniversary of the Stonewall riot, which ushered in a new age of coming out and political activism. Men in the third, post-Stonewall cohort felt more free to express themselves in gay-affirmative ways, and gay neighborhoods like Greenwich Village in New York and Castro in San Francisco grew in size and visibility. There was mass coming out and an ethic of "free love" and recreational sex.

The AIDS epidemic ushered in the most recent cohort in the early 1980s, bringing radical changes in sexual behaviors and lifestyles. Martin Levine (1991) describes the new sexual ethic of the gay community: "Most men now perceive coupling, monogamy, and celibacy as healthy and socially acceptable." At the same time, gay communities began to make concerted efforts to support young gay men in the process of coming out. The sieges of AIDS and homophobic backlash appear to have brought the gay community together, and gay life is increasingly marked by a service orientation to the rest of the community and a renewed political activism (Pharr, 1997a). Laud Humphreys (quoted in Levine, 1991) describes the products of gay community transformation:

> The dozen largest urban areas of North America now have readily identifiable gay neighborhoods with heavy populations of same-sex couples. Each of these districts features not only openly gay bars and restaurants, but clothiers, bookstores, laundromats, a variety of shops, doctors, lawyers, dentists, and realtors that cater to a gay clientele." (p. 74)

Martin Levine (1991) contends that gay lifestyles are largely shaped by the culture and social structures that surround it. The relative social and geographical separation of many gay communities from mainstream cultures is a response to the heterosexual assumptive world of the mainstream culture and the stigma that it continues to attach to gay roles and behavior.

Attitudes toward Homosexuality

The social acceptance or nonacceptance of homosexuality varies from culture to culture and from one historical era to another (Gregersen, 1982). The beliefs that gays are mentally ill, immoral, vulgar, or dangerous are probably connected to the strong conservative Christian roots of mainstream United States culture. Early Catholic theologians, most notably Augustine, pronounced that sexual activity had procreation, not pleasure or self expression, as its purpose (Nelson, 1997). Since homosexual behavior could not possibly produce offspring, it was seen as immoral. The Victorian ethic of repressed sexuality led one to ask, "Why would a person have sex if he or she did not 'have to'?" There is no good answer, from the perspectives of these values, except to vilify the homosexual. Some social conservatives such as the Religious Right have characterized homosexuality as immoral and a sin against God (Rosin & Edsall, 1998). Some psychologists have developed a "therapy" designed to convert gays to heterosexuality (Edwards, 1996). This treatment is called "reparative therapy," connoting that homosexuality is a pathological condition in need of rectification.

There have been some fluctuations in attitudes toward gays in mainstream United States culture. In the 1970s, support for gay legal rights increased, perhaps as a function of more generally liberal political and sexual attitudes. The 1980s witnessed a resurgence of negative attitudes toward gays. AIDS struck the gay male community first, and there was a tendency among some people to believe that this horrible disease was a result of gays' lack of morality. Some prominent fundamentalist Christian leaders publicly stated that AIDS was a punishment from God for homosexuals' sins. People tend to believe in a "just world"—that bad things happen to bad people (Aronson, 2012), and gays became a convenient scapegoat for this deadly disease.

Some seem to believe that same-sex erotic orientation is a "choice." In light of the kinds of phenomena described above, who would choose a life in which one encounters threats of physical, psychological, and institutional violence on a daily basis? In our view, it is remarkably insensitive to believe that gay people can and should change their sexual orientations. If you asked the typical heterosexual man, he would probably say that he believes strongly that his sexuality is determined by his biology in a powerful way. There is no reason to believe that a gay man's sexuality originates from a different source.

Homophobia and Masculinity

Homophobia is the irrational fear and intolerance of homosexuality and homosexual persons (Smith, 1971). It is a widespread phenomenon that manifests itself in a variety of ways, including the avoidance of nonsexual intimate behaviors between men, derogatory terms for and jokes about gays, societal bigotry against homosexuals, and even unprovoked violence against persons perceived as gay.

Box 6.1 illustrates a few extreme reactions to homophobic feelings. These descriptions attest to the deep levels of anxiety that tend to arise when men consider the possibility of same-sex erotic feelings. One method of dealing with this anxiety is to defend against it by placing very rigid boundaries between the self and other men. The man who claims to have absolutely no clue about male attractiveness or who becomes violent when dealing with gay men wants it to be absolutely clear to everyone (including himself) that he does not have an ounce of homosexuality in his body.

Why would men go to such great lengths to deny even the slightest possibility of homosexual feeling and thought? After all, it's not like we have been given a huge sexual partner "menu" in this life. You can love men, women, or both. It would make sense that the possibility has at least crossed the minds of even the most heterosexual of men. Yet these experiences are so disturbing to many men that they feel compelled to use somewhat desperate measures to protect the self from the perceived threat of homosexuality.

We have come to believe that homophobia may be at least partly an unconscious view of the homophobe's feelings about the self projected on to gay men. At base, homophobia is about the fear of unwanted sexual attention. (One might think that this fear would give men empathy for women, who often get this kind of attention, but that

---

Box 6.1   Homophobic Behavior

The depth of homophobia reaches almost incredible proportions in many men. Consider the following true stories:

1. A teenage boy received disapproval from the male peer group because he revealed that he had kissed his girlfriend after she had performed oral sex on him. The message was that you do not want any connection between your mouth and a penis, even if the contact is indirect, and even if the penis is your own!

2. A businesswoman having lunch with a colleague (in his thirties) pointed out a man in the restaurant and commented that he was attractive. Her male colleague replied, "I wouldn't know."

3. Many men, especially young men, have been heard to comment that they would become violent if approached by a gay man.

4. During the 1992 controversy around allowing gays and lesbians to serve openly into the military, a military man wrote a letter to the editor of a small town newspaper. He spoke against integrating the military with persons of alternate sexual orientations, saying, "Military personnel have the right to live in a nonthreatening environment." He seems to have forgotten that a large part of the military mission is to face threat. Perhaps being on a battlefield is experienced as less threatening than being in the same room with a gay man. The Don't Ask; Don't Tell law was repealed in 2011 (defense.gov, 2011), and has been accompanied by very few problems, indicating remarkable progress in the reduction of homophobia (Packard, 2014).

seems not to be the case.) Behind this fear may be some assumptions about male sexuality. First is the belief that male sexuality is indiscriminate. Why else would, e.g., a middle-aged, overweight, balding man who isn't particularly attractive to most women believe that, given the opportunity, any gay man would be sexual with him? Second is the belief that male sexuality is predatory in nature—that males will seek out people on whom to impose their sexualities without regard for that person's wishes. From this belief arises another, that men are not sexually desirable, and that therefore they have to be predatory or at least devious, to get people to be sexual with them. This belief is communicated culturally in films such as the 2005 *Wedding Crashers*, in which men lie in an attempt to obtain sexual access to women. A self-loathing attitude is behind these kinds of behaviors: If she really knew who I am, she would not be interested.

Homophobia is both the *substance* and the *enforcer* of culturally dominant forms of masculinity (Lehne, 1998), patriarchy, and sexism (Pharr, 1997b). You might recall from Chapter Two that one of the central messages of masculine socialization is "don't be like a girl." Any "feminine" behavior casts doubts on one's masculinity. Some people claim that they do not even know any people who are not heterosexual. If you do not believe that you know a gay or lesbian person, it would seem that homophobia is less likely to stem from actual experiences with gay people and more likely to be based on stereotypes (Herek, 1994).

The childhood male peer group uses homophobia to enforce gender conformity (Plummer, 2001). The male who behaves in stereotypically unmasculine ways is often labeled a "queer" or "fag," and ostracized from the social group. He may be given these pejorative homosexual labels for sexual behavior such as getting an erection in the boys' locker room, but more commonly he is labeled for failing to live up to masculine role norms. Regardless of the boy's sexual orientation, his heterosexuality may be called into question if he refuses to be violent, express a love of sports, or participate in the derogation of females. Males who want to maintain the approval of other males often find it necessary to display rigid, defensive attitudes toward homosexuality and homosexuals.

On a personal level, homophobia functions to trap men into rigid gender roles and limit their friendships with other men. Gay men are not immune to homophobia, and the anxiety created by these feelings sometimes compounds an already difficult process of understanding the sexual self in the context of a heterosexist culture. The gay man who has learned to hate homosexuality in his childhood may find himself dealing with feelings of self-hatred in adulthood. On one level, he knows that these feelings are irrational. On another, they seem quite real and difficult to ignore.

The intolerance of homosexuality is thought by many to be a way of projecting unacceptable sexual feelings onto others. Vague feelings of same-sex attraction threaten the sense of masculinity, and ultimately self esteem. If the person can psychologically place these unacceptable feelings outside of the self, then he can hate the feelings without hating himself. Herek (1986) reported that people who hold defensive attitudes toward gays also showed a generalized tendency toward this externalizing defensive style. It is not surprising that we see this style often in males, who are usually socialized to deal with conflicts externally rather than to "look inside" and think about how they feel (Lynch & Kilmartin, 2013).

The hypothesis that homophobia is a defense against homoerotic feelings received some support in an important study by Adams, Wright, and Lohr (1996), who measured physiological responses to erotic stimuli. These researchers used the results from a homophobia questionnaire to divide self-reported heterosexual men into two groups: men with high levels of homophobia and men with low levels. Then, they showed these men videotapes of heterosexual, lesbian, and male homosexual sex. Using a device known as a *penile plethysmograph*, which records changes in the circumference of the penis, they measured research participants' physiological arousal in response to the videotapes. Although both groups of men showed signs of sexual arousal while viewing the heterosexual and lesbian tapes, only the high homophobia group showed arousal in response to the male homosexual tapes. The researchers surmised that homophobic men deny or are unaware of their own homoerotic arousal.

The external defensive style prevents a man from learning anything about himself and encourages him to react to the pressure of masculine insecurity by overconforming to the masculine gender role (Pleck, 1981a). This hyperconformity is dehumanizing and has serious negative implications for physical health, psychological health, and relationships with other people. When men lower their defenses against homophobia, they often find that homosexuality is not the huge threat they once perceived, and they feel somewhat freed from the pressure of constantly proving to themselves and others that they are masculine (heterosexual) men. Homophobia is highly emotional and deeply rooted (see Box 6.2). Some suggestions for dealing with homophobic feelings are presented in Box 6.3.

AGING MEN

What is the pattern of continuity and change in the gendered behavior of men as they age? If you think about the older men that you know, you may be acquainted with some who have seemed to change and some who have not. Actor Jack Palance, in his seventies, demonstrated his physical fitness by doing one-armed pushups on stage after receiving an Academy Award, a "macho" display that one does not expect to see from an old man. On the other hand, there are many older men who seemed to have shifted from this kind of behavior as they have aged into styles that we might describe as androgynous. And, of course, as we have stated many times, there are many who never really fit the mainstream masculine image in the first place.

There is some evidence of adult developmental changes in gendered behavior that appear to be driven by significant changes in family status, physical changes, social position, career, or health. Middle-aged and elderly men are likely to encounter several psychologically transformative events such as parents' deaths, retirement, changes in parental status, and adjustments in relationships. These gradual and abrupt life changes have the potential to affect their gender ideologies and behaviors.

A common misunderstanding about adult developmental change is the belief that men encounter a predictable "midlife crisis," and that they then make profound changes in the ways that they approach their work, relationships, and leisure pursuits as a result of the psychological pressure produced by this emotional upheaval. Two very popular books in the 1970s (D. J. Levinson, Darrow, Klein, M. H. Levinson,

---

Box 6.2   Are You Homophobic?

Like any form of prejudice, homophobia has cognitive, emotional, and behavioral components. These sometimes conflict with one another. For example, you might believe that gay people should not be treated any differently from others, but at the same time, you might feel uncomfortable around openly gay people and avoid them. A parallel in racial prejudice would be a white person's discomfort around people of color. Although one may be very egalitarian in one's ideology, racism, sexism, and heterosexism often operate at emotional and/or unconscious levels.

Most of us were raised in a heterosexist, homophobic environment. Therefore, one should not be ashamed for having emotional reactions to gay people. On the contrary, the openness to these reactions reveals a willingness to be honest with oneself, to learn something about others who are perceived as different, and to work toward dealing with homophobic anxiety.

In assessing your feelings and attitudes toward sexual orientation, think about the following:

1. How and when did you first learn about homosexuality? What attitudes toward gays were conveyed by your family and your peer group? What nicknames for gays did you learn when you were growing up? What connotations for these names did you perceive? How did you feel about homosexuality when you were a child?

2. Imagine that you are having a conversation with several friends and someone tells a disrespectful joke about gays. How do you react, emotionally and behaviorally? Do you feel pressured to join in, to confront the person, to withdraw?

3. Imagine that a family member or close friend has just revealed to you that he or she is gay. How do you react? Will your relationship change, and if so, in what ways? Does your reaction differ depending on whether you imagine a male or a female?

4. If you are heterosexual, role play or imagine that you are gay or bisexual and "coming out" (revealing your sexual orientation) to a close friend. How do you go about the task? What feelings are present? If you are gay, lesbian, or bisexual, you may have had this experience or at least thought about it. What feelings come up? How would (or did) you deal with the emotions and with the task?

& McKee, 1978; Sheehy, 1976) proposed and popularized the idea that this "crisis" is universal and based on chronological age. In other words, one could expect that, around age 40, a man is very likely to do things like change jobs, get divorced, buy a sports car, and find a young woman to date. Subsequently, researchers demonstrated that the so-called male midlife crisis is non-normative. Although some men's behavior at midlife might be characterized in this way, no such crisis occurs among *most* men (Kilmartin, 2004a). When there is a crisis during this time of life, the chances are that it is brought on by changes in the man's job situation or relationships, not merely by the fact that he is aging. Even crisis-level changes in important areas such as these are no guarantee that a full-blown life crisis will ensue. Most psychologically healthy people manage to handle a crisis in one area of their life without causing crises in others.

Box 6.3   Dealing with Homophobic Feelings

What can an individual do to work against homophobia at a personal level and against heterosexism (the cultural-institutional manifestation of homophobia)? Below are several suggestions:

1. If you are heterosexual, do not avoid contact with gay people. Like everybody else, gays and lesbians are also students, sons and daughters, teammates, coworkers, friends, etc. You may find that you have something in common with a gay person. Direct interpersonal contact with feared people tends to reduce that fear (Aronson, 2012), Don't wait for your homophobia to go away before having contact with a gay person. Do it *despite* these uncomfortable feelings.

2. Work toward understanding that occasional same-sex erotic feelings are probably more a rule than an exception, and that homophobic feelings are a consequence of growing up in a heterosexist culture.

3. Support gay rights.

4. Refuse to participate in interpersonal or institutional gay-bashing and challenge those who participate.

5. Learn about the gay rights movement and gay and lesbian people's struggles.

6. Work to understand the freeing effects of breaking out of homophobia and rigid gender roles.

Psychoanalyst Carl Jung believed that people's gendered sense of self tends to expand during the second half of life (Hall, Lindzey, & Campbell, 1998). Jung's belief came largely from essentialist notions about personality development, but it is also quite possible to assess gender shift (or lack of it) as a result of social environmental forces. For instance, most men encounter several life changes in their 40s or 50s that may affect their gender ideologies and behavior. Physical declines are inevitable and may include minor hearing loss, graying hair, decreased muscularity, weight gain, and more frequent aches and pains. Men who are athletes see their abilities diminish and/or have to "retire" from some sports. There may be changes in workplace status, such as big promotions or declines in duties. Men whose work involves physical labor may find themselves having more difficulty keeping up with younger men or avoiding injury on the job. Children grow up and move out of the house. There may be a realization that some of the things they dreamed about as younger men are not going to take place. Rybarczyk (1994) summarizes the impact of these events: "The consequences of these changes can be positive (e.g., new roles, new goals) and negative (e.g., feelings of disappointment). For men whose self-concepts rely heavily on youth-oriented masculine traits, these changes undoubtedly force a redefinition of their gender identities" (p. 114).

We have to be cautious with generalizations about older men from research, because of the inevitable confounding of generation (also known as *cohort*) and age. Comparisons of the current generation of older adults and the current generation of younger adults cannot demonstrate age differences, only age and cohort differences as they occur together. The level to which each factor contributes is a matter of speculation. For example, we could assume that older men are less likely to exercise than younger men because this is currently the case. However, it is quite possible that this generation of younger men might exercise at the same level when they become older. Separating cohort and age effects is difficult, if not impossible (Rybarczyk, 1994).

There is also a lack of research on all but White, middle-class United States men. Minority men may experience aging in very different ways. There is very little examination of the interactions between these statuses and adult psychological development. For example, many working class retirees may not fit the stereotype of the person who spends a lot of time traveling, playing golf, and enjoying other leisure activities, as they may not have the money to do so.

Gutmann (1987) proposed that gender role differentiation becomes minimal in later life and that this gender shift is a universal, not a culture-specific phenomenon. Based on anthropological studies of several different cultures, he concludes that women tend to become more powerful and assertive as they age and men tend to become more passive and more involved in domestic matters. Like sociobiologists, Gutmann believed that these changes are a result of evolutionary adaptation, however he never considered the possibility that cultural redundancy could produce this universal phenomenon, if in fact it is universal.

A number of researchers disagree with Gutmann's proposed universal midlife gender transformation. Peskin (1992) followed a small sample of college graduates for more than 25 years and found little evidence of such a shift. Huyck (1992) found that these gender changes tended to be confined to relationships between spouses, with men and women becoming more similar in their behaviors as time went on. Feldman, Biringen, and Nash (1981) demonstrated that gender changes were more related to parenting status than to a person's chronological age.

These contradictory findings have led some theorists to conclude that age-related shifts in gendered behavior result largely from the expansion of social role opportunities for older men. For example, most men can spend more time at home after they retire, and thus they are freer to pursue more activities associated with traditional femininity, like cooking and gardening. Social forces that encourage men to be traditionally masculine may not apply as much to older men, and, even if they do, older men may become less invested in maintaining a masculine image (O'Rand, 1987).

Aging men face special challenges in dealing with the influence of masculine social demands. Even those who were once "successful" in traditional masculine realms often find it difficult to live up to dominant gender standards. Traditional masculinity is defined as very physical, work-oriented, and independent, yet older men experience physical decline, retirement, and the increasing need to depend on others and ask for help. It seems that very few older men can hold on to the macho ethic and survive, either physically or psychologically.

Considerable evidence points to the negative effects of certain aspects of traditional masculinity on the lives of older men. They are less likely than women to see a physician or psychotherapist (Addis & Mahalik, 2003), more likely to downplay their symptoms even if they seek help (Komiya, Good, & Sherrod, 2000), and overwhelmingly more likely to commit suicide (Arias, 2004). Men who attempt to deal with old age using the psychological approach of traditional masculinity often find themselves lonely, ill, and depressed. We often refer to "macho old men" as *developmentally unsuccessful*, as they have not learned the behaviors they need to negotiate this stage of adult development.

But the picture of elderly men is not usually so bleak, as most adjust well to changes in gender identity. They take on new social roles and often come to appreciate aspects of their lives that were previously "off-limits" because they were defined as feminine (Gutmann, 1987). As a result, they report a wider range of self-expression and less worry about whether or not they are being masculine enough to suit others' wishes.

Masculinity becomes more complicated when it intersects with other identities. We have described a number of social, economic, cultural, and historical factors that affect social conceptions of masculinity, and yet have barely scratched the surface of the richness of these topics, which are being explored at the cutting edges of social science. The writers of these many disciplines are convincing in their argument that gendered behaviors, self-concepts, and social institutions are not formed by a unitary path from singular cause to singular effect, and that a full understanding of our gendered world can only be gained through a full understanding of the effects of cultural forces.

SUMMARY

1. Gender stereotypes are somewhat variant at different levels of education, occupation, and income. Lacking the central masculine characteristic of economic power, low-income men may turn to other sources of power and dominance. Socioeconomic class is often intertwined with race and sex, as average incomes are widely discrepant among groups.

2. The dominant definition of United States masculinity includes heterosexuality as one of its central characteristics. Therefore, men of other sexual orientations tend to construct their identities in ways that are different than mainstream masculine ideologies. Besides the sexual behavior of the person, minority sexualities also involve considerations of personal identity and lifestyle. Gay, bisexual, and transgendered men are more likely than heterosexual men to consider and adopt a broader range of gendered behavior.

3. Individual and group identity goes through a series of transformations for gay men as they learn more about themselves and deal with both mainstream and gay cultures. Coming out is an important process for gay men. Historical events such as the Stonewall riot and the AIDS epidemic had powerful effects on individual and community gay identities. Large urban areas contain gay neighborhoods that provide support and community.

4. Because men sometimes confuse sexual and intimate feelings, they may feel very anxious when natural feelings of closeness to other men arise. Homophobia, the irrational fear of homosexuality and homosexuals, results in a number of negative personal and social consequences, including gay bashing, institutional bigotry toward gays, and the limiting of male-male friendships. The threat of being labeled homosexual enforces conformity to traditional masculine gender role prescriptions under the threat of ostracization from the male

peer group. Because we live in a heterosexist culture, most people experience some degree of homophobia.

5. Aging may be connected to changes in gendered ideologies and behavior. These may be driven by significant changes in family status, physical changes, social position, career, or health. Age-related shifts in gendered behavior may also result from the expansion of older men's social role opportunities. The so-called "male mid-life crisis" is not a normative event.

Chapter Seven

The Inner Reality: Phenomenological Perspectives on Male Development

Every man lives in two worlds. One is the physical, external world with which he interacts. The other is a unique, private, inner world where he feels, thinks, perceives, and interprets, and where he ascribes meaning to his life. It is here that he experiences himself as nobody else can, and it is here that he constructs his own reality. His self awareness and private world are unique; he is a phenomenon.

Phenomenological psychologists emphasize the importance of the person's subjective psychological environment. At any given moment, an individual may experience perceptions, sensations, interpretations, ideas, and feelings about the self, others, or objects. For the phenomenologist, the subject of study is the totality of the subjective, immediate experience of the individual, termed the *phenomenal field*, and its effect on behavior. For men, the application of phenomenological theory provides a rich avenue for the enhancement of gender awareness and self-understanding.

Phenomenological theories stress the ability of the person to create and fulfill the self by following inner nature and making choices that affect his or her life in a positive way. In this chapter, we apply two phenomenological theories to the understanding of men: the humanistic approach of Carl Rogers, and the existential theories of Rollo May and others.

HUMANISTIC THEORY

As we have seen, biological and psychoanalytic theories emphasize the primitive, survival aspects of the person. These theories often characterize human nature as animalistic and selfish. Social learning theories emphasize the aspects of the person that are shaped by the environment. These theories tend to describe human nature as essentially neutral.

In contrast, humanistic theory emphasizes the person's ability to create and express the self. Humanists are unabashedly optimistic about human nature. They believe that the most powerful force in a person's life is *self-actualization*, the fulfillment of an individual's positive, unique, human potential. In other words, the core motivation of the human being is to become whatever his or her nature is to become.

Carl Rogers (1961) believed that all living things, if given the right environmental conditions, would grow and thrive. He termed this drive toward fulfillment the *actualizing tendency* and theorized that it is biologically-based. There is a genetic blueprint not only to survive and reproduce (as analytic and biological theories stress), but also to grow and develop.

Self-actualization is the psychological outgrowth of the biological actualizing tendency (Rogers, 1959). Just as a healthy plant grows larger and extends itself, a healthy person progressively and vigorously expresses a unique self. Just as a plant will grow on its own in a favorable environment, so will a human being. You do not have to seize control of a plant or a person for growth to occur. It is enough to merely provide the right conditions.

All organisms need physical nutrients to set the actualizing tendency into motion, and people need a "psychological nutrient" to become self-actualized. The approval of important people early in the person's life allows him or her to develop approval of the self, or *self-esteem*. The person who has a solid, positive sense of self is able to be aware of and fulfill his or her potential.

When children first come into the world, they tend to get a lot of approval. Parents and others hold them, attend to their needs, smile at them, and communicate joy about their existence. Rogers called this basic approval *positive regard*. It is roughly equivalent to a non-possessive love. The child who experiences positive regard feels valued by others. Later in life, he or she internalizes these attitudes and comes to value the self. In other words, the person develops *positive self-regard*.

As a child grows, he or she acquires a larger behavioral repertoire as a result of the actualizing tendency that causes the body and the brain to develop. Behaviors are a way of expressing the self, but some of these expressions may not be particularly pleasing to others. For instance, a two-year-old boy who expresses his curiosity about some expensive object may grab and inadvertently break it. If parents or caretakers respond by communicating disapproval of the child (not merely the child's behavior, but his value as a person), they have, in effect, withdrawn their love from the child because of his behavior. They can do this by striking the child, by saying "bad boy" (which says "you are a bad person"), or by saying something like, "Daddy doesn't like you when you do that." These expressions of disapproval can also be indirect or non-verbal, as when the parent gives the child a "dirty look" or becomes emotionally cold. Children are remarkably sensitive to parents' expressions of disgust at a very early age (Carver and Vaccaro, 2007).

Rogers called this kind of parental behavior *conditional positive regard*, or placing *conditions of worth* on the child. It is a communication to the child that he or she is only worthwhile under certain conditions. As a result, the child begins to construct the self in terms of actions, thoughts, and feelings which have been approved. If events like the one described above were to happen repeatedly, the boy would come to deny the parts of himself that are associated with curiosity.

A healthier environment is one in which the child experiences *unconditional positive regard*, which is a warmth, respect, and acceptance that does not depend on the behavior of the child. It is possible to communicate disapproval of a behavior while communicating approval of the person. In effect, the parent is saying, "You are valuable no matter what you do" (without conditions). The child is worthwhile for the mere reason that he or she has shown up on the planet. You should not confuse this position with *laissez-faire* parenting, where the parent provides no guidance to the child. Rogers' position is that parents can make a clear distinction between disapproving of a behavior and disapproving of the personhood of one who enacts the behavior.

There are several negative consequences for the person who experiences conditions of worth in large doses. First, feelings of inadequacy result in anxiety and defensiveness as the person denies and rejects the disapproved parts of the self. Second, self-actualization is blocked because the self-concept is narrowed. Rogers believed that the full experience of the self provided the vital information needed to strive toward human potential. It is difficult to fully express the self when one has lost touch with significant parts of it. Third, defensiveness against and rejection of these aspects of the self render the individual less able to appreciate others, and misunderstandings in relationships often ensue.

The net result of conditional regard is that the self-actualizing tendency becomes misguided and full functioning is inhibited. The following example will serve to illustrate Rogers' theory: A child who grows up with an overprotective parent receives disapproval for any minor risk taking, such as going outside if it is a little cold or trying something for the first time. This child denies the parts of the self that are associated with exploring new environments and with healthy assertion of the self. When this person becomes an adult, he or she does not develop a satisfying career or relationships outside the family (despite having the resources to do so), because he or she has internalized the parent who disapproved of the independent parts of the self. The person feels an undue amount of anxiety around what most people find to be reasonable risks, and thus he or she fails to activate a good deal of his or her potential.

Humanistic Theory and Masculinity

The application of Rogers' theory to male development provides an excellent framework for understanding the negative aspects of masculine gender roles. Often, boys are socialized in a way that is fraught with conditional positive regard. As a result, a great many men have hidden away large parts of themselves, sometimes with dire consequences.

The gender role strain model (Pleck, 1975; O'Neil, 1982) presented in Chapter Two is based in humanistic theory. Gender role strain occurs when cultural gender demands conflict with naturally occurring tendencies in the person. This conflict creates a discrepancy between the "real self" and the "ideal self-concept" (Garnets & Pleck, 1979). In other words, gender role strain occurs when "who I am" is not consistent with "who I should be."

In Rogerian terms, gender role demands are enforced by conditional positive regard. In the typical scenario of male socialization, a boy's "masculine" behavior meets with approval and other behavior results in the withdrawal of approval. The boy learns that he is valued when he acts masculine, and that he loses some of his worth when he does not. He may cry when he is sad and be told, "Don't be a sissy; big boys don't cry." He then withdraws value from this emotion.

As a result of consistent disapproval of certain aspects of his experience and behavior, the boy begins to deny the part of the real self that is considered unmasculine by important people in his life. He attempts to match his behavior to the gender demands that allow him to gain the positive regard of these significant others in his life, and later, himself. The price that he pays is in self-alienation. As the full experience of the true self is necessary for self-actualization, the attempt to live up to gender demands that are not a part of the self limits the potential for full functioning. The gender role strain position is that, for the most part, a man often cannot be himself and "be a man" (as culturally defined) at the same time. The more a man comes to value traditional masculinity, the more he will lose his individuality and his path to fulfillment. Loss of significant parts of the self results in behavior that is destructive to the self and/or others (O'Neil, 1990).

Because every man is unique, and because some men are raised with harsher gender demands than others, the degree to which an individual man experiences gender role strain will vary. For example, there is generally an expectation for boys to participate in athletics. For a boy who is naturally athletic and drawn to sports, this demand would not create much strain. However, a boy who is not athletic or interested in sports would experience a high degree of strain, which might be accompanied by feelings of low self-esteem and misgivings about his masculinity. If his parents and other important people in his life are especially harsh in pressuring the boy to be athletic, he experiences even more strain. The level of gender role strain is a function of the level of gender role demand in interaction with the degree of conflict between naturally-occurring tendencies and gender role.

Gay and bisexual men find themselves in the position of having to deal with considerable gender role strain. They are sexually oriented toward men, but society defines masculinity as antifemininity and attraction to males as feminine. Therefore, they face social disapproval for expressing themselves in a homophobic society and/or the self-alienation of denying a sexuality that is central to their identities.

Pleck (1981b) advanced the theory that gender role strain can lead a male to exaggerate his masculinity. Unable to gain approval because he does not naturally fit the cultural ideal, he tries to overcompensate by forcing himself into the gender role. This high level of gender role strain and the hypermasculine reaction to it result in an extreme degree of self-alienation. There would seem to be a great many men who compulsively conform to masculine standards of behavior because they do not want to risk the social disapproval (and the internalized self-disapproval) for behaving in unmasculine ways. Paradoxically, they receive approval for behaving in ways that fulfill the masculine values of independence and courage, yet they find it extremely difficult to be truly independent or emotionally courageous by defying a gender demand when they sense that it is important for them to do so.

Even though the level of gender role strain varies from person to person, certain gender role demands would seem to conflict with naturally-occurring tendencies in every man. It is impossible for a real self to be congruent with the inhuman aspects of traditional masculinity. There are also certain gender role demands that conflict with naturally occurring tendencies in many, though perhaps not all, men.

Emotion is universal. Various structures in the brain have the function of processing emotional experiences. In Rogerian terms, feelings are a part of the "true self" for everyone. It is as natural to express them as it is to express every part of the self. Strong emotion is accompanied by strong physical sensations. One can feel emotions virtually demanding expression from the most primal part of one's organism. For many young boys, however, the expression of emotion (except for anger, and, later, sexual feelings) is met with disapproval, and the boy denies the parts of the self connected with most vulnerable emotions. As he incorporates gender role demands into his ideal self-concept, the experience of emotion becomes associated with lowered self-esteem, and he is motivated to move away from his feelings. As a result of this undervaluing of the emotional self, many men report difficulties in expressing their feelings (Englar-Carlson, 2006).

Emotion is a huge part of human experience. Denying this primal aspect of the self requires a great deal of psychological effort, and the amount of strain and self-alienation that results can be considerable (O'Neil, 1990). In fact, the problems associated with restrictive emotionality require an entire chapter (Chapter Eight) to detail. For now, it will suffice to say that this issue pervades virtually every aspect of many men's lives. As O'Neil (1982) put it, "the capacity for accurate recognition and communication of feelings is a prerequisite for coping with life's problems" (p. 24). Yet many men have been stripped of this basic capacity by social forces that seek to make them into machines.

Safety is another universal human need. Part of the actualizing tendency is to protect the self from physical harm. Many males, however, are taught to deny this basic human need in the service of striving to meet standards of masculinity (Jourard, 1971). The conflict here is between the self-protective aspects of the real self and the masculine demand to "take it like a man." This eschewal of safety needs is related to the earlier issue of emotion. Fear is an information sense. It is the emotional experience that tells us that we are in a situation where our safety is threatened. If the male's self-worth is undermined when he feels fearful, then he is motivated to deny or suppress that fear. For example, if a large man is running at you at full speed, your basic self-protective instinct makes you fearful and tells you to get out of the way. However, if you are a middle linebacker and the man coming at you is carrying a football, then you are motivated to do the very opposite.

The denial of safety needs affects men's physical health (see Chapter Nine). The fact that a man can be reluctant to acknowledge a symptom, even a life threatening one, attests to the depth to which masculine conditional positive regard has moved him away from his real (self- protecting) self. He would rather die than be considered unmanly. It is quite common for men to ignore other physiological needs in the areas of sleep, diet, exercise, and alcohol intake (Courtenay, 2011).

Many a man has risked physical harm to preserve his sense of masculinity. You can see gender role strain in a typical school or neighborhood situation where a bigger, stronger, boy challenges a smaller, weaker one to a fight. The human part of the smaller boy tells him to run away, but the masculine part tells him to stay and defend his "honor," even though he is nearly certain to be hurt.

Contact sports and war are two arenas where men have traditionally tested their masculinity. Football is dangerous, and it hurts. Playing this game requires that one suppress the self-protective and pain-avoiding parts of the self. Even as young boys, athletes are encouraged to play in spite of pain and to risk their bodies to win games. Winners receive a great deal of approval, whereas losers are often shamed or ignored.

War, of course, is the ultimate in the suppression of the self-preservation instinct. Although there may be more reasons to fight in a war than just to prove one's masculinity, men who have refused to do so have historically been branded as cowards and shamed as unmanly (Levy, 1992). Young men in war find themselves living with abject fear in virtually every moment. It is probably not a coincidence that modern men's movements began near the end of the Vietnam War, when thousands of men experienced the ultimate in gender role strain.

Many theorists argue that a degree of dependence on others is also a universal human need (Jourard, 1971). Here again there is a conflict between the human and parts of the masculine, and again we find a connection to emotionality. A man can never be completely independent and thus he will sometimes feel helpless and alone. Gender role strain results from these feelings, which the man must deny if he accepts traditional standards of masculinity.

There are several other areas where gender role strain is evident for many men:

1. *Power, control, and competition.* The socialized tendency for men is to dominate others. Doing so requires a man to bury the parts of the self that are associated with empathy, mutuality, and cooperation. Many theorists believe that this orientation leads to damaged interpersonal relationships (Burn & Ward, 2005), role strain (O'Neil, 1990), and sexual conflicts (Gross, 1992).

2. *Homophobia.* The role demand for men to restrict interpersonal closeness to males due to the risk of being labeled homosexual requires one to deny naturally affectionate feelings toward other men (R. J. May, 1988). Many theorists believe that homophobia has the effect of severely limiting the intimacy of male-male relationships (see Chapter Six).

3. *Achievement, success, and money.* Many people associate men's personal value with their accomplishments and social standing. At the extreme, this involves a denial of the parts of self associated with pleasure, relaxation, and family life (Skovholt, 1990). Validation of masculinity from this source is dependent on economic conditions, social position, and talent, as well as education and access to resources (Pleck, 1981a). Many socially marginalized men experience the demand for economic success but have few avenues for achieving it.

4. *"Femiphobia"* (term coined by O'Donovan, 1988). Men are encouraged to avoid any behavior that might be considered feminine. This demand requires them to suppress any parts of their personalities that are culturally associated with women's characteristics. O'Neil (2008) believes that fear of femininity is at the root of all other role strain.

5. *Athletic prowess.* Boys are often shamed and ridiculed if they do not play sports or do not play them well. Athletic participation is the most important factor in boys' high school social status (a form of positive regard), and non-athletic boys are more likely than athletic ones to doubt their masculinity (Morris, 2012).

6. *Sexual initiative and performance.* Men are expected to seek sex actively, and to be insatiable, promiscuous, indiscriminate, and sexually goal-oriented. This masculine sexual orientation involves denial of the parts of self that make affectional ties to others (Nelson, 1997) and the more sensual aspects of the man. Engaging in unwanted sexual activity is normative for men. Most college men report that they have had sex when they did not want to because of male peer pressure or the desire to be popular (Berkowitz, 1997). Sexually aggressive men, who are considered to be under a great deal of role strain (Pleck, 1981a) tend to set nearly impossible sexual expectations for themselves and may feel chronically unsatisfied with their amount of sexual experience.

The bottom line of gender role strain is that conditional positive regard leaves the male out of touch with his "inner world" and over-concerned with the external world. His socialization has impaired his ability to deal with psychological conflicts, except by denying that they exist.

However, the self-actualizing tendency is a potent human force. Going back to the comparison between humans and plants, Rogers (1980) says:

> I remember that in my boyhood the bin in which we stored our winter's supply of potatoes was in the basement, several feet below a small window. The conditions were unfavorable, but the potatoes would begin to sprout—pale white sprouts, so unlike the healthy green shoots they sent up when planted in the soil in the spring. But these sad, spindly sprouts would grow two or three feet in length as they reached toward the distant light of the window. The sprouts were, in their bizarre, futile growth, a sort of desperate expression of the directional tendency I have been describing… in dealing with clients… I often think of these potato sprouts…. The clue to understanding their behavior is that they are striving, in the only ways that they perceive as available to them, to move toward growth, toward becoming…. They are life's desperate attempt to become itself… this potent constructive tendency. (p. 118–119)

Despite unfavorable conditions, most men strive, in the only ways that they experience as available to them, to achieve some degree of emotional expression, intimacy, self-care, and sexual satisfaction. Most men put their power, status, and competitive needs into some kind of perspective with the rest of their identities. In other words, most men cling to their humanness in spite of the forces that seek to wrest it away and turn them into machines. Rogers would say that this tenacity is the manifestation of the self-actualizing tendency.

Rogers would also be optimistic with regard to the ability of men to deal with the effects of their harsh childhood socialization and adult environments. Because he believes that the self-actualizing tendency exists in every man, Rogers also believes that it will emerge under the right conditions, just as the potato shoots he described would turn healthy if deposited in rich soil. Given an environment in which men can discover and express their true selves, they can drop their masculine facades and make the transition from "seeming" to "being."

At least two factors work against this potential change. First, the emotional "scar tissue" from childhood and adolescence is considerable for many men, making it difficult for them to feel safe in dealing with this inner world that has become so alien. Second, we live in a sexist culture which continues to base approval on traditional masculine characteristics and behavior. Nevertheless, the primacy of this psychological work has encouraged many men to deal with these obstacles.

EXISTENTIAL THEORY

Existential theory of personality is based on the writings of existentialist philosophers such as Sartre, Kierkegaard, Heidegger, and Nietzsche. It bears a strong resemblance to humanistic theory in many regards, but it departs in others. The existential view of the person provides an interesting perspective on men, particularly with regard to the positive attributes of traditional masculinity.

The major similarities between humanistic and existential theories are the emphases on self-awareness and self-determination. Like humanistic theorists, existentialists believe in the importance of being in touch with the inner life and using it as a guide for action. The major difference in these two theories is in the area of conflict within the person. For the humanist, the self-actualizing tendency is only stifled by conditional positive regard, a force that originates from outside of the person. If the environment supports the real self, then the person can move unencumbered toward fulfillment. Growth only entails risk if positive regard is conditional. In contrast, existential theorists see conflict within the person as an inevitable feature of the human condition. For them, growth always entails risk.

Existentialists like Rollo May (1958) believe that moving toward fulfillment is not just a matter of a person following his or her actualizing tendency. It requires more effort than that. Because the person has many different possibilities and potentials for growth, he or she must decide which ones to pursue and which ones to leave by the wayside. It is in these decisions that conflict emerges. At every moment, the person is forced to make choices that involve giving something up. If you decide to go to class, you cannot stay in bed. If you decide to stay in bed, you cannot go to class. If you decide to spend an afternoon with other people, you cannot spend it by yourself.

Although these are relatively trivial choices, other decisions are more profound in their effect on our lives. If you decide to marry, you can not stay single, and vice versa. Maybe you can experience the other alternative later on, but maybe there will not be a "later on." Since we have a limited amount of time to spend in this world, our choices are finite and vitally important. For the existentialist, it is the pattern of choice that determines the personality, and the person is wholly responsible for his or her decisions. This reality means that you are what you do, and that you create who you are. By making choices, a person ascribes purpose and meaning to his or her life. It is an intensely personal meaning, not some meaning that is bestowed by outside forces such as biology or other people.

Life is a frightening thing, because we must continually make choices without having all the necessary information on which to base these decisions (May, 1958). When you chose a college to attend, you probably gathered information about aspects of several schools, but you could not know everything about every school and be able to perfectly predict the outcome of attending one or the other. You made your best guess and you lived with it. For the existentialist, life is a series of such guesses; hopefully they are educated ones. These choices are made every day and at every moment. Not only did you choose to attend a college, you chose to be in school every day that you stay. If you choose to marry, you will also opt to stay with your partner (or not) every day.

Decisions are satisfying when we make good ones, although we can never know with absolute certainty whether or not we have made the best one. To do so, we would need to see into the future and see into an alternate future that resulted from a different path. Even when you make a choice that turns out well, you may be left with a lingering feeling that perhaps another alternative might have been better. When you make a poor decision, you are left with the negative feeling that you had a chance but did not take advantage of it.

Every choice involves two basic alternatives: you could choose to face the unknown future, or you can stick with the routine, predictable past. For example, you can face the problems of going out on your own and defining your world (future), or you can define your world simply by what your parents or other people tell you is important (past).

Choosing the future is a frightening thing because it always involves risk. You might make a decision that does not turn out right, and this could result in your losing something valuable. If you left home to go to college, you probably felt pretty apprehensive when you first arrived there. After all, you might not like it, you might not do well, and you might lose touch with your friends at home. You had to risk the loss of peace of mind, self-esteem, and the companionship of people whom you value. Existential psychologists call this feeling of apprehension *ontological anxiety*, or fear of the unknown (Maddi, 2001).

Choosing the routine, predictable past is not frightening, but it is boring. When you merely stick with what you know, you get the feeling that you are missing out on something, and that the routine does not seem to have any meaning in life. For instance, you could choose to work for the rest of your life at a job that is unfulfilling and unchallenging. If you did, you might find that your life had become unsatisfying and meaningless. Existentialists call this feeling of boredom and regret *ontological guilt*. It is the stifling sense of missed opportunity.

Ontological anxiety and ontological guilt are the painful and inescapable realities of the human condition (May, 1958). Ontological anxiety will always be with us because we are faced with the necessity of making new choices every moment, and our prediction of the outcomes of our decisions is always imperfect. Ontological guilt is inescapable because we have too many potentials to be fulfilled in one lifetime. Choosing one thing always involves giving up another, and we are always left with the sense that we might have missed something important.

Although it never goes away completely, we can minimize ontological guilt by making wise choices and vigorously participating in our lives (Tillich, 1952). If you are pursuing a rewarding and interesting career, you do not feel so badly about the other things you could have done. If you are courageous enough to assert your being in the face of ontological anxiety, then ontological guilt will not rear its ugly head very often.

Courage is the hallmark of psychological health for the existentialist (Frankl, 1960). Choosing to grow despite the uncertainty of one's decisions is what allows a person to be most fully human and fulfilled. It is "daring to be great." Courage should not be confused with bravado. Courage involves taking a risk to attain something valuable. Bravado is pretended courage; it is often seen in "macho" behavior, where a man is facing risk solely to avoid being considered unmasculine. Courage is risk taking because one values the outcome; bravado is risk taking as an end in itself. Bravado is born of fear; courage is born of commitment.

Existential values should not be misconstrued as a prescription for recklessness. Existential psychology places value on the willingness to make your best guess and go with it, not the willingness to make a random guess, or to fail to consider the consequences of your actions. Spontaneity is not the same as impulsivity, and making an educated guess is much more than merely "rolling the dice."

But from where does the "educated" in "educated guess" come? If one's being is so unique and individual, what information can a person use to guide decision making? The answers to these questions come back to humanistic theory. If the person's being is unique and individual, then he or she must use it as a guide for decision making. The full experiencing of the self involves a vigorous sense of body, emotions, thoughts, sensations, an appreciation of the physical world, and an ability to examine the self in a nondefensive way. The person who has a full experience of self is said to be living an "authentic" life.

Authenticity helps point the way to existential choice. Intentionality and courage actualizes the choice. For instance, occasionally people leave high paying jobs, even if they are good at what they do. When asked why they left, they often say, "That job just wasn't me." Their self-awareness told them that their job no longer had a place in their lives, and they were courageous enough to search for something more important.

Existentialism and Masculinity

From the existential perspective, traditional masculinity has a number of marked advantages and disadvantages (as does traditional femininity). Men are socialized in some ways that help them assert their existential selves. Other influences get in the way of this process. Because responsibility for the self is inescapable, each man is charged with the struggle for overcoming these negative influences and living an authentic life.

We can conceptualize these negative influences in much the same way as in the application of humanistic theory. If the vigorous experience of the self provides the data on which to base existential decision, then many men are basing their decisions on limited information. The socialization of boys to avoid emotion leaves a large gap in the experience of the self. This lack of awareness allows men to see emotional situations only in intellectual terms and may often force them to wallow in emotional problems.

Masculine gender roles contain a wide variety of prescriptions for behaviors that emphasize the outward appearance of the man: emotional constriction, job status, wealth, material possessions, control, dominance, achievement, and independence. Traditional masculinity is defined by how the man looks, not by his inner experience.

Many men who chase the masculine dream find it to be disillusioning and self-alienating. This is especially true for men who have reached middle adulthood. Some have exerted considerable effort in attempting to live up to the masculine mystique, and they may have done fairly well at it. Others have given up on trying to reach the harsh standards of masculinity.

In middle adulthood, the body begins to decline and the man must acknowledge his mortality and vulnerability. At the same time, he may have become tired of holding up the heavy burden of the masculine facade in his work and social life. These changes may prompt him to re-examine traditional masculine values. One of Vaillant's (1977) middle-aged interviewees described his crisis: "One part of me wants power, prestige, recognition, success; the other part feels all of this is nonsense and chasing the wind" (p. 228).

Many men choose to emphasize family and leisure roles at midlife (R. J. May, 1988) or to otherwise reevaluate their lives (Levinson, Darrow, Klein, Levinson, & Mckee, 1978). In existential terms, their self-experience tells them that they need to make adjustments in their choices for their lives to remain meaningful. Choosing to define himself by gender role standards may prevent a man from pursuing options in many areas such as work, leisure, relationships, and sexuality. Some men gather the courage to break out of the narrow definition of self and exercise options that they previously avoided.

There are a number of positive aspects to traditional masculinity from the existential perspective. Courage is surely one of them. Throughout history, men have been willing to face challenges and overcome obstacles. Again, however, we need to make a clear distinction between real courage and engaging in a dangerous behavior as an end in itself (such as participating in the running of the bulls in Pamplona, Spain). Men have poured themselves into physically and psychologically dangerous ventures, and pushed the limits of their capabilities, because they believed that what they were doing was worthwhile. To do so is to risk failure to attain fulfillment. Men have also been raised to believe in the necessity of decision making and action, which are also existential ideals. Sometimes the most courageous thing a person can do is to get to work and do what must be done.

Many of men's accomplishments have required them to tolerate a good deal of discomfort, which the existential person must do to carry out difficult decisions. Millions of working men have suffered horrible physical conditions to support their families. From an existential standpoint, these men made the choice to stay in these circumstances moment after moment and day after day, because they defined their purpose as the role of provider and breadwinner.

The healthy existential person is someone with vision who can imagine possibilities and future. In boys' play, problem solving, and other aspects of their socialization, the culture often encourages this kind of imagination (Block, 1984). The fact that males are encouraged to go out into the world independently and deal with it helps them to see and choose from a wide variety of options. But as we mentioned earlier, if these socialized tendencies are healthy for person and/or society under the right circumstances, then they will be healthy for both men and women. Thus they should be defined as human, not just masculine.

An existential men's studies perspective would argue for an expansion rather than an eradication of traditional masculinity. The existential man who wants to move beyond the constraints of traditional gender roles can do so by expanding masculine ideals into psychosocial realms. To be truly independent means that he sometimes goes against what others define as appropriately masculine. Risk-taking does not only include things like running into burning buildings—we can expand it to include emotional risk-taking, like telling someone that you are afraid and need his or her support. The value of providing for a family can expand beyond material providing into including emotional nurturing and the kinds of daily caretaking activities that have traditionally been relegated solely to mothers. From a base of independence, courage, and risk taking, men can expand to becoming independent from unreasonable gender role demands, having the courage to enter the traditional realm of the feminine, and taking emotional risks.

We return to the discussion of gender as a set of "default options" from Chapter One. In moving from "going along with the program" to making informed choices about one's behavior and life, it is very helpful to have an awareness of what the program is. If gender is a cultural pressure that it sometimes makes sense to oppose, it is very difficult to resist a pressure that one cannot name. Gender awareness gives men a language for symbolizing their experience, and this language is a helpful guide to existential choice.

SUMMARY

1. Phenomenological psychology emphasizes the importance of the individual's sense of self and the ability of the human being to attain personal fulfillment. Carl Rogers believed that all living things have an actualizing tendency which propels the organism toward growth. Self-actualization is the psychological outgrowth of the actualizing tendency in human beings. Under the right environmental conditions, self actualization allows a person to fulfill his or her unique potential.

2. The healthiest psychological environment is one in which important others communicate loving and valuing to the person in all circumstances (unconditional positive regard). When a person gets messages that the self is not of value when certain types of behavior are evident, they experience conditional positive regard.

3. Because feedback from others is critical in shaping the personality, the person who receives a great deal of unconditional positive regard will internalize this attitude and come to value the self. Large doses of conditional regard cause the person to deny the parts of the self associated with disapproval. Because

vigorous experiencing of all parts of the self is necessary for self actualization, conditional regard inhibits the fulfillment of human potential.

4. The application of Rogers' theory to masculine socialization reveals that many males grow up with a good deal of conditional regard. "Masculine" behaviors often meet with approval and "feminine" behaviors with disapproval. Boys begin to value the masculine parts and deny the feminine parts of the self. This denial leads to self-alienation.

5. The gender role strain model is based in humanistic theory. Boys whose naturally occurring personalities contradict social standards of masculinity tend to experience many negative consequences. They may become hypermasculine and force themselves to strive for the cultural ideal.

6. The denial of emotion is central to many masculine gender roles and creates a good deal of strain for many men. Other areas of strain include safety needs, the avoidance of physical pain, dependence, power needs, homophobia, femiphobia, achievement, athletics, and sexuality. Despite this strain, most men are able to assert their unique human selves. Rogers would be optimistic about men's healing.

7. Existential theory resembles humanistic theory in its emphases on self-awareness and self-determination, but it departs in its emphases on personal responsibility, conflict, and risk. From the existential perspective, self-definition is a matter of individual choice, which always involves the possibility of losing something valuable. The human condition is one of ontological anxiety, or fear of the unknown, and ontological guilt, the sense of missed opportunity. Although both are unavoidable, one can minimize the latter by choosing to push forward despite the experiences of fear and uncertainty. The authentic person is one who is attuned to the self and courageous enough to make difficult choices.

8. From the existential viewpoint, traditional masculinity contains positive and negative influences. The negative influences are the encouragement to deny the emotional self and the emphasis on the outward appearance of the man. The positive aspects include the masculine willingness to face challenges, overcome obstacles, take action, make decisions, take risks, endure discomfort, and push the limits of one's potential. Because these aspects are positive, they should not be limited to males.

Chapter Eight

It Never Lies, and It Never Lies Still: Emotion and Masculinity

Few human experiences are as basic and ubiquitous as emotion. A person responds to almost any internal or environmental event with some degree of feeling, and the experience of positive emotions is probably one of the most important motivators in life. People seek money, love, knowledge, physical pleasure, relationships, or human service because they believe that these things will provide some degree of emotional fulfillment. The United States Declaration of Independence holds the "pursuit of happiness," an emotion, as an inalienable human right. Just as the brain structures associated with emotion are at the center of the brain, emotion is at the center of human experience.

As an old psychoanalytic saying goes, "Emotion never lies, and emotion never lies still." Directly or indirectly, feelings tend to find some sort of manifestation. Strong emotions seem to have a life of their own. You can feel them physically; they seem to cry for expression. If you accept the premise that emotional *experience* strongly encourages emotional *expression*, then it must take even stronger forces to suppress the outward display of emotion. These powerful influences can be found in masculine gender socialization, masculine ideologies, and situational expectations for men to avoid the expression of vulnerable feelings.

Even the casual observer will notice that many men have difficulty understanding, dealing with, and expressing emotions. Restrictive emotionality is one of the most frequently discussed issues in men's studies, and it is thought to underlie a number of other problems for men, including relationship difficulties, physical illness, mental health problems, and violence (O'Neil, 2008). Masculine gender roles often encourage men to resist the awareness of affect, avoid emotional vulnerability, and disguise their feelings, especially when those feelings involve hurt, fear, sadness, or any experience that signals weakness or lack of control. Some men believe that tear ducts on men are like nipples—we only have them through a biological accident.

In this chapter, we explore the origins and consequences of, and remedies for restrictive emotionality by addressing the following important questions:

- What do sex and gender comparisons in emotional experience, expression and self-disclosure tell us?
- What typical masculine socialization experiences and social situations lead to restrictive emotionality?
- What have researchers learned about the effects of emotional constriction on the person?
- What are the possibilities for helping men and boys improve the quality of their emotional lives?

SEX AND GENDER COMPARISONS IN EMOTIONAL EXPRESSION

We must keep in mind that, although every culture exerts pressure on its members to handle emotion in prescribed ways, these "rules" vary widely from culture to culture. For instance, many Asian cultures expect both men and women to control their emotions. Many Middle Eastern and South American cultures expect both men and women to express their emotions. Some cultures expect women, but not men, to express emotions. And in some cultures, men are considered more expressive of certain emotions than women (Tavris & Wade, 2001).

It is also worthwhile to repeat an important consideration from earlier chapters. Although a culture exerts pressure on people to feel, think, and act in certain ways, individual responses to cultural influences are widely variable. Even in cultures that expect women to be highly emotional and men to be less so, there are very expressive men and very inexpressive women.

Leslie Brody and Judith Hall (2010) delineate several important conceptual categories in the study of gender and emotion. First, many researchers have studied gender *stereotypes* of emotionality. These studies describe people's *beliefs* about men's and women's emotional lives. There is also a body of research on *self-descriptions* of emotionality—people's reports about their experiences. And there is an important distinction between the *experience* and the *expression* of emotion. A person might feel quite strongly but try not to communicate that feeling for any number of reasons.

It is no surprise that, in studies of gender stereotypes, most people believe that women are more emotional than men. Fischer and Manstead (2000) noted that this stereotype exists in 30 of the 33 cultures that they observed. In fact, this difference in emotionality is one of the central defining features of the masculinity-femininity dimension (O'Neil, 1981a; Bem, 1981). These findings are especially robust for judgments of emotional *expression*. Although people tend to also believe that women *experience* stronger emotions than men, they do not see the gulf between the sexes as being as large as that for expression of feelings (Brody & Hall, 2010). Actually, there is little evidence that men-as-a-group experience emotion less often than women-as-a-group (Shields, 2005). Therefore, the prevalent beliefs are that women feel a little bit more than men, but that they display their emotions a great deal more than men.

Self-descriptive studies may be strongly biased by gender stereotypes. Psychologists have known for a long time that *social desirability* affects self-report, even in basically honest people (Kenrick, Neuberg, & Cialdini, 2005). People are motivated to present themselves in a positive light. As gender stereotypes carry with them strong values, males and females are more likely to portray themselves as masculine and feminine, respectively. Thus it is no surprise that women, on average, report greater intensity of emotion than men. We also know that retrospective reports are subject to memory distortion, and that gender ideologies affect memory. Reports asking how one felt in the past day, week, or month tend to reflect gender stereotypes, but when people are asked to chronicle their feelings in real time, their reports tend not to be stereotypical (Shields, 2010).

With these limitations in mind, we find a number of researchers who have demonstrated that women report greater experiences of positive emotions (happiness, well-being, joy) than men. At the same time, females also report higher levels of many negative feelings, especially those that are *intropunitive* (self-punishing), such as shame, guilt, sadness, anxiety, and fear. Although males reported feeling contempt more often, there was no difference between men and women in the intensity of contempt. Studies on sex comparisons in the experience of anger show mixed results, with some finding no differences and others finding differences depending on the target of the anger (Brody & Hall, 2010).

An important finding is that there is a strong correlation between the reported experience of positive feelings and the reported experience of negative feelings (Diener, Larsen, Levine, & Emmons, 1985). According to self-descriptions, it is apparent that high emotionality is a mixed blessing, allowing one to fully experience joy, satisfaction, awe, gratitude, amusement, interest, inspiration, and contentment, but also leaving the person vulnerable to intense negative feelings like sadness, loneliness, embarrassment, and anxiety. The same is true for low emotionality—it allows a person to escape from intense feelings of fear and anxiety, but apparently at the cost of sacrificing positive emotional experiences. Positive and negative emotions are therefore a kind of package deal, or perhaps more accurately, a pact with the Devil.

Within the domain of emotional expression, there is little doubt that males tend to display most feelings less frequently and less intensely than females. Interesting data have emerged from developmental studies in this area. Infant boys appear to actually be more expressive than infant girls (Brody & Hall, 2010). Preschool children show no sex differences in expression, but consistent differences begin to emerge by age six and these differences become well established by middle adolescence (Adams, Kuebli, Boyle, & Fivush, 1995). In an older study, Stapely & Haviland (1989) found that adolescent boys were much more likely than girls to deny that they *ever* had emotional experiences.

Although females tend to display generally higher levels of emotions than males, the expression of anger, pride, and loneliness are more frequent in males (Brody & Hall, 2010). However, psychological gender is more predictive of level of emotional expression than biological sex. In other words, knowing a person's level of stereotypical masculinity and femininity allows for a better understanding of his or her emotional expressiveness than simply knowing whether the person is male or female. People who believe in the stereotype that men are "naturally" unemotional are more likely to report stereotypical emotionality for themselves (Deaux, 2000). Likewise, men's high levels of adherence to masculine ideology, which includes the belief that men *should be* unemotional, are associated with low expressiveness (Bruch, Berko, & Haase, 1998).

There are also average sex differences in the manner of emotional expression. Among North American adults, women smile and touch others more, use more expressive hand and body movements, and talk about their feelings more (Tavris & Wade, 2008). Males are more likely to act out their feelings (Brody & Hall, 2010; Lynch & Kilmartin, 2013). Females also tend to be better than males at identifying others' feelings from facial, body, and voice cues (Manstead, 1992). These findings indicate that women, on the average, are more sensitive than men to people's feelings, even when those feelings are expressed indirectly. But we need to keep in mind that there are enormous within-group sex variations; some women are not very sensitive to others' emotions, and some men are. After a thorough review of the available research on sex and emotion, one group of scholars (Wester, Vogel, Pressly, & Heesacker, 2002) concluded that patterns of men's and women's emotionality are much more similar than they are different.

We should also keep in mind that context is a critical factor in the display of emotion (Brody & Hall, 2010). Masculine men may embrace one another when they are teammates and win the game, cry with one another at funerals or war veterans' reunions, and may otherwise show feelings usually defined as unmasculine by the culture when the immediate social setting allows for such display. Social forces exert influence on people both in immediate context and the "big picture" of the larger culture (Deaux, 2000). In fact, situational characteristics often influence emotional expression to a much greater degree than gender factors (LaFrance, Hecht, & Paluck, 2003).

The Special Case of Anger

Although masculine stereotypes and ideologies contain the expectation for men to be in control of their emotions, the expression of anger is a notable exception. Curiously, in contrast to the vulnerable emotions that are assumed to be in complete control, men's anger is often seen as being completely *out of* control. Moreover, an angry man is expected to express his anger through acting out, sometimes in violent ways. Because anger is socially acceptable for men, traditionally gender-typed men tend to convert most other emotions into anger, often resulting in destructive behavior and a lack of awareness of the original, more vulnerable emotion (e.g. jealousy, sadness, disappointment) that gave rise to the anger (Lynch & Kilmartin, 2013). Don Long (1987) referred to anger as the "male emotional funnel system." One group of researchers noted that men's expressions of anger are associated with their fear of experiencing vulnerable emotional states (Jacupak, Tull, & Roemer, 2005), and men who evidence restrictive emotionality on the gender role strain measure show a greater likelihood to engage in aggressive behavior when their masculinity is threatened (Cohn, Seibert, & Zeichner, 2009). Parents have a tendency to highlight the experiences of anger and the related emotions of contempt and disgust with their sons much more often than with their daughters (Brody & Hall, 2010), and psychological masculinity is associated with aggressive, unacknowledged, and uncontrolled anger (Kopper & Epperson, 1996).

Although emotional expression can have positive health and mental health consequences, the expression of anger is quite risky from a health perspective. Carol Tavris (1989) noted that giving vent to anger is sometimes dangerous and self-destructive. Many people believe that, when a person is angry, he or she needs to "blow off steam"—to act out the anger in some way. But a conventional belief can be wrong. In many circumstances, the unrestrained expression of anger tends to make a person angrier, and also tends to damage relationships. In extreme situations, the expression of anger can put the person at risk, as in "road rage," in which more than 95 percent of the participants are boys and men (Katz, 2013).

Researchers have identified chronic anger as an important contributor to a number of physical health problems: hypertension, heart attack, and stroke (Williams, et. al., 2002) (see Chapter Nine). The research on anger expression tells us that "counting to ten" is often a much better strategy than "blowing off steam," in both the long and the short term (Lynch & Kilmartin, 2013).

Self-disclosure

Self-disclosure is the verbal communication of personal information from one person to another (Cozby, 1973). It includes an important emotional component. There is ample evidence that self-disclosure is basic to mental health (Pennebaker, 2002). The person who is able to reveal his or her thoughts and feelings to others has the opportunities to express the self, receive social support, gain insight into the self, understand his or her emotional nuances, and form close relationships. To do so, however, the person must tolerate some degree of vulnerability. In other words, the revelation of the self to important others involves some interpersonal risk, but it also helps the person to be understood, connected, and in touch with the self.

There also appears to be differences in topics that males and females disclose about as well as the sex of the person who more often receives the disclosure. Stapely and Haviland (1989) reported that adolescent boys disclosed more about their activities and achievements than girls, and that they found these areas (where performance is assessed) to be more emotionally charged than other areas. Girls reported relationships to be more emotionally charged, and they disclosed more in this area. In general, girls tend to reveal personal information and boys tend to reveal what they are doing or thinking (Polce-Lynch, 2002).

The "target" of a self-disclosure refers to the person to whom the disclosure is directed. Here the data are unambiguous. People of both sexes disclose more often to females than to males (Timmers, Fischer, & Manstead, 1998). Gender-typed males tend to reveal very little personal information to other males, although they disclose about the same to females as androgynous men do (Winstead, Derlega, & Wong, 1984). Males overwhelmingly express more affection toward women than toward men (Brody, 1993).

Overall, we can make the following conclusions about sex, gender, and emotion. Men and women are overwhelmingly more similar than they are different; emotional restrictiveness varies widely among men and among women; most men are not significantly restrictive, but most significantly restrictive persons are men, especially men who subscribe strongly to stereotypical masculine ideologies, and both sexes tend to disclose more to women than to men. There is little doubt that many cultures discourage males from expressing their emotions, but as with all gender pressures, individual responses to that pressure are widely variable. There is little evidence that males are naturally unemotional or incapable of improving the quality of their emotional lives (Wong & Rochlen, 2008).

ORIGINS OF RESTRICTIVE EMOTIONALITY

Emotional constriction is one of the hallmarks of traditional masculinity. Males are often socialized to deny and suppress feelings from an early age. The masculine values of toughness, self reliance, task orientation, logic, fearlessness, and confidence are usually perceived to be antithetical to the expression of emotions, especially those associated with vulnerability. Anger would seem to be a potentially empowering emotion, and therefore it is socially allowable for men (Shields, 2010).

There are a number of cultural and social forces that encourage men to restrict their emotionality. O'Neil (1981a) believes that the antifemininity norm is at the heart of men's fears of emotional expression. He describes the following four commonly held masculine beliefs:

1. Emotions, feelings, and vulnerabilities are signs of femininity and therefore to be avoided;
2. Men seeking help through emotional expressiveness are immature, weak, dependent, and therefore feminine;
3. Interpersonal communication emphasizing emotions, feelings, and intuitions are considered feminine and to be avoided;
4. Emotional expression may expose inner fears and conflicts that could portray the man as unstable, immature, and unmanly. (p. 206)

Some psychoanalytic interpretations of masculine inexpression appeal to the early childhood denial of psychological identification with the mother. Because boys are often raised by their other-sex parent, they must put rigid boundaries between themselves and their mothers to define themselves as masculine. If the boy's mother is emotionally expressive and his father is not (a fairly common case), then emotions are experienced as "feminine" and they threaten masculine identification. When the boy feels something, he becomes anxious about his masculinity and learns to deny and devalue these emotions. Theoretically, girls' gender identity is based on attachment to the mother, whereas that of boys is based on separation from her (Chodorow, 1978). As a result, girls tend to become more relationship-oriented and boys more task-oriented.

Relationships do not really have outcomes, per se. They are experiences, just as emotions are, and the maintenance of attached, intimate relationships requires emotional self-disclosure (Jourard, 1971). On the other hand, tasks are often defined by outcome. They tend to be more cognitive in nature, and the important thing is not to experience the task, but rather to get it done. A task-oriented approach to the world may often involve the view that emotions are a nuisance to be disposed of as soon as possible.

If the boy's father is emotionally inexpressive, then this style may become a part of the boy's identification with the father. Sons whose fathers are highly involved parents are more emotionally expressive than other boys, and sons of emotionally expressive fathers display their feelings at similar levels to girls (Brody, 1999). In families where both parents are expressive, boys will not tend to view emotional expression as an exclusively feminine trait, and therefore the natural inclination to display feelings will emerge, since it is not associated with threats to masculinity.

We could also easily view the finding that expressive fathers tend to have expressive sons as merely a product of imitation. Fathers tend to use more demanding language than mothers and, especially with sons, use more pejorative language ("You knucklehead!") (Brody & Hall, 2010), hardly a style conducive to the display of vulnerable feeling. If we look at the availability of male role models in mainstream United States culture, it is easy to see how inexpressiveness perpetuates itself generation after generation. Fathers' inexpressiveness is imitated, and male heroes in popular culture are often paragons of traditional masculinity. Movies and television often contain male characters who are task oriented, tough, inexpressive, and violent.

An interesting research finding is that parents display a wider range of their own emotions to their daughters than to their sons (Brody, 2000). Therefore, girls usually have more opportunities than boys to observe and imitate expressive models. In one longitudinal study (in which a group of children is followed over a number of years), Adams, Kuebli, Boyle, & Fivush (1995) demonstrated that parents' more frequent use of emotional language with girls appeared to create a sex difference in children's use of similar language. The researchers found no sex differences at 40 months of age, but clear differences emerged by 70 months. These 30 months are a time of highly accelerated language acquisition, and parents' reluctance to speak to boys about their emotions may communicate the belief that feelings are not important.

There is also considerable evidence that interpersonal and behavioral influences within the family lead boys away from the world of emotion. Parents talk about emotion more to daughters than to sons, except for anger and disgust. When children feel badly, mothers are more likely to talk directly about the feeling with daughters and to talk about the causes and consequences of the feeling with sons. The former encourages expression; the latter, control (Brody & Hall, 2010). In these interactions that highlight certain aspects of experience, pattern-seeking children learn which of these aspects deserve their attention. For girls, it is often the emotional world. For boys, it is likely to be the world of task, control, and detached analysis.

When a girl comes home from school and says, "the kids are picking on me," parents are more likely to engage her in a discussion of how she *feels* about it (emotion-focused coping). When a boy makes the same statement, parents are more likely to talk about what he is going to *do* about it (task-focused coping). Thus we sometimes encourage girls to solve problems within themselves and boys outside of themselves. In the extreme, either style can be maladaptive, as people need to do both to cope effectively.

Rewards and punishments for self-disclosure may also affect the frequency of this behavior. It is clear that "unmasculine" behaviors such as crying often meet with disapproval from parents and peers (Brody, 2000). Many men have a storehouse of memories of times when their emotional expression was punished. The crying little boy whose father says to him threateningly, "*I'll* give you something to cry about," can quickly extinguish that behavior. There is solid research evidence that the extensive socialization to control emotional expression can lead to an *overlearning* of this tendency (Barr & Kleck, 1995). In other words, emotional inhibition can become a habit that is applied automatically across a variety of situations.

The male peer group can be especially brutal in its enforcement of the restrictive emotionality norm (Polce-Lynch, 2002). In extreme groups, such as street gangs, this standard is rigidly enforced with threats of violence. Besides punishing expressiveness, male groups may also reward emotional inexpressiveness. For instance, in some fraternity initiation rites, a group symbol is burned into the arm of the initiate, and he is applauded for remaining unresponsive. Many male initiation rites around the world encourage emotional suppression, an important skill for warriors (Herdt, 1982).

We can see from the above research findings and examples that restrictive emotionality is not only the product of a *history* of these sanctions. Gendered reward and punishment contingencies exist in many settings in which adult men find themselves. Not only did men get punished for emoting when they were children, they often get punished for displaying their feelings as adults. From blue collar to corporate workplaces, for example, emotions other than anger are not often tolerated in men.

Women in the corporate world sometimes find that expression of vulnerable feeling is disadvantageous to their careers. A female banking executive relates that, among her female colleagues, the rule is, "you die before you cry." We suspect that, for males in these and other work settings, this rule goes without saying. Our experience of the corporate culture is that, for many women executives, emotional restriction is situation-specific. They tend to confine inexpressiveness to the workplace because it is defined as appropriate there, but they continue to view expressiveness as useful elsewhere. For many men however, emotional constriction may be more cross-situational. There are precious few settings when they feel safe enough to disclose. For women, "die before you cry" is a hyperbole that stresses the career importance of avoiding the display of weakness in a male-dominated setting. For men, dying may be literally what they are doing (see Chapter Nine).

Role Theory

As we have noted several times, social roles are powerful determinants of behavior. It is in this theoretical area that we find one of the most convincing explanations of male inexpressiveness. People tend to assume roles in organizing their behavior, and they tend to avoid out-role behavior. As we have seen, masculine and feminine roles are generalized social roles that function to influence a wide variety of social behaviors. This may be especially true for gender-schematic people, who tend to rigidly organize their worlds into male and female categories (Bem, 1993).

Masculine roles involve a set of expectations for task-oriented behaviors that emphasize logic and rationality, and de-emphasize emotional experience. From early childhood, social forces encourage boys to value masculine traits and behaviors and devalue feminine ones. The ideal of masculinity is physical courage, toughness, risk taking, competitiveness, and aggression, traits seen as incompatible with emotional expression (Balswick, 1988). For example, men are socialized to view all other men as competitors. One does not exhibit vulnerability to a competitor (Skovholt & Hansen, 1980). Since self-disclosure often involves vulnerability, males tend to avoid it, especially in the company of other males.

Besides being incompatible with masculine expectations, emotional expression is defined as feminine. Consider what your reaction might be if you overheard the following conversation (Brannon, 1985, p. 307):

> "Mike, I've been so upset since we had that argument, I could
> hardly sleep last night. Are you *sure* you're really not mad at me?"

> "Heck, Jim, I'm so relieved... I was just afraid that you'd be mad at *me*!"

For many, this example is comical—so out of the ordinary that it seems absurd. But it is important to note that, even if this conversation might not take place, these two men may well *experience* this kind of upset even if they do not *display* it. Because of the social dominance of men, out-role behavior is viewed as a loss of masculine power and privilege, and not to be tolerated. Hence, pejorative terms like "sissy" or "wimp" are applied to men who exhibit emotionality, submissiveness, or dependence. Masculine privilege not only devalues and restricts women, it devalues and restricts the feminine-defined parts of men as well as making it difficult for others to connect with the person. James Nelson (1997) likens emotional constriction to armor: "It seems to protect us, but it also keeps us from leaping, dancing, and being seen."

We can also understand emotional expression within the context of relationships. One broad social expectation is for *reciprocity*, the tendency to respond to other people as they behave toward us (Baron & Branscome, 2011). For example, when someone expresses anger toward you, you tend to respond with anger. When haggling over the price of something, a salesperson who reduces an asking price influences a buyer to increase his or her offer. With regard to self-disclosure, the reciprocity norm influences people to disclose at a level similar to that which they receive. Since males are less often the targets of disclosure than females, then it is not surprising that they tend to disclose less. Males exhibit higher levels of emotional disclosure to females than to other males, perhaps reflecting the influence of the reciprocity norm.

Jack Sattel's (1998) explanation of male inexpressiveness is very different than those presented thus far. He argues that men are inexpressive simply because they want to maintain power. By being emotionally withholding, men force women to "draw them out" and do the emotional work in the relationship. Sattell notes that some men are quite expressive in the early stages of romantic relationships with women. Later on, they sometimes become inexpressive as a way of asserting control, since masculinity and male privilege demand dominance. He goes so far as to suggest that inexpressiveness is directly related to the power of a person's role. Husbands are more likely than wives to respond to marital conflict by "stonewalling"—minimizing their

"Ideally, I'd like a guy whose eyes will well up but who doesn't actually cry."

facial expressions, eye contact, and willingness to listen (Levenson, Carstensen, & Gottman, 1994).

Lakoff (1990) contends that men's and women's typical communication patterns are better understood in terms of superior and subordinate, noting that similar patterns develop between supervisors and workers, Whites and People of Color, prisoners and guards. Both women and men in positions of authority use power-assertive language, reveal their feelings less often (except for anger), and display similar non-verbal behaviors (Tavris, 1992). Social status and power are extremely important variables in the study of emotional expression (Deaux, 2000), with gender often operating as a generalized power variable.

In summary, it seems that there are a variety of social, cultural, and interpersonal forces that influence men to be inexpressive. The available evidence is that these forces can do a pretty good job of inhibiting what seems to be a natural, often healthy inclination to disclose and express feelings. Since emotion is pervasive, the results of compulsively restricting it may also be pervasive.

CONSEQUENCES OF RESTRICTIVE EMOTIONALITY

Emotion never lies, and emotion never lies still. Affective experience is central to human experience, regardless of whether or not one attempts to deny its existence. Feelings that are not expressed directly often find indirect forms of expression. Many men deal with emotions by placing feelings outside of themselves, through externalizing defenses, by "acting out" emotional conflicts, and/or through physical symptoms.

We have seen that, from early childhood, girls are encouraged to look inside of themselves and think about how they feel, and boys are encouraged to look outside of themselves and think about what to do (Brody & Hall, 2010). Strong "feminine" emotions are experienced as threats to masculinity, and these threats are sometimes difficult to ignore. The traditional male deals with these feelings with strategies that allow him to perceive them as nonexistent. In this way, he preserves his masculinity by defending against feminine experience and behavior.

Families' acceptance of emotion in children is associated with higher levels of social and psychological adjustment (Bronstein, Briones, Brooks, & Cowan, 1996). It is critical to children's mental health for their families to allow them to experience and express their feelings. Although some families squelch emotions in children of both sexes, they are much more likely to do so with sons than with daughters.

James Mahalik and his colleagues (1998) found that men with rigid masculine expectations used more immature and neurotic ego defenses than more gender-flexible men. Some psychologists see the main function of masculinity itself as a generic defense against vulnerable feelings (Lynch & Kilmartin, 2013). An example will help to clarify these styles. If you are rejected by a romantic partner, that event can precipitate painful feelings of sadness due to the loss of the valued person, as well as anxiety due to doubts about your adequacy. There are several ways to deal with these feelings. You could talk about them with a close friend and gain support, express the sadness through "having a good cry," convert these feelings into anger and engage in some aggressive behavior, or deal with the feelings as though they were an intellectual problem. The latter two strategies are preferred by masculine men. The former two are feminine styles which, despite their effectiveness, cannot be accessed by these men, because doing so would constitute a threat to masculinity.

Because of the overwhelming quality of these emotions, the traditionally gender-typed man might punch a wall, drink heavily, or compulsively and desperately seek a new partner. In all of these strategies, solutions come from outside of the self. The man can take out his frustrations on an object or find something (alcohol or another person) that will hopefully soothe him, as he is not good at soothing himself.

There are several negative consequences to this external style. First, if the soothing person or object is not available, the man may find it very difficult to deal with his loss. Second, little new learning can take place. He does not have the skills to introspect and think about himself, and thus he has difficulty in learning what caused the troubling situation and how he might behave differently. If he always deals with emotions externally, he can learn little about what is inside. Third, these kinds of behaviors may have a tendency to alienate other people.

A relationship breakup involves a powerful experience of emotional loss, and one must assimilate that loss into one's sense of self to recover healthy functioning. This course of recovery from loss is known as *grieving*. It is a process by which one expresses, works through, eventually accepts the feelings that have accompanied the loss, and comes to a point of resolution that allows one to move on with one's life. John Lynch and Christopher Kilmartin (2013) describe the problem that traditional masculinity creates for the grieving process:

Grieving has a life of its own. It is quite natural to feel and behave in certain ways—such as crying, reminiscing, and expressing a wish that one had treated the person better—in response to loss. Every culture has funeral rituals that help people to initiate the grief process following the ultimate loss, death. The grieving process takes time; one cannot spend an hour grieving and be done with it once and for all. Depending on the loss, it can take months or even years. The man who has lost his partner is aware that something is wrong, but many men avoid grieving because it involves the expression of vulnerable feelings, and also involves acknowledging that he feels connected to her. These two behaviors are culturally defined as unmasculine, and so he tends to make efforts to distract himself so that he does not have to deal with his pain. He pays a price for doing so, as he is likely to develop symptoms, which are his body's and his mind's way of telling him that something is wrong. If he does not heed these signals, he will continue to have these symptoms. When there comes a time for him to again become involved in a relationship, he will be predisposed to acting out the psychological issues that arise from an incomplete grieving process. (p. 176)

Alexithymia

Acting like one has no feelings over many years may result in the loss of ability to experience emotion. Sifneos (1972) coined the term *alexithymia* to describe the style of habitual inexpressiveness. It comes from the Greek (*a* = lack, *lexis* = words, as in lexicon, and *thymos* = emotions). Literally, the word alexithymia means "no words for feelings." Alexithymic persons have such an impoverished emotional life that they can not even identify feelings, much less express them. Nemiah, Fryberger, and Sifneos (1976) described alexithymia as having four features: "a) difficulty identifying and describing feelings; b) difficulty distinguishing feelings from bodily sensations; c) reduction or absence of symbolic thinking (lack of imaginative ability); d) an external, operative cognitive style" (pp. 227–228).

A large body of research provides strong support for the hypothesis that emotion never lies still. People who do not deal with feelings directly do not make them go away. The alexithymic style often becomes destructive to the person either physically, psychologically, or both. Although only a small percentage of men are truly alexithymic, and some women also suffer from this problem, the connections between alexithymia and masculinity can hardly be denied. In a large, four-city, multicultural sample, Ronald Levant and his colleagues (2003) found a strong relationship between alexithymia and masculinity ideology. Using meta-analysis, a statistical technique that combines findings from a group of studies, researchers found small but consistent sex differences across 45 studies, with males more likely to show evidence of alexithymia (Levant, Hall, Williams, & Hasan, 2009).

Other Consequences

The hypothesis that "emotion never lies; emotion never lies still" is supported by a number of studies indicating that men are more likely than women to express negative emotions through physiological processes such as heart rate reactivity and elevated blood pressure. When this style of reaction becomes ingrained and habitual, it can have a negative effect on men's physical health (Jansz, 2000) (see Chapter Nine), the quality of their relationships (Wong & Pituch, & Rochlen, 2006), their ability to be effective as parents (Lynch & Kilmartin, 2013), and their willingness to seek medical or psychological help (Addis & Mahalik, 2003).

Restrictive emotionality also has societal consequences. *Empathy* is the emotional awareness of another person's distress and thus an inhibitor of violence. In other words, if you can put yourself in the victim's place in an emotional way, you will be less likely to hurt him or her intentionally. However, it is impossible to understand someone else's feelings if you do not understand your own. David Lisak (1997) coined the term *empathy for the self* in his work with male victims of childhood abuse. Lisak found that those men who were able to acknowledge the emotional and physical pain of their experience as victims showed a strong tendency to not become violent as adults. In contrast, those who denied their pain tended to later act it out in a violent way. For a survivor of childhood abuse, being able to understand his own vulnerable feeling—having empathy for the self—allowed him to have empathy for other people, and thus not harm them. In other words, it appears that a person must have an experiential referent to connect emotionally to others' pain.

Men who have embraced task-oriented and inexpressive gender role characteristics may find it easy to perceive people as if they were things, and subordinate human welfare to a task that they define as more important. When such men are in power, their potential for destruction is great. War, racism, sexism, violence, exploitive business practices, the pollution of the planet, and other forms of victimization are all at least partly the result of a failure of compassion and empathy. Men have not been the exclusive perpetrators of these human wrongs, but they have certainly contributed more than their share. The social encouragement to become unfeeling machines, together with the disproportionate allotment of power to males, shoulders some of the responsibility for this state of affairs.

Toward Solutions

We have seen that restrictive emotionality has many psychological, physical, interpersonal, and societal consequences. The good news is that we are not doomed to live with them. A number of therapeutic, educational, and social interventions have been designed to help men become more comfortable with affect. Because feelings such as satisfaction, love, and emotional connectedness are critical to quality of life, and because restrictive emotionality has negative consequences, it is not surprising that many men desire to become more aware and expressive of their emotional worlds (Levant, 1997a).

We have already seen that inexpressiveness arises, at least in part, from situations in which males are discouraged from being emotional. Therefore, one solution is to create environments that give men permission to break the social norm of non-disclosure, thus allowing the natural human propensity for expression of feeling to emerge. One popular method for creating such settings has been through the establishment of men's support or therapy groups, where men who want to learn expressive skills come together into an unusual all-male situation. Rather than having the common men's group norms of competition, task orientation, and macho rigidity, group members strive to create an atmosphere of cooperation, empathy, and self-disclosure. In summarizing more than 25 years of leading such groups, Frederic Rabinowitz (2011) concluded that, "Men are deep, but they need a place to explore that depth, and they need time to do it."

Therapists and researchers have designed other interventions and accumulated some evidence of their effectiveness. Ronald Levant (2003) developed a five step, skill-based model for individual treatment of men who display normative male alexithymia. He informs his client that "We're going to learn the skills that nine year old girls learn as a matter of course," (Levant, 1997a) but that the culture has conspired to prevent men from attaining. In the first phase, the therapist educates the client about the connection between masculine socialization and inexpressiveness and helps the client develop the ability to tolerate emotions. Step two is the development of an emotional vocabulary. Levant has the client list as many words for feelings that he can generate over the course of several days. The third step is practice in identifying others' emotions by learning to read their facial expressions, vocal tone, and body language. He can do this in conversations and in watching movies and television and attempting to take the perspective of the characters. In the fourth stage, the client keeps a daily log where he tracks his emotional responses, concomitant physical sensations, and the contexts in which the feelings arise. The final step involves practice to reinforce the emotional skills he has learned. Levant (1998) reports that this new emotional awareness is empowering and exciting for many men. One client remarked that "it was as though I had been living in a black-and-white television set that had suddenly gone to color" (p. 48).

Y. Joel Wong and Aaron Rochlen (2008) suggest an approach based on Solution-focused therapy (SFT). Although most therapy tends to focus on reducing problem behavior and experience, SFT focuses on "successful exceptions" to the problem. A therapist treating a man for restrictive emotionality would explore instances when he was able to express vulnerable feeling such as sadness or gratitude, situations in which and people with whom he feels more comfortable with expression, and types of feelings that he tends to be able to express. This approach helps the client to identify the situational and other factors that affect his emotional expression and to expand his emotional competence to a wider variety of settings.

Increases in male expressiveness can also be realized through societal changes. We are seeing some movement in this direction in the United States in recent years. As women increasingly share the involvement in economic activities, many men are increasing their family involvement, with its emphasis on expressive activities, albeit at a slower pace (Marsiglio & Pleck, 2005). Balswick (1988) first suggested that, in the traditional structure of the family, women are economically dependent on men, while men are emotionally dependent on women. Just as many women are beginning to attain economic independence, many men are beginning to work toward emotional independence. This kind of self-sufficiency does not refer to disconnection, but rather to the man's expressive management of his emotions in the context of relationships, self-awareness, and attainment of his life goals.

SUMMARY

1. Even though emotion is at the center of human experience, masculine gender roles define it as feminine and discourage it in men, with the exception of the expression of anger. However, the display "rules" for emotion vary with changing social contexts.

2. There is some evidence that men, especially gender-typed men, tend to be less expressive and self-disclosing than women.

3. The origins of restrictive male emotionality are in the gender role definitions of vulnerability, inner conflict, dependence, and the definition of feeling as an unmasculine experience. These norms are often enforced by family and peers, as well as by media images of masculinity.

4. Emotional constriction may have a number of negative consequences for men and those around them. Men who are uncomfortable with their feelings are prone to using external defenses and acting out. These methods of coping are often less effective and efficient than self-disclosing and asking for help.

5. The extreme of inexpressiveness is alexithymia, which involves a poor awareness of and ability to describe feeling states. Alexithymia has been associated with a wide variety of physical and mental health problems. The hypothesis that "emotion never lies, and emotion never lies still" is supported by the research in this area. Restrictive emotionality also appears to have negative effects on relationships and parenting skills.

6. There are many men who have expressed a desire to improve their abilities to express and disclose. Interventions for this purpose have met with significant success.

7. Male expressiveness should also increase as a function of more progressive gender roles. Because restrictive emotionality is strongly influenced by the expectations of social settings, the creation of nontraditional settings with alternative expectations holds a great deal of promise for improving the quality of men's emotional lives.

Chapter Nine

Surviving and Thriving: Men and Physical Health

In the not-too-distant past, before it was possible to know a baby's sex before birth, it was common to ask expectant parents if they had a preference for either a boy or a girl. One of the most frequent responses to this inquiry was, "We don't care as long as 'it's' healthy." As it turns out, "it" has a greater chance to be healthy if she is a girl, as sex and gender have a significant relationship to physical well-being. As we will see, the reference to females as "the weaker sex" is misleading when it comes to serious health problems and longevity.

There are sex differences in the epidemiologies (statistical incidences within a population) of many physical problems. For example, males are more likely than females to contract early-onset heart disease, emphysema, and most forms of cancer. On average, men die at a significantly earlier age than women. Many researchers believe that these sex differences in disease and longevity cannot be explained solely by biological differences between the sexes.

A good deal of evidence has led scholars to suggest that certain aspects of traditional masculinity are at least partially responsible for men's problems with disease and longevity. In this chapter, we describe some of these problems and review the relevant psychological literature on sex and gender as it relates to physical health.

SEX DIFFERENCES IN LONGEVITY

The most recent available United States statistics for life expectancy are for the year 2010. The National Center for Health Statistics (CDC, 2013) reported that the average life expectancy for Black males born in the United States in 2010 was 71.8 years, compared with 78.0 years for Black females (The descriptor Black is used in these reports rather than the term African American). For Whites, the expectancies were 76.5 years and 81.3 years for males and females, respectively. Overall Hispanic rates were 78.5 and 83.5 (Murphy, Xu, & Kochanek., 2013).

As you can see from these data, relative to their female counterparts, Black men are especially at risk for early death. They are more likely than majority men to live in hazardous, stressful, and/or impoverished environments, as well as to lack access to

153

health care (Ro, Casares, Treadwell, & Thomas, 2004). In poor urban areas, two-thirds of African American males fail to reach the age of 65. According to health scholar Arline Geronimus (quoted in Blitstein, 2009), "American minorities face a bevy of chronic obstacles that Whites and the socioeconomically advantaged cope with far less often: environmental pollution, high crime, poor health care, overt racism, concentrated poverty" (p. 51). Homicide is the eighth leading cause of death for Black males in the United States (CDC, 2013).

Although life expectancies for all groups rise steadily over the years, men in the United States have died an average of five to eight years sooner than women since the decade of the 1950s (Arias, 2005). This "mortality gap" varies internationally, from a low of 3.3 (Israel) to a high of 13.3 (Russian Federation) (National Center for Health Statistics, 2008). In the United States, the mortality gap between the sexes has declined from around 7.7 years in 1980 to around 5 years in 2010.

Table 9.1 details sex ratios for U.S. deaths in 2010. As you can see, more males than females die at every stage of life until age 85 (the ratio changes directions at that point because so many more women than men have survived to that age). At ages 15 to 24, the ratio of male to female deaths is a staggering 296:100. At best, U.S. males die "before their time" at about a 6 to 5 ratio to females. At worst, the ratio is nearly 3 to 1. Contrary to the social belief that males are heartier and more resistant to disease, the evidence is indisputable that males are more vulnerable than females at every age.

At birth, there is a slight imbalance in the ratio of males to females. Conception favors males because Y-chromosome bearing sperm (androsperm) are more motile than X-chromosome bearing sperm (gynosperm), and thus they are more likely to fertilize the ovum. There are somewhere between 120 and 160 males for every 100 females at conception (Stillion, 1995). However, male fetuses are more likely to have problems *in utero*, leading to spontaneous abortion (miscarriage). By birth, the large sex imbalance that was produced at conception has shrunken considerably; there are between 104 and 106 male births for every 100 female births (Stein, 2005). Because

Table 9.1   Ratio of Male to Female Deaths by Age (2010 U.S. Data)

Age in Years	Male: Female Death Ratio
1 to 4	133:100
5 to 9	132:100
10 to 14	142:100
15–19	260:100
20–24	294:100
25–34	223:100
35–44	170:100
45–54	157:100
55–64	156:100
65–74	129:100
75–84	99:100
over 85	56:100

Calculated from data from National Vital Statistics Reports (Heron, 2013)

males die at higher rates than females, parity (an equal number of males and females in the age group population) is reached somewhere between the ages of 25 and 34 (Basow, 1992). From this age range and up, women outnumber men. Women are nearly twice as likely as men to survive beyond age 85 (derived from Heron, 2013), and nearly three times as likely to live to be 100 (Arias, 2005).

SEX DIFFERENCES IN DISEASE

There is some evidence to suggest that women get ill more often and report feeling sicker than men on a day-to-day basis. For instance, they are more likely than men to report being bothered by headaches, bladder infections, arthritis, corns and calluses, constipation, hemorrhoids, and varicose veins. We cannot be sure to what extent these differences are real, and to what extent they reflect the social permission for women to report illness. But when it comes to serious (life threatening) diseases, men outnumber women in almost every category (Arias, 2005).

The two diseases that most often cause death are heart disease and cancer. About 24 percent of all people eventually die of heart disease. The male:female ratio for cause of death by heart disease is about 106:100 (Heron, 2013), a fairly small sex difference. When one looks at these data *by age group*, however, a very different picture emerges. Between the ages of 25 and 44, the ratio of male to female deaths from heart disease in 2004 was 260:100. Thus, although many people die of heart disease, males tend to die much earlier than females. Males are also nearly three times more likely than females to have a non-fatal heart attack or to be diagnosed with heart disease before age 65 (American Heart Association, 2014).

With regard to cancer, sex ratios differ depending on the location of the cancerous tumor in the body. As a cause of death, men lead women in every category except breast and hormonal cancers. Sex ratios for cancers of the mouth and throat (247:100), genitals (256:100, including prostate cancer, which accounts for nearly one in three cancers in men) and urinary organs (220:100) show the most lopsided sex differences (derived from American Cancer Society, 2014). Table 9.2 details sex ratios for leading causes of "early" (before age 65) deaths. Although data from all ages tends to obscure

Table 9.2   Ratio of Male to Female Deaths Before Age 65: Selected Causes of Death

Cause of Death	Male: Female ratio
Suicide	354:100
Homicide	459:100
Heart disease	227:100
Accidents	285:100
Diabetes	388:100
Malignant neoplams (cancer)	112:100
Liver failure, including cirrhosis	225:100

Calculated from Heron, 2013

sex ratios due to the greater number of females alive at older ages, this table provides a good picture of the causes of deaths that we might consider premature, and males lead females in every category.

Table 9.2 also includes data for causes of early death other than diseases: accidents, suicide, and homicide. You will note that the sex differences in these areas are very large. Thus, an alarming number of physically healthy men die from causes that are somewhat preventable. In fact, homicide is the leading cause of death for African American males between the ages of 15 and 34 and the second leading cause for 10- to 14-year-olds (Heron, 2013). Males are more than six times as likely as females to die from a firearm injury (including self-inflicted injuries) in the United States, and this proportion is nearly nine to one for Black males (derived from Heron, 2008).

WHY ARE MEN'S LIVES SHORTER THAN WOMEN'S?

Around the beginning of the twentieth century, men's lives and women's lives, on average, were about the same length. In modern industrial nations such as the United States, there has been a dramatic reduction in the risk of death from pregnancy and childbirth, which were relatively dangerous at the beginning of the twentieth century (Stillion, 1995). The decrease of this risk resulted in the lifespan sex differential. It could be said that both women's and men's lives were shortened 100 years ago, and that we have found ways to prevent many early deaths for women. Hopefully, the same can be done for men. However, it may become apparent to you that this is a complicated process.

There are two basic types of explanations for the sex difference in average lifespan. The first is a *biogenic* explanation. From this viewpoint, men die earlier because of genetic, hormonal, or other biological differences between the sexes. The second type of explanation is a *psychogenic* one, in which sex differences in lifespan are attributed to gender differences in psychological and social areas such as behaviors, socialization, and methods of problem solving.

Note that these two types of explanations do not necessarily compete with each other. It is possible for both biogenic and psychogenic factors to contribute to sex differences in longevity. In fact, there is good evidence to suggest that both factors are operating in many cases. The question is one of the relative contribution of each factor. There has been a trend among researchers in recent years to speak of *biopsychosocial* models that take biology, individual psychology, and the effects of other people and social systems into account in constructing comprehensive pictures of behavioral phenomena.

It is also possible for biogenic and psychogenic factors to interact with one another. For instance, a man who is at high risk for heart disease because of his physiology (biogenic factor) might be less likely than a woman to see a physician for regular checkups because he sees doing so as an admission of weakness and vulnerability, which he considers unmasculine and therefore undesirable (psychogenic factor). The man in this example might have a shorter life than would be the case if either factor were operating in isolation.

In the above example, the biogenic factor might be the major contribution. It would also be possible for a psychogenic factor to make a major contribution while still interacting with a biogenic factor. For instance, a man might drink alcohol heavily in response to the pressure of meeting masculine gender role demands, thus damaging his body and shortening his life, or he might use tobacco to enhance his masculine image, with a similar result.

BIOGENIC EXPLANATIONS

As we mentioned earlier, male fetuses are more vulnerable *in utero* than female fetuses, and the death rate for males aged 1 to 4 exceeds that of females. These data are ample evidence that biological factors operate in the lifespan sex differential, as it would be difficult to argue that masculine socialization could have an effect on mortality at such an early age. Explanations of biological factors include genetic and hormonal sex differences.

Genetic Differences

The difference in males' and females' genetic makeup is that females have two X-chromosomes and males have one X- and one Y-chromosome. When there are recessive disease genes on the X-chromosome, having a second X-chromosome turns out to be a genetic advantage. The second X-chromosome often contains a dominant corresponding gene that protects the female from contracting the genetic disease. For example, if there is a gene for hemophilia on one X-chromosome, the female will not contract the disease unless there is also a hemophilia gene on the other X-chromosome, an extremely rare occurrence.

Because the form of the Y-chromosome does not correspond exactly with that of the X-chromosome, the male is not always afforded such protection. In fact, the Y-chromosome is far and away the smallest of the 46, containing about 60 genes compared with about 800 on the X chromosome (Eliot, 2009). Genetic abnormalities on the X-chromosome are much more likely to appear in the male because of the absence of a second (corrective) X-chromosome. Some "X-linked" abnormalities like color blindness or baldness are relatively innocuous. Others are more serious. For instance, there is some speculation that dyslexia (a learning disability) and hyperactivity might be X-linked. A few genetic abnormalities, such as hemophilia, can be life threatening.

In the search for explanations of the sex differential in longevity, genetic differences make a very small contribution because of the rarity of life-threatening X-linked diseases. As Waldron (quoted in Dolnick, 1991) stated, "Most of the common X-linked diseases aren't fatal, and most of the fatal X-linked diseases aren't common" (p. 12).

Hormonal Differences

A major sex difference in hormones is in males' higher levels of testosterone and females' higher levels of estrogen. These two hormones account for physiological sex differences in average muscle size, body fat percentage, and metabolic speed. There is evidence to suggest that testosterone may render men somewhat more vulnerable to certain diseases, and that estrogen may have some protective effect.

The most demonstrable effect of these two hormones is in the area of heart disease. In recent years, the effect of cholesterol on heart disease has been the subject of much research and discussion. There are two kinds of cholesterol, high density lipoprotein (HDL), called "good cholesterol" because it protects against heart disease, and low density lipoprotein (LDL), called "bad cholesterol" because of its damaging effects.

In prepubescent males and females, HDL levels are about equal. At puberty, HDL levels drop rapidly in boys, but they hold steady in girls. This change coincides with the large surge of testosterone in boys and estrogen in girls. It is assumed that adolescent testosterone production is responsible for the reduction of HDL cholesterol, while estrogen has little or no effect on HDL levels (Dolnick, 1991).

LDL ("bad") cholesterol begins to rise in both males and females after puberty. However, males show a more rapid increase, leaving them more susceptible to heart disease. After menopause, when women's estrogen level is greatly reduced, LDL levels show this same kind of sharp increase. Therefore, researchers assume that estrogen has a protective effect against LDL cholesterol, while testosterone probably has little effect (Kevorkian & Cepeda, 2007). These hormonal effects are important ones because heart disease is the leading cause of death. However, there is also some evidence that testosterone may shorten men's lives in other ways that are not fully understood.

PSYCHOGENIC EXPLANATIONS

There are at least four ways in which psychological processes can contribute to illness, injury, and/or premature mortality. First, behaviors can be directly self-destructive. Suicide is obviously the best example of this type of psychogenic factor, but one might also consider the use of tobacco products or the excessive use of alcohol and other drugs in this category. These behaviors involve the person's active harm of his or her body. It is also possible for the person to passively harm his or her health by neglecting to perform behaviors that maintain health. For example, a man with high blood pressure who refuses to take prescribed medication to control it, or someone who does not see a physician even though he has detected a symptom of cancer (when he has medical resources available to him) adversely affects his health through his behavior.

Third, some behaviors involve physical risk of illness, injury, or death. These behaviors include: sharing needles in intravenous drug use, drunk driving, and engaging in dangerous sports. Fourth, some psychological processes seem to have adverse effects on the body. For instance, the effects of stress on physical health are well documented, and there are also certain personality characteristics that are predictive of some physical conditions. We have separated these four categories of psychogenic factors for purposes of discussion.

Self-Destructive Behaviors

Suicide. Suicide is, of course, the ultimate self-destructive behavior, and the overwhelmingly most common motive for it is to escape from one's pain. Although females in the United States are more likely than males to make suicidal gestures or attempts, U.S. males complete suicide attempts more than three times more often than females (Heron, 2013). Among older people, the ratio of male to female suicides is striking. U.S. men over 65 commit suicide at more than seven times the rate of women; at age 85, the ratio is more than eleven to one (National Center for Health Statistics, 2008).

There is some conjecture that more women than men use suicide attempts to "cry for help" rather than as determined efforts to die, which are more common in men (Harrison, Chin, & Ficaratto, 1995). Women are also more likely to use suicide methods that have relatively low potential for death, such as overdose or wrist slashing, whereas men are more likely to use violent and highly lethal methods such as firearms or motor vehicles (Nolen-Hoeksema, 1998). Firearm suicides accounted for 60 percent of all male suicides, compared to 39 percent of all female suicides (Anderson & Smith, 2005) and among U.S. older men, 80 percent of completed suicides are with firearms (Kaplan, Huguet, McFarland, & Mandle, 2012). White males commit four out of five firearm suicides (National Institute of Mental Health, 2003). The lethality of method does not account for the whole difference, however. Males complete more suicides with every method (Canetto, 2000).

Traditional masculinity has several connections to suicidal behavior. Foremost among these is a gender-differentiated socialization for dealing with psychological pain. Whereas women have been taught to think about and express feelings, gain social support, and take care of themselves, men are socialized to act on problems, be hyperindependent, and disdain emotional self-care. The hypermasculine man in severe emotional distress is often alone with his pain. He cannot express it, and he cannot ask for help with it. If the pain becomes great enough, it may seem to him that suicide is his only option. A second factor is the success, status, problem-solving orientation in gender-typed males. The masculine value of "getting the job done" may actually relate to the "job" of taking one's life. Finally, there is the masculine norm of independence. Needing and requesting help is antithetical to traditional masculinity. Teenagers who feel connected to their families are much less likely to engage in suicidal behavior (or violence and drug abuse), and the adolescent suicide sex differential may be related to families' demands for hyperindependence in boys (Pollack, 1998). Despondent men often feel alone with problems that seem unsolvable and pain that seems intractable. For these men, suicide may seem like the only alternative. It is apparent that, more often than females, males are unwilling to ask for help either before their problems escalate to the point of suicide contemplation, or by giving messages through a suicide gesture rather than a serious attempt.

It is also interesting to speculate about the two periods of development in which the suicide sex ratios are most unbalanced: adolescence and old age. Adolescence is the most gender-typed time of life, the time in which the boy begins to establish himself as a man, sometimes without healthy guides for doing so. Males who feel "unsuccessful" at meeting masculine demands may be at high risk for depression and suicide. In part because masculinity and heterosexuality are so intertwined, gay male teenagers may be particularly at risk.

In old age, the traditional hallmarks of masculinity begin to fade away. Men are culturally defined by physical abilities and the work role. The older man must face the facts that his body is declining and, after he retires, that he is no longer a valued contributor in the working world. If his sense of self is overly consumed by this narrow standard of masculinity, body and work role decline can seriously undermine his sense of self-worth. Additionally, the man may also be faced with a loss of independence at some point during his physical decline, which is also antithetical to the traditional masculine role.

The combination of pain and masculine bravado can indeed be a quite volatile one. In a strongly worded statement, Stillion and McDowell (1996) describe this association:

> If we wanted to write a prescription for increasing suicide risk, we could not improve on the traditional male socialization pattern. Take one male child, who has higher levels of aggression and activity than his female peers. Put the child into competitive situations. Tell him he must win at all costs. Teach him that to admit fear or doubt is weakness and that weakness is not masculine. Complete the vicious circle by assuring him that his worth is dependent on winning games, then salary and promotion competitions, and you have the perfect recipe for enhanced suicide risk. (p. 243)

William Pollack (2000a) pointed out that, although more people die from suicide than from homicide in the United States, homicide prevention accounts for ten times the financial expenditure of suicide prevention.

Use of tobacco. Tobacco products are the only commodities legally sold in the United States that, when used as intended, will usually kill the consumer. The most common results of extended tobacco use are bronchitis, emphysema, asthma, and cancers of the respiratory system, mouth, and throat. Male smokers tend to engage in more dangerous smoking habits than women, including smoking more than 25 cigarettes a day, inhaling deeply, using products with high tar and nicotine content and/or cigarettes without filters (Courtenay, 2000a). Will Courtenay (2000b) summarizes the connections between gender and tobacco use:

> Cigarette smoking is considered the single most preventable cause of illness and death in the United States... Tobacco use accounts for roughly one in five deaths overall, and one in four deaths among those aged 35 to 64 years. *Twice as many male as female deaths are attributed to smoking,* and men's higher lifetime use of tobacco is considered a primary reason for their higher rates of cardiovascular disease and stroke. One quarter of all heart disease deaths are associated with smoking. The risk of heart disease and stroke among smokers is more than double the risk for nonsmokers, and the risk of sudden cardiac death is up to 4 times greater... Three of four men who get *any* kind of cancer are smokers. The lung cancer death rate for men is 2 ½ times higher than the rate for women, and 9 of 10 male lung cancer deaths can be directly attributed to cigarette smoking. Men who smoke double their risk of prostate cancer. Regularly smoking cigars doubles a man's risk of lung cancer and increases his risk of oral cancer between 5 and 10 times. Smokeless tobacco users increase their risk of developing oral cancer by *nearly 50 times.* (pp. 8–9, emphases added)

"Smokeless" tobacco (chewing tobacco and snuff) is used by males almost exclusively. According to a Public Health Service survey, one out of six males had used these products within the past year. The average first use of smokeless tobacco is at age nine, and one quarter of users had their first taste of chewing tobacco before age five! There are 30,000 new cases of oral cancer each year in the United States, with a mortality rate of one-half of new cases within five years of diagnosis. Males are diagnosed with mouth and throat cancer two and a half times more often than females and account for two thirds of all deaths from this cause (American Cancer Society, 2014).

Socialization of destructive masculine behaviors can certainly be implicated in tobacco use. Advertisers have long used masculine mystique approaches to sell their products by associating tobacco with desirable images of masculinity (self-assuredness, independence, and adventurousness). About 6 times more males than females smoke on prime time television, and *Sports Illustrated*, the number one magazine read by adolescent males, contains more tobacco advertisements than any other magazine (Courtenay, 2000a). Advertisers know that they can sell a great deal by playing on people's insecurities and then offering a product that promises to remove their misgivings about their adequacy. When one is asked to live up to vague and impossible standards of masculinity, what man would not feel insecure? This advertising is both reflective and encouraging of certain cultural values for men: Do whatever you want; don't worry about dying.

Neglectful Behaviors

Men sometimes shorten their lives or become ill because they fail to perform the behaviors necessary to maintain their health. For example, 30 to 50 percent of hypertension (high blood pressure) patients stop taking their medication, leaving them at increased risk for heart attack (Hackett, Rosenbaum & Cassen, 1985). Men are disproportionately represented in this group.

Men can also create problems by failing to seek help or take time off from work when it is advisable, such as when they are injured, sick, emotionally distraught, or when they have not had a physical examination for a long time. Traditionally masculine men may see taking necessary medication and seeking help as admissions of weakness, vulnerability, and dependence, which go against the masculine cultural prescriptions to handle problems on one's own, focus outside of the self, be strong and invulnerable, and "take it like a man." Negative or extreme masculinity is related to poor health practices (Courtenay, 2000a). Men's perception of the normativity of other men's health behaviors (i.e., their beliefs about what most men do to safeguard their health) also affects their health behavior. Therefore it may be possible to improve men's health behavior by changing their perceptions of masculine health norms (Mahalik, Burns, & Syzdek, 2007).

In a national survey conducted by the American Medical Association and the Gallup Poll, 40 percent of physicians endorsed the belief that over one-half of men aged 50 or older undermine potential lifesaving treatment for prostate or colorectal cancer (which kill an estimated 200,000 men per year in the United States), by ignoring symptoms, delaying treatment, or refusing to discuss symptoms. Embarrassment was cited as the major reason for failing to discuss medical problems (Royner, 1992).

Men who adhere to stereotypical masculine ideologies are less likely than other men to do this: have regular medical checkups.
Photo: Bettman / Corbis

Women give more information and ask more questions during doctor visits than men. The average number of questions that a woman asks during a 15-minute visit is six; men average zero (Pleck, 1995)! Half of men do not know the symptoms of prostate and colorectal cancer, nor those of prostate enlargement, which affects half of men over the age of 50 (Fortin, 2007).

Men are also less likely than women to practice preventive health care such as taking vitamins, eating a healthy diet (Wardle, et. al., 2004), performing self-examinations, having regular physicals (Courtenay, McCreary, & Merighi, 2002), taking prescriptions as directed, and returning to physicians for follow-up visits (Helgeson, 2011). A recently published cookbook is entitled *Eat What You Want and Die like a Man: The World's Unhealthiest Cookbook* (Graham, 2008). There is also emerging evidence that social support is protective of health (Karren, Smith, Hafen, & Gordon, 2009), and therefore men who adopt a rugged individualist version of masculinity may incur increased risk.

Risk Behaviors

Men sometimes choose to engage in behaviors that involve the risk of injury, death, or legal sanction. For instance, habitual excessive drinking puts one at increased risk for liver disease and accidents. Drunk driving, drug dealing, sharing hypodermic needles, use of firearms, high speed driving, engaging in gang violence, and working in dangerous jobs are other risky behaviors. Again, many more males than females participate in these behaviors (Courtenay, 2011). For instance, males are twice as likely to abuse alcohol as females (Nolen-Hoeksema & Hilt, 2006), and are more than 80 percent of those arrested for alcohol and drug abuse violations (Schwartz, 2008). Males die in car accidents more than twice as often as females and are nearly three times more likely to die in an accident in which they are driving while drunk. They drown more than four times as often (National Safety Council, 2010). Males account for 82 percent of spinal cord injuries (National Spinal Cord Injury Association, 2005). United States males are eighteen times more likely than females to die on the job (derived from National Center for Health Statistics, 2008). As early as preschool, gender stereotype conformity is a predictor of injury risk behaviors (Granie, 2010). Although their college-aged sons are more likely to be hurt than their daughters, parents are less concerned for their sons' than for their daughters' safety (Schwartz, et. al., 2009).

Risk behaviors associated with masculinity are summarized in Box 9.3. Males are less knowledgeable than females about health in general and about symptoms of specific diseases, less responsive to health information, and less likely to utilize the health care system (Courtenay, 2011). Men who subscribe to traditional masculine gender ideologies show a greater willingness than other men to engage in a wide range of risk behaviors (Courtenay, McCreary, & Merighi, 2002). Our discussion will focus on three areas of risk: dangerous sports, war, and unsafe sexual practices.

Dangerous Sports

To say that sports and masculinity are strongly interconnected in U.S. culture seems like an understatement. The almost religious fervor with which many men approach athletics is evidence that sports have more importance to men than mere physical fit-

Table 9.3   Masculine Risk Behaviors

overuse of alcohol	tobacco use
dangerous sports	criminal activity
refusing to see a physician	use of recreational drugs
refusing to wear a seat belt	engaging in physical fights
carrying weapons	consuming high amounts of fat
sleep deprivation	physical overexertion
refusing to wear sunscreen	failing to obtain health information
risky sexual practices	ignoring symptoms of disease
taking risks in the workplace	lacking basic nutritional knowledge
eschewing social support	consuming high levels of dietary cholesterol
physical inactivity	neglecting to do testicular self-examinations
dangerous driving practices	using anabolic steroids
driving drunk	refusing to wear a motorcycle helmet
working in dangerous occupations	

Source: Courtenay (2011)

ness. The sports that are most dominated by male participation are those with high risks of injury (Courtenay, 2011). Males sustain around 70 percent of the sports injuries that result in emergency room visits (Flores, Haileysus, & Greenspan, 2008).

An unfortunate minority of men and boys have suffered debilitating injuries and even death as a result of overexertion, physical contact, or accidents in sporting events. The most dangerous sports would seem to be auto racing and professional boxing. The object of the latter is to pummel one's opponent into unconsciousness. Between 1950 and 2007, 339 professional boxers died as a direct result of brain injuries suffered in the ring (Baird, et. al., 2010). Others—such as former heavyweight champion Muhammad Ali, who now suffers from Parkinsonian symptoms—have suffered irreparable brain damage as the cumulative result of many years of repeated head traumas. For several years prior to his death in 1999, former heavyweight Jerry Quarry needed help putting on his shoes and cutting his food because of neurological impairment. It is estimated that 20 percent of professional boxers suffer some degree of permanent brain damage (Trafford, 1996), resulting in symptoms such as "memory loss, inattention, impaired hearing, paranoid ideas, and a decrease in general cognitive functions" (Newfield, 2001, p. 20).

Few men participate in auto racing and boxing relative to other violent sports such as ice hockey and football. The populations that engage in risky sports such as sky diving, hang gliding, scuba diving, mountain climbing, hunting, and contact sports is overwhelmingly male (Courtenay, 2011). An average of 12 high school and college players die each year from football injuries or heat-related illnesses sustained in football practice or games (*Daily News*, 2013). More than a half-million high school boys and college men are injured playing football every year (Shankar, Fields, Collins, Dick, & Comstock, 2007).

The average number of concussions in the National Football League (NFL) is between two and four per game (Fainaru-Wada & Fainaru, 2013). A concussion is a traumatic brain injury (where the brain is thrown against the inside of the skull) that disrupts the functioning of the brain. It renders the victim more susceptible to subsequent concussions, and multiple concussions can result in permanent neurological damage. Former Jets wide receiver Al Toon estimated that he suffered as many as 13 concussions during his 8–year professional career (Alloy, Jacobson, & Acocella, 1999) and reported that his head "has never been clear" since that time (ESPN, 1994).

As many as 50 percent of high school football players report having had symptoms of concussions (Schwarz, 2007) and there are an estimated 250,000 head injuries to football players annually (Mueller, 2001). Many high school and college football players say that they do not report their head injuries to team trainers or coaches because they do not think their symptoms are serious and/or because they do not want to be taken out of the game (Schwarz, 2007). Some football programs test their players' cognitive skills to assess the possibility of unreported concussions and to evaluate injured players' recovery (Williams, 2008).

Dementia is a general term to describe cognitive impairments such as memory failures, language disturbances, and problems in planning and abstract thinking (Sue, et. al., 2014). A recent survey of retired NFL players showed a dramatic difference in reported dementia between the former players and their age peers in the general population. Retired players over 50 years old were more than four times more likely to report dementia symptoms than non-players (6.1 percent to 1.2 percent). In the relatively rare case of dementia before age 50, retired players showed a 19–fold increased risk (1.9 percent to 0.1 percent) (Weir, Jackson, & Sonnega, 2009). Although this research cannot demonstrate a causal link between football playing and later cognitive disturbances, the possibility of such a link appears strong. In the same study, researchers noted that retired players are more likely to be non-smokers and to have higher rates of physical activity than men in the general population, and perhaps as a result, they have better cardiovascular fitness as a group and are less likely to have diabetes. At the same time, they also report more arthritis and pain and greater problems with mobility.

Football is one of the ultimate expressions of hypermasculinity in the United States. It involves sacrifice of the body for a task and denial of basic instincts for self-preservation and safety. The average NFL player engages in thousands of impacts per season, the worst of which are the equivalent of a 25 mile per hour head-on automobile accident (Gugliotta, 2003), and the median age of death of NFL veterans, is the early-to-mid-50s (Baron, Hein, Lehman, & Gersic, 2013). Today, linemen weighing 300 pounds or more are more the rule than the exception, and it was estimated that the momentum generated by a 340–pound player running at 15 miles per hour (the equivalent of the 40 yard dash in 5.1 seconds, average for these players) is the same as a 17–pound bowling ball shot from a cannon at 30 miles per hour (Mihoces, 2002). Many retired players report chronic headaches and dementia symptoms, but the NFL has been reluctant to provide medical services, saying that the players cannot prove that their symptoms are directly related to football (Leahy, 2008). However, in 2013, the NFL offered to settle a class action lawsuit filed on the behalf of former players for $765 million without admitting responsibility. A federal judge denied approval of the settlement in 2014, assessing it as too small (*Sports Illustrated*, 2014).

Television commentary of football injuries (and sports injuries in general) almost always involves reference to the task: "Will he return in the second half?" "How will they contain the pass rush without their best blocker?" "Will the other team exploit the substitute?" Imagine a television commentator reacting to an injury with "That must be disappointing and painful; I wonder how he feels about that?"

Contrary to popular belief, men are no more physically active than women, and the health risks from sedentary lifestyles are well documented. Among those who are physically active, men are much more likely than women to engage in "weekend warrior" kinds of exercise—infrequent but strenuous activity—that actually increases the risk of death from heart attack, perhaps as much as 100 times (Courtenay, 2000b). Another recent trend is the use of anabolic steroids to enhance muscle mass and athletic performance. It is estimated that 260,000 high school students and half of all NCAA Division I football players have used steroids. These substances are associated with a number of health problems, including high blood pressure, elevated cholesterol levels, liver damage, hyperthyroidism, cancers of the kidney and prostate, shrinkage of the testicles, obstructive lung disease, baldness, acne, mental health symptoms, and sterility (Sabo, 2005).

War

Generation after generation, we have marched young men off to be killed in wars. In U.S. society, dying or being maimed in war is considered an act of heroism rather than as the victimization of a young man. Although participating in the defense of one's country might be considered to be a loving thing to do, only relatively recently have U.S. men been given a choice as to whether or not they would serve in the armed forces.

The wars of the twentieth century have been described as "holocausts of young men" in which millions of men were killed and over 100 million were injured. The average age of World War I and II casualties was 18.5 years (Kimbrell, 1991). Thus, the victims of war tend to be the youngest men, who feel (and often are) less powerful, and who feel the strongest need to establish a sense of masculinity. Poor men and men of color, who are marginalized by mainstream U.S. culture, have also been disproportionately represented among the war dead. Many men who survived the modern, technological war in Vietnam returned with physical and emotional scars of profound proportions. It is perhaps no coincidence that some men began to question the dictates of cultural masculinity at about this time, when it was becoming obvious that soldiers were finding it difficult to "take it like a man."

Those hardships continued into the recent wars in the Middle East where women were serving in unprecedented numbers and the American public became aware of the shameful levels of soldier-on-soldier sexual assault against service members of both sexes. Although men's risk (1.2 percent annually) is lower relative to women (6.1 percent), because about 85 percent of U.S. military are men, they accounted for approximately 53 percent of an estimated 26,000 victims in 2012 (SAPRO, 2012). Survivors of sexual assault show very high rates of posttraumatic stress disorder (PTSD) (Sue, et. al., 2014)

Unsafe Sexual Practices

Males are nearly four times more likely than women to contract AIDS (Avert, 2005). It is only possible to get this disease through introduction of the Human Immunodeficiency Virus (HIV) into the bloodstream. This may happen by unfortunate accidents such as receiving an HIV-tainted blood transfusion, but the overwhelming majority of HIV infections occur through the sharing of hypodermic needles by intravenous drug users and through unsafe sexual practices.

It is not difficult to find connections between sexual risk behaviors and cultural prescriptions for masculinity. Foremost among these are the expectations that males will be sexually promiscuous and adventurous. Condom use reduces the risk of infection, but there is a good deal of resistance to using condoms, perhaps because their use involves an acknowledgment of one's vulnerability, as well as a caring for the self and the sexual partner. These orientations go against masculine norms. Poppen (1995) found that, among college students, males were much more willing than females to engage in risky sexual behavior, both with regard to partner choice (e.g., having more partners and partners they did not know well) and sexual risk behaviors (e.g. non-use of contraceptives and condoms). Men tend to underestimate their health risks across every domain of dangerous behavior (Courtenay, McCreary, & Merighi, 2002).

Adverse Physical Effects of Psychological Processes

The relatively young field of behavioral medicine is focused on understanding and treating physical disorders that are thought to be strongly influenced by the person's psychological functioning. Masculine socialization may well contribute to some physical disorders that are disproportionately experienced by men. Chief among these are cardiovascular disorders.

Cardiovascular Disorders

It has long been suspected that coronary artery disease and hypertension have strong relationships to stressful work settings and certain behavioral patterns of response to those environments. Hypertension is quite common among workers in highly stressful occupations (e.g., air traffic controllers, police officers). It is also common among those described as projecting an image of being easygoing but at the same time suppressing a good deal of anger (Hackett, Rosenbaum, & Cassen, 1985).

Several decades ago, cardiologists Meyer Friedman and Ray Rosenhan coined the term *Type A behavior* to describe a personality pattern commonly found in people who had suffered myocardial infarction (heart attack). This pattern described the classic compulsive, hostile, competitive, emotionally inexpressive "workaholic." Friedman (cited in Hackett, et. al., 1985) defined *Type A* as, "a characteristic action-emotion complex which is exhibited by those individuals who are engaged in a relatively chronic struggle to obtain an unlimited number of poorly defined things from their environments in the shortest period of time and, if possible, against the opposing efforts of other things or persons in this same environment" (p. 1154). Recent research indicates that the hostility component of Type A is more predictive of coronary heart disease than the other characteristics (Benson, 2003), and chronic anger and hostility is estimated to increase the risk of heart attack by a factor of three (Smith, 2003). Hostile personality is associated with four to five times the risk of death from all causes for the age group 25 to 50, thus it also carries risks beyond heart disease, most notably, stroke (Williams et. al., 2002).

Again we see vestiges of the destructive aspects of traditional masculinity in this pattern: the aggressive attempt to measure up to vague standards of achievement and competition. Type A individuals tend to be hyperindependent; they seize authority and dislike sharing responsibility. Contrary to popular belief, they tend to be less successful than those who are more relaxed and less aggressive (Hackett, et. al., 1985). Type A behaviors are significantly related to masculine gender typing (Grimm & Yarnold, 1985). Negative or extreme masculinity is also related to heart attack severity (Helgeson, 1990). Higher femininity scores in men are predictive of decreased death risk from coronary heart disease after controlling for other risk factors (Hunt, Lewars, Emslie, & Batty, 2007).

Vicki Helgeson (1995) proposed that certain aspects of traditional masculinity interact with biological factors to produce high levels of coronary risk. Not only is traditional masculinity associated with Type A behavior, but it is also linked with low levels of social support and poor health care practices, which are both linked with masculine hyperindependence as well as with coronary risk. African heritage men who endorse nontraditional masculinity ideologies also engage in more positive health behaviors than their counterparts who do not (Wade, 2008a, 2008b).

It is clear that men are biologically predisposed toward certain physical health problems. This predisposition interacts with certain aspects of masculine socialization, as well as with the negative effects of dangerous, historically male environments. Women who expose themselves to these environments and exhibit traditionally masculine behaviors increase their health risks (Rodin & Ickovics, 1990). Thus, it is hazardous to be male, and it is also hazardous to be negatively masculine. Lippa, Martin, and Friedman (2000) found that people of both sexes who score high on measures of masculinity were more likely to die at every age than those who scored low. Thus, in addition to sex, gender is a significant factor in mortality. In fact, this relationship is a strong one. As the researchers note, "The increase in mortality risk in masculine individuals... was comparable to increases in mortality risk associated with physiological factors such as elevated blood pressure" (p. 1568).

Moreover, according to Stanistreet, Bambra, and Scott-Samuel (2005), who undertook a comparative study of 51 countries, high levels of patriarchy in a society are associated with higher mortality in men. The authors opine that, "The same practices that represent men's capacity to oppress women and promote their interest in doing so are also systematically harming men" (p. 874). A specification of these factors awaits further research; we do not yet know exactly how patriarchy harms men's health.

Sidney Jourard said it best in his landmark 1971 article, "Some Lethal Aspects of the Male Role." Jourard described a set of human needs: to know and be known, to depend and be depended upon, to love and be loved, and to find some purpose and meaning in one's life. The masculine role is poorly designed to fill these human needs. It requires us to hide our feelings, be hyperindependent, and to focus more on external achievements than relationships or feelings about the self. Jourard's belief was that this style not only limited the quality of our emotional lives, but that it also had the effect of slowly destroying us physically. Only recently have researchers and practitioners begun to address the gendered aspects of health and well-being for men.

SUMMARY

1. There are many health problems that are more common in men than in women. Men's average lifespan is more than five years shorter than that of women as a result of a number of factors.

2. Biogenic explanations for sex differences in disease and longevity include male chromosomal vulnerability, the damaging effects of testosterone, and the protective effects of estrogen.

3. Psychogenic explanations for sex differences in disease and longevity include the masculine denial of vulnerability, self-destructive behaviors, eschewal of self-care, risky sexual behaviors, and the cultural expectation to take part in dangerous sports and in war.

4. Stressful work environments and typical masculine responses to them also take their toll on health and longevity. There is a growing awareness that living up to masculine gender demands involves the denial of some basic human needs, and that the results may be illness, injury, and/or premature death.

Chapter Ten

Men at Work:
Jobs, Careers,and Masculinity

If there is anything that men have been about throughout history, it is work. From the assembly line worker to the chief executive officer, most men in the Western world define themselves according to their jobs (e.g., Deutsch & Saxon, 1999). An important part of the masculine socialization process is oriented toward preparing males for the working world. Many scholars (e.g. Basow, 1992; Eagly, Wood, & Diekman, 2000) have argued that gender roles are mainly a result of the historical division of labor between men and women. From this perspective, it is not surprising that the last several decades have witnessed changes in the ways that people think about gender as the working world undergoes significant evolution. Women are entering the paid work force in record numbers and rightfully demanding that they be treated as equals. Some men are having trouble adjusting to increasingly mixed-sex environments, especially those in which women are in positions of authority. More and more labor-saving devices are becoming available, and the competition-oriented, individualistic working culture is giving way to team building and environments where cooperation is valued. As a result, there are fewer and fewer places for the physically powerful working man or the hard-nosed manager, and more and more places for the technician and the executive with "people skills."

Although much of the mainstream masculine value system encourages being a good worker, it may do so at a considerable cost. Additionally, some aspects of masculine gender role socialization are counterproductive to functioning in many modern workplaces. Changing gender roles also create considerable stress for many, as well as providing exciting opportunities for men (and women) in the working world. In this chapter, we investigate the relationships between masculinity and work. To provide a context, we look first at changes in the sex-based division of labor, with special attention to relatively recent economic developments in the United States.

A HISTORY OF WORK AND THE SEXES

You will often hear people speak of the "traditional" (heterosexual) family in which the husband works outside of the home and the wife works full-time on child care and other domestic duties. Stephanie Coontz (1997) points out that this conception of the family has only existed for about 150 years. Moreover, a substantial proportion of U.S. families do not and have not fit this pattern. In the 1950s, when the male earner, female homemaker model hit its peak in the United States, approximately two-thirds of American families had this arrangement. Today, approximately one-quarter of families have one (male) earner, and the number is expected to fall to approximately one-sixth (17 percent) by 2030 (Clay, 2005).

In a section of her book entitled "The Late Birth and Short Life of the Male Breadwinner Family," Coontz (1997) dispels the myth that sex-based labor division is traditional, except in a very narrow historical frame: "One of the most common misconceptions about modern marriage is the notion that coprovider families are a new invention in human history. In fact, today's dual-earner family represents a return to older norms, after a very short interlude that people mistakenly identify as 'traditional'" (p. 54).

For the vast majority of human history, labor chiefly consisted of hunting animals and gathering edible vegetation. Societies based on other forms of labor are a relatively recent phenomenon, comprising only about two percent of the time in which people have inhabited the Earth (Collins, 1979). In these hunter-gatherer societies, which still exist in some parts of the world, women nearly always contributed equal or larger amounts of the community food supply compared to men. There is some evidence that gender roles in these societies tended to be more egalitarian and cooperative than in most modern cultures, as men and women worked together as economic partners. As Nancy Bonvillain (2001) notes, "In many foraging bands, women's and men's interdependent contributions to their households were reflected in equality of social relations and social status" (p. 17).

When people learned to plow, plant, and domesticate animals, some 6,000 years ago, the character of gendered labor arrangements changed. Plowing required one to be relatively far from home, thus it became largely the man's job. Producing offspring meant more help in the fields, and thus children became an economic asset. Therefore, it became economically advantageous to control women's sexuality and reproduction (Lerner, 1986).

Another important change characterized agrarian societies. There was no longer a need for people to be nomadic. In hunter-gatherer societies, survival depended on moving to where vegetation and game were available. In agrarian societies, people could stay in one place and produce food with a little cooperation from nature. There was a certain harmony with the earth, and husbandry, the cultivation and respect of nature, became a dominant value (Keen, 1991). Sons spent a good deal of time working with and learning from their fathers. Thus, there was a sense of intergenerational continuity (Stearns, 1991). Civilizations and communities took on a relatively permanent, and therefore more elaborate, character.

Land was now useful and valuable for long periods of time, generation after generation. It became something a person owned, dealt, protected, and willed to heirs. Land meant food, and food meant wealth. Institutions were created to deal with land transactions. The most notable of these was *patriarchy*, the system by which males dominated public and private life. *Primogeniture* was the patriarchal arrangement by which sons inherited property from their fathers and passed it on to their sons. This system established male social and economic dominance, as well as the control of women's sexuality by men (Lerner, 1986).

Susan Basow (1992) described changes in the !Kung society of Africa, a foraging society which has moved to the agrarian way of life during the last few decades. She noted that women's mobility became more restricted and that they contribute less to the food supply than before. Children's play groups became more sex-segregated, and aggression increased. Basow argues that agrarian society is historically responsible for gender inequity, and that these types of societies are the bases for every industrialized society in the world.

Property ownership and patriarchy changed masculinity in important ways. Men created institutional laws to protect their land, but physical force also came to be used, hence the transition of man the planter to man the warrior. In hunter-gatherer societies, men bonded together to share resources in the hunt, and the kill was shared by all the community. After property ownership, men's bonds were in the service of killing other men. Therefore, organized violence became a hallmark of masculinity. Sam Keen (1991) speculated that the masculine ethic of cooperation gave way to an ethic of conquest at this time, and that the quest for harmony became a quest for control. He also noted that men from victorious armies routinely raped the women of the conquered territories. Thus, we see in these societies the origins of negative masculinity: violence, over-competitiveness, dominance over women, and physical risk-taking.

Patriarchy also dictated that men should control their children's (especially their son's) lives. Fathers had to see that their sons learned to act properly, since they would someday control the family wealth. In Western cultures, this need gave rise to an ethic of discipline, which was sometimes administered physically. The punitive nature of their relationship created a tension between affection and resentment for both father and son (Stearns, 1991).

The division of labor in agrarian societies was not nearly as sharp as it has been in the last one and a half centuries in the industrialized world. Typically, family members worked alongside each other in farming or small businesses. The co-provider family remained the norm, as it has been throughout most of human history (Coontz, 1997). But the turn of the nineteenth century witnessed the dawn of the Industrial Revolution. Hand tools were increasingly replaced by machines, and production became more large-scale and centralized in factories. Industrialization continues to spread throughout the world.

Since patriarchy was firmly established by this time, since the vast majority of industrial work was at a distance from the home, and since a good deal of this labor required upper body strength, factory work became largely men's work. Women were expected to withdraw from the paid labor force following marriage and to work full-time at domestic duties and child care. Men began to specialize in paid employment outside of the home and abdicated their traditional child care duties to their wives. In times of male labor shortages, more women worked outside of the home, but their work was devalued, and they were pushed aside by men when jobs became scarce.

In the transition from co-provider to single-earner families, women's contributions to economic life tended to become less direct. Although most families could no longer survive by farming, crafting, and trading, they could not rely solely on ready-to-use goods that they purchased from the husband's earnings. Many families could afford fabric but not clothing, flour but not bread, seeds but not vegetables. Among many other duties, the wife's work was to turn these raw materials into useable goods with her cooking, sewing, gardening, and other skills. Thus, women's work was critical for family functioning, but men's work became increasingly associated with wage earning (Coontz, 1997).

The development of many masculine gender role norms can be laid at the doorstep of industrialization. First and foremost is the establishment of the breadwinner role, which Gould (1974) described as the beginning of "measuring masculinity by the size of a paycheck." Socially, masculine attractiveness is based largely on economic power. Many men attempt to project a masculine image through external success, not internal fulfillment. Gould suggested if a man "flashed a roll of bills, no one would see how little else there was of him" (p. 97).

A second and equally important development of industrialization was a renewal of the antifeminine element of masculinity. The increased polarization of men's and women's work led to a belief that work outside and inside the home are the natural environments for men and women, respectively, an ideology that many writers refer to as "the doctrine of separate spheres." Doing "women's work" became an increasing threat to men, as did spending too much time in the home and in the company of women. Exclusively male lodges and other social and recreational organizations became popular as avenues for fulfilling a perceived need for safe haven from women's "sphere." Men became increasingly hostile to femininity, and, by extension, to women themselves. Scott Coltrane (1998) and other anthropologists have noted that cultures with higher levels of sex segregation tend to have higher levels of men's violence against women.

The Industrial Revolution ushered in the age of specialization. In agrarian societies, a man plants, reaps, takes care of animals, and is able to see the fruits of his labor. In contrast, the industrial worker may spend the better part of a lifetime putting a single bolt on each of a million machines. Karl Marx (1872) first described the dehumanizing character of such a job. Although agrarian man could take pride in the *process* of planting, growing, and harvesting, industrial man is focused on *outcome*, the amount of money (and goods) produced.

For most men, this was not a lot of money, as the few powerful men exploited the many less powerful men. Most men became (and still are) "work objects" (the term "object" in reference to a person was first coined by Marx). Objectification is the denial of the person's humanness. Just as many women have historically been treated as sex objects, men have been exploited as work objects. However, women were, and are, also work objects, as their domestic labor went largely unpaid and viewed as secondary to men's labor (Coontz, 1997).

Men have also been war objects. When the work of the wealthy and powerful involves organized, state-sponsored violence, it often becomes the task of poor young men. Most victims of recent wars are young, sometimes even teenaged boys, the least powerful males in the society. A disproportionate number of victims were men of color. More privileged men were (and are) often allowed to opt out of combat, or of military service altogether.

The stereotype of men as socially and economically powerful does not fit the experience of most men. Although men-as-a-group retain much more economic power than women-as-a-group, the vast majority of men have jobs, not careers. They sacrifice and labor day after day, under the pressure to be a good provider for their families. Their work is "quietly useful," in the words of World War II photographer Ernie Pyle (Faludi, 1999). Moreover, the necessity of earning a living makes many men vulnerable to exploitive employers.

Perhaps the most profound effects of industrialization on masculinity were that it effectively banished men from their homes (Keen, 1991) and devalued domestic work. It is no surprise that many men who subscribe to the breadwinner ideology are not very relationship-oriented. In his workplace, emotional expression and connection are of little value. When the father returns home at the end of the day, he finds it difficult to flip the switch that turns on all of the emotional and relationship attitudes that he has suppressed all day at work. As Robert Bly (1990) put it, "When a father, absent during the day, returns home at six, his children receive only his temperament, and not his teaching." The result is the disconnection of father and child (Keen, 1991) and an intergenerational pattern of masculine alienation.

The ethic of paternal discipline carried over from agrarian societies, but now fathers had to assert this role after coming home from the industrial workplace. This perceived need for control may have involved more physical punishment both as a function of diminished contact with children and work strain on the father (Stearns, 1990, 1991). Many sons now had to deal with fewer positive contacts with fathers in addition to harsher discipline.

Far from being a "natural" economic arrangement, the male breadwinner role was a relatively recent development, a historical artifact of the transition from agricultural to industrial society. Although the ideal of male wage earner-female homemaker began to take hold early in the nineteenth century, a majority of families did not have this arrangement until industrialization and urbanization reshaped American society in the 1920s, and, despite many people's nostalgia for the 1950s, only about 60 percent of children in the United States grew up in this kind of family even during that decade. As a result of a decrease in real wages and a sharp increase in the cost of housing, the single-income arrangement is now untenable for most families. Married women who are employed full-time now contribute more than 40 percent to the family income. In historical context, no sooner had the male as sole wage earner family arrived on the scene that it began to disappear (Coontz, 1997). Gender roles are (and will most likely continue to) change in conjunction with changes in the sex-based division (or increasingly, the non-division) of labor. Contrary to popular belief, there is mounting evidence that the majority of two-earner families find considerable satisfaction in both work and domestic life (Barnett & Rivers, 1996).

Although many people throughout the world continue to be employed in industrial and preindustrial settings, large segments of the population are involved in work that is characterized as postindustrial. This recent trend is a movement away from the production of goods and toward the provision of information and services. In these settings, upper body strength is not highly valued, as labor-saving devices have been developed and thus men have no biologically-based advantage over women. Because a single income is no longer sufficient for most families, and because many women want to claim their right to be full economic partners in society, these settings are becoming increasingly heterogeneous. Moreover, most of the fastest growing vocations and professions do not rely on "traditional" male attributes like strength or physical stamina, but rather "traditional" female attributes like working affably with other team members or clients.

Work outside the home is no longer the exclusive province of men, and thus social changes are taking place. We will return to a discussion of these changes later in this chapter. Before doing so, a description of men's issues around work seems appropriate.

NET WORTH EQUALS SELF WORTH: THE SOCIALIZATION TO WORK

Masculine gender socialization is largely oriented toward preparing boys for work. Boys are often asked at a young age, "What do you want to be when you grow up?" They learn that the right answer is not "a husband, father, and friend," but rather a worker of some kind. Boys tend to develop an occupational "dream" in childhood and strive to attain it in adulthood (Levinson, et. al., 1978). They are taught very early in life that gainful employment is manly. The masculine values of competition, task completion, and independence serve to provide attitudes conducive to functioning in a wide variety of work settings.

Sports and play are a training ground for the world of work. Sports usually have elaborate sets of rules, score keeping, and clear cut winners and losers (Pasick, 1990). Athletic results are quantifiable in terms of wins and losses, batting averages, and other statistics that invite comparisons among players and teams. The amount of adulation a boy receives for being an athletic success is matched by the amount of adulation a man receives for being a career success. We see connections between sports and work in the language of the business world: "Who are the players?" "They have a good batting average," "Let's see if we can get them to play ball with us." An easy business deal is sometimes referred to as a "slam dunk."

The messages are clear. In the sports world, you are a valued person if you are a winner. Later, being a winner translates into being a *bread*winner—a vocational success. In fact, many men's very definition of their masculine value depends on their occupational statuses. As Pasick (1990) pointed out, "For males in our culture, simply passing through puberty is not sufficient to enter adulthood" (p. 39). Although providing for one's family is a long-standing criteria for proving one's manhood (Gilmore, 1990), having real economic power through high earnings qualifies one as The Man." The important factor is the outcome, not the process. Success for men is often defined in terms of being "better" by getting promotions, having high job status, and making

Men's physical labor has traditionally been a source of pride and an opportunity for male camaraderie.

Photo © Bettman / Corbis

more money. Women tend to be more oriented toward providing a helpful service (Bridges, 1989), although there is a great deal of variability in occupational values both within the population of men and within the population of women.

The man-as-breadwinner association of masculinity with work and money can hardly be denied. Anybody who works knows that it is a two-edged sword with both advantages and disadvantages. The work tradition has gotten men where they are today, in both a positive and a negative sense.

"Positive Masculinity" and Work

Ruth Hartley's classic (1959) essay on masculine socialization includes the statement that, "On the positive side, men mostly do what they want and are very important" (p. 463). The social status and economic power that men-as-a-group have enjoyed from work is unmistakable. The fact that men are less often the victims of job discrimination than women has given many men opportunities for self-determination. It has even been argued that, just as many women face a "glass ceiling" (an invisible barrier to entry into powerful and lucrative positions), majority men have sometimes had the advantage of a "glass escalator" of quicker promotion (Williams, 2007). This may be part of the reason why men continue to hold the majority of industrial and political power. In 2014, there were a record number of women who served as Chief Executive Officer (CEO) of Fortune 500 companies and served as U.S. Senators. Although women are approximately half of the population, they represented only 4.8 percent of Fortune 500 CEOs and 20 percent of Senators (Fairchild, 2014). As of 2005, women made up only 14.7 percent of members of Fortune 500 Boards of Directors, a 5 percent increase from 1995 (Catalyst, 2006). Of course, this gendered workplace advantage is rarely in evidence for minority men, who have been occupationally marginalized throughout U.S. history.

Work can be quite satisfying. People who are fortunate enough to have careers (reimbursable means of expressing an important part of the self) as opposed to jobs (labor done solely for economic survival) may find the challenge and satisfaction of their work to be one of the most fulfilling aspects of their lives. It also goes without saying that money goes a long way toward making life easier and more enjoyable. Traditionally, men's orientation toward task completion and self-reliance, together with work opportunity, has made economic and career success a strong possibility for many. The "winners" may get some of the best that life has to offer: status, material wealth, and the opportunity to make a difference.

Men who have not been able to enjoy satisfying work have nevertheless been able to take pride in fulfilling the breadwinner role, a traditional expression of masculine love. Historically, many men have felt a deeply emotional investment toward this role, which also has clear social value (Stearns, 1991). Mark Kiselica (2005) describes his feelings about his father's work ethic:

> My father is the most wonderful man I have ever known. He overcame a tragic childhood—including the death of his dear mother when he was only about 8 years old, a neglectful and exploitive alcoholic father, debilitating injuries to his leg and hip, poverty, and a lack of education—to be the most wonderful parent any child could ever wish for. My father worked two jobs—one as a maintenance mechanic in a factory, the other as a painter—always in excruciating pain, and literally had to drag himself out of bed every day in order to limp off to work so that he could earn a living to support our family, consisting of my mom and my four siblings and me. And he did all of this, never once complaining, all out of his love for his family. He is a truly heroic man, and I will always adore him.

Negative Masculinity and Work

Although vocational success carries with it great rewards, they can come at a cost to the man's relationships, leisure pursuits, and health. It is also important to note that many, perhaps most, men do not feel successful, and the association of success and masculinity for these men may lead to chronic feelings of inadequacy. Following is a list of some potentially damaging effects of the masculine gender role in the world of work:

1. *You only hurt the ones you love:* Many men work in frustrating environments, for example the assembly line worker who is bored and unable to find much job satisfaction, the mechanic who faces difficult problems and time pressure, or the middle manager who faces pressure from both his subordinates and his superiors. Some have not learned how to deal with the emotional aspects of work frustration. They have been raised to ignore emotion, especially if it is connected to feelings of weakness or powerlessness. Some of these men deal

with these feelings by projecting them outside of the self. Since spouses and other family members are most available for these projections, they may bear the brunt of these negative emotions, and this can lead to strained family relationships. A spouse interviewed for Weiss's (1990) study illustrates the effects of "bringing work home":

> He is so proud, telling people that he works things out for himself and he doesn't worry his family… Well, that really isn't the case. Because what happens is, (if) he has a problem, whatever it is, whether it's a business slowdown or a difficult supplier or whatever, he is just a *bear*… to live with until he has worked it out… If we say, 'What is the problem?,' he will say, 'What do you mean, what is the problem?' (p. 99)

2. *What price glory?:* The competitive, pressure-packed nature of masculine occupational striving is associated with a wide variety of physical and mental health problems such as heart disease, back pain, alcoholism, and suicide (Harris, 1992). Men are much more likely than women to work in hazardous environments, and an overwhelming proportion of workplace injuries and deaths involve male victims (National Center for Health Statistics, 2008). When they are hurt, men are less likely than women to seek medical help (Courtenay, 2011).

3. *The burden of proof:* A conventionally-gendered man proves his masculinity by succeeding in work and being "number one." However, a single success, no matter how significant, does not last. There is always another goal to set and accomplish. If a man is fortunate enough to become "number one" at something, he can only remain in this position by continuing to compete with and vanquish his opponents. Thus, the validation of masculinity involves attempting to prove something that is essentially impossible to prove. Satisfaction, for many men, becomes a dangerous feeling, because it may inhibit further competition. In the world of sports (the leading masculine metaphor for work), we hear sportscasters lauding players and coaches who can never be satisfied. We hear athletes talking about next year's season less than an hour after they have won the championship!

4. *You've got to break a few eggs to make an omelet:* A man who wishes to "work his way up" in an organization may have to subordinate his individuality to the wishes of his superiors. Of course, nearly everybody alters their behavior to adapt to social situations, so it is a matter of degree. To what extent are men willing to move against their personalities and values to "fit in" at work?

   Many business organizations expect gender stereotypical behavior from men, and men who do not display such behavior often forfeit the opportunity for advancement. Therefore, the man who refuses to act like "one of the boys" may not succeed, regardless of his level of competence. If he plays the masculine role to gain approval, he may experience a high level of gender role strain. In corporate culture, a large part of this strain is based in the organization's encouragement for men to emphasize the work role over the family role (Bowen & Orthner, 1991).

The extent to which a man will compromise his behavior to fit the work environment involves a decision that each individual must make. Is he willing to engage in derogatory humor, wear ties and white dress shirts, and/or lie to customers? Because men are socialized against introspective skills, they may have difficulty in accessing the information necessary to make these decisions. Alternately, some men may subordinate their own ethics to fulfill the breadwinner role.

Crites and Fitzgerald (1978) described the constriction of human qualities to meet organizational demand as a "straitjacket of success" that requires the man to "be able to obey rules and follow orders, regardless of how silly and unnecessary they may seem... to control and hide true feelings when faced with an incompetent superior... (to be) intensely loyal to an employer, yet able to transfer that loyalty when you change jobs." These prescriptions produce men who are "expedient, shallow, conforming but competitive, and ultimately ruthless" (p. 44).

According to humanistic theory, extreme conformity to outside demands leaves one feeling alienated and out of touch with the self-actualizing tendency. The man may sacrifice some of his human potential to strive for external success. This conflict is common among working men (Cournoyer & Mahalik, 1995; O'Neil, 1981a, 1981b).

5. *Cast your fate to the wind:* Job or career success is often dependent upon factors that are beyond the man's control, and perhaps his understanding. The mainstream U.S. cultural belief that working hard enough always brings success may be a reality for the talented and privileged, but the "average Joe" depends at least partly on opportunity and the vicissitudes of the market. The combination of subscribing to the myth and equating economic success with masculinity leaves the average man feeling powerless and thus emasculated.

6. *You can't win if you don't play:* Equating masculinity with vocational accomplishment has especially damaging effects on men who encounter significant barriers to meaningful employment. In many poor segments of society, few opportunities for work, education, or training are provided, yet the men in these subcultures tend to subscribe to the "money equals masculinity" value (Liebow, 1969). Is it any wonder that some of these men turn to illegal activities such as drug dealing (Majors & Billson, 1992; Kiselica & Kiselica, 2014)? They may see such activities as their only opportunity to validate their masculinity through economic success. The high rates of incarceration, violence, and drug use among economically disadvantaged men of color are the result of the oppressive nature of mainstream U.S. culture, which imparts its masculine values to these men while at the same time blocking most avenues for them to participate in the dream of occupational success.

Employed men who lose their jobs through economic downturn, injury, or even retirement face a battle to retain their masculine self esteem. Mirra Kamarovsky (1940/1971) published a classic study of 59 unemployed men and their families. Many of these men were ridiculed, blamed, and rejected by their fami-

---

Box 10.1 *Death of a Salesman*

Arthur Miller's classic (1949) play, *Death of a Salesman*, is a brilliantly insightful examination of the relationships among masculinity, work, and family. Willy Loman, the lead character, is a salesman in his sixties. His job skills are deteriorating, and thus his value to his employer is decreasing rapidly.

Because Willy is relatively poor, and because his self-esteem is almost wholly invested in his work identity, he is suffering emotionally. He is a traditional man who refuses to admit vulnerability, and so he tries to delude himself into believing that the best is yet to come. He frequently fantasizes about his brother Ben, a financially successful and adventurous man who reminds Willy of the differences between the brothers' wealth: "When I was seventeen I walked into the jungle, and when I was twenty-one I walked out. And by God I was rich."

Willy Loman wholly subscribes to the value that wealth equals masculinity and self-worth. Underneath, he has the painful feeling that he has not been courageous or industrious enough. He says, "The world is an oyster, but you don't crack it open on a mattress." To make matters worse, Willy's two sons, Biff and Happy, are also unsuccessful. Because Willy cannot deal directly with his feeling of failure, he deals with it indirectly through his sons, alternately berating them for their irresponsibility and pumping them up with unrealistic dreams of instant success.

Biff occasionally tries to fight through his father's denial, but the effect is to flood Willy with overwhelming pain.

Willy's feelings of emasculation and depression peak in intensity when he loses his job and can no longer deny that his sons are also not on the path to success. He takes the provider role so seriously that he contemplates suicide so that he can bequeath $20,000 (a huge sum of money in the 1940s) in insurance money to his family. In an imaginary conversation with Ben, Willy says, "A man can't go out the way he came in, Ben, a man has got to add up to something." Willy has come to feel that he has only added up to an insurance policy, and thus that he is worth more dead than alive.

Because of his sense of loss and hopelessness, his feelings of failure as a father and worker, and his ardent desire to live up to the masculine ideal of the good provider, Willy finally commits suicide by intentionally crashing his car. Ironically, he does so during the same week that the final payment on the family house is made, a joyous occasion for most families. In some ways, Willy was a success: he provided an acceptable standard of living for years, and purchased a house "free and clear." But traditional standards of masculine success demand much more, and Willy did not feel free or clear. *Death of a Salesman* details the tragedy of a man who would rather die than re-define his masculinity.

---

lies for failing to fulfill the provider role. They also tended to blame themselves and to suffer from depressive symptoms. Retirement presents a difficult transition for many men, as they must leave the activity through which they have defined themselves for most of their lives. Box 10.1 depicts the tragic story of an unsuccessful man at retirement.

7. *What have you done for me lately?:* As we pointed out in Chapter Four, early masculine socialization shapes behavior, but ongoing social contingencies

maintain it. Successful men have their masculinity affirmed frequently across many social settings while less than successful men are socially devalued. Men with high levels of wealth and occupational status are defined as the most desirable partners for dating and marriage (Schmitt, 2005). It is not surprising that men learn to connect sexuality with money. A business deal is sometimes referred to as, "getting into bed with" the partner. In a classic article on work and masculinity, Gould (1974) remarked on the association of men's money and their sexual desirability:

> Women have been taught that men who achieve success are the best 'catches' in the marriage market. Women have also been taught that the right motives for marriage are love and sexual attraction. Thus, if a woman wants to marry a man with money, she has to believe she loves him; that he is sexually appealing—even if the real appeal is his money… Many women learn to make this emotional jump: to feel genuinely attracted to the man who makes it big, and to accept the equation of moneymaking power with sexual power. There are many phenomenally wealthy men in the public eye who are physically unattractive by traditional criteria; yet they are surrounded by beautiful women and an aura of sexiness and virility. (p. 97)

8. *When enough is never enough:* Men who overemphasize the work role sometimes fall prey to what are commonly referred to as workaholism or work addiction. Current definitions of a *workaholic* define it as a person who invests more time and energy in work than is required; the key being the combination of both time and energy, not simply number of hours (Andreassen, 2014). Men and women are equally likely to be workaholics (Taris, van Beek, & Schaufeli, 2012), who are at risk for a number of negative outcomes. Physically, they tend to experience high levels of physical symptoms of stress, such as irritability and high blood pressure, as well as insomnia and chronic fatigue. Psychologically, they often report higher levels of work-family conflict and relatively poorer functioning in non-work settings (Andreassen, 2014). The work-family conflict is likely the result of decreased time with family as well as their irritability and poorer functioning in non-work settings. Workaholism is more common in some fields than others. Men dramatically outnumber women as construction workers, which has some of the highest rates of workaholism. Yet relatively low rates are found among male-dominated law enforcement and the military. Blue-collar or manual labor jobs tend to have higher rates of workaholism than pink-collar (i.e., secretarial) or white-collar (professional) positions (Taris, van Beek, & Schaufeli, 2012). Box 10.2 describes the relationship of a workaholic and his family.

9. *The lonely hunter:* A singular striving for success is often incompatible with the formation of relationships. We have already pointed out the negative aspects of the success-masculinity connection on the family. This connection also inhibits the formation of close relationships with other men.

   Ochberg (1988) describes an interesting pair of role demands on a group of career men he interviewed. He investigated aspects of these men's relationships

Box 10.2   The Blue Collar Workaholic

A therapist related the story of a woman who "dragged" her husband into marital therapy under threat of divorce. He was an automobile mechanic who worked a 40- hour per week job and had a free-lance business in his home garage on evenings and weekends. His side business provided more than enough work and a good deal of money, but he rarely spent more than a few minutes with his wife or family before the phone would ring or someone would pull into the driveway in need of repairs.

When the therapist asked him why he worked such long hours, the man said, "I don't want to retire at 65 like my father; I'm going to retire at 45." It was clear that this man was chasing a quantifiable and probably mythical definition of success, to the detriment of his family. One has to question the rationality of extreme overwork towards reaching a goal of *not working.*

with male coworkers and concluded that men are encouraged to present the *illusion* that they are personal with one another while at the same time maintaining limits. Friendliness is expected, but men who get too close to one another are seen as losing control of their situations. According to Ochberg, "Striking this balance between detachment and the appearance of friendliness is actually more of a strain than being either genuinely personal or genuinely indifferent" (p. 11). Although most of the men Ochberg interviewed reported a desire for personal relationships with their colleagues, they work hard to resist it because the man who is a colleague today may be a subordinate tomorrow, and they believe it to be difficult to discipline or give orders to a friend. Ochberg reports studies indicating that "successful executives show that they have an unusual ability to cultivate friendships with those who are ahead of them on the corporate ladder, and disentangle themselves from attachments to people who once were their peers, but whom they have since left behind" (p. 11). Male-male friendships are discussed further in Chapter Thirteen.

WORKING IN THE MODERN WORLD

The world of work in the postindustrial world has undergone many changes in recent years. There are increases in women's participation in nearly every segment of the paid labor force, and these increases are accompanied by slight decreases in men's participation. Several men's issues have arisen in response to these changes.

Probably the most important development in the work arena for men is that financial providing can no longer be considered exclusively masculine. In modern societies, most men have not gained much satisfaction from their work. They validated their masculinity through the *results* of their work: money and providing. In some large United States cities, unmarried childless women in their 20s earn more than their unmarried childless male peers (Sharockman, 2014). As women continue to make gains in the amount they earn as a group, men who hold antifeminine ideologies will often have to find masculine validation elsewhere, although many do not know where to turn. As Bernard wrote in 1981, "The good-provider role may be on its way out, but its legitimate successor has not yet appeared on the scene" (p. 12); three decades later, the issue persists. Men who have been marginalized (e.g., men of color and older men) have experienced the greatest difficulty living up to the breadwinner role demand (Wilkie, 1991). There is a small but positive movement toward men's gender-egalitarian beliefs as a result of a decreasing emphasis on the provider role (Zuo, 1997).

Male-Female Relationships in the Workplace

The dominance and antifemininity norms of traditional masculinity can cause men difficulty when their work peers, superiors, or subordinates are women. Gender-typed men tend to react to a woman in a "man's job" with some mixture of anger, fear, confusion, and anxiety (Astrachan, 1992; Eisler, 1995). The traditional view of woman as underling and sex object is dysfunctional in a number of increasingly common work situations, a few of which are detailed below:

1. When a man and woman are required to work together cooperatively, unreasonable dominance by the man is damaging to employee relationships and the quality of the work.

2. When a man and a woman are competing for promotion, he may feel emasculated if she wins and claim that she got the job because she's a woman, not because she's better qualified.

3. When organizations engage in hiring, promotion, and pay increase decisions in which they discriminate against women, individuals are victimized and organizations suffer emotional distress, lowered productivity, and sometimes economic hardships brought on by litigation or job action.

4. When a man's supervisor is a woman, he may be uncooperative, anxious, resentful, or disrespectful if he holds a traditional perspective on gender (Eisler, 1995). These behaviors and attitudes may result in poorer job performance and thus harm the organization. As a group, men tend to have negative attitudes toward female managers (Schein, 2001), especially when the manager acts in a stereotypically masculine way (Rudman & Glick, 2001).

5. Sexual harassment in the workplace is pervasive (Holland & Cortina, 2013; Rospenda, Richman, & Shannon, 2009). The man who sexually objectifies women at work and acts on this attitude is engaging in an illegal act, harming other human beings and the organization, and sometimes damaging his potential for vocational success.

SEXUAL HARASSMENT

In October of 1991, a United States Senate committee held hearings on the confirmation of Judge Clarence Thomas to the Supreme Court. Anita Hill, a University of

Oklahoma law professor, testified that Thomas had pressured her for dates and made frequent lewd comments in the workplace while he was her supervisor in the early 1980's. Hill's accusations and the reactions to them by the all-male Senate Judiciary Committee elevated public awareness of sexual harassment (Jaschik-Herman & Fisk, 1995). In 1992, several women reported similar behaviors by Oregon Senator Bob Packwood (who resigned because of the scandal) (Taylor, 1995), and the allegations of sexual harassment by Paula Jones against President Bill Clinton (along with his "consensual" sexual affair with Monica Lewinsky) cast a pall on his entire presidency. In 2007, former New York Knicks executive Anucha Browne Sanders won an 11.6 million dollar judgment against Madison Square Garden because she was fired from her job for refusing the sexual advances of then-coach Isiah Thomas (ESPN, 2007). In the 1990s, Mitsubishi Motors lost a pair of harassment lawsuits related to inappropriate behavior at its plant in Normal, Illinois. While the Equal Employment Opportunity Commission (EEOC) was investigating, Mitsubishi officials shut down the plant for a day, rented 59 buses, and transported 2500 employees on a six-hour bus ride to Chicago to protest at the EEOC building. The costs of the plant shutdown and trip were estimated at 21 million dollars (Grimsley & Brown, 1996). Mitsubishi eventually settled two lawsuits for a total of 43.5 million dollars, a record amount for a sexual harassment suit, and undertook a vigorous corporate program to correct sexual harassment in the workplace (Grimsley, 1998; Grimsley & Swoboda, 1997).

The Equal Employment Opportunity Commission (EEOC) (1980) defines sexual harassment as:

> Unwelcome sexual advances, requests for sexual favors and other verbal or physical conduct of a sexual nature when submission to such conduct is made either explicitly or implicitly a term or condition of an individual's employment; submission or rejection of such conduct by an individual is used as the basis for employment decisions affecting the individual; or such conduct has the purpose or effect of unreasonably interfering with an individual's work performance or creating an intimidating, hostile, or offensive working environment"(p. 25024).

For a behavior to be considered sexual harassment, it must meet the following criteria. First, it must be sexual or gender-focused. For example, repeated requests for dates are sexual in nature; frequent derogatory comments about women or men are gender-focused. Second, it must be unwanted. Conduct is sexually harassing if the person who is the target of the sexual behavior feels uncomfortable, attacked, offended, or intimidated. If the person enjoys or is not bothered by sexual comments, flirting, or requests for romantic attention, then there is no sexual harassment in these behaviors. Third, the conduct must occur in the workplace. In this case, "workplace" is broadly defined. If someone is having a drink at a bar after work and a co-worker approaches him or her with unwanted sexual attention, then we can reasonably assume that the negative impact of this conduct will not just go away when the person returns to work the next day. Although the behavior has not occurred in the physical workplace, it has nonetheless occurred in the workplace.

There are two types of sexual harassment. *Quid pro quo* ("this for that") sexual harassment involves an attempt to gain sexual cooperation through threats of negative job-related consequences and/or promises of positive ones. It is a proposed exchange of influence in return for sex. This category includes *sexual extortion* (e.g., "Have sex with me or I'll fire you") and *sexual bribery* (e.g., "Have sex with me and I'll give you a raise"). Threats can be implicit or explicit. A supervisor can say, "You'll do well in your career if you know how to 'play ball,' if you know what I mean," and this statement can be construed as a kind of offer.

Quid pro quo harassment need happen only once to be chargeable. In fact, sometimes officials can also bring other charges under laws that cover bribery, extortion, or sexual assault. This type of harassment is fairly cut-and-dried—when quid pro quo harassment results in a formal complaint, the dispute usually centers on whether or not the behavior actually occurred, not whether or not it was harassing.

Hostile environment sexual harassment involves unwelcome and offensive, pervasive and frequent sex-related verbal and/or physical behavior that has the effect of creating discomfort in the working environment. Examples include unwanted touching of a sexual nature, sexually-oriented jokes and conversations, asking about sexual experiences, repeated pressure for dates, staring at a person's body, making derogatory gender-related comments, displaying pornographic pictures in the workplace, and a variety of other behaviors.

In contrast to quid pro quo harassment, which needs to happen only once to be chargeable, hostile environment harassment must be severe, persistent, and/or pervasive to be chargeable. One of the most frequent questions from male employees to sexual harassment prevention trainers is, "What if I slip up and say something inappropriate? Will I lose my job and ruin my career?" They seem to have a fear that the "sexual harassment police" will come around the corner and arrest them if they exhibit even a momentary lapse of discretion. Nothing could be further from the truth. The word "environment" within the phrase "hostile environment" means that behavior must have the effect of coloring a person's entire experience within the workplace to sustain a legal charge. At the same time, making an inappropriate sexual comment violates the *principle* of workplace respect that underlies sexual harassment policies, and so the person who "slips" would do well to apologize to anyone he or she has offended and make efforts to avoid repeating the behavior.

Legally, sexual harassment law is subsumed under Title VII of the Civil Rights Act of 1964 that forbids discrimination in employment based on sex (and a variety of other characteristics such as race and religion). The U.S. Supreme Court has upheld the right of individuals to protection from same-sex sexual harassment (Biskupic, 1998). A campus is a student's workplace, and Title IX of the Education Amendments of 1972 entitles all students to a harassment-free environment. This right extends to protection from the unwanted sexual attention from faculty, administrators, staff, other students, vendors, visitors, and any person who might potentially interfere with the student's learning environment. It also extends to travel away from the campus on school-sanctioned business such as athletic teams' games on other campuses and interns' work at off-campus sites. Schools and employers are legally required to take all reasonable steps to prevent sexual harassment and to provide a swift remedy when given notice of its occurrence. They face legal liability when they knew or should have known that sexual harassment was occurring, yet took inadequate steps to deal with it.

Workplace sexual harassment is fairly common. In the U.S., the Equal Employment Opportunity Commission (EEOC) and Federal Employment Protection Agencies received an average of about 12,000 new complaints per year in the 2010s, approximately 15 percent of which come from men, a decrease from the 15,000 new complaints filed annually in the late 1990s (EEOC, undated). More than 50 percent of women and 40 percent of men reported being harassed at some point in the most recent year, and one sample of women reported a rate of nearly 80 percent (Holland & Cortina, 2013; Rospenda et al., 2009). Women who work in "traditionally male" blue-collar fields (e.g., construction or industrial work) and women in the military are especially likely to experience sexual harassment (Sandler & Shoop, 1997; Saunders & Easteal, 2013; Stockdale & Bhattacharya, 2009; Willness, Steel, & Lee, 2007).

Thirty to 50 percent of female college students report having been sexually harassed by male professors or other staff members (Sandler & Shoop, 1997; Fitzgerald, 1993) and approximately 80 percent of male undergraduates reported being sexually harassed at least once in their lifetime, mostly by other students (Kearney & Rochlen, 2007). Sexual harassment has been particularly problematic at American military academies. In 1991, approximately 97 percent of female students reported having been sexually harassed ("Nearly all Women at Academies are Harassed, Study Says," 1994). In 2005, the rate had "improved" to only 96 percent at West Point and 93 percent at the Naval Academy. The Air Force Academy showed a little more progress, with 82 percent of female cadets reporting unwanted sexual behavior (White, 2005).

The impact of sexual harassment on the victim is enormous and affects both his or her job and mental health. Victims typically report a decrease in job satisfaction, with the focus primarily on co-workers and supervisors and not as much on the work itself. Victims' commitment to their employers, work performance, and productivity also suffer, and they often quit their jobs (e.g., Raver & Gelfand, 2005; review by Willness, Steel, & Lee, 2007). As such, sexual harassment directly affects a company's performance by decreasing workers' effectiveness and productivity while also increasing turnover. It can also have a direct cost; businesses pay approximately $50 million per year in cases settled with the EEOC (EEOC, undated). Cases in which employees sue their employers are not included in this estimate and as we noted earlier, Mitsubishi paid approximately $43.5 million to settle two cases, close to the same amount as all cases settled with the EEOC up to that point in time. In the U.S. Federal Government alone, sexual harassment is estimated to cost 135 billion dollars annually (Foote & Goodman-Delahunty, 2004). Reliable estimates of cost in the private sector are difficult to obtain, but one older report included an estimate of $6.7 billion annually for every Fortune 500 company (Wagner, 1992).

Victims typically report general declines in their mental health, often indicated by greater rates of depression and/or anxiety. They also report somewhat lower levels of life satisfaction (Willness et al., 2007). Masculinity directs men to be invulnerable, not admit weakness, and avoid help seeking, perhaps the reason why male victims may be more likely to drink to the point of intoxication but report no changes in their mental health statuses (Rospenda, Richman, & Shannon, 2009). Compared with women who were frequently sexually harassed, men with similar experiences were more than ten times less likely to seek mental health services (Shannon, Rospenda, & Richman, 2007).

In a large-scale study, researchers found that most harassers are male: 95 percent of female victims and 22 percent of male victims said that they had been harassed exclusively by males (Tangri, Burt, & Johnson, 1982). Men who subscribe to traditional masculine ideologies are more likely to harass than other men (Wade & Brittan-Powell, 2001). Kearney, Rochlen, and King (2004) found that men who report high gender role conflict are also more likely than other men to harass. This study lends support to Pleck's (1981a) hypothesis that cultural changes in gender roles, as well as witnessing individuals violate the "old" roles, leads some men to overconform to gender roles. Thus the sex difference in perpetrating harassment is tied to various aspects of masculinity.

Sexual harassment depends on whether or not the target of the behavior experiences the conduct as offensive. This "eye of the beholder" criterion has left many men confused about what they can and cannot do and say in the workplace. It is clear to most people that saying, "Have sex with me or you're fired" to a subordinate constitutes an illegal act, but most sexual harassment is not so blatant. Many men are wondering, at what point does "normal" flirting, sexual discussion, or complimenting cross the line into harassment? Can a man say, "Let's go have a drink after work," "How are things going with your boyfriend?" "You look especially good today," or "I think you have nice legs?"

We see a gender role-related problem in the mere understanding of the behavior. Most men are raised with the sense that rules should be clear and unambiguous. Sports, that basic training ground for masculinity, have clear, rigid rules. "Guidelines" like those established by the EEOC, tend to make conventionally-gendered men uncomfortable.

More importantly, the "eye of the beholder" definition means that men have to make judgments about what another person is feeling. As we have already discussed, many have little experience with this sort of interpersonal orientation. Not surprisingly, men (especially traditionally masculine ones) are much less likely to perceive sexual harassment than women (Fitzgerald, 1993), however it may be possible to use educational interventions to make men more sensitive to the problem (Kearney, Rochlen, & King, 2004). Both men and women who hold traditional gender beliefs often react to sexual harassment policies and training with resistance (Tinkler, 2013).

Other aspects of the masculine gender role contribute to a sexual harassment proclivity. The view of women as subservient sexual objects is a primary one. Men who see women as sexual objects first and human beings (or coworkers) second, are at greater risk for committing harassment. The sense that one has to be dominant to be a man (Pryor, 1987) and generally negative attitudes toward women (Robinson & Schwartz, 2004) are associated with higher likelihood of sexual harassment. These behaviors are embedded within an abuse of power, most often perpetrated by people with high status in an organization against subordinates (Basow, 1992). In speaking of verbal harassment on the street (which does not amount to workplace sexual harassment, but has the same kinds of emotional effects), Benard and Schlaffer (1997) described the issue of sexually-based harassing behavior and power: "Whether you wear a slit skirt or are covered from head to foot in black chador [(the garb of Muslim and Hindu women who are only allowed to have their eyes uncovered in public)], the message is not that you are attractive enough to make a man lose his self-control but that the public realm belongs to him and you are there by his permission as long as you follow his rules and as long as you remember your place" (p. 396).

The traditional roles of man as sexual initiator and woman as sexual gatekeeper also set the stage for sexual harassment. Men who subscribe to the belief that sexual activity is a matter of power and conquest believe that they must persistently pressure women, and the workplace provides opportunities to do so. Men who hold adversarial sexual beliefs—that sexual relationships are a matter of exploitation and manipulation—are more likely than other men to harass. Foote & Goodman-Delahunty (2004) described three types of male harassers:

> *Misperceiving harassers* seek sexual relationships and believe that the workplace is an appropriate location for doing so. They misconstrue women's friendliness or dress as invitations for sexual behavior and also tend to hold the belief that relationships between men and women are adversarial and aggressive.

> *Exploitive harassers* associate sexuality with social power and believe that women enjoy being dominated by men. When in positions of organizational power, they use provocative sexual behavior to intimidate women, and they also tend to subscribe to the beliefs that women invite rape by the way they dress or that women like being raped.

> *Misogynistic harassers* hold hostile attitudes toward women and express these attitudes through displays of pornography, derogatory language in reference to women, denigration of women's abilities, and sometimes direct sexual taunting of women.

These characteristics of sexual harassers are not unlike those of acquaintance rapists. Again we find evidence that underlying masculine inadequacy may be related to damaging others and perhaps the self. Sexual harassment is a men's issue, and it is intertwined with other issues involving men's power, emotionality, sexuality, relationships, antifemininity, and gendered self-definition.

As with all gendered victimizing behaviors, sexual harassment takes place within a context of patriarchal male dominance. One of us (C. K.) was struck by the expectation of male sexual privilege when an older colleague told him that when he had arrived on campus as a new professor in the 1980s, the college president invited all new faculty members to his house for a welcoming party, and remarked, "Professor, I see that you are a single man. Many of our male faculty members have found their wives from among our student body—I hope you will be as fortunate." Thus, the president not only condoned sexual relationships between people of vastly different power levels on the campus, he encouraged them.

There is good evidence that the risk of sexual harassment is greater for both women and men who violate traditional gender standards than for those who do not (Stockdale & Bhattacharya, 2009). Therefore, sexual harassment can be an organizational practice that polices the boundaries of acceptable gendered behavior, and thus ending restrictive gender norms is a key step toward ending the practice. The implementation of organizational policies and procedures that clearly define and prohibit sexual harassment are also a particularly effective way to reduce it (Willness et al., 2007).

Solutions to the problem of sexual harassment include education, prevention programs, legal and government policy changes, and effective efforts to hold perpetrators responsible for their actions. Organizations must make strong statements that they will not tolerate the behavior and then follow through with effective institutional policies and strategies (Willness et al., 2007). Communicating respect for women in the structures and activities of the organization will be helpful in working against the attitudinal undercurrent of the problem. In the big picture, sexual harassment is an agent of social control of women by men (Fitzgerald, 1993), and thus efforts to end it also involve social change in the gender and the structure of patriarchy, as well as in the lives of individual men.

MALE-FEMALE RELATIONSHIPS IN DUAL-EARNER HOMES

The continued influx of women into the paid labor force is changing the ways in which couples manage work and family roles. Women who are equal economic partners usually expect their spouses to become equal domestic partners. A sense of fairness would seem to dictate that a shared provider role means that men's household responsibilities should increase.

Pasick (1990) points out several problems for many men in this area. First, there is sometimes a skill deficit. Some men have little training in cleaning, cooking, and especially child care. Second, gender-typed men may resist learning these skills because they consider them unmanly. Third, wives may be reluctant to relinquish control of what has traditionally been women's domain. A man may sometimes feel that he is in a double-bind situation. He feels the demand to contribute, yet he may receive frequent criticism that he is not doing the task well enough. Finally, many employers do not offer much support to men who are trying to adopt nontraditional roles. For example, a man who leaves work to care for a sick child may be subject to much more disapproval than a woman who does the same thing (see also Hochschild & Machung, 1989)

As a result of these difficulties, women tend to do more housework and child care than men, even when both partners work equally long hours (DeLatt, 2007). Most people still consider this work to be primarily a woman's responsibility, as evidenced by some men's remarks that they "help out" in their own homes and "babysit" their own children (Deutsch & Saxon, 1998). Only about one-fifth of husbands are fully involved in household chores like cooking and cleaning, compared with virtually all wives (Starrels, 1994). In the United States, wives initiate about three of every four divorces (Marguiles, 2004). Explanations for this sex difference are likely complicated, but it may be related to many wives' dissatisfaction with having to do a disproportionate amount of domestic work despite working outside the home just as much of their husbands, a burden that Hochschild & Machung (1989) termed *the second shift*.

Traditional men in co-provider families also tend to feel threatened if their wives earn more money than they do. Clearly, subscribing to the belief that money means power and masculinity would cause problems for the man whose wife earns more than him. The incredible power of gender roles is illustrated by some men's reactions to their wives' getting a raise—they feel strong resentment and feelings of being unmanly, and they would rather get along with less money than deal with these feelings and their underlying attitudes. On the other hand, some men become stay at home fathers because the arrangement makes economic sense for them (Dunn, Rochlen, & O'Brien, 2013; Rochlen, McKelley, & Whitaker, 2010). We describe these men in more detail in Box 10.3.

Although the increased entry of women into the paid workforce has complicated the lives of men both at home and at work, the benefits of these changes often outweigh the costs, at least for egalitarian men (Rudman & Phelan, 2007). First, the man can share the provider pressure with his partner. Second, because outcome (earning) can no longer be defined as traditionally masculine, men can pay more attention to process (day-to-day experiences within the workplace) and seek satisfaction from the work itself. Third, egalitarian roles at work and home enhance the appreciation of

---

Box 10.3   Stay-at-Home Fathers

Some men do the majority of child care in their families and do not work outside the home. There are approximately 2 million stay-at-home-fathers (SAHFs, also known as stay-at-home-dads or SAHDs), representing approximately 16 percent of all stay-at-home-parents (Livingston, 2014). Researcher Aaron Rochlen and his team conducted a series of studies to help us better understand these men's lives.

SAHFs gave multiple reasons for choosing to become primary caretakers. The most common of these were that the couple strongly believed one parent should be home to raise the child (i.e., no paid childcare), consideration of the adults' personalities and preferences, and employment or wage earning factors. About half of them, and three-quarters of their partners, said the fact that the woman earned more was an important consideration (Dunn, Rochlen, & O'Brien, 2013; Rochlen, McKelley, & Whittaker, 2010; Rochlen, Suizzo, McKelley, & Scaringi, 2008).

These fathers also talked about feeling both excited and anxious about being their child(ren)'s primary caretaker, at least initially. By the time they participated in the research, most were very confident of their parenting abilities. Perhaps more importantly, most were highly satisfied with this non-traditional role (Rochlen, McKelley, Suizzo, & Scaringi, 2008; Rochlen, Suizzo, et al,. 2008). Although there was quite a bit of variability among the men who participated in the research, most were psychologically healthy in general, reported good relationships with their partners, and had slightly lower than average masculinity ideology scores (Rochlen, et al., 2008). At the same time, approximately half reported at least one event in which they had been stigmatized, most commonly because they were violating gender roles (Rochlen et al., 2010).

Although these findings are quite positive, it is important to note that the majority of participants were European-American, highly educated, and had relatively high family incomes (equivalent to upper-middle class or better). The majority of research participants had chosen to become stay at home parents, but most men who adopt this role do so because they are unable to find work, are ill or disabled, are in school or retired, or for some other reason (Livingston, 2014).

women as human beings and improves the quality of relationships between women and men. Rather than living in the parallel lives of the 1950s model, partners can claim common ground both at work and at home. Fourth, men may have opportunities to enter new realms of rich experience as they expand the view of themselves beyond that of functional work machines. We describe some of these issues for long-term romantic couples in Chapter Thirteen (Relationships)

There is some evidence that ideologies about men's and women's work and family roles are changing. In 2004 at Match.com, one of the largest heterosexual on-line dating services, 53 percent of men under age 30 asked to meet women who earned a certain amount of money, double the percentage from only three years earlier. In 2001, 70 percent of women subscribers to this service specified a minimum income for potential mates but this percentage fell to 50 in 2004 (Wen, 2004). If Match.com is a trend indicator (clearly, more research is needed), men and women are increasingly looking for the same things in potential marriage partners, as gender becomes less and less of an organizing principle in both the workplace and the home.

In the heterosexual relationship that people have come to view as traditional, the woman experienced success vicariously through the man, who experienced emotions and relationships vicariously through the woman. Now that women are more often succeeding financially for themselves, men may have important opportunities to rediscover their emotional lives and reinvolve themselves in the lives of their families and friends.

SUMMARY

1. Work has defined men's identities throughout history, and the masculine socialization process is strongly oriented toward producing workers. The character of work and the sexual division of labor has changed throughout human history.

2. The man-as-provider, woman-as-homemaker arrangement was a temporary transition from agricultural to industrial societies. It does not characterize most of human history, and it is changing. Similarly to the transition to single-earner families, the return to co-provider families is a result of economic exigencies. Women's participation as full economic partners is associated with gender egalitarian values. Sex segregation is associated with the oppression of women.

3. As a consequence of industrial demands, most men were effectively removed from their homes and often specialized in some small part of the production process. As a result, they were alienated from both their work and their families, and they had to rely on the financial outcome of work for the validation of masculinity. The provider role requires sacrifice and emotional restrictiveness. These aspects of masculinity continue to live on in many men.

4. The masculine values of task orientation, competition, and independence are conducive to a wide variety of work settings. Boys' sports and play, with their emphasis on outcome and quantification, socialize males toward work.

5. The advantages of this socialization for men are social status, opportunity, and work satisfaction, but many men who lose jobs or do not succeed feel emasculated. Even men who do well at work may encounter difficulties in relating to family and coworkers, maintaining physical and mental health, dealing with the pressures of competition, and coping with gender role strain.

6. Sexual harassment is pervasive in the workplace, and most perpetrators are men. This problem is costly in both human and financial terms, and it is tied to masculine issues of power and sexual privilege. Solutions to the problem involve a wide range of social, legal, organizational, and personal changes.

7. In recent times, economic and social conditions have led to work changes for families. Men who adhere to gender-typed attitudes may encounter significant problems at work and at home as they find it necessary to adjust to newer, more egalitarian gender roles. Issues around the loss of the masculine breadwinner role, sexual harassment, and the sharing of domestic duties have come to the fore. Although the result is a more complicated life for working men, the benefits may outweigh the costs, as many men are expanding their senses of self beyond their occupational roles.

Chapter Eleven

Pleasure and Performance: Male Sexuality

Few areas of human behavior are as fraught with emotion as sexuality. Dealing with oneself as a sexual person can involve a wide array of experiences, including pleasure, mystery, wonder, lust, love, anxiety, guilt, repression, and confusion. During social-ization, people receive quite a few messages about sexual feelings and relationships, presumed differences between male and female sexuality, sexual orientation, seduc-tion, intimacy, and sexual communication. Many of these messages are highly value-laden and specify morally correct ways to behave. Some messages, particularly from abstinence-only programs, involve misinformation, half-truths, and highly stereotyped presentations of masculinity and femininity (Guttmacher Institute, 2012; Santelli et al., 2006). These messages influence how biological sexual tendencies are shaped into sexual behaviors and feelings, as well as how the person experiences his or her sexual-ity within the larger picture of the total self-concept (Marston & King, 2006).

Anthropological evidence indicates that there is wide cross-cultural variation in the social rules for handling sexuality. For example, some cultures value marital fidel-ity, but some peoples in the Arctic consider it proper etiquette for a man to offer to make his wife sexually available to a male visitor. Kissing is unpopular in some soci-eties. Some cultures encourage sexual experimentation in adolescence while others punish it severely (Rathus, Nevid, & Fichner-Rathus, 2008). And, adolescent boys in some tribes on Papua, New Guinea are expected to perform oral sex on the older men of the tribe as a rite of passage into manhood (Gilmore, 1990).

In the United States, the Victorian era of the early twentieth century was very sexu-ally repressive, in sharp contrast to the sexually permissive values of the late 1960s (Strong, DeVault, Sayad, & Yarber, 2007) and the so-called "hookup culture" of today (Bogle, 2008). One outcome of this shift is a change in the ideal expression of male sexuality from men who were faithful to their wives and fathered several children to men who had multiple short-term sexual partners (Smiler, 2013).

In this chapter, we explore the connections between masculinity and sexuality, as well as men's actual practices of and experiences with sex. We start by discussing comparisons between males and females, then examine direct links between masculinity and sexuality, including risk-taking, competition, and intimacy. We then address changes in sexuality related to different points in the lifespan and the effects of online pornography, and end with a discussion of sexual orientation. Some topics related to sexuality are addressed elsewhere, including romantic relationships (Chapter Thirteen), sexual harassment in the workplace (Chapter Ten), and rape (Chapter Twelve).

MALE-FEMALE COMPARISONS

There are several well-documented differences between males and females regarding sexual behavior. In *attitudinal* research, males have been more accepting of teen, pre-marital sex, and non-relational sex than females since the 1920s, at least among U.S. samples (Fass, 1977; Oliver & Hyde, 1993). Men are much more likely than women to view sex as a physical activity that is relatively unconnected to relationships (Laumann, Gagnon, Michael, & Michaels, 2001). They also report higher levels of sexual desire (Schmitt, 2005) although the popularly held belief that men have *biologically* stronger sex drives than women is not supported by any available scientific evidence (Rathus et al., 2008). Remember that these are aggregate, average differences between males and females and that there is substantial variability within each of those groups.

Studies of sexual *behavior* also reveal several differences and again, many of these differences have been documented as far back as the 1950s and earlier. Specifically, men and boys are more likely to report that they masturbate and evidence indicates that among all those that do, males do so more frequently (Strong et al., 2007). In fact, the difference in masturbation rates is among the largest and most consistently documented sex differences in sexual behavior (Oliver & Hyde, 1993). Men are more likely to "hook up" or have sex with someone they have recently met (Bogle, 2008; Maticka-Tyndale, Herold, & Mewhinney, 1998) and are more likely to "cheat" or have an extra-dyadic partner without approval from their primary partner (Humblet, Paul, & Dickson, 2003). Although boys have often had their first sexual intercourse or "lost their virginity" at a younger average age than girls (Oliver & Hyde, 1993), a small number of recent studies have reported no meaningful difference in *average* age of first sexual experience.

You may have also heard or been taught that girls usually do not enjoy their first heterosexual intercourse but boys typically do. This statement is inaccurate. Both girls and boys evaluate the experience more positively than negatively with scores suggesting that most people describe the experience as "good with little-to-no bad" or "more-good-than-bad." In those same studies, boys rated their experience both more positively and less negatively than girls (Bauserman & Davis, 1996; Smiler, Ward, Caruthers, & Merriwether, 2005).

SEX AND MASCULINITY

Gendered expectations and ideologies pervade virtually every area of experience, and sexuality is no exception. The traditional masculine gender role contains many prescriptions for sexual behavior and experiencing, and these are embedded in the larger context of masculine values and ideologies. Being a "real man" has often included expectations for certain ways of being a sexual man.

These male vs. female differences, combined with a cultural emphasis on male promiscuity, teach both boys and girls how men are expected to behave. Many see this set of sexual behaviors as central to definitions of masculinity, in part because of double standards that prescribe differences in male and female sexual behaviors (Brooks, 1995; Crawford & Popp, 2003).

Promiscuous sexuality may be central to current definitions of masculinity because, unlike some other masculine expectations, adolescent boys can achieve it. Manhood rituals have typically revolved around the 3 P's: providing, protecting, and procreating (Gilmore, 1990), also known as the 3 F's: feeding, fighting, and fornicating. Current-day United States culture does not allow most teen boys to meaningfully protect or provide for their families. But they can procreate—or be promiscuous, at any rate—and that behavior has become one way to demonstrate masculinity.

Regardless of the rationale(s), the idea that males should be sexually promiscuous is connected to other aspects of gender (David & Brannon, 1976). One link is the close connection between masculinity and being not-homosexual, a theme we've discussed throughout the book. Another is the value that being promiscuous can qualify a boy or man for a high level of status among other males, or at least among others who adhere to the hegemonic definition of masculinity. Today, we might call a promiscuous male a "player." In the past he's also been called a "stud" or a "Don Juan," among other terms (Smiler, 2006a, 2013).

This ideal of heterosexual promiscuity is so central that several masculinity ideology measures such as the *Conformity to Masculine Norms Index* (CMNI; Mahalik et al., 2003) and the *Male Role Norms Index* (MRNI; Levant et al., 2007) explicitly include it as a component of masculinity. In fact, promiscuity subscale scores are strongly related to measures of aggression, dominance, and emotional restriction (Levant et al., 2007; Mahalik et al., 2003).

Perhaps, then, it is no surprise that teen boys and undergraduate men with higher scores on these and other scales report having more total sexual partners and having their first sexual experience at a younger age (Pleck, Sonenstein, & Ku, 1993; Smiler, 2008), as well as more partners per year, than other men (Sinn, 1997; Smiler, 2013). In fact, even among young men who entered college with no sexual experience, those with higher masculinity scores had intercourse sooner than their less masculine virginal male peers (Forste & Haas, 2002).

A younger age of first sexual experience and the total number of partners one has had are seen as ways to compete with others. Both of these numbers feed into the traditional masculine emphasis on getting something accomplished rather than on the experience of doing something. Masculine achievements are, by definition, things that have happened in the past that contribute to the sense of gendered identity. They are also quantifiable; masculine success means "putting up numbers." Carrying this orientation over into sexual behaviors has often created problems for traditional men and those around them.

This goal-oriented attitude toward sex focuses the man on the good feelings that come from having "conquered" someone and leads to a focus away from enjoying the sexual experience. Some men even want to hurry sex so that they can go and tell their friends about having "scored," and thus gain admiration and status. The sexual partner, however, is often a victim of disrespect. She (or he) is dehumanized by being treated as merely an avenue to achievement for the "player."

Philosopher and men's studies pioneer Harry Brod (2005) stated, "Unless you are as concerned with your partner's free will as you are with your own, you are treating her as less than human and therefore you are the only person in the room. We have a name for solitary sex. You are not having sexual intercourse, so don't congratulate yourself."

Risk-Taking

Taking risks is also sometimes necessary to achieve the goal of more partners or a younger age of first sex. Farrell (1986) summarized the social message young men receive: "Be prepared to risk rejection about 150 times between eye contact and sexual contact. Start all 150 over again with each girl" (p. 126). Because men are expected to be tough and strong, rejection is not supposed to hurt.

The directive to take sexual risks also harms men in other ways. Generally, those with higher masculinity ideology scores, especially those who endorse stereotypical gender beliefs, tend to underestimate the risks involved in sexual behaviors (Courtenay, McCreary, & Merighi, 2002). Heterosexual boys with higher masculinity scores report lower levels of intentions to use condoms, in part because they believe pregnancy prevention is a woman's responsibility (Pleck, Sonenstein, & Ku, 1993, 1994). Failure to use condoms also puts them at greater risk for contracting sexually transmitted infections (STIs) and research indicates that many men do not defy the odds for long. Men who do not use condoms and are more promiscuous are more likely to have an extra-dyadic sexual interaction without approval from their partners, contract a sexually transmitted infection, and initiate an unintended pregnancy (Dariotis et al., 2008; Humblet et al., 2003). One result of these ideologies is that the U.S. has notably higher rates of unplanned teen pregnancy and teens with STIs than any other industrialized nation (Weinstock, Berman, & Cates, 2004; World Health Organization, 2004).

Competition

One aspect of the sexual double standard is that promiscuous boys and men are rewarded for having a lot of partners while girls and women are shamed for the same behavior (Crawford & Popp, 2003). A promiscuous male is often praised as "The Man," at least among teen boys and young adult men (Brooks, 1995; Kimmel, 2008; Smiler, 2013).

To compete in this "game," men learn to equate sex with physical pleasure and diminish or at least control their desire to experience a sense of emotional intimacy with their sexual partner(s) (Levant, 1997b; Smiler, 2013). The result is an approach that positions partnered sex as a physical release or an adventure (Blumstein & Schwartz, 1983) and may explain why one expert was astonished by men's frequent reports that they do not enjoy sex (Zilbergeld, 1992). This approach makes it easier for men to engage in "hook up" sex (Bogle, 2008; Bradshaw, Kahn, & Saville, 2010), defined as a one-time sexual encounter with someone the individual is not currently dating and does not intend to date (Epstein, Calzo, Smiler & Ward, 2009; Garcia, 2012). It likely also explains why men are more likely than women to interpret an ambiguous event, such as an invitation from a woman to have a cup of coffee together, as indicating sexual interest or availability (Fisher & Walters, 2003).

In Chapter Three, we discussed sexual strategies theory (SST) (Buss & Schmitt, 1993; Schmitt, 2005), which positions male promiscuity as evolutionarily derived. Proponents of this theory argue that men who spread their seed widely and eschew long-term commitments with women are more likely to produce children and thus propagate their genes. However, one anthropological review of foraging tribes (i. e., hunter-gatherers) demonstrated that children who were raised by both biological parents were more likely to survive to puberty than children whose fathers were not involved (Quinlan, 2008). If your children fail to reproduce, is that really a "win" in evolutionary terms?

Others have criticized the methodology and interpretation of results. SST research relies on long-documented male vs. female differences. It also focuses heavily on evidence that men are more likely than women to say they would like two or more sexual partners in the next 30 days (Schmitt, 2005), a gender difference David Schmitt and his colleagues demonstrated in every one of 52 nations (Schmitt et al., 2003). The data, which rely heavily on unmarried undergraduate students age 18 to 22, showed that approximately 25 percent of young men and 6 percent of young women wanted multiple partners. As critics have pointed out, that is a minority of men who completed anonymous surveys and who have extensive access to unmarried young women without meaningful adult supervision, at least in Western nations. If there were ever a group who could have—or admit to wanting to have—high numbers of partners, this is it (Diamond & Hazan, 2000; Smiler, 2011).

The research regarding actual number of partners is fairly consistent and indicates that most men have few partners. Only an estimated 15 percent to 20 percent of young men have three or more partners per year. When the time frame is expanded to three years or longer, the percentage of men who consistently have three or more partners per year drops to 5 percent or lower (Dariotis et al., 2008; Humblet et al., 2003; Offer, Offer, & Ostrove, 2004).

Researchers exploring the attitudes that support male promiscuity have revealed a set of ideologies that are consistent with mainstream U.S. definitions of masculinity such as competition with other men, "stealing" a friend's girlfriend (Messner, 1992), endorsement of sexual double standards, a desire for power over women, and the belief that lying to women during seduction is "fair play" (Smiler, 2013). Moreover, endorsement of this approach to masculinity is associated with endorsement of various rape myths (e.g., "Only bad girls are raped.") and the use of aggression in sexual scenarios (Murnen, Kaluzny, & Wright, 2002).

Intimacy

According to researchers who examine the subjective understanding of sex, most men do not conform to stereotypical expectations (Smiler, 2013). Men routinely report that their experiences are grounded in love, or at least affection, for their partners (Fiering, 1996; Smiler, 2008; Smiler, Ward, Caruthers, & Merriwether, 2005). An emphasis on physical intimacy combined with emotional intimacy can shift the center of sexual activity away from penetrative sex and on to other forms of sexual activity that emphasize pleasure and may or may not include orgasm. In addition to the focus on a broader array of physical pleasures, men desire and often attain this sensuality. We discuss other aspects of romantic relationships, such as emotional support, in Chapter Thirteen.

Many adult men report making a transformation away from a "selfish," penis-based sexuality to a couples-based approach emphasizing sensuality. By the time a man reaches his 60s or 70s, his sexual activity may have shifted from being focused on penetrative sex to cuddling and mutual masturbation (Potts, Grace, Vares, & Gavey, 2006; Sandberg, 2013). This approach seems more similar to many women's experiences of sex, which often include caressing, intimate conversation, or other aspects of sensuality. It would also seem to minimize the heterosexual women's oft-expressed frustration with male partners who seem overly focused on the physical aspects of sex.

SEXUAL DEVELOPMENT

The sexual behaviors in which boys and men engage can change over the lifespan. In this section, we address some of those age-related changes.

A boy discovers his penis very early in life. Compared with the girl's vagina and clitoris, the penis is more external and visible. Once he is out of diapers or learns to take them off by himself, his penis is easily accessible to his hands, and he finds that touching it produces very pleasurable sensations. A boy will often learn his culture's beliefs about sex before he learns to seek out sexual information. That knowledge comes from parents, peers, and media (Sutton et al., 2002) and these sources provide different amounts of input and variant messages. According to American teens, parents provide the least amount of information and media the most; parents tend to be most negative and media almost exclusively positive (Epstein & Ward, 2008). At the same time, most parents want their children to have healthy sex lives in adulthood (Vernacchio, 2013).

Media-based messages about sex tend to be fairly stereotypical, emphasizing male promiscuity, performance, and initiative as well as female attractiveness, inexperience, and responsiveness (or passivity). These themes can be found in the television programs, movies, and music videos most popular with children and teens (Cope-Farrar & Kunkel, 2002; Jhally, 2007; Montemurro, 2003; Morrison & Halton, 2009; Turner, 2011; Ward, 1995). Magazines like *Maxim, Rolling Stone, Cosmopolitan*, and even *Golf Digest* (Hatton & Trautner, 2011; Joshi, Peter, & Valkenburg, 2011; Krassas, Blauwkemp, & Wesselink, 2003; Vokey, Tefft, & Tysiaczny, 2013) also reinforce these stereotypes, as do romance novels (Clawson, 2005) and pornography (Picker & Sun, 2008). Very few media messages promote a healthy sexuality characterized by mutual respect, good communication, condom use, and explicit consent (Hust, Brown, & L'Engle, 2008).

Box 11.1   The Circumcision Debate

The cutting and removal of the penile fore-skin (prepuce) is performed on more than half of male infants in the United States, which is the only Western country where this practice is routine (Zak, 2009). Perhaps because of heightened awareness of its risks and/or beliefs that it is unnecessary, circumcision rates have decreased in much of the world. In 1975, 93 percent of U.S. newborn boys were circumcised. That figure fell dramatically to 56 percent by 2006 (Zak, 2009), although there are significant variations among religious affiliations and regions. Globally, the practice is much less common, with an estimated 85 percent of male infants not circumcised (Goldman, 1992). In Australia and Canada, for example, approximately 20 percent of boys undergo the procedure as infants, and the neonatal circumcision rate in Britain is only one percent (Laumann, 1999).

A century ago, circumcised men were also a small minority in the United States. The rise to the high rate of circumcision in the mid-twentieth century was fueled by beliefs about its value for hygiene, disease avoidance, reduction of cancer risks, and other concerns (Hussey, 1989). Circumcision also has ritual meaning within some religions (Allgeier & Allgeier, 2000). However, complications from circumcision such as hemorrhage, infection, or mutilation, occur in as much as four percent of cases (Niku, Stock, & Kaplan, 1995).

In 1989, the American Academy of Pediatrics (AAP) recommended that parents carefully weigh the risks and benefits of circumcision before deciding whether to subject their newborn boys to it (Rathus, Nevid, & Fichner-Rathus, 2008). A decade later, in 1999, the AAP issued a statement saying that the benefits of circumcision do not outweigh its risks, and that therefore the operation should not be carried out routinely (Rathus et al., 2008). In 2004, The Circumcision Resource Center stated that, "no med-ical organization in the world recommends routine circumcision of male infants." Why, then, does circumcision remain the majority experience in the U. S.? Milos (1992) cited several persistent myths about the value of circumcision:

Myth: A circumcised penis is cleaner than an uncircumcised penis. Although circumcision may reduce the frequency of urinary tract and other kinds of infections (Wiswell & Geschke, 1989), an uncircumcised penis is easy to care for. Infections can easily be avoided by simple hygiene procedures, which most men around the world use routinely.

However, there is newly-emerging evidence that circumcision may offer a significant measure of protection from Human Immunodeficiency Virus (HIV) and that therefore it is possibly a valuable tool for fighting the worldwide AIDS pandemic. The World Health Organization and UNAIDS now recommend it (WebMD, 2009). Safer sexual practices would have the same effect, however condoms and proper safer sex information are not always available, especially in non-industrialized nations.

Myth: Babies don't remember the pain. In a review of the controversy around circumcision, Laumann (1999) stated that, "Even four to six months later, babies circumcised without anesthesia exhibit greater pain reactions to vaccination than uncircumcised boys or babies whose circumcision pain was attenuated by anesthetics" (p. 70). This finding tells us that infants certainly are affected by the experience for at least a period of several months.

> *Myth: A boy needs to look like his father or the other boys in the locker room.* This belief did not appear to be a concern when, from 1870–1900, most U.S. boys were circumcised and their fathers were not (Hussey, 1989). Milos (1992) suggests that boys readily accept the explanation that "When I was a boy, they thought circumcision was necessary for health, but now we know better" (p. 15). However, for U.S. parents, the circumcision status of the father is strongly related to the decision of whether or not to subject the baby boy to the procedure. Ninety percent of sons of circumcised fathers undergo the operation compared with 23 percent of sons of uncircumcised fathers (Laumann, 1999).

Puberty

Puberty is the process of physical and sexual maturation. Some changes are specifically related to reproduction, including growth in genital size and production of semen, called "primary sexual characteristics." Other changes, such as development of facial hair and deepening of voice, are called "secondary sexual characteristics" and can be understood as signals that the boy is sexually mature (or soon will be).

Puberty includes a series of hormonal changes. Perhaps most relevant here is a dramatic increase in the level of testosterone. We note that girls' level of testosterone also increases (but not as much as boys), and that levels of estrogen also increase for both sexes, although more for girls (Dorn & Biro, 2011; Saucier & Ehresman, 2010). Changes also occur at the neurological level. The shift in hormones appears to both reorganize neural circuitry and activate those newly reorganized systems, especially those specifically related to sexual behavior. Ultimately, the interaction between pubertal hormones, adolescent brain structure, and a boy's experiences all influence his sexual behavior (Sisk, 2006).

Another change is an increase in penis size. Pre-pubertal boys' penises are smaller than those of adult men's, which average approximately 14 to 15 cm (5.5 to 5.9 inches) when erect (Reece, Herbenick, & Dodge, 2009). When asked about their ideal penis length, men tend to say they'd like a longer penis. Depending on the format of the question, they say they'd like to have a slightly longer penis (2.0 cm, or .8 inches) or specify a length of approximately 18.5 cm (7.25 inches). Very few men tell researchers they would prefer shorter penises (Johnston, McLellan, & McKinlay, 2014; Lever, Frederick, & Peplau, 2006). Women consistently provide lower estimates of actual and ideal length than men and the vast majority (approximately 85 percent) are satisfied with the size of their partner's penis (Johnston et al., 2014; Lever et al., 2006). Statements like "it's not the size of the wand, it's the magic in the magician" or "it's not the size of the ship, it's the motion of the ocean" provide little comfort to men who think their penises are too small.

Boys often describe puberty as both exciting and somewhat embarrassing, and in the media, male puberty is almost always depicted as funny (Hust, Brown, & L'Engle, 2008). Although parents know they should talk to their sons about puberty and first ejaculation before these events occur, few do (Frankel, 2002; Stein & Reiser, 1994). Boys say puberty is exciting because they want to be and be seen as more mature. Yet it is also embarrassing because their bodies behave differently and in ways that remind the boy (and others) that he is not in full physical control (Frankel, 2002; Stein & Reiser, 1994). The most embarrassing moments seem to be the spontaneous erections that occur for no conscious reason. These events are most likely a manifestation of growth and biological "system checks" that have little to do with either conscious or unconscious desire, but that bulge in a boy's pants may be visible all the same. Math class is rarely *that* interesting.

In industrialized nations, and among the middle- and upper-middle classes of non-industrialized ones, older teens and undergraduates typically report entering puberty at age 12 or 13 with some evidence that the average age of pubertal onset has become younger during the last century (Bhalla, 2003; Ponton & Judice, 2004; Goldstein, 2011).

On average, sexual behaviors start soon after the onset of puberty. Many boys report that their first open-mouthed kisses with girls took place around age 13 or 14. This experience is typically followed by increasingly more intimate sexual behaviors such as manual-genital contact and first intercourse around age 16 (Regan et al., 2004; Smiler, Frankel, & Savin-Williams, 2011). Most boys follow this sequence (Jakobsen, 1997). Or, more precisely, most boys follow this sequence when they have female partners (Smiler et al., 2011). First "serious" relationships with girls typically occur around age 16 or 17 (Smiler et al., 2011). We discuss romantic relationships in Chapter Thirteen.

For boys with male sexual partners, average age of these firsts and the sequences in which they experience them is much more variable. On average, first sexual penetration (oral or anal) occurs around age 16, alongside manual-genital contact, with first kiss following at age 16 or 17. For these boys, the most common sequence is to have one's first kiss and first sex at the same age. First "serious" relationships often begin around age 18 (Smiler et al., 2011).

Adulthood & Older Age

The typical U.S. man reports having sex between two to three times per week and once every few months. For most, sexual activity becomes less frequent as they get older than during their 20s and more often occurs with long-term partners (Laumann et al., 2001). Unfortunately, with older age also comes a greater likelihood of experiencing sexual problems such as difficulties with sexual desire, functioning, or enjoyment. Clinicians often use the terms sexual dysfunction or sexual disorder to describe these problems. The term dysfunction seems to imply that the "equipment" is not working; disorder implies a pathological condition. Since male sexuality is not only in the penis, and since sexual difficulties do not necessarily mean that there is something fundamentally wrong, the term "problem" seems more appropriate. Generally speaking, problems become more common as men age; men with poorer health and lower levels of happiness also tend to report sexual difficulties at higher rates than their age-mates (Laumann et al., 2001).

The *Diagnostic and Statistical Manual of Mental Disorder* (DSM-V) (American Psychiatric Association, 2013) directs clinicians to consider if sexual problems are lifelong or acquired as well as generalized or situational. Most diagnoses, including those reviewed here, require the problem to be present in at least 75 percent of (attempted) sexual experiences over the course of at least six months. In addition, the problem cannot be the result of an issue related to one's partner, the relationship, other characteristics or mental conditions in the individual (such as high anxiety), cultural or religious practices, or a medical condition (such as high blood pressure), and it must also be associated with distress. These considerations are important with regard to treatment. If a condition is longstanding and global, it usually presents a more serious problem than transient or situational difficulties. A problem that is largely biogenic usually points to different interventions than a problem of psychological origin. And there is no need to treat a condition when it is not associated with distress.

The overall incidence of sexual problems is difficult to estimate because sex is usually such a private matter, but it is probably the case that most people have, at some time in their lives, experienced sexual disinterest, arousal difficulties, and/or sexual performance problems (Laumann et al., 2001). Males are also much more likely than females to develop sexual arousal to atypical or deviant stimuli such as children, inanimate objects or parts of the body not usually associated with sex, pain and suffering of self and/or partner, exhibitionism, and voyeurism (American Psychiatric Association, 2013). The following discussion centers on problems with arousal and performance.

Male Hypoactive Sexual Desire Disorder. Male Hypoactive Sexual Desire Disorder focuses on a lack of interest in sex. It only becomes a problem if it is distressing to the man and/or his partner. The gender prescriptions that a man should always want, need, and be ready for sex may produce negative feelings in the man when he experiences even a normal ebb in his sexual appetite. Fewer than 2 percent of men report a persistent, lifelong lack of interest in sex (American Psychiatric Association, 2013).

Low levels of sexual desire can stem from physiological causes such as fatigue, drug use, or illness, and/or from psychological/interpersonal causes. Other problems, such as work stress or conflicts in the relationship with the man's sexual partner, might also lead to a decrease in sexual desire. Declines in testosterone levels after midlife, which are a common part of aging (Saucier & Ehresman, 2010), may also play a role. Occasional experiences of low sexual desire appear to affect approximately 15 percent of men age 49 or younger and 22 percent of men in their 50s. It is estimated that approximately 6 percent of men age 18 to 24 and approximately 40 percent of those age 66 to 74 have severe and persistent enough symptoms to qualify for diagnosis (American Psychiatric Association, 2013).

Erectile Dysfunction. Transient or longstanding difficulties in attaining or maintaining erection are relatively common in men, and these problems often produce significant distress. Historically, the term "impotent" was used to refer to men who experience these difficulties. Literally, this word means "powerless" and parallels the conception of erection as a cultural symbol of man's strength. Clinically, these problems are now referred to as erectile dysfunctions to more specifically describe the problem and to avoid implicit value judgments about the man's personality (just as the term "frigid" is no longer used to describe a woman with orgasmic difficulty).

It is estimated that 5 to 10 percent of men age 49 or younger suffer from occasional erectile problems, with the rate increasing to approximately 20 percent of men in their 50s (Laumann et al., 2001). The DSM-V indicates that erectile problems are severe enough to be diagnosed in approximately 2 percent of men younger than age 40, with rates rising to between 40 and 50 percent of those beyond age 70. Although the exact contributions of physical and psychological causes is not known, the estimate of physical origin has increased in recent years, and some researchers believe that close to half of erectile problems are based more in biology than psychology (Shabsigh, Fishman, & Scott, 1988), a view that has become more popular since the release of drugs like Viagra and Cialis in the late 1990s (Potts et al., 2006). Physical causes include illness, disease, high blood pressure, use of some types of prescription and nonprescription drugs, injury, hormonal imbalance, fatigue, or vascular problems (Allgeier & Allgeier, 2000; Crooks & Baur, 2007).

Emotional factors can also play a role in erectile difficulty. Anxiety is probably the most common one (Zilbergeld, 1992). Many men feel a good deal of pressure to penetrate their partners with their erect penises (or else it's not "really" sex). Paradoxically, the fear of losing one's erection can result in dysfunction. Men who think of intercourse as the only mode of sexual expression often believe that they must have an erection for sexual pleasure to occur for both self and partner. Something of a vicious cycle may result: he feels self-induced pressure to attain an erection and perform, which leads to anxiety, which leads to erectile difficulty, which results in more pressure, more anxiety, etc. As Nelson (1988) opined "[Erectile dysfunction] is a man's threat, always waiting in the wings while he is on stage" (p. 33).

There are several treatments for erectile problems, including vascular medications such as Viagra, Cialis, and Levitra. One could argue that these drugs, or the advertising around these drugs, has reinforced the concept of male sexuality being all about penetrative sex and not a broader sensuality (Potts et al., 2006). Men with intractable physiological barriers to erection can opt for penile implants, which produce erections by the pumping of liquid into a cylinder that has been surgically implanted in the penis (Wienke, 2005).

Psychological treatments for erectile problems usually involve turning attention away from penis, intercourse, and performance, and toward sensuality, the partner's pleasure, and sexual communication. Among men whose erectile problems are largely psychogenic, most can achieve erections when the pressure to do so is removed. Erectile problems specifically related to (Internet) pornography viewing are addressed below and in the final chapter.

Ejaculatory Problems. Many experts believe that premature (early) ejaculation is the most common sexual complaint for men (Zilbergeld, 1992), with 20 to 30 percent of adult men reporting some concern of this type (American Psychiatric Association, 2013; Laumann et al., 2001). The DSM-V specifies a time frame of less than one minute after penetration and sooner than desired. The two-part definition is important because it is difficult to define the problem in absolute terms. How soon is too soon?

A subjective criterion of "sooner than desired" may simply be more practical: if the man and/or his partner are unhappy with the man's level of ejaculatory control, some attention may be warranted.

Although the cause or causes of premature ejaculation are not well understood, sex therapists have developed reliable treatments for this problem. Pharmacological treatments using low doses of antidepressant drugs have been somewhat successful (Forster & King, 1994; Wise, 1994). Behavioral techniques involve the starting, stopping, and restarting of stimulation at various points of arousal, the squeezing of the base or glans of the penis, and a number of other exercises that the man can do alone or with a partner. These treatments are also highly effective. Success rates are estimated at between 80 and 98 percent (Zilbergeld, 1992).

Fewer than one percent of men experience an opposite problem: the inability to ejaculate during a reasonable period of time, or sometimes at all, known as delayed ejaculation (American Psychiatric Association, 2013). This problem is thought to be anxiety-based, perhaps related to a fear of impregnating the partner or a discomfort with one's own erotic pleasure. Sex therapists have prescribed a number of techniques for increasing arousal (Zilbergeld, 1992).

Online Pornography & Sexual Dysfunction.   Viewing online pornography is a common activity among males. Estimates suggest that one-quarter to one-third of 14-year-old boys have intentionally viewed sexually-explicit media online (Brown & L'Engle, 2009; Sabina, Wolak, & Finkelhor, 2008) and nearly all young men have done so by age 18 (Brown & L'Engle, 2008; Steeves, 2014). Among younger boys, the primary reason given is to "learn about sex" (Cameron et al., 2005). Although there is no official diagnostic category for "Internet addiction," "online pornography addiction," or even "sexual addiction," the terms are widely used, and many seek treatment for these problems (Cantor et al., 2013; Griffiths, 2012). Men's primary complaints often focus on inability to perform sexually with a live partner, specifically erectile difficulties and premature ejaculation, as well as negative effects from spending so much time looking at online sexually-explicit media (e.g., not enough time for other tasks, including work, school, and hobbies) (Cantor et al., 2013; Shaeer, 2013).

Assuming there are no physical problems that lead (or contribute) to the erectile and ejaculatory issues, then the problem may be that the individual has effectively "re-wired" his arousal system through watching large quantities of pornography while masturbating. One part of the problem is that his is seeing more naked and sexual bodies in a week than humans evolved to see in a lifetime (Wilson, 2011). Teens who start watching pornography at younger ages, do so at relatively high rates, and continue to watch at this level for several years also tend to support more regressive and traditional gender role attitudes and report younger ages at first sex (Brown & L'Engle, 2009). Another part of the problem is that more frequent viewers may have trained themselves to become aroused almost exclusively to visual stimuli instead of the combination of tactile and other sensory inputs involved with partnered sex. In many cases, this set of inputs occurs in a single place and physical position (e.g., seated in front of a desktop computer in the bedroom). Among physically healthy young men, treatment that consists of avoiding all pornography, decreasing the frequency of masturbation, and varying the ways in which the individual masturbates, can lead to a return of sexual functioning in approximately three months (Shorrock, 2012).

SEXUAL ORIENTATION

As we have noted frequently, heterosexuality—or rather, being not-homosexual—is an important part of the dominant definition of masculinity. As we discussed in Chapters Three and Four, this idea is rooted in the acceptance of a gender binary, stereotypes of gay men as effeminate (Green & Ashmore, 1998; Madon, 1997), and religious and moral perspectives (DeBlock & Adriaens, 2013). Researchers Michael Parent and Bonnie Moradi (2009) have argued that some masculinity ideology scales measure the importance of presenting oneself as heterosexual more than they measure homophobia per se, as their authors claim (e.g., Mahalik et al., 2003). We discuss the relationship experiences of gay men in Chapter Thirteen.

Origins

Although some people believe homosexuality is a choice and thus can be changed (see Box 11.2), research increasingly points to a significant level of biological causation. Factors linked with sexual orientation include genetics, brain structure, and hormones (Saucier & Ehresman, 2010), although the latter two may be effect, cause, or both. Gay men tend to have more older brothers than heterosexual men and are less likely to be right-handed, although the birth order effect may be limited to right-handed men. There is no effect for number of older sisters (Blanchard, Cantor, Bogaert, Breedlove, & Ellis, 2006). The data are also clear that family structure, such as being raised by a single mother or gay (or lesbian) parents is not predictive of homosexuality (American Association of Pediatrics, 2013; Lamb, 2012).

In some ways, discussions of the causes of homosexuality are somewhat offensive in and of themselves. After all, we do not ask people "What do you think caused your heterosexuality?" or "If you have never slept with a person of the same sex, is it possible that all you need is a good gay lover?" (Rochlin, 1982, p. 1). For years, researchers did not include people with other-sex attractions in their studies, so there are relatively little data on how heterosexuals determine that they are "straight." Yet an examination of the available evidence tells us that by age six, some boys are clearly attracted to girls while others are clearly attracted to boys. Some do not report any attractions until their teen years (Eliason, 1995; Savin-Williams, 1998). These similarities and others suggest that we need to understand what causes sexual orientation, not just what causes homosexuality.

Current-day sexuality researchers rarely ask the categorical question "Are you gay, heterosexual, or bisexual?" Instead, many use some version of Alfred Kinsey's 7–point scale, which is anchored by "completely heterosexual" (score: 0) and "completely homosexual" (score: 6). A score of 3 indicates someone who is equally heterosexual

Box 11.2   Sexual Conversion "Therapies"

Can sexual orientation be changed? Should it change? A small group of psychologists and psychiatrists answer both questions in the affirmative, but only with regard to homosexual orientation; no one seems to be interested in converting people from heterosexuality to homosexuality. Efforts to reorient people to heterosexuality are viewed as remarkably offensive by most gay and lesbian people and their heterosexual allies.

Jack Drescher (2002) notes that there are three prevalent types of theories on the origins of homosexuality. *Normal variant* theories define homosexuality as a minority but naturally-occurring orientation, analogous to left-handedness (e.g., Money, 1987a). *Pathology* theories define homosexuality as an abnormal condition, and *immaturity* theories regard this orientation as a (perhaps passing) phase. Although the American Psychological Association (APA) once endorsed a pathology theory, it changed to a normal variant theory in 1973. Thus, adherents to either of the other two theories are clearly outside the psychology mainstream in the United States. However, there are many people who continue to believe that homosexuality is a pathology, and in recent years, some have sought to change it in individuals, mainly because of a perceived contradiction with fundamentalist Christian religious beliefs. Moberly (1983) coined the term "reparative therapy" to describe these efforts. The title obviously implies that something is broken and needs repair, a claim that many find profoundly offensive. A broad collection of professional organizations, including the American Psychological Association, American Psychiatric Association, American Counseling Association, and National Association of Social Workers, have taken the official position that therapy to change an individual's sexual orientation is inappropriate and unethical (Just the Facts, 2008). States such as California and New Jersey have made it explicitly illegal.

The research study that most strongly supported the effectiveness of reparative therapy (RT) was published by Robert Spitzer in 2003. Relying on self-reports from 143 men and 57 women who had experienced RT, he concluded that it helped some people change their sexual orientations, although never from strictly homosexual to strictly heterosexual. No subsequent researcher was able to replicate Spitzer's findings, his research methodology was (rightly) questioned, and in 2012 he published a statement saying that his results were likely erroneous. He apologized to the gay community and "any gay person who wasted time and energy undergoing some form of reparative therapy because they believed that I had proven that reparative therapy works with some 'highly motivated' individuals" (Spitzer, 2012, p. 757).

and homosexual, or in current terms, bisexual (Kinsey et al., 1948). Assessing categories of sexual orientation can be further compounded by the distinction between the partners an individual wants and the ones they have, as well as evidence that some men change categories (Baumeister, 2000; Savin-Williams & Vrangalova, 2013; Smiler et al., 2011).

Rates

Given the different ways to measure sexual orientation, it should not be surprising that there is no accurate count of exactly how many people fall into any particular category. Assessing the presence of homosexual and heterosexual men within the populations becomes even more complicated when we acknowledge that many self-identified gay males have some type of sexual experience with females and that some self-identified heterosexual men have some type of sexual experience with males (Laumann et al., 2001; Savin-Williams, 1998; Savin-Williams & Vrangalova, 2013; Smiler, Frankel, & Savin-Williams, 2011). For example, if a heterosexual man kisses another man because he is dared to do so (Anderson, McCormack, & Lee, 2012), or simply because he wants to "experiment" and see what it's like "the other way," does that one-time behavior say anything about his orientation? The same questions might be asked of a gay man with a female partner. And how should we classify men who have wives but also have male lovers "on the down low" (King & Hunter, 2004)?

Yet results are somewhat consistent. To demonstrate that "mostly heterosexual" (1 on Kinsey's scale) is a distinct group, researchers Ritch Savin-Williams and Zhana Vrangalova (2013) evaluated data from 53 studies of men's and women's sex-of-partner preferences. In 43 of them, at least 90 percent of men said they were strictly heterosexual; for most of the remaining studies, the rate was between 85 percent and 89 percent. Mostly heterosexual was the next largest group of men, consisting of approximately 3.5 to 4.1 percent of the population. In most studies, between one and three percent of men identified as exclusively homosexual.

In this chapter, we have addressed sex and gender comparisons in sexual attitudes and behaviors, the connections between masculinity and sexuality, sexual development throughout the lifespan, and sexual orientation. As we have seen, there is a strong cultural and individual emphasis on male promiscuity and penetrative sex. This focus obscures the actual experiences of boys and men, which tend to highlight emotional and relational connection, including a more sensual approach to sexuality. As Gary Brooks and Ronald Levant (1997) concluded, "The fundamental problem is the approach to sexuality that we teach to adolescent boys and young men. Until we reconstruct the traditional standards for male sexual conduct, we will continue to be plagued with men behaving badly" (p. 258), or at least in ways that may be less than optimal for men and their partners.

SUMMARY

1. The ways people understand, behave, and respond to male sexuality have varied among cultures and historical eras.

2. Many differences between men and women exist regarding both sexual attitudes and behaviors, and several of these differences reflect double standards that praise men and punish women for the same activities.

3. The dominant masculine role encourages (especially young) men to support promiscuous attitudes and engage in sex with multiple partners. Teen boys and young men with higher masculinity ideology scores report younger ages of first sex, more total sexual partners, and more sexual partners per year.

4. Masculine role norms that encourage risk taking appear to encourage boys and men to engage in dangerous sexual practices, especially failing to use condoms,

which contributes to high rates of unplanned pregnancies and sexually transmitted infections (STIs) within the United States.

5. Masculine injunctions against emotional expression and intimacy run counter to most men's desire for emotional connection with their sexual partners. Yet as men age and gain sexual experience, they often shift towards a more sensual approach to sexuality that is less dependent on penetrative sex.

6. Puberty involves a series of hormonal and neurological transformations. These two changes interact with a male's experience to shape his behavior.

7. The majority of males have their first sexual experiences during their teen years. Average ages and specific patterns vary based on whether his partners are male or female.

8. At midlife, men report having sex less frequently than during their 20s. In addition, the likelihood of experiencing some type of sexual problem increases.

9. Frequent viewing of online sexually-explicit media contributes to endorsement of more traditional gender roles among teen males. Frequent masturbation while using online pornography can lead to sexual problems such as erectile difficulty and premature ejaculation.

10. Sexual orientation appears to be a biologically-based phenomenon, akin to handedness. Efforts to change an individual's orientation, known as "reparative therapy," are unethical and ineffective.

11. Sexual orientation categories are somewhat difficult to define and some individuals change categories during their lifetimes. Despite the challenges of categorization, the proportion of individuals who identify themselves as belonging to any particular category appears to be relatively stable.

Chapter Twelve

Boys will be Boys:
Men and Violence

In the United States, we hate violence. We think that people who commit violent crimes should go to jail for a long time, and some even think they should be executed. We shake our heads in disbelief at "senseless" violence like drive-by shootings, boys who kill their classmates and teachers, serial killings, and mass murderers like those committed by Seung-Hui Cho, who killed 32 people on the Virginia Tech campus in 2007, and Elliot Rodgers, who murdered six and wounded 13 in Isla Vista, California in 2014. The horrific terrorist attacks of September 11, 2001 will remain in people's minds for many years to come.

In the United States, we love violence. We spend large amounts of time and money watching exhibitions like football, boxing, "mixed martial arts," and "professional wrestling" (which is neither professional, nor is it wrestling), in which men inflict pain on other men. We love to see "adventure" film heroes who get the job done with their guns and their fists. We have executed more than 1300 convicted murderers since the death penalty was reinstated in 1976, and more than 3000 others are awaiting execution (Death Penalty Information Center, 2014). And we are increasingly tolerant of psychological violence on "reality TV" shows in which those in power bully and humiliate people.

There may be no other place in the world where the culture seems to have such a powerful love-hate relationship with aggression. Although we abhor "senseless" violence, we often feel or think that there are times when violence makes a lot of sense. We seem comfortable with destructive acts as long as they are performed for the "right" reasons, against those who "deserve" to be victimized. We glorify those who are willing to "fight the good fight." It is a well-documented fact that men and boys commit the vast majority of violent acts (Erne, 2014). One of the most central issues in the gender-aware study of men is the connection between masculinity and violence.

We explore this link in this chapter, beginning with a brief description of the extent of male violence, followed by a summary of theories about its origins. Then, we pay special attention to two specific forms of gender-based violence, domestic violence and rape, with regard to origin and potential solutions. Finally, we will turn to a discussion of the effects of violence on male victims.

ORIGINS OF MALE VIOLENCE

Although no researcher has documented sex differences in aggressive behavior in infants and toddlers, clear sex differences emerge by preschool age, with males displaying more physical aggression and females displaying more verbal and indirect aggression (Loeber & Stouthamer-Loeber, 1998). Men commit about 81 percent of violent crimes in the United States, including about 88 percent of murders. If men were no more violent than women, there would be 14 fewer murders per day (derived from arrest records at FBI, 2011). Male partners or ex-partners beat more than half a million U.S. women every year (Catalano, 2012), and males are the virtually exclusive perpetrators of sexual assaults (FBI, 2011). Although sex comparison research has demonstrated nonexistent or nonsignificant differences between males and females in most areas, violence is a glaring exception. The good news for the United States is that both violent crime in general and intimate partner violence have fallen nearly 50 percent between 1994 and 2010 (Catalano, 2012).

At the same time, it is important to say that the vast majority of males are not violent. Recall from Chapter Two the discussion of normal curve overlap between the two sexes and variability within the population of males and within that of females. There is a small difference in physical aggression at the mean (arithmetic average) of the distribution, but this small difference translates to a large difference at the tail

Although most males are not violent, more violent people are males.
Photo © Bettman / Corbis

(extreme end) of the distribution. In other words, most men are not violent, but most violent people are males.

The search for the connections between masculinity and violence leads us back to the old nature-nurture question. Many people believe that men are biologically predisposed toward aggression. It is certainly also true that gender socialization and cultural support encourage violent behaviors for males more than for females. We probably will never know the relative contributions of nature and nurture to violence, but it is important to consider the roles of each of these types of forces.

The Biological Perspective

Sociobiologists argue that male aggression is tied to reproductive competition. In many different animal species, males engage in violent, confrontational, and sometimes mortal competition for breeding access to females (Daly & Wilson, 1985). Dominant males overcome other males through ritualized violence (such as rams butting horns), and these dominant males mate with more females than their submissive counterparts, who sometimes do not mate at all.

Daly & Wilson (1985) argue that violence among human males can be explained by this evolutionary pattern of ritualized competition. As evidence, they cite a 1958 study in which it was judged that 37 percent of the cases in which a male murdered another male were precipitated by "trivial" (ritualized) events, such as the killer's "saving face" when another man had insulted him. Daly's and Wilson's contention is that these types of killings are the result of the competition for dominance, and that this competition is most fierce among young, poor men who have little status. Men with higher socioeconomic status, they say, tend to be less violent because they are higher on the dominance hierarchy and thus able to attract suitable mates.

Daly and Wilson are accurate in their description of the population who are most at risk for being involved in violence—young, poor males. And, in fact, they are probably also correct in describing much of this violence as taking place for reasons that most people would consider trivial. However, to say that this kind of behavior is a result of breeding competition seems to be quite a leap of logic. In fact, even in other animals, male aggression is not always associated with increased breeding opportunities, nor is it universal (Basow, 1992). Would there be so many angry, aggressive young men if we took better care of their emotional and material needs, ceased to expose them to so many violent models, and stopped holding them to impossible standards of masculinity? As we shall see, other explanations of male violence (and young, poor men's violence) are at least as plausible as the sociobiological one.

Researchers who study biological influences on behavior are often interested in hormonal factors. Because males and females differ greatly both in levels of sex hormones and in levels of violence, it would make sense to look to these hormones for a possible link.

Some speculate that the male sex hormone testosterone may be related to aggression, and there is some evidence in support of this hypothesis. For example, in some animal species, males with high positions in social dominance hierarchies (which are often established by fighting) have higher testosterone levels than lower status males.

But there are complicating data. First, testosterone levels drop when an animal falls in the hierarchy. Therefore, although testosterone level may be a cause of aggression (or lack of it), it may also be an effect. Second, the excretion of high levels of testosterone in the urine of the animal may stimulate other animals to aggress toward him, and he must then fight back to protect himself. This evidence comes from an older study in which male rats were more likely to attack a castrated male rat after it had been coated with the urine of a dominant male (Pleck, 1981a).

The extent to which testosterone is a cause, effect, or simply a marker of aggression is a continuing subject of inquiry. Of course, the degree to which animal studies relate to human behavior is always a matter of debate. In a classic study by Kreuz and Rose (1972), testosterone levels were measured in prison inmates who were labeled as either "fighters" or "nonfighters" on the basis of prison records of aggressive incidents. There were no significant differences in testosterone levels between these two groups of men, casting considerable doubt on the straightforward testosterone-aggression hypothesis. Angier (1999b) reported a study in which testosterone replacement therapy actually resulted in an increase in friendliness in men.

Kemper (1990) reviewed the extensive literature on testosterone and concluded that, in animals and in humans, there exists a "socio-bio-social chain" in the effects of testosterone on behavior. When males gain *dominance*, testosterone levels increase, and the male is, in turn, affected by these hormonal surges in various ways. In other words, the social affects the biological, which in turn affects the social. Kemper described a complicated causal chain which included connections between testosterone, dominance, social structure, sexual behavior, and aggression. Mazur's (1983) contention is that dominance, not aggression, is the primary motive, with physical aggression as a frequent avenue for dominance. Therefore, aggression and testosterone may be linked, but only if aggression produces dominance.

Endocrinologist Robert Sapolsky (1997) in an essay entitled *The Trouble with Testosterone* echoes some of these findings and summarizes recent research. He asks a crucial question, "Does the action of this hormone tell us anything about *individual* differences in levels of aggression, anything about why some males, some human males, are exceptionally violent? Among an array of males—human or otherwise— are the highest testosterone levels found in the most aggressive individuals?" (p. 151, emphasis original). The answer is no. Changes in testosterone levels over time within an individual do not predict levels of aggression, or, as Sapolsky puts it, there is no *dose-response effect*. Although the removal of testosterone in an animal (through castration) drastically lowers aggression, restoring that animal to 20 percent of the original testosterone level returns aggression to the previous level, and increasing testosterone to 200 percent of original has no effect (although there is somewhat of an increase at 400 percent).

Sapolsky's conclusion is that testosterone has a "permissive effect" on aggression—some of the hormone must be present, but the level of the hormone is not a critical factor. Moreover, animals' aggressions are not random. Among monkeys, males most often fight with the males who are immediately above and below them in the dominance hierarchy, and so the aggression is instrumental in holding the animal's position within the troop or moving up in the hierarchy. Sapolsky makes two important conclusions: "testosterone isn't causing aggression, it's *exaggerating* the aggression that's already there" (p. 155, emphasis original), and "the more social experience an individual has prior to castration, the more likely that the behavior persists [after castration]. *Social conditioning can more than make up for the hormone*" (p. 156, emphasis added).

It is also important to repeat what we said in Chapter Three—that aggression is not the only path to dominance in animal hierarchies. Frans de Waal (2005) dispelled the stereotype of the primate "alpha male" (the animal at the top of the troop's dominance hierarchy) as a bully who attains his status by aggression or the threat of it. Although some alphas fit this description, they usually do not maintain their positions for very long, as other animals will form coalitions and overthrow them. The most successful alphas are what de Waal terms "populists" who keep the peace among the troop by, for instance, breaking up fights and helping with food sharing. The Darwinian "survival of the fittest" is often interpreted as an ability to eliminate the unfit, but the successful alpha's fitness is more in the service of helping with the troop's harmony and survival (de Waal, 2007).

Researchers have also investigated the role of genes in violence. Genetic factors may affect emotional arousal, perception, and neurotransmitter levels, some of which may predispose one to aggression (Huesmann, Dubow, & Boxer, 2011). One study of five generations of violent Dutch men found an apparent genetic marker on the X-chromosome (Richardson, 1993). People with close relatives who are antisocial personality disordered are at increased risk for developing the disorder, even when they have no contact with the antisocial relative (Sue, et. al. 2014). There is also evidence of brain abnormalities in some violent people (Densen, 2011).

One more point is very important: male-female differences in aggression are much more pronounced for *physical* aggression (violence) than for other forms of aggression, such as insults or social ostracizing (Pepler & Slaby, 1994), and even these differences do not exist prior to preschool age (Loeber & Stouthamer-Loeber, 1998). Therefore, the major difference is not in the experience of aggression or even the frequency of its expression, but rather in the *mode* of expression. Males and females show relatively large differences in how their aggressive experience is channeled, and it is very likely that the mode of aggressive expression is strongly influenced by gendered forces. Pepler's and Slaby's (1994) conclusion is that "there is a growing recognition that biology is not the primary determinant of gender differences in aggression" (p. 44).

Three other pieces of evidence cast considerable doubt on the hypothesis that biology causes violence in males in a straightforward and universal way. First, as already mentioned, the majority of males are *not* violent. If males' biology causes violence, then social forces have done a pretty good job at inhibiting these "natural" tendencies in the vast majority of the male population. Second, violence is confined to rather narrow settings for many men. The best example of situationally-based physical aggression is domestic violence. The most common type of wife batterer is violent only in his own home and has little or no problem controlling his aggression elsewhere (Holtzworth-Munroe & Stuart, 1994). Finally, there are considerable cross-cultural variations in the frequency of violence within the male population (Lepowsky, 1998). Ideologies of masculinity as antifemininity and unequal social statuses between the sexes are especially strongly associated with male dominance over (Coltrane, 1998) and violence toward (Lepowsky, 1998) women.

Claims about the biological universality of male violence provide a measure of justification for it and leave us with few options for resolving the problem besides punishment and confinement. The view that it is natural and normal to be physically aggressive if you are male is disrespectful to men, most of whom deserve a dignity that goes beyond that of violent animals. But even if there is a biological propensity toward aggression, we should keep in mind that there is also a biological propensity to resist violent impulses—the instincts to protect the self and to empathize with others.

The answer to the nature-nurture debate is not either/or; it is both/and. In evaluating the biological bases for male violence, there is little argument that biology appears to set thresholds for many behaviors. Possibly because of temperamentally-based higher average activity levels, hormones, neurotransmitters, or some yet undiscovered biological forces, it may take less stimulation to push the average male over the aggression threshold than it does for the average female. It would be difficult to change biology, and so the entire debate is moot, in a way. We know that biology and social forces both affect behavior, and so we should do whatever we can to work against the social forces that push a person over the threshold into violent behavior. We turn now to an examination of how these "pushes" are created through socialization and culture.

Psychosocial Perspectives

Adhering to traditional masculine gender roles has been consistently associated with aggression (Cohn & Zeichner, 2006; Cohn, Zeichner, & Seibert, 2008) and the willingness to endorse the use of violence (Mahalik, et. al., 2003; Moore & Stuart, 2004). A variety of male socialization experiences encourage violence. If we look at masculine norms, we see the seeds of aggression in many aspects. Brannon's classic (1985) description of the structure of traditional masculinity is useful in understanding male violence:

1. *Antifemininity* ("No Sissy Stuff"): the avoidance of stereotypically feminine behaviors. Women are often viewed as caring, nurturing, compassionate, and vulnerable, the very antitheses of aggression. The hallmark of the "sissy" (the feminine man, as traditionally defined) is backing down from a fight. Men may engage in physical aggression, not because they want to dominate, but because they fear being dominated by another male, which is viewed as feminine.

2. *Achievement* ("The Big Wheel"): success and status. Two factors operate here. First, dominance through aggression is one way of rising in status in some male social groups. Second, the male who does not succeed often suffers from doubts about his masculinity, and violence is both a way of proving to himself that he is a "real man" as well as a way of venting his anger at having to live up to masculine norms. Poor and oppressed men tend to be more violent than other men. This is not surprising, given that they feel the pressure to be a "big wheel" while at the same time being prevented from many of the avenues for status attainment that privileged men enjoy.

3. *Self-reliance* ("The Sturdy Oak"): the expectation to be tough and unemotional. In a fight, men try their best. If they are beaten, they "take it like a man." Anger, the emotion that usually precedes aggression, is rarely present by itself. Normally, there are other, more vulnerable feelings associated with it (Lynch & Kilmartin, 2013). Much anger would seem to be a reaction to unacknowledged threat or uncomfortable emotional states. In one study, a team of researchers found that "macho" males respond to a crying baby with less compassion and more anger than other males. Thus, conformity to masculine ideologies is empirically associated with the propensity for converting most emotional experiences into anger (Gold, Burke, Prisco, & Willett, 1992).

We can see the conversion of vulnerability into anger in the world of athletics. Most sports fights seem to be triggered by one athlete's perception that another is trying to hurt him. Because fear is considered unmasculine, especially on the field of play, the player's fear becomes anger, and he expresses it through an act of violence. But it is important to note that this expression takes place within a violence-supportive cultural context. Fighting in many sports (especially professional sports) is condoned and sometimes encouraged by the league and the public. Referees do not intervene in professional ice hockey fights as long as only two players are involved. The punishment for fighting is five minutes in the penalty box. (Note that there are very few fights in Olympic hockey, where fighting results in ejection from the game.) In professional sports, the same assaultive behaviors occurring in the game would meet with legal penalties on the street. Yet, players are prosecuted for their behavior only in the most extreme instances, despite the fact that this violence is often captured on videotape and takes place before thousands of witnesses, including police officers.

4. *Aggression* ("Give 'em Hell): physical risk taking and violence. Aggression is one of the primary defining features of traditional masculinity. Hockey players with the strongest levels of endorsement of traditional masculine ideologies are more likely to fight than other players. Moreover, teammates and coaches in youth hockey leagues judge players' competence more on their willingness to engage in violence (especially fist fighting) than on their playing and skating skills (Weinstein, Smith, & Wiesenthal, 1995).

Just as there are probably biological forces that work against violence and those that work toward it, there are psychosocial forces that work in both directions. Physical aggression, then, is a behavior that can be either encouraged or inhibited in various ways. We can look at violent men as men who have experienced encouragement and/or a lack of discouragement for aggressive behavior.

Understanding a behavior is not the same as excusing it, and so this approach should not be construed as absolving men from responsibility for their own behavior. As a man matures, he becomes increasingly capable of providing his own inhibitors and of resisting the encouragement to act aggressively. Violent men choose their behavior, and thus they are accountable for it, perhaps with the rare exception of the psychotic person who cannot discern right from wrong. Still, a look at how gender socialization sets the stage for violence helps us in constructing solutions. Simply put, solutions to male violence involve reducing encouragers and increasing inhibitors. In practice, of course, this is not always easily done.

Violence-Encouraging Factors

1. *Separation:* According to Chodorow (1978), girls' early experiences involve connection and attachment, while boys' experiences involve the construction of a "self in separation." If a person experiences the self as unconnected to others, he or she can tolerate the other's being hurt. Lepowsky (1998) noted that overt anger and physical aggression are less prevalent in societies that have cultural ideologies of gender egalitarianism and low levels of separation between the sexes. Insecure attachment style, which develops in childhood, is associated with a higher likelihood to perceive dangers and threats within relationships, which then leads to anger, hostility, and often, violence (Shaver, Segev, & Mikulincer, 2011).

2. *Objectification:* Male privilege and the masculine mystique encourage men to see other people as objects. It is easier to aggress against someone if he or she is not accorded the status of being a real person. Gender-based violence—rape, domestic violence, and gay bashing—are fueled by this kind of insensitivity, as there is a strong masculine socialization to view women and gay men as less than human.

3. *Externalizing defensive style:* Males are not socialized to "look inside" and think about how they feel. Instead, they are taught to deal with what is "out there" in the world. Therefore, when bad feelings about the self arise, men frequently deal with them in an external way. For example, a man's female partner leaves him, and he feels unlovable and worthless. Experiencing this vulnerability threatens his masculinity, so he projects all of his bad feelings onto the woman and deals with these emotions symbolically by being violent toward her. When women move out of the house or threaten to do so following intimate partner violence, their risk of escalating violence, including murder, increases significantly (Stith, & McMonigle, 2009). Nearly 90 percent of school shootings are preceded by some type of social rejection (Leary, Kowalski, Smith, & Phillips, 2003) and rather than dealing with the pain of being excluded, the killer responded with violence. Men who have difficulty understanding vulnerable emotional states and regulating these experiences show a tendency to react aggressively in response to strong feelings (Cohn, Jakupcak, Hildenbrandt, & Zeichner, 2010).

4. *Overattention to task:* Men are raised to view the world as competitive and hierarchical (Messner, 1995). They are taught to get the job done regardless of the consequences for others. When tasks become more important than people, violence is sometimes a problem-solving measure. Examples of this mindset are not hard to find: the football player who intentionally hurts the other team's star player to put him out of the game, the gangster who has his rival killed to

eliminate the competition, the man who rapes his date to "score," and the armed services commander who allows many men to be killed to secure a strategic position.

A college football player who had caused a shoulder separation in the other team's quarterback remarked, "You don't just hit people to tackle them. You tackle them so they don't get up. I say that respectfully." ("Notre Dame Stuns No. 9 Tennessee," 2004, p. E14). Steve Watkins (1997) describes the culture of violence in a (hopefully atypical) college football team's practice sessions:

> [Two days a week], the players ran until they dropped, did exhausting agility drills, and went into 'the Room', a converted locker area that had been stripped bare except for old wrestling mats and a chicken-wire 'ceiling' hanging down from cables four feet off the floor. Surrounded by their teammates and by a battery of assistant coaches, all screaming, two players at a time were required to fight under the chicken wire until one was clearly beaten and lying on the floor. The winner moved on; the loser fought the next player in line, and the next one after that... until he finally won and could crawl out of the cage.... [A player described the scene:] 'I've seen people with blood completely covering their shirts...You could be standing there puking blood and the coaches would just holler louder, 'Get tough. Get tough.' Everyone was so desperate to win we kicked, slugged, hit each other in the groin, did everything and anything.... You could be out there with your best friend, and you'd be trying to kill him." (pp. 85–86)

5. *Reinforcement:* Simply, behaviors that are rewarded tend to increase in frequency. More than one boy has returned home from beating up another boy to receive the glowing approval of his father. Classroom aggression by boys often meets with loud reprimands from the teacher. All of the action in the room stops, and attention (which has a strong social reward quality) focuses on the boy. Girls' aggression is usually reprimanded more quietly (Maccoby, 1988a, 1988b). In some circles, especially sports and war, highly aggressive men reap social and material rewards. Culturally, male violence maintains patriarchal privilege through dominance and intimidation.

6. *Violent models and vicarious reinforcement:* Males may pattern their behavior after violent male role models, who are not hard to find. Sons of aggressive fathers tend to become aggressive themselves. When they grow up, they tend to produce aggressive sons of their own (Holtzworth-Munroe & Stuart, 1994), and so imitation is a strong factor in this intergenerational pattern of violence. The son of a violent father sees his father re-establish power and control through beating his wife. In the short run, the batterer gets what he wants, and so the boy is vicariously reinforced.

One does not have to be a keen social observer to see that a great many media idols are violent. In the movies, many actors have built lucrative careers portraying extremely violent characters in the "action-adventure" genre where violence is generally portrayed as an effective solution to problems. Theater audiences will cheer for violent actions, identifying with the aggressor. The depiction of male violence in sports, cartoons, Western and war movies, and "cop shows" is a longstanding tradition of the glorification of masculine aggression. Boys who imitate these characters in their play engage in rehearsal for later violence. In an analysis of top-grossing U.S. movies over the course of more than a half century (1950–2006), Bleakley, Jameison, and Romer (2012) found that 89 percent contained violence and that the proportion of characters engaging in violence increased over time.

Nearly 80 percent of video games include violence; 28 percent depict women as sex objects, and 21 percent depict violence directly toward women (Dietz, 1998). Adolescents exposed to sexualized media are more likely to than their less-exposed peers to view women as sex objects, i.e., less than human (Peter & Valkenburg, 2007), an attitude that strongly supports gender-based violence. Males play violent video games at least twice as often as females (Gentile & Anderson, 2003). In contrast to passive forms of entertainment, the aggression in violent video games is participative, to the point of "first person shooter" games where the user can upload a photo of his/her face on to the body of the character wielding the firearm. Frequent use of violent video games among children is associated with increased defiance of teachers, greater risk of being involved in a physical fight or engaging in relational aggression, an increase in aggressive cognitions, and a decrease in positive social behaviors (Gentile, Coyne, & Walsh, 2011).

Television and movie violence is rampant, and male characters are much more likely to perpetrate violence than female ones. By the time an average U.S. child finishes elementary school, he or she will have witnessed 8,000 murders and 100,000 other acts of violence on television (Gentile, 2003). Fifty-seven percent of television shows depict violence; one-third of these average at least nine acts of violence per program (Seppa, 1996). More often than not, characters show no remorse for their violent actions, and rarely do scripts portray the long-term physical, emotional or financial consequences of violence (Murray, 1998). Although 0.2 percent of real world crimes in the United States are murders, 50 percent of television crimes are murders. If real life were as violent as television, it would take only 50 days to exterminate the entire U.S. population (Bartholomew, Dill, Anderson, & Lindsay, 2003).

"Good" characters (attractive role models whom children are likely to imitate) commit 40 percent of violent television acts (Murray, 1998). Simon Moore and Tracey Cockerton (1996) summarize the impact of these types of portrayals: "when the 'bad guys' are punished, the violence used by the 'good guys' to achieve this is often portrayed as justified... rather than inhibiting aggression, these programs serve to facilitate it... the viewer attributes 'good guy' violence as a justified means to an end, and in the same way, their own aggressive actions can be permissible as long as these achieve the same end" (p. 932). Thus justified violence tends to allow a person not to consider the moral dimension of his/her actions. Media violence that is carried out by attractive heroes provides the "best prescription for encouraging imitation of violent scripts and adoption of proviolence beliefs and attitudes" (Bartholomew, Dill, Anderson, & Lindsay, 2003, p. 5).

Television specifically aimed at child audiences are among the worst offenders. Prime time television shows contain an average of five violent acts per hour, but children's programming contains an average of 20 (Strasburger, Wilson, & Jordan, 2014). Many of these shows not only portray violence as an acceptable way to solve problems, and as having no long-term consequences, but they also portray it as being *fun!* Boyatzis, Matillo, and Nesbitt (1995) documented a sevenfold increase in children's violent play immediately after they watched *Mighty Morphin Power Rangers*. In general, mass media depicts violence as masculine and fails to communicate the terrifying and painful aspects of violence, thus rarely encouraging viewers to identify with the suffering of victims or to inhibit their aggression.

Bandura and Walters (1963) first demonstrated that behaviors were more likely to be acquired from a model if one observes that the model is rewarded for the behaviors. In movies and television, aggressive men (who engage in what is perceived as "legitimate" violence) obtain the love of women, the admiration of others, and a feeling of self-righteous satisfaction.

In other early research by Bandura (1973), girls and boys were compared with regard to their willingness to imitate a physically aggressive model. Boys were more likely to do so. However, when the researchers provided rewards for imitating the model, there were no sex differences. It would be reasonable to speculate, then, that the higher incidence of male violence is at least partly the product of the differential reinforcement of physical aggression for males and females. People are also more likely to imitate models who are perceived as being similar to the self (Bandura & Walters, 1963). It is indisputable that there are vastly more violent male models than female ones.

Violent media are not likely to turn an otherwise nonviolent person into a highly aggressive one any more than smoking a single cigarette is going to give someone lung cancer or eating junk food once is going to make someone obese, but as with smoking and unhealthy food, the effects of violent media are indirect and cumulative, and small effects add up in large populations (Gentile & Sesma, 2003). Because violence is a low frequency behavior that has profound effects, even a small reduction of media violence can have important quality of life implications.

Beyond reducing children's exposure to violence, it is also possible to teach them to be critical of the messages they view. A team of researchers (L. Rosenkoetter, S. Rosenkoetter, Osretich, & Acock, 2004) engaged third and fourth grade children in brief lessons to help them understand how television contains distorted messages about violence. They identify low-probability outcomes (such as Wile E. Coyote having an anvil dropped on him from a high cliff and recovering by the next frame in a Road Runner cartoon) and alternative conflict resolution. Over time, girls, but not boys, began to watch less violent television, however the boys' levels of playground and classroom aggression decreased, so that even though they were watching as much violent television as before the intervention, they were less affected by it.

7. *Drug use:* Some drugs have the effect of reducing the inhibition toward violence. The most notable of these is alcohol. Intoxicated people tend to overestimate threats to the self, to choose aggressive solutions when they are frustrated, and to be more sensitive to social pressure to either increase or to decrease aggression (Gustafson, 1986). Drinking is a cultural symbol of masculinity (Lemle & Mishkind, 1989), and male social groups are almost certainly more likely to encourage physical aggression compared with female social groups. However, we must be careful not to imply that alcohol causes violence, as most people who use alcohol are not violent. The relationship between alcohol and violence can be compared to throwing gasoline on a fire. If there is no propensity for aggression, there will be no violence. Rather than causing aggression, alcohol has the effect of exaggerating the pre-existing propensity toward violence.

8. *Social expectations:* We expect males to be aggressive and we communicate these expectations to young males. The phrase, "boys will be boys" captures it well. Sometimes a young boy who is aggressive will elicit the comment, "he's all boy." Classroom teachers expect boys to be rough with one another and intervene in boys' aggressive play less often than they do with girls. Thus, boys' aggression meets with a higher degree of tolerance by the classroom authority figure (Maccoby, 1998).

These social-cognitive links between aggression and masculinity carry over into the evaluation of adult men. Miedzian (1991) argued that political leaders are often willing to engage in war to affirm masculinity and gain the approval of the populace. During the George W. Bush administration, the bodies of United States servicemen killed during the Persian Gulf and Iraq wars were quietly buried with little media coverage or government ceremony. As a result, Americans were able to revel in the "glory" of war without experiencing its human tragedy or grieving for loss.

9. *Low masculine self-esteem:* The man who is unsure of his status or identity is prone toward violence as a compensation for feelings of worthlessness (Toch, 1992). The more powerless a man feels, and the more he equates masculinity with dominance, the more likely he is to make attempts to seize power, thus preserving his masculinity through desperate means. This type of violent man is like the stereotypical schoolyard bully who beats up other kids to cover his insecurity and vent his anger toward those who will not love him. Peer rejection is strongly correlated with bullying (Coie, Dodge, & Kupersmidt, 1990), and James O'Neil (2008) reports that gender role conflict is linked to self-reports of violent behavior as well as a variety of violence-encouraging characteristics, including sexually aggressive behaviors, dating violence, hostility toward women, rape myth acceptance, and tolerance for sexual harassment.

The traditional masculine gender role emphasizes that a man is valued for what he does, not for who he is. Therefore, many men feel that they must prove their masculinity, to themselves and to others, over and over again. The man who is unsuccessful by traditional social standards, the man who succeeds but feels empty inside, and the man who is enraged by a sense that he is not valued, is more likely to be violent. The diminishment of others draws attention away from feelings of a diminished self. The relegation of women, gays, poor men, and men of color to a social underclass serves a precarious sense of defensive masculinity in majority men.

10. *Peer support:* A male peer group usually has powerful influence over its members and not surprisingly, teenagers who associate with delinquent peers are several times more likely than those who do not to engage in criminal behaviors (Huizinga, Weiher, Espiritu, & Esbensen, 2003). Peers can reinforce the ideology that violence is an appropriate way to solve problems, directly encourage a member to fight, and display hateful attitudes that underlie violence. School boys are more than twice as likely as girls to engage in physical fights, three times as likely to carry a weapon to school, and nearly twice as likely to threaten or injure someone with a weapon (Grunbaum, et. al., 2004).

Violence-Inhibiting Factors

Several social forces may have the effect of making violence less likely. It is therefore important to look at these factors in the context of masculine socialization.

1. *Empathy:* Some of the foremost inhibitors of aggression are the abilities to be sensitive to, identify with, and be concerned about the pain of others. Girls are often socialized to think about how other people feel and to be connected to them. For example, playing with dolls is a rehearsal for being attuned to another's needs and caring for a child.

   Culturally, there seems to be less concern for building these violence-inhibiting qualities in boys. First and foremost, boys are socialized away from the emotional life. It would seem to be nearly impossible to understand and experience someone else's emotions without a referent of one's own feelings. The masculine emphasis on competition and task completion does not emphasize the consideration of others. In team sports, players often feel for and protect their teammates, but it is a byproduct of the task of winning, which is always defined as more important than relationships among teammates.

2. *Modeling:* Just as aggressive models can be imitated, control of aggression can also be imitated. It is vital for fathers to model this control for their sons, and many fathers do.

3. *Punishment:* Behaviors that are punished tend to decrease in frequency. Appropriate (non-physical and non-shaming) and consistent punishment of aggression clearly communicates that this type of behavior is unacceptable. In some social systems, this is done well.

4. *Social and Political Systems:* Increasingly, people are speaking out against the institutional violence of war. Governments are paying more attention to holding perpetrators responsible for domestic violence. Boycotts of violent films and

television can be helpful, as can support of women's empowerment and fair treatment for historically marginalized groups.

5. *Therapeutic interventions:* Individual men who have problems with control of violent behaviors can learn how to inhibit explosive urges through a variety of techniques such as anger management and communication skill development (Kivel, 1992). Some men who have histories of violence within their homes have achieved full recoveries (Acker, 2013).

6. *Reduced access to weapons:* Gun control probably does not reduce the frequency of physical aggression, but there is strong evidence that it reduces the amount of physical injury and mortality. In the United States, someone dies from a gunshot wound (many by accident or suicide) once every 17 minutes (derived from Webster & Vernick, 2013). A criminal murders someone with a firearm about once every 45 minutes in the United States (derived from Miller, Azrael, & Hemenway, 2013), and the risk of homicide or suicide is several times higher if a gun is kept in the home (Miller, Lippmann, Azrael, & Hemenway, 2007). The handgun homicide rate fell from 14,150 to 9,390 following the enactment of the "Brady Law" (which imposes background checks and a waiting period for potential gun purchasers) in 1994 ("Pulling the Trigger," 1998). By 2010, when firearm laws had become significantly more lax, the annual firearm homicide rate had risen to 11,780 (Miller, Azrael, & Hemenway, 2013) even though the overall violent crime rate had fallen considerably. Compared with children in comparably developed countries, U.S. children are 13 times more likely to be murdered and 8 times more likely to commit suicide with a firearm (Miller, Azrael, & Hemenway, 2013). Although we cannot attribute a causal link between the law and the reduction of firearm murders, the evidence is compelling. Moreover, there are about 925 nonfatal violent crimes committed with a firearm every day (derived from Miller, Azrael, & Hemenway, 2013).

7. *Education:* Learning about gender and acquiring alternative means for dealing with frustration and conflict can be powerful tools for reducing violence. Increasingly, educational programs about violence cast the behavior in the context of toxic masculinity (Kilmartin & Allison, 2007; Kilmartin & Berkowitz, 2005).

8. *Withdrawal of male peer support:* When violent behavior or the display of its underlying attitudes meet with disapproval from valued male peers, restraint becomes more likely. Canada's White Ribbon Campaign is a good example of men working to end men's violence against women (see Box 12.1).

The elimination of male violence involves the reduction of the needs and the incentives for this kind of behavior, the increase of disincentives, and the provision of alternative ways for dealing with the feelings that precede the aggression (Toch, 1992). Violence is deeply ingrained in traditional masculinity and in many cultures. Therefore, efforts toward violence reduction must cover a broad range of settings, including parenting practices, education, the legal system, politics, economics, and therapeutic settings. Because violence is so much a part of the masculine gender role, the very fabric of masculinity must change if violence is to be reduced.

Box 12.1   The White Ribbon Campaign

For a week in December, 1991, tens of thousands of Canadian men wore small white ribbons pinned to their clothing on the anniversary of the 1990 "Montreal Massacre," when Mark Lepine murdered 14 women at L'ecole Polytechnique in Montreal, Canada before committing suicide. The White Ribbon Campaign was an effort to get men to show their support for ending men's violence against women. It was the first large-scale initiative ever developed by men to speak out on a subject usually considered to be a "women's issue."

Supporters of the campaign distributed the ribbons at schools, churches, shops, and places of employment. The Prime Minister, several celebrities, and some corporate heads were among the men who participated. Canadian men of conscience also raised money for rape crisis centers, domestic violence shelters, batterer treatment programs, and other organizations that deal directly with the consequences of men's violence against women. As the campaign became highly visible, men's violence against women became a subject for publicity, discussion, and debate. Many men across Canada were talking seriously about the problem for the first time.

One of the goals of the campaign organizers was to break the silence on the issue.

In that regard, the effort was an unqualified success. A larger goal is to build a permanent national men's antiviolence organization. That effort is now well underway.

I brought the White Ribbon Campaign to my campus in 1994 (Kilmartin, 1996). Detractors of the campaign voiced the opinion that it is a "feel-good" effort fueled by men's guilt, and that it has no positive effect. We were able to answer these critics with two pieces of evidence. First, we raised a significant amount of money for the local rape crisis and domestic violence agencies, a very tangible contribution. Second, we recognized the contention that the White Ribbon Campaign is ineffective as an *empirical* question (one that can only be answered by collecting data). Our research indicated that students' awareness of the problem of men's violence against women and their attitude toward the problem both improved as a direct result of the campaign (Kilmartin, Chirico, & Leemann, 1997).

The White Ribbon Campaign is significant in that it is a grass roots movement by men in the direction of dealing with a central men's social issue. It provides a stimulus for men to begin to understand the impact of gender socialization and sexist culture on their lives (Sluser & Kaufman, 1992).

INTIMATE PARTNER VIOLENCE

It is sad to say that perhaps the most frequent site of men's violence is in the home. Finding the true prevalence of intimate partner violence (IPV) is difficult because as many as 75 percent of assaults by partners or former partners are never reported to police (Tjaden & Thonnes, 2000). Male partners victimize more than 20 percent of women with physical violence and nearly 8 percent with sexual violence in the United States (Arias & Ikeda, 2006). For people in dating relationships, the rates of violence may be even higher (Straus, 2004). Male partners and ex-partners murder more than 1,000 women every year in the United States. These women are one-third of all female murder victims. Males murdered by female partners are about three percent of all male murder victims (United States Department of Justice, 2008).

This rate of about three murders per day of female partners or ex-partners is equivalent to a Virginia Tech massacre every 11 days or a set of September 11, 2001 attacks every 1000 days, and yet victims of this violence rarely get much attention from the public, perhaps reflecting the belief that they are partly responsible for their own victimization, and that therefore their deaths do not raise concern about our own safety the way that random violence does (Kilmartin, 2010). IPV is a serious problem in most parts of the world (McCue, 2008).

Somewhat surprisingly, research indicates that women use physical violence against their partners as much or even more than men (Straus, 2004; Archer, 2000). However, for many theorists, this finding does not imply gender symmetry in violence in the home. Researchers usually used the *Conflict Tactics Scale* (CTS; Strauss, 1990) in demonstrating men's and women's similar levels of aggression. The CTS counts acts of violence but does not measure the context or the meaning of each act (Kimmel, 2001). To illustrate, Person A threatens to hit Person B in the head with a baseball bat and rushes toward Person B, who tries to push Person A away as Person A strikes Person B with the bat and causes a severe brain injury which leads to death. Under the CTS, each person's aggression counts as one. Michael Kimmel (2001) uses an even more striking example, "if she punches him to get him to stop beating the children, or pushes him away after he has sexually assaulted her, it would count one for her, none for him" (p. 9). Kimmel goes on to say that ignoring the context of injury is like "observing that death rates have soared for males between 19 and 30 without observing that a country has declared war" (p. 9).

Several researchers have documented gender asymmetry in IPV. Women's aggression against men usually results in less fear and much less physical damage than men's domestic violence (Kilmartin & Allison, 2007). Therefore, although female domestic physical aggression is common and should not be ignored, it is male aggression that engenders the highest levels of terror and danger. More than 40 percent of female IPV victims sustain injuries (Arias & Ikeda, 2006).

Men's violence in the home has a long history. For many years, the exercise of the man's authority over his family via physical abuse was accepted and tolerated (Landes, Squyres, & Quiram, 1997). The patriarchal tradition of woman as property allowed the man to do whatever he wanted with his wife. In 1996, after a man shot and killed his wife when he found her in bed with another man, a Maryland judge apologized for sentencing him to time in jail because of mandatory sentencing guidelines (Childress, 1996). His remarks gave the clear impression that this man's homicidal behavior was natural and acceptable.

Research into the characteristics of male batterers reveals that, in general, they tend to be overconforming to the traditional masculine role and the culture of violence (Gondolf, 1988). They have a high need for power and control and tend to blame their partners for their own violent behavior (Arias & Ikeda, 2006). Thus, they often think that they beat their wives, not because they have trouble controlling their tempers or feel threatened by their partners' independence, but because their wives behaved wrongly or "don't know how to listen." The blaming of the victim allows the man to abdicate responsibility for and downplay the impact of his violent behavior. When a man perceives the source of his problems to be outside of himself, he sees no reason to explore his inner world or change his behavior. Male batterers also tend to be insecure and have difficulty regulating negative emotional states. As Donald Dutton (2011) describes it, their anger is born of fear. Nearly half of the time when a man murders his female partner, she is either leaving him or threatening to do so (Dutton & Golant, 1995). These data support the hypothesis that violence is a compensatory measure for feelings of masculine failure.

One of the most striking (but not surprising) risk markers of male domestic violence is the presence of a physically aggressive father in the family of origin. Perpetrators are often survivors of some form of childhood abuse and usually witnessed violence within their parents' relationship (Dodge, 2011). Sugarman & Hotaling (1989) described the following childhood experience of the typical male batterer and its connection to dominance: "Essentially, the individual not only witnessed his father physically aggress against his mother and be reinforced for this behavior (the individual's mother often gave in to the father's demands), but his own violent behavior goes unpunished and is reinforced by his partner's surrendering to his will" (p. 1035).

We should be careful not to forget that domestic violence takes place in a cultural context that supports it. Former football star O. J. Simpson, who pleaded "no contest" to a charge of assaulting his wife, was directed to attend counseling sessions (which he did over the telephone), pay a small fine, and perform some community service. Later, he was charged in the double murder of his wife and a companion. (He was acquitted in a criminal trial but was found to be responsible for these two deaths in civil court.) Simpson's status as a masculine, powerful former athlete was probably a factor in the leniency of the original sentence and the failure of the legal system to take an interest in rehabilitating him. Football is the quintessential hypermasculine and violent pursuit, and so it is not surprising that a disproportionate number of football players (Brubaker, 1994) and other contact sport athletes are involved in domestic violence and rape (Crosset, Benedict, & McDonald, 1998). We should be careful not to characterize all of these athletes as assaultive, as most are not. At the same time, participation in contact sports is associated with the risk of physical violence off the field.

In summary, male batterers tend to be angry, hypermasculine, and disenfranchised men who often see violence as natural and normal. They are unable to deal with vulnerable emotions and so they convert these feelings into anger. They also have learned that engaging in violence gets them what they want: dominance, power, and control. And their behavior takes place within a patriarchal social-cultural context that condones and even encourages physical aggression.

Toward Solutions

The reduction of such a widespread problem as domestic violence requires a comprehensive, coordinated effort. The city of Duluth, Minnesota launched such a program in 1982. It involved the establishment of a women's shelter, stricter criminal penalties for spousal assault, and mandatory participation in rehabilitation programs for offenders. Police officers who have probable cause that an assault has taken place are required to

A poster from the "Strength Campaign" of *Men Can Stop Rape*, a social activist organization in Washington D.C. Public information efforts such as this one are attempts to encourage men's respect for women. Additional information about this organization can be found at http://www.mencanstoprape.org.

Photo: © 2006 Men Can Stop Rape, Inc. Photography by Lotte Hansen make an arrest, effectively redefining IPV as a crime against the community, not just against the victim (Hoffman, 1992). Seminars, trainings, and resource materials are offered for prosecutors, human service providers, community leaders, and educators (Duluth Domestic Abuse Intervention Project, undated).

The Duluth project has met with some degree of success, particularly in the city-wide reduction of domestic homicide, and it has been used as a model in many other cities. At the same time, recidivism in offenders is high (about 40 percent), and even the director of the program doubts that it has a strong deterrent effect on men as they consider engaging in violence (Hoffman, 1992). Holtzworth-Munroe and Stuart (1994) note that a substantial proportion of battering men have antisocial personality tendencies or full blown sociopathic disorders. These men do not respond well to the kind of self-control treatment approaches that batterer programs often use. Unfortunately, many do not respond at all to any psychological interventions, and these men must be controlled through the legal system.

Many male batterers, however, are treatable, and a number of strategies for intervention have emerged in recent years. Among these are social skills training, therapy groups, and educational programs. The goals of these programs are to sensitize men to the personal and interpersonal consequences of their violence, to help them take responsibility for their violence, and to teach them ways of changing their thinking, emotional responses, and behaviors in conflict situations. In one study, researchers found that the combination of more severe criminal penalties and an emphasis on rehabilitation resulted in a 10 percent increase in arrests and a 50 percent decrease in recidivism (Gover, MacDonald, & Alpert, 2003).

As with any violence, the best solutions are in prevention. Lower levels of intimate partner violence result from greater gender equality, lower poverty and overcrowding, and better education. Public policy changes can influence social norms, and workplaces are good entry points for prevention efforts (Parks, Cohen, & Kravitz-Wirtz, 2007).

RAPE AND OTHER SEXUAL ASSAULT

Rape is sexual penetration without consent. Sexual assault is a broader term; it includes any form of nonconsensual touching of areas of the body that are associated with sexuality (Kilmartin & Allison, 2007). These violent crimes are alarmingly common. In large scale studies, researchers have found that rapists have victimized or attempted to victimize at least one of every six United States females at some point in their lives (Seidman & Pokorak, 2011). In a large study of female Navy recruits, the reported rape or attempted rape rate was 39 percent. Thirteen percent of male recruits admitted to perpetrating sexual violence (Stander, Merrill, Thomsen, Crouch, & Milner, 2008). One out of 12 college men has reported that he has sexually penetrated a woman against her will on at least one occasion (Koss, Gidycz, & Wisniewski, 1987). Sexual assault perpetrators also victimize other males at a much higher rate than is generally believed (see the section below on male victims and survivors). Very few rapists are ever incarcerated for their crimes (Lisak & Miller, 2002).

The stereotypical rapist is the evil stranger who attacks in public, but in fact, in more than three-quarters of rapes, the victim knows the attacker (Vobejda, 1995). These acquaintance rapes have been the subject of increased research and publicity within the past 30 years. This crime of violence takes place in incredibly high frequency on college and university campuses. And yet many institutions of higher learning have been slow to respond to the problem, perhaps for fear that acknowledging it would bring adverse publicity. In 2014, Missouri Senator Claire McCaskill surveyed colleges and universities to evaluate their policies and responses and found that 22 percent allowed athletic departments to oversee cases involving athletes, a clear conflict of interest. More than 40 percent of schools had not conducted a single investigation within the past five years. About 20 percent provided no training for faculty and staff, and more than 30 percent provided no training for students. Only 16 percent conducted surveys to address the prevalence of sexual assault on their campuses, an essential measure, as sexual assault is a notoriously underreported crime (Anderson, 2014).

One common misconception about rape is that it is primarily motivated by sexual arousal. For some people, the image of the rapist is one of a lusty, sex-starved man whose frustrated urges get the best of him. However, most experts believe that the primary motivation for rape is not sexual, but aggressive (Burt, 1991). It is the use of sex in the expression of power, control, anger, and hate. Groth (1979) referred to rape as a "pseudosexual act." In describing the relationship between rape and sex, we might ask the following question: If I hit you over the head with a frying pan, would you call it cooking? Across several different cultures, men who engaged in sexual violence had more consensual sexual partners than men who did not (Heilman, Hebert, & Paul-Gera, 2014). An estimated 91 percent of rapes are committed by serial offenders and are premeditated (Lisak & Miller, 2002). These findings undercut the myth of the rapist as sexually deprived and/or as overcome by his lust in the heat of the moment.

Rape and Masculinity

Sexual aggression is part and parcel of the socialization of males. Lisak (1997) cites fourteen studies demonstrating that hypermasculine characteristics are strongly connected to sexualized violence. In the search for an understanding of why men rape, it is useful to identify the rape-supporting cultural messages that boys receive as they grow up:

1. *Femiphobia and misogyny*: Males are raised to be separate from women and the culturally-defined feminine within themselves. The result is a fear of femininity. One way of dealing with this fear is to overpower and control the woman. From this perspective, derogatory nicknames, misogynist jokes, and other behaviors that disrespect women create the social atmosphere that encourages rape. One group of researchers (Sadler, Booth, Cook, & Doebbeling, 2003) found that, when ranking military officers allowed others to make demeaning comments or gestures in servicewomen's presence, women under their command were at a 600 percent increased risk of rape than when officers did not tolerate these kinds of behaviors.

   Many feminist theorists believe that rape is a symptom of economic and political systems in which women have been rendered relatively powerless by men (Kilmartin & Allison, 2007). Mainstream United States culture tradition-ally encourages men to dominate women, and victimizing a woman with some-thing as emotional and intimate as sexuality is extreme domination. Sexual aggression in men is related to stereotyped views of gender roles, among them the belief that women and men are sexual adversaries, and that therefore a het-erosexual date is a kind of competition in which the male attempts to obtain sex and the female attempts to obtain affection and/or persuade the male to spend money on her (Knight & Sims-Knight, 2013). This belief is an extreme distortion of what is supposedly a pleasurable event in which two people enjoy each other's company, but cultural ideologies like "the battle of the sexes" and linguistic constructions like "the opposite sex," both of which portray men and women as enemies, encourage this kind of distortion.

2. *Emotional denial*: As with any violence, rape is a failure of empathy. The so-cialized inability to be sensitive to one's own feelings makes it difficult to be sensitive to the feelings of another person. Lisak (1997) summarizes the con-nection: "it can be argued that the very fact of being disconnected from emo-tional experience dramatically increases the likelihood that someone would be able and willing to exploit and abuse the sexuality of another person. Separated from its emotional associations, unlinked from its relationship to human con-nection, sexuality is more likely to be experienced as simply another physical sensation... the 'other' can be experienced as pure object" (p. 163).

3. *Two exceptions of emotional control*: Although men are encouraged to deny and control emotions, the expression of two feelings, anger and lust, is socially condoned. Interestingly, cultural ideologies consider these two emotions to be *completely out of the man's control*. It is not unusual to hear that a "man's gotta do what a man's gotta do" when he gets angry, that a "man's gotta have it" sexu-ally, and that an erect penis "has no conscience."

   With anger and lust being the only two culturally permissible emotions, it is not surprising that they can become combined with each other. In fact, probably the most frequently used slang term for sexual intercourse (fuck) is also one of the most frequently used terms for victimization. Violence is sexualized time and time again in movies, television, Internet pornography, and other media.

   Western culture encourages men to *act out* emotion rather than deal with it in other ways (Lynch & Kilmartin, 2013). This may be a partial explanation for the striking difference between East and West in the incidence of rape and other violent crimes (Sue, Bernier, Durran, Feinberg, Pedersen, Smith, & Vasquez-Nattall, 1982).

4. *Rape myths*: Some men believe that women secretly want to be raped, say "no" when they mean "yes," and "ask for it" by dressing or acting provocatively, or by putting themselves in risky situations (Burt, 1980; Johnson, 1994). Male undergraduates who viewed films depicting rape myths were more likely to subscribe to the myths, less likely to identify with victims, and less likely to agree that rapists deserves punishment (Briere & Malamuth, 1983; Koss, Leon-ard, Beezley, & Oros, 1985). One need not see an actual rape depicted in media

to accept rape myths. The sexual domination of the woman, followed by her giving in and becoming aroused, conveys the same message in milder form. A typical scene is a leading man who forcefully kisses an unwilling woman, who then "melts into his arms" and falls in love with him. Many romantic comedies portray erotic love as an outcome of conflict between a man and a woman. In these films, the man's persistence often pays off, whereas in real life, it is more likely to result in a no-contact order. There is some evidence that certain kinds of pornography may also encourage violence toward women. See the final chapter on contemporary topics in masculinity for a discussion of the effects of pornography.

5. *Performance and quantification over experience:* Cultural masculinity emphasizes that a man's worth is measured by deeds and results, not by his emotional satisfaction or feelings about himself. We also tend to judge men in quantifiable terms ("more is better"). In the sexual arena, this attitude is played out by the encouragement of men to have intercourse with as many women as possible. "Stud" and "Playboy" are complimentary terms, and the "macho mentality" values the man who "goes after what he wants" and "won't take no for an answer."

6. *Poor sexual communication:* One of the questions that Biernbaum and Weinberg (1991) ask men in their campus rape prevention workshops is, "How do you know when your friend wants to kiss on a date?" Most men respond, "it's in her eyes… she leans toward me and I lean toward her… it's in the air… I just know… body language" (p. 22). When asked, "Have you ever thought that she wanted to kiss you and been wrong?" most men acknowledge that they have. In most jurisdictions, kissing someone against his or her will is a misdemeanor sexual assault, and so this normative mistake is in fact a crime. In response to Biernbaum and Weinberg's question, few men say, "I ask her," or "I tell her I would like to kiss her and see how she responds."

But we should not be fooled into thinking that most rapes are the result of mere misunderstandings between two people. The vast majority of rapes are the result of intentional victimization on the part of male perpetrators, who frequently isolate women and sometimes incapacitate them with alcohol or other drugs as part of planned predatory behavior. In an interview with David Lisak (2005), a rapist describes a methodical sequence in which he identifies a female college student as a potential victim, obtains her trust ("grooms" her, much as a child sex offender does), reduces her resistance with alcohol, isolates her, and then physically overpowers her. He refers to her as a "target" and as "prey" that he has "staked out." This rapist was never charged with any crime.

Interestingly and disturbingly, relative to their gender-egalitarian counterparts, both college males and females who hold traditional gender ideologies tend to minimize the impact of rape on a victim who is described as a current life partner or even an ex-partner (Ben-David & Schneider, 2005). Benevolent sexist attitudes are related to lower sympathy for acquaintance rape victims in general and a tendency to assign blame for the attack to the victim rather than the offender (Abrams, Viki, Masser, & Bohner, 2003).

Rape requires three conditions: a social-cultural context that supports it, individual pathology, and a decision to engage in the harmful act (Kilmartin, 2014). We turn now to the second set of influences in a discussion of the differences between rapists and healthy men.

Rapist Characteristics

Rape-encouraging attitudes and socialization experiences are rather common and pervasive, yet it is clear that the vast majority of men do not rape. Recent research and theory has resulted in descriptions of the psychology of the rapist. Although these violent men are not all alike, some typical characteristics emerge among them.

Groth (1979) described three basic patterns in incarcerated rapists. The most common one was *power rape,* in which the major motive of the rapist seems to be to conquer and control the victim. The power rapist's main goal is to possess the person sexually. Sexual penetration is taken as evidence of conquest, and the rapist uses whatever force he deems necessary to subdue the victim.

The power rapist uses sex as a way of "compensating for underlying feelings of inadequacy and serves to express issues of mastery, strength, control, identity, and capability" (Groth, 1979, p. 25). In other words, the rapist makes a desperate attempt to demonstrating his masculinity. He is desperate because his underlying feelings are so painful, and because he has no emotional resources to use in dealing with his pain. About 55 percent of convicted offenders are judged to be primarily motivated by power.

The second most common pattern is the *anger rape,* which comprises about 40 percent of imprisoned rapists. The anger rapist's primary objective is to harm the victim. He typically uses more force than he needs to overpower the victim and includes verbal abuse in his attack, as his goal is to make the victim feel as badly as possible, both psychologically and physically. Typically, the anger rapist feels that he has been wronged and hurt by women and rape is his revenge. Any woman is a symbol of the source of his pain.

Like the power rapist, the anger rapist is not usually sexually aroused at the time of the attack, nor does he derive much sexual pleasure from his crime. Often, he does not attain an erection without masturbating or forcing the victim to stimulate him. Many anger rapists do not have orgasms during the assault, and some even have trouble remembering whether or not they ejaculated.

The least frequent pattern is the *sadistic rape,* in which power and violence are eroticized. For this type (about 5 percent of incarcerated rapists), sexual gratification comes from hurting another person. The sexual motive is more connected to the assault for the sadistic rapist, unlike the other two patterns. A similarity to the other types is underlying feelings of masculine inadequacy.

Groth's study described men who had been arrested, convicted, and imprisoned as a result of having raped. However, these are a very small minority of rapists, estimated at around only one percent of actual offenders (Lisak & Miller, 2002). It remained to be seen whether or not unincarcerated rapists are different from convicted rapists in significant ways.

Lisak and Roth (1988) compared questionnaire responses of college men who reported having engaged in sexually aggressive behavior with those who reported that they had not. Sexually aggressive men were more likely to perceive themselves as having been hurt, betrayed, or dominated by women. They were highly sensitive to being teased or manipulated by women, and they often experienced angry feelings in connection with interactions with women. The conclusion of the researchers was that the motivations for college men's sexual aggression are similar to those of incarcerated rapists.

As we paint the picture of the rapist as an insecure, hypermasculine man, it seems important to search for the origins of masculine inadequacy in the sexual aggressor. Lisak (1991) collected data from psychological measures and conducted in-depth interviews with fifteen men who admitted to acquaintance rape and fifteen matched control subjects in a college population. Although this was neither a large nor a representative sample of the population of men, this study provides some important clues to the origins of rape within the individual.

Lisak's findings confirm what we have already described. Rapists scored significantly higher than other men on "standardized measures of hostility toward women, underlying anger motivation, dominance as a motive for sexual interactions, underlying power motivation, and on two indices of hypermasculinity" (Lisak, 1991, p. 248). Hypermasculinity has been found to be related to callous sexual attitudes and misogyny in other studies (Mosher & Tomkins, 1988).

In Lisak's (1991) interviews, one striking finding was that the rapists invariably expressed bitter feelings and clear disappointments toward their fathers, whom they described as both emotionally and physically distant. Some rapists reported having suffered significant physical violence at the hands of their fathers. Although the other participants in the study also reported having wanted to be closer to their fathers, the underlying bitter feelings were not there, and they made positive statements about their fathers much more often than the rapists. Feelings about mothers were much more variable. These men, who have not been accepted by the most important male figure in their lives, are most likely to lash out against women (although it is important to say that all men with bitter feelings toward their fathers are not rapists).

In a five-nation study sponsored by the international activist organization *Promundo*, Heilman, Hebert, and Paul-Gera (2014) reported that the biggest risk factors for perpetration of sexual violence were the childhood experiences of witnessing violence against their mothers and/or being abused or neglected themselves. Attitudes of male privilege or entitlement also emerged as a correlate, and one marker of these attitudes is the willingness to purchase sexual access. Men who had hired prostitutes were much more likely than men who had not to have engaged in sexual violence.

Without an internal sense of positive masculinity, these men are more likely to be drawn into and contribute to hypermasculine peer groups that are aggressive and misogynist (Koss & Dinero, 1988). They use these groups to protect themselves from their insecurities by identifying with the group and having women as an underclass. The street gang is the most common of these negative male peer cultures. It has also been argued that some fraternities (Sanday, 1996, 2007), and athletic teams, especially in contact sports like football, hockey, and basketball (Crosset, 2000) serve this function on college campuses. The sense of some college athletes that they are somehow privileged contributes to the atmosphere of victimization, and male college athletes tend to have more traditional gender role attitudes than non-athletes (Houseworth, Peplow, & Thirer, 1989). The most extreme example of sexual violence in negative cultures of masculinity is the gang rape. Fraternities and athletic teams are disproportionately involved in these crimes (O'Sullivan, 1991).

Boswell and Spade (1996) carried out an interesting study of fraternity male peer culture. Based on surveys of campus women's awareness of sexual assault incidents, they identified four fraternities that were perceived as relatively safe places for women (low-risk fraternities) and four that were perceived as relatively dangerous (high-risk fraternities). Then, they observed fraternity parties and described differences between these two types of organizations.

Typical parties in low-risk fraternities tended to have a friendly atmosphere and a good deal of social interaction between men and women. Music was not so loud as to make it difficult to have conversation. There was very little cursing, yelling, or jokes and comments that degrade women, and bathrooms provided for women were clean and well-supplied. In contrast, parties at high-risk houses were marked by separation of the sexes, heavier drinking, louder music, and fewer conversations between men and women. There was more crude behavior and open hostility toward women, and women's bathrooms were filthy, sometimes with vomit in the sinks and clogged toilets. Men at high-risk houses gathered on porches the morning after parties and shouted derogatory comments to women who were walking home after spending the night there. In contrast to low-risk fraternities, men in high-risk fraternities had few long-term relationships with women, and in fact, the fraternity brothers actively discouraged such relationships. In some fraternities, sexual coercion is viewed as a contest or game rather than a crime, and members of the fraternities collude to facilitate sexual assault as well as to hide it if there is any legal or official investigation (Martin & Hummer, 2009).

The findings from this study support the conclusions of anthropological studies by Sanday (1981; 1996) and Lepowsky (1998) that link violence against women to the social separation of the sexes and the lack of gender-egalitarian attitudes. One group of scholars summarized the cultural supports for rape: "Rape is associated with male fraternal interest groups, warfare, gender antagonism, constraints on women's sexuality, and generally low status of women." (Lalumiere, Harris, Quinsey, & Rice, 2005, p.13).

In the high-risk fraternities, men denigrated women and kept them at a distance except for sex. The power distinction between the sexes was very evident, with clear messages that women are subordinate to men, who are in control of the situation, and that respectful relationships with women are a threat to the fraternal brotherhood. Martin and Hummer (2009) conclude that many fraternities "create a sociocultural context in which the use of coercion in sexual relations with women is normative and in which the mechanisms to keep this pattern of behavior in check are minimal at best and absent at worst" (pp. 471–472).

Thus, sexual violence in the context of hypermasculinity is related to patriarchal culture. Whiting (1965) was one of the first to argue that the internal sense of masculinity is only necessary when the culture demands that men be different, more important, and more powerful than women. When the man feels powerless, he denigrates and attacks women in an attempt to affirm this cultural definition of masculinity, an act which Whiting labeled "masculine protest." Researchers have found a link between masculine gender role stress and sexual aggression (O'Neil, 2008).

Thus viewed, rape is an extreme compensatory reaction to the gender role strain created by patriarchy. There would be no motivation to rape if men did not feel the need to prove themselves superior by virtue of being men. Sanday (1981) reports that rape is virtually nonexistent in 44 nonpatriarchal societies, and that only 18 percent of cultures are "rape prone." She includes mainstream U.S. culture in the latter category.

Toward Solutions

The reduction of rape can involve a variety of strategies, including those that thwart the attempted rapist, prevent the rapist from committing repeated crimes, prevent potential rapists from ever committing the crime, and change the rape-supportive aspects of the culture. These varied interventions can involve legal, educational, economic, family, community, therapeutic, and political systems. To describe all of the possibilities would require several volumes, but we can outline some ideas here.

Preventing a rapist from committing repeated crimes is a critical component of rape prevention, as perpetrators tend to commit multiple rapes as well as other crimes, and only an estimated one percent are ever incarcerated (Lisak & Miller, 2002). These efforts include vigorous legal enforcement and rehabilitative interventions such as facilitating the rapist's acceptance of responsibility for the crime, building the criminal's empathy for the victim, developing social skills, and decreasing sexual arousal to rape. Attempts to thwart the potential rapist have historically taken the forms of rendering environments less conducive to rape, and of educating potential victims. Lighting of dark areas, police patrols, and teaching self-defense skills are strategies in this area. On some college campuses, risk reduction strategies such as escort services, danger avoidance education (i.e., don't walk alone at night, make sure windows and doors are locked, learn what kinds of men are likely to assault), alcohol rules, and fraternity policies are fairly common.

Police and prosecutor education is critical for rapes that are reported to the legal system. Untrained police investigators sometimes approach complainants with skepticism about their truthfulness, especially when the victim had been drinking, had engaged in consensual behaviors such as kissing, had no physical injuries, and was not threatened with a weapon. They tend to believe that sexual motives are paramount in rape, and that therefore attractive, charming, socially-skilled men would never commit this crime. Educating investigators about rape myths, the psychology of the victim, and more sensitive approaches to questioning can be helpful in improving the quality of police work in this area (Kilmartin, 2007). Prosecutors also need to educate jurors about these issues. Legal advances are also helpful. These include "rape shield" laws that prevent defense attorneys from bringing up irrelevant topics like the victim's past sexual behavior, and "affirmative consent" laws that define consent as the presence of "yes" rather than the absence of "no" (Caringella, 2009).

When these kinds of strategies are the sole interventions, there are implicit assumptions that men will rape if given the chance, that there is little we can do to stop them short of incarceration, and that therefore we must deal with the problem largely by helping potential victims to be prepared and making environments less conducive to rape opportunity. Carole Corcoran (1992) described these approaches as "victim control" strategies. She argued that they subtly place the responsibility for rape prevention on women. Alan Berkowitz (Kilmartin & Berkowitz, 2005) strongly suggested that the term *risk reduction* should be used when educating women, and that the term *rape prevention* be reserved for male audiences, to give the clear message that women are not responsible for preventing rape.

Although there is no argument that safety measures can and should be implemented, they are not enough. Broader rape prevention efforts involve changing the behaviors and underlying motivations of men. Rape prevention services for men are a relatively recent development.

The alarming estimates of the incidence of acquaintance rape at colleges and universities have stimulated a number of programmatic efforts to decrease violence against women. Services designed specifically for men include rape awareness programs (Brod, 2005), experiential workshops (Allison, 2005; Foubert, 2005; Heppner, 2005), peer education and counseling (Allison, 2005), and specialized workshops for fraternity members (Mahlstedt, 1998; Kilmartin & Ring, 1991) or athletes (Katz, 1995; Stevens, 2005). The most effective efforts include convincing people to challenge the gender-based norms that encourage sexual violence and to build the skills necessary to intervene as bystanders in dangerous situations (Gidycz, Orchowski, & Edwards, 2013).

Some programs are "one-shot" or annual events, others are ongoing, comprehensive, institutional efforts. The goals of all of these rape prevention efforts include: sensitizing men to the negative consequences of sexual violence for the perpetrator, facilitating empathy for victims of sexual assault, educating men about the rape-encouraging aspects of socialization, culture, and patriarchy, and teaching them to intervene as bystanders. Parrot (1991) first pointed out that a major goal is to effect an understanding of the continuum of sexual violence against women. Sexist behavior, objectification, and exploitation of women have the effect of desensitizing men to the seriousness and deep pain of sexual assault.

Recent efforts in sexual assault prevention have emphasized the role of male peer support (Kilmartin & Berkowitz, 2005; DeKeseredy & Schwartz, 2013, Foubert, 2005). When men remain silent or "go along with the joke" when their peers make derogatory comments about women, they contribute to a social atmosphere that makes sexual assault possible. When men learn to confront other men's sexist behavior, they can be effective in undermining the peer cultural support of sexual assault. Doing so requires a good deal of courage and a willingness to be independent enough to resist the cultural pressure to express indifference or hatred toward women when in an all-male group. Both courage and independence are traditionally masculine attributes, yet traditionally masculine men show extreme levels of conformity to sexist behavior.

Most men underestimate the degree to which their peers are made uncomfortable by other men's sexism and bragging about sexual conquest (Kilmartin, Conway, Friedberg, McQuoid, Tschan, & Norbet, 1999; Kilmartin, Smith, Green, Kuchler, Heinzen, & Kolar, 2008). Correcting the misconception that men are not bothered by sexist behavior in all-male groups may be useful in helping men to break the silence, as pressure for group conformity is sharply reduced when a group member perceives that he or she has an ally within the group (Asch, 1965) and men show a greater willingness to confront perpetrators when they believe that they share their concerns with other men (Berkowitz, 2010). As many as 75 percent of college men report discomfort with male peers' sexist behavior (Berkowitz, 1994). Therefore, the attitude that rape prevention strategists wish to impart already exists in large part, and so increasing the positive influence of this attitude is a matter of leadership (Berkowitz, 1997), another traditionally masculine attribute. Courageous, independent, risk-taking college men must take the lead by speaking out against their peers' sexist behavior.

In the United States military, where sexual assault is more rampant than in the mainstream society, comprehensive solutions are being implemented. At Naval Station Great Lakes, sexual assault decreased by 60 percent over a two year period (Shanker, 2013) and training of the top leaders has proven to be an essential component of the solution (Stern, 2014), as commanders have great power to influence the climate of respect within their units (Sadler, et. al., 2003).

Michael Kimmel (2008) tells a story of a successful intervention at an elite private college in the Northeastern United States, where members of one fraternity verbally harassed women as they walked home from fraternity houses on Saturday or Sunday mornings, presumably having spent the night and had sex (widely referred to as the "walk of shame"). In meetings with Kimmel, several fraternity members privately expressed disapproval and even disgust with the practice. Kimmel suggested that they look around at the group and seek out a fellow member who also seemed uncomfortable to talk with privately. Members soon discovered that there was a significant disapproval of the practice and called a meeting of the fraternity, where they agreed to end the ritual.

John Foubert (2011) and his colleagues deliver a peer education effort called "The Men's Program," which consists of four young male presenters educating college men about the extent of the problem of sexual assault and its effects on victims, and helping audience members to learn how they can help someone who survives an assault (they have also recently introduced a risk reduction program for women). The Mentors in Violence Prevention (MVP) program employs a similar bystander-to-ally approach. Gail Stern and Christian Murphy's interactive play, *Sex Signals*, has had remarkable success in educating audiences around the world, and the organization Men Can Stop Rape coordinates comprehensive efforts in prevention education. The international organization Promundo is reducing gender-based violence by educating men and getting them more connected with their families.

It is obvious that the rapist causes a great deal of pain for the victim. The awareness that the rapist is also in pain needs to be addressed as well. In fact, these violent men nearly all have histories of physical and/or sexual victimization as children (Knight & Sims-Knight, 2013). If the pain can be prevented, or the potential rapist can learn to deal with his pain in a different way, then sexual assault should decrease. In addition to better efforts to hold offenders responsible for their behavior, efforts to help men understand themselves as gendered beings, to facilitate the improvement of positive relationship skills, and to support attempts for men to change the destructive aspects of masculinity are positive steps. We also very much need to improve the efforts of the legal system to hold violent men accountable for their behavior. Since most rapes are by serial offenders, effective intervention can constitute effective prevention through lowering the likelihood that the offender will have further access to potential victims. There is no contradiction between understanding what might influence a person to be violent and at the same time holding the person responsible for the decision to engage in violence. The overall efforts of men's gender awareness and change should contribute to dealing with the specific problem of sexual assault and the general problem of men's violence.

In the big picture, sexual assault against women and girls is a toxic product of societal sexism, which is in turn a product of inequality between the sexes (Kilmartin, 2014). Therefore it will end when women's status is equal to men, and in fact, there is evidence that increases in gender equality within a culture are accompanied by decreases in sexual violence (Yodanis, 2004).

MALE VICTIMS AND SURVIVORS

The lopsided sex ratio of male to female violence and the incredible frequencies of domestic violence and rape can obscure the fact that males are victims of violence in significant numbers. Males are four times more likely than females to be murdered in the United States (U.S. Dept. of Justice, OJP, 2008). Homicide is the second leading cause of death for males aged 15 to 24 and the third leading cause for males aged 25 to 34 (Anderson & Smith, 2005). Males comprise 75 percent of all gunshot murder victims in the United States, an average of one every hour (derived from Miller, Azrael, & Hemenway, 2013). Males' greater willingness to fight, use firearms, and engage in criminal activity all contribute to a higher risk of being injured or killed by violent means (Courtenay, 2011).

Males comprise about 93 percent of the U.S. jail and prison population of 2.5 million people (Sabol & Coture, 2008), and prison violence is rampant (Toch, 1998). These institutions receive reports of sexual abuse for one out of every twenty inmates, and as is the case with other sexual assault, this statistic is widely considered to be a gross underestimate. Former President Bush authorized the creation of The National Prison Rape Elimination Commission in 2003 and former Attorney General Eric Holder set national mandatory standards in 2010 (Johnson, 2009).

There is a growing awareness that men are also victims of rape in greater numbers than people would have ever believed. It is estimated that sexual assault perpetrators victimize as many as one in 8 men at some point during his life (Bolton, Morris, & MacEachron, 1989) and the incidence of prison rape is much higher (Johnson, 2009). Recently, the sexual assault of U.S. military personnel by others within their ranks has been identified as a major problem. Although men's statistical risk of being victimized (1.2 percent per year) is much lower than that of women (6.1 percent), because men are a large majority (6 of every 7) of military personnel (Active Duty Gender Distribution, 2013), in terms of raw numbers they are actually a slight majority (53 percent) of victims. Military male sexual assault victims are even less likely than female victims to report the assault to military authorities (Scarborough, 2013), and there is virtually no research on the offenders or victims of male sexual crimes in the services.

Most male rapes are committed by heterosexual men against homosexual men (King, Coxell, & Mezey, 2000). Michael Scarce (1997a) considers these types of attacks as hate crimes against gay men. Similar to the rape of women, the rape of men is an expression of power, not of sexuality. Rus Ervin Funk (1997) described his chilling victimization at the hands of several men who gang-raped him because of his involvement in feminist causes. Thus we see the use of coercive sexuality to maintain hypermasculine privilege, just as in men's sexual assaults on women.

Male rape survivors experience some similar responses to female survivors. They may suffer from posttraumatic stress disorder (PTSD) and experience various psychological symptoms, including depression, anxiety, anger, shame, relationship difficulties, suicidal thoughts, sexual problems, sleep disturbances, increased alcohol use, and psychosomatic symptoms (Isely & Gehrenbeck-Shim, 1997). They also experience difficulties that are somewhat unique to male survivors: doubts about their masculinity and sexuality, extreme isolation, and even fewer resources for treatment and support than female victims have available (Isely, Isely, Freiburger & McMackin, 2008). It is estimated that 90 percent of male survivors never report the rape to police or hospitals, and 70 percent never tell anybody at all (VAASA, 1989). Research into the specific effects of sexual assault on men is sorely lacking (Isely, Busse, & Isely, 1998).

Several researchers have made suggestions for dealing with the largely hidden problem of male-on-male rape. Scarce (1997a; 1997b) recommends lobbying for gender-neutral rape laws where they do not currently exist, providing referrals and information tailored specifically to male survivors, training emergency room and rape crisis workers on the reality and unique character of male victimization, and educating the general public about the extent of the problem. Paul Isely and his colleagues (Isely, Busse, & Isely, 1998) suggest that school counselors and health services professionals be trained to recognize symptoms of sexual victimization and learn how to respond appropriately, as untreated symptoms often develop into chronic behavioral and psychological difficulties. In a subsequent article on men who were abused as children by Catholic clergy, Isely and colleagues (Isely, Isely, Freiburger & McMackin, 2008), described child sexual victimization as a "developmental insult with a high likelihood of compromising social, relational, and intrapsychic functioning in later life" (p. 209).

Traumatic psychological experience also increases the risk that a male survivor will become a perpetrator if he fails to acknowledge his pain. The refusal to deal directly with vulnerable emotions like fear and shame is central to mainstream cultural masculinity. Lisak (1997) noted that men who have been abused in some way as children *and* have accepted masculinity's traditional values are more likely to become violent adults, in comparison to other child abuse survivors. His contention is that, as children, these men have experienced powerful and painful emotional events. At the same time, they have gotten the social message that expressing vulnerable feelings is taboo for males—the classic "big boys don't cry" dictum. These boys find that they can follow one of two paths: they can reject traditional masculinity and deal with the tragedy of their victimization, or they can accept it and act out their intense rage by becoming abusive themselves and/or by self-abuse, such as risk taking or drug use. Violence to the self and others appears to lie at the confluence of victimization and masculinity.

Many men have experienced varying levels of victimization at the hands of their fathers, other adult men, or peers. Harsh masculine socialization is victimizing in and of itself. When it is combined with hypermasculinity, this inhumane treatment can lead to inhuman behavior (Lynch & Kilmartin, 2013). In extensive interviews with death row inmates, Lisak and Beszterczey (2007) found remarkably high levels of childhood histories of physical and sexual abuse.

The male abuse survivor who seals over his pain cannot feel empathy for his victims because he is so unaware of his own feelings of shame and vulnerability. In other words, it is impossible for a person to feel for others when his own emotional life is impoverished. He has no frame of reference for emotional pain because his defenses against his own pain are so rigid.

David Lisak (1997) suggests that re-humanizing men entails helping them to recover the vulnerable emotionality that accompanied their victimization. He refers to full awareness of one's vulnerable emotions as *empathy for the self* and tells the heart-rending story of a death row inmate who refused to deal with the painful reality of his childhood victimization until, after 10 years in prison, he finally began to acknowledge his pain. One day, during a prison psychotherapy session, he began to cry, perhaps for the first time in his adult life, and sobbed uncontrollably for 45 minutes as he relived the horrors of multiple abuses in his youth. He recovered from this episode and, 15 minutes later, became anguished again as, for the first time, he came to a full emotional awareness of the pain that he had inflicted on his victims. Lisak saw the connection between empathy for the self and empathy for others in this dramatic hour.

Men's violence has biological, historical, economic, social, and cultural roots that interact with the personal histories and ideologies of individual men, and with their decisions to act violently. The cross-cultural variation and striking differences in men's and women's violence lead us to the conclusion that violence is largely centered in the social meanings attached to gender. Solutions to the problems created by men's violence must be broad in scope, encompassing economic, educational, legal, institutional, and social activist strategies.

SUMMARY

1. Men commit the vast majority of violent crimes, and this fact leads researchers to investigate the origins of violence and the connections between aggression and masculinity.

2. Sociobiologists view male aggression as an evolutionary strategy for propagating one's genes, yet aggression is not always associated with an increase in breeding access, even in non-human animals.

3. The hormone testosterone is another possible biological link to male violence. Although testosterone may set the stage for aggression, implicating it as the singular cause of male violence ignores the complexity of human behavior and

the powerful influence of psychosocial forces. Cross-cultural variations in the character of violence make singular biological explanations untenable.

4. Socioculturally, aggression is a defining feature of masculinity. A number of factors encourage aggression in men, including the privilege of patriarchy, a socialized external defensive style, unmitigated attention to task, violent modeling, and rewards for aggressing. Compared with females, violence-inhibiting factors such as empathy, nonaggressive modeling, and consistent punishment for aggression are less in evidence for males. Male violence is thought by many to be a compensation for the inadequate feelings that sometimes result from masculine gender role strain.

5. Men who are violent in the home often show this compensatory pattern. They have exaggerated needs for power and control as well as the externalizing style of blaming their partners for their own negative feelings and behaviors. Domestic violence often follows an intergenerational pattern against the backdrop of a patriarchal system that tolerates violence against women and even children. A number of interventions are focused on legal, therapeutic, and educational systems.

6. Research and debate about the commonplace crime of rape has increased dramatically during the past two decades. Many researchers believe that rape is fueled by aggressive, not sexual motivations. The social construction of masculinity, with its emphasis on misogyny, sexual promiscuity, performance, and homophobia, is both cause and effect of a rape-tolerant social climate.

7. As with other violent behaviors, rape is perpetrated by men who are desperately attempting to compensate for feelings of masculine inadequacy through hypermasculine displays of dominance, anger, and control. For many acquaintance rapists, low masculine self-esteem may be related to poor relationships with emotionally and/or physically distant or abusive fathers.

8. Interventions for decreasing rape include more vigorous law enforcement, rehabilitative efforts, safety measures, and the education of potential victims. However, rape is a men's issue, and men need to address it. Recent interventions have included bystander approaches to men, especially in college populations, where acquaintance rape is rampant. Men who can understand, at a deep level, the negative consequences of rape, the origins of male violence, the pain of victims, and the continuum of violence against women, will be less likely to rape or to support violent peers. Education with powerful people within institutions like the military also shows great promise.

9. Male victimization occurs at alarming levels, especially with regard to murder in the United States. Male-on-male rape is much more common than is generally believed, and male rape survivors face a unique set of recovery issues. Males with a history of any kind of victimization are at increased risk for becoming perpetrators if they embrace traditional masculine gender role norms.

Chapter Thirteen

No Man is an Island:
Men in Relationships with Others

Humans are inherently social animals (Maslow, 1943). We live with other people and interact with others on a daily basis. Relationship problems are one of the most common reasons that people seek psychotherapy. There is strong evidence that lack of social support has severe negative effects, such as greater levels of major depression (Courtenay 2011; Kendler, Myers, & Prescott, 2005).

Yet our stereotypical image of (United States) men is that their relationships focus on doing things together and tend to be emotionally shallow. We often imagine them as loners who do not confide in others, drawing on images of gunslingers in old Westerns like *Shane* or current day superheroes like Wolverine or Spiderman (see also Strate, 1992). When we think about all-male groups, American stereotypes tell us they take risks and get into trouble (or barely escape it) as in movies like *American Pie* and *The Hangover*, as well as television shows like *The Suite Life of Zack & Cody* and *Fineas and Ferb*.

But this is not how male-male friendship is seen across cultures. In some parts of the world, same-sex best friends go through a ceremony similar to a marriage to formalize their commitment to each other. When one of the friends dies, people express more sympathy to his best friend than to family members. In Java and parts of Ghana, and in some native North American tribes, the man turns to his best friend for fulfillment of his primary emotional needs, and husband-wife relationships are marked by less emotional intensity. The romantic ideal of mainstream U.S. culture dictates that a spouse meets all the emotional needs of his or her partner, an ideology that makes deep friendships more difficult (Williams, 1992).

As is often the case, the stereotypes disguise the reality. Most boys and men have, want, and value close connections with others (Smiler & Heasley, in press; Vasquez et al. 2014; Way, 2011). When 18-year-old Ethan described his best friend to researcher Judy Chu (2004, p. 96), he said "We're like, very different. But at the same time, I have a very strong bond with him. Every time I see him, it's just the greatest time ever. It's just, he's the best." In this chapter, we examine the reality of men's relationships, beginning with a discussion of some aspects of male social development (see also Chapter

Four) and the aspects of masculinity that directly affect how boys and men experience relationships. Then we shift to particular types of relationships, including both male-male and male-female friendships, romantic relationships, and father-son relationships.

THE MALE EXPERIENCE

As we have seen throughout the book, even though there is great similarity and within-sex variability, there are also some average differences between the sexes. Those general trends contribute to and are reflected in the interpersonal relationships typical of boys and men. We begin our discussion by focusing on those gendered experiences and then examine how the definition of masculinity connects to relationships.

Male Social Development

Developmental psychologist Eleanor Maccoby (1998) has described distinct, gender-typed interaction patterns that emerge early in life. She contends that these are largely a function of children's preferences for same-sex interaction. By the age of six and a half, children choose to spend the majority of their time with same-sex peers. They will play in sex-integrated groups when adults force them to but will return to sex-segregated groups when adults withdraw. This segregation is not limited to gender-typed activities such as playing with dolls or trucks. It also occurs in gender-neutral activities such as drawing or playing with clay.

Martin and Fabes (2001) found that sex-differentiated behavior is a consequence of the frequency of same-sex play. Often finding themselves in the company of male peers, most boys develop a way of relating to others that is distinctly masculine. This style involves an orientation toward dominance, competition, and rough-and-tumble play (Maccoby, 1998). Boys also tend to play in larger (Levant, 1995), less intimate (Maccoby, 1990), and more publicly visible groups (Thorne, 2009).

In these all-male groups, we see boys interrupting each other, bragging, telling stories, ridiculing others, and using commands much more frequently than girls. Their conversations are more like turn-taking monologues, with one boy telling a story, followed by another boy (who often tries to "top" the first boy's story). Girls' conversation rely more on a give-and-take format. The tendency is to request rather than demand, express interest in others' stories, perspective, or feelings, and a variety of other strategies that non-verbally communicate a desire to connect to the other person instead of competing with him or her. Maccoby's (1998) view is that typically masculine conversation tends to be self-assertive and self-promotional whereas typically feminine speech serves the dual purpose of collaboration and self-assertion.

These manners of relating to others begin in childhood. By the second grade, female best friends' conversations begin to center around personally significant events, while boys' conversations focus on activities. By early adolescence, friendships are somewhat less stereotypical (Golombok & Fivush, 1994). Still, many gender-typed communication patterns continue into adulthood (Tannen, 1990). Since interpersonal interactions serve to form and maintain relationships, men's long-established pattern of communication colors the character of their social ties with women, children, and other men.

Masculinity. When we think about relationships, the things that indicate closeness are sharing secrets, feelings, hopes and fears (Smiler & Heasley, in press; Way, 2011). In a series of interviews with the same boys throughout their teens, boys repeatedly told Niobe Way and her research team (2011) that the most important attributes of a close or best friend was knowing that he would be there for you, stand up for you, and that he could be trusted with your deepest secrets (see also Kaplan & Rosemann, 2014). These attributes are also among the most important characteristics of a romantic partner (Buss, Shackelford, Kirkpatrick, & Larsen, 2001). Yet masculinity ideologies dictate that boys not do any of these things because they require being somewhat emotionally open, vulnerable, and non-competitive. Reflecting on these patterns, James Nelson (1988) suggested that for traditionally masculine men "There is a deep tension between intimacy and masculinity. He wants both, and each seems to be purchased at the price of the other" (p. 42).

This strategy works for some men, at least to an extent. For example, many men who buy into traditional concepts of masculinity report relatively high levels of relationship satisfaction (Wade & Donis, 2007). Men on athletic teams, in military units, or those who work together often form close bonds (Kaplan & Rosenmann, 2014; Messner, 1992; Migliaccio, 2009). But other researchers have found that men who subscribed to stereotypical masculine ideologies reported fewer close friends, were more likely than other men to experience loneliness, and experienced more conflict around psychological intimacy (Blazina, Eddins, Burridge, & Settle, 2007; Shepard, Nicpon, Haley, Lind, & Liu, 2011). Many men experience relationship dissatisfaction even with their best friends (Elkins & Peterson, 1993).

Research illustrates some of this cost. Boys and men with higher masculinity scores perceive less need to ask for assistance and tend to be less emotionally expressive within their friendships (Cunningham & Newkirk, 2004; Migliaccio, 2009). Moreover, men with greater gender role conflict scores tend to have poorer quality relationships. They report lower levels of intimacy and less self-disclosure, as well as fewer friends (O'Neil, 2008). Women tend to desire high levels of intimacy (McAdams, Lester, Brand, McNamara, & Lensky, 1988), but gender-typed men tend to be emotionally inexpressive and unempathic.

Competition. Boys and men are taught to be competitive with one another. The establishment of intimacy rests partly on revealing one's weaknesses and vulnerabilities to another (Kaplan & Rosemann, 2014; Way, 2011). It is not wise to reveal these to a perceived competitor who might well exploit the weakness. You probably wouldn't make a $20 bet with a friend that you can win at any Xbox game, tell your friend your weakest one, and then ask which game he would like to play. Men who feel competitive with other men tend to have friendships that are inhibited by an undercurrent of distrust, which may help to explain why adolescent boys find it harder to trust their same-sex friends than girls do (Berndt, 1992).

Independence.   The masculine demand for independence and self-sufficiency also inhibits self-disclosure. Taken to the extreme, a man might come to believe that he should not need others and that he should always be able to get by on his own. But we are members of a variety of social systems and are dependent on others for information, resources, support, and human contact. Imagine what your life would look like if you had to produce your own food, clothing, and electricity, could not use the Internet (because other people maintain it and create webpages), and if you did not have conversations with the same people day after day (in person, by text, through social media, etc.). The masculine focus on independence does not exactly discourage relying on others for goods and services, but it does seem to look down on men's needing interpersonal connection. One study with African-American teens found that boys who had higher masculinity scores saw less need to talk to others when they had problems (Cunningham & Newkirk, 2004).

Emotional Restriction.   Masculine directives to avoid emotional expression are also problematic for creating deep friendships. One characteristic of more substantive friendships is the sharing of our deepest hopes and fears, as well as moments of joy and sadness (Migliaccio, 2009; Vasquez et al., 2014; Way, 2011). In fact, men with closer relationships report lower levels of isolation, depression, and violence (Courtenay, 2011; Levant & Richmond, 2007), while men with higher levels of masculine gender role conflict report having more problems achieving and maintaining intimacy (O'Neil, 2008).

Yet masculinity directs men to avoid sharing feelings. Even when they do, their upbringing shortchanges them: on average, their emotional vocabularies tend to be smaller than women's, and thus their understanding of feelings tends to be poorer (Adams et al., 1995; see Chapter Four). As you might expect, men who do not experience intimacy as children or teens have difficulty demonstrating it as adults (Garfield, 2010).

Homophobia.   Homophobia is perhaps the greatest barrier to friendships between men (Reid & Fine, 1992). Because some men have difficulty making a clear distinction between sexual and nonsexual intimacy, becoming emotionally close to another man may feel similar to being sexual with him. The antifemininity demand of masculinity then rears its ugly head, and panic—or at least some anxiety and discomfort—sets in. To avoid these feelings, men often keep other men at arm's length, both physically and psychologically. The friendships of highly homophobic men are significantly less intimate than those of other men (Devlin & Cowan, 1985). Greg Lehne (1998) illustrated the role of homophobia in distancing heterosexual men from one another:

> I've asked men to describe their relationships with their best male friends. Many offer descriptions that are... filled with positive emotions and satisfaction.... However, if I suggest that it sounds as if they are describing a person whom they love, they become flustered....'Well, I don't think I would like to call it love, we're just best friends. I can relate to him in ways I can't with anyone else. But, I mean,

we're not homosexuals or anything like that.'…The social stigma of homosexual love denies these close relationships the validity of love in our society. This potential loss of love is a pain of homophobia that many men suffer because it delimits their relationships with other men. (p. 246)

According to Thorne and Luria (1986), U.S. boys begin to use homophobic labels such as "queer" or "fag" as insults by the fourth grade. As sociologist C. J. Pascoe (2007) documented, male and female teens use these terms to refer to any behavior they find distasteful, especially those that violate the masculine gender role. In fact, most of the adolescents Pascoe spoke with said they would not use these terms to refer to their openly gay peers (see also Slaatten, Andersson, & Hetland, 2014). Thorne and Luria theorized about the impact of homophobic labeling on boys' physical contact:

As 'fag' talk increases, relaxed and cuddling patterns of touch decrease among boys. Kindergarten and first-grade boys touch one another frequently and with ease, with arms around shoulders, hugs, and holding hands. By fifth grade, touch among boys becomes more constrained, gradually shifting to mock violence and the use of poking, shoving, and ritual gestures like 'giving five' (flat hand slaps) to express bonding. (p. 182)

Thus, males appear to have strong desire to maintain interpersonal contact with other males, but (historically and developmentally) the threat of homophobic labeling increasingly forces this contact to become highly ritualized and sometimes aggressive.

Researcher Eric Anderson and his colleagues (Anderson, McCormack, & Lee, 2012) recently argued that young men are becoming less homophobic. They observed the initiation rituals of the rugby and (male) field hockey teams over a seven-year span at a single British University, and also interviewed several of the participants. Initiates were often required to drink large quantities of alcohol during this process, and one of the teams was put on probation due to their extreme levels of drinking. During the time frame, the researchers found that young men became less squeamish about being required to wrestle each other while nude or nearly nude, and they were increasingly willing to engage in open-mouthed kissing with one another. One participant said he would rather kiss his friend than be required to drink another beer when already intoxicated. Given the circumstances, it is hard to know if this finding represents a larger trend or is specific to this particular setting.

There is reason to believe that decreases in homophobia may reflect generational change and cultural differences. History reveals that maintaining physical separation to validate heterosexuality is a relatively recent phenomenon. In the United States, it seems to have begun in the early twentieth century at about the time when the label "homosexual" moved from a definition of *behavior* (something one does) to one of *identity* (something one is) (Rotundo, 1993). Given that acceptance of homosexuality tends to be stronger among younger generations (Savin-Williams, 2005), efforts to validate heterosexuality by not touching other males and adding the disclaimer "no homo" when admiring another man may vanish in the next few decades.

Outcomes. The result of these masculine injunctions is that men tend to experience more loneliness than women (Brody & Hall, 2000), probably because they experience lower levels of social support. This is unfortunate because self-disclosure has demonstrable positive mental health benefits (Pennebaker, 1995). Men who place a high value on traditional masculinity tend to avoid self-disclosure (Cunningham & Newkirk, 2004; Shepard et al., 2011), so when a problem arises, they tend to rely solely on their own resources even when others are available and willing to help. The familiar situation where a man who is lost refuses to ask for directions is a good illustration of how some men will solve problems inefficiently to maintain a manly image.

The handshake is symbolic of men's ambivalence around being close to one another. Young boys whose fathers refuse to kiss, hug, or cuddle them, or tell them that they are loved, deprive their sons of the important human needs for touching and valuing. In addition, these fathers model unaffectionate behavior as a distinctive feature of masculinity. As a result, these boys may well grow up to be distant fathers to their own sons. This pattern is reflected in "G" rated movies, where males are twice as likely as females to be depicted as emotionally disconnected, and this difference is even more pronounced for characters who are males of color (Kelly & Johnson, 2009). Thus media models also encourage children to think of males in less relationship-oriented terms than females.

Social norms constrain behavior in significant ways. Both women and men behave in more gender-stereotypical ways in public than they do in private (Burn, 1996; Heasley, 2005) even though many males express a desire to be more disclosing (Chu, 2004; Way, 2011). These findings suggest that masculine and feminine styles of friendship are at least partly a function of the social expectations that women and men tend to bring into interactions with others.

It may not be unusual for two male friends to both have a desire for greater levels of intimacy with each other but continue to keep each other at an emotional arm's length because both overestimate the degree to which the other expects gender-stereotypical behavior (Wade & Donis, 2007; Way et al., 2014). Masculinity inhibits them from talking about their expectations (which would be intimate in itself) and therefore their distorted views of each other's masculinity prevent the friendship from moving in the direction that both would like to go. As we have mentioned repeatedly throughout the text, boys who behave in gender-inconsistent ways are likely to experience disapproval from their friends and lose popularity or see themselves pushed to the margins of the social hierarchy (Carver, Egan, & Perry, 2004; Kehler, 2007). One outcome is that many boys who would like to have more emotionally connected relationships with their male friends are unable to find other boys who share that desire because no one is "allowed" to say so (Way et al., 2014).

Although it provides a measure of social support, "male bonding" tends to be a poor substitute for the deeper connections of intimate friendships. For boys and men who have a decades-long pattern of being buddies rather than true friends, shifting to a deeper version of friendship may be very difficult. Box 13.1 describes techniques for doing so.

Box 13.1   Guerilla Tactics for Making a Friend

Letich (1991) makes some excellent, step by step suggestions for working on deeper friendships:

1. First, you have to want it: Breaking patterns not only causes anxiety, it is hard work. "You have to remind yourself that there's nothing weird or effeminate about wanting a friend" (p. 87).

2. Identify a possible friend: Seek someone who seems to want to question the values of traditional masculinity.

3. Be sneaky: Get involved in a comfortable, nonpressured activity. Get used to spending time with this man.

4. Invite him to stop for a beer or a cup of coffee: Try to make honest, personal conversation at these times.

5. Call just to get together.

6. Sit down and talk about your friendship.

Letich calls these suggestions "guerilla tactics" because they seem extreme and difficult for traditional men in a culture that discourages male-male intimacy. The last two suggestions are especially antithetical to male gender role norms. Men who try these "tactics" will feel awkward, but as with any skills, they improve and become more comfortable with practice.

As we have seen repeatedly, context matters. The contours of men's relationships can vary dramatically depending on the type of relationship. Next, we talk about common patterns in male-male friendships, male-female friendships, dating relationships (with women and men), and long-term and marital relationships, before turning to the father-son dyad.

Male-Male Friendships

Although boys and men may report having more friends than girls and women (Vigil, 2007), they usually report less support and intimacy from their friends (Bank & Handford, 2000; Claes, 1992; Kendler et al., 2005). Generally speaking, women often spend time talking about their experiences and feelings while men share activities (Lips, 2008).

It is sometimes said that men have many "buddies" but few true friends. Buddies are people you bond with around an object or activity (sports, work, drinking, etc); friends are people with whom you are intimate. The formation of warm feelings between men is many times the result of an indirect process of spending time in a mutual pursuit or interest rather than a more direct process of emotional self-disclosure. These relational patterns are sometimes described as "side-by-side" (masculine) and "face-to-face" (feminine) relationships. The expression of closeness between men often takes the form of continuing to spend time with each other and helping each other with tasks rather than more direct expressions such as touching, or saying "I like you," "I'm glad you're my friend," or "I feel close to you." In one recent study, researchers asked Israeli men, for whom military service is mandatory, to rate the men in their military units and their best male friend. Although scores were higher for best friends than unit peers, the six highest rated characteristics (of twelve) were identical: enjoying doing things together, comradeship, chemistry and shared language, desire to be together, admiration, and seeking validation. Love was in seventh (unit) and eighth (best male friend) place (Kaplan & Rosenmann, 2014). These findings tell us men see relationships with best male friends and military unit members in very similar ways, including experiencing these relationships as not particularly involving love.

Male-Female Friendships

Earlier in the chapter, we described boys' typical interactional style as boisterous and competitive and girls' as quieter and relational. Friendships are based partly on reciprocity, or mutual influence (Youniss & Haynie, 1992). Among boys, especially preteens, influence tends to be exerted through direct demands. By contrast, girls of the same age are more likely to use polite suggestions. Although girls' styles work well with adults, they are not very effective with boys. Therefore, girls may find it quite frustrating and unpleasant to interact with boys who will not respond to their influence attempts (Maccoby, 1998).

While boys' interaction style keeps girls away from them, the antifemininity norm keeps boys away from girls. The boy who acts like a girl in any way, including being friends with girls, risks losing his place in the masculine dominance hierarchy (Carver et al., 2004). When a boy has low social status compared with other boys, he finds it difficult to exert any influence on his male peers. As a result, his interactions with them may also become aversive. Thus, the masculine culture does not foster egalitarian relationships with females. Boys' interactions are often geared toward competition, they are barraged with messages that they should not act like girls, and they are encouraged to value girls and women only as sexual objects. These patterns do not facilitate the creation of cross-sex friendships.

Yet male-female friendships have become increasingly common among adolescents and adults over the last few decades. In the late 1970s, only about 18 percent of American adults reported having a close friend of the other sex. That figure grew to between 25 to 40 percent by the mid-1980s (Basow, 1992). As late as 1992, one leading friendship researcher speculated that male-female friendships were rare and would continue to be uncommon (Hartup & Overhauser, 1991). Today, cross-sex friendships have become increasingly common and having at least one cross-sex friendship may now be the norm among teens and young adults (Kimmel, 2011; Smiler, 2013).

Both males and females tend to self-disclose more often to female friends, so a cross-sex friendship frequently offers a man something that may well be lacking in his friendships with other men. Not surprisingly, women have a stronger tendency than men to describe their cross-sex friendships as less satisfactory than their other friendships (Parker & De Vries, 1993).

ROMANTIC RELATIONSHIPS

We now shift from friendship to romantic relationships because they share many features, including companionship, emotional intimacy, trust, and shared interests

(Connolly, Craig, Goldberg, & Pepler, 1999; Sprecher & Regan, 2002). Romantic relationships that include a strong friendship between dating partners tend to last longer (Giordano, Manning, & Longmore, 2010; VanderDrift, Wilson, & Agnew, 2013). We discuss relationships separately from sexual activity even though most males prefer their sexual contact with a known partner (Bradshaw, Kahn, & Saville, 2010; Smiler, 2013). See Chapter Eleven for a detailed discussion of sexual behavior.

Male-Female Dating Relationships

The average United States male has his first "real" or "serious" relationship with a female at age 16 or 17 (Regan, Durvasula, Howell, Ureno, & Rea, 2004; Smiler, Frankel, & Savin-Williams, 2011). Many of these relationships last for relatively long periods of time; almost half of 10th grade boys reported a relationship of 12 weeks or longer and approximately one-sixth of high school seniors reported a relationship of 11 months or longer (Connolly & Johnson, 1996; Fiering, 1999).

Many men, and some women, believe that "nice guys finish last"—that women are only interested in dominant men, and that men who are kind, sympathetic, attentive, or caring are viewed as less desirable. But one group of researchers (Jensen-Campbell, Graziano, & West, 1995) found little support for this belief. In fact, women rated men who were described as being kind, cooperative, and attentive as more desirable—sexually, physically, and socially—than those described as less agreeable or less caring. In fact, the "nice guys" cliche may tell us more about the label than the reality of dating. One research project included the same survey protocol repeatedly from 1939 through 1996 in asking undergraduate women and men to rate the characteristics they most desired in a mate. The top four (of eighteen) characteristics were almost identical in every round of surveying: dependable character, emotional stability/maturity, pleasing disposition, and mutual attraction/love (Buss, Schackelford, Kirkpatrick, & Larsen, 2001). In other words, women want nice, stable guys.

By contrast, women tend to report lower levels of relationship satisfaction when they judged their partners to be emotionally restricted and highly concerned with success, power, and competition (Rochlen & Mahalik, 2004). More broadly, men with higher masculinity ideology scores tend to be less respectful of women and report lower levels of relationship satisfaction (Levant & Richmond, 2007; Smiler, 2013).

One interesting research finding is that heterosexual males tend to "fall in love" faster than females (Huston & Ashmore, 1986), contrary to the popular belief that women are more emotional and love-hungry. We can make some guesses about the origins of this tendency. First, men tend to place more value than women on a partner's physical attractiveness (Buss et al., 2001). Thus they may be more likely to report being in love largely on the basis of this attraction, which of course can happen very early in the relationship (or even from across the room). Second, men have not been socialized to understand and manage their emotional lives except through suppression. Feelings that are difficult to squelch may be experienced as a "flood" of emotion. Third, the level of intimacy in a romantic relationship is likely to be very different from that of a male's other relationships, which are often centered on activities. This level of intimacy is likely to be less different from the intimacy level of the female's other relationships, which are often focused on feeling and disclosure. The man's hunger for intimacy is greater because he has few or no other places to get this need met. The heterosexual relationship becomes the only safe haven from the masculine demands for independence and inexpressiveness, the only place where he can show the "softer" side of himself. A man might well experience the normal feminine style of reciprocity and consideration as love.

These tendencies may explain why men often perceive sexual interest from a woman when it is not present. Men are more likely than women to interpret her suggestion of getting together for coffee, and even her agreement to meet for coffee when he asks, as a prelude to sexual activity (Fisher & Walters, 2003), which may explain why it can be difficult to convince other-sex romantic partners that an other-sex friend is only a friend (Swain, 1992). Men's readiness to sexualize behavior may result in men misperceiving friendliness as flirtation, making it difficult to establish nonsexual cross-sex relationships.

Male-Male Dating Relationships

In some ways, the experiences of boys who are romantically attracted to other boys are the same as the experiences of boys who are attracted to girls. As Ritch Savin-Williams (1995) pointed out, "The intimacy needs of gay and bisexual youth are common, even normative" (p. 159). Yet their day-to-day experience is one in which homophobic insults like "dude, you're a fag" are common (Pascoe, 2007; Slaatten, Anderssen, & Hetland, 2014), school events are geared towards male-female couples (homecoming court, Sadie Hawkins day), and they may fear rejection by their parents, friends, and others in their community. A boy who has overcome these challenges and publicly acknowledged his same-sex attractions may still have difficulty finding a partner because there might not be very many other out gay boys in his school or town, let alone one he is romantically attracted to (Savin-Williams, 1998; Smiler, 2013).

Given this context, it should not be surprising that only a minority of gay youth find romantic partners at school; instead, they are more likely to find partners at gay bars, gay organizations or clubs, or online (DeHaan, Kuper, Magee, Bigelow, & Mustanski, 2013; Savin-WIllilams, 1998). Many, perhaps most, gay boys do not have their first romantic relationships until age 18 or later. Despite their difficulty finding dating partners, many report having fleeting sexual encounters with other boys and a sizable minority find partners who are more than a decade older (Savin-Williams, 1998, 2005). In studies, 16- and 17-year-old gay boys often indicate that first sex occurred at age 13 or 14, while in studies with advanced undergraduates and graduate students, reports for age of first male-male sexual contact average at 16 (Savin-Williams, 1998, 2005; Smiler et al., 2011).

The combination of early sexual experiences outside of a relational context, combined with masculine norms, may contribute to some gay men's difficulties in finding relationship partners. As one teen explained, "I'm looking for someone very special, but it is really hard to meet such a guy. They all just want sex" (Savin-Williams,

2005, p. 137). Adult gay men have echoed this concern (Sanchez, Greenberg, Liu, & Vilain, 2009). They also expressed beliefs that masculine norms adversely affect their relationships by encouraging gay men to prefer "macho" or "butch" men and avoid effeminate ones, as well as by restricting emotional sharing and intimacy. Although most of these masculine norms provided no help to gay male relationships, a minority identified the provider role as a benefit (Sanchez et al., 2009).

Marriage & Long-Term Romantic Relationships

We now turn to the factors associated with long-term relationships. Maccoby (1990) described successful couples as ones who have "develop[ed] a relationship that is based on communality rather than exchange bargaining. That is, they have many shared goals and work jointly to achieve them. They do not need to argue over turf because they have the same turf" (p. 518).

There is a substantial body of literature with examinations of long-term relationships among heterosexual couples and a growing number of studies of same-sex couples. Among both groups, several factors have been repeatedly identified as important to maintaining the relationship over the long term: affection, dependability, shared interests, similar religious beliefs, liking, and loving. For men, their partners' physical attractiveness also influences their comfort in the relationships regardless of whether the partner is male or female. Sexual satisfaction, which is closely connected to frequency of sex, is also positively correlated with relationship satisfaction. The most frequent topics of disagreement are also unrelated to sexual orientation: money, affection (or lack thereof), sex, criticism (of partner/self), and distribution of household tasks. It is also worth noting that in addition to love for and satisfaction with one's partner, having access to alternative partners and having few barriers to separation (e.g., not needing a legal divorce, not needing to address child support and custody, etc.) also affect a couple's decision to stay together and again, these factors influence both same- and mixed-sex couples (Peplau & Fingerhut, 2007).

Gender norms and socialization patterns also affect long term couples, albeit differently for hetereosexual and gay couples. It is important to note that all of the research on gay male couples, including the information above, relies heavily on studies of male-male couples who are often highly educated and highly paid and those in which European-Americans are over-represented (Peplau & Fingerhut, 2007). This is not the case with research on male-female couples.

Male-Female Couples. Perceived equality (or lack thereof) can affect many aspects of a couple's experience. Although men earn more than women on average, there are a growing number of couples in which this is not the case. Not surprisingly, men who adhere to traditional masculine ideologies, including the provider role, place greater importance on earning more than their partners while men who are more flexible place less importance on this disparity. These emphases come with relational costs, as more dogmatic men report lower levels of relationship satisfaction than their more progressive peers (Bradbury, Campbell, & Fincham, 1995; Couglin & Wade,

2012). At the other extreme, many men who are stay-at-home-fathers report that they chose this role and that they are quite satisfied with their relationships as long as they receive relatively high levels of support from their partners and their families (Rochlen, Suizzo, McKelley, & Scaringi, 2008). We describe stay at home fathers in more detail in Chapter Ten.

Couples who hold more egalitarian ideals tend to be more equal in their division of household labor than more traditional couples (Schwartz, 1994). At the same time, women in egalitarian couples still tend to do more housework than their husbands (Hochschild & Machung, 1989). It's important to note that men's subscription to egalitarian ideals has a greater effect on the couple's relationship than that of his partner. Among other things, more egalitarian men report higher levels of sexual satisfaction in their long term relationships; women's perception of their partners' egalitarianism is related to both her relationship and sexual satisfaction (Rudman & Phelan, 2007).

Communication is also a key predictor of relationship satisfaction (Perren, Von Wyl, Burgin, Simoni, & Von Klitznig, 2005). This should not be surprising: talking to your partner may be the only activity you undertake together every single day. Yet men and women demonstrate group-level differences in a number of aspects of communication (McHugh & Hambaugh, 2010).

These differences in interactional styles, which date back to childhood patterns of socialization, can create problems. Males are often not responsive to the typical feminine influence style of polite suggestion, are more likely to interrupt, and more likely to use profanity, all of which may lead females to feel somewhat powerless (McHugh & Hambaugh, 2010). By contrast, the masculine preference for direct requests or demands may feel aversive and overpowering to women. At the extreme, masculine expectations of dominance and power over women may encourage some men to ignore even direct influence attempts by their partners.

Men's lower levels of intimacy with their male friends may lead them to rely heavily, and possibly entirely, on their wives for intimacy. Not only do men tend to have less intimate friendships (Bank & Handford, 2000; Kendler et al., 2005), married men tend to be less intimate than single men with their male friends (Tschann, 1988) and they often have difficulty filling their intimacy needs should their long-term relationships end (Nolen-Hoeksema & Girgus, 1994). Ultimately, these interactional patterns may create the "masculine dilemma" that John Lynch and Christopher Kilmartin (2013) called "not too close; not too far away," in which the man comes closer when he fears abandonment but then distances his partner when he fears engulfment.

Disparities in income and housework, levels of emotional support directed toward the partner, beliefs about egalitarian gender roles, and styles of communication may ultimately lead the couple to dissolve the relationship. Given that many of these factors are related to aspects of the masculine gender role that dictate how he interacts, it should be little surprise that wives tend to report lower levels of relationship satisfaction when their husbands endorse traditionally masculine ideologies or that wives are more likely than husbands to file for divorce (Bradbury, Campbell, & Fincham, 1995; Brinig & Allen, 2000).

Male-Male Couples. Gender roles affect male-male couples as well. For example, gay men appear to experience lower levels of some forms of masculine gender role conflict. Coupled gay men tend to report lower levels of restricted affective behavior between men than single gay men, and also possibly lower levels of restricted emotionality (Wester, Pionke, & Vogel, 2005). Power within the relationship may play out in similar ways to male-female relationships, with greater influence being determined by income, although this pattern may only reflect a minority of gay male couples (Peplau & Fingerhut, 2007).

Masculine norms regarding promiscuity play an important role among male-male couples, who are sometimes more willing to explore and practice non-monogamy than male-female or female-female couples (Parsons, Starks, Gamarel, & Grov, 2012). As we noted earlier, sexual satisfaction within a relationship is often related to relationship satisfaction, and relationships endure longer when partners are more satisfied (Greene & Britton, 2013). On average, gay men's relationship satisfaction was higher among those who were less interested in casual sex (Sanchez, Bocklandt, & Vilain, 2009) and higher in monogamous and "monogam-ish" than in "open" relationships (Parsons et al., 2012). Although it is unclear which comes first—open relationship status or lower levels of relationship satisfaction—it is clear that gay male couples, as well as the mental health professionals who work with them, would do well to discuss the sexual boundaries of their relationships (Houts & Horne, 2008; Sanchez et al., 2009).

FATHERS AND SONS

Although there is debate as to whether or not there was ever a single, universally agreed upon definition of what it means to be a good or successful father, it is clear that the idea of father as financial provider and disciplinarian is no longer the standard, at least in the United States. Although some individuals still prefer this formulation, the trend is toward a more emotionally involved father than in the past (Cabrera, Tamis-LeMonda, Bradley, Hofferth, & Lamb, 2000; Genesoni & Tallandini, 2009; Stewart & Newton, 2010). As one research team summarized, "It now appears that fathers generally perceive that they are expected to assume the twin responsibilities of providing economical and emotional support for their family" (Genesoni & Tallndini, 2009, p. 315). Levant and Wimer (2009) call this image the "good family man."

For heterosexual adult couples, the "transition to parenthood," but not the event of getting married, is typically associated with a shift to more traditional roles in which the man becomes the primary earner and the woman the primary caretaker (Burke & Cast, 1997). Even in couples where both adults work outside the house for at least 20 hours per week and both adults are responsible for solo childcare at least 15 hours per week, partners describe their activities in term of the man "helping" with the kids and the woman providing "extra" income (Deutsch & Saxon, 1998). This shift may be accounted for by the finding that mothers are more likely than fathers to be involved in basic child care activities: feeding, dressing, washing clothes, and bathing. Fathers spend more time playing with children (Lips, 2008).

For many families, the reality includes two working parents and may include a man as the primary or stay-at-home parent (Department of Labor, 2005; Livingston & Parker, 2011; Rochlen et al., 2008). This definitional variability reflects the fact that while women's roles as mothers are fairly well-defined on a societal level, men's roles as fathers are much more subject to negotiation, the boundaries much more flexible, with their participation requiring less time than mothers (Cabrera et al., 2000; Marsiglio & Pleck, 2005). We discuss stay-at-home fathers in Chapter Ten.

For some men, living out the provider role and actively being a father may signify and validate masculinity. For others, impregnating someone may serve this purpose, especially for young men living in poverty (Lohan, Cruise, O'Halloran, Alderdice, & Hyde, 2010). Historically and cross-culturally, procreation has often been viewed as one way to demonstrate masculinity (Gilmore, 1990).

Who Becomes a Father?

Approximately three-quarters of United States men become fathers prior to age 40; the average age at first childbirth is 25 (and 23 for women). Almost half have had a child outside of marriage, usually as part of a cohabiting couple (Martinez, Daniels, & Chandra, 2012).

Approximately 180,000 teens become fathers each year in the U.S., and they account for about 20 percent of all births in any given year (Kiselica & Kiselica, 2014; Martinez et al., 2012). The vast majority have been in romantic relationship with their partners, often those exceeding one year in length (Kiselica & Kiselica, 2014). Although half of teen fathers are of European descent, young men of African and Latino heritage are more likely to become teen fathers than their European heritage peers (Kiselica & Kiselica, 2014). Teen fathers are more likely to have come from poverty, done poorly in school or dropped out entirely, engaged in delinquent behaviors, struggle with mental health problems, come from a single parent home, had a mother who had her first child at a relatively young age, had at least one parent who is depressed, had impoverished or non-existent relationships with their fathers, and/or multiple large-scale transitions (e.g., residential moves, changes in parental employment, changes in adults in parenting roles) (Kiselica & Kiselica, 2014; Martinez et al., 2012). By the time they reach their mid-30s, these men tend to be less educated, earn less money, live in poverty, and have been in jail than their age-mates who did not become fathers during their teens (Dariotis et al., 2011).

Anticipating Fatherhood

When faced with news of pregnancy and impending fatherhood, most young males see this potential change as a negative event that limits their current freedoms as well as their future aspirations and goals. A minority of young men see the event as an opportunity to change their lives for the better. This ambivalence, at both the group level and among individuals, is quite common (Lohan et al., 2010; Kiselica & Kiselica, 2014).

Adult men, for whom pregnancy is often at least somewhat planned or not actively prevented (Kaye, Suellentrop, & Sloup, 2011) tend to say that the experience of having a pregnant partner brings a different version of ambivalence. There is often an excitement about being a parent and an active partner to the pregnant woman, as well as a sense of unreality before the pregnancy is visible. Ambivalence is also furthered by other changes and transitions, including those within the couple's relationship, creation of the new identity as a father, a sense of powerlessness over the pregnancy, difficulty connecting emotionally to a fetus inside their partner's body, and reorganization of social life, including the loss of free time (Genesoni & Tallandini, 2009).

Across studies, males under age 24 who unintentionally impregnate their partners often say they want to keep the child and that they want to be involved in the decision to keep, abort, or adopt the child (Lohan et al., 2010). Both men's involvement in prenatal care (e.g., attending doctor's appointments with their pregnant partners) and their presence in the household at the time the child is born predict involvement in the child's life at five years of age. In one large-scale study, only half of men who were not involved in their children's prenatal care were still involved with their children three months after birth. By contrast, almost two-thirds of men who were involved and residing with the child's mother remained so by the time the children reached their fifth birthdays (Shannon, Cabrera, Tamis-LeMonda, & Lamb, 2009).

Becoming a Father

The realities of parenting can be quite difficult. Most parents appear to learn their parenting skills "on the job" and women usually spend more time on this job than men (Lamb, 2012). In contrast to most women, many men have no childhood parent-like experience, such as babysitting or playing with dolls, nor were they taught the psychological skills of nurturing or empathy (Levant, 1990). Despite the general lack of training prior to childbirth, most parents raise children who are relatively well-adjusted (Lamb, 2012; Pleck, 2007).

These challenges may be compounded by the father's wage-earning work. Many men report feeling strong conflicts between work and family roles (O'Neil, 2008), and employers have been slow to accommodate employed parents who wish to participate more fully in family roles through, for example, "flex time" arrangements that allow them to synchronize the workday and school day schedules (Bem, 1993). This is unfortunate because the more time a father spends at work, the less involved he tends to be with his children, which is not true for mothers (Hofferth & Anderson, 2003).

Fathers' perceptions of what it means to be a good parent are derived from a variety of sources, including their own parents and grandparents, their wives and her parents, and their parenting peers (Masciardelli, Pleck, & Stueve, 2006). A man's beliefs about what constitutes a good father, in terms of both providing and caretaking, are a key determinant of how he acts as a father; those beliefs may reflect his own assessment, his understanding of his wife's expectations, his understanding of other fathers his age, or some combination of these factors (Masciardelli et al., 2006; Maurer & Pleck, 2006). A man's experience of his own father is also important. Men whose childhood experiences were with highly involved fathers are more likely to be actively involved themselves. Men who perceived their fathers as less-than-positive models, and who display a commitment to doing better, also tend to be highly involved. Those who report having been involved in child care responsibilities as boys or adolescents (and having responded positively to these experiences) are also more involved. There is some cross-cultural evidence that boys who provide early infant care tend to become involved fathers (Pleck, 1997).

Reviews of studies demonstrating fathers' influences on their child's development include consistent findings that those who are actively involved have children whose development is more positive. Fathers who are emotionally invested in and attached to, and who provide resources for their children, tend to have children who have better cognitive development, educational outcomes, and emotional outcomes from early childhood through adolescence. Both quantity and quality of interaction matter, and fathers' impact is both direct in father-child interactions as well as indirect through partner, socioeconomic status, or other factors (Cabrera et al., 2000; Lamb, 2012; Stevenson & Black, 1988).

The structure of a child's family—who makes up that unit and what role each fulfills—is much less important than what takes place within the family. Studies of infants, young children, elementary-aged children, and teens all point to the importance of a warm relationship between the child and at least one parent, a warm relationship between the adults living in the household, and adequate economic and physical security (Lamb, 2012; Pleck, 2007). Moreover, children, especially boys, do not need to have an adult male in the house, exactly two adults in the house, or heterosexual parents, to develop into healthy adults or heterosexual adults, or endorse gender roles in a similar manner as their peers (Golombok et al., 2014; Lamb, 2012).

For example, one recent study of parents' sexual orientation on child development included approximately 150 adoptive two-parent families in England, with nearly equal numbers of gay male, lesbian, and heterosexual couples. On average, their adoptive children were approximately six years old and had been adopted between their second and third birthdays (often younger for mixed- than for same-sex parents). There were no differences between children in gay male and lesbian households. Comparisons of gay male and heterosexual households indicated that children being raised by gay male couples were less likely to demonstrate conduct problems or show signs of hyperactivity, which are "classic" boy problems. Compared to heterosexual couples, gay male couples reported less parenting stress, reported lower levels of depression, were less likely to use aggressive discipline approaches, showed more warmth towards their children, and were more responsive to their children's needs. Children's endorsement of traditional gender roles were similar across households (Golombok et al., 2014).

Although current research indicates that the absence of a (biological) father does not necessarily harm children's adjustment, a negative impact had been documented for prior generations (Stevenson & Black, 1988), although those studies often confounded father absence and poverty. However, father absence does appear to have a lasting impact on men's understanding of themselves and their lives. This feeling is sometimes referred to as "father hunger" (Bly, 1991) or even as "the wound" (Lee, 1991). One author positioned the death of one's father as a rite of passage in which a "son's reaction may surprise both himself and others... [and] propel a son toward despondency and even self-destruction... [or] inspire in the son a new appreciation for his life and move him with urgency to make the most of his remaining years" (Chethik, 2001, p. 2). The monumental nature of this event may help to explain why men's autobiographies regularly mentioned the loss of a father, but rarely mentioned a father who was (still) alive, wives, or children (Gergen & Gergen, 1993).

Despite the new model of fatherhood that emphasizes greater paternal involvement and emotional connection, masculine injunctions against emotional expression may hamper the fulfillment of this role. In fact, men with higher levels of gender role conflict typically report connections with their sons (O'Neil, 2008). But beginning with very young children may help fathers overcome gendered challenges. When men are allowed to interact with their children shortly after birth, they react similarly to mothers, showing strong emotional reactions and becoming enthralled with the baby (Parke & Tinsley, 1981). Storey, Walsh, Quinton, & Wynne-Edwards (2000) demonstrated that new and expectant mothers and fathers showed similar physiological reactions to infant-related stimuli. In these early interactions, fathers thus form a paternal bond that resembles the mother-child attachment.

Teen fathers have relatively low levels of education compared to other fathers, and their jobs and income opportunities are more limited, increasing the likelihood that they will turn to illegal activities to earn money and thus increasing their chances of becoming incarcerated during their twenties (Dariotis, Pleck, Astone, & Sonenstein, 2011; Kiselica & Kiselica, 2014). Young fathers also face difficulties that prevent them from receiving services. Some barriers are structural, such as programs that are designed for mothers but even though fathers are allowed to participate, while other barriers are inaccurate stereotypical beliefs among providers or policymakers, such as the beliefs that men are incompetent or uninterested parents (Bellamy & Banman, 2014; Devault, 2014; Kiselica & Kiselica, 2014). In effect, these problems leave young men, especially those from impoverished backgrounds, in "double jeopardy" because they may not have the resources needed to become good fathers and they are often unable to obtain the supports they need (Devault, 2014).

Men engage in various relationships as friends, romantic partners, and parents. The interactional patterns that are common among all-male groups, and men's adherence to masculinity ideologies may affect the quality of these relationships, often in negative ways. In particular, men's ability and willingness to express their intimate thoughts and feelings are often under-developed and meet with disapproval, leading many men to find their intimate relationships to be not-quite-enough. But we should not overemphasize the negative; most men and boys achieve satisfying and healthy relationships despite gendered barriers.

SUMMARY

1. Boys' development, particularly in all-boys groups, teaches them an interactional style that is self-promoting and dominant but not responsive or attentive to other's feelings, wants, and needs.

2. Masculine norms of emotional restriction and independence encourage boys and men not to share their inner thoughts and feelings, thus diminishing their opportunities for intimacy.

3. Homophobia exacerbates this dynamic in male-male friendships. It also serves to diminish physical contact between males.

4. These factors combine to leave men with relationships that often are not as intimate as men would like them to be, and frameworks that give them little opportunity to deepen their relationships without risking their masculine status.

5. Friendships and romantic relationships share many of the same characteristics: intimacy, trust, sharing of secrets, and loyalty. These attributes are the same for both male-male and male-female dyads.

6. Although male-male friendships are often deep and carry great importance to their participants, they are rarely described as "loving," possibly because shared time is often spent in side-by-side activities where the emphasis is on doing rather than direct interaction.

7. Male-female friendships have become commonplace. They face challenges from masculine directives to dominate women as well as from some men's tendency to sexualize intimacy. At the same time, males often place great value in the intimacy and support offered by their female friends.

8. Male-female dating relationships usually begin to appear in mid-adolescence. They too are negatively affected by men's adherence to masculine norms, including the erroneous belief that "nice guys finish last."

9. Male-male dating relationships often do not appear until later adolescence, in part due to lack of available partners. Gay men say that the masculine role is more of an impediment to relationships than it is a support.

10. Long-term romantic relationships, including marriage, often rely on factors such as affection, dependability, shared interests, sexual satisfaction, and a man's appreciation for his partner's appearance. These findings apply to both homosexual and heterosexual men.

11. Long-term heterosexual couples' satisfaction is also related to practices of equality within the relationship, as well as their ability to communicate effectively.

12. Long-term gay male couples' satisfaction is also related to their ability to negotiate (and maintain) sexual boundaries.

13. Becoming a father involves a series of transitions for the man, which may reinforce the provider role while challenging his sense of competence in caring for an infant or young child.

14. Fathers' perceptions of what it means to be a good father, as well as their actual parenting practices, depend on models to which they have had access and to their memories and perceptions of the fathering they received. Access to resources such as education, money, and partner support also has great influence over their behaviors as fathers.

Chapter Fourteen

Coping in a Difficult World:
Men and Mental Health

A middle-aged man gets so distraught after his wife leaves him that he has to be admitted to a psychiatric hospital. A teenaged boy commits frequent robberies and assaults. A young man cannot resist the urge to expose his genitals to pubescent girls. A senior citizen, despondent from loneliness and the decline of his body, contemplates suicide. An alcoholic experiences significant difficulties with his job, relationships, finances, and the law.

The problems that these men have in dealing with their life problems have become unmanageable. All of them are experiencing a good deal of psychological discomfort, although some might be able to hide it. Many would have trouble admitting to others, or even to themselves, that they need help, or believing that they could benefit from treatment. Even if they come to an awareness that their problems are out of control, they might be very reluctant to ask for assistance from professionals or even their closest friends.

Throughout this book, we have described many of the negative psychological effects of uncritically adhering to rigid and unreasonable gender demands. On the other hand, certain aspects of traditional masculinity may also contribute positively to mental health. In this chapter, we explore in more depth the relationships between gender and psychological well-being for men. The chapter is structured in four parts. First, we look at definitions of mental health and their connections with cultural conceptions of gender. Second is a discussion of mental health problems that boys and/or men experience disproportionately in relation to girls and/or women and the associations of these disorders with gender role characteristics. Third, we examine life experience factors that either protect men from mental illness or put them at increased risk. Finally, we explore the special issues around men in counseling and psychotherapy.

DEFINING MENTAL HEALTH

Virtually every abnormal psychology textbook begins with a chapter on the definitions of mental health and mental illness. If these were easy concepts to define, it would not

259

take an entire chapter to cover the territory. Setting forth criteria for mental health and illness turns out to be a rather complicated enterprise. Nearly everyone agrees that a person who hallucinates frequently or cannot remember his or her name is suffering from a mental disturbance. On the other hand, when does "normal" sadness become "abnormal" depression? What if a person is satisfied with a lifestyle that others consider "sick?" How about the person who is a member of an oppressed group—if he or she is suspicious of others' motives, is that "paranoia," or is it "accurate reality testing?" (Sue, et. al., 2014).

Some major definitional difficulties lie in the culture-bound character and historical context of definitions of mental health and illness. For instance, suppose that you were visiting the United States without knowing anything about the mainstream culture. You find out that every Saturday and Sunday during autumn, men get together, run as fast as they can, and knock each other down. Some of these men become severely injured and are carried off on stretchers. Others experience a good deal of lingering pain from these frequent violent collisions, and occasionally some even suffer catastrophic spinal cord injuries. Moreover, tens of thousands of people gather to watch these spectacles, and sometimes they even cheer when someone gets hurt.

As an outside observer, you wonder if the term for "war" in the United States is "football," yet you see the players shaking hands afterwards. You might be likely to go back to your native land and describe these "crazy," self-destructive men who engage in these exhibitions and the "sadistic" people who watch and cheer. If you did, you would be making a judgment about the mental health of these people that few U.S. inhabitants would make.

Even the professional community has difficulty agreeing on criteria for mental illness, and in fact these standards change over time. In 1968, the American Psychiatric Association published the second edition of the *Diagnostic and Statistical Manual of Mental Disorders* (DSM-II), a guide for labeling psychological disturbances. In this version of the manual, homosexuality was defined as a mental disorder. When the next revision (DSM-III) (American Psychiatric Association, 1980) was published, the diagnostic category was called "ego-dystonic homosexuality," which meant that if you were gay, you had a mental disorder only if you were dissatisfied with being gay and wanted to become heterosexual.

This development prompted psychiatrist Thomas Szasz to describe himself as having "ego-dystonic chronological disorder" because he was older than he wanted to be! His point was well taken. Everybody has some aspects of themselves with which they are dissatisfied. Why have we chosen only sexual orientation to pathologize? Perhaps as a result of convincing arguments by Szasz and others, this diagnostic category disappeared in the next three editions (DSM-III-R; DSM-IV, DSM-V, American Psychiatric Association, 1987; 1994; 2013).

Landrine (1988) pointed out the cultural bias in defining mental health and illness:

> Contemporary concepts of normalcy and psychopathology perpetuate the construction of the behavior of minorities and women as pathological along with the view that culture is peripheral to psychopathology.... The term normal suggests, among other things, an individual who exhibits abstract and logical thinking, emotional control, independence, delay of gratification, happiness, a concern with

developing one's own potential to the fullest, and a sense of self as an autonomous individual who exerts personal control over self and environment... the sense of self described above—from which many other characteristics derive—is not how the poor experience the self... how Blacks experience the self... how Asian Americans experience the self... how women experience the self... or how most people throughout the world experience the self.... This concept of normalcy, held by U.S. public and professionals alike... is largely synonymous with the characteristics of upper income White men in this country... and is firmly rooted in the social meanings shared by middle-class White Americans. (p. 40)

Especially since the publication of DSM-III in 1980, some feminist scholars have argued that the mental health establishment pathologizes women for the way that they have been socialized (e.g., to be interdependent, emotional, and self-sacrificing). Pantony and Caplan (1991) suggested that a diagnostic category of "Delusional Dominating Personality Disorder" be used to describe people who have an "inability to establish and maintain meaningful interpersonal relationships, an inability to identify and express a range of feeling in oneself and others, and difficulty responding empathically to the feelings and needs of close associates and intimates" (p. 120). This proposed diagnosis is, of course, a description of a hypermasculine interpersonal style. Rather than labeling the behavior as emotionally disturbed, it is more often cast in a language of moral failure. As Prior (1999) stated, there is a tendency to see women as "mad" and men as "bad."

These objections to gender bias in the diagnostic criteria focus on the negative social consequences of being labeled as "disordered," and psychiatry has a rather long history of bias against women that constitutes a serious issue. However, we should not overlook the fact that it is not the purpose of diagnosis to stigmatize and blame people for their problems. Stigmatization is an unfortunate byproduct of diagnosis in a society that is prejudiced against the mentally ill.

The real purpose of diagnosis is to identify problems that require attention. In most cases, the willingness of health insurance providers to pay for treatment hinges on the diagnos-ability of the person seeking mental health services. Failing to label the hypermasculine behaviors described above as disturbed therefore has at least two consequences. First, it reinforces masculine privilege by tacitly approving the behavior. In other words, it says to the mental health community that it is all right to be emotionally withholding, aggressive, and unempathic. Second, it says that men who behave in such a way merit no attention. There is a denial that such behavior limits the quality of the man's life to a significant enough extent that we should do something for him.

The concepts of gender role conflict and strain show some promise in the study of gender and men's psychological adjustment. Gender role conflict is a negative psychological state that results from the contradictory and\or unrealistic demands of the gender role. The hypothesis of the gender role conflict and strain model is that men who accept traditional gender ideologies, yet do not feel that they fulfill the prescriptions inherent in the role, will experience the highest levels of psychological conflict and negative health consequences. For example, a man thinks that being unemotional means being manly, but he finds it difficult to suppress his emotions. This man would experience more role conflict than either: a) a man who accepts low emotionality as manly but has no difficulty suppressing his feelings; or b) an emotional man who does not experience much pressure from the masculine prescription for emotional restrictedness. There is a growing body of evidence linking male gender role conflict with negative psychological states (O'Neil, 2008).

MEN, MASCULINITY AND MENTAL DISORDERS

There are significant variations in the proportions of men and women who are diagnosed within several categories of mental illnesses. Researchers believe that a number of factors contribute to these sex differences, including gender socialization, which may strongly affect how a person expresses his or her psychological distress. For instance, a gender-typed woman who experiences psychological pain may often become depressed. A gender-typed man might react to the same kind of pain by abusing alcohol. These tendencies may be at least partly fueled by the woman's socialization to "act in" or internalize—to introspect and think about how she feels—and the man's gender-typed encouragement to deny vulnerability and "act out" or externalize—to look to the environment for solutions to his problems. Some theorists (e.g., Lynch & Kilmartin, 2013; Real, 1997) maintain that a depressive psychological base underlies many common symptoms in men, but that diagnostic criteria reflect a feminine mode of depression (more on this subject later).

A related possibility is that gender socialization sometimes prevents a person from acquiring certain coping skills (O'Neil, 1981b). A highly gender-typed man may not have learned well how to deal with emotions and relationships. A highly gender-typed woman may not have learned well how to deal with independence. Thus, gender socialization can contribute to behavioral deficits as well as to negative patterns of behavior.

People use psychological *defense mechanisms* to protect themselves from perceived threats to the self (Clark, 1998). Sometimes, their use is very adaptive. For instance, it is quite common for a person who has recently lost a loved one through death to experience some level of initial *denial* about the death. If the person were to come to a full emotional realization of such a profound loss, he or she might be flooded with anxiety and sadness and become completely incapacitated. The defense mechanism allows the person to protect the self and deal with the loss over time. On the other hand, all defenses involve distortion of reality, and so overusing them results in impaired psychological functioning.

Largely because of early gender socialization, males and females tend to develop somewhat distinct defensive styles. When defensiveness becomes problematic, these gendered styles express themselves in a differential vulnerability to several mental disorders. The masculine-feminine externalizing-internalizing dimension leads men to use the defense of *projection* (attributing one's own conflicts to others) more frequently than women (Clark, 1998). Faced with psychological discomfort such as low self-esteem, a man is more likely than a woman to project his negative feelings on to others and deal with these feelings in a distorted way. As we discussed in Chapter Thirteen, violent behavior is often a projection of unacceptable negative feelings about the self on to another person. Unfortunately, projection leaves the person who is experiencing the conflict with no avenue for dealing with it directly and no process for improving his or her functioning. A person is unlikely to see the need for a change in behavior when that person experiences the problem as external to the self.

As with many areas of investigation, gender is a better predictor of defensive behavior than sex. Men who experience high levels of rigid beliefs around masculinity as it relates to success, power, competition, and emotional expression are significantly more likely than other men to use immature defenses—those that are common in three- to 15-year olds and people who are personality disordered (Mahalik, Cournoyer, DeFranc, Cherry, & Napolitano, 1998). In other words, high levels of gender role conflict and strain tends to result in grown men acting like children.

There is a tendency to think that individuals are predisposed toward certain types of mental disorders only because of the way they were raised. In addition to the contribution of past socialization to current behavior, we should also remember that, in an important sense, men and women live in different gendered cultural worlds. We saw in Chapter Thirteen that sex-segregated social groups tend to have gender-characteristic interpersonal styles. In the sociocultural context, different behaviors are anticipated, rewarded, and punished on the basis of sex. For example, expressions of sadness and helpless feelings by a woman might be met with sympathy and emotional support. The same behavior in a man might result in social isolation and loss of status.

Researchers have observed the following sex differences in mental illness:

1. Males experience a disproportionate number of most childhood disorders, such as Attention Deficit Hyperactivity Disorder and Conduct Disorder.

2. Women are somewhat more likely to be diagnosed with depression and most anxiety-based disorders, and much more likely than men to have eating disorders. However, there is a growing awareness of body image disturbances in boys and men (see Box 14.1).

3. Males constitute a majority of substance abusers, sexual deviates, and people with behavior control problems such as pyromania, compulsive gambling, and intermittent explosive disorder (a pattern of rageful outbursts) (Sue, et. al., 2014).

4. There are unequal sex proportions for a variety of personality disorders: more men than women are diagnosed as paranoid, schizoid, schizotypal, narcissistic, obsessive-compulsive, and antisocial; more women than men are diagnosed as borderline (Sue, et. al., 2014).

5. Men are much more likely than women to commit suicide (Heron, 2013), although women make more incomplete suicide attempts (Stillion & McDowell, 1996) (see Chapter Nine for a discussion of suicide and masculinity).

MENTAL HEALTH ISSUES FOR MEN

There has been much speculation about the relationships between some aspects of masculinity and the disorders listed above. The following discussion will focus on a few areas of diagnosis (substance abuse, personality disorder, and depression) and mental health issues (the role of marriage in men's mental health, and the psychological effects of parental divorce and father absence on sons).

Box 14.1   Body Image Disturbances in Men

The drive for thinness and resultant risk of eating disorders in females is a well-documented phenomenon that is strongly associated with cultural standards of beauty that emphasize body types that are impossible to achieve for most women. As Jackson Katz (2013) points out in the documentary film *Tough Guise II*, cultural standards for male body types also appear to be changing, but in the opposite direction—hypermuscularity is more and more in evidence in media portrayals of men. Katz displays the contrast between the somewhat flabby "professional wrestlers" of the 1960s and today's overdeveloped performers. During approximately the same period of time, the "action figure" (doll) G. I. Joe has changed from having the equivalent of 13 inch biceps (estimated by their proportion to the rest of the body) to 28 inch ones. The action-adventure film star known as "The Rock," a very muscular man, has 20 inch biceps, and so these figurines present a virtually impossible standard of manliness, much as Barbie dolls do with female thinness. *Star Wars* figurines have undergone a similar transformation from commonplace male bodies to hypermuscular ones. Other action figures have undergone similar transformations (Baghurst, Hollander, Nardella, & Haff, 2006). Katz believes that this cultural change reflects a crisis of masculinity accompanied by high anxiety in men around their desirability and manliness.

Do changing societal demands for muscular physiques have negative effects on men in similar ways that standards of thinness have on women? Emerging evidence suggests that this is indeed the case. In the same fashion in which eating disordered women are dissatisfied with their bodies and evidence body distortions in which they believe that they are fatter than they actually are, young men often perceive themselves as thinner and less muscular than objec-

tive assessments indicate (Raudenbush & Zellner, 1997). This body dissatisfaction and resultant pattern of pathological behaviors has been called *bigorexia* or the *Adonis Complex* (Pope, Phillips, & Olivardia, 2002).

Donald McCreary & Doris Sasse (2000) coined the term *drive for muscularity* and demonstrated negative phenomena associated with this characteristic. Not surprisingly, males are much more motivated to gain weight and muscle than females, and boys with a high drive for muscularity tend to have lower self-esteem and greater levels of depression than other boys. Moreover, they are more likely to binge eat and to use anabolic androgenic steroids, which entails risks to the heart, kidneys, liver, and immune system (Olivardia, Pope, Borowiecki, & Cohane, 2004). Many steroid users also share hypodermic needles, thus risking infection. An estimated three percent of adolescent boys in the United States abuse these substances (Irving, Wall, Neumark-Sztainer, & Story, 2002). Morrison, Morrison, and Hopkins (2003) discovered that high levels of exposure to idealistic images of men's bodies (e.g., in muscle and fitness magazines) and the tendency to compare one's body with these images were associated with high drive for muscularity. In addition, steroid use is associated with having friends who emphasize muscularity and parents who tease boys about their size (Smolak, Murnen, & Thompson, 2005).

Researchers have found links between gender role conflict and the drive for muscularity (McCreary, Saucier, & Courtenay, 2005), specifically in conflicts centering around success, power, and competition. It is not surprising that gender role conflict has a strong relationship to body image in men (O'Neil, 2008). The negative effects of drive for muscularity can be added to the list of the toxic consequences of uncritical adherence to the hypertrophied version of masculinity that is being sold to boys and men by cultural forces. Only by educating males about gender and providing alternate models of health can we inoculate boys and men against these negative influences.

Substance Abuse

Men are more than twice as likely as women to have difficulty with alcohol (Grant, et. al., 2004) or other drug abuse or dependence (Sue, et. al., 2014). Alcoholism is one of the most serious mental health problems in the world. In the United States, nearly 14 percent of people have these disorders at some point during their lives (American Psychiatric Association, 2013). Brooks & Silverstein (1995) report that alcoholics occupy half of all U.S. hospital beds at any given time, that they attempt suicide 75 to 300 percent more often than non-abusers, and that as many as one in 10 men become alcoholic (compared with one in 50 women). Alcohol abuse is also strongly related to violence, crime, accidents, work absenteeism, relationship problems, and disease (Lex, 1995).

David Sue and his colleagues (2014) note that there is considerable cultural variation in rates of alcoholism. Although there are possible genetic factors in alcoholism, e.g. many Native Americans and Asians often have highly sensitive physiological reactions to alcohol (Butcher, Hooley, & Mineka, & 2014), the cross-cultural variability in rates of problem drinking suggests that cultural values also play an important role in the prevalence of the disorder.

Gender is one of the central organizing principles of mainstream U.S. culture, and we do not have to look far to find social connections between masculinity and alcohol abuse. Following are a few of these connections:

1. *Externalizing defensive style:* As noted earlier, men are encouraged to look outside of themselves for solutions to problems. Being in any kind of psychological pain is considered unmanly, as it implies emotional vulnerability. Drinking can function as self-medication. Alcohol reduces anxiety and clouds the person's consciousness so that he or she will be both emotionally and physically numb. Men who rely on avoidant forms of coping with negative emotions are more likely to exhibit abusive drinking patterns (Cooper, Russell, Skinner, Frone, & Mudar, 1992).

2. *Toughness and risk-taking:* Some men perceive becoming dead drunk to be a way of demonstrating one's masculinity, since "real men" can hold their liquor (de Visser & Smith, 2007; Peralta, 2007). Binge-drinking men have been known to continue drinking *after* throwing up (a body's signal that it has had enough, if ever there were one). Driving and taking other risks while drunk are ways of demonstrating a masculine disregard for safety. In the United States, men are nearly four times as likely as women to be arrested for drunken driving (Halsey, 2009).

3. *The quantification of experience:* Men are often socialized into the world of sports, where it is important to count things like home runs, touchdowns, and points. Drinking can become a competition whereby the man who drinks the

most "wins." Drinking games, where players are forced to drink, bring a masculine sport-like structure into the social arena.

4. *Dealing with emotions and relationships indirectly:* A friend once told Chris Kilmartin about an experience he had at a party. He decided to go out on the deck to get some fresh air, and there he found two men, dead drunk, having an argument about which one of them loved the other one more. Imagine these men having that same conversation when they were sober. Alcohol allows men to lower their masculine inhibitions and behave in affectionate ways with each other (Blazina & Watkins, 1996). Men feel that they can walk down the street with their arms around each other when they are drunk, but not at other times. The next day, they can maintain their interpersonal distance by not mentioning their affectionate behavior or attributing it to their drunkenness. Therefore, alcohol abuse enables men to deal with their feelings of attachment while at the same time maintaining a façade of masculine independence (Capraro, 2000).

5. *Modeling and social group factors:* Males are more likely than females to have same-sex peers who are heavy drinkers (Brooks & Silverstein, 1995), and some male social groups actively promote binge drinking. Chiefly among these groups on college campuses are fraternities. Nearly 40 percent of fraternity members went from being low level drinkers in high school to being high level drinkers in college (compared with 17 percent of non-members) (Lo & Globetti, 1995). Heavy drinkers tend to seek fraternity membership (Wechsler, Kuh, & Davenport, 1996), and the majority of fraternity members are binge drinkers (Smith & Mathews, 1997).

6. *The cultural association of masculinity with alcohol:* Drinking is interconnected with the social meanings attached to being masculine (Uy, Massoth, & Gottdiener, 2014). Male television actors are portrayed drinking significantly more often than females, and alcohol advertisements are largely oriented toward the associating masculine fantasy with alcohol use. Traditional gender attitudes are associated with alcohol-related problems in adult men (McCreary, Newcomb, & Sadava, 1999) and adolescent males (White & Huselid, 1997).

Beer advertisers present images of their products as "related to challenge, risk, and mastery over nature, technology, others, and the self" (Fejes, 1992, p. 14). Men in these commercials are usually portrayed in occupational and leisure pursuits, especially in outdoor settings and sometimes with an element of danger. Beer is often presented as a substitute for the overt communication of affection between men, a rite of passage into manhood, and as a reward for hard work. Men are often shown participating in activities that involve speed and coordination, like race-car driving, skiing, and calf-roping, despite the fact that drinking would severely decrease one's performance in these pursuits and increase the risk of injury. (Strate, 1992). When women are portrayed, they are often presented as an audience for men (Fejes, 1992), or as sexual objects (Hall & Crum, 1994). Advertisers often imply that alcohol is a means of sophistication and heterosexual seduction (Barthel, 1992).

In an article titled "Beer Commercials: A Manual on Masculinity," Strate (1992) sums up the impact of this advertising: "No other industry commercials focus so exclusively and exhaustively on images of the man's man…in reflecting the myth, the commercials also reinforce it" (pp. 78–79). Fejes (1992) adds: "Men who are sensitive, thoughtful, scholarly, gay, or complex are not present in beer commercials" (p. 14). Beer commercials also portray a sanitized version of drinking—there is never any smoke in the bar, nobody ever pays for a drink, and nobody ever gets drunk (Strate, 1992).

7. *Gender role conflict and strain:* Men use alcohol to deal with the pressures of social masculinity. Researchers have found that men with high levels of gender role conflict also had higher levels of reported alcohol use (Uy, Massoth, & Gottdiener, 2014) and alcohol-related problems (McCreary, Newcomb, & Sadava, 1999) than men with lower levels of gender role conflict.

Williams and Ricardelli (1999) describe two basic gendered dimensions to men's alcohol use. First, alcohol is clearly associated with traditional masculinity. Therefore, drinking is a way to display one's manliness (the *confirmatory* function). Second, drinking can help men to handle the stress and strain of living up to difficult standards of masculinity (the *compensatory* function).

Personality Disorders

Personality is a relatively stable set of behavioral predispositions that characterize a human being's typical functioning (Funder, 2010). In the case of the person who is *personality disordered*, the generalized ways in which he or she approaches the world are marked by an inflexible and self-defeating style that results in poor mental stability (T. Millon, C. F. Millon, Meagher, Grossman, & Ramnath, 2005). The ingrained ways of relating to others that personality disordered individuals use almost always cause them problems in their work and social functioning. They also tend to produce a good deal of personal distress.

The DSM-V (American Psychiatric Association, 2013) lists 10 of these disorders. Five affect men more often than women and one affects women more often. The remaining four disorders are distributed fairly equally between the sexes and the overall sex ratios of personality disorders taken together are fairly equal (Rosenberg & Kosslyn, 2014). A description of the male-dominated diagnoses follows.

Schizoid Personality Disorder is characterized by flat emotionality and interpersonal aloofness. These people seem to lack the capacity to experience emotion and lead dull, joyless, and solitary lives.

Schizotypal Personality Disorder is characterized by peculiarities of thinking and behavior. These oddities of experience and action result in highly impaired interpersonal relationships.

People with *Narcissistic Personality Disorder* display a grandiose sense of self-importance and absorption. They present themselves as exceptionally talented, accomplished, and "special." Narcissists are easily hurt by any kind of criticism and believe that they are entitled to special favors by virtue of being so wonderful. They feel shamed and enraged when others react negatively to them and when they do not receive a steady source of admiration and attention (American Psychiatric Association, 2013). Underneath this grandiose exterior is a fragile sense of self-worth.

Antisocial Personality Disorder is characterized by a long history of behaviors that violate the rights of others, such as lying, stealing, and assaulting. Antisocial people feel little remorse for having mistreated others. They are frequently in legal trouble and fail to sustain any close relationships (American Psychiatric Association, 2013). Many antisocial people are dangerous criminals.

People with *Obsessive-compulsive Personality Disorder* are stereotypical perfectionists. They often demand that others conform to their unreasonable standards of order and devotion to details, thus they tend to be interpersonal bullies.

One could characterize many of the traits described in these disorders as caricatures of negative masculinity. All of these personality types are marked by some mixture of self-absorption, indifference toward others' feelings, and an overemphasis on independence. Narcissistic and antisocial people are interpersonally exploitive, using others to reach their own goals. All of these styles are characterized by extreme difficulty in relationships, another stereotypically masculine characteristic.

There is also pronounced emotional restrictedness in antisocial, obsessive-compulsive, and schizoid disorders. Schizoids feel nothing or next to nothing. Antisocials and obsessive-compulsives express little emotion except for anger, which is stereotypically masculine. The combination of hostility and hyperindependence in antisocial disorder is an especially volatile one. Lacking a sense of self-compassion, they have no point of reference for empathizing with others, and thus they are prone to violence (see Chapter Twelve). Antisocial personality disorder is the only one that has demonstrated biological heritability, and so the sex difference in this disorder may be a reflection of a differential vulnerability combined with gender socialization and adverse childhood experiences (Rosenberg & Kosslyn, 2014).

Although mental illnesses are caused by multiple factors, dysfunctional interaction styles in the family of origin are strong influences in the development of personality disorders (Millon, et. al., 2005). If we consider hypermasculinity to result from harsh masculine socialization, we could speculate that men who exhibit the above personality disorders may well have received an exaggerated "dose" of overly stern gender socialization in addition to other dysfunctional developmental patterns such as childhood maltreatment and/or neglect.

Depression

Depression involves pervasive feelings of hopelessness, helplessness and worthlessness accompanied by a family of behavioral symptoms like social isolation, sleep problems, and loss of interest or pleasure in activities (American Psychiatric Association, 2013). It has been called the "common cold of mental illness" (Seligman, 1990a), affecting approximately one in five people in the United States at some point during their lives.

Rates of depression have risen steeply in the U.S. during the twentieth century (Nolen-Hoeksema, 1998), prompting psychologist Martin Seligman (1990b), who has spent much of his professional career studying this mental disorder, to label it an epidemic.

Females are diagnosed with clinical depression twice as often as males in the United States. Susan Nolen-Hoeksema (1998) believes that women are more depressed than men because of two basic factors: the patriarchal oppression of women, and the tendency for women to be socialized into a *ruminative coping style* in which the depressed person dwells on his or her distress in passive ways that are not oriented toward problem solving, which tends to make the depression more severe and longer-lasting (Nolen-Hoeksema, 2006). On the other hand, males are more likely to deal with negative emotions by distracting themselves from their feelings.

Several theorists believe that the epidemiology of depression in men as a group approaches that of women, but that men tend to have different, gendered styles of expressing their problem. The reported sex difference in depression may be misleading due to a number of factors. First, women may be more likely than men to seek treatment or to report their depression to others (Sue, et. al., 2014). Males have a tendency to underreport most physical and psychological treatment, as having symptoms implies unmasculine vulnerability (Pollack, 1998). Second, the diagnostic system may be gender-biased. Third, males may manifest depression in different ways from females, leading to different diagnoses. For instance, men are more disposed toward externalizing symptoms such as heavy drinking, angry outbursts, and aggression in response to sad feelings (Real, 1997; Lynch & Kilmartin, 2013, Cochran & Rabinowitz, 2000; Kilmartin, 2005).

In an exhaustive review of the research literature on men and depression, Michael Addis (2008) concludes that acceptance of traditional masculine ideologies puts men at risk for both conventional depression and for externalizing symptoms that co-occur with depression, but that there is significant variability in symptom patterns among men. Mariola Magovcevic and Addis (2008) developed a scale to assess masculine depression. Adherence to gender norms like competitiveness, homophobia, and hyper-independence also are associated with a lower likelihood of help seeking for one's symptoms. O'Neil (2008) noted that in 24 of 27 studies, researchers have linked men's gender role conflict with depressive symptoms, and a link to low self-esteem is demonstrated in several other studies.

Regardless of the debate around the true prevalence rates of depression for men and women, we should avoid being drawn in to a competition between the sexes to claim the title of "most depressed." All troubled people are in need of help. At the same time, the sex differential in diagnosis may provide important clues to the connections between gender demands and mental illness. It might well be that the roots of the illness are different for the average depressed woman and the average depressed man. In other words, it is possible that rigid gendering is a risk factor for depression, but that the character of that gendering may also produce markedly different modes of expression in the two sexes.

Several pieces of evidence lend credence to the hypothesis that depression is under-diagnosed in males. The strongest is that males commit suicide, the ultimate expression of depression, four times more often than females (see Chapter Nine). There are also very high rates of psychiatric hospitalization in divorced men compared with divorced women, suggesting that female partners may have a strong role in helping men defend from their underlying depressive senses of self (see the discussion below on the protective function of marriage for men). And, serious psychogenic physical diseases, which are related to psychological conflicts, are more common among men (Lynch & Kilmartin, 2013).

While women are prone toward the aforementioned ruminative coping style for dealing with negative emotions, men's externalizing tendencies lead them to gravitate toward distracting themselves and acting out. Alcohol abuse is a major way to hide one's depression, even from the self, and there is ample evidence linking alcohol problems to underlying depression. As Real (1997) stated, "While the capacity to externalize pain protects some men from *feeling* depressed, it does not stop them from *being* depressed; it just helps them to disconnect further from their own experience" (p. 82, emphasis original).

Masked depression is also in evidence in a number of other typically masculine problems, including violence, overinvolvement in sports or work, narcissism, criminal behavior, and relationship difficulties. Addressing the underlying depressive dynamics of these problems is a key component of effective treatment (Lynch & Kilmartin, 2013; Kilmartin, 2005; Cochran & Rabinowitz, 2000).

The Role of Marriage in Mental Health

A stereotypical scene: A man and a woman have been dating for an extended period of time. The relationship is monogamous and mutually satisfying. They love each other. The woman expresses a desire to marry but the man shies away. She asks, "Why don't you want to get married?" He doesn't really know. He asks, "Why is getting married so important?" She doesn't really know.

For many heterosexual men, committing to and being intimate with one woman for the rest of their lives feels very dangerous. He may lose his independence and freedom, and then he would become very unhappy. For many heterosexual women, committing to and being intimate with one man for the rest of their lives seems like the "thing to do." Remaining unmarried after extended dating feels dangerous. The cultural myth is that marriage fulfills women and restricts men. Cultural stereotypes reflect this bias—the happy and devoted housewife, the lonely spinster or old maid, the carefree bachelor, and the henpecked husband (note that there is no cultural slang equivalent for a woman whose husband dominates her) (Johnson, 2001).

Social scientists have investigated the accuracy of this bias by examining mental illness rates for married men, single men, married women, and single women. If marriage has damaging or beneficial effects for any of these groups, these effects should be reflected by mental illness rates that are at variance with contrasted groups.

In general, the results of this research cast considerable doubt on the accuracy of the cultural myth. An extensive survey of mental hospital patients revealed that single and divorced men were hospitalized at about three times the rate of married men, and also at a higher rate than single or divorced women. Married women were hospitalized at a higher rate than married men. Married people in general were hospitalized less often than single people, but the size of that difference was much greater for men than for women (Rosenstein, Steadman, McAskill, & Manderscheid, 1987).

Although one can not say from these data that marriage *causes* better mental health in men, there certainly are relationships between being married and staying out of the hospital, avoiding mental illness, reduction in physical risk-taking, and avoiding stress-related physical illnesses. These relationships hold for women, but they are much stronger for men (Denmark, Rabinowitz, & Sechzer, 2000).

One can make sense of these data by looking at the functions of marriage for men and women. For both partners, marriage would seem to provide opportunities for intimacy and companionship, as well as fulfilling a social obligation—95 percent of people in the United States get married at some time during their lives (Casteneda & Burns-Glover, 2004). We have already discussed in Chapter Eight the gender role prohibitions against intimacy and self-disclosure for men. Yet these are human needs, and failing to attend to them has adverse effects on the person. Although marriage does not necessarily involve psychological intimacy, it certainly sets the stage for it. For many men, then, marriage is an opportunity to fill a void that has been created by harsh masculine socialization.

Women need intimacy too but they are more likely than men to experience it in relationships with friends (see Chapter Thirteen). In the realm of psychological intimacy, marriage tends to be less novel for women than for men. Men may also tend to be less responsive to women's disclosures. As a result, fewer psychological benefits accrue for women than for men.

The social role aspects of marriage are also worthy of mention. The traditional Christian marriage ceremony begins by asking, "Who gives this woman to be married to this man?" It is an exchange of property from father to son-in-law. The celebrant ends by saying, "I now pronounce you man and wife." The man keeps his identity ("man"), and the woman's identity ("wife") seems to become defined by her relationship to the man. As Anthony Porter (Bunch & Porter, 2003) describes it, "She went down the aisle as a piece of property; she came back with a job." Then the celebrant says, "you may now kiss the bride," as if she is not doing any kissing; she is merely the passive recipient of the kiss. The bride relinquishes her last name and sometimes even gives up her first name ("Mrs. John Smith"). Historically, marriage was a legal agreement by which the husband took possession of his wife's property (Herttell, 1839/1992). In fact, the woman herself became her husband's property—rape laws were originally property crimes against a husband or father (Basow, 1992). Clearly, society has historically expected wives to adapt to their husbands and take responsibility for the relationship.

This part of the social role is slowly changing. Some marriage ceremonies have become more egalitarian, with language like, "I now pronounce you *husband* and wife," and "you may now kiss *each other*." We are also seeing many more women retaining their last names, which is emblematic of their having identities apart from their husbands. The social myth that women are incomplete unless they are married is slowly undergoing modification.

Despite their stereotypical resistance to getting married, it appears that considerable benefits are associated with being a husband. The fact that most men eventually marry (despite gender role demands for hyperindependence and promiscuity) is good evidence that men want and need intimacy. Pleck (1995) reported that men usually experience their family roles as more important in their lives than their work roles, and that satisfaction with family roles is strongly associated with psychological well-being.

Divorce and Father Absence

Marital separation and divorce are becoming increasingly prevalent in the United States. Although much research has been done in the context of what John Hill (1987) called "Dick and Jane" families (those with a father who works outside of the home, a housewife mother, and two or more children, none of whom are from the parents' previous relationships), these families constitute less than three percent of U.S. households (U.S. Department of Labor Statistics, 2005). One in every two or three U.S. marriages ends in divorce, and the average length of a marriage that ends in divorce is 6.3 years (Coontz, 2005). Social scientists have become interested in how children are affected by parental conflict, divorce, remarriage, and family blending.

The breakup of a marriage is rarely, if ever, easy on any of the people involved. Children of divorce have a higher risk than other children of psychological difficulties for several years, although most children of divorce are mentally healthy (Hetherington, Stanley-Hagen, & Anderson, 1989). Some researchers have discovered that the process and aftermath of marital dissolution has an especially negative impact on boys.

Researchers Jeanne and Jack Block began to follow a cohort of young children in the late 1960s in a longitudinal study designed to investigate several developmental hypotheses. They and their colleagues collected data on the same youngsters year after year. During that time, some of these children's parents divorced, and together with another colleague, they investigated the effects of parental conflict and divorce on children (Block, Block, & Gjerde, 1986). This study is an especially important one because it is *prospective*, meaning that the researchers were able to gather data on these children prior to the marital breakup, often for several years. They did not have to rely on children's memories of what happened to them and how they felt.

Comparisons of 60 intact families with 41 subsequently divorced or separated families revealed that sons are more vulnerable than daughters to the negative effects of parental conflict. Boys from subsequently divorcing families showed more aggression, more difficulty in controlling impulses, less cooperation, and higher anxiety in novel situations than boys from intact families. These characteristics also stood in contrast to girls from subsequently divorcing families, who showed different and milder symptoms than boys.

Another important finding from this study was that parents were much more likely to engage in marital conflict in the presence of boys than in the presence of girls. If you think about the experience of your parents fighting with each other when you were a child, you might recall (or imagine) it to be very frightening indeed. The sex difference in witnessing parental conflict may be a critical factor in explaining the significantly more negative impact of marital difficulties on sons. It is also important to note that these effects are not simply a result of divorce, per se, but from the conflict preceding the divorce. The researchers observed these sex differences in symptomatology for years prior to the marital separation.

The fact that parents in conflict are much more comfortable with expressing their animosity in front of their sons may reflect the beliefs that boys can "take it" and that boys' emotions are nonexistent or less important than those of girls. One can see that childhood gender role strain in interaction with family stress can have pronounced negative effects on the personality development of the boy. Boys who have internalized dominant masculine norms tend to have more difficulty adjusting to the separation and divorce of their parents (DeFranc & Mahalik, 2002).

However, we should not overstate the problem and neglect the wide range of effects in marriage dissolution. Many children of divorced parents adjust very well with a minimum of symptoms, especially when their mothers and fathers cooperate with each other in parenting tasks. Although divorce doubles the risk of emotional and behavioral problems, it raises that risk from about 10 percent to about 20 percent (and part of the difficulty can be attributed to relocating and economic stress). Therefore, about 80 percent of children do well in spite of the unfavorable environment that parental conflict produces (Hetherington & Stanley-Hagen, 1997). Moreover, these risk differences reduce sharply within two to three years following the divorce. Children of divorce who live with a competent single parent are only one-half at risk for problems compared with children living in two-parent conflicted families (Coontz, 1997). The social conservative movement to make divorce more difficult ignores the fact that staying married against one's will perpetuates a conflictual environment that may have adverse effects on children. Although divorce has negative effects on children when it results in the dissolution of a low-conflict marriage, divorce benefits children when it removes them from high-conflict situations (Amato & Booth, 2001).

The effects of father absence on boys are difficult to separate from the effects of parental conflict, economic changes, relocation, and other stressors that accompany marital dissolution. Although parental separation is probably the most prevalent cause of father absence, fathers may also be gone from the home because of death, or due to military service or other work. Additionally, many males have complained about fathers who, although physically present, are psychologically absent because of their emotional unresponsiveness. At the same time, there are physically absent fathers who may be somewhat psychologically present through telephone and email communication, letters, and visits. Father absence may be especially damaging when the father refuses to contribute to his children's economic support, as do an estimated one-quarter of non-custodial fathers (Hetherington & Stanley-Hagen, 1997).

There may well be variant effects of father absence depending on the type of absence (physical, psychological, or both), the circumstances around which the father left the home, the characteristics of the mother or other caretaker, the gender-typing of father and son, and/or other factors. Although there is a widespread societal assumption that father absence is damaging to males, researchers studying the connections between father absence and mental health have not demonstrated that it is necessary for boys to have same-sex role models to develop healthily. On the other hand, it has not been demonstrated that same-sex role models are unnecessary either (Silverstein & Auerbach, 1999). A good deal more investigative work in this area remains to be done.

Whatever the effects of father absence on boys are, we can be quite certain that relationships with fathers and feelings about fathers are of profound importance to sons. In an extensive research study of men, Barnett, Marshall, and Pleck (1992) found that the quality of the adult son's relationship with his father was significantly associated with the son's level of mental health, and a later meta-analysis indicates that both sons and daughters are better adjusted when their fathers remain active as parents after a divorce (DeAngelis, 2005). These conclusions support an earlier finding from an equally extensive study by Kamarovsky (1976) that male college seniors with psychological adjustment problems tended to report low levels of satisfaction in their relationships with their fathers. You may also recall from Chapter Twelve Lisak's (1991) finding of a connection between negative father-son relationships and the risk of sexual assault perpetration.

In all of these studies, the son's relationship to the father was much more predictive of mental health than his relationship to his mother. This research corroborates a great deal of anecdotal evidence from therapists and men's studies educators that feelings about the father constitute a major psychological issue in men's lives.

COUNSELING AND PSYCHOTHERAPY WITH MEN

Everyone will benefit if we can find ways to alleviate the suffering of people who struggle with mental health problems. The processes for doing so include counseling (psychotherapy), education, and social change. The latter two are saved for the final chapter of this book. The following discussion centers on the treatment of individual men in a psychotherapeutic context.

Men as a Special Population

Carl Rogers (1957) first popularized the idea that a counselor's understanding of the client's subjective psychological environment is a critical first step in the therapeutic process. If the therapist is to be helpful, he or she must gain a deep awareness of how the client experiences the self and the world. Rogers was an important early influence in defining the field of *Counseling Psychology,* which is founded on the appreciation and respect of individual differences and perspectives.

One of the important ways in which therapy clients differ is in their identifications with, and memberships in, different sociocultural groups. For example, people of color, physically challenged people, gays, and lesbians have almost always had some different experiences than Caucasians, people without significant physical challenges, and heterosexuals. Some of these experiences have important effects on the person's sense of self and view of the world. When these people see counselors, especially ones who are dissimilar to them, it is important for the counselor to be sensitive to the typical psychological and political issues associated with memberships in various groups.

With this basic assumption in mind, many counselors began to undergo formal and informal training in understanding diversity in the 1960s and 1970s, and this kind of education continues today. One of the basic categories of individual difference is, of course, the sex of the person seeking treatment. In 1979, the American Psychological

Association's (APA) Counseling Psychology division published a list entitled "Principles Concerning the Counseling and Therapy of Women." The preamble to these principles begins:

> Although competent counseling/therapy processes are essentially the same for all counselor/therapist interactions, special subgroups require specialized skills, attitudes, and knowledge. Women constitute a special subgroup. (Division 17, 1979, p. 21)

The psychologists who drafted this document believed that it is essential for counselors who treat women to be knowledgeable about biological, psychological and social issues affecting women, to be aware of their own values and biases about women, and to develop skills that are particularly suited to female clients.

Around the same time this document was published, therapists were beginning to realize that men also have typical styles and psychological issues that they bring to the therapeutic setting. Therapists also began to recognize and examine their values and biases about men, and some realized that a gender-aware perspective on masculine socialization would be helpful in their treatment of male clients.

A number of excellent books and journal articles have been published in the past two decades on the subject of men as a special population in psychotherapy. Some of these have integrated men's issues with those of special subpopulations of men such as ethnic, older, divorced, gay, and bisexual men (see Brooks & Good, 2001; Englar-Carlson & Stevens, 2006; Englar-Carlson, Evans & Duffey, 2014, and Rochlen & Rabinowitz, 2014).

MEN'S ISSUES IN COUNSELING AND PSYCHOTHERAPY

Counselors are becoming increasingly aware that men constitute a special subgroup of clients. They have identified a number of psychotherapeutic men's issues and developed some specialized treatments for male clients. Traditional individual psychotherapy is a set of methods that were developed by mostly male therapists to treat mostly female clients. If we look closely at the counseling relationship, we see that very little of traditional masculinity is conducive to requesting treatment, sustaining the therapeutic effort, or performing the activities required of clients.

Help Seeking

People who request psychotherapeutic services have often been stereotyped as "crazy," weak, or out of control. This stigma makes it difficult for almost anyone to come to counseling, but it is especially difficult for men, who often place a special value on being rational, self-sufficient, strong, and in control. The act of telephoning or walking into a counseling center and asking for an appointment may feel like the equivalent of a declaration that, "I am weak, afraid, dependent, and vulnerable. I don't know what is going on with me, even though I should, and I can't handle my problems on my own. I need help."

One would be hard-pressed to find statements that reflect perceived masculine failure more than these. Given the social expectations to work it out for oneself, "take it like a man," and control one's feelings, it is not surprising that men utilize psychological services considerably less often than women (Addis & Mahalik, 2003). Since entering counseling is often perceived as a threat to masculine self-esteem, men frequently resist asking for services until they experience a very deep level of psychological pain and until their problems reach crisis proportions. If they begin treatment, they may drop out when their discomfort reaches a barely manageable level. After dropping out their pain may worsen. At that time, it may be even more difficult for them to return and ask for assistance, because they now admit two failures by doing so: the one that initially brought them to counseling, and the failure on the first attempt as a therapy client (Kilmartin, 2004b; 2005).

Michael Addis and James Mahalik (2003) call for a contextual analysis of help seeking in men across several dimensions including the perceptions of normality and ego-centrality. People are more likely to seek help if they think that their problem is shared by others (normality) and does not affect the core of their perceptions of self (ego-centrality). The National Institute of Mental Health (NIMH) has undertaken an extensive public information campaign called *Real Men, Real Depression* in an effort to re-cast this increasingly common mood disorder as normal for males and not reflective of one's level of masculinity (Rochlen, Whilde, & Hoyer, 2005). The slogan, "It takes courage to ask for help" is an attempt to re-define a positive masculine attribute as reflective of a culturally proscribed but useful behavior.

Counseling Activities

Counseling is an activity in which clients are usually expected to perform certain behaviors thought to be helpful in solving emotional problems. These behaviors often include emotional self- disclosure, exploration of feelings, nondefensive introspection ("looking inside" of oneself), and emphasizing interpersonal material. Men sometimes have little experience in these areas, which are culturally defined as feminine. Therefore, the counseling setting tends to be a rather poor match of person and environment for many men (Bruch, 1980). In other words, asking a man to do these things may make him feel like a fish out of water, and this discomfort may well be another factor that contributes to the high male dropout rate.

Because many counseling activities are uncomfortable for them, men often ask for masculine kinds of help, such as a logical analysis of the problem, an emphasis on thinking over feeling, or help with defending against rather than experiencing the problem. For instance, typically masculine strategies for dealing with the breakup of a romantic relationship might be to find a substitute lover, to use thoughts to master feelings, or to learn how to not think about the former partner (Kilmartin, 2005).

In the above scenario, the counselor might think that it is more important for the man to deal with powerful feelings and go through the process of grieving for the lost lover. This would not fit very well with a client who expects directive, analytical, problem solving. Thus, counselors find themselves in quandaries when these kinds of situations arise. They do not want to reinforce a maladaptive strategy, yet they also do not want their client to terminate treatment. In these cases, counselors should address the client's needs and expectations in the context of feelings about control, independence, and vulnerability. They should also discuss the man's ambivalent feelings about the process of counseling itself. To do so requires sensitivity to men's issues.

Men's skill levels in these emotionally-focused activities are another consideration. Many have had their emotional experience systematically removed from their lives. Not only are they uncomfortable with the expression of feeling, they are understandably not very good at it. Asked how he feels, a man might often reply, "about what?" The counselor might then say, "about your girlfriend breaking up with you." The man tells the counselor what he *thinks*, "I feel she shouldn't have done it." He may feel sad, disappointed, angry, etc., but these emotion-descriptive words are not in his working vocabulary.

It is also vitally important for counselors to introduce the topic of gender very early in the therapeutic relationship. Because masculinity is an important context in which the male client experiences his symptoms and expectations for therapeutic process and outcome, counselors should assess the client's level of gender conformity, educate him about masculinity, and help him find alternative, more adaptive ways of framing his experiences (Kilmartin, 2004b; 2005).

For counselors, it is an extraordinary challenge to reach a man in the context of questions like, "How do you feel?" when the man has been socially manipulated to the point that the question does not even make sense. The good news is that men who can learn emotion-focused coping in the therapeutic setting may gain a skill that will be helpful to them in virtually every area of their lives.

One way to approach emotional awareness and expression in the therapeutic setting is to help the client to see them as skills which improve with practice. Recall Ronald Levant's (1997a) program described in Chapter Eight. Clients may believe that emotional competence is an inborn ability and/or one that is found only in women. Christopher Kilmartin's (2005) approach is to find some skill that the client has mastered and say, "Remember the first time you e.g., swung a golf club, played a chord on the guitar, ran a business meeting? It felt awkward at first, but if you stuck with it, you got better at it, and over time it began to feel like second nature." And when do we invest time and effort in learning a skill? When we value the outcome.

PSYCHOLOGICAL SERVICES FOR MEN

The specific techniques that a counselor would use with a male client are dependent on the individual's problem and the theoretical orientation of the therapist, among other factors. As all men are different, it is hard to make sweeping generalizations about what techniques work with male clients. At the same time, some writers have identified certain approaches that are helpful in the treatment of many male therapy clients.

Because the counseling environment feels threatening for many men, several theorists have suggested that structured and psychoeducational approaches be considered as alternatives to traditional individual psychotherapy. John Robertson and Louise Fitzgerald (1992) found that college men were more likely to say they would utilize workshops or seminars than personal counseling. Psychoeducational programs that offer self-help and problem-solving approaches allow men to do some psychological work in a masculine and structured context. Men in corporate settings may respond more positively to psychological work if it is called "executive coaching" rather than "therapy." In this approach, the executive's job performance is explored in relationship to his psychological well-being and relationship skills (Hills, Carlstrom, & Evanow, 2001).

It is important to help men understand the effects of gender on their lives. In therapy, the client's presenting problem can often be viewed in terms of masculine socialization or gender role strain. For example, a man who is feeling very lonely following a breakup could understand his loneliness in the context of the social demands to be independent, non-disclosing, and task-oriented. The mental health practitioner can help the man identify what he believes about masculinity and the sources of these beliefs during this process. Then, the client can start to understand the ways in which he has been restricted by narrow definitions of masculinity and begin the difficult task of freeing himself from gender conformity. In this way, the counselor lets the man know that his problems are understandable, that he need not feel shamed because he has problems, and that he can work toward feeling better.

In addition to helping male clients learn about the danger of avoiding certain behaviors, therapists can help men understand the value of behaviors that they have not learned. When men become clients, counselors often perform the educative role of helping their clients understand that self-disclosure and other nonsexual intimate behaviors are important for the person's mental health. The therapist communicates to the client that these behaviors are expected of him, but also acknowledges that they are difficult and anxiety provoking.

A major therapeutic task is to reintroduce men to the worlds of emotion and connectedness. At the most elementary level, men often need to incorporate "feeling words" into their working vocabulary. Men who need structure in doing so can keep diaries in which they identify emotional reactions and record the situations in which the feelings occurred. Some men need a checklist of possible emotions because the identification of feeling is such a new task (Levant, 1997a). Some men at the most basic level need to start with the most elementary emotions (e.g., mad, sad, glad, afraid), and build their affective vocabulary from there. Importantly, men need to explore the vulnerable emotions underneath their anger (Lynch & Kilmartin, 2013).

Therapists can also facilitate men's emotional education by confronting intellectualized interpretations of events, and by communicating the expectation of emotional reaction. This can be done in a very matter-of-fact fashion, by saying in a nonjudgmental way, "I would think you'd have some feelings about [whatever is being discussed]." Again, because most men need a little structure, the therapist is more successful if he or she talks about feelings in the context of some event, rather than in the abstract (Kilmartin, 2005).

One other strategy for helping men access their feelings is by attending to the physiological sensations that accompany emotions (Rabinowitz & Cochran, 2002). The therapist can ask, "What's going on inside your stomach?" or "Can you feel the tension in your forehead?" A jumpy stomach usually accompanies anxiety; a smile reflects pleasure. When the client is able to understand these connections and become more accepting of his natural emotional life, he may be able to resist the masculine propensity to dissociate the self from feeling. Eventually, he may learn to spontaneously identify his affective responses.

Therapists can also be helpful to their male clients by tapping into masculine modes of experience. For instance, men value independence, and the therapist can help the man view nonconformity to stereotypical masculinity as a kind of independence. Men who value risk taking can learn to take risks with emotional self-disclosure. Men who value assertiveness can see objecting to sexist jokes or telling a male friend that he is valued as assertive communications. Men who are good at goal setting can set goals that are related to family, relationships, or play.

Group therapy is increasingly popular as an approach to men's issues. Men in groups can experience other men in completely new ways, and the process of intimate connection to other men can have strong therapeutic effects (Rabinowitz, 2010). Group approaches for men who share a common problem or experience can deal with the interactions between masculine role demands and those experiences. Therapists and educators have recently developed group techniques for working with men of color (Caldwell & White, 2001; Cervantes, 2006), teenage fathers (Kiselica, 2006), survivors of trauma (Crete & Singh, 2014), older men (Robertson, 2014), sexual minority men (Sanabria, 2014), and sex offenders (Becker, 1996; Lazur, 1996), to name only a few. A number of gender-aware self-help books have also appeared in recent years with focuses on subjects such as depression (Real, 1997; Lynch & Kilmartin, 2013), sexuality (Brooks, 1995), anger (Lynch, 2004), and grieving for a father who has died (Chethik, 2001).

A gender-aware approach to therapy with men involves giving them permission to be who they are and providing a safe atmosphere in which they can express the socially prohibited parts of the self. The therapy room can become a haven from the harsh demands of masculinity. In his exploration, the male client can discover which of these demands have been internalized and self-imposed, and work toward a less restricted experience of the self. He becomes more prepared to take the changes he has made in counseling and expand them into other parts of his life.

Summary

1. Mental health problems are related to gender from several perspectives. Definitions of mental health are culture bound, and gender stereotypes are a central feature of culture.

2. The proportions of males and females diagnosed in some categories of mental disorder vary significantly. Gender seems to be an important factor in determining how psychological distress finds expression. For adult men, the diagnoses of substance abuse, sexual disorders, behavior control problems, and certain personality disorders are more common than for women.

3. Typically male personality disorders tend to share the masculine characteristics of hyperindependence, emotional restrictedness, self absorption, and interpersonal exploitiveness. Men who exhibit these disorders display the most dysfunctional and destructive aspects of traditional masculinity.

4. Although depression is diagnosed twice as often in women as in men, there is evidence that men's depression is underdiagnosed and misunderstood.

5. Contrary to stereotypical beliefs, marriage seems to have the effect of protecting the mental health of men. The marital relationship may offer the man's only avenue for meeting his intimacy needs. When marriages and other intimate relationships dissolve, men tend to have more psychological difficulties than women.

6. Boys are especially at risk for suffering negative effects from parental conflict and family separation. Sons witness more of their parents' marital conflict than daughters, and this experience is thought to be a critical factor in the development of psychological distress. Although connections between childhood father absence and mental health problems have not been convincingly demonstrated, it is clear that sons usually have powerful psychological issues around their relationships with their fathers.

7. Approaches to treating men in counseling and psychotherapy have recently placed an emphasis on the view of men as a special subgroup of clients. Well-trained therapists recognize that men bring characteristic issues to counseling, examine personal and societal biases about men and masculinity, and are aware of the impact of gender on the therapeutic relationship.

8. Individual psychotherapy does not provide a masculine environment. Vulnerability, emotional self-disclosure, and asking for help are connected with the sense that one is unmanly.

9. Because the counseling environment is uncomfortable for many men, other approaches to doing male psychological work have been developed. Workshops, seminars, and discussion groups provide for a structured examination of men's issues. Mental health practitioners can help men to understand the effects of gender on their lives through these activities, as well as in the traditional therapy setting.

10. Many men have difficulty in dealing with emotions and relationships. In counseling, a man can begin to reconnect with his feelings and intimacy needs. As a result, he can achieve a fuller experience and expression of the self.

Chapter Fifteen

Masculinity and Sports

By Matthew R. Yeazel

Anne Arundel Community College

It goes without saying that athletics and masculinity are strongly linked and that the sports are ubiquitous within mainstream U.S. culture. The athletic arena is a physical and psychological battlefield in which many men see their manhood judged by others as well as themselves. In this chapter, we explore the ways in which sports permeate men's lives both physically and psychologically.

YOUTH SPORTS: WHERE IT ALL BEGINS

For many young men, sports provides a safe place to do things that they may not feel comfortable doing in other spheres, such as bonding with and showing affection for other boys, which might violate the "boy code" in other settings. For some boys, athletics provides the positive experiences of developing important connections between teammates and adults (McNeal, 1995), learning values such as sportsmanship and healthy competition (Jeziorski, 1994), and gaining an avenue for the senses of self-esteem and competence in both physical and social spheres (Ewing, Gano-Overway, Branta, & Seefeldt, 2002). It is cliché to say that "sports builds character." As coach Joe Ehrmann (2011) has noted, this assertion is supported for some if they have a coach who possess character himself or herself and actually teaches it to the players. Some have the good fortune to have this experience.

But others do not have such positive outcomes. As Kreager (2007) noted,

> Rather than building socially competent young men and women... the conditions of contemporary athletics embed youth in value systems marred by homophobia, sexism, racism, and ruthless competition. Within these contexts, middle-class white males have the most to gain, while disadvantaged minority and female athletes are either marginalized or forego long-term attainment in favor of short-term status benefits and illusory professional careers" (p. 706).

Comments such as "you throw like a girl," "he's black so he must be good at sports," or "you are playing like a bunch of wussies" are part of the everyday back-and-forth on some field or court every day.

The racist stereotype that athletic prowess is predetermined by the very color of one's skin is not only untrue (Kerr, 2010), but it is often accompanied by the false belief that people of color are lacking in intellectual ability. And what does it mean to throw "like a girl?" In 2014, a 13-year-old girl, Mo'Ne Davis was such a standout baseball pitcher that she almost took her team to the Little League World Series (Wise, 2014). Are those who use that comment referring to her? Obviously, not, but antifeminine shaming has a lengthy history in sport.

The two competing positions on the effects of sport on boys are *social control theory* and *social learning theory* (Kreager, 2007). Social control theory appeals to the structures that create bonds and a sense of belongingness, making delinquent or antisocial behavior less likely. In other words, sports, like school, provide an environment where boys can connect and build relationships with other boys and their coaches with the net effect of keeping them out of trouble.

Some researchers have provided support for social control theory. For example, Mahoney and Cairns (1997) found that sports increases the likelihood that athletes will stay in school. Eccles & Barber (1999) noted that sports played a role in increasing the chance that an athlete would attend college or refrain from antisocial behavior (Langbein & Bess, 2002). There are some critics to this position, however, who voice concern regarding most of the research's lack of focus on violence (Kreager, 2007), which has garnered more attention from social learning theory. To maximize the chances that sports will have a positive effect, a growing number of youth organizations have adopted a program called *coaching effectiveness training* (Smith, Smoll, & Curtis, 1979) in which youth coaches learn to utilize cognitive-behavioral techniques to develop healthy approaches with their team and move outside an exclusive focus on winning at any cost (Smith, Smoll, & Curtis, 1979).

The social learning perspective is an attempt to describe the complex relationship between sports and aggressive behaviors, positing that a boy operates in many different systems on a daily basis such that, even though there are bonds that may exist on a team that encourage the learning of sportsmanship and ethics, there may be other systems in which aggression and antisocial behavior meet with approval (Kreager, 2007). A player may learn prosocial values at practice every day, but interact with friends whose values are not so positive on the way home.

Even the most casual observer of youth sports will note that team environments are not always so positive. Although a boy may learn about teamwork, maximization of effort, and perseverance, he may also learn that, e.g., in football, "giving your best" might be tackling with maximum effort, which often raises the potential for significant injury or head trauma. A basketball player might be directed by a coach to foul the other team's best player aggressively to slow him down or intimidate him. These less-than-sportsmanlike behaviors are rationalized because they might give the team a strategic advantage.

He's Just a Boy by Chaplain Bob Fox was written 70 years ago but has again become frequent sight at some little league fields (Allen, K. (2013).

Hughes and Coakley (1991) called this justification *positive deviance*—things learned through sports that are viewed as deviant in society but as positive on the field or court. The player may engage in those harmful behaviors out of a sense of loyalty and duty to his team. In a study of middle school boys, coaches often encouraged players to engage in violent behaviors so as not to appear "soft" (Eder, Evans, & Parker, 1997). Family members and others within a boy's social network may also play a role in romancing overly aggressive play (Messner, 1995).

Media are also very strong influences that, in general, transmit values through what Messner, Dunbar, and Hunt (2000) call the *Televised Sports Manhood Formula* which is comprised of ten reoccurring themes:

1. White males are the voices of authority.

2. Sports is a man's world.

3. Men are foregrounded in commercials.

4. Women are sexy props or prizes for men's successful sport performances or consumption choices.

5. Whites are foregrounded in commercials.

6. Aggressive players get the prize. Nice guys finish last.

7. Boys will be (violent) boys.

8. Give up your body for the team.

9. Sports is war.

10. Show some guts.

SPORTS AND PRIVILEGE

The locker room sometimes may seem like a sacred space where players can share parts of themselves with the assurance that they will stay within the team constellation. Kane & Disch (1993) define the locker room as an "inner sanctum of male privilege" (p. 331). Bonding occurs that for many men seems almost impossible elsewhere (Messner, 1990). In this place, physicality can define men as separate from women in a way that is viewed positively within the culture (Kane & Snyder, 1989).

But, of course, not all locker rooms are so noble. Miami Dolphins football player Jonathan Martin left the team in October, 2013, for "emotional reasons" (Associated Press, 2013), later discovered to be a result of the frequent harassment of teammate Richie Incognito (ESPN Wire Services, 2013). One example included a voicemail obtained and confirmed by ESPN's Adam Schefter:

> Hey, wassup, you half n—— piece of s——. I saw you on Twitter, you been training 10 weeks. [I want to] s— in your f—ing mouth. [I'm going to] slap your f—ing mouth. [I'm going to] slap your real mother across the face [laughter]. F— you, you're still a rookie. I'll kill you. (ESPN Wire Services, 2013, para. 3)

As more damning reports began to emerge via the exposure of texts and off-the-field demands by Incognito, a fierce resistance arose from some teams, media, and fans in which they rejected the assertion that Incognito had done anything wrong. In fact they supported the hazing of rookies as an important sports tradition—a rite of passage to incorporate the player into team culture—eventually leading to universal acceptance from the team for those who pass the test (Trotter, 2013). In its investigation, the league uncovered other significant abuse and harassment toward Martin that extended beyond those of Incognito and into the heart of the Dolphin's locker room culture (Rosenthal, 2014). Still, many criticized Martin's public voicing of his concerns as a violation of a sacred code (Byrd, 2013). The hazing went well beyond more benign traditions of having rookies carry veterans' bags or sing their college's fight song at a team dinner into psychologically damaging abuse (Rosenthal, 2014).

Unfortunately, this kind of locker room culture is not unique and it can also serve as a place where the demeaning of women is allowed and where players are required to demonstrate lockstep conformity to other rigid and destructive norms (Kane & Disch, 1993; Curry, 1991). Michael Messner (1990) theorized that, for many men, sports provides a meaningful shelter to the threat posed by the progress of women in society (and in athletics).

SPORTS AND HEGEMONIC MASCULINITY

Up until the beginning of the 20th century, many men were part of long-standing family businesses, but the Industrial Revolution largely transported economic bases into larger workplaces (Tolson, 1977). As most work moved into factories owned by a small cadre of rich men, workers were faced with what sociologist Michael Kimmel (1987b) called the "crisis of masculinity," accelerated by the fact that other institutions such as public schools seemed increasingly dominated by women. Men compensated for feelings of powerlessness by placing a greater emphasis on physicality and toughness (Wilkenson, 1984). Institutionalized sports provided athletes with a sense of superiority and gave male spectators that same feeling vicariously. In the United States, football especially provided a mythology that excluded and marginalized women (Oriard, 1981) whose presence was limited to that of sex objects in the form of cheerleaders (Messner, 1988).

The case of Jonathan Martin and of the few others who chose to make their concerns public provides an example of *hegemonic masculinity* which, according to Hanke (1990), "refers to the social ascendancy of a particular version or model of masculinity that operates in the terrain of 'common sense' and conventional morality, defines 'what it means to be a man'" (p. 232). In the time since football overtook baseball as the national pastime in the 1970s, the message that masculinity encouraged aggression, violence, and patriarchal ideals became even more clear (Real, 1975). In addition to being violent, football players must also refuse to show pain or display vulnerable emotions, lest they be seen as weak or incompetent (Fagan, 2013). Nick Trujillo (1991) identified the distinguishing characteristics of hegemonic masculinity as physical force and control, occupational achievement, familial patriarchy, frontiersmanship, and heterosexuality (Trujillo, 1991; Brod, 1987b; Connell, 1990; Jeffords, 1989; Kaufman, 1987).

The athlete demonstrates physical force and control by overpowering and intimidating his opponent. (Fagan, 2013). In 2014, Baltimore Ravens NFL football star Ray Rice was videotaped by an elevator security camera at an Atlantic City, New Jersey casino striking his girlfriend so hard that she was rendered unconscious. The public was aghast at seeing him then drag her out of the elevator and place her onto the floor. The video was leaked onto YouTube and almost immediately and widely reported by news networks (Hensley, 2014).

The ensuing events provided a good example of how use of physical power and control by men is seen as permissible and how the impact on the victim is minimized. Months later, NFL Commissioner Roger Goodell suspended Rice for only two regular season games in contrast to a full season (16 game) suspension for a player who drove while intoxicated and failed a drug test (Cash, 2014). It was quite clear that the Commissioner, many other NFL insiders such as Rice's head coach, and many members of the general public did not understand the issues surrounding domestic violence. In their comments, they marginalized the incident and, in some cases, praised the offender for how he handled the whole situation. ESPN reporter Stephen A. Smith blamed women for provoking men into violence. Sports journalist Dave Zirin (2014) noted that, "Unfortunately, the only lessons that kids are going to learn from this episode is that the vaunted "shield" of the NFL protects perpetrators of violence against women, for the sake of what it sees as the greater good" (paragraph 5).

The occupational achievement form of hegemonic masculinity manifests itself in the need to succeed on the field or court, which results in reward and good will from large segments of society (Lumpkin, Stoll, & Beller, 2003). Those who do not display a failure to live up to the "culturally idealized form of masculine character" (Connell, 1990, p. 83) risk being social misfits or even outcasts.

As noted in Chapter One, patriarchy is a system that provides greater levels of economic power, influence, and prestige to the aggregate of men over that of women. Familial patriarchy is reflected and reinforced by the coaching ideology of "making boys into men." College football coaches often present themselves as father figures to young athletes as a selling point to parents, particularly when a boy comes from a father-absent household. They assure the athlete's parent(s) that they will provide the necessary lessons for the son to take his place in the world as a man. Unfortunately, many coaches fail to provide such lessons. Former Texas Tech head football coach Mike Leach was fired in 2009 after it was discovered that he had mistreated a player suffering from a severe concussion (ESPN News Services, 2009) and that he had sent another to a storage shed as punishment (Zinser, 2013).

The history of college basketball coach Bobby Knight is rife with stories of his demeaning treatment of players. In a striking example of Knight's antifemininity, he put a box of tampons in a player's locker as a message that he was underperforming (Simmons, Klosterman, Leavy, & Weinreb, 2011). With a collection of frightening stories about his coaching habits and general personality, one would think that parents would steer clear of him. Surprisingly, many families continued to view playing for Knight as a dream-come-true. For them, Knight was the father figure and family patriarch (Trujillo, 1991) they desired for their sons when they were away from home. Because his teams were winners, many boys from the state dreamed of playing for Knight at Indiana University (Hutton, 2000).

The frontiersmanship aspect of hegemonic masculinity can be seen in Trujillo's (1991) examination of the legacy of professional baseball pitcher Nolan Ryan, who set many records over the course of his 27-year career. Growing up in Texas, Ryan's life made cowboy metaphors quite easy to produce in the spreading of his Texas legend, such as in comparing him to an "old gunslinger" or cowboy or identifying close games as "showdowns at the OK Corral." Similarly, the media construction of former NFL Quarterback Brett Favre included his image as a small town "man's man" who came from the backwoods of Mississippi and spent his off-seasons hunting and fishing (Weir, 2010).

Heterosexuality is also a central feature of hegemonic masculinity. Although there now seem to be some inroads into challenging this belief, it is clear that much work has yet to be done. Of course, there are numerous gay professional athletes now and in the past. However, until basketball player Jason Collins (2013) and football player Michael Sam (2014) came out during their active careers, gay athletes did not reveal their sexual orientations during their playing days (Collins, 2013). Only a few, such as John Amaechi (basketball), Billy Bean and Glen Burke (baseball), and Esera Tualolo, Dave Kopay and Roy Simmons (football), came out after their athletic careers were over (Cotton, 2012; Dreier, 2010). In some cases, teams were aware that a player was gay and would take grand steps to avoid its becoming public knowledge. In the late 1970s, the Los Angeles Dodgers baseball team offered Glenn Burke a world-class honeymoon vacation if he would marry a woman to conceal his sexual orientation (Burke, Sherman, & Sherman, 1995). Former Dodgers manager Tommy Lasorda would continue to make homophobic comments despite having a gay son who would later die of AIDS-related complications (Bean, 2004; Richmond, 1992).

Without question, the biggest story surrounding the 2014 NFL draft of college players was the coming out of Michael Sam during an interview with ESPN's Chris Connelly (Connelly, 2014). Shortly thereafter, *Sports Illustrated* writer Peter King reported that "unnamed" front office personnel from various teams were stating that they would not draft Sam because of his sexual orientation. *Sports Illustrated's* Pete Thamel (2014) provided what was a common response from front office personnel:

> 'I don't think football is ready for (an openly gay player) just yet,' said an NFL player personnel assistant. 'In the coming decade or two, it's going to be acceptable, but at this point in time it's still a man's man game. To call somebody a [gay slur] is still so commonplace. It'd chemically imbalance an NFL locker room and meeting room.' (paragraph 5)

This response was curious because the NFL had a history of having few or no problems with drafting players with on- or off-the-field conduct issues, including Lawrence Phillips, who was drafted sixth overall despite having a history of violence against women. The St. Louis Rams drafted Sam in the seventh round, making him one of only two former Southeast Conference Defensive Players of the Year to be drafted after the first two rounds (Lisk, 2014).

Former head coach and current television sportscaster Tony Dungy, who encountered a great deal of resistance in his quest to become only the sixth African American NFL head coach, said "I wouldn't have taken him. Not because I don't believe Michael Sam should have a chance to play, but I wouldn't want to deal with all of it.… It's not going to be totally smooth.… Things will happen" (Jones, 2014, paragraph 8). Ironically, Dungy is viewed by many as someone who stands up for the underdog (Wetzel, 2014). After quarterback Michael Vick was released from prison in 2009 because of his abuse of dogs, Dungy was the first to voice support of him and ask NFL teams to give him a second chance (Jones, 2014). Quarterback Johnny Manziel was drafted at the end of the first round in 2014 despite the concerns of many that he was undisciplined and had a history of off the field troubles, but Dungy was at the forefront of encouraging teams to draft him (Jhabvala, 2014). Still, he wanted no part of any openly gay player and the growing pains that might occur for a coach in the player's first year. Thus, his statement and history highlight the continued existence of hegemonic masculinity in its acceptance of only those players perceived as heterosexual.

Parts of the Michael Sam story show us that many things are changing and many athletes are showing their undivided support for gay athletes. When basketball great Magic Johnson's son came out in 2013, his father took the opportunity to reaffirm his continued support of the LGBT community (Fisher, 2014). In fact, an increasing

---

Box 15.1 Athlete LGBT Allies

Despite the growing support within sports for the LGBT community, those athletes who speak out against homophobia continue to take significant risks professionally and in the larger society. When football player Brendan Ayanbadejo became a strong advocate for Maryland marriage equality, he was faced with opposition from politicians (Rosenwald, 2012) and some of his teammates (Morgan, 2012). Football player Chris Kluwe (2014), also an outspoken supporter of marriage equality, wrote an article on the website *Deadspin* claiming that he was released from the Minnesota Vikings in retaliation and stated that assistant coach Mike Priefer made repeated homophobic remarks, a claim that was corroborated by an independent investigation. Kluwe is contemplating a lawsuit against the Vikings for workplace discrimination (Associated Press, 2014b).

---

number of current and former athletes have been heterosexual allies, including basketball player Kenneth Faried, who was raised by lesbian parents (Erby, 2013) and is an ambassador for Athlete Ally, an organization of professional athletes that seeks to take an active role in fighting homophobia and transphobia. Others involved in this organization include football players Mercedes Lewis, D'Qwell Jackson, and Connor Barwin, and former tennis great Andy Roddick (Athlete Ally, 2014). Even baseball legend Yogi Berra, a member of a generation in which non-heterosexuals suffered much more prejudice, is an active supporter of the LGBT community (Footer, 2014).

Legendary Green Bay Packers football coach Vince Lombardi was a stalwart in preaching the importance and acceptance of diversity in the locker room. Lombardi was clear with his players that they accept men of color and gay men. In fact, in reference to a player suspected to be gay, Lombardi told his assistant coaches, "If I hear one of you people make reference to his manhood, you'll be out of here before your ass hits the ground" (Maraniss, 1999, p. 471).

SPORTS AGGRESSION AND MASCULINITY

During the entire history of sport, "violent contests affirmed a masculine ethos of individual prowess and physical courage" (Rader, 2009, p. 3). Aggression takes two forms (Cox, 2011). *Instrumental aggression* occurs within the context of the game with no real intent to harm another player, for example when an ice hockey player hits his opponent, causing him to fall face first onto the ice. The player's goal was to take the puck away, but it caused his opponent to fall awkwardly and resulted in injury. *Hostile aggression* takes place when a player hurts a competitor in a way that has nothing to do with gaining an advantage in competition. For example, after being embarrassed by a hitter's home run, the baseball pitcher deliberately tries to hit him with a pitched ball the next time he comes to bat. Players are sometimes ejected and/or suspended for hostile aggression, but it is sometimes difficult to distinguish hostile from instrumental aggression (Diaz, 2012). Male athletes generally view aggressive acts as much more acceptable than female athletes (Tucker & Parks, 2001; Bredemeier, 1985; Silva,

Boston Celtics' Kevin McHale "clotheslines" Los Angeles Lakers' Kurt Rambis. Was this aggression instrumental or hostile?

Photo: *Los Angeles Times*

1983) beginning in childhood (Bredemeier, 1985; Conroy, Silva, Newcomer, Walker, & Johnson, 2001) as they are more likely to view it as a routine part of sports.

CONCUSSIONS AND BRAIN DAMAGE IN SPORTS

Dr. Bennet Omalu is a neuropathologist who in 2002 performed an autopsy on Mike Webster, who died at age 50 and who had played for over 15 years in the NFL, sustaining major injuries throughout (Breslow, 2013). Omalu was stunned to find out that the brain he was viewing was from a 50 year old because it looked like it was from someone who was much older. Omalu observed the first evidence that playing football could lead to permanent brain damage in the form of *chronic traumatic encephalopathy* (CTE) (Omalu, DeKosky, Minster, Hamilton, & Wecht, 2005), the cumulative result of multiple concussions and subconcussions.

Webbe (2006) describes the brain trauma thus:

> Cerebral concussion is a closed head injury that represents a usually transient alteration in normal consciousness and brain processes as a result of traumatic insult to the brain. The alterations may include loss of consciousness, amnesia, impairment of the reflex activity, and confusion regarding orientation. Although most symptoms resolve within a few days in the majority of cases, some physical symptoms such as memory dysfunction, may persist for an undetermined time. (p. 48)

Repeated traumas to the brain bring about CTE, which is "associated with memory disturbances, behavioral and personality changes, Parkinsonism, and speech and gait abnormalities" (McKee et al., 2009, p. 709). For Webster, an intelligent individual before becoming symptomatic, normal functioning was not only compromised, but became almost nonexistent as he aged and began to show remarkable anger, depression, and paranoia. He began to live in his truck or in train stations despite having numerous former teammates who were willing to take him in (Laskas, 2014).

The Mike Webster tragedy was just the start of the discovery of what football does to men's brains over the long term of using the body as a weapon by which they assert themselves in competition (Messner, 1992), and of playing with pain and sacrificing the body for the sake of winning, which is viewed as heroic by teammates and fans. Weir, Jackson, & Sonnega (2009) found that former professional football players were nineteen times more likely to have early-onset (before age 65) dementia than non-players.

College football, lacrosse, and soccer players have higher rates of concussions than their non-playing counterparts (Institute of Medicine of the National Academies, 2013) and all sports in which head trauma is a frequent are played almost exclusively or predominantly by men. Studies connecting boxing with CTE date back to the early part of the twentieth century (Stone, 2013) and historically were known as being "punch drunk" or having "boxer's dementia." Although amateur boxing organizations instituted the use of headgear many years ago, these are not as protective as once believed (Stone, 2013). According to the American Association of Neurological Surgeons, more than 90 percent of boxers sustain concussions, sometimes multiple ones, at some point during their careers, and thus the number of potential future cases of CTE is considerable (Stone, 2014). Moreover, men who sustain concussions take longer to recover than women (Fakhran, Yaeger, Collins, & Alhilali, 2014).

After looking at the devastation that CTE does to athletes who have sustained multiple concussions over the years, one might ask, "If we know so much about the impact of concussions, why haven't we taken more steps to protect athletes?" There are perhaps two reasons. First, aggression and toughness, especially in the world of sports, are hallmarks of masculinity. Second, organizations have been slow to act to protect athletes. Even after researchers completed numerous reputable studies on the connections between football and CTE, the NFL continued to be in denial of the problem. In 1994, then-commissioner Paul Tagliabue reduced the mounting evidence to a "pack journalism issue." At one point, the NFL named Dr. Ira Casson head of its Traumatic Brain Injury Committee. In a May, 2007 interview, Casson vehemently denied any link between prolonged head injuries and CTE (Ezell, 2013).

ATHLETE OFF-THE-FIELD AGGRESSION

It is a common assumption that male college and professional athletes are more apt than other men to be violent in other settings. The issue is complex, with competing findings from various studies, but in the aggregate, the available data call into question the connection between on-field and off-field violence. It is not in dispute that the vast majority of athletes are not violent, so the question is not whether participation in aggressive sports causes violence; clearly it does not. But does it contribute to violence when combined with other risk factors?

There are several complex issues related to research in this area. First, many studies have significant limitations because it is difficult to control for other factors such as athletes' use of alcohol or their attitudes toward women (Woods, 2011). Second, small sample sizes often limit the explanatory power of the study (Crosset, Benedict, & McDonald, 1998). Crosset (1999) found that, although athletes, especially in the contact sports, have greater risk of committing sexual assault than non-athletes, one cannot infer from that correlation that being an athlete causes one to be sexually violent. Blumstein and Benedict, noting a concern that high status of professional football players would be more likely to attract police attention, still found it interesting that the NFL players, who earn a living largely through the exercise of their physical strength—and who may even be seen to thrive on their violent encounters on the football field—still seem to have a lower rate of off-the-field violence than the comparable population (page 15).

So why are we under the impression that NFL players are so much more apt to commit domestic violence or aggressive offenses? In an Internet poll in the late 1990s, 51 percent of participants said they believed that there was a connection between being an athlete and some type of deviant behavior (Crosset, 1999). Media attention to extreme cases may fuel beliefs that athlete violence is commonplace. Perhaps the best example is the trial of former football star O. J. Simpson in the early 1990s, where the media competed to attract viewers and covered every angle of the story possible.

A group particularly at risk for media exploitation is African American males. Because they represent more than 66 percent of NFL and 77 percent of National Basketball Association (NBA) players, the domestic violence arrest of one is likely to fuel racist stereotypes of Black men as dangerous (Woods, 2011). On one hand, it is important to report the news. On the other, because of the plethora of media outlets, random and peripheral issues begin to dominate coverage rather than a larger discussion on the issue of domestic violence and sexual assault, with the result being that no real understanding of the dynamics can take place.

In his book on race and sport, Dr. Richard Lapchick (1999) interviewed Joyce Williams-Mitchell, at the time executive director of the Massachusetts Coalition of Battered Women's Service Groups. Williams-Mitchell voiced considerable displeasure at the characterization of African American male athletes as violent monsters who are prone to inordinate amounts of aggression, stating "It is a myth! Most batterers are men who control women through their profession, and they include police officers, clergymen, dentists, and judges. Athletes get the headlines, though, and an unfair public rap. Men from every profession (regardless of race) have the potential to be batterers" (Lapchick, 1991, p. 275).

SUMMARY

1. *Social control theory* includes an analysis of social structures that may create bonds that discourage delinquent or antisocial behavior.

2. Proponents of *social learning theory* posit that an adolescent male operates in many different systems in addition to athletics, some of which encourage and some of which discourage aggression (Kreager, 2007).

3. The concept of *positive deviance* is that there are certain things learned through sports that are deviant in society but are viewed as positive in sports. Adolescent males will engage in those harmful behaviors when they believe that doing so fulfills obligations of loyalty and duty to teammates.

4. *Televised sports manhood formula* is a set of ten recurring themes that provide the basis by which young men see the sports world.

5. *Hegemonic masculinity* refers to widely accepted beliefs about the definition of manhood within a society. This dominant form of masculinity is in strong evidence in the sporting world.

6. Homophobia is rampant in sports but there are trends toward its reduction, as gay athletes and heterosexual allies become more visible.

7. *Instrumental aggression* is that which occurs within the context of the game with no intent to harm. *Hostile aggression* takes place when harm is intentional and unrelated with gaining an advantage in competition.

8. Contact sports, especially football and boxing, carry serious risks of *chronic traumatic encephalopathy* (CTE), a long term compromise of the brain and associated functioning as a result of repeated head traumas sustained in the context of the sport.

9. The link between on-field and off-field violence has not been firmly established by researchers.

Chapter Sixteen

Struggles and Changes: Contemporary Topics on Men and Masculinity

It seems that gender roles as we now know them are slowly becoming archaic because the economic and cultural forces that maintained them are changing, and because they have aspects which limit human potential in modern living. Some gender-based expectations have negative effects on men, women, and children, and thus the need for transitions in gendered traditions is a quality of life issue for everyone. This chapter includes a discussion of various recent developments related to gender and masculinity and their effects in the mainstream of United States culture and elsewhere.

In the first three editions of this book, the final chapter was a description of what were often termed "men's social movements"—attempts to either reify traditional masculinity or to transform it through political action, consciousness-raising, or education. In the United States, these movements were largely a phenomenon of the 1990s (although one of them, the profeminist movement, began in the 1970s). The groups that advocate for these various movements are still in existence, but they tend to be small and isolated. When they have captured the attention of the mainstream, none could sustain it for more than a few years. Therefore, the fourth edition included a description of these movements but also an expansion into other contemporary topics, as does this edition.

Kenneth Clatterbaugh (2000) describes the decrease of attention and support for these movements: "All of the men's movements have probably suffered because there are larger social forces at work, and it is with these forces that men and women will make their accommodations with one another" (pp. 891–892). In other words, because gender is deeply ingrained in individuals, families, social customs, laws, and institutions—indeed in virtually every facet of living—social movements that seek to change it will need to be sustained across generations, as in the United States civil rights movement. However, unlike the civil rights movement, there is no consensus about whether masculinity should be transformed, or if so, into what. Clatterbaugh (2004) later stated that, "lack of unanimity [in men's movements] should not be surprising.

Men are divided by race, class, education, religion, and even different masculinities, and they have no explicit oppressive structures around which to rally" (p. 531).

Even though there is scant attention to any social movement around masculinity, a brief discussion of these movements will help us to understand the historical context and cultural ambivalence around changing continuity and transformation. Some people think that social problems are a result, not a cause, of changing gender roles—that we would all be better off if we would return to the time when, as fictional character Archie Bunker put it, "girls were girls and men were men." Among those who advocate gender transformation, some believe that men should reclaim "deep masculinity"; some think that gender roles should disappear altogether; some decry sexism against men and resist feminism; some believe that the answers can be found in fundamentalist Christianity, and some just want men to "buck up" and take more responsibility.

VERSIONS OF MEN'S REALITY

Beliefs about whether or not masculinity should change, and if so, how it should be transformed, are embedded in beliefs about the nature of social problems surrounding gender. There is widespread disagreement about the ideologies expressed in the following statements:

1. Modern men are a group of people who are alienated from their "true nature."
2. The innate differences between males and females go well beyond reproductive roles.
3. Men are oppressed, mistreated victims of sexism.
4. Gender roles are a reflection of a natural order in which men are dominant.
5. Men should focus most on discovering and changing themselves.
6. Men should focus most on eliminating sexism and patriarchy in the larger society.
7. Men should focus on eliminating sexism against men.
8. Men should gain a fuller appreciation of their privileged status, work to understand the worlds of people who do not have such status, and strive to help women achieve equality.
9. Fundamental changes in masculinity are not possible.
10. Feminism is men's ally.

Theorists have taken differing positions on these issues, and thus there are varying perspectives on men's nature and agendas for change or conservation. Kenneth Clatterbaugh (1997) described some of these:

1. *Conservatives* believe that male dominance and traditional masculinity are natural and desirable. They often see feminism as dangerous. Therefore, they either oppose gender role reforms or see these reforms as impossible.

2. *Profeminists* believe that traditional masculinity is destructive to women and men, in that order. They believe that men ought to work to end patriarchy and men's violence and foster equal rights for women. Somewhat secondarily, they believe that men should also deal with the limitations of gender roles in their personal lives. The largest profeminist men's group is the National Organization of Men Against Sexism (NOMAS), which undertakes political activities and has sponsored annual conferences on Men and Masculinity for nearly four decades. Without a doubt, this is the longest organized tradition of gender-aware dialogue about men.

NOMAS is based on four principles: "pro-feminist, gay-affirmative, anti-racist, and enhancing men's lives" (NOMAS, 2014). The efforts of this group involve understanding the effects of masculine privilege, working to end injustices experienced by women, people of color, non-heterosexuals, and other oppressed groups, and challenging the self-destructive aspects of traditional masculinity. Over the years, NOMAS has participated in social protest, monitored legislation related to sexism, and filed *amicus* ("friend of the court") opinions in legal cases related to its cause.

3. *Men's rights advocates* see men as victims of social and legal sexism. They believe that men are more oppressed than women. Their agenda is toward changing divorce, child custody, rape, sexual harassment, and domestic violence laws that they view as favoring women at men's expense. They also complain about "male bashing." The men's rights perspective has a sense of adversarial sexual beliefs—that men and women are enemies, and thus men lose when women gain. The most extreme of these activists subject feminist bloggers to rape and death threats (Hess, 2014).

Historically, the most visible of men's rights activists was Warren Farrell (1986), who described men as victims of "the new sexism," a general lack of respect for men and lack of understanding for their struggles. He cast feminism as an effort to vilify and overpower men. In 2005, Farrell published *Why Men Earn More*, taking the position that men make more money because they deserve it for working longer hours in more dangerous environments than women.

The men's rights movement takes the position that men are the victims of cultural, social, legal, and psychological injustices, and that men's victimization outweighs that of women. This view is clearly anti-feminist, as every feminist analysis begins with the position that women-as-a-group are vastly disadvantaged compared with men-as-a-group (Clatterbaugh, 1997).

The men's rights social change strategy is to resist feminist objectives and counterattack with social action efforts that are perceived as advancing the cause of justice for men. The subtext of much men's rights rhetoric seems to be that women and men are political enemies. The historical roots of this movement are in divorce and child custody reform efforts. When divorce began to skyrocket in the 1960s, many men believed that courts unfairly sided with divorcing wives in awarding alimony and child custody, and they founded organizations to combat these perceived inequities. At a recent men's rights conference, one discussion involved the economic disadvantages for men while their ex-wives live in luxury, ignoring the fact that custodial mothers are about twice as likely to be living below the poverty line as custodial fathers (Hesse, 2014).

Among groups that embraced this thinking, the view that emerged was of men as a victimized and oppressed segment of the population. Their position is that men should not accept women's interpretations of their experience. Feminists complain that men have too much power, yet these individual men do not feel powerful (recall from Chapter One the discussion of the invisibility of privilege). Feminists claim that men are not oppressed, yet these men experience themselves otherwise in what Michael Kimmel (2013a) refers to as "'windchill' psychology: it doesn't really matter what the actual temperature is; what matters is what it feels like" (p. 16). Not unsympathetic to these men's pain, Kimmel believes it stems from a sense of "aggrieved entitlement"—the beliefs that they are not getting the privileges that they take to be their birthrights and that their suffering is due to the special considerations that are given to women in the courts, workplaces, and society in general.

Men's rights advocates have long lists of complaints, such as the demand that men always take the initiative, and therefore risk rejection, in heterosexual relationships (Farrell, 1986), the lack of attention to male victims of spouse abuse, prison rape, war, and false accusations of rape or sexual harassment (despite very reliable evidence that these false accusations are exceeding rare and pale in comparison to unreported victimizations). At their recent conference, conservative columnist Barbara Kay (quoted in Hesse, 2014, p. C1) stated, "Ordinary people know [that] the vast majority of women crying rape on campus are actually expressing buyer's remorse from alcohol-fueled promiscuous behavior involving murky consent on both sides." It was unclear how "ordinary people" came to "know" this information.

The men's rights movement is highly controversial and has been the target of criticism and ridicule. Feminists and profeminists tend to see the members of these organizations as men who do not understand or appreciate the cultural privilege of men-as-a-group and the legitimate anger of women. They view men's rights types as working to reinforce a patriarchy that is perceived as eroding. After undertaking in-depth interviews with several Canadian fathers' rights activists, Bertoia and Drakich (1998) concluded that these men seemed much more interested in regaining control of their ex-wives, children, and money than they were in sharing parenting duties.

4. *Mythopoetic* types believe that males in modern society have been disconnected from their "deep masculinity." They seek to reclaim this male essence through an agenda of self-development. This movement leaped into the national spotlight in the early 1990's with two best selling books: Robert Bly's (1990) *Iron John*, and Sam Keen's (1991) *Fire in the Belly*. Bly is by far the most central figure in this movement.

The philosophical position of the mythopoetic movement is that modern men have lost the archetypal masculine essence that was established and passed on from generation to generation since the dawn of humankind. This "deep masculinity" involves a fierce (but not violent), mysterious, distinctly male energy. Being disconnected from this energy means being alienated from one's nature, and this self-alienation is thought to have negative psychological consequences.

The mythopoetic contention is that deep masculinity has been eroded by several forces: the industrial revolution (which banished men from their homes and disconnected them from the land), the loss of male initiation rites, the growing social disrespect of men, and the frequent psychological distance between men and their fathers (Bly, 1990, 1991). Some mythopoetic types seem to think that feminism has made things worse by devaluing the natural "wild man" quality of males. According to many mythopoetic types, men who buy into the feminist view of the world become "soft," female dominated, self-alienated "mama's boys."

For mythopoetic men, the agenda for change is mainly a personal one. They must separate from their mothers and be initiated into the world of men through all-male group activities such as "wildman weekend" retreats in the service of exploring the deep masculine. These meetings involve a variety of activities, including story telling, poetry reading, drumming, face painting, "sweat lodges," and other rituals. The philosophical position of the mythopoetics is that shared male ritual is the major avenue for accessing and reclaiming the rich inner experience of being a man. One of the major controversies concerns the mythopoetic doctrine of *essentialism* (see Chapter One). The definition of deep masculinity as a guide to experience takes the position that there is a singular, important, innate (essential) masculine quality. This position conflicts with the social constructionist view that gender is more of a social artifact than a "hardwired" reality.

Mythopoetic leaders tend to blame "the system" (Keen, 1991) and the industrial revolution (Bly, 1990), two social forces, for men's self-alienation. However, their early solutions were exclusively personal ones, not attempts to transform the societal arrangements that purportedly lie at the root of the problem (Johnson, 1997). In response to this criticism, a more recently-formed mythopoetic organization, the ManKind Project, encourages its members to participate in community activities in addition to personal explorations (Burke, Maton, Anderson, Mankowski, & Silvergleid, 2004).

5. The *evangelical Christian* men's movement sees the contemporary crisis of masculinity as a product of the diminishing role of Christian religion in men's lives. Advocates of this position want a return to a style of traditional families where fundamentalist Christianity is at the center of experience. The evangelical Christian men's movement *Promise Keepers* was very popular in the 1990s. Its aim was to encourage men to recommit themselves to being good fathers and husbands as defined by "biblical principles." The most visible events were rallies held in football stadiums (Abraham, 1997), and a 1997 rally in Washing-

ton, DC that attracted an estimated 500,000 men (Wheeler, 1997; Escobar & Murphy, 1997).

Promise Keepers is based on three major premises. First is the Christian doctrine that men are sinners who must atone and resist temptation to lead moral lives. Promise Keepers strive for "sexual purity," meaning that they condemn extramarital and premarital sex, use of pornography, sexual fantasy, "habitual" masturbation, and homosexuality (and yet, according to *Internet Filter Review*, 2009, 53 percent of Promise Keeper men view Internet pornography at least once in an average week). Clatterbaugh (1997) describes the Promise Keepers' view of men's sexuality as the religious conservative parallel to the sociobiological view that men are naturally barbaric, promiscuous, and inclined toward short-term gratification, and that these tendencies must be actively curtailed for the good of society.

The second major premise is that society has become hostile and adversarial to Christians. Sexual promiscuity, pornography, single parenthood, homosexuality, divorce, and decreased church attendance are cited as evidence of this decline. Promise Keepers founder Bill McCartney (quoted in Mann, 1997) characterized their activities as a Holy War, and this rhetoric was accompanied by a view of Jesus Christ as a heroic warrior who leads soldiers into battle, reviving the "muscular Christianity" of the mid-nineteenth, and then the early twentieth century by leaders such as evangelist Billy Sunday, who described Christ as "no dough-faced, lick-spittle proposition [but rather] the greatest scrapper who ever lived."

The traditionally masculine theme of men as dominant and aggressive (but for the right reasons) also finds its expression in the frequent reference to sports in Promise Keepers rallies. The ties to athletics are unmistakable. McCartney (a former head football coach at the University of Colorado) referred to the Bible as "God's playbook." At the 1997 Washington, DC rally, there was a striking presence of sports and other masculine themes on tee shirts and baseball caps, such as "real men follow God," "live pure, train hard," "cross trainers," "soldiers of the cross," and a shirt that said "Lord's gym" on the top, accompanied by a figure of Jesus on his back with a crown of thorns and a cross across his chest reading "sins of the world." Underneath the drawing, the shirt read, "Bench press this!"

The third major premise is the doctrine that men and women are essentially different, with complementary but distinct functions ordained by God. Promise Keepers see men as the natural leaders in the family. They frequently cite New Testament bible verses stating that women were created *for men* and that wives should submit to their husbands, who hold authority in the world. As you can imagine, this rhetoric is especially troubling to feminists and profeminists.

The leaders of Promise Keepers frequently described their movement as apolitical, and yet some of their main financial supporters were well-known leaders of the Christian conservative political movement. McCartney was very involved in anti-gay and other conservative political action. In 1992, he called homosexuality "an abomination against Almighty God" (Abraham, 1997) and supported Colorado's Amendment Two, which called for a ban on making any law that would grant gay and lesbian people civil rights protection, a law that National Organization for Women (NOW) official Rosemary Dempsey called, "in effect, a license for gay bashing" (quoted in Recer, 1995, p. 14).

Masculinities in the Mainstream

Very little gender-aware dialogue on masculinity has taken place in the United States mainstream after the turn of the twenty-first century. Perhaps part of this lack of cultural conversation can be laid at the doorstep of the U.S. marketplace, which effectively censors dialogue that does not sustain significant profit. One manifestation of market-driven gendering can be seen in the evolution of the magazine *Men's Health*, which began as an effort to help men learn to take better care of their bodies but quickly morphed into a reinforcement of traditionally-gendered attitudes: physical strength, sexual performance, and antifemininity. In 2000, *Men's Health* published a list of the best and worst colleges for men. It described the best colleges as those with good athletic programs and many available women, and the worst as those with strong Women's Studies departments and sexual assault policies, implying that sexual assault was good for men's health and that feminism is not.

Arran Stibbe (2004) cites numerous examples of the reinforcement of stereotypical masculinity (guns, political conservatism, beer drinking, hypermuscularity, disdain for cats, sexual promiscuity, chivalry, calling women "girls," etc.) and concludes that *Men's Health* is "a lifestyle magazine that gives advice on every aspect of living, from sex to shoes and, [only] incidentally, health" (p. 32). A recent visit to the magazine's website (menshealth.com, 2014) included stories on how to build "monster muscle," tone abdominals, and banish your "man boobs." There were also stories on the "best bikini bodies of the last century," "pickup lines that don't sound like pickup lines," and "how to have more oral sex." The magazines *Men's Journal* (mensjournal.com, 2014) and the more misogynistic *Maxim* magazine (maximonline.com, 2014) appear to be little more than manuals for traditional masculinity.

We can see from these and many other cultural manifestations of masculinity that transformative gender perspectives for men are censored by the marketplace. It is much more profitable to reinforce dominant masculinity than to challenge it. Jackson Katz's (2013) contention is that the increase in media portrayals of misogynistic and irresponsible masculinity caters to a significant population of men who feel threatened by gender changes and cannot deal with their anxiety in any other way except to reinforce their aggression and self-absorption.

Gail Dines (2013) asks the rhetorical question: "How many industries would collapse if, tomorrow morning, American women woke up and decided that they liked their bodies the way they are?" to point out how much profit is to be made by inferring that people are defective and offering the product as the way to restore them. We could ask a similar question: How many industries would collapse if, tomorrow morning, men woke up and decided that they were adequately masculine?

Although large-scale cultural efforts to redefine gender for men have stalled in the early twenty first century, we are seeing the emergence of several social change efforts and contemporary developments related to gender. Following is a brief description of some major ones.

The Advancement of Gay Rights in the United States

President Barack Obama's parents married in 1961, at a time when it would have been illegal to do so in many states because they were of different races. All of these laws were invalidated by civil rights legal challenges based on the equal protection clause of the fourteenth amendment to the United States Constitution. Advocates of same-sex marriage cited the same clause as the basis for overturning the United States ban on their rights to marry, resulting in rapid changes in these laws in the United States and many other parts of the world.

In 2009, President Obama extended some employment benefits to same-sex partners of federal employees by executive order (Wilson, 2009), and Secretary of State Clinton did the same with Foreign Service personnel (Kessler, 2009). Also in 2009, President Obama and the Office of Personnel Management (OPM) began working toward legislation that would guarantee full domestic benefits to same-sex partners of federal employees (Davidson, 2009). And in 2013, the Supreme Court ruled unconstitutional the 1996 Defense of Marriage Act (DOMA) (freedomtomarry.org, 2013) which banned same-sex couples from having rights that they did not have in the first place (Rauch, 2004).

In 2004, the American Psychological Association (APA) adopted a resolution supporting equal legal rights for gay and lesbian people, including the right to marry and adopt (Farberman, 2004), noting that there is no credible research indicating that same-sex marriage and family arrangements are detrimental to anyone. APA also cited a United States General Accounting Office study which identified more than one thousand federal statutory provisions in which marital status is a factor. A few of these are:

- Rights to community property
- Custody and visitation rights with children for partners and former partners living apart
- Employment benefits such as insurance, pension, and family leave
- The right to make health care decisions for an incapacitated partner
- The right to file a wrongful death suit if a partner dies as the result of negligence or wrongdoing
- No transfer tax applied to spouse on inheritance but applied to "unrelated" heir
- The right to make decisions about the disposition of bodily remains of a deceased spouse
- The legal right to refrain from testifying against a spouse in a criminal trial
- Conjugal prison visitation
- The choice to file joint income taxes
- Protection against deportation for a non-citizen partner
- Social security survivors' and disability insurance

- Protection from local statutes forbidding unrelated individuals from cohabiting
- Automatic ownership of a deceased partner's copyrights (Strasser, 2007)

Therefore, same-sex marriage is more than a symbolic step; it has a number of very tangible and important consequences.

One of the major arguments against same-sex marriage is that the state has an interest in maintaining heterosexual marriage because it needs to regulate issues around procreation. However, there is no legal marriage license requirement or expectation for having children, and fertility is neither a requirement for marriage nor grounds for divorce. Heterosexuals can marry even if they are incapable of reproducing. In fact, an immobile person can marry someone of the other sex on his or her deathbed (Bonauto, 2007). If the government believes that marriage offers a protection for children, it ought to support same-sex marriage, as fully one-third of these couples are raising or have raised children (Phy-Olsen, 2006). In a related discrimination case, Supreme Court Justice Ruth Bader Ginsberg stated, "A prime part of the history of our Constitution... is the story of the extension of constitutional rights and protections to people once ignored or excluded" (quoted in Bonauto, 2007, p. 19). Because it violates the rights to equal protection and free association, the exclusion of same-sex couples to the right to marry will likely be legally rectified, as has been the exclusion of mixed-race couples.

Prison

In the United States, there are now more than two million men in federal and state prisons or local jails (The Sentencing Project, 2014), a fourfold increase since 1980 (Elsner, 2004). By 1985, a new federal or state prison opened an average of once a week to house the growing inmate population (Mauer, 2006) which includes 73 out of every 1000 citizens (Jones & Mauer, 2013). The United States has about five percent of the world's population but nearly 25 percent of the world's incarcerated population (Webb, 2009)—more prisoners than any other industrialized country in the world, both by raw numbers and by percentage. It has more incarcerated persons than China, which has five times its population (Aizenman, 2008), and there are more prisoners in the United States than there are farmers (Tucker, 2003). Since males are about 90 percent of those in prisons and jails (The Sentencing Project, 2014), incarceration is by definition a men's issue. In fact, approximately one of about every 56 adult males in the United States is incarcerated (calculated from West, 2010, Golinelli & Minton, 2013, and United States Bureau of the Census, 2014).

A disproportionate number of prisoners are men of color, including one out of every nine African American men between the ages of 20 and 34 (Aizenman, 2008). Minority drivers are more likely than whites to be stopped and searched and there is a higher level of police surveillance in poor minority neighborhoods. Minority persons charged with felonies were more likely to be detained and less likely to be offered bail or pretrial release. They have less access to drug addiction treatment, a significant cause of racial disparity in the criminal justice system, as more than 60 percent of federal inmates are incarcerated because of drug offenses. Although African heritage people use illegal drugs at about the same rate as their European heritage counterparts, they are many times more likely to be incarcerated for drug offenses (The Sentencing Project, 2014). Racial minority clients tend to have many fewer resources to negotiate the criminal justice system (Mauer, 2006) and the discrimination against African Americans in this system is so egregious as to be labeled as "the new Jim Crow." (Alexander, 2012). The incarceration of African American men lies at the confluence of race, class, and gender.

Because of the economic crisis which began in 2008, states have explored alternatives to the costly incarceration of drug offenders, as treatment and parole have been demonstrated to be cost effective (Richburg, 2009). It remains to be seen whether economic recovery will lead to a new increase in the prison and jail population.

In 2003, Congress unanimously passed the Prison Rape Elimination Act, which provides funding for studying and producing remedies for the very common occurrence of sexual assault behind bars (Tucker, 2003), and the National Prison Rape Elimination Commission was established in 2009 (Johnson, 2009). The Commission on Safety and Abuse in America's Prisons is also attempting to provide solutions to the problems of inadequate physical and mental health care for prisoners (Slevin, 2005). And emerging data indicates that family and friends also suffer when someone is incarcerated (Munsey, 2009).

The risk of criminality and incarceration is certainly one of the most profoundly negative aspects of cultural masculinity, and yet sex and gender are rarely addressed in news stories about prison and crime. The acceptance of toxic gender ideologies, with its emphasis on dominance, control, wealth, and power, is doubtless an important factor in the decision to steal, use illegal drugs, or commit violent acts, especially for marginalized men such as the poor and racial minorities, who are disproportionately represented among the prison population. As James Messerschmidt (1993) put it, "Crime is not simply an extension of the 'male [masculine] sex [gender] role.' Rather crime by men is a form of social practice invoked as a resource, when other resources are unavailable for accomplishing masculinity" (p. 85). Moreover, these men are less likely than others to have adequate legal representation or to be offered plea bargaining that would allow them to avoid incarceration (The Sentencing Project, 2014).

Once they are behind bars, men learn quickly that "Prison is an ultramasculine world where nobody talks about masculinity." (Sabo, Kupers, & London, 2001, p. 1). Donald Sabo (2000) described prison as the penultimate patriarchal institution, marked by hierarchy, sex segregation, and violence. A small but committed group of reformers is trying to make inroads into prison reform, including gender-aware work with male juveniles (Katz, 2001), support groups (Brieman & Bonner, 2001), prison labor reform (Parenti, 2001), mental health services (Kupers, 1999), and efforts to find viable alternatives to incarceration (Kupers, 2004). It would seem that education about toxic masculinity is a key factor in inoculating boys and men against committing criminal acts in the first place or in avoiding recidivism following incarceration.

Pornography and Prostitution

The sale of sexually explicit material worldwide is a $56 billion per year industry (Dines, 2005). In the United States, this $13 billion industry brings in more revenue than the National Football League, the National Basketball Association, and Major League Baseball *combined* and more than the three major television networks *combined*. There are 4.2 million pornography websites (12 percent of all websites) containing 420 million pages (89 percent from the United States), and 25 percent of search engine requests are for sexually explicit material (Internet Filter Review, 2009). Robert Jensen (2007) reported that the pornographic film industry released 13,588 new films in 2005, an average of 37 per day, and that pornographic film revenues in the United States are larger than those generated by the Hollywood film industry. Mainstream corporations like General Motors, AT&T, and Time Warner own subsidiary companies that produce pornographic material (Dines, 2005).

One of the difficulties in evaluating the effects of pornography is terminology. When the U.S. Supreme Court first considered legal challenges to explicit erotic material, it had a serious problem with constructing the definition of "obscenity." This difficulty prompted Justice Potter Stewart to say that, "I can't define it, but I know it when I see it." (quoted in Green, 1987, p. 437). Explicit photographs and films can depict clothed people in provocative pose and situation, nudity, consensual sexual activity, the dominance of one sex over the other, or the violence and degradation of a person in a sexual situation. In the latter two types of material, it is nearly always the depiction of men dominating, objectifying, and raping women. Most researchers make an effort to distinguish erotica (sexually explicit but not exploitive material) and legitimate sex education materials from pornography.

The Campaign Against Pornography and Censorship (CPC) offers this definition:

> the graphic, sexually explicit subordination of women through pictures and/or words, that includes one or more of the following: women portrayed as sexual objects, things or commodities, enjoying pain, humiliation or rape, being tied up, cut up, mutilated, bruised or physically hurt, in postures of sexual submission or servility or display, reduced to body parts, penetrated by objects or animals, or presented in scenarios of degradation, injury, torture, shown as inferior, bleeding, bruised or hurt in a context which is sexual. (Smith, 1993, pp. 71–72)

One could expand this definition beyond its sex-specific boundaries to include the sexual exploitation of men and children. Although not all sexually explicit material fits the CPC definition, a great deal of it does. As Gail Dines (2005) states, "Pictures of naked women... popularized by *Playboy* have been replaced by videos that compete to see which can use and abuse the female body in new and more creative ways" (p. 110). Robert Jensen (2007) explains the rise in violence and cruelty in the industry: "Men typically consume pornography to avoid love and affection. That means pornography has a problem. When all emotion is drained from sex it becomes repetitive and uninteresting... Because the novelty of seeing sex on the screen wears off, pornography needs an edge. Pornography has to draw on some emotion, hence the cruelty" (p. 76).

Does pornography cause men to become violent toward women? Not directly, but evidence is emerging that, among men and boys who have other risk factors such as histories of child maltreatment and association with deviant peers, regular pornography viewing multiplies the risk of sexual aggression by about 400 percent (Ybarra and Mitchell, 2005). This finding should not be surprising, as there is more than 60 years of research on the negative effects of viewing violent media (see Chapter 12). Sexually explicit media has become widely available via the Internet and, as with nonsexual violent media, its effects on children is especially of concern. About 70 percent of children's first exposure is accidental (Kaiser Family Foundation, 2012) and the average first exposure for boys is at age 11 (Johnson, 2013).

In a study of fraternity men, Foubert, Brosi, and Brannon (2011) found that pornography users reported being less likely to intervene as bystanders in dangerous situations, more likely to endorse rape myths, and more likely to report a behavioral intent to rape compared with non-users. Beauregard, Lussier, and Proulx (2004) discovered a link between youth pornography use and adult deviant sexual interest, and Peter and Valkenburg (2007) found a strong relationship between pornography use and objectification of women. Another group of researchers found a strong relationship between pornography use and repeated criminal behavior in men previously convicted of a crime (Kingston, Fedoroff, Firestone, Curry, & Bradford, 2008).

Opponents of the pornography-violence hypothesis often cite cross-cultural research that shows a decrease (or lack of increase) in sex crimes for countries such as Denmark and the former West Germany following the legalization of sexually explicit material. Still, these are correlational data. The fact that two events occur together does not mean that one has caused the other. Theorists on this side of the issue also point out that violent pornography and depictions of consensual sex (often referred to as "erotica") produce different effects on viewers (Green, 1987).

Long before Internet pornography became available, several feminist theorists expressed strong disapproval of exploitive sexualized images. Susan Brownmiller (1975) argued that pornography is degrading by its very nature because it creates a social climate for the tolerance of sexual assault. Catherine MacKinnon (1985) stated that pornography "eroticizes hierarchy, it sexualizes inequality... institutionalizes the sexuality of male supremacy, fusing the eroticization of dominance and submission with the social construction of male and female" (p. 1). There are several studies demonstrating that a significant number of male pornography consumers use the material to intimidate their wives and girlfriends as well as their female co-workers, neighbors, and social contacts (Russo, 1998).

Does pornography cause rape? Not directly. There are many men who view pornography and are not sexually aggressive and men who are sexually aggressive and do not view pornography. But as Jensen (2007) points out, the important question is does pornography constitute a factor that contributes to rape? Evidence suggests that it does, as it "can perpetuate, reinforce, and be part of a wider system of woman-hating" (p. 103). If other predispositions to rape are present (see Chapter Twelve.), aggressive pornography has the potential of activating or reinforcing these predispositions (Malamuth, Addison, & Koss, 2000). Acknowledging that sexually explicit material is quite compelling but nonetheless harmful if aggressive, Gail Dines (2006) stated, "I don't believe that most boys and men come to pornography because they hate women. But if they stay, they learn to hate women."

Pornography researchers have documented instances of extreme violence against women in sexually explicit films. Pornography producers defend their industry by saying that films are very diverse and that anti-pornography activists point to only the most extreme examples of violence and degradation. Ana Bridges and her research team (2008) randomly selected scenes from the 250 most popular sexually explicit films and coded randomly-selected segments of them for aggressive acts. They found that 82.8 percent of the 304 scenes had physical aggression (such as slapping, hair pulling, or spitting), that 95 percent of the aggression was directed toward women, and that the female performers were almost always depicted as enjoying these acts. Thus, whether or not sexually-explicit films are diverse, the ones that are viewed most often contain elements of violence against women.

Although nonviolent erotica probably has no direct link to violence against women, there has long been evidence that it may have a damaging effect on relationships between men and women. Male research subjects who viewed *Playboy* and *Penthouse* magazine centerfolds tended to give lower ratings of their female partners' attractiveness and individual worth (Malamuth, 1984). Moreover, they reported being less in love with their partners than men who did not view these pictures (Kenrick, Gutierres, & Goldberg, 1989). Thus, those who view the physical "perfection" (enhanced with lighting and photograph retouching) of these magazine models seem to make comparisons of centerfolds with other women. The fact that they report being less in love reveals that erotica reinforces the patriarchal notion that relationships between men and women depend on the woman's sexual desirability.

Anti-pornography activist Gail Dines (2013) described women in pornography as being viewed as having "no past, future, biography, goals, or aims," and as being disposable. The average length of their careers is about three months because they become injured and/or diseased. In an interesting development, the State of California, which houses most United States pornography production companies, passed a bill requiring condom use on pornography film sets in 2013. Activists worked with the state's Occupational and Safety Health Administration (OSHA) to define the film set as a workplace that needs to meet safety standards. People in the pornography industry argued that most performers are willing to work without condoms (one wonders if they would be hired if they were not willing) but OSHA countered with the analogous situation of a construction worker willing to work without a hard hat but who nonetheless is required to wear one. Not surprisingly, some pornographers threatened to move their businesses to other states (bizjournals.com, 2014). Dines (2013) opined that the industry fought the condom law because performers wearing condoms disrupts the "porn narrative" that women are disposable because wearing a condom is an act of caring for one's sexual partner.

What direct effects does pornography have on the male viewer? Just as they compare sexualized women with their own partners, pornography viewers compare themselves with male performers, many of whom are handsome, fit, and have large genitalia. Viewing idealized and sexualized men has a tendency to make the heterosexual male viewer more self-conscious of his own body, decreases his estimation of his sexual desirability, and makes him less likely to interact with women (Aubrey, 2007). Internet hypersexualized media viewing is associated with a higher likelihood of engaging in risky sexual behavior, increased loneliness, and the acceptance of the negative gender stereotype of men as dominant and women as submissive (Johnson, 2013).

There is evidence emerging that Internet pornography has an adverse effect that was not present for a previous generation of men whose early exposure to images of naked women were from paper magazines. Neuroscientist Gary Wilson (2014) explains that, because it is now possible to click images quickly and open multiple windows at a time, men can now view more naked bodies in sexual motion in a half hour than humans evolved to experience in a lifetime. As a result, the brain becomes habituated to the images and significant numbers of men are having extreme difficulty in becoming aroused with their real-life partners, a condition called Pornography Induced Erectile Dysfunction (PIED).

Wilson explains that men can recover from this condition by abstaining from viewing Internet pornography for a period of months, a process he calls "rebooting the brain." Interestingly, men in their 50s recover faster and better than men in their 20s despite having less testosterone, older blood vessels and, well, older everything. He surmises that the older men's better recoveries are due to the fact that they did not grow up with Internet pornography and thus did not view it until their brains were fully developed, but the younger men's early exposure resulted in more durable changes to the structure and function of the brain.

Ana Bridges (quoted in Jensen, 2007) notes that compulsive pornography viewers tend to require increasingly deviant material to attain arousal, and that they often pressure their partners to engage in unpleasant or degrading sexual acts that they viewed on video. Their female partners report a decline in their feelings of intimacy and connection to these men. Pamela Paul (2005) interviewed young men and found that, for many, frequent pornography use resulted in their being distracted from their partners and diminished their sexual pleasure. As Robert Jensen (2007) notes, "Pornography opens a path to a door that opens into a prison" (p. 180). Men's and boys' sexualities are being manipulated and distorted by other men for profit.

Prostitution is similar to pornography in that it involves the objectification and disrespect of human beings and the buying and selling of bodies for sexual purposes. Nearly all those who hire prostitutes also view pornography on a regular basis (Malarek, 2009). Pimps are (nearly all) men who deal in the trafficking of women and sometimes children and men. They are notoriously exploitive and sometimes violent. Pimps are akin to pornographic film producers, as they exploit the sexualities of human beings for profit. "Johns" are men who purchase sex from prostitutes; they are akin to consumers of pornography. Like pornography and all sex industry workers, prostitutes often have impoverished backgrounds, few other avenues for employment, and a history of childhood abuse. Many are brought into prostitution as young children. Two-thirds of prostitutes have symptoms of posttraumatic stress disorder (PTSD) (Farley, Cotton, Lynne, Zumbeck, & Spiwack, 2003), many are clinically depressed, have been seriously injured by pimps or customers, and/or have significant drug abuse problems. Nearly half have attempted suicide (Carter & Giobbe, 2006), and overall they are 40 times more likely to die than people in other occupations (Malarek, 2009).

Victor Malarek (2009) and other anti-prostitution researchers and activists note that prostitution cannot be separated from human trafficking. Wherever there is a demand for prostitutes and a market that can be exploited, unscrupulous pimps will transport poor and desperate women and children and sell their bodies for profit. There are an estimated 800,000 such victims worldwide, netting organized crime an estimated $12 billion per year. There are an estimated 10 million prostituted women and children in the world.

Malarek (2009) describes the mentality of the johns who rent bodies for sexual purposes: "The search for paid sex is all about entitlement, power, and control... His wants, needs, and desires reign supreme. He doesn't have to worry about anybody else's... He can give or take without the burden of reciprocity" (p. 10). Some johns who have the financial wherewithal will travel to locations where prostitution is legal or unprosecuted, and cheap. These are areas of the world where crippling poverty results in people having few choices for survival except to face the danger and humiliation of renting their bodies. An estimated 5.1 million men per year travel to Thailand to purchase prostitutes, accounting for at least 10 percent of that country's gross domestic product. Other popular destinations for this euphemistically-titled "sex tourism" are Cambodia, Costa Rica, Columbia, Brazil, Ghana, Kenya, Russia, and Ukraine. Because of the easy access and anonymity of the Internet, johns now have extensive networks where they recommend places to travel and strategies for avoiding law enforcement.

Johns have varying motivations for purchasing and exploiting human beings for sexual purposes. Some are lonely men who believe that they cannot attract women for consensual sex. Some do not want to deal with what they perceive as the "hassle" of dating and relationships. The most dangerous johns are those who seek out prostitutes because they have sadistic tendencies and a deep hatred of women. These men are often physically abusive with the prostitutes they hire. And some want the false affection provided by "the girlfriend experience" in which the prostitute plays the role of a woman who is falling in love with the john. He can spend the weekend in this fantasy and then return to his life without having to deal further with the woman. One prostitute described the end of the weekend: "Oh, I play the girlfriend role to the hilt. I pout a bit. I tell them that I'll miss them and I can't wait to see them again soon, and once they're out the door I take a long, cold shower" (Malarek, 2009, p.79).

Because some view prostitution as an inevitability of life that fills an important need for some men, some countries such as Germany, the Netherlands, and Australia, and municipalities such as Las Vegas have legalized or decriminalized the practice, believing that doing so may allow better regulation of the industry and even add tax money to the economy. However, legalization has had disastrous effects. It has resulted in an increase in illegal prostitution, an increase in the presence of organized crime, and an increase in the number of prostituted people trafficked into the region to meet the increased demand that results from johns' impunity. It has not resulted in better health or safety for prostituted women. In effect, legalization turns the state into a pimp (Malarek, 2009). In an amazing development, the organization Amnesty International, whose mission it is to protect the least powerful people in the world, proposed in 2013 that purchasing sex (i.e., renting the genitalia of a human being) is a fundamental human right, ignoring the considerable evidence of the damage that prostitution wreaks (change.org, 2014). Amnesty also takes no stand on age of consent, thus condoning child sexual exploitation.

Historically, law enforcement has targeted prostituted women for prosecution much more frequently than johns. Eleven times as many prostitutes as johns are arrested in Boston, and in New York and Chicago, the ratios are 6:1 and 9:1, respectively. Legalization has clearly not been the answer to the problem of prostitution, but more successful efforts have resulted from decriminalizing the act of selling sex—based on the assumptions that prostituted people are victims, not perpetrators of the crime—but at the same time increasing negative legal consequences for those who purchase sex, the johns, a strategy known as the Nordic Model (Korsvik & Sto, 2013).

Philosophically, this approach is grounded in the beliefs that prostitution is an extension of slavery, that the basic worth and dignity of a human being means that no person should be treated as merchandise, and that prostitution, historically and currently, is one of the most salient symbols of women's subordination to men (Korsvik & Sto, 2013). Sweden adopted the Nordic Model in 1999 and now defines prostitution as a violation of human rights and an act of gender-based violence by men who hire prostitutes. As a result the number of prostitutes trafficked into the region dropped by half within four years, resulting in dramatic differences between Sweden and the other Scandinavian countries, which do not do as effective a job at prosecuting johns (Malarek, 2009).

In the United States, some cities have tracked first-time offenders into "john school" as an alternative or addition to criminal penalties. In these education programs, johns learn about the health and legal risks of participating in prostitution and also hear from former prostitutes about the misery that was brought to them by being in this occupation. The johns begin to see prostitutes as human beings and the combination of enlightened self-interest and victim empathy has resulted in significant decreases in subsequent offending (Malarek, 2009). For prostitution to end, prostitutes also need help to access better viable avenues for employment and johns need support to learn how to manage their lives without buying sex (Korsvik & Sto, 2013).

Regardless of whether an individual who consumes pornography or hires a prostitute harms the self or others directly, he or she is nevertheless participating in a system that generates significant harm. John Foubert (2007) raises the moral issue for men who choose to do so: "Can you mentally justify for your own pleasure watching someone pretend to experience pleasure but in reality they are suffering inside anyway? Do you care? Is that something that matches your values?"

The "Boy Crisis"

The late 1990s and early twenty-first century witnessed a good deal of dialogue in the popular culture on the emotional lives of boys. Led by William Pollack's (1998) bestseller, *Real Boys: Rescuing Our Sons from the Myths of Boyhood*, a number of writers began to explore emotional, scholastic, and criminality problems that show a highly imbalanced sex ratio. Laura Bush, wife of the then-President of the United States, spoke publicly about concerns over boys' problems, thus giving the debate a very high profile (NPR, 2005) as Pollack and others offered solutions to difficulties boys encounter in managing their emotional lives and achieving in a culture that expects emotional constriction, violence, and hyperindependence (see also Gurian & Stevens, 2005, and Polce-Lynch, 2002).

One of the debates that emerged was whether boys are shortchanged by schools relative to girls, with one author (Sommers, 2001) even claiming that "feminism" is waging a "war" against boys by demanding that boys behave like girls. As evidence, supporters of this position cite statistics indicating that boys achieve lower average grades in school and are a shrinking minority in the college student population (Gurian, 2005). Behind this argument are the assumptions that feminism is males' enemy and that the sexes are adversarial (i.e., attention paid to girls' problems leads boys to be "shortchanged"). On the other hand, males' standardized test scores and working-world achievement are as strong as they ever were (Sadker, 2000), demonstrating that, if there is a war, it is clearly not a very successful one.

One interesting part of the debate is the growing disproportion of male to female college students, with women making up 57 percent of all students, which at first glance makes it appear that there is a higher education crisis among young men. However, when one looks more closely at the data, a very different picture emerges. Among students of all races who come from relatively affluent families, male students are proportional to the male population (49 to 51 percent). But males from middle and lower income families comprise only 36 to 42 percent of college students within their demographic, with the exception of Asian males (50 percent of students from middle income and 47 percent from lower income families). The lowest proportions of males in college are found for Blacks (36 percent) and Hispanics (39 percent) from lower income families (Marklein, 2005). Therefore, income and race appear to interact strongly with sex and gender.

It is also important to note that more people of both sexes are going to college compared with two decades ago relative to their proportions in the general population, with the exception of White, non-Hispanic people, whose college attendance increased by 5.5 percent for males and 11.3 percent for females between 1990 and 2007, when the population of the United States increased by about 17 percent (calculated from USBC, 2009). During that same time period, Indigenous people's enrollments increased by 42.1 percent for males and 48.3 percent for females, and other non-White groups also showed dramatic increases (Asian: 47.6 percent males, 57.7 percent females; Black, non-Hispanic: 42.2 percent males, 50.7 percent females; Hispanic: 58.9 percent males, 64.7 percent females). Among all groups taken together, the college population grew by 19.6 percent for males and 27.8 percent for females (calculated from *The Chronicle of Higher Education*, 2009). Therefore, male enrollments are increasing at a rate slightly higher than the population growth, and the dwindling percentage of male college students is not a product of fewer men going to college; it is a product of their increases in enrollments not being as sharp as women's increases.

Males-as-a-group earn more than females-as-a-group at every level of education, and so one possibility is that males have more avenues to employment than females without college. However, going to college continues to add significantly to earning potential throughout life. Therefore, choosing not to go to college when one has the resources to do so is not a rational choice for many. One group of scholars notes that labor market considerations do not explain the sex imbalance of the college student population. Rather, males are more likely than females to place a high value on self-sufficiency and earning as opposed to long-term investment and the relatively dependent role of college student (Leicht, et. al., 2007). This gender identity conflict hypothesis and its interaction with race and class await further study.

The debates about how boys are harmed by various social forces will likely continue, but as many scholars (Sadker, 2000; Kimmel, 2013b; Pollack, 2000; Morris, 2011), have pointed out, we should be careful not to be lulled into playing a game of "boys against the girls." It is clear that both boys and girls face problems that are somewhat specific to their sexes. Addressing the typical male problems of poor school achievement, criminality, bullying, impoverished emotional lives, and suicide need not come at the expense of a focus on girls' struggles.

Men's Advocacy Organizations

In recent years, as men's studies scholars have identified a set of health vulnerabilities specific to males, organizations have begun attempts to address the health needs and problems of this population. In the United States, the most visible group is the Men's Health Network (www.menshealthnetwork.org), a nonprofit organization that supports education, research, and political action (such as lobbying Congress to establish an Office of Men's Health) to improve men's wellness. Institutions such as the Mayo Clinic (mayoclinic.com) provide information on health and mental health concerns specific to men. In recognition of the increased risk for negative health outcomes for poor and ethnic minority men, other organizations have attempted to address race and class issues in men's health care (Ro, Casares, Treadwell, & Thomas, 2004; Rich & Ro, 2002). The World Congress on Men's Health (wcmh.info) has a similar mission in the international context., as does the organization Movember (www.movember.com).

Men are also becoming more involved in gender equality movements, including efforts to end gender-based violence. We detailed some of these approaches in Chapter Twelve. Internationally, organizations such as Oxfam, Promundo, and the World Health Organization have taken the lead in supporting these men's movements (Ferguson, et. al., 2004; Krug, et. al., 2002; Ruxton, 2004; Heilman, Hebert, & Paul-Gera, 2014). Much remains to be accomplished in the quest to reduce men's violence against women, and men's involvement in this effort, although it is increasing, remains rather sparse.

Men's Studies

During the last 50 years, modern feminist scholars have convincingly demonstrated that gender affects virtually every area of life, including politics, family organization, literature, art, individual psychology, international relations, and views of history. Women's Studies has emerged as a legitimate field of multidisciplinary intellectual inquiry. College and university courses, research programs, and even entire academic departments have been developed to place gender and women's perspectives into the previously male-dominated body of knowledge. As men began to understand that gender has colored their views of the world, it became important to understand the effects of masculinity on the individual and society. The relatively new field of Men's Studies has emerged as an effort in this direction.

Critics have questioned the need for men's studies. The most frequent objection is that nearly all study already *is* men's study, because of the pervasive dominance of men in academia and literature. Kimmel (1987), Brod (1987b), and others have responded to this objection by drawing a distinction between the study of men in the context of specific functions—as scientists, historical figures, artists, etc.—and the study of men *as men*. In the former approach, masculinity is a (usually unarticulated) backdrop of intellectual discourse. The latter approach brings masculinity into the *center* of inquiry. Recall Box 1.5 for an analogy to describe the importance of men's studies.

The field of Men's Studies cuts across traditional academic disciplines. These courses are being taught in a wide variety of academic departments, including psychology, sociology, English, religion, classics, history, education, anthropology, and philosophy. It was conservatively estimated that there were more than 500 such courses being taught in the United States as of the late 1990s (Dobbin, 1997).

The American Psychological Association (APA) is comprised of many divisions (e.g. counseling psychology, abnormal psychology, addictions, and psychology of women), where members are organized around common interests. In 1995, APA recognized the Society for the Psychological Study of Men and Masculinity (SPSSM) as an official division (Brooks & Levant, 1995), giving it legitimate status within mainstream psychology. The following year, *The Washington Post* carried a front-page headline reading "Men's Studies Coming of Age in New Campus Rite of Passage" (Sanchez, 1996). Harry Brod (Laker, Davis, Kellom, & Brod, H., 2005) cited the publication of two encyclopedias of men's studies as evidence that researchers and theorists in this field have assembled a critical mass of scholarship. It seems that Men's Studies has attained a small but significant and legitimized place in mainstream academe.

James Doyle and Sam Femiano (1998) traced the history of two organized men's studies associations. In the early days of NOMAS (then the National Organization for Men), there were several members with an interest in gender research. Led by Harry Brod, Martin Acker, Michael Messner, and others, they formed the Men's Studies Task Group (MSTG), later renamed the Men's Studies Association (MSA), which began to sponsor sessions during the annual NOMAS conferences. In 1991, several scholars broke from MSA, partly because of the timing of the annual conference, but largely because they rejected the premise that men's studies should be guided exclusively by feminist principles. They formed the American Men's Studies Association (AMSA) and held their first conference in 1993.

Two interdisciplinary journals, *Men and Masculinities* (sponsored by MSA) and *The Journal of Men's Studies* (sponsored by AMSA), are wholly devoted to men's studies scholarship. In addition, SPSSM began publishing its own journal, *Psychology of Men and Masculinity*, in 1999. The journals *Sex Roles* and *Gender Issues* are dedicated to gender scholarship in general, and they also carry many articles that fit within the field of men's studies. Many other journals, such as the *Journal of Marriage and the Family*, the *Journal of Counseling Psychology*, the *Journal of Social Issues, Child Development*, and the *Journal of Homosexuality*, to name only a few, also carry masculinity articles as they relate to the central focus of the particular journal. This proliferation of masculine gender scholarship into the mainstream attests to the ever-widening acceptance of Men's Studies.

Following are some examples of broad Men's Studies questions:

1. How have concepts of masculinity changed throughout history?
2. What do images of men in literature, art, and film tell us about masculinity?
3. How do we make sense of the reality of male patriarchal power and its seeming contradiction with the sense of powerlessness in the lives of so many men (Kimmel, 2013b)?
4. What are the connections between masculinity and power, racism, sexism, heterosexism, and social class?
5. How has masculinity affected religious institutions and practices?
6. What are the effects of male initiation rites in various cultures, and how are these rites similar or dissimilar (Herdt, 1992)?
7. How can the various "men's movements" be understood in historical, psychological, and political perspective (Clatterbaugh, 2000)?
8. How does masculinity affect a nation's willingness to enter or avoid war (Connell, 2005)?
9. What kinds of techniques are useful in facilitating men's understanding of the impact of gender on their lives?
10. How does masculinity change and evolve in mid-life and old age?

Most Men's Studies scholars come from profeminist or mythopoetic frames of reference. The general approach is to take seriously the influence of gender on men and articulate its effects. Profeminist-oriented writers are mainly interested in studying the changing character of masculinity and its consequences for individual men and social systems. Mythopoetic writers are mostly involved in writing (or writing about) stories, poems, and rituals that can be used to get closer to the symbolic experience of masculinities.

A Final Word

Cultural constructions of masculinity will continue to change in response to economics, legal changes, shifting ideologies, and various other social forces. And yet there is also strong resistance to change. As one Nicaraguan woman (quoted in de Keizer (2004), put it "Men are looking for women who don't exist *any more* and women are looking for men who don't exist *yet*" (p. 32, emphasis original). Men in the industrialized world who attempt to apply their fathers' and grandfathers' strategies to reaching life goals will find these approaches increasingly untenable in a modern world where gender is becoming less of an organizing principle in society.

James Nelson (1997) describes a basic dilemma for men in the donning of masculine "armor," which "seems to protect us, but it also prevents us from leaping, dancing, and being seen." What is the future of masculinity? With hope, it is a new generation of men who feel less pressure to look, feel, and act like "real men," and more of an urgency to look, feel, and act like the people whom they truly are. It is men who can hear the voices of women, children, other men, nature, and the self, and who can connect more deeply with all of them. It is men who can retain a vigorous masculine energy and direct it into breaking the cycles of violence and self-destructiveness that have stood in place for centuries. It is a new generation of men who can love, work, and play in different and healthier ways. It is the reconnection of the masculine self with the human self.

Summary

1. There is a good deal of controversy around whether masculinities should change or not. Among those who think that they should change, there are disagreements about the nature and direction these changes should take.

2. As gender is deeply ingrained in all social systems, the alteration of gender roles is a painstaking process. Differing opinions on men's social reality result in differing opinions on the necessity and nature of change.

3. No men's movement has captured the attention of mainstream cultures for very long. Currently, a number of new social issues have emerged in the public eye, including same-sex marriage, male criminality and incarceration, pornography and prostitution, social and academic struggles for young boys, men's health, and men's movements to achieve gender equality and end men's violence around the world.

4. There is a growing amount of research and scholarship on men and masculinity from a variety of perspectives. The academic interest in Men's Studies cuts across traditional disciplines and has established itself as a legitimate area of scholarship.

5. Cultural constructions of masculinity will continue to change in response to various social forces.

References

Abraham, K. (1997). *Who are the Promise Keepers? Understanding the Christian men's movement.* New York: Bantam Doubleday Bell.

Abrams, D., Viki, G. T., Masser, B., & Bohner, G. (2003). Perceptions of stranger and acquaintance rape: The role of benevolent and hostile sexism in victim blame and rape proclivity. *Journal of Personality and Social Psychology, 84*, 111–125.

Acker, S. E. (Ed., 2013). Unclenching our fists: Abusive men on the journey to nonviolence. Nashville, TN: Vanderbilt University Press.

Active Duty Gender Distribution (2013). U. S. Military Active Duty Demographic Profile. Retrieved August 26, 2013 from http://www.slideshare.net/pastinson/us-military-active-duty-demographic-profile-presentation.

Adams, H. E., Wright, L. W., & Lohr, B. A. (1996). Is homophobia associated with homosexual arousal? *Journal of Abnormal Psychology, 105*, 440–445.

Adams, S., Kuebli, J., Boyle, P. A., & Fivush, R. (1995). Gender differences in parent-child conversations about past emotions: A longitudinal investigation. *Sex Roles, 33*, 309–323.

Addis, M. E. (2008). Gender and depression in men. *Clinical Psychology: Science and Practice, 15*, 153–168.

Addis, M. E. & Mahalik, J. R. (2003). Men, masculinity, and the contexts of help seeking. *American Psychologist, 58 (1)*, 5–14.

Adler, L. L. (Ed.) (1993). *International handbook on gender roles.* Westport, CT: Greenwood.

Adorno, T., Frenkel-Brunswik, E., Levinson, D., & Sanford, R.N. (1950). *The authoritarian personality.* New York: Harper.

Aizenman, N. C. (2008, February 29). New high in U. S. prison numbers: Growth attributed to more stringent sentencing laws. *The Washington Post, A1.*

Alexander, M. (2012). *The new Jim Crow: Mass incarceration in the age of color blindness.* New York: New Press.

Allison, J. (2005). *Violence response and prevention at Pittsburg State University.* Paper presented in symposium: Sexual assault prevention for men (C. Kilmartin, chair) at the Annual Convention of the American Psychological Association, Washington, DC.

Alloy, L. B. Jacobson, N. S., & Acocella, J. (1999). *Abnormal psychology: Current perspectives* (8th ed.). Boston: McGraw-Hill.

315

Amato, P. & Booth, A. (2001). The legacy of parents' marital discord: Consequences for children's marital quality. *Journal of Personality and Social Psychology, 81 (4)*, 627–638.

American Cancer Society (2014*). Estimated number of new cancer cases and deaths by sex, U. S., 2014.* Retrieved May 29, 2014 from http://www.cancer.org/acs/groups/content/@research/documents/document/acspc-041780.pdf.

American Heart Association (2014). *Heart disease and stroke statistics: 2010 update.* Retrieved May 29, 2014 from *my.americanheart.org/idc/groups/aha-mah-public/.../ucm_424455.*

American Psychiatric Association (1980). *Diagnostic and statistical manual of mental disorders* (3rd ed.) (DSM-III). Washington, DC: American Psychiatric Association.

American Psychiatric Association (1987). *Diagnostic and statistical manual of mental disorders* (3rd ed. - revised) (DSM- III-R). Washington, DC: American Psychiatric Association.

American Psychiatric Association (1994). *Diagnostic and statistical manual of mental disorders* (4th ed.) (DSM-IV). Washington, DC: American Psychiatric Association.

American Psychiatric Association (2000). *Diagnostic and statistical manual of mental disorders* (4th ed., text revision) (DSM-IV-TR). Washington, DC: American Psychiatric Association.

American Psychiatric Association (2013). *Diagnostic and statistical manual of mental disorders* (5th ed.) (DSM-V). Washington, DC: American Psychiatric Association.

American Psychological Association (2005). Resolution on sexual orientation and marriage and resolution on sexual orientation, parents, and children. *American Psychologist, 60 (5)*, 494–496.

Anderson, E., McCormack, M., & Lee, H. (2012). Male Team Sport Hazing Initiations in a Culture of Decreasing Homo-hysteria. *Journal of Adolescent Research,* 427–448.

Anderson, N. (2014, July 10). McCaskill questions handling of campus sexual assault. *The Washington Post,* A3.

Anderson, R. N. & Smith, B. L. (2005). Deaths: Leading causes, 2002. *National Vital Statistics Reports, 53 (17)*, 1–90.

Andreassen, C. S. (2014). Workaholism: An overview and current status of the research. *Journal of Behavioral Addictions, 3*(1), 1–11.

Angier, N. (1999a). *Woman: An intimate geography.* Boston: Houghton-Mifflin.

Angier, N. (1999b). *The beauty of the beastly: New views on the nature of life.* Boston: Houghton-Mifflin.

Archer, J. (1984). Gender roles as developmental pathways. *British Journal of Social Psychology, 23*, 245–256.

Archer, J. (2000). Sex differences in aggression between heterosexual partners: A meta-analytic review. *Psychological Bulletin, 126 (5)*, 651–680.

Archer, J. (2006). Testosterone and human aggression: An evaluation of the challenge hypothesis. *Neuroscience and Biobehavioral Reviews, 30*(3), 319–345.

Arciniega, G.M., Anderson, T. C., Tovar-Blank, Z. G., & Tracey, T. J. G. (2008). Toward a fuller conception of machismo: Development of a traditional machismo and caballerismo scale. *Journal of Counseling Psychology, 55*, 19–33.

Arias, E. (2005). United States life tables 2002. National Vital Statistics Reports, Center for Disease Control. Retrieved June 10, 2009 from http://www.cdc.gov/nchs/data/nvsr/nvsr53/nvsr53_06.

Arias, I. & Ikeda, R. M. (2006). Etiology and surveillance of intimate partner violence. In J. R. Lutzker (Ed.). *Preventing violence: Research and evidence-based intervention strategies.* Washington, DC: American Psychological Association.

Aronson, E., with Aronson, J. (2012). *The social animal* (11th ed.). New York: Worth.

Asch, S. E. (1965). Effects of group pressure upon the modification and distortion of judgments. In H. Proshansky & B. Seidenberg (Eds.), *Basic studies in social psychology*. New York: Holt, Rinehart, and Winston.

Associated Press (2014). Here's the status of gay marriage in all 50 states. Retrieved October 9, 2014 from http://www.washingtonpost.com/national/heres-the-status-of-gay-marriage-in-all-50–states/2014/10/07/4c4ed7ac-4e7f-11e4–877c-335b53ffe736_story.html.

Astrachan, A. (1992). Men and the new economy. In M. S. Kimmel & M. A. Messner (Eds.), *Men's lives* (2nd ed., pp. 221–225). New York: Macmillan.

Aubrey, J. S. (2007). The Impact of Sexually Objectifying Media Exposure on Negative Body Emotions and Sexual Self-Perceptions: Investigating the Mediating Role of Body Self-Consciousness. *Sex Roles, 10*, 1–23.

Avert (international AIDS charity) (2005). HIV and AIDS Statistics. Avert.org.

Axson, S. (2014, August 25, 2014). Mo'ne Davis on this week's national *Sports Illustrated* cover. *Sports Illustrated*.

Baca Zinn, M. (1995). Chicano men and masculinity. In M. S. Kimmel & M. A. Messner (Eds.), *Men's lives* (3rd ed., pp. 33–41). Boston: Allyn and Bacon.

Baghurst, T., Hollander, D. B., Nardella, B., & Haff, G. G. (2006). Change in sociocultural ideal male physique: An examination of past and present action figures. *Body Image, 3*, 87–91.

Baird, L. C., Newman, C. B., Volk, H., Svinth, J. R., Conklin, J., & Levy, M. L. (2010). Mortality resulting from head injury in professional boxing. Neurosurgery, 67, 1444–1450.

Balswick, J. (1988). *The inexpressive male*. Lexington, MA: D.C. Heath.

Bandura, A. (1989). Social cognitive theory. In P. H. Mussen (Ed.), *Annals of child development (Vol. 6)* (pp. 1–60). Greenwich, CT, USA: JAI Press.

Bandura, A., Ross, D., & Ross, S. (1961). Transmission of aggression through imitation of aggressive models. *Journal of Abnormal and Social Psychology, 63*, 575–582.

Bandura, A., Ross, D., & Ross, S. A. (1963a). Imitation of film-mediated aggressive models. *The Journal of Abnormal and Social Psychology, 66*(1), 3–11.

Bandura, A., Ross, D., & Ross, S. A. (1963b). Vicarious reinforcement and imitative learning. *The Journal of Abnormal and Social Psychology, 67*(6), 601–607.

Bandura, A., & Walters, R. H. (1963). *Social learning and personality development*. New York: Holt, Rinehart, and Winston.

Bank, B. J., & Hansford, S. L. (2000). Gender and friendship: Why are men's best same-sex friendships less intimate and supportive? *Personal Relationships, 7*(1), 63–78.

Barash, D. P., & Lipton, J. E. (1997). *Making sense of sex: How genes and gender influence our relationships*. Washington, DC: Island.

Barnett, R. C., Marshall, N. L., & Pleck, J. H. (1992). Adult son-parent relationships and their associations with sons' psychological distress. *Journal of Family Issues, 13*, 505–525.

Barnett, R. C., & Rivers, C. (1996). *She works/he works: How two-income families are happier, healthier, and better-off*. New York: Harper San Francisco/Harper Collins.

Baron, R. A. & Branscome, N. R. (2011). *Social psychology* (13th ed.). Boston: Pearson.

Baron, S. L., Hein, M. J., Lehman, E., & Gersic, C. M. (2013). Body mass index, playing position, race, and the cardiovascular mortality of retired football players. *American Journal of Cardiology, 109*, 889–896.

Barr, C. L., & Kleck, R. E. (1995). Self-other perception of the intensity of facial expressions of emotion: Do we know what we show? *Journal of Personality and Social Psychology, 68*, 604–618.

Barthel, D. (1992). When men put on appearances: Advertising and the social construction of masculinity. In S. Craig (Ed.), *Men, masculinity, and the media* (pp. 137–153). Newbury Park, CA: Sage.

Bartholomew, B. D., Dill, K. E., Anderson, K. B., & Lindsay, J. J. (2003). The proliferation of media violence and its economic underpinnings. In D. A. Gentile (Ed.), *Media violence and children: A complete guide for parents and professionals.* Westport, CT: Praeger.

Basow, S. (1992). *Gender: Stereotypes and roles* (3rd ed.). Monterey, CA: Brooks/Cole.

Baumeister, R. F. (2000). Gender differences in erotic plasticity: The female sex drive as socially flexible and responsive. *Psychological Bulletin, 126*(3), 347–374.

Bauserman, R., & Davis, C. (1996). Perceptions of early sexual experiences and adult sexual adjustment. *Journal of Psychology and Human Sexuality, 8*, 37–59.

Beauregard, E., Lussier, P., & Proulx, J. (2004). The role of sexual interests and situational factors on rapists' modus operandi: Implications for offender profiling. *Legal and Criminological Psychology, 10*, 265–278.

Becker, J. V. (1996). Outpatient treatment of adolescent male sexual offenders. In M. P. Andronico (Ed.), *Men in groups: Insights, interventions, and psychoeducational work* (pp. 377–388). Washington, DC: American Psychological Association.

Bellamy, J. L., & Banman, A. (2014). Advancing research on services for adolescent fathers: A commentary on Kiselica and Kiselica. *Psychology of Men & Masculinity, 15*(3), 281–283.

Bem, S.L. (1974). The measurement of psychological androgyny. *Journal of Consulting and Clinical Psychology, 42*, 155–162.

Bem, S. L. (1981). Gender schema theory: A cognitive account of sex-typing. *Psychological Review, 88*, 354–364.

Bem, S. L. (1989). Genital knowledge and gender constancy in preschool children. *Child Development, 60*(3), 649–662.

Bem, S. L. (1993). *The lenses of gender: Transforming the debate on sexual inequality.* New Haven, CT: Yale University Press.

Bem, S. L. (1998). Gender schema theory and its implications for child development: Raising gender-aschematic children in a gender-schematic society. In D. L. Anselmi & A. L. Law (Eds.), *Questions of gender: perspectives and paradoxes* (pp. 262–274). Boston: McGraw-Hill.

Benard, C., & Schlaffer, E. (1997). "The man in the street: Why he harasses." In L. Richardson, V. Taylor, & N. Whittier (Eds.), *Feminist frontiers* IV (pp. 395–398). Boston: McGraw-Hill.

Ben-David, S. & Schneider, O. (2005). Rape perceptions, gender-role attitudes, and victim-perpetrator acquaintance. *Sex Roles, 53*, 385–399.

Benson, E. (2003). Hostility is among the best predictors of heart disease in men. *Monitor on Psychology, 34 (1)*, 15.

Bergman, S. J. (1995). Men's psychological development: A relational perspective. In R. F. Levant & W. S. Pollack (Eds.), *A new psychology of men.* New York: Basic.

Berkowitz, A. D. (Ed.) (1994). *Men and rape: Theory, research, and prevention programs in higher education.* San Francisco: Jossey-Bass.

Berkowitz, A. D. (1997). Effective sexual assault prevention programming: Meeting the needs of men and women. Paper presented at the Seventh International Conference on Sexual Assault and Harassment on Campus, Orlando, FL.

Berkowitz, A. D. (2010). Fostering healthy norms to prevent violence and abuse: The social norms approach. In K. L. Kaufman (Ed.), *The prevention of sexual violence: A practitioner's sourcebook.* Holyoke, MA: NEARI Press.

Bernard, J. (1981). The good-provider role: Its rise and fall. *American Psychologist, 36*, 1–12.

Berndt, T. J. (1992). Friendship and friends' influence in adolescence. *Current Directions in Psychological Science, 1*, 156–159.

Bertoia, C. E., & Drakich J. (1998). The fathers' rights movement: Contradictions in rhetoric and practice. In M. S. Kimmel & M. A. Messner (Eds.), *Men's lives* (4th ed., pp. 548–564). Needham Heights, MA: Allyn and Bacon.

Best, D. L. & Williams, J. E. (1993). Cross-cultural viewpoint. In A. E. Beall & R. J. Sternberg (Eds.), *The psychology of gender* (pp. 215–248). New York: Guilford.

Bhalla, A. K. (2003). Sexual maturation in well-off Chandigarh boys: A longitudinal study. *Mankind Quarterly, 44*, 175–184.

Biernbaum, M., & Weinberg, J. (1991). Men unlearning rape. *Changing Men, 22*, 22–24.

Biskupic, J. (1998, March 5). Court says law covers same-sex harassment: Justices unanimous in civil rights case. *The Washington Post*, pp. A1, A8.

Bizjournals.com (2014). Pornographers threaten to flee California over condom bill. Retrieved on July 17, 2014 from bizjournals.com/sacramento/news/2014/05/29/pornographers-threaten-to-flee-california-over.html?page=all.

Blackstone, A., Houle, J., & Uggen, C. (2014). "I didn't recognize it as a bad experience until I was much older": Age, experience, and workers' perceptions of sexual harassment. *Sociological Spectrum, 34*(4), 314–337.

Blanchard, R., Cantor, J. M., Bogaert, A. F., Breedlove, S. M., & Ellis, L. (2006). Interaction of fraternal birth order and handedness in the development of male homosexuality. *Hormones and Behavior, 49*(3), 405–414.

Blazina, C., Eddins, R., Burridge, A., & Settle, A. G. (2007). The relationship between masculine ideology, loneliness, and separation-individuation difficulties. The *Journal of Men's Studies, 15*, 101–109.

Blazina, C., & Watkins, C. E. (1996). Masculine gender role conflict: Effects on college men's psychological well-being, chemical substance usage, and attitudes toward help-seeking. *Journal of Counseling Psychology, 43*, 461–465.

Bleakley, A.., Jameison, P., & Romer, D. (2012). Trends of sexual and violent content by gender in top-grossing U. S. films, 1950–2006. Journal of Adolescent Health, 51, 73–79.

Bleier, R. (1984). *Science and gender: A critique of biology and its theories on women*. New York: Pergamon.

Blitstein, R. (2009). Weathering the storm. *Miller-McCune: Turning Research into Solutions, 2(4)*, 48–57.

Block, J. H. (1984). *Sex role identity and ego development*. San Francisco: Jossey-Bass.

Block, J. H., Block, J., & Gjerde, P. F. (1986). The personality of children prior to divorce: A prospective study. *Child Development, 57*, 827–840.

Blumenfeld, W. J. (1992). Squeezed into gender envelopes. In W. J. Blumenfeld (Ed.), *Homophobia: How we all pay the price* (pp. 23–38). Boston: Beacon.

Bly, R. (1990). *Iron John*. Reading, MA: Addison Wesley.

Bly, R. (1991). Father hunger in men. In K. Thompson (Ed.), *To be a man: In search of the deep masculine* (pp.189–192). Los Angeles: Tarcher.

Bogle, K. A. (2008). *Hooking up: Sex, dating, and relationships on campus*. NY: New York University Press.

Bonauto, M. (2007). Massachusetts: Cradle of liberty. In M. Strasser, (Ed.), *Defending same-sex marriage: "Separate but equal" no more: A guide to the legal status of same-sex marriage, civil unions, and other partnerships* (pp. 1–28). Westport, CT: Praeger.

Bolton, F. G., Morris, L. A., & MacEachron, A. E. (1989). *Males at risk*. Newbury Park, CA: Sage.

Bonvillain, N. (2001). *Women and men: Cultural constructs of gender* (3rd ed.). Upper Saddle River, NJ: Prentice-Hall.

Boswell, A. A., & Spade, J. Z. (1996). Fraternities and collegiate rape culture: Why are some fraternities more dangerous places for women? *Gender and Society, 10(2)*, 133–147.

Bowen, G. L., & Orthner, D. K. (1991). Effects of organizational culture on fatherhood. In F. W. Bozett & S. M. H. Hanson (Eds.), *Fatherhood and families in cultural context* (pp. 187–217). New York: Springer.

Boyatzis, C. J., Matillo, G. M., & Nesbitt, K. M. (1995). Effects of the "Mighty Morphin Power Rangers" on children's aggression with peers. *Child Study Journal, 25*, 45–55.

Bradbury, T. N., Campbell, S. M., & Fincham, F. D. (1995). Longitudinal and behavioral analysis of masculinity and femininity in marriages. *Journal of Personality and Social Psychology, 68*, 328–341.

Bradshaw, C., Kahn, A. S., & Saville, B. K. (2010). To hook up or date: Which gender benefits? *Sex Roles, 62*, 661–669.

Brannon, R. (1985). Dimensions of the male sex role in America. In A.G. Sargent, *Beyond sex roles* (2nd ed., pp. 296–316). New York: West.

Bridges, A. J., Wosnitzer, R., Scharrer, E., Sun, C., & Liberman, R. (2010). Aggression and sexual behavior in best-selling pornography videos: A content analysis update. *Violence Against Women, 16*, 1065–85.

Bridges, J. S. (1989). Sex differences in occupational values. *Sex Roles, 20*, 205–211.

Brieman, H. & Bonner, T. P. (2001). Support groups for men in prison: The fellowship of the king of hearts. In D. Sabo, T. A. Kupers, & W. London (Eds.). *Prison masculinities*. Philadelphia: Temple University Press.

Briere, J., & Malamuth, N. M. (1983). Self-reported likelihood of sexually aggressive behavior: Attitudinal versus sexual explanations. *Journal of Research in Personality, 17*, 315–323.

Brod, H. (1987a). A case for men's studies. In M. S. Kimmel (Ed.), *Changing men: New directions in research on men and masculinity* (pp. 263–277). Newbury Park, CA: Sage.

Brod, H. (Ed.) (1987b). *The making of masculinities: The new men's studies*. Boston: Allen and Unwin.

Brod, H. (2005, April 2). Working with men against violence: Strategies for date rape prevention. Annual conference of the Amercian Men's Studies Association, Nashville, TN.

Brody, L. R. (1999). Gender, emotion, and the family. Cambridge, MA: Harvard University Press.

Brody, L. R. (2000). The socialization of gender differences in emotional expression: Display rules, infant temperament, and differentiation. In A. H. Fischer (Ed.), *Gender and emotion: Social psychological perspectives*. Cambridge, UK: Cambridge University Press.

Brody, L. R., & Hall, J. A. (2010). Gender and emotion in context. In M. Lewis, J. M. Haviland, & L. F. Barrett (Eds.), *Handbook of emotions* (3rd. ed.). New York: Guilford.

Bronstein, P., Briones, M., Brooks, T., & Cowan, B. (1996). Gender and family factors as predictors of late adolescent emotional expressiveness and adjustment: A longitudinal study. *Sex Roles, 34*, 739–765.

Brooks, G. R. (1995). *The centerfold syndrome: How men can overcome objectification and achieve intimacy with women*. San Francisco: Jossey-Bass.

Brooks, G. R. & Good, G. E. (2001). *The new handbook of psychotherapy and counseling with men: A comprehensive guide to settings, problems, and treatment approaches*. San Francisco: Jossey-Bass.

Brooks, G. R., & Levant, R. F. (1995, July). We've done it! SPSSM becomes APA's Division 51. *SPSSM Bulletin*, pp. 1–7.

Brooks, G. R., & Levant, R. F. (1997). Toward the reconstruction of male sexuality: A prescription for the future. In R. F. Levant & G. R. Brooks (Eds.), *Men and sex* (pp. 257–272). New York: Wiley.

Brooks, G. R. & Silverstein, L. B. (1995). Understanding the dark side of masculinity: An interactive systems model. In R. F. Levant & W. S. Pollack (Eds.), *A new psychology of men*. New York: Basic Books.

Brown, J., & L'Engle, K. L. (2009). X-rated: Sexual attitudes and behaviors associated with U.S. early adolescents' exposure to sexually explicit media. *Communication Research, 36*, 129–151.

Brownmiller, S. (1975). *Against Our Will: Men, Women, and Rape*. New York: Simon and Schuster.

Brubaker, B. (1994, November 13). Violence in football extends off field. *The Washington Post*, pp. A1, A24–25.

Bruch, M. A. (1980). Holland's typology applied to client/counselor interactions: Implications for counseling with men. In T. M. Skovholt, P. Schauble, & R. David (Eds.), *Counseling men* (pp.101–119). Monterey, CA: Brooks/Cole.

Bruch, M. A., Berko, E. H., & Haase, R. F. (1998). Shyness, masculine ideology, physical attractiveness, and emotional inexpressiveness: Testing a mediational model of men's interpersonal competence. *Journal of Counseling Psychology, 45*, 84–97.

Bunch, T. & Porter, A. (2003). Ending domestic violence: A call to men. Presentation at Congreso Nacional Sobre Violencia Domestica Agresion Sexual, Acecho y Violencia en Cita, San Juan, Puerto Rico.

Bureau of Labor Statistics (undated). Table 11. Employed persons by detailed occupation, sex, race, and Hispanic or Latino ethnicity. Retrieved August 1, 2014, from http://www.bls.gov/cps/cpsaat11.pdf

Burger, J. M. (2009). Replicating Milgram: Would people still obey today? *American Psychologist, 64*, 1–11.

Burke, C. K., Maton, K. I., Anderson, C. A. Mankowski, E., & Silvergleid, C. (2004). The ManKind Project. In M. Kimmel & A. Aronson (Eds.), *Men and masculinities: A social, cultural, and historical encyclopedia*. Santa Barbara, CA: ABC-Clio.

Burke, P. J., & Cast, A. D. (1997). Stability and change in the gender identities of newly married couples. *Social Psychology Quarterly, 60*, 277–290.

Burn, S. M. (1996). *The social psychology of gender*. Boston: McGraw-Hill.

Burn, S. M., & Ward, A. Z. (2005). Men's conformity to traditional masculinity and relationship satisfaction. *Psychology of Men and Masculinity, 6*, 254–263.

Burt, M. R. (1991). Rape myths and acquaintance rape. In A. Parrot & L. Bechofer (Eds.), *Acquaintance rape: The hidden crime* (pp. 26–40). New York: Wiley.

Buser, S. J., & Sternes, G. F. (2009). *The guys-only guide to getting over divorce and on with life, sex, and relationships*. Houston: Bayou.

Buss, D. M. (1989). Sex differences in human mate preferences: Evolutionary hypotheses tested in 37 countries. *Behavioral and Brain Sciences, 12*, 1–49.

Buss, D. M., & Schmitt, D. P. (1993). Sexual strategies theory: An evolutionary perspective on human mating. *Psychological Review, 100*, 204–232. doi: 10.1037/0033-295X.100.2.204

Buss, D. M., Shackelford, T. K., Kirkpatrick, L. A., & Larsen, R. J. (2001). A half century of mate preferences: The cultural evolution of values. *Journal of Marriage and the Family, 63*, 491–503.

Buss, K. A., Brooker, R. J., & Leuty, M. (2008). Girls most of the time, boys some of the time: Gender differences in toddlers' use of maternal proximity and comfort seeking. *Infancy, 13*(1), 1–29.

Bussey, K., & Bandura, A. (1992). Self-regulatory mechanisms governing gender development. *Child Development, 63*, 1236–1250.

Bussey, K., & Bandura, A. (1999). Social cognitive theory of gender development and differentiation. *Psychological Review, 106*, 676–713.

Butcher, J. N., Dahlstrom, W. G., Graham, J. R., Tellegen, A., & Kaemmer, B. (1989). *Minnesota Multiphasic Personality Inventory-2 (MMPI-2): Manual for administration and scoring*. Minneapolis: University of Minnesota Press.

Butcher, J. N., Hooley, J. M., & Mineka, S. (2014). *Abnormal psychology* (16th ed.). Boston: Pearson.

Cabrera, N. J., Tamis-LeMonda, C. S., Bradley, R. H., Hofferth, S., & Lamb, M. E. (2000). Fatherhood in the twenty-first century. *Child Development, 71*(1), 127–136.

Caldera, Y. M., Huston, A. C., & O'Brien, M. (1989). Social interactions and play patterns of parents and toddlers with feminine, masculine, and neutral toys. *Child development, 60*, 70–76.

Caldwell, L. D. & White, J. L. (2001). African-centered therapeutic and counseling interventions for African American males. In G. R. Brooks & G. E. Good (Eds.). *The new handbook of psychotherapy and counseling with men: A comprehensive guide to settings, problems, and treatment approaches.* San Francisco: Jossey-Bass.

Cameron, K. A., Salazar, L. F., Bernhardt, J. M., Burgess-Whitman, N., Wingood, G. M., & DiCilemente, R. J. (2005). Adolescents' experience with sex on the web: Results from online focus groups. *Journal of Adolescence, 28*, 535–540.

Campbell, J. L., & Snow, B. M. (1992). Gender role conflict and family environment as predictors of men's marital satisfaction. *Journal of Family Psychotherapy*, 6, 84–87.

Canetto, S. (2000). The paradox of male suicidal behavior. Symposium: Boys, men, depression, and suicide: Cutting-edge research and practice (J. Mahalik & M. Addis, chairs). Annual Convention of the American Psychological Association, Washington, DC.

Cantor, J. M., Klein, C., Lykins, A., Rullo, J. E., Thaler, L., & Walling, B. R. (2013). A treatment-oriented typology of self-identified hypersexuality referrals. *Archives of Sexual Behavior, 42*(5), 883–893.

Capraro, R. L. (2000). Why college men drink: Alcohol, adventure, and the paradox of masculinity. *Journal of American College Health, 48*, 307–315.

Caringella, S. (2009). *Addressing rape reform in law and practice.* New York: Columbia University Press.

Carlson, P. (2004). A hunger for victory: Sonya Thomas is competitive eating's next small thing. *The Washington Post*, January 31, pp. A1, A14.

Carothers, B. J., & Reis, H. T. (2013). Men and women are from Earth: Examining the latent structure of gender. *Journal of Personality and Social Psychology, 104*(2), 385–407.

Carter, V. & Giobbe, E. (2006). Duet: Prostitution, racism, and feminist discourse. In J. Spector (Ed.), *Prostitution and pornography: Philosophical debate about the sex industry.* Stanford, CA: Stanford University Press.

Carver, K., Joyner, K., & Udry, J. R. (2003). National estimates of adolescent romantic relationships. In P. Florsheim (Ed.), *Adolescent romantic relations and sexual behavior: Theory, research, and practical implications* (pp. 23–56). Mahwah, NJ: Erlbaum.

Carver, L. J. & Vaccaro, B. G. (2007). 12 month old infants allocate increased neural resources to stimuli associated with adult negative emotion. Developmental Psychology, 43, 54–69.

Carver, P. R., Egan, S. K., & Perry, D. G. (2004). Children who question their heterosexuality. *Developmental Psychology, 40*, 43–53.

Casteneda, D. & Burns-Glover, A. (2004). Gender, sexuality, and intimate relationships. In M. A. Paludi (Ed.), *Praeger guide to the psychology of gender.* Westport, CT: Praeger.

Catalano, S. (2012). Intimate partner violence, 1993–2010. Retrieved June 3, 2014 from http://www.bjs.gov/content/pub/pdf/ipv9310.pdf.

Catalyst (2006). 2005 Catalyst census of women board directors of the fortune 500. New York: Author.

Centers for Disease Control (CDC) (2013). Leading causes of death and numbers of death by sex, race, and Hispanic origin: United States, 1980 and 2010. Retrieved May 29, 2014 from http://www.cdc.gov/nchs/data/hus/2013/022.pdf.

Cervantes, J. M. (2006). A new understanding of the macho male image: Explorations of the Mexican American man. In M. Englar-Carlson & M. Stevens (Eds.), *In the room with men: A casebook of therapeutic change.* Washington, DC: American Psychological Association.

Chan, J. (2004). Asian American Men's Studies. In M. Kimmel & A. Aronson (Eds.), *Men and masculinities: A social, cultural, and historical encyclopedia.* Santa Barbara, CA: ABC-Clio.

Change.org. (2014). Listen to survivors: Reject the proposal to decriminalize all aspects of prostitution. Retrieved July 16, 2014 from change.org/petitions/amnesty-international-listen-to-survivors-reject-the-proposal-to-decriminalize-all-aspects-of-prostitution.

Chethik, N. (2001). *FatherLoss: How sons of all ages come to terms with the deaths of their dads.* New York: Hyperion.

Childress, D. M. (1996, May 4). Md. judge cleared of bias in remarks at sentencing: He expressed degree of understanding toward trucker convicted of killing unfaithful wife. *The Washington Post*, p. B3.

Chodorow, N. (1978). *The reproduction of mothering: Psychoanalysis and the sociology of gender.* Berkely, CA: University of California Press.

Chomsky, N. (1957). *Syntactic structures.* The Hague, Netherlands: Mouton.

Chronicle of Higher Education (2009). The nation: Students, enrollments and demographics, 41 (1), 10.

Chu, J. Y. (2004). A relational perspective on adolescent boys' identity development. In N. Way & J. Y. Chu (Eds.), *Adolescent boys: Exploring diverse cultures of boyhood* (pp. 78–105). NY: New York University press.

Circumcision Resource Center (2004). Current position statements of medical societies in English-speaking countries. Self-published.

Claes, M. E. (1992). Friendship and personal adjustment during adolescence. *Journal of Adolescence, 15*, 39–55.

Clark, A. J. (1998). *Defense mechanisms and the counseling process.* Thousand Oaks, CA: Sage.

Clark, R. D., & Hatfield, E. (1989). Gender differences in receptivity to sexual offers. *Journal of Psychology & Human Sexuality, 2*(1), 39–55.

Clatterbaugh, K. (1997). *Contemporary perspectives on masculinity: Men, women, and politics in modern society* (2nd ed.). Boulder, CO: Westview.

Clatterbaugh, K. (2000). Review essay: Literature of the U. S. men's movements.

Signs: Journal of Women in Culture and Society, 25 (3), 883–894.

Clatterbaugh, K. (2004). Men's movements. In M. Kimmel & A. Aronson (Eds.), *Men and masculinities: A social, cultural, and historical encyclopedia.* Santa Barbara, CA: ABC-Clio.

Clawson, L. (2005). Cowboys and schoolteachers: Gender in romance novels, secular and Christian. *Sociological Perspectives, 48*, 461–479.

Clay, R. A. (2005). Making working families work: As the number of dual wage-earner families soars, psychologists focus on families' strategies for success. *Monitor on Psychology, 36 (11)*, 54–55.

Cochran, S. V. & Rabinowitz, F. E. (2000). Men and depression: Clinical and empirical perspectives. San Diego: Academic Press.

Cohen, T. F. (1998). What do fathers provide? Reconsidering the economic and nurturant dimensions of men as parents. In D. L. Anselmi & A. L. Law (Eds.), *Questions of gender: perspectives and paradoxes* (pp. 569–581). Boston: McGraw-Hill.

Cohen-Bendahan, C. C. C., van de Beek, C., & Berenbaum, S. A. (2005). Prenatal sex hormone effects on child and adult sex-typed behavior: Methods and findings. *Neuroscience and Biobehavioral Reviews, 29*(2), 353–384.

Cohn, A. M., Seibert, A., & Zeichner, A. (2009). The role of restrictive emotionality: Trait anger, and masculinity threat in men's perpetration of physical aggression. *Psychology of Men and Masculinity, 10*, 218–224.

Cohn, A. M., Jakupcak, M., Seibert, L. A., Hildebrandt, T. B., & Zeichner, A. (2009). The role of emotion dysregulation in the association between men's restrictive emotionality and use of physical aggression. *Psychology of Men and Masculinity, 11*, 53–64.

Cohn, A. M. & Zeichner, A. (2006). Effects of masculine identity and masculine gender role stress on aggression in men. *Psychology of Men and Masculinity, 7*, 1–10.

Cohn, A. M., Zeichner, A., & Seibert, L. A. (2008). Labile affect as a risk factor for aggressive behavior in men. *Psychology of Men and Masculinity, 9,* 29–39.

Collins, G. (1979, June 1). A new look at life with father. *The New York Times Magazine,* pp. 30–31.

Coltrane, S. (1998). Theorizing masculinities in contemporary social science. In D. L. Anselmi & A. L. Law (Eds.), *Questions of gender: perspectives and paradoxes* (pp. 76–88). Boston: McGraw-Hill.

Comas-Díaz, L. (1993). Hispanic/Latino communities: Psychological implications. In D. R. Atkinson, G. Morten, & D. W. Sue (Eds.), *Counseling American minorities: A cross-cultural perspectiv*e (4th ed., pp. 245–263). Madison, WI: Brown and Benchmark.

Committee on Psychosocial Aspects of Child and Family Health (2013). Promoting the well-being of children whose parents are gay or lesbian. *Pediatrics, 131*(4), 827

Connell, R. W. (1995). *Masculinities.* Berkeley, CA: University of California Press.

Connell, R. W. (2005). *Masculinities* (2nd ed.). Berkeley, CA: University of California Press.

Connolly, J., Craig, W., Goldberg, A., & Pepler, D. (1999). Conceptions of cross-sex friendships and romantic relationships in early adolescence. *Journal of Youth and Adolescence, 28,* 481–494.

Connolly, J. A., & Johnson, A. M. (1996). Adolescents' romantic relationship and the structure and quality of their close interpersonal ties. *Personal Relationships, 3,* 185–195.

Constantinople, A. (1973). Masculinity-femininity: An exception to a famous dictum? *Psychological Bulletin, 80*(5), 389–407.

Coontz, S. (1997). *The way we really are: Coming to terms with America's changing families.* New York: Basic Books.

Coontz, S. (2005). *Marriage, a history: From obedience to intimacy, or how love conquered marriage.* New York: Viking.

Cooper, M. L., Russell, M., Skinner, J. B., Frone, M. R., & Mudar, P. (1992). Stress and alcohol use: Moderating effects of gender, coping, and alcohol expectancies. *Journal of Abnormal Psychology, 101,* 139–152.

Cope-Farrar, K. M., & Kunkel, D. (2002). Sexual messages in teens' favorite prime-time television programs. In J. D. Brown, J. R. Steele & K. Walsh-Childers (Eds.), *Sexual teens, sexual media: Investigating media's influence on adolescent sexuality* (pp. 59–78). Mahwah, NJ: Lawrence Erlbaum.

Corcoran, C. B. (1992). From victim control to social change: A feminist perspective on campus rape prevention programs. in J. Chrisler & D. Howard (Eds.), *New directions in feminist psychology* (pp. 130–140). New York: Springer.

Cosenzo, K. A., Franchina, J. J., Eisler, R. M., & Krebs, D. (2008). Effects of masculine gender-relevant task instructions on men's cardiovascular reactivity and mental arithmetic performance. *Psychology of Men and Masculinity, 5,* 103–111.

Coughlin, P., & Wade, J. C. (2012). Masculinity ideology, income disparity, and romantic relationship quality among men with higher earning female partners. *Sex Roles, 67*(5–6), 311–322. doi: 10.1007/s11199–012–0187–6

Cournoyer, R. J., & Mahalik, J. R. (1995). Cross-sectional study of gender role conflict examining college-aged and middle-aged men. *Journal of Counseling Psychology, 42,* 11–19.

Courtenay, W. H. (2000a). Constructions of masculinity and their influence on men's well-being: A theory of gender and health. *Social Science and Medicine, 50 (10),* 1385–1401.

Courtenay, W. H. (2000b). Behavioral factors associated with disease, injury, and death among men: Evidence and implications for prevention. *Journal of Men's Studies, 9 (1),* 81–142.

Courtenay, W. H. (2011). *Dying to be men: Psychosocial, environmental, and biobehavioral directions in promoting the health of men and boys.* New York: Routledge.

Courtenay, W. H., McCreary, D. R., & Merighi, J. R. (2002). Gender and ethnic differences in health beliefs and behaviors. *Journal of Health Psychology, 7 (3)*, 219–231.

Cozby, P. C. (1973). Self-disclosure: A literature review. *Psychological Bulletin, 79*, 73–91.

Crawford, M., & Popp, D. (2003). Sexual double standards: A review and methodological critique of two decades of research. *The Journal of Sex Research, 40*, 13–26.

Crete, G. K. & Singh, A. A. (2014). Counseling men with trauma histories: Developing foundational knowledge. In M. Englar-Carlson, M. P. Evans, & T. Duffey (Eds., 2014), *A counselor's guide to working with men*. Alexandria, VA: American Counseling Association.

Crites, J. O., & Fitzgerald, L. F. (1978). The competent male. *The Counseling Psychologist, 7*, 10–14.

Crooks, R. & Baur, K. (2007). *Our sexuality* (10th ed.). Belmont, CA: Wadsworth.

Crosset, T. W. (2000). Athletic affiliations and violence against women: Toward a structural prevention project. In J. McKay, M. A. Messner, & D. F. Sabo (Eds.), *Masculinities, gender relations, and sport*. Thousand Oaks, CA: Sage.

Crosset, T. W., Benedict, J. R., & McDonald, M. A. (1998). Male student-athletes reported for sexual assault: A survey of campus police departments and judicial affairs offices. In M. S. Kimmel & M. A. Messner (Eds.), *Men's lives* (4th ed., pp. 194–204). Needham Heights, MA: Allyn and Bacon.

Cunningham, M., & Newkirk Meunier, L. (2004). The influence of peer experiences on bravado attitudes among African American males. In N. Way & J. Y. Chu (Eds.), *Adolescent boys: Exploring diverse cultures of boyhood* (pp. 219–234). New York: New York University Press.

Daily News (2013, April 6). Average 12 high school and college football players die each year, study says. Retrieved June 2, 2014 from http://www.nydailynews. com/life-style/health/average-12-school-football-players-die-year-study-article-1.1309671.

Daly, M. & Wilson, M. (1983). *Sex, evolution, and behavior* (2nd ed.). Boston: Willard Grant.

Daly, M., & Wilson, M. (1985). Competitiveness, risk taking, and violence: The young male syndrome. *Ethology and Sociobiology, 6*, 59–73.

Dariotis, J. K., Sonenstein, F. L., Gates, G. J., Capps, R., Astone, N. M., Pleck, J. L., Zeger, S. (2008). Changes in sexual risk behavior as young men transition to adulthood. *Perspectives on Sexual and Reproductive Health, 40*.

Darwin, C. (1871). *The descent of man, and selection in relation to sex*. New York: Appleton & Co.

David, D., & Brannon, R. (1976). The male sex role: Our culture's blueprint for manhood and what it's done for us lately. In D. David & R. Brannon (Eds.), *The forty-nine percent majority: The male sex role* (pp. 1–48). Reading, MA: Addison-Wesley.

Davidson, J. (2009, July 9). OPM 'wholeheartedly' endorses benefits for same-sex partners. *The Washington Post*, A17.

Davis, K., Christodoulou, J., Seider, S., & Gardner, H. (2011). The theory of multiple intelligences. In R. J. Sternberg & S. B. Kaufman (Eds.), *The Cambridge handbook of intelligence*. (pp. 485–503). New York, NY, US: Cambridge University Press.

DeAngelis, T. (2005). Stepfamily success depends on ingredients. *Monitor on Psychology, 36 (11)*, 58–61.

Death Penalty Information Center (2014). Facts about the death penalty. Retrieved June 3, 2014 from http://www.deathpenaltyinfo.org/documents/FactSheet.pdf.

Deaux, K. (1985). Sex and gender. *Annual Review of Psychology, 36*, 49–81.

Deaux, K. (2000). Gender and emotion: Notes from a grateful tourist. In A. H. Fischer (Ed.), *Gender and emotion: Social psychological perspectives*. Cambridge, UK: Cambridge University Press.

Deaux, K., & LaFrance, M. (1998). Gender. In D. T. Gilbert, S. T. Fiske & G. Lindzey (Eds.), *The handbook of social psychology* (Vol. 4th, pp. 788–827). Boston, MA, USA: McGraw-Hill.

DeBlock, A., & Adriaens, P. R. (2013). Pathologizing sexual deviance: A history. *Journal of Sex Research, 50*, 276–298.

DeFranc, W. & Mahalik, J. R. (2002). Masculine gender role conflict and stress in relation to parental attachment and separation. *Psychology of Men and Masculinity, 3*, 51–60.

Defense.gov (2011, July 22). "Don't ask; don't tell" repeal certified by President Obama. Retrieved July 10, 2014 from www.defense.gov/news/newsarticle.aspx?id=64780.

DeHaan, S., Kuper, L. E., Magee, J. C., Bigelow, L., & Mustanski, B. S. (2013). The interplay between online and offline explorations of identity, relationships, and sex: A mixed-methods study with LGBT youth. *Journal of Sex Research, 50*(5), 421–434.

DeNavas-Walt, C., Proctor, B. D., & Smith, J. (2007). Income, poverty, and health insurance coverage in the United States: 2006. Washington DC: U. S. Census Bureau Current Population Report P60–233.

Dekeseredy, W. S., & Schwartz, M. D. (2013). *Male peer support and violence against women: The history and verification of a theory.* Boston: Northeastern University Press.

de Keizer, B. (2004). Masculinities: Resistance and change. In S. Ruxton, (Ed.). *Gender equality and men: Learning from practice.* Oxford, UK: Oxfam.

DeLatt, J. (2007). *Gender in the workplace: A case study approach* (2nd ed.). Thousand Oaks, CA: Sage.

Denmark, F., Rabinowitz, V., & Sechzer, J. (2000). *Engendering psychology.* Boston: Allyn & Bacon.

Densen, T. F. (2011). A social neuroscience perspective on the neurobiological bases of aggression. In P. R. Shaver & M. Mikulincer (Eds.), *Human aggression and violence: Causes, manifestations, and consequences.* Washington, DC: American Psychological Association.

Deutsch, F. M., & Saxon, S. E. (1998). Traditional ideologies, nontraditional lives. *Sex Roles, 38*, 331–362.

Devault, A. (2014). Commentary on The complicated worlds of adolescent fathers: Implications for clinical practice, public policy, and research. *Psychology of Men & Masculinity, 15*(3), 275–277.

Devlin, P. K., & Cowan, G. A. (1985). Homophobia, perceived fathering, and male intimate relationships. *Journal of Personality Assessment, 49*, 467–473.

de Visser, R. O. & Smith, J. A. (2007). Alcohol consumption and masculine identity among young men. *Psychology and Health, 22*, 595–614.

de Waal, F. B. M. (1997, June 27). Bonobos are from Venus. *The Chronicle of Higher Education*, 43, B8–B9.

de Waal, F. B. M. (2005). Our inner ape: What primate behavior tells us about human nature. Paper presented at the Annual Convention of the American Psychological Association, Washington, DC.

de Waal, F. B. M. (2007, September 21). Our inner ape: What primate behavior tells us about human nature. Presentation at the University of Mary Washington, Fredericksburg, VA.

Diener, E., Larsen, R. J., Levine, S., & Emmons, R. A. (1985). Intensity and frequency: Dimensions underlying positive and negative affect. *Journal of Personality and Social Psychology, 48*, 1253–1265.

Dines, G. (2005). Unmasking the pornography industry: From fantasy to reality. In E. Buchwald, P. R. Fletcher, & M. Roth (Eds.), *Transforming a rape culture* (revised ed.). Minneapolis: Milkweed.

Dines, G. (2006, May 18). Dirty sexy money. Presentation at the Virginia Colleges Against Sexual Assault Conference, Virginia Beach, VA.

Dines, G. (2013, May 20). Discussion comments at the Blue Ribbon Panel on Hypersexualized Media, Richmond, VA.

Division 17, American Psychological Association (1979). Principles concerning the counseling and therapy of women. *The Counseling Psychologist, 8,* 21.

Dobbin, B. (1997, July 20). Men will be men... maybe: University hopes courses will dispel myths of manhood. *Richmond Times-Dispatch,* p. C1.

Dodge, K. A. (2011). Social information processing patterns as mediators of the interaction between genetic factors and life experiences in the development of aggressive behavior. In P. R. Shaver & M. Mikulincer (Eds.), *Human aggression and violence: Causes, manifestations, and consequences.* Washington, DC: American Psychological Association.

Dolnick, E. (1991, August 13). Why do women outlive men? *Washington Post Health,* pp. 10–13.

Dorn, L. D., & Biro, F. M. (2011). Puberty and Its Measurement: A Decade in Review. *Journal of Research on Adolescence (Wiley-Blackwell), 21*(1), 180–195.

Doyle, J., and Femiano, S. (1998). Reflections on the early history of the American Men's Studies Association and the evolution of the field. *Men's Studies News, 7(1),* 8–11.

Doyle, J. A., & Paludi, M. A. (1998). *Sex and gender: The human experience* (4th ed.). Boston: McGraw-Hill.

Drescher, J. (2002). Sexual conversion ("reparative") therapies: History and update. In B. E. Jones & M. J. Hill (Eds.), *Mental health issues in lesbian, gay, bisexual, and transgender communities.* Washington, DC: American Psychiatric Publishing.

Duluth Domestic Abuse Intervention Project (undated). *Creating a public response to private violence.* Duluth, MN: self.

Dunn, M. G., Rochlen, A. B., & O'Brien, K. M. (2013). Employee, mother, and partner: An exploratory investigation of working women with stay-at-home fathers. *Journal of Career Development, 40*(1), 3–22.

Dutton, D. G. (2011). Attachment and violence: An anger born of fear. In P. R. Shaver & M. Mikulincer (Eds.), *Human aggression and violence: Causes, manifestations, and consequences.* Washing-

ton, DC: American Psychological Association.

Dutton, D. G., & Golant, S. K. (1995). *The batterer: A psychological profile.* New York: Basic.

Eagly, A. H. (1987). *Sex differences in social behavior: A social-role interpretation.* Hillsdale, NJ: Erlbaum.

Eagly, A. H. & Wood, W. (1999). The origins of sex differences in human behavior: Evolved dispositions versus social roles. *American Psychologist, 54,* 408–423.

Eagly, A. H., Wood, W., & Diekman, A. B. (2000). Social role theory of sex differences and similarities: A current appraisal. In T. Eckes & H. M. Trautner (Eds.), *The developmental social psychology of gender* (pp. 123–174). Mahwah, NJ: Lawrence Erlbaum.

"Eating Champ Downs 44 Lobsters in Win" (2005). *The Washington Post,* B3.

Edwards, R. (1996). Can sexual orientation change with therapy? APA ponders its stance on a therapy designed to convert gay men and lesbians into heterosexuals. *APA Monitor, 27(9),* 49.

Ehrenreich, B. (1983). *The hearts of men: American dreams and the flight from commitment.* Garden City, NY: Anchor.

Eisler, R. M., & Skidmore, J. R. (1987). Masculine gender role stress: Scale development and component factors in the appraisal of stressful situations. *Behavior Modification, 11,* 123–136.

Eliason, M. J. (1995). Accounts of sexual identity formation in heterosexual students. *Sex Roles, 32,* 821–834.

Eliot, L. (2009). Pink brain, blue brain: How small differences grow into troublesome gaps—and what we can do about it. Boston: Houghton Mifflin Harcourt.

Elkins, L. E., & Peterson, C. (1993). Gender differences in best friendships. *Sex Roles, 29,* 497–508.

Else-Quest, N. M., Hyde, J. S., & Linn, M. C. (2010). Cross-national patterns of gender differences in mathematics: A meta-analysis. *Psychological Bulletin, 136*(1), 103–127.

Elsner, A. (2004, January 24). America's prison habit. *The Washington Post*, A19.

Englar-Carlson, M. (2006). Masculine norms and the therapeutic process. In M. Englar-Carlson & M. Stevens (Eds.), *In the room with men: A casebook of therapeutic change*. Washington, DC: American Psychological Association.

Englar-Carlson, M., Evans, M. P., & Duffey, T. (Eds., 2014). *A counselor's guide to working with men*. Alexandria, VA: American Counseling Association.

Englar-Carlson, M. & Stevens, M. A. 2006). *In the room with men: A casebook of therapeutic change*. Washington, DC: American Psychological Association.

Epstein, M., Calzo, J. P., Smiler, A. P., & Ward, L. M. (2009). "Anything From Making Out to Having Sex": Men's Negotiations of Hooking Up and Friends with Benefits Scripts. *Journal of Sex Research, 46*, 414–424.

Epstein, M., & Ward, L. M. (2008). "Always use protection": Communication boys receive about sex from parents, peers, and the media. *Journal of Youth and Adolescence, 37*, 113–126.

Equal Employment Opportunity Commission (EEOC) (1980). Discrimination because of sex under Title VII of the Civil Rights Act 1964, as amended; adoption of interim interpretive guidelines. *Federal Register, 45*, 25024–25025.

Equal Employment Opportunity Commission (nd). Sexual Harassment Charges EEOC & FEPAs Combined: FY 1997 - FY 2011. Retrieved October 1, 2014, from http://www1.eeoc.gov//eeoc/statistics/enforcement/sexual_harassment.cfm?renderforprint=1

Erne, R. (2014). Is serious violence almost exclusively male? *Violence and Gender, 1*, 90–93.

Escobar, G., & Murphy, C. (1997, October 5). Promise Keepers answer the call: Christian men flock to the Mall for rally massive and moving. *The Washington Post*, pp. A1, A18.

Espiritu, Y. L. (2008). *Asian American men and women: Labor, laws, and love* (2nd ed.). Lanham, MD: Rowman & Littlefield.

Espiritu, Y. L. (2007). All men are *not* created equal: Asian American men in U.S. history. In M. S. Kimmel & M. A. & Messner (Eds.), *Men's lives* (7th ed). Boston: Allyn and Bacon.

ESPN (1994, October 23). *Outside the Lines* (television documentary).

ESPN (2007). Jury rules Thomas harassed ex-executive; MSG owes her $11.6M. Retrieved June 17, 2009 from sports.espn.go.com/nba/news/story?id=3046010

Evans, L., & Davies, K. (2000). No sissy boys here: A content analysis of the representation of masculinity in elementeray school reading textbooks. *Sex Roles, 42*, 255–270.

Fagot, B. I., & Hagan, R. (1985). Aggression in toddlers: Responses to the assertive acts of boys and girls. *Sex Roles, 12*, 341–351.

Fainaru-Wada, M., & Fainaru, S. (2013). *League of denial: The NFL, concussions, and the battle for truth*. New York: Crown Archetype.

Fairchild, C. (2014, June 3, 2014). Number of Fortune 500 Women CEOs Reaches Historic High. *Fortune, 5*.

Falicov, C. J. (2005). Mexican families. In M. McGoldrick, J. Giordano, & N. Garcia-Preto (Eds.), *Ethnicity and family therapy* (3rd ed.). New York: Guilford.

Farberman, R. (2004). Council actions include gay-marriage resolution. *Monitor on Psychology*, 36 (9), p. 24.

Farley, M., Cotton, A., Lynne, J., Zumbeck, S., & Spiwack, F. (2003). Prostitution in nine countries: Update on violence and posttraumatic stress disorder. *Journal of Trauma Practice, 2*, 33–74.

Farrell, W. (1986). *Why men are the way they are: The male-female dynamic*. New York: McGraw-Hill.

Farrell, W. (2005). *Why men earn more: The startling truth behind the pay gap, and what women can do about it*. New York: AMACOM.

Fass, P. S. (1977). *The Damned and the Beautiful: American Youth in the 1920s.* NY: Oxford University Press.

Fassinger, R. E. (1998). Lesbian, gay, and bisexual identity and student development theory. In R. L. Sanlo (Ed.), *Working with lesbian, gay, bisexual, and transgender college students: A handbook for faculty and administrators* (pp. 13–22). Westport, CT: Greenwood.

Fausto-Sterling, A. (1996). The five sexes: Why male and female are not enough. In K. E. Rosenblum & T. C. Travis (Eds.), *The meaning of difference: American constructions of race, sex and gender, social class, and sexual orientation* (pp. 68–73). Boston: McGraw-Hill.

Fausto-Sterling, A. (2000). *Sexing the body: Gender politics and the construction of sexuality.* New York: Basic Books.

Fazio, R. H. & Olson, M. A. (2003). Implicit measures in social cognition research: Their meaning and use. *Annual Review of Psychology, 54,* 297–327.

Federal Bureau of Investigation (FBI) (2011). Uniform Crime Reports: Crime in the United States, 2011: Ten year arrest trends by sex, 2002–2011. Retrieved June 3, 2014 from http://www.fbi.gov/about-us/cjis/ucr/crime-in-the-u.s/2011/crime-in-the-u.s.-2011/tables/table-33.

Federal Bureau of Investigation (FBI) (2012). Uniform Crime Reports: Crime in the United States, 2012. Retrieved June 3, 2014 from http://www.fbi.gov/about-us/cjis/ucr/crime-in-the-u.s/2012/crime-in-the-u.s.-2012/offenses-known-to-law-enforcement/expanded-homicide/expanded_homicide_data_table_6_murder_race_and_sex_of_vicitm_by_race_and_sex_of_offender_2012.xls.

Feiring, C. (1996). Concepts of romance in 15–year-old adolescents. *Journal of Research on Adolescence, 6,* 181–200.

Feiring, C. (1999). Other-sex friendship networks and the development of romantic relationships in adolescence. *Journal of Youth and Adolescence, 28,* 495–512.

Fejes, F. J. (1992). Masculinity as fact: A review of empirical mass communication research on masculinity. In S. Craig (Ed.), *Men, masculinity, and the media* (pp. 9–22). Newbury Park, CA: Sage.

Feldman, S. S., Biringen, Z. C., & Nash, S. C. (1981). Fluctuations of sex-related self-attributions as a function of stage in the family life cycle. *Developmental Psychology, 17,* 24–35.

Ferguson, H., Hearn, J., Holter, O. G., Jalmert, L., Kimmel, M., Lang, J., & Morell, R. (2004). *Ending gender based violence: A call for global action to involve men.* Sweden: SIDA Productions.

Ferrar, K. E., Olds, T. S., & Walters, J. L. (2012). All the stereotypes confirmed: Differences in how Australian boys and girls use their time. *Health Education & Behavior, 39*(5), 589–595.

Fischer, A. H., & Manstead, A. S. R. (2000). The relation between gender and emotion in different cultures. In A. H. Fischer (Ed.), *Gender and emotion: Social psychological perspectives.* Cambridge, UK: Cambridge University Press.

Fisher, T. D., & Walters, A. S. (2003). Variables in addition to gender that help to explain differences in perceived sexual interest. *Psychology of Men and Masculinity, 4,* 154–162.

Fitzgerald, L. F. (1992). *Sexual harassment in higher education: Concepts and issues.* Washington, DC: National Education Association.

Fitzgerald, L. F. (1993). Sexual harassment: Violence against women in the workplace. *American Psychologist, 48,* 1070–1076.

Flores, A. H., Haileysus, T., & Greenspan, A. I. (2008). National estimates of outdoor recreational injuries treated in emergency departments, United States, 2004–2005. *Wilderness and Environmental Medicine, 19,* 91–98.

Foote, W. E. & Goodman-Delahunty, J. (2004). *Evaluating sexual harassment.* Washington, DC: American Psychological Association.

Forste, R., & Haas, D. W. (2002). The transition of adolescent males to first sexual intercourse: Anticipated or delayed. *Per-*

spectives on Sexual and Reproductive Health, 34, 184–190.

Forster, P., & King, J. (1994). Fluoxetine for premature ejaculation. *American Journal of Psychiatry, 151,* 1523.

Fortin, J. (2007). Enlarged prostate common in older men. Retrieved June 17, 2009 from www.cnn.com/2007/HEALTH/10/22/hm.prostate.qa/index.html.

Foubert, J. D. (2011). *The men's and women's programs: Ending rape through peer education.* New York: Routledge.

Foubert, J. D. (2007). Pornography: Fighting it with feminist thought and scholarly research. Paper presented at Safe Society Zone Conference; October, 2007.

Foubert, J. D., Brosi, M. W., & Bannon, R. S. (2011). Pornography viewing among fraternity men: Effects on bystander intervention, rape myth acceptance and behavioral intent to commit sexual assault. *Sexual Addiction & Compulsivity, 18,* 212–231.

Frankel, L. (2002). "I've never thought about it": Contradictions and taboos surrounding American males' experiences of first ejaculation (semenarche). *The Journal of Men's Studies, 11,* 37–54.

Frankl, V. (1960). *The doctor and the soul.* New York: Knopf.

Freedomtomarry.org (2013). The Defense of Marriage Act. Retrieved July 14, 2014 from freedomtomarry.org/states/entry/c/doma.

French, K. & Poska, A. (2006). *Women and gender in the Western past.* Boston: Houghton-Mifflin.

Freud, S. (1905/1963). *Dora: An analysis of a case of hysteria.* New York: Collier.

Freud, S. (1910/1989). Leonardo da Vinci and a memory of his childhood. In P. Gay (Ed.), *The Freud reader* (pp. 443–481). New York: Norton.

Freud, S. (1915/1989). Three essays on the theory of sexuality. In P. Gay (Ed.), *The Freud reader* (pp. 239–293). New York: Norton.

Freud, S. (1924/1989). The dissolution of the Oedipus complex. In P. Gay (Ed.), *The*

Freud reader (pp. 661–669). New York: Norton

Freund, K., Nagler, E., Langevin, R., Zajac, A., & Steiner, B. (1974). Measuring feminine gender identity in homosexual males. *Archives of Sexual Behavior, 3,* 249–260.

Funder, D. C. (2010). *The personality puzzle* (5th ed.). New York: Norton.

Funk, R. E. (1997). Men who are raped: A profeminist perspective. In M. Scarce, *Male on male rape: The hidden toll of stigma and shame* (pp. 221–231). New York: Plenum.

Garcia, J. R., Reiber, C., Massey, S. G., & Merriwether, A. M. (2012). Sexual hookup culture: A review. *Review of General Psychology, 16,* 161–176. doi: 10.1037/a0027911

Garcia-Preto, N. (2005). Latino families: An overview. In M. McGoldrick, J. Giordano, & N. Garcia-Preto (Eds.), *Ethnicity and family therapy* (3rd ed.). New York: Guilford.

Garfield, R. (2010). Male emotional intimacy: How therapeutic men's groups can enhance couples therapy. *Family Process, 49*(1), 109–122.

Garnets, L., & Pleck, J. H. (1979). Sex role identity, androgyny, and sex role transcendence: A sex role strain analysis. *Psychology of Women Quarterly, 3,* 270–283.

Gastil, J. (1990). Generic pronouns and sexist language: The oxymoronic character of masculine generics. *Sex Roles, 23,* 629–643.

gaymarriage.procon.org (2014). 19 states with legal gay marriage and 31 states with same-sex marriage bans. Retrieved July 10, 2014 from gaymarriage.procon.org/view.resource.php?resourceID=004857.

Gelles, R. J. (1997). *Intimate violence in families* (3rd ed.). Thousand Oaks, CA: Sage.

Gelman, S. A. (2003). *The essential child: Origins of essentialism in everyday thought.* New York, NY, US: Oxford University Press.

Genesoni, L., & Tallandini, M. A. (2009). Men's psychological transition to fatherhood: An analysis of the literature, 1989–

2008. *Birth: Issues in Perinatal Care, 36*(4), 305–318.

Gentile, D. A. (Ed., 2003), *Media violence and children: A complete guide for parents and professionals.* Westport, CT: Praeger.

Gentile, D. A. & Anderson, C. A. (2003). Violent video games: The newest media violence hazard. In D. A. Gentile (Ed.), *Media violence and children: A complete guide for parents and professionals.* Westport, CT: Praeger.

Gentile, D. A., Coyne, S., & Walsh, D. A. (2011). Media violence, physical aggression, and relational aggression in school-age children: A short-term longitudinal study. *Aggressive Behavior, 37*, 193–206.

Gentile, D. A. & Sesma, Jr., A. (2003). Developmental approaches to understanding media effects on children. In D. A. Gentile (Ed.), *Media violence and children: A complete guide for parents and professionals.* Westport, CT: Praeger.

Gergen, M. M., & Gergen, K. J. (1993). Autobiographies and the shaping of gendered lives. In N. Coupland & J. F. Nussbaum (Eds.), *Discourse and lifespan identity* (pp. 28–54). Newbury Park, CA: Sage.

Gibbs, J. T. (1994). Anger in young black males: Victims or Victimizers? In R. G. Majors & J. U. Gordon (Eds.), *The American Black male: His present status and his future* (pp. 127–143). Chicago: Nelson-Hall.

Gidycz, C. A., Orchowski, L. M., & Edwards, K. M. (2013). Primary prevention of sexual violence. In M. P. Koss, J. W. White, & A. E. Kazdin (Eds*.), Violence against women and children, Volume 2: Navigating solutions.* Washington, DC: American Psychological Association.

Gilder, G. (1986). *Men and marriage.* London: Pelican.

Gilmore, D. D. (1990). *Manhood in the making: Cultural concepts of masculinity.* New Haven, CT: Yale University Press.

Giordano, J., McGoldrick, M. & Guarino Klages, J. (2005). Italian families. In M. McGoldrick, J. Giordano, & N. Garcia-Preto (Eds.), *Ethnicity and family therapy* (3rd ed). New York: Guilford.

Giordano, P. C., Manning, W., & Longmore, M. A. (2010). Affairs of the heart: Qualities of adolescent romantic relationships and sexual behavior. *Journal of Research on Adolescence, 20*, 983–1013.

Glick, P. (2005). Ambivalent gender ideologies and perceptions of the legitimacy and stability of gender hierarchy. Paper presented in Symposium: New weave sexism research – Tangled webs of feminism, romance, and inequality (S. T. Fiske, Chair). Annual Convention of the American Psychological Association, Washington, DC.

Glick, P. & Fiske, S. T. (2001). An ambivalent alliance: Hostile and benevolent sexism as complementary justifications for gender inequality. *American Psychologist. 56*(2), 109–118.

Glick, P., Lameiras, M., Fiske, S. T., Eckes, T., Masser, B., Volpato, C., Manganelli, A. M., Pek, J., Huang, L., Sakalli-Ugurlu, N., Castro, Y. R., D'Avila Pereira, M. L., Willemsen, T. M., Brunner, A., Six-Materna, I., & Wells, R. (2004). Bad but bold: Ambivalent attitudes toward men predict gender inequality in 16 nations. *Journal of Personality and Social Psychology, 86*, 713–728.

Goffman, E. (1963). *Stigma.* Englewood Cliffs, NJ: Prentice-Hall.

Gold, S. R., Burke, C. H., Prisco, A. G., & Willett, J. A. (1992). Vicarious emotional responses of macho college males. *Journal of Interpersonal Violence, 7*, 165–174.

Goldberg, H. (1977). *The hazards of being male.* New York: New American Library.

Goldfoot, D. A. & Neff, D. A. (1987). Assessment of behavioral sex differences in social contexts: Perspectives from primatology. In J. M. Reinisch, L. A. Rosenbaum, & S. A. Sanders (Eds.), *Masculinity/femininity: Basic perspectives* (pp. 179–195). New York: Oxford University Press.

Goldman, R. F. (1992). Questioning circumcision: A growing movement. *Wingspan, 6 (2)*, 12–13.

Goldstein, J. R. (2011). A secular trend toward earlier male sexual maturity: Evidence from shifting ages of male young adult mortality. *PLoS ONE, 6*

Golinelli, D. & Minton, T. D. (2013). Jail inmates at midyear-2013: Statistical tables. Retrieved July 14, 2014 from bjs.gov/index.cfm?ty=pbdetail&iid=4988.

Golombok, S., & Fivush, R. (1994). *Gender development.* New York: Cambridge University Press.

Gondolf, E. W. (1988). Who are those guys? Toward a behavioral typology of batterers. *Violence and Victims, 3,* 187–203.

Gough, H. G. (1957). *Manual for the California Psychological Inventory.* Palo Alto, CA: Consulting Psychologists Press.

Gould, R. E. (1974). Measuring masculinity by the size of a paycheck. In J.H. Pleck & J. Sawyer (Eds.), *Men and masculinity* (pp. 96–100). Englewood Cliffs, NJ: Prentice-Hall.

Gould, S. J. (1981). *The mismeasure of man.* New York: W. W. Norton.

Gould, S. J. (1987). *An urchin in the storm.* New York: W. W. Norton.

Gover, A. R., MacDonald, J. M., & Alpert, G. P. (2003). Combating domestic violence: Findings from an evaluation of a local domestic violence court. *Criminology and Public Policy, 3,* 109–132.

Graham, S. H. (2008). *Eat what you want and die like a man: The world's unhealthiest cookbook.* New York: Citadel.

Granie, M. A. (2010). Gender stereotype conformity and age as determinants of preschoolers' injury risk behaviors. *Accident Analysis and Prevention, 42,* 726–733.

Grant, B. F., Dawson, D. A., Stinson, F. S., Chou, S. P., Dufour, M. C., & Pickering, R. P. (2004). The 12–month prevalence and trends in DSM-IV alcohol abuse and dependence: United States, 1991–1992 and 2001–2002. *Drug and Alcohol Dependence, 74,* 223–234.

Green, R. (1987). Exposure to explicit sexual materials and sexual assault: A review of behavioral and social science research. In M. R. Walsh (Ed.), *The psychology of women: Ongoing debates* (pp. 430–440). New Haven, CT: Yale University Press.

Green, R. J., & Ashmore, R. D. (1998). Taking and developing pictures in the head: Assessing the physical stereotypes of eight gender types. *Journal of Applied Social Psychology, 28,* 1609–1636.

Gregersen, E. (1982). *Sexual practices: The story of human sexuality.* New York: Franklin Watts.

Grimm, L., & Yarnold, P. R. (1985). Sex typing and the coronary-prone behavior pattern. *Sex Roles, 12,* 171–178.

Grimsley, K. D. (1998, June 12). Mitsubishi settles for $34 million: Amount is record in harassment suits. *The Washington Post,* p. A1.

Grimsley, K. D., & Brown, W. (1996, April 23). Mitsubishi workers march on EEOC: UAW alleges, company denies "pressure" to protest suit. *The Washington Post,* p. A1.

Grimsley, K. D., & Swoboda, F. (1997, August 30). Mitsubishi settlement said to total $9.5 million: Company still faces larger suit filed by EEOC. *The Washington Post,* pp. F1, F3.

Gross, A. E. (1992). The male role and heterosexual behavior. In M. A. Kimmel & M. S. Messner (Eds.), *Men's lives* (2nd ed., pp. 424–432). New York: Macmillan.

Grossman, D. (1995). *On killing: The psychological cost of learning to kill in war and society.* Boston: Little, Brown.

Groth, A. N. (1979). *Men who rape: The psychology of the offender.* New York: Plenum.

Groth-Marnat, G. (2003). *Handbook of psychological assessment* (4th ed.). New York: Wiley.

Grunbaum, J. A., Kann, L., Kincen, S. A., Hawkins, J., Ross, J. G., Lowry, R., Harris, W. A., McManus, T., Chyen, D., & Collins, A. (2004). Youth risk behavior surveillance: United States, 2003. *Morbidity and Mortality Weekly Report, 53 (2),* 1–96.

Gugliotta, G. (1994, May 16). Institute finds that a number that adds up, has meaning on the streets. *The Washington Post,* p. A3.

Gugliotta, G. (2003, October 11). Concussions, impact studied by the NFL. *The Washington Post*, p. D3.

Gurian, M. (2005). Where have the men gone? No place good. *The Washington Post*, p. B1.

Gurian, M. & Stevens, K. (2005). *The minds of boys: Saving our sons from falling behind in school and life*. San Francisco: Jossey-Bass.

Gustafson, R. (1986). Threat as a determinant of alcohol-related aggression. *Psychological Reports*, *58*, 287–297.

Gutierrez, F. J. (1990). Exploring the macho mystique: Counseling Latino men. In D. Moore & F. Leafgren (Eds.), *Men in conflict* (pp. 139–151). Alexandria, VA: American Association for Counseling and Development.

Gutmann, D. (1987). *Reclaimed powers*. New York: Basic Books.

Guttmacher Institute (2012). State policies in brief: Sex and HIV education.

Hackett, T. P.; Rosenbaum, J. F. & Cassen, N. H. (1985). Cardiovascular disorders. In H. I. Kaplan & B. J. Saddock (Eds.), *Comprehensive textbook of psychiatry/IV* (pp. 1148–1159). Baltimore: Williams and Wilkins.

Hall, C. S., Lindzey, G., & Campbell, J. B. (1998). *Theories of personality* (4th ed.). New York: Wiley.

Halsey, III, A. (2009, August 20). Rise in drunken-driving arrests of women deplored. The Washington Post, A2.

Hamilton, M. C. (1991). Masculine bias in the attribution of personhood: People=male, male=people. *Psychology of Women Quarterly*, *15*, 393–402.

Hammer, J. H., & Good, G. E. (2010). Positive psychology: An emprical examination of beneficial aspects of endorsement of masculine norms. *Psychology of Men and Masculinity, 11*, 303–318.

Hampl, A. (2014, August 15, 2014). Mo'Ne Davis becomes first girl to throw a shutout in LLWS. *Sports Illustrated*.

Haney, C., Banks, C., & Zimbardo, P. (1973). Interpersonal dynamics in a simulated prison. *International Journal of Criminology and Penology*, *1*, 69–97.

Hantover, J. (1978). The boy scouts and the validation of masculinity. *Journal of Social Issues, 34*, 184–195.

Hare-Mustin, R. T., & Marecek, J. (1990a). Gender and the meaning of difference: Postmodernism and psychology. In R. T. Hare-Mustin & J. Marecek (Eds.), *Making a difference: Psychology and the construction of gender* (pp. 22–64). New Haven, CT, USA: Yale university press.

Hare-Mustin, R. T., & Marecek, J. (1990b). On making a difference. In R. T. Hare-Mustin & J. Marecek (Eds.), *Making a difference: Psychology and the construction of gender* (pp. 1–21). New Haven, CT, USA: Yale University Press.

Harrison, J.; Chin, J., & Ficarotto, T. (1995). Warning: Masculinity may be dangerous to your health. In M. S. Kimmel & M. A. Messner (Eds.), *Men's lives* (3rd ed., pp. 237–249). Boston: Allyn and Bacon.

Hartley, R. E. (1959). Sex role pressures and the socialization of the male child. *Psychological Reports, 5,* 457–468.

Hartup, W. W., & Overhauser, S. (1991). Friendships. In R. M. Lerner, A. C. Petersen & J. Brooks-Gunn (Eds.), *Encyclopedia of Adolescence* (pp. 378–384). NY: Garland Publishing.

Hathaway, C. R. & McKinley, J. C. (1951). *Minnesota Multiphasic Personality Inventory*. New York: Psychological Corporation.

Hatton, E., & Trautner, M. N. (2011). Equal opportunity objectification? The sexualization of men and women on the cover of Rolling Stone. *Sexuality & Culture, 15*, 256–278.

Hax, C. (2009, March 8). Carolyn Hax (advice column). *The Washington Post*, C7.

Hazan, C., & Diamond, L. M. (2000). The place of attachment in human mating. *Review of General Psychology, 4*, 186–204.

Heasley, R. (2005). Queer Masculinities of Straight Men: A Typology. *Men and Masculinities, 7*(3), 310–320. doi: 10.1177/1097184X04272118

Hebl, M. R., King, E.B., McGuire, J., & Turchin, M. (2008). The grapefruit race: Demonstrating the influence of competition on gender differences in intimacy. *Teaching of Psychology, 35*, 18–20.

Hedges, L. V., & Nowell, A. (1995). Sex differences in mental test scores, variability, and numbers of high-scoring individuals. *Science, 269*(5220), 41–45.

Heilman, B., Hebert, L., & Paul-Gera, N. (2014). The making of sexual violence: How does a boy grow up to commit rape? Evidence from five IMAGES countries. Washington, DC: International Center for Research on Women (ICRW), and Promundo.

Helgeson, V. S. (1990). The role of masculinity in a prognostic predictor of heart attack severity. *Sex Roles, 22*, 755–774.

Helgeson, V. S. (1995). Masculinity, men's roles, and coronary heart disease. In D. Sabo & D. F. Gordon (Eds.), *Men's health and illness: Gender, power, and the body* (pp.68–104). Thousand Oaks, CA: Sage.

Helgeson, V. S. (2011). *The psychology of gender* (4th ed.). Boston: Pearson.

Henderson, N. (2014, October 9). White men hold 65% of U. S. elected offices. *The Washington Post*, A4.

Heppner, M. (2005). *Theoretically driven rape prevention programming for men.* Paper presented in symposium: Sexual assault prevention for men (C. Kilmartin, chair) at the Annual Convention of the American Psychological Association, Washington, DC.

Herdt, G. (1982). *Rituals of manhood.* Berkeley, CA: University of California Press.

Herdt, G., & Boxer, A. (1991). Introduction: Culture, history, and life course of gay men. In G. Herdt (Ed.), *Gay culture in America: Essays from the field* (pp. 1–28). Boston: Beacon.

Herek, G. M. (1985). On doing, being, and not being: Prejudice and the social construction of sexuality. *Journal of Homosexuality, 12*, 135–151.

Herek, G. M. (1986). On heterosexual masculinity: Some psychical consequences of the social construction of gender and sexuality. *American Behavioral Scientist, 29*, 563–577.

Herek, G. M. (1991). Stigma, prejudice, and violence against lesbians and gay men. In J. C. Consiorek & J. D. Weinrich (Eds.), *Homosexuality: Research implications for public policy* (pp. 60–80). Newbury Park, CA: Sage.

Herek, G. M. (1994). Assessing heterosexuals' attitudes toward lesbians and gay men. In B. Greene & G. M. Herek (Eds.), *Lesbian and gay psychology: Theory, research, and clinical applications.* Thousand Oaks, CA: Sage.

Heron, M. P. (2013). Deaths: Leading causes for 2010. *National vital statistics reports, 62 (6).* Retrieved May 29, 2014 from http://www.cdc.gov/nchs/data/nvsr/nvsr62/nvsr62_06.pdf.

Herttell, T. (1839/1992). The right of married woman to hold and control property. (pp. 76–78). In M. S. Kimmel & T. E. Mosmiller, *Against the tide: Pro-feminist men in the United States, 1776–1990.* Boston: Beacon.

Hess, A. (2014). Women aren't welcome here. *Pacific Standard, 7 (1)*, 37–47.

Hesse, M. (2014, July 1). Men's rights activists say society has wronged them. *The Washington Post*, C1–3.

Hetherington, E. M., Cox, M., & Cox, R. (1985). Long term effects of divorce and remarriage on the adjustment of children. *Journal of the American Academy of Child Psychiatry, 24*, 518–530.

Hetherington, E. M., & Stanley-Hagen, M. M. (1997). The effects of divorce on fathers and their children. In M. Lamb (Ed.), *The role of the father in child development* (3rd ed., pp. 191–211). New York: Wiley.

Hetherington, E. M., Stanley-Hagen, M., & Anderson, E. R. (1989). Marital transitions: A child's perspective. *American Psychologist, 44*, 303–312.

Hewlett, B. S. (2005). The cultural nexus of father-infant bonding. In C. B. Brettell and C. F. Sargent (Eds.), *Gender in cross-cultural perspective* (4th ed.). Upper Saddle River, NJ: Prentice-Hall.

Heyl, B. S. (1996). Homosexuality: A social phenomenon. In K. E. Rosenblum & T. C. Travis (Eds.), *The meaning of difference: American constructions of race, sex and gender, social class, and sexual orientation* (pp. 120–129). New York: McGraw-Hill.

Hines, P. M. & Boyd-Franklin, N. (2005). Families of African origin. In M. Mc-Goldrick, J. Giordano, & N. Garcia-Preto (Eds.), *Ethnicity and family therapy* (3rd ed). New York: Guilford.

Hill, J. P. (1987). Research on adolescents and their families: Past and prospect. *New Directions for Child Development, 37*, 13–31.

Hilliard, L. J., & Liben, L. S. (2010). Differing levels of gender salience in preschool classrooms: Effects on children's gender attitudes and intergroup bias. *Child Development, 81*, 1787–1798.

Hills, H. I., Carlstrom, A., & Evanow, M. (2001). Consulting with men in business and industry. In G. R. Brooks & G. E. Good (Eds.). *The new handbook of psychotherapy and counseling with men: A comprehensive guide to settings, problems, and treatment approaches.* San Francisco: Jossey-Bass.

Hochschild, A., & Machung, A. (1989). *The second shift.* New York: Avon.

Hofferth, S. L. & Anderson, K. G. (2003). Are all dads equal? Biology versus marriage as a basis for paternal investment. *Journal of Marriage and the Family, 65 (1)*, 213–232.

Hoffman, J. (1992, February 16). When men hit women. *The New York Times Magazine*, pp. 23–27, 64–66, 72.

Hoffman, R. M., & Borders, L. D. (2001). Twenty-five years after the Bem Sex-Role Inventory: A reassessment and new issues regarding classification variability. *Measurement and Evaluation in Counseling and Development, 34*, 39–55.

Hofstede, G. (1998). Comparative studies of sexual behavior: Sex as achievement or as relationship? In G. Hofstede (Ed.), *Masculinity and femininity: Taboo dimensions of national culture* (pp. 153–178). Thousand Oaks, CA: Sage.

Holland, K. J., & Cortina, L. M. (2013). When sexism and feminism collide: The sexual harassment of feminist working women. *Psychology of Women Quarterly, 37*(2), 192–208.

Holtzworth-Munroe, A., & Stuart, G. L. (1994). Typologies of male batterers: Three subtypes and the differences among them. *Psychological Bulletin, 116*, 476–497.

Horne, A. M., Jolliff, D. L., & Roth, E. W. (1996). Men mentoring men in groups. In M. P. Andronico (Ed.), *Men in groups: Insights, interventions, and psychoeducational work* (pp. 97–112). Washington, DC: American Psychological Association.

Horney, K. (1932). The dread of women: Observations on a specific difference in the dread felt by men and women respectively for the opposite sex. *International Journal of Psychoanalysis, 13*, 348–360.

Houseworth, S., Peplow, K., & Thirer, J. (1989). Influence of sport participation upon sex role orientation of Caucasian males and their attitudes toward women. *Sex Roles, 20*, 317–325.

Houts, C. R., & Horne, S. G. (2008). The role of relationship attributions in relationship satisfaction among cohabiting gay men. *The Family Journal, 16*(3), 240–248.

Hubbard, R. (1998). The political nature of "human nature." In In D. L. Anselmi & A. L. Law (Eds.), *Questions of gender: perspectives and paradoxes* (pp. 146–153). Boston: McGraw-Hill.

Huizinga, D., Weiher, A. W., Espiritu, R., & Esbensen, F. (2003). Delinquency and crime: Some highlights from the Denver Youth Survey. In T. P. Thornberry & M. D. Krohn (Eds.), *Taking stock of delinquency: An overview of findings from contemporary longitudinal studies.* New York: Kluwer Academic/Plenum.

Huesmann, L. R., Dubow, E. F., & Boxer, P. (2011). The transmission of aggressiveness across generations: Biological, contextual, and social learning processes. In P. R. Shaver & M. Mikulincer (Eds.),

Human aggression and violence: Causes, manifestations, and consequences. Washington, DC: American Psychological Association.

Humblet, O., Paul, C., & Dickson, N. (2003). Core group evolution over time: High-risk sexual behavior in a birth cohort between sexual debut and age 26. *Sexually Transmitted Diseases, 30*, 818–824.

Hunt, K., Lewars, H., Emslie, C., & Batty, G. D. (2007). Decreased risk of death from coronary heart disease amongst men with higher "femininity" scores: A general population cohort study. *International Journal of Epidemiology, 36*, 612–620.

Hurt, B. (2006). *Hip-hop: Beyond beats and rhymes* (documentary film). Northampton, MA: Media Education Foundation.

Hussey, A. (1989). Neonatal circumcision: A uniquely American ritual. *Transitions, 9 (4)*, 18–22.

Hust, S. J. T., Brown, J. D., & L'Engle, K. L. (2008). Boys will be boys and girls better be prepared: An analysis of the rare sexual health messages in young adolescents' media. *Mass Communication & Society, 11*, 3–23.

Huston, T. L., & Ashmore, R. D. (1986). Women and men in personal relationship. In R. D. Ashmore & R. K. Del Boca (Eds.), *The social psychology of female-male relations* (pp. 167–210). New York: Academic Press.

Huyck, M. (1992). Evaluating the parental imperative in Parkville. Paper presented at the Annual Meeting of the American Gerontological Society, Washington, DC.

Hyde, J. S. (1984). Children's understanding of sexist language. *Developmental Psychology, 20*, 697–706.

Hyde, J. S. (2005). The gender similarities hypothesis. *American Psychologist, 60*, 581–592.

Hyde, J. S., & Plant, E. A. (1995). Magnitude of psychological gender differences: Another side to the story. *American Psychologist, 50*, 159–161.

Internet Filter Review (2009). 2006 and 2005 pornography United States Industry revenue statistics. Retrieved July 16, 2009 from internet-filter-review.toptenreviews.com/internet-pornography-statistics.

Intersex Society of North America (undated). How common is intersex? Retrieved July 3, 2014, from http://www.isna.org/faq/frequency.

Irving, L., Wall, M., Neumark-Sztainer, D., & Story, M. (2002). Steroid use among adolescents: Findings from Project EAT. Journal of Adolescent Health, 30, 243–252.

Isely, P. J., Busse, W., & Isely, P. (1998). Sexual assault in males in late adolescence: A hidden phenomenon. *Professional School Counseling, 2*, 153–160.

Isely, P. J., Isely, P., Freiburger, J., & McMackin, R. (2008). In their own voices: A qualitative study of men abused as children by Catholic clergy. *Journal of Child Sexual Abuse, 17*, 201–215.

Isely, P. J., & Gehrenbeck-Shim, D. (1997). Sexual assault of men in the community. *Journal of Community Psychology, 25*, 159–166.

Jacupak, M., Tull, M. T., & Roemer, L. (2005). Masculinity, shame, and fear of emotions as predictors of men's expressions of anger and hostility. *Psychology of Men and Masculinity, 6*, 275–284.

Jakobsen, R. (1997). Stages of progression in noncoital sexual interactions among young adolescents: An application of the Mokken Scale Analysis. *International Journal of Behavioral Development, 21*, 537–553.

James, S. (1984). *A dictionary of sexist quotations*. Totowa, NJ: Barnes and Noble.

Jansz, J. (2000). Masculine identity and restrictive emotionality. In A. H. Fischer (Ed.), *Gender and emotion: Social psychological perspectives*. Cambridge, UK: Cambridge University Press.

Jaschik-Herman, M. L., & Fisk, A. (1995). Women's perceptions and labeling of sexual harassment in academia before and after the Hill-Thomas hearings. *Sex Roles, 33*, 439–446.

Jenkins, S. (2005). The age-old question: How young is too young? *The Washington Post*, July 6, pp. E1, E7.

Jensen, R. (2007). *Getting off: Pornography and the end of masculinity*. Cambridge, MA: South End.

Jensen-Campbell, L. A., Graziano, W. G., & West, S. G. (1995). Dominance, prosocial orientation, and female preferences: Do nice guys really finish last? Journal of *Personality and Social Psychology, 68*, 427–440.

Jhally, S. (2007). Dreamworlds 3: Desire, sex, & power in music video.

Johnson, A. G. (1997). *The gender knot: Unraveling our patriarchal legacy*. Philadelphia: Temple University Press.

Johnson, A. G. (2001). *Privilege, power, and difference*. Mountain View, CA: Mayfield.

Johnson, C. (2009, June 23). Panel sets guidelines for fighting prison rape. *The Washington Post, A4*.

Johnson, J. A. (2013, May 20). The effects of hypersexualized media: A review of empirical evidence. Presentation at the Blue Ribbon Panel on Hypersexualized Media, Richmond, VA.

Johnson, K. L., Lurye, L. E., & Tassinary, L. G. (2010). Sex categorization among preschool children: Increasing utilization of sexually dimorphic cues. *Child Development, 81*(5), 1346–1355.

Johnston, L., McLellan, T., & McKinlay, A. (2014). (Perceived) size really does matter: Male dissatisfaction with penis size. *Psychology of Men & Masculinity, 15*(2), 225–228. doi: 10.1037/a0033264

Jones, S. & Mauer, M. (2013). *Race to incarcerate: A graphic retelling*. New York: New Press.

Joshi, S. P., Peter, J., & Valkenburg, P. M. (2011). Scripts of sexual desire and danger in US and Dutch teen girl magazines: A cross-national content analysis. *Sex Roles, 64*, 463–474.

Jourard, S. M. (1971). *The transparent self*. New York: Van Nostrand.

Joyce, A. (2005, June 6). Workplace improves for gay, transgender employees, rights group says. *The Washington Post*, A5.

Jung, C. G. (1959/1989). Concerning the archetypes with special reference to the anima concept. In C. G. Jung, R. F. C. Hull (Translator) & J. Beebe (Ed.), *Aspects of the masculine* (pp. 115–122). Princeton, NJ: Princeton University Press.

Kahn, J. S. (2009). *An introduction to masculinities*. Oxford, UK: Wiley-Blackwell.

Kaiser Family Foundation (2012). Generation RX.com: How young people use the Internet for health information. Accessed December 27, 2012 from kff.org/entmedia/loader.cfm?url=/commonspot/security/getfile.cfm&pageid+13719.

Kamarovsky, M. (1940/1971). *The unemployed man and his family: The effect of unemployment upon the status of the man in fifty-nine families*. New York: Dryden Press/Arno Press.

Kaplan, D., & Rosenmann, A. (2014). Toward an empirical model of male homosocial relatedness: An investigation of friendship in uniform and beyond. *Psychology of Men & Masculinity, 15*(1), 12–21. doi: 10.1037/a0031289

Kaplan, M. S., Huguet, N., McFarland, B. H., & Mandle, J. A. (2012). Factors associated with suicide by firearm among U. S. older men. *Psychology of Men and Masculinity, 13*, 65–74.

Karraker, K. H., Vogel, D. A., & Lake, M. A. (1995). Parents' gender-stereotyped perceptions of newborns: The eye of the beholder revisited. *Sex Roles, 33*, 687–701.

Karren, K. J., Smith, L., Hafen, B. Q., & Gordon, K. J. (2009). *Mind body health: The effects of attitudes, emotions, and relationships* (5th ed.). San Francisco: Benjamin Cummings.

Katz, J. (2001). Boys are not men: Notes on working with adolescent males in juvenile detention. In D. Sabo, T. A. Kupers, & W. London (Eds.). *Prison masculinities*. Philadelphia: Temple University Press.

Katz, J. (2013). *Tough guise 2: Violence, manhood, and American culture* (documentary film). Northampton, MA: Media Education Foundation.

Kaufman, M. (1994). Men, feminism, and men's contradictory experiences of power. In H. Brod and Michael Kaufman (Eds.), *Theorizing masculinities* (pp. 142–163). Thousand Oaks, CA: Sage.

Kawakami, K., Dovidio, J. F., Moll, J., Hermsen, S., & Russin, A. (2000). Just say no (to stereotyping): Effects of training in the negation of stereotypic associations on stereotype activation. *Journal of Personality and Social Psychology, 78 (5),* 871–888.

Kaye, K., Suellentrop, K., & Sloup, C. (2009) The Fog Zone: How misperceptions, magical thinking, and ambivalence put young adults at risk for unplanned pregnancy. Washington DC: The National Campaign to Prevent Teen and Unplanned Pregnancy.

Kearney, L. K., & Rochlen, A. B. (2012). Mexican-American and Caucasian university men's experience of sexual harassment: A preliminary report. *Psychology of Men & Masculinity, 13*(3), 264–269.

Kearney, L. K., Rochlen, A. B., & King, E. B. (2004). Male gender role conflict, sexual harassment tolerance, and the efficacy of a psychoeducative training program. *Psychology of Men and Masculinity, 5 (1),* 72–82.

Keen, M. (1984). *Chivalry.* New Haven, CT: Yale University Press.

Keen, S. (1991). *Fire in the belly: On being a man.* New York: Bantam.

Kelly, J. & Johnson, L. A. (2009, January 13). It's hard out here for a pop: Stereotypes, silence, and the socialization of future fathers. Presentation at the Minnesota Fatherhood Summit, St. Cloud, MN.

Kemper, T. D. (1990). *Social structure and testosterone.* New Brunswick, NJ: Rutgers University Press.

Kendler, K. S., Myers, J., & Prescott, C. A. (2005). Sex Differences in the Relationship Between Social Support and Risk for Major Depression: A Longitudinal Study of Opposite-Sex Twin Pairs. *The*

American Journal of Psychiatry, 162(2), 250–256.

Kenrick, D. T., Gutierres, S. E., & Goldberg, L. L. (1989). Influence of popular erotica on judgments of strangers and mates. *Journal of Experimental Social Psychology, 25,* 159–167.

Kenrick, D. T., Neuberg, S. L., & Cialdini, R. B. (2005). *Social psychology: Unraveling the mystery* (3rd ed.) Boston: Pearson.

Kessler, G. (2009, May 25). Clinton to extend benefits to gay partners: Draft memo outlines new foreign service policies for all unmarried couples. *The Washington Post,* A8.

Kevorkian, R. T. & Cepeda, O. A. (2007). The biologic basis for longevity differences between men and women. In B. Lunenfeld, L. J. Gooren, A. Morales, & J. E. Morley (Eds.), *Textbook of men's health and aging* (2nd ed.). London: Informa.

Kilmartin, C. T. (1996). The White Ribbon Campaign: Men working to end men's violence against women. *Journal of College Student Development, 37 (3),* 347–348.

Kilmartin, C. T. (2004a). "Midlife crisis". In M. Kimmel & A. Aronson (Eds.), *Men and masculinities: A social, cultural, and historical encyclopedia.* Santa Barbara, CA: ABC-Clio.

Kilmartin, C. T. (2004b). Masculinity as a cultural variable in psychotherapy. Paper presented in Symposium: Men and mental health: New directions in marketing and treatment (M. E. Addis & J. M. Lane, Chairs). Annual Convention of the American Psychological Association, Honolulu, HI.

Kilmartin, C. T. (2005). Depression in men: communication, diagnosis, and therapy. *Journal of Men's Health and Gender, 2 (1),* 95–99.

Kilmartin, C. (2007, February). Polizei und Sexuelle Übergriffe: Wie Sie helfen können (Police and sexual assault: How you can help). *Polizei Kärnten. Das Info-Magazin des Landespolizeikommandos* (Austria). Translated by Bettina Pirker.

Kilmartin, C. (2010). Incremental terrorism: Cultural masculinity, conflict, and violence against women. In W. Berger, B. Hipfl, K. Mertlitsch, & V. Ratkovic (Eds.): *Kulturelle Dimensionen von Konflikten (Cultural dimensions of conflicts)*. Baden Baden, Germany: Nomos.

Kilmartin, C. (2014). Counseling men to prevent sexual violence. In M. Englar-Carlson, M. P. Evans, & T. Duffey (Eds.), *A counselor's guide to working with men*. Alexandria, VA: American Counseling Association.

Kilmartin, C. T., & Allison, J. (2007). *Men's violence against women: Theory, research, and activism*. Mahwah, NJ: Erlbaum.

Kilmartin, C. T., & Berkowitz, A. D. (2005). *Sexual assault in context: Teaching men about gender*. Mahwah, NJ: Erlbaum.

Kilmartin, C. T., Chirico, B., & Leemann, M. (1997). *The White Ribbon Campaign: Evidence for Social Change on a College Campus*. Paper presented at the Spring Convention of the Virginia Psychological Association, Roanoke, VA.

Kilmartin, C. T., Conway, A., Friedberg, A., McQuoid, T., Tschan, T., & Norbet, T. (1999, April). Using the social norms model to encourage male college students to challenge rape-supportive attitudes in male peers. Paper presented at the Virginia Psychological Association Spring Conference, Virginia Beach, VA.

Kilmartin, C. T., McDermott, R., & Wright, C. (under review). Sexual violence and masculinities: A map of the territory. Under submission to *Psychology of Men and Masculinity*.

Kilmartin, C., Smith, T., Green, A., Kuchler, M., Heinzen, H., & Kolar, D. (2008). A real time social norms intervention to reduce male sexism. *Sex Roles: A Journal of Research, 59*, 264–273.

Kilmartin, C. T., & Ring, T. E. (1991). Understanding and preventing acquaintance rape on college campuses: Services for men. Paper presented at the annual meeting of the Maryland College Personnel Association, College Park, MD.

Kimbrell, A. (1991, May/June). A time for men to pull together. *Utne Reader*, pp. 66–74.

Kimmel, M. S. (1987). Rethinking masculinity: New directions in research. In M. S. Kimmel (Ed.), *Changing men: New directions in research on men and masculinity* (pp. 9–24). Newbury Park, CA: Sage.

Kimmel, M. S. (1994). Masculinity as homophobia: Fear, shame, and silence in the construction of gender identity. In H. Brod and Michael Kaufman (Eds.), *Theorizing masculinities* (pp. 119 -141). Thousand Oaks, CA: Sage.

Kimmel, M. S. (2001). Male victims of domestic violence: A substantive and methodological research review. Report to the Equality Committee of the Department of Education and Science.

Kimmel, M. S. (2006). *Manhood in America: A cultural history* (2nd ed.). New York: Oxford University Press.

Kimmel, M. S. (2008). *Guyland: The perilous world where boys become men. Understanding the critical years between 16 and 26*. New York: Harper Collins.

Kimmel, M. S. (2013a). *Angry white men: American masculinity at the end of an era*. New York: Nation.

Kimmel, M. S. (2013b). A war against boys? In M. S. Kimmel & M. A. Messner (Eds.), *Men's Lives* (9th ed.). Boston: Pearson.

Kimmel, M. S., & Mosmiller, T. E. (1992). *Against the tide: Pro-feminist men in the United States, 1776–1990*. Boston: Beacon.

King, J. L., & Hunter, K. (2004). *On the down low: A journey into the lives of "straight" black men who sleep with men*. New York: Harlem Moon.

King, M. B., Coxell, A., & Mezey, G. (2000). The prevalence and characteristics of male sexual assault. In G. C. Mezey & M. B. King (Eds.), *Male victims of sexual assault* (2nd ed., pp. 1–16). New York: Oxford University Press.

Kingston, D. A., Fedoroff, P., Firestone, P., Curry, S., & Bradford, J. M. (2008). Pornography use and sexual aggression: The impact of frequency and type of pornography use on recidivism among sexual offenders. *Aggressive Behavior, 34*, 341–351.

Kinsey, A. C., Pomeroy, W. B., & Martin, C. E. (1948). *Sexual behavior in the human male*. Philadelphia: W. B. Saunders.

Kipling, R. (1940). *Rudyard Kipling's Verse: Definitive Edition*. Garden City, NY: Doubleday.

Kiselica, M. S. (2005, May 14). Personal communication.

Kiselica, M. S. (2006). Helping a boy become a parent: Male-sensitive psychotherapy with a teenage father. In M. Englar-Carlson & M. Stevens (Eds.), *In the room with men: A casebook of therapeutic change*. Washington, DC: American Psychological Association.

Kiselica, M. S., & Kiselica, A. M. (2014). The complicated worlds of adolescent fathers: Implications for clinical practice, public policy, and research. *Psychology of Men & Masculinity, 15*(3), 260–274.

Kivel, P. (1992). *Men's work: How to stop the violence that tears our lives apart*. Center City, MN: Hazleden.

Knight, R. A. & Sims-Knight, J. (2013). Risk factors for sexual violence. In M. P. Koss, J. W. White, & A. E. Kazdin (Eds.), *Violence against women and children, Volume 1: Mapping the terrain*. Washington, DC: American Psychological Association.

Komiya, N., Good, G. E., & Sherrod, N. (2000). Emotional openness as a contributing factor to reluctance to seek counseling among college students. *Journal of Counseling Psychology, 47*, 138–143.

Kopper, B. A., & Epperson, D. L. (1996). The experience and expression of anger: Relationships with gender, gender role socialization, depression, and mental health functioning. *Journal of Counseling Psychology*, 43, 158–165.

Korobov, N. (2004). Inoculating against prejudice: A discursive approach to homophobia and sexism in adolescent male talk. *Psychology of Men and Masculinity,* 5, 178–189.

Korsvik, T. R. & Sto, A. (2013). *The Nordic model*. Copenhagen, Norway: The Feminist Group.

Koss, M. P., & Dinero, T. E. (1988). Predictors of sexual aggression among a national sample of male college students. In R. A. Prentky & V. L. Quinsey (Eds.), *Human sexual aggression: Current perspectives* (pp. 133–147). New York: New York Academy of Sciences.

Koss, M. P., Gidycz, C. A., & Wisniewski, N. (1987). The scope of rape: Incidence and prevalence of sexual aggression and victimization in a national sample of higher education students. *Journal of Consulting and Clinical Psychology, 55*, 162–170.

Koss, M. P., Leonard, K. E., Beezley, D. A., & Oros, C. J. (1985). Nonstranger sexual aggression: A discriminant analysis of the psycholotical characteristics of undetected offenders. *Sex Roles, 12*, 981–992.

Kreuz, L. E., & Rose, R. M. (1972). Assessment of aggressive behavior and plasma testosterone in a young criminal population. *Psychosomatic Medicine, 34*, 321–332.

Krishnamurthy, K. (1998, June 17). No pomp, but honor student gets diploma. *The Free-Lance Star*, p. C1.

Krug, E. G., Dahlberg, L. L., Mercy, J. A., Zwi, A. B., & Lozano, R. (Eds., 2004). *World report on violence and health*. Geneva: World Health Organization.

Kruger, D. J., & Nesse, R. M. (2004). Sexual selection and the Male:Female mortality ratio. *Evolutionary Psychology, 2*, 66–85.

Kruger, D. J., & Nesse, R. M. (2006a). An evolutionary framework for understanding sex differences in Croatian mortality rates. *Psihologijske Teme, 15*(2), 351–364.

Kruger, D. J., & Nesse, R. M. (2006b). An evolutionary life-history framework for understanding sex differences in human mortality rates. *Human Nature, 17*(1), 74–97.

Kupers, T. A. (1999). *Prison madness: The mental health crisis behind bars and what we must do about it*. San Francisco: Jossey-Bass.

Kupers, T. A. (2004). Prisons. In M. Kimmel & A. Aronson (Eds.), *Men and masculinities: A social, cultural, and historical encyclopedia*. Santa Barbara, CA: ABC-Clio.

Kurdek, L. A. (1988). Correlates of negative attitudes toward homosexuals in heterosexual college students. *Sex Roles, 18,* 727–738.

LaFrance, M., Hecht, M. A., & Paluck, E. L. (2003). The contingent smile: A meta-analysis of sex differences in smiling, *Psychological Bulletin, 129,* 305–334.

Laker, J., Davis, T., Kellom, G., & Brod, H. (2005). (En)Gendering men on campus: A state of field discussion on college men. Panel discussion: American Men's Studies Association 13th Annual Conference, Nashville, TN.

Lakoff, R. T. (1990). *Talking power: The politics of language.* New York: Basic Books.

Lalumiere, M. L., Harris, G. T., Quinsey, V. L., & Rice, M. E. (2005). *The causes of rape: Understanding individual differences in male propensity for sexual aggression.* Washington, DC: American Psychological Association.

Lamb, M. E. (2012). Mothers, fathers, families, and circumstances: Factors affecting children's adjustment. *Applied Developmental Science, 16*(2), 98–111.

Landrine, H. (1988). Revising the framework of abnormal psychology. In P. Bronstein and K. Quina (Eds.), *Teaching a psychology of people: Resources for gender and sociocultural awareness* (pp. 37–44). Washington, DC: American Psychological Association.

Lash, S. J., Eisler, R. M., & Southard, D. R. (1995). Sex differences in cardiovascular reactivity as a function of the appraised gender relevance of the stressor. *Behavioral Medicine, 21,* 86–94.

Lash, S. J., Gillespie, B. L., Eisler, R. M., & Southard, D. H. (1991). Sex differences in cardiovascular reactivity : Effects of the gender relevance of the stressor. *Health Psychology, 10,* 392–398.

Laumann, E. O. (1999). The circumcision dilemma: Physicians in the U. S. are at odds over neonatal circumcision. Is it preventive medicine, cosmetic surgery, or inhumane mutilation? *Scientific American Presents, 10 (2),* 68–72.

Laumann, E. O., Gagnon, J., Michael, R. T., & Michaels, S. (2nd ed., 2001). *The social organization of sexuality: Sexual practices in the United States.* Chicago: University of Chicago Press.

Lazur, R. F. (1996). Managing boundaries: Group therapy with incarcerated adult male sexual offenders. In M. P. Andronico (Ed.), *Men in groups: Insights, interventions, and psychoeducational work* (pp. 389–410). Washington, DC: American Psychological Association.

Leahy, M. (2008, February 3). The pain game. The Washington Post Magazine, 8–13, 21–26.

Leary, M. R., Kowalski, R. M., Smith, L., & Phillips, S. (2003). Teasing, rejection, and violence: Case studies of the school shootings. *Aggressive Behavior, 29,* 202–214.

Lee, C. C. (1990). Black male development: Counseling the "native son." In D. Moore & F. Leafgren (Eds.), *Men in conflict*. Alexandria, VA: American Association for Counseling and Development.

Lee, J. (1991). *At my father's wedding: Reclaiming our true masculinity.* New York: Bantam.

Lehne, G. (1998). Homophobia among men: Supporting and defining the male role. In M. S. Kimmel and M. A. Messner (Eds.), *Men's lives* (4th ed., pp. 237–249). Needham Heights, MA: Allyn and Bacon.

Leicht, K. T, Thompkins, D., Wildhagen, T., Rogalin, C. L., Soboroff, S. D., Kelley, C. P., Long, C., & Lovaglia, M. J. (2007). Women's predominance in college enrollments: Labor market and gender identity explanations. In S. J. Correll (Ed.), *Social psychology of gender* (pp. 283–310). Amsterdam: Elsevier.

Lemann, N. (1991). *The promised land.* New York: Knopf.

Lemle, R., & Mishkind, M. E. (1989). Alcohol and masculinity. *Journal of Substance Abuse Treatment, 6*, 213–222.

Lepowsky, M. (1998). Women, men, and aggression in an egalitarian society. In D. L. Anselmi & A. L. Law (Eds.), *Questions of gender: perspectives and paradoxes*). Boston: McGraw-Hill.

Lerner, G. (1986). *The creation of patriarchy*. New York: Oxford University Press.

Letich, L. (1991, May/June). Do you know who your friends are? *Utne Reader*, pp. 85–87.

Levant, R. F. (1990). Coping with the new father role. In D. Moore & F. Leafgren (Eds.), *Men in conflict* (pp. 81–94). Alexandria, VA: American Association for Counseling and Development.

Levant, R. F. (1995). *Masculinity reconstructed: Changing the rules of manhood -- at work, in relationships, and in family life*. New York: Dutton.

Levant, R. F. (1996). The new psychology of men. *Professional Psychology: Research and Practice, 27*, 259–265.

Levant, R. F. (1997a). Men and emotions: A psychoeducational approach. New York: Newbridge Professional Programs.

Levant, R. F. (1997b). Nonrelational sex. In R. F. Levant & G. R. Brooks (Eds.), *Men and sex* (pp. 9–27). New York: Wiley.

Levant, R. F. (1998). Desperately seeking language: Understanding, assessing, and treating normative male alexithymia. In W.S. Pollack & R. F. Levant (Eds.), *New psychotherapy for men* (pp. 35–56). New York: Wiley.

Levant, R. F. (2003). Treating male alexithymia.. In L.B. Silverstein & T. J. Goodrich (Eds). *Feminist family therapy: Empowerment in social context* (pp. 177–188). Washington, DC: American Psychological Association.

Levant, R. F., Hall, R. J., Williams, C. M., & Hasan, N. T. (2009). Gender differences in alexithymia. *Psychology of Men and Masculinity, 10*, 190–203.

Levant, R. F., & Richmond, K. (2007). A review of research on masculinity ideologies using the Male Role Norms Inventory. *The Journal of Men's Studies, 15*, 130–146.

Levant, R. F., Smalley, K. B., Aupont, M., House, A. T., Richmond, K., & Noronha, D. (2007). Initial validation of the Male Role Norms Inventory-Revised. *The Journal of Men's Studies, 15*, 83–100.

Levant, R. F., & Wimer, D. J. (2010). The new fathering movement. In C. Z. Oren & D. C. Oren (Eds.), *Counseling fathers* (pp. 3–21). New York: Routledge.

Levenson, R., Carstensen, L., & Gottman, J. (1994). The influence of age and gender on affect, physiology, and their interrelations: A study of long-term marriages. *Journal of Personality and Social Psychology, 67*, 56–68.

Lever, J., Frederick, D. A., & Peplau, L. A. (2006). Does size matter? Men's and women's views on penis size across the lifespan. *Psychology of Men and Masculinity, 7*, 129–143.

Levinson, D. J., Darrow, C. N., Klein, E. B., Levinson, M. H., & McKee, B. (1978). *The seasons of a man's life*. New York: Knopf.

Levine, H. J., & Evans, N. J. (1996). The development of gay, lesbian, and bisexual identities. In K. E. Rosenblum & T. C. Travis (Eds.), *The meaning of difference: American constructions of race, sex and gender, social class, and sexual orientation* (pp. 130–136). New York: McGraw-Hill.

Levine, M. P. (1991). The life and death of the gay clone. In G. Herdt (Ed.), *Gay culture in America: Essays from the field* (pp. 68–86). Boston: Beacon.

Levine, M. P. (1998). *Gay macho: The life and death of the homosexual clone*. New York: New York University Press.

Levy, C. J. (1992). ARVN as faggots: Inverted warfare in Vietnam. In M. S. Kimmel & M. A. Messner (Eds.), *Men's lives* (2nd ed., pp. 183–197). New York: Macmillan.

Lewis, R. A. (1986). Men's changing roles in marriage and the family. In R. A. Lewis (Ed.), *Men's changing roles in the family* (pp. 1–10). New York: Haworth.

Lex, B. W. (1995). Alcohol and other psycho-active substance dependence in women and men. In M. V. Seeman (Ed.), *Gender and psychopathology* (pp. 358). Washington, DC: American Psychiatric Press.

Liebow, E. (1967). *Talley's corner.* Boston: Little, Brown.

Lindberg, S. M., Hyde, J. S., Petersen, J. L., & Linn, M. C. (2010). New trends in gender and mathematics performance: A meta-analysis. *Psychological Bulletin, 136*(6), 1123–1135.

Lippa, R. A., Martin, L. R., & Friedman, H. S. (2000). Gender-related individual differences and mortality in the Terman longitudinal study: Is masculinity hazardous to your health? *Personality and Social Psychology Bulletin, 12*, 1560–1570.

Lips, H. (2008). *Sex and gender: An introduction* (6th ed.). Boston: McGraw-Hill.

Lisak, D. (1991). Sexual aggression, masculinity, and fathers. *Signs, 16*, 238–262.

Lisak, D. (1997). Male gender socialization and the perpetration of sexual abuse. In R. F. Levant & G. R. Brooks (Eds.), *Men and sex* (pp. 156–177). New York: Wiley.

Lisak, D. (2005). The undetected rapist. Videotaped re-enactment of an interview with a sexual assault perpetrator. Available from legal momentum.org.

Lisak, D. & Beszterczey, S. (2007). The cycle of violence: The life histories of 43 death row inmates. *Psychology of Men and Masculinity, 8*, 118–128.

Lisak, D. & Miller, P. M. (2002). Repeat rape and multiple offending among undetected rapists. *Violence and Victims, 17 (1)*, 73–84.

Lisak, D., & Roth, S. (1988). Motivational factors in nonincarcerated sexually aggressive men. *Journal of Personality and Social Psychology, 55*, 795–802.

Little League World Series. (2014). Schedule and Results 2014. Retrieved November 12, 2014, from https://gc.com/tmt/summer-2014/little-league-baseball-world-series-539f4a5315f9ba-5fdb6b94b4/schedule

Liu, W. M. (2002). Exploring the lives of Asian American men: Racial identity, male role norms, gender role conflict, and prejudicial attitudes. *Psychology of Men and Masculinity, 3 (2)*, 107–118.

Livingston, G. (2014). Growing Number of Dads Home with the Kids: Biggest Increase Among Those Caring for Family. Washington DC: Pew Research Center's Sociaal and Demographic Trends project.

Livingston, G., & Parker, K. (2011). A tale of two fathers: More are active, but more are absent.

Lo, C. C., & Globetti, G. (1995). The facilitating and enhancing roles Greek associations play in college drinking. *International Journal of the Addictions, 30*, 1311–1322.

Loeber, R., & Stouthamer-Loeber, M. (1998). Development of juvenile aggression and violence: Some common misconceptions and controversies. *American Psychologist, 53*, 242–249.

Lohan, M., Cruise, S., O'Halloran, P., Alderdice, F., & Hyde, A. (2010). Adolescent men's attitudes in relation to pregnancy and pregnancy outcomes: A systematic review of the literature from 1980–2009. *Journal of Adolescent Health, 47*(4), 327–345.

Long, D. (1987). Working with men who batter. In M. Scher, M. Stevens, G. Good, & G. A. Eichenfield (Eds.). Handbook of counseling and psychotherapy with men. Newbury Park, CA: Sage.

Lorber, J. (1986). Dismantling Noah's ark. *Sex Roles, 14*, 567–580.

Lorber, J. (1994). *Paradoxes of gender.* New Haven, CT: Yale University Press.

Loughery, J. (1998). The other side of silence: Men's lives and gay identities: A twentieth century history. New York: Henry Holt.

Lutz, T. (2001). *Crying.* New York: Norton.

Lynch, J. (2004). *When anger scares you: How to overcome your fear of conflict and express your anger in healthy ways.* Oakland, CA: New Harbinger.

Lynch, J., & Kilmartin, C. T. (2013). *Overcoming masculine depression: The pain behind the mask (2nd. Ed.).* New York: Routledge/Taylor & Francis.

Lynn, D. B. (1959). A note on sex differences in the development of masculine and feminine identification. *Psychological Review, 66*, 126–135.

Lynn, D. B. (1966). The process of learning parental and sex-role identification. *Journal of Marriage and the Family, 28*, 466–477.

Lynn, D. B. (1969). *Parental and sex role identification: A theoretical formulation.* Berkeley, CA: McCutchan.

Lytton, H., & Romney, D. M. (1991). Parents' differential socialization of boys and girls: A meta-analysis. *Psychological Bulletin, 109*, 267–296.

Maccoby, E. E. (1987). The varied meanings of "masculine" and "feminine." In J.M. Reinisch, L.A. Rosenblum, & S.A. Sanders (Eds.), *Masculinity/femininity: Basic perspectives* (pp. 227–239). New York: Oxford University Press.

Maccoby, E. E. (1988a). Gender as a social category. *Developmental Psychology, 24*, 755–765.

Maccoby, E. E. (1988b). Gender as a social construct. Paper presented at the Annual Meeting of the Eastern Psychological Association, Buffalo, NY.

Maccoby, E. E. (1990). Gender and relationships: A developmental account. *American Psychologist, 45*, 513–520.

Maccoby, E. E. (1998). *The two sexes: Growing up apart, coming together.* Cambridge, MA: Harvard University Press.

Maccoby, E. E. & Jacklin, C. N. (1974). *The psychology of sex differences.* Stanford, CA: Stanford University Press.

MacKinnon, C.A. (1985). Pornography, civil rights, and speech. *Harvard Civil Rights-Civil Liberties Law Review, 20*, 1–70.

Maddi, S. R. (2001). *Personality theories: A comparative analysis* (6th ed.). Prospect Heights, IL: Waveland.

Magovcevic, M. & and Addis, M. E. (2008). The masculine depression scale: Development and psychometric evaluation. *Psychology of Men and Masculinity, 9*, 117–132.

Mahalik, J. R., Burns, S. M., & Syzdek, M. (2007). Masculinity and perceived normative health behaviors as predictors of men's health behaviors. *Social Science and Medicine, 64*, 2201–2209.

Mahalik, J. R., Cournoyer, R. J., DeFranc, W., Cherry, M., & Napolitano, J. M. (1998). Men's gender role conflict and use of psychological defenses. *Journal of Counseling Psychology*, 45, 247–255.

Mahalik, J. R., Locke, B. D., Ludlow, L. H., Diemer, M. A., Scott, R. P. J., Gottfried, M., & Freitas, G. (2003). Development of the Conformity to Masculine Norms Inventory. *Psychology of Men and Masculinity, 4 (1)*, 3–25.

Mahlstedt, D. (1998). Getting started: A dating violence peer education program for men. West Chester, PA: self.

Majors, R., & Billson, J. M. (1992). *Cool pose: The dilemmas of black manhood in America.* New York: Lexington.

Malamuth, N. M. (1984). Aggression against women: Cultural and individual causes. In N. M. Malamuth & E. Donnerstein (Eds.), *Pornography and sexual aggression* (pp. 19–52). Orlando, FL: Academic Press.

Malamuth, N. M., Addison, T., & Koss, M. P. (2000). Pornography and sexual aggression: Are there reliable effects and can we understand them? Annual Review of Sex Research, 11, 26–91.

Malarek, V. (2009). The johns: Sex for sale and the men who buy it. New York: Arcade.

Mann, J. (1997, October 1). Promise Keepers marching backward. *The Washington Post*, p. E13.

Manstead, A. S. R. (1992). Gender differences in emotion. In M. A. Gale & M. W. Eysenck (Eds.). *Handbook of individual differences: Biological perspectives.* Chichester, UK: Wiley.

Margulies, S. (2004). *Man's guide to civilized divorce.* Emmaus, PA: Rodale.

Marklein, M. B. (2005). College gender gap widens: 57% are women. Retrieved July 16, 2009 from usatoday.com/news/education/2005–10–19–male-college-cover.

Marsiglio, W. & Pleck, J. H. (2005). Fatherhood and masculinities. In M. S. Kimmel, J. Hearn, & R. W. Connell (Eds.), *Handbook of studies on men and masculinities.* Thousand Oaks, CA: Sage.

Martin, C. L. (1995). Stereotypes about children with traditional and nontraditional gender roles. *Sex Roles, 33,* 727–751.

Martin, C. L. & Fabes, R. A. (2001). The stability and consequences of young children's same-sex peer interactions. *Developmental Psychology, 3,* 431–446.

Martin, C. L., & Ruble, D. N. (2010). Patterns of gender development. *Annual Review of Psychology, 61,* 353–381.

Martin, C. L., Ruble, D. N., & Szkrybalo, J. (2002). Cognitive theories of early gender development. *Psychological Bulletin, 128*(6), 903–933.

Martin, E. (1991). The egg and the sperm: How science has constructed a romance based on stereotypical male-female roles. *Signs, 16,* 485–501.

Martin, P. Y., & Hummer, R. A. (2009). Fraternities and rape on campus. In V. Taylor, N. Whittier, & L. J. Rupp (Eds.), *Feminist frontiers* (8th ed., pp. 471–479). Boston: McGraw-Hill.

Martinez, G., Daniels, K., & Chandra, A. (2012). Fertility of men and women aged 15–44 years in the United States: National Survey of Family Growth, 2006–2010. (pp. 29). Washington DC: National Center for Health Statistics.

Marx, K. (1872). *Das Kapital.* Hamburg, Germany: Meissner.

Masciadrelli, B. P., Pleck, J. H., & Stueve, J. L. (2006). Fathers' Role Model Perceptions: Themes and Linkages with Involvement. *Men and Masculinities, 9*(1), 23–34.

Maslow, A. H. (1943). A theory of human motivation. *Psychological Review, 50,* 370–396.

Mauer, M. (2006). *Race to incarcerate.* New York: The Sentencing Project.

Maurer, T. W., & Pleck, J. H. (2006). Fathers' caregiving and breadwinning: A gender congruence analysis. *Psychology of Men & Masculinity, 7*(2), 101–112.

Maximonline.com (2014). Retrieved on July 14, 2014 from maximonline.com.

May, R. (1958). Contributions of existential psychotherapy. In R. May, E. Angel, & H. F. Ellenberger (Eds.), *Existence: A new dimension in psychiatry and psychology.* New York: Basic Books.

May, R. J. (1988). The developmental journey of the male college student. In R. J. May & M. Scher (Eds.), *Changing roles of men on campus* (pp. 5–18). San Francisco: Jossey-Bass.

Mazur, A. (1983). Hormones, aggression, and dominance in humans. In B. B. Svare (Ed.), *Hormones and aggressive behavior* (pp. 563–576). New York: Plenum.

McAdams, D. P., Lester, R. M., Brand, P. A., McNamara, W. J., & Lensky, D. B. (1988). Sex and the TAT: Are women more intimate than men? Do men fear intimacy? *Journal of Personality Assessment, 52,* 397–409.

McCreary, D. R. (1994). The male role and avoiding femininity. *Sex Roles, 31,* 517–531.

McCreary, D. R., Newcomb, M. D., & Sadava, S. W. (1999). The male role, alcohol use, and alcohol problems: A structural modeling examination in adult women and men. *Journal of Counseling Psychology, 46,* 109–124.

McCreary, D. R. & Sasse, D. K. (2000). An exploration of the drive for muscularity in adolescent boys and girls. *Journal of American College Health, 48,* 297–304.

McCreary, D. R., Saucier, D. M., & Courtenay, W. H. (2005). The drive for muscularity and masculinity: Testing the association among gender role traits, behaviors, attitudes, and conflict. *Psychology of Men and Masculinity, 6,* 83–94.

McCue, M. L. (2008). *Domestic violence: A reference handbook* (2nd ed.). Santa Barbara, CA: ABC-Clio.

McHugh, M. C., & Hambaugh, J. (2010). She said, he said: Gender, language, and power. In J. C. Chrisler & D. R. McCreary (Eds.), *Handbook of gender research in psychology, Vol 1: Gender research in general and experimental psychol-*

ogy. (pp. 379–410). New York, NY, US: Springer Science + Business Media.

McIntosh, P. (2009). White privilege: Unpacking the invisible knapsack. In V. Taylor, N. Whittier, & L. J. Rupp (Eds.), *Feminist frontiers* (8th ed., pp. 120–126). Boston: McGraw-Hill.

Mead, M. (1935). *Sex and temperament in three primitive societies.* New York: Morrow.

Mead, M. (1949). *Male and female: A study of the sexes in a changing world.* New York: Morrow.

Menshealth.com (2014). Homepage. Retrieved on July 14, 2014 from menshealth.com.

Mensjournal.com (2014). Homepage. Retrieved on July 14, 2014 from mensjournal.com.

Messerschmidt, J. W. (1993). *Masculinities and crime: Critique and reconceptualization of theory.* Lanham, MD: Rowman & Littlefield.

Messner, M. A. (1992). Like family: Power, intimacy, and sexuality in athletes' friendships. In P. M. Nardi (Ed.), *Men's friendships* (pp. 215–237). Newbury Park, CA: Sage.

Messner, M. A. (1995). Boyhood, organized sports, and the construction of masculinity. In M. A. Kimmel & M. S. Messner (Eds.), *Men's lives* (3rd ed., pp. 102–114). Boston: Allyn and Bacon.

Miedzian, M. (1991). *Boys will be boys: Breaking the link between masculinity and violence.* New York: Doubleday.

Migliaccio, T. (2009). Men's friendships: Performances of masculinity. *Journal of Men's Studies, 17,* 226–241.

Mihoces, G. (2002, January 18). Two big guys are key to success. *USA Today,* 1A.

Milgram, S. (1963). Behavioral study of obedience. *Journal of Abnormal and Social Psychology, 67,* 371–378.

Miller, A. (1949). *Death of a salesman.* New York: Viking.

Miller, M., Azrael, D., & Hemenway, D. (2013). Firearms and violent death in the United States. In D. W. Webster & J. S. Vernick (Eds.), *Reducing gun violence in America: Informing policy with evidence and analysis.* Baltimore, MD: Johns Hopkins University Press.

Miller, M., Lippmann, S. J., Azrael, D., & Hemenway, D. (2007). Household firearm ownership and rates of suicide across the 50 United States. *Journal of Trauma, Injury, Infection, and Critical Care, 62,* 1029–1034.

Miller, S. (2013, January 3). Meet the New Class: The Senate Swears in a Historic 20 Female Senators. Retrieved October 1, 2014, from http://abcnews.go.com/Politics/meet-class-senate-swears-historic-20-female-senators/story?id=18113363

Millon, T., Millon, C. F., Meagher, S., Grossman, S., & Ramnath, R. (2005). *Personality disorders in modern life.* New York: Wiley.

Milos, M. F. (1992). Circumcision: Don't be conned by the pros. *Journeymen,* 14–16.

Moberly, E. (1983). *Homosexuality: A new Christian ethic.* Cambridge, UK: Clarke.

Money, J. (1987). Sin, sickness, or status? Homosexual gender identity and psychological neuroendocrinology. *American Psychologist, 42,* 384–399.

Moore, T. M., & Stuart, G. L. (2004). Effects of masculine gender role stress on men's cognitive, affective, physiological, and aggressive responses to intimate conflict situations. *Psychology of Men and Masculinity, 5,* 132–142.

Morawski, J. G. (1985). The measurement of masculinity and femininity: Engendering categorical realities. *Journal of Personality, 53,* 196–223.

Morris, E. W. (2012). *Learning the hard way: Masculinity, place and the gender gap in education.* New Brunswick, NJ: Rutgers University Press.

Morrison, T. G., Morrison, M. A., & Hopkins, C. (2003). Striving for bodily perfection? An exploration of the drive for muscularity in Canadian men. *Psychology of Men and Masculinity, 4 (2),* 111–120.

Mosher, D. L., & Tomkins, S. S. (1988). Scripting the macho man: Hypermasculine socialization and enculturation. *Journal of Sex Research, 25*, 60–84.

Movember.com (2014). Homepage. Retrieved July 17, 2014 from www.movember.com.

Minnesota Public Radio (MPR) (2007). Sen. Larry Craig: "I am not gay." Retrieved June 10, 2009 from minnesota.publicradio.org/display/web/2007/08/28/craig/.

Mueller, F. O. (2001). Catastrophic head injuries in high school and collegiate sports. *Journal of Athletic Training, 36*, 312–315.

Munsey, C. (2009). The lesser-known health costs of incarceration. Monitor on Psychology, 40 (7), 12.

Murdock, G. P. (1967). *Ethnographic Atlas*. Pittsburgh, PA: University of Pittsburgh.

Murnen, S. K., Wright, C., & Kaluzny, G. (2002). If "boys will be boys," then girls will be victims? A meta-analytic review of the research that relates masculine ideology to sexual aggression. *Sex Roles, 46*, 359–375.

Murphy, S. L., Xu, J. Q., & Kochanek, K. D. (2013). Deaths: Final data for 2010. *National vital statistics reports, 61 (4)*. Retrieved May 29, 2014 from http://www.cdc.gov/nchs/data/nvsr/nvsr61/nvsr61_04.pdf.

Murray, B. (1998). Study says TV violence still seen as heroic, glamorous: Psychologists call on television executives to embed antiviolence messages in programming. *APA Monitor, 29 (6)*, p. 16.

Myers, B. (1997). NOW promises "No surrender" to right-wing Promise Keepers. *National NOW Times, 29(4)*, pp. 1, 16.

Myers, D. G. (2008). *Social psychology* (9th ed.). Boston: McGraw-Hill.

Nathan, S. (1981). Cross-cultural perspectives on penis envy. *Psychiatry, 44*, 39–44.

National Center for Education Statistics (2010, 2010). Table 212. Enrollment rates of 17– to 24– year olds in degree-granting institutions, by type of institution and sex and race/ethnicity of student: 1967 through 2009. from http://nces.ed.gov/programs/digest/d10/tables/dt10_212.asp?referrer=list

National Center for Health Statistics (2008). Health, United States 2008 with chartbook on trends in the health of Americans. Hyattsville, MD: Center for Disease Control.

National Institute of Mental Health (2003). Suicide in the United States. Retrieved June 17, 2009 from www.policyalmanac.org/health/archive/suicide.shtml.

National Safety Council (2010). *Injury facts* (2010 ed.). Itasca, IL: self.

National Spinal Cord Injury Association (2005). More about spinal cord injury (fact sheet). Retrieved July 30, 2005 from www.spinalcord.org.

"Nearly all Women at Academies are Harassed, Study Says" (1994, February 4). *The Washington Post*, p. D3.

Nelson, J. B. (1988). *The intimate connection: Male sexuality, masculine spirituality*. Philadelphia: Westminster.

Nelson, J. B. (1997). Male sexuality, masculine spirituality. Paper presented at the 22nd Conference on Men and Masculinity, Collegeville, MN.

Nemiah, J. C., Fryberger, H., & Sifneos, P. E. (1976). Alexithymia: A view of the psychosomatic process. In O.W. Hill (Ed.), *Modern trends in psychosomatic medicine*, Vol. 3. London: Butterworths, 430–439.

Neu, T. W. & Weinfeld, R. (2007). *Helping boys succeed in school*. Waco, TX: Prufrock.

Newfield, J. (2001, November 12). The shame of boxing. The Nation, pp. 13–22.

Niku, S. D., Stock, J. A., & Kaplan, G. W. (1995). Neonatal circumcision. *Common Problems in Pediatric Urology, 21*, 57–65.

Nolen-Hoeksema, S. (1998). Gender differences in coping with depression across the lifespan. *Depression, 3*, 81–90.

Nolen-Hoeksema, S. (2006). Thinking too much about trauma: The detrimental effects of rumination. Paper presented at the American Psychological Association Convention, August 10, New Orleans, LA.

Nolen-Hoeksema, S. & Girgus, J. S. (1994). The emergence of gender differences in depression during adolescence. *Psychological Bulletin, 115*, 424–443.

Nolen-Hoeksema, S. & Hilt, L. (2006). Possible contributors to the gender differences in alcohol abuse and problems. *Journal of General Psychology, 133*, 357–374.

NOMAS (National Organization for Men Against Sexism) (2014). NOMAS Statement of Principles. Retrieved July 14, 2014 from www.nomas.org.

"Notre Dame Stuns No. 9 Tennessee" (2004, November 7). *The Washington Post,* E14.

NPR (National Public Radio) (2005, February 9). Laura Bush: Putting boys into the spotlight. Radio interview.

Ochberg, R. (1988). Ambition and impersonality in men's careers. *Men's Studies Review, 1*, 10–13.

O'Donovan, D. (1988). Femiphobia: Unseen enemy of intellectual freedom. *Men's Studies Review, 5*, 14–16.

Olivardia, R., Pope, Jr., H. G., Borowiecki III, J. J., & Cohane, G. H. (2004). Biceps and body image: The relationship between muscularity and self-esteem, depression, and eating disorder symptoms. *Psychology of Men and Masculinity, 5,* 112–120.

Oliver, M. B., & Hyde, J. S. (1993). Gender differences in sexuality: A meta-analysis. *Psychological Bulletin, 114*, 29–51.

O'Neil, J. M. (1981a). Patterns of gender role conflict and strain: Sexism and fear of femininity in men's lives. *Personnel and Guidance Journal, 60*, 203–210.

O'Neil, J. M. (1981b). Male sex role conflicts, sexism, and masculinity: Psychological implications for men, women, and the counseling psychologist. *Journal of Counseling Psychology, 9*, 61–80.

O'Neil, J. M. (1982). Gender role conflict and strain in men's lives. In K. Solomon & N. Levy (Eds.), *Men in transition: Theory and therapy* (pp. 5–43). New York: Plenum.

O'Neil, J. M. (1990). Assessing men's gender role conflict. In D. Moore & F. Leafgren (Eds.), *Men in conflict* (pp. 23–38). Alexandria, VA: American Association for Counseling and Development.

O'Neil, J. M. (2008). Summarizing 25 years of research on men's gender role conflict using the gender role conflict scale: New research paradigms and clinical implications. The Counseling Psychologist, 36, 358–445.

O'Rand, A. M. (1987). Gender. In G. L. Maddox (Ed.), *The Encyclopedia of Aging* (p. 271). New York: Springer.

O'Sullivan, C. S. (1991). Acquaintance gang rape on campus. In A. Parrot & l. Bechofer (Eds.), *Acquaintance rape: The hidden crime* (pp. 140–156). New York: Wiley.

Packard, G. A. (2014). Gays in the military: Why the all-volunteer force didn't "break" with the repeal of "Don't Ask; Don't Tell." Invited address, University of Mary Washington.

Pantony, K. L., & Caplan, P. J. (1991). Delusional dominating personality disorder: A modest proposal for identifying some consequences of rigid masculine socialization. *Canadian Psychology, 32*, 120–135.

Parenti, C. (2001). Rehabilitating prison labor: The uses of imprisoned masculinity. In D. Sabo, T. A. Kupers, & W. London (Eds.). *Prison masculinities*. Philadelphia: Temple University Press.

Parke, R. D., & Tinsley, B. R. (1981). The father's role in infancy: Determinants of involvement in caregiving and play. In M. Lamb (Ed.), *The role of the father in child development* (2nd ed., pp. 429–457). New York: Wiley.

Parker, S., & De Vries, B. (1993). Patterns of friendship for women and men in same- and cross-sex relationships. *Journal of Social and Personal Relationships, 10*, 617–626.

Parks, L. F., Cohen, L., & Kravitz-Wirtz, N. (2007). *Poised for prevention: Advancing promising approaches to primary prevention of intimate partner violence*. Princeton, NJ: Prevention Institute.

Parrot, A. (1991). Recommendations for college policies and procedures to deal with acquaintance rape. In A. Parrot & L. Bechofer (Eds.), *Acquaintance rape: The hidden crime* (pp. 368–380). New York: Wiley.

Parsons, J. T., Starks, T. J., Gamarel, K. E., & Grov, C. (2012). Non-monogamy and sexual relationship quality among same-sex male couples. *Journal of Family Psychology, 26*(5), 669–677.

Pascoe, C. J. (2007). *Dude, You're a Fag: Masculinity and sexuality in high school.* Berkeley, CA: University of California Press.

Pasick, R. S. (1990). Raised to work. In R. L. Meth & R. S. Pasick, *Men in therapy: The challenge of change* (pp. 35–53). New York: Guilford.

Patterson, G. R., Reid, J., & Dishion, T. (1992). *Antisocial boys.* Eugene, OR: Castalia.

Paul, P. (2005). Pornified: How pornography is damaging our lives, our relationships, and our families. New York: Holt.

Pellegrini, A. D. (2004). Sexual segregation in childhood: A review of evidence for two hypotheses. *Animal Behaviour, 68*(3), 435–443.

Pennebaker, J. W. (2002). *Emotion, disclosure, and health.* Washington, DC: American Psychological Association.

Peplau, L. A., & Fingerhut, A. W. (2007). The Close Relationships of Lesbian and Gay Men. *Annual Review of Psychology, 58,* 405–424.

Pepler, D. J., & Slaby, R. G. (1994). Theoretical and developmental perspectives on youth and violence. In L. D. Eron, J. H. Gentry, & P. Schlegel (Eds.), *Reason to hope: A psychosocial perspective on violence and youth* (pp. 27–58). Washington, DC: American Psychological Association.

Peralta, R. L. (2007). College alcohol use and the embodiment of hegemonic masculinity among European American men. *Sex Roles, 56,* 741–756.

Perren, S., Von Wyl, A., Bürgin, D., Simoni, H., & Von Klitzing, K. (2005). Intergenerational Transmission of Marital Quality Across the Transition to Parenthood. *Family Process, 44*(4), 441–459.

Perry, D. G., & Bussey, K. (1979). The social learning theory of sex differences: Imitation is alive and well. *Journal of Personality and Social Psychology, 37,* 1699–1712.

Peskin, H. (1992). Shifts in uses of the past in the Intergenerational Longitudinal Studies. Paper presented at the Annual Meeting of the Gerontological Society of America, Washington, DC.

Peter, J. & Valkenburg, P. M. (2007). Adolescents' exposure to a sexualized media environment and their notions of women as sex objects. *Sex Roles, 56,* 381–395.

Pharr, S. (1997a, July 19). Our search for liberation in the time of the Right. Paper presented at the 22nd National Conference on Men and Masculinity, Collegeville, MN.

Pharr, S. (1997b). *Homophobia: A weapon of sexism.* (Expanded Edition). Little Rock, AR: Chardon.

Phy-Olsen, A. (2006). Historical guides to controversial issues in America: Same-sex marriage. Westport, CT: Greenwood.

Picker, M. & Sun, C. (2008). *The price of pleasure: Pornography, sexuality, and relationships.* Documentary film, Open Lens Media.

Pleck, J. H. (1975). Masculinity-femininity: Current and alternative paradigms. *Sex Roles, 1,* 161–178.

Pleck, J. H. (1981a). *The myth of masculinity.* Cambridge, MA: MIT Press.

Pleck, J. H. (1981b, September). Prisoners of manliness. *Psychology today,* 24–27.

Pleck, J. H. (1987). The theory of male sex-role identity: Its rise and fall, 1936 to the present. In H. Brod (Ed.), *The making of masculinities: The new men's studies* (pp. 21–38). New York: Routledge.

Pleck, J. H. (1988). Letter to the editor. *APA Monitor, 18 (11),* 2.

Pleck, J. H. (1995). The gender role strain paradigm: An update. In R. F. Levant & W. S. Pollack (Eds.), *A new psychology of men* (pp. 11–32). New York: Basic Books.

Pleck, J. H. (1997). Paternal involvement: Levels, sources, and consequences. In M. E. Lamb (Ed.), *The role of the father in child development* (3rd ed., pp. 66–103). New York: Wiley.

Pleck, J. H. (2007). Why could father involvement benefit children? Theoretical perspectives. *Applied Developmental Science, 11*(4), 196–202.

Pleck, J. H., Sonenstein, F. L., & Ku, L. C. (1993). Masculinity ideology: Its impact on adolescent males' heterosexual relationships. *Journal of Social Issues, 49 (3)*, 11–29.

Pleck, J. H., Sonenstein, F. L., & Ku, L. C. (1994). Attitudes toward male roles: A discriminant validity analysis. *Sex Roles, 30*, 481–501. doi: 10.1007/BF01420798

Plummer, D. C. (2001). The quest for modern manhood: Masculine stereotypes, peer culture, and the social significance of homophobia. *Journal of Adolescence, 24 (1)*, 15–23.

Polce-Lynch, M. (2002). *Boy talk: How you can help your son express his emotions.* Oakland, CA: New Harbinger.

Pollack, W. (1998). *Real boys: Rescuing our sons from the myths of boyhood.* New York: Random House.

Pollack, W. (2000). Real boys' voices. Paper presented at the Annual Convention of the American Psychological Association, San Francisco, CA.

Pomerleau, A., Bolduc, D., Malcuit, G., & Cossette, L. (1990). Pink or blue: Environmental stereotypes in the first two years of life. *Sex Roles, 22*, 359–367.

Pope, H. G., Phillips, K. A. & Olivardia, R. (2000). *The Adonis complex: The secret crisis of male body obsession.* New York: Free Press.

Poppen, P. J. (1995). Gender and patterns of sexual risk taking in college students. *Sex Roles, 32*, 545–555.

Prior, P. M. (1999). *Gender and mental health.* New York: New York University Press.

Promundo (2014). Program areas and activities. Retrieved May 21, 2014 from http://www.promundo.org.br/en/activities/programs/.

Pryor, J. B. (1987). Sexual harassment proclivities in men. *Sex Roles, 17*, 269–290.

"Pulling the Trigger" (1998, April 4). *The Washington Post*, p. A18.

Quinlan, R. J. (2008). Human pair-bonds: Evolutionary functions, ecological variation, and adaptive development. *Evolutionary Anthropology, 17*, 227–238.

Rabinowitz, F. E. (2010). Group therapy for men. Paper presented at the Annual Convention of the American Psychological Association, Washington, DC.

Rabinowitz, F. E. & Cochran, S. V. (2002). *Deepening psychotherapy with men.* Washington, DC: American Psychological Association.

Ramsey, L. R. (2005). Personal communication.

Raphael, R. (1988). *The men from the boys: Rites of passage in male America.* Lincoln, NB: University of Nebraska Press.

Rathus, S. A., Nevid, J. S., & Fichner-Rathus, L. (2008). *Human sexuality in a world of diversity* (7th ed.). Boston: Pearson/Allyn & Bacon.

Rauch, J. (2004, June 13). Virginia's new Jim Crow. *The Washington Post*, B7.

Raudenbush, B. & Zellner, D. A. (1997). Nobody's satisfied: Effects of abnormal eating behaviors and actual and perceived weight status on body image satisfaction in males and females. *Journal of Social and Clinical Psychology, 16*, 95–110.

Raver, J. L. & Gelfand, M. J. (2005). Beyond the individual victim: Linking sexual harassment, team processes, and team performance. *Academy of Management Journal, 48*, 387–400.

Real, T. (1997). *I don't want to talk about it: Overcoming the secret legacy of male depression.* New York: Scribner.

Recer, J. (1995). Whose promise are they keeping? *National NOW Times, 27(5)*, p. 14.

Regan, P. C., Durvasula, R., Howell, L., Ureno, O., & Rea, M. (2004). Gender, ethnicity, and the developmental timing of first sexual and romantic experiences. *Social Behavior and Personality, 32*, 667–676.

Reid, H. M., & Fine, G. A. (1992). Self-disclosure in men's friendships. In P. M. Nardi (Ed.), *Men's friendships* (pp. 132–152). Newbury Park, CA: Sage.

Rich, J. A. & Ro, M. (2002). *A poor man's plight: Uncovering the disparity in men's health*. Battle Creek, MI: W. K. Kellogg Foundation.

Richardson, L. (2009). Gender stereotyping in the English language. In V. Taylor, N. Whittier, & L. J. Rupp (Eds.), *Feminist frontiers* (8th ed., pp. 120–126). Boston: McGraw-Hill.

Richardson, S. (1993). A violence in the blood: Five generations of aggressive men in a Dutch family have led researchers to a gene that seems to lie at the root of violence. *Discover, 14(10)*, 30–31.

Richburg, K. B. (2009, July 13). States seek less costly substitutes for prison: Treatment, parole are gaining favor. *The Washington Post*, A1.

Ro, M. J., Casares, C., Treadwell, H. M., & Thomas, S. (2004). *A man's dilemma: Heathcare of men across America: A disparities report*. Atlanta, GA: The National Center for Primary Care at the Morehouse School of Medicine.

Robertson, J. M. (2014). Counseling older men. In M. Englar-Carlson, M. P. Evans, & T. Duffey (Eds., 2014), *A counselor's guide to working with men*. Alexandria, VA: American Counseling Association.

Robertson, J. M., & Fitzgerald, L. F. (1992). Overcoming the masculine mystique: Preferences for alternative forms of assistance among men who avoid counseling. *Journal of Counseling Psychology, 39*, 240–246.

Robinson, D. T., & Schwartz, J. P. (2004). Relationship between gender role conflict and attitudes toward women and African Americans. *Psychology of Men and Masculinity, 5 (1)*, 65–71.

Rochlen, A. B. & Mahalik, J. R. (2004). Women's perceptions of male partners' gender role conflict as predictors of psychological well-being and relationship satisfaction. *Psychology of Men and Masculinity, 5*, 147–157.

Rochlen, A. B., McKelley, R. A., Suizzo, M.-A., & Scaringi, V. (2008). Predictors of relationship satisfaction, psychological well-being, and life satisfaction among stay-at-home fathers. *Psychology of Men & Masculinity, 9*(1), 17–28.

Rochlen, A. B., McKelley, R. A., & Whittaker, T. A. (2010). Stay-at-home fathers' reasons for entering the role and stigma experiences: A preliminary report. *Psychology of Men & Masculinity, 11*(4), 279–285.

Rochlen, A. B., Suizzo, M.-A., McKelley, R. A., & Scaringi, V. (2008). 'I'm just providing for my family': A qualitative study of stay-at-home fathers. *Psychology of Men & Masculinity, 9*(4), 193–206.

Rochlen, A. B. & Rabinowitz, F. E. (Eds., 2014). *Breaking barriers in counseling men: Insights and innovations*. New York: Routledge.

Rochlen, A. B., Whilde, M. R., & Hoyer, W. D. (2005). The Real Men, Real Depression Campaign: Overview, theoretical implications, and research considerations. *Psychology of Men and Masculinity, 6*, 186–194.

Rochlin, C. (1982). The heterosexual questionnaire. *Changing Men, 13*, 1.

Rodin, J., & Ickovics, J. R. (1990). Women's health: Review and research agenda as we approach the 21st century. *American Psychologist, 45*, 1018–1034.

Rogers, C. R. (1957). The necessary and sufficient conditions of therapeutic personality change. *Journal of Consulting Psychology, 21*, 95–103.

Rogers, C. R. (1959). A theory of therapy, personality, and interpersonal relationships, as developed in the client-centered framework. In S. Koch (Ed.), *Psychology: A study of a science: Volume 3: Formulations of the person and the social context* (pp. 184–256). New York: McGraw-Hill.

Rogers, C. R. (1961). *On becoming a person*. Boston: Houghton-Mifflin.

Rogers, C. R. (1980). *A way of being*. Boston: Houghton Mifflin.

Rosenberg, R. S. & Kosslyn, S. M. (2014). *Abnormal psychology* (2nd ed.). New York: Worth.

Rosenblum, K. E. & Travis, T. C. (2003). Framework essay: experiencing difference. In K. E. Rosenblum, & T. C. Travis (Eds.), *The meaning of difference: American constructions of race, sex and gender, social class, and sexual orientation* (3rd ed., pp. 182–202). Boston: McGraw-Hill.

Rosenblum, L. A. (1987). The study of masculinity/femininity from a comparative developmental perspective. In J. M. Reinisch, L. A. Rosenblum, & S. A. Sanders (Eds.), *Masculinity/femininity: Basic perspectives*. New York: Oxford University Press.

Rosenkoetter, L. I., Rosenkoetter, S. E., Osretich, R. A., & Acock, A. C. (2004). Mitigating the harmful effects of violent television. Journal of Applied Developmental Psychology, 25, 25–47.

Rosenstein, M. J., Steadman, H. J., McAskill, R. L., & Manderscheid, R. W. (1987). *Characteristics of admissions to Veterans Administrations medical center psychiatric inpatient services, United States, 1980*. Rockville, MD: Department of Health and Human Services.

Rosin, H., & Edsall, T. B. (1998, July 15). Religious right targets homosexuality: Ad, fund-raising drive coordinated. *The Washington Post*, pp. A1, A13.

Rospenda, K. M., Richman, J. A., & Shannon, C. A. (2009). Prevalence and mental health correlates of harassment and discrimination in the workplace: Results from a national study. *Journal of Interpersonal Violence, 24*(5), 819–843.

Rotundo, E. A. (1993). *American manhood: Transformations in masculinity from the Revolution to the modern era*. New York: Basic Books.

Rowlands, A. V., Pilgrim, E. L., & Eston, R. G. (2008). Patterns of habitual activity across weekdays and weekend days in 9–11–year-old children. *Preventive Medicine: An International Journal Devoted to Practice and Theory, 46*(4), 317–324.

Royner, S. (1992, February 4). What men won't tell. *Washington Post Health*, p. 10.

Ruble, D. N., & Martin, C. L. (1998). Gender Development. In W. Damon & N. Eisenberg (Eds.), *Handbook of Child Psychology* (Vol. 5th, pp. 933–1016). NY: John Wiley & Sons.

Rudman, L. A. & Glick, P. (2001). Prescriptive gender stereotypes and backlash toward agentic women. *Journal of Social Issues, 57 (4)*, 743–762.

Rudman, L. A., & Phelan, J. E. (2007). The interpersonal power of feminism: Is feminism good for romantic relationships? *Sex Roles, 57*(11–12), 787–799.

Russo, A. (1998). Feminists confront pornography's subordinating practices: Politics and strategies for change. In G. Dines, R. Jensen, & A. Russo, *Pornography: The production and consumption of inequality* (pp. 9–35). New York: Routledge.

Ruxton, S. (Ed., 2004). *Gender equality and men: Learning from practice*. Oxford, UK: Oxfam.

Rybarczyk, B. (1994). Diversity among American men: The impact of aging, ethnicity and race. In C. T. Kilmartin, *The masculine self*. New York: Macmillan.

Sabo, D. (2000). Men in prison. Paper presented at the annual conference of the American Men's Studies Association, Nashville, TN.

Sabo, D. (2005). The study of masculinities and men's health. In M. S. Kimmel, J. Hearn, & R. W. Connell (Eds.), *Handbook of studies on men and masculinities*. Thousand Oaks, CA: Sage.

Sabo, D., Kupers, T. A., & London, W. (Eds., 2001). *Prison masculinities*. Philadelphia: Temple University Press.

Sabol, W. J., & Coture, H. (2008). Prison inmates at midyear 2007. Retrieved on June 22, 2009 from www.ojp.usdoj.gov/bjs/pub/pdf/pim07.pdf.

Sadker, D. (2000, July 31). Gender games. *The Washington Post*, A19.

Sadker, M., & Sadker, D. (1985). Sexism in the classroom of the '80s. *Psychology Today, 3*, 54–57.

Sadler, A. G., Booth, B. M., Cook, B. L., & Doebbeling, B. N. (2003). Factors associated with women's risk of rape in the military environment. *American Journal of Industrial Medicine, 43,* 262–273.

Sanabria, S. (2014). Affirmative therapy with sexual minority men. In M. Englar-Carlson, M. P. Evans, & T. Duffey (Eds., 2014), *A counselor's guide to working with men.* Alexandria, VA: American Counseling Association.

Sánchez, F. J., Bocklandt, S., & Vilain, E. (2009). Gender role conflict, interest in casual sex, and relationship satisfaction among gay men. *Psychology of Men & Masculinity, 10*(3), 237–243.

Sanchez, F. J., Greenberg, S. T., Liu, W. M., & Vilain, E. (2009). Reported effects of masculine ideals on gay men. *Psychology of Men and Masculinity, 10,* 73–87.

Sanchez, R. (1996, November 17). Men's studies coming of age in new campus rite of passage: Female attendance attests: It's not just a guy thing. *The Washington Post,* pp. A1, A11.

Sanday, P. R. (1981). The socio-cultural context of rape: A cross-cultural study. *Journal of Social Issues, 37,* 5–27.

Sanday, P. R. (1996). *A woman scorned: Acquaintance rape on trial.* New York: Doubleday.

Sanday, P. R. (2007). *Fraternity gang rape: Sex, brotherhood, and privilege on campus.* New York: New York University Press.

Sandler, B. R. & Shoop, R. J. (1997). What is sexual harassment? In B. R. Sandler & R. J. Shoop (Eds.), *Sexual harassment on campus: A guide for administrators, faculty, and students.* New York: Allyn & Bacon.

Sapolsky, R. M. (1997). The trouble with testosterone: Will boys just be boys? In R. M. Sapolsky, *The trouble with testosterone and other essays on the biology of the human predicament* (pp. 147–159). New York: Touchstone.

SAPRO (2012). Department of Defense annual report on sexual assault in the military, fiscal year 2012: Volume 1. Retrieved June 3, 2014 from http://www.sapr.mil/public/docs/reports/FY12_DoD_

SAPRO_Annual_Report_on_Sexual_Assault-VOLUME_ONE.pdf.

Sattel, J. (1998). Men, inexpressiveness, and power. In B. M. Clinchy & J. K. Norem (Eds.), *The gender and psychology reader* (pp. 498–504). New York: New York University Press.

Saunders, S., & Easteal, P (2013). The nature, pervasiveness and manifestations of sexual harassment in rural Australia: Does 'masculinity' of workplace make a difference? *Women's Studies International Forum, 40,* 121–131.

Savin-Williams, R. C. (1995). An exploratory study of pubertal maturation timing and self-esteem among gay and bisexual male youths. *Developmental Psychology, 31,* 56–64.

Savin-Williams, R. C. (1998). *"...and then I became gay".* NY: Routledge.

Savin-Williams, R. C. (2005). *The New Gay Teenager.* Cambridge, MA: Harvard University press.

Sax, L. (2009). *Boys Adrift: The Five Factors Driving the Growing Epidemic of Unmotivated Boys and Underachieving Young Men.* New York: Basic Books.

Scarborough, R. (2013). Victims of military sexual assault are mostly men; Women are more likely to speak up. The Washington Times, Retrieved August 26, 2013 from http://www.washingtontimes.com/news/2013/may/20/victims-of-sex-assaults-in-military-are-mostly-sil/.

Scarce, M. (1997a). *Male on male rape: The hidden toll of stigma and shame.* New York: Plenum.

Scarce, M. (1997b). Same-sex rape of male college students. *Jounal of American College Health, 45,* 171–173.

Schein, V. E. (2001). A global look at psychological barriers to women's progress in management. *Journal of Social Issues, 57 (4),* 675–688.

Schmitt, D. P. (2005). Fundamentals of human mating strategies. In D. M. Buss (Ed.), *Handbook of Evolutionary Psychology* (pp. 255–291). Hoboken, NJ: Wiley.

Schwartz, P. (1994). *Love between equals: How peer marriage really works.* New York: Free Press.

Schwarz, A. (2007, September 15). Silence on concussions raises risk of injury. Retrieved June 2, 2014 from http://www.nytimes.com/2007/09/15/sports/football/15concussions.html?pagewanted=all&_r=0.

Schwartz, J. (2008). Gender differences in drunk driving prevalence rates and trends: A 20–year assessment using multiple sources of evidence. *Addictive Behaviors, 33,* 1217–1222.

Schwartz, S. J., Zamboanga, B. L., Ravert, R. D., Kim, S. Y., Weisskirch, R. S., Williams, M. K., Bersamin, M., & Finley, G. E. (2009). Perceived parental relationships and health-risk behaviors in college-attending emerging adults. *Journal of Marriage and Family, 71,* 727–740.

Seidman, I. & Pokorak, J. J. (2011). Justice responses to sexual violence. In M. P. Koss, J. W. White, & A. E. Kazdin (Eds.*),* *Violence against women and children, Volume 2: Navigating solutions.* Washington, DC: American Psychological Association.

Seligman, M. E. P. (1990a). Attributional style and depression. Paper presented at the annual meeting of the Eastern Psychological Association, Philadelphia, PA.

Seligman, M. E. P. (1990b). *Learned optimism: How to change your mind and your life.* New York: Simon & Schuster.

The Sentencing Project (2014). Incarceration. Retrieved July 14, 2014 from sentencingproject.org/template/page.cfm?id=107.

The Sentencing Project (2004). Facts about prisons and prisoners. Retrieved June 22, 2009 from www.sentencingproject.org/pdfs/1035.pdf.

Settles, I. H., Buchanan, N. T., & Colar, B. K. (2012). The impact of race and rank on the sexual harassment of Black and White men in the U.S. military. *Psychology of Men & Masculinity, 13*(3), 256–263.

Shabsigh, R., Fishman, I, & Scott, F. (1988). Evaluation of erectile impotence. *Urology, 32,* 83–90.

Shannon, C. A., Rospenda, K. M., & Richman, J. A. (2007). Workplace harassment patterning, gender, and utilization of professional services: Findings from a US national study. *Social Science & Medicine, 64*(6), 1178–1191.

Shankar, P. R., Fields, S. K., Collins, C. L., Dick, R. W., & Comstock, D. (2007). Epidemiology of high school and collegiate football injuries in the United States, 2005–2006. *American Journal of Sports Medicine, 35,* 1295–1303.

Shanker, T. (2013, July 8). For Navy recruits, basic training now targets sexual assault. *The New York Times,* A1.

Shannon, J. D., Cabrera, N. J., Tamis-LeMonda, C., & Lamb, M. E. (2009). Who stays and who leaves? Father accessibility across children's first 5 years. *Parenting: Science and Practice, 9*(1–2), 78–100.

Sharockman, A. (2014). What pay gap? Young women out-earn men in cities, conservative pundit claims. Retrieved October 1, 2014, from http://www.politifact.com/punditfact/statements/2014/apr/09/genevieve-wood/what-pay-gap-young-women-out-earn-men-cities-gop-p/

Shaver, P. R., Segev, M., & Mikulincer, M. (2011). A behavioral systems perspective on power and aggression. In P. R. Shaver & M. Mikulincer (Eds.), *Human aggression and violence: Causes, manifestations, and consequences.* Washington, DC: American Psychological Association.

Sheehy, G. (1976). *Passages.* New York: Dutton.

Shepard, S. J., Nicpon, M. F., Haley, J. T., Lind, M., & Liu, W. M. (2011). Masculine norms, school attitudes, and psychosocial adjustment among gifted boys. *Psychology of Men & Masculinity, 12*(2), 181–187. doi: 10.1037/a0019945

Shields, S. A. (2005). The politics of emotion in everyday life: "Appropriate" emotion and claims on identity. *Review of General Psychology, 9,* 3–15.

Shields, S. A. (2010). *Speaking from the heart: Gender and the social meaning of emotion.* Cambridge, UK: Cambridge University Press.

128000

Sifneos, P. E. (1972). *Short-term psychotherapy and emotional crisis*. Cambridge, MA: Harvard University Press.

Sigelman, C. K., & Rider, E. A. (2009). *Lifespan Human Development* (Vol. 6th). Belmont, CA: Wadsworth.

Silverstein, L. B. & Auerbach, C. F. (1999). Deconstructing the essential father. *American Psychologist, 54*, 397–407.

Skinner, B. F. (1974). *About behaviorism*. New York: Alfred A. Knopf.

Skovholt, T. M. (1990). Career themes in counseling and psychotherapy with men. In D. Moore & F. Leafgren (Eds.), *Men in conflict* (pp. 39–53). Alexandria, VA: American Association for Counseling and Development.

Skovholt, T. M., & Hansen, A. (1980). Men's development: A perspective and some themes. In T. M. Skovholt, P. Schauble, & R. David (Eds.), *Counseling men* (pp. 1–39). Monterey, CA: Brooks/Cole.

Slaatten, H., Anderssen, N., & Hetland, J. (2014). Endorsement of male role norms and gay-related name-calling. *Psychology of Men & Masculinity, 15*(3), 335–345.

Slevin, P. (2005, July 26). Prison experts see opportunity for improvement. *The Washington Post*, A3.

Sloane, M., Hanna, J., & Ford, D. (2013, September 3). 'Never, ever give up:' Diana Nyad completes historic Cuba-to-Florida swim. Retrieved July 3, 2014, from http://www.cnn.com/2013/09/02/world/americas/diana-nyad-cuba-florida-swim/

Smiler, A. P. (2004). Thirty years after the discovery of gender: Psychological concepts and measures of masculinity. *Sex Roles, 50*, 15–26.

Smiler, A. P. (2006). Conforming to masculine norms: Evidence for validity among adult men and women. *Sex Roles, 54*, 767–775.

Smiler, A. P. (2011). Sexual Strategies Theory: Built for the short term or the long term. *Sex Roles, 64*, 603–612.

Smiler, A. P. (2013). *Challenging Casanova: Beyond the Steroetype of Promiscuous Young Male Sexuality*. San Francisco: Jossey-Bass.

Smiler, A. P. & Epstein, M. (2010). Issues in the measurement of gender. In J. Chrisler & D. R. McCreary (Eds.), *Handbook of gender research in psychology*. New York: Springer.

Smiler, A. P., Frankel, L., & Savin-Williams, R. C. (2011). From kissing to coitus? Sex-of-partner differences in the sexual milestone achievement of young men. *Journal of Adolescence, 34*, 727–735.

Smiler, A. P. & Gelman, S. (2008). Determinants of gender essentialism in college students. *Sex Roles*, 58, 864–874.

Smiler, A. P., & Heasley, R. (in press). Boys and Men's Intimate Relationships: Friendships and Romantic Relationships. In J. Wong & S. R. Wester (Eds.), *Handbook of Men and Masculinities*. Washington, DC: American Psychological Association.

Smiler, A. P., Kay, G., & Harris, B. (2008). Tightening and loosening masculinity's (k)nots: Masculinity in the Hearst press during the interwar period. *Journal of Men's Studies, 16*, 266–279.

Smiler, A. P., Ward, L. M., Caruthers, A., & Merriwether, A. (2005). Pleasure, empowerment, and love: Factors associated with a positive first coitus. *Sexual research and social policy: Journal of NSRC, 2*, 41–55.

Smith, A. M. (1993). "What is pornography?: An analysis of the policy statement of the Campaign Against Pornography and Censorship. *Feminist Review, 43*, 71–87.

Smith, D. (2003). Angry thoughts, at risk hearts. *Monitor on Psychology, 34 (3)*, 46–48.

Smith, K. (1971). Homophobia: A tentative personality profile. *Psychological Reports*, 29, 1091–1094.

Smith, L., & Mathews, J. (1997, December 7). In Va., a sobering lesson doesn't sink in: Binge drinking remains common on college campuses, despite recent tragedies. *The Washington Post*, pp. B1, B7.

Smolak, L., Murnen, S. K., & Thompson, J. K. (2005). Sociocultural influences and muscle building in adolescent boys. *Psychology of Men and Masculinity, 6 (4)*, 227–239.

Snow, M. E., Jacklin, C. N., & Maccoby, E. E. (1981). Birth- order differences in peer sociability at thirty-three months. *Child Development, 52,* 589–595.

Sodomylaws.org (2009). Sodomy laws around the world. Retrieved June 10, 2009 from http://www.sodomylaws.org/index.htm.

Sommers, C. H. (2001). *The war against boys: How misguided feminism is harming our young men.* New York: Simon & Schuster.

Spence, J. T., & Helmreich, R. L. (1978). *Masculinity and femininity: Their psychological dimensions, correlates and antecedents.* Austin, TX: University of Texas Press.

Spence, J. T., Helmreich, R. L., & Holahan, C. K. (1979). Negative and positive components of psychological masculinity and femninity and their relationships to self-reports of neurotic and acting out behaviors. *Journal of Personality and Social Psychology, 37,* 1673–1682.

Spitzer, R. L. (2003). Can some gay men and lesbians change their sexual orientation? 200 participants reporting a change from homosexual to heterosexual orientation. *Archives of Sexual Behavior, 32*(5), 403–417.

Spitzer, R. L. (2012). Spitzer reassesses his 2003 study of reparative therapy of homosexuality. *Archives of Sexual Behavior, 41*(4), 757–757.

Sports Illustrated (2014). Judge Anita Brody denies preliminary approval for NFL concussion settlement. Retrieved June 20, 2014 from http://nfl.si.com/2014/01/14/nfl-concussion-lawsuit-settlement-2/.

Sprecher, S., & Regan, P. C. (2002). Liking some things (in some people) more than others: Partner preferences in romantic relationships and friendships. *Journal of Social and Personal Relationships, 19,* 463–481.

Stander, V. A., Merrill, L. L., Thomsen, C. J., Crouch, J. L., & Milner, J. S. (2008). Pre-military adult sexual assault victimization and perpetration in a Navy recruit sample.

Journal of Interpersonal Violence, 23, 1636–1652.

Stanistreet, D., Bambra, C., & Scott-Samuel, A. (2005). Is patriarchy the source of men's higher mortality? *Journal of Epidemiological Community Health, 59,* 873–876.

Stapely, J. C., & Haviland, J. M. (1989). Beyond depression: Gender differences in normal adolescents' emotional experiences. *Sex Roles, 20,* 295–308.

Starrels, M. E. (1994). Husbands' involvement in female gender-typed household chores. *Sex Roles, 31,* 473–491.

Stearns, P. N. (1990). *Be a man! Males in modern society.* New York: Holmes and Meier.

Stearns, P. N. (1991). Fatherhood in historical perspective: The role of social change. In F. W. Bozett & S. M. H. Hanson (Eds.), *Fatherhood and families in cultural context* (pp. 28–52). New York: Springer.

Steeves, V. (2014). Young Canadians in a Wired World, Phase III: Sexuality and Romantic Relationships in the Digitial Age. Ottawa: MediaSmarts.

Stein, R. (1998). Brain scan suggests some are born with violent tendencies. *The Washington Post,* p. A3.

Stein, R. (2005, June 20). Report shows drop in baby boys. *The Washington Post,* p. A5.

Stern, G. (2014). Personal communication.

Sternberg, R. J. (1999). The theory of successful intelligence. *Review of General Psychology, 3*(4), 292–316.

Stevenson, M. R., & Black, K. N. (1988). Paternal absence and sex-role development: A meta-analysis. *Child Development, 59,* 793–814.

Stewart, A. J., & Newton, N. J. (2010). Gender, adult development, and aging. In J. C. Chrisler & D. R. McCreary (Eds.), *Handbook of gender research in psychology, Vol 1: Gender research in general and experimental psychology.* (pp. 559–580). New York: Springer Science and Business Media.

Stibbe, A. (2004). Health and the social construction of masculinity in *Men's Health* magazine. *Men and Masculinities, 7 (1)*, 31–51.

Stillion, J. M. (1995). Premature death among males. In D. Sabo & D. F. Gordon (Eds.), *Men's health and illness: Gender, power, and the body* (pp. 46–67). Thousand Oaks, CA: Sage.

Stillion, J. M., & McDowell, E. E. (1996). *Suicide across the life span* (2nd ed.). Washington, DC: Taylor and Francis.

Stith, S. M. & McMonigle, C. L. (2009). Risk factors associated with intimate partner violence. In D.J. Whitaker & J. R. Lutzker (Eds.). Preventing partner violence: Research and evidence-based strategies. Washington, DC: American Psychological Association.

Stockdale, M. S. & Bhattacharya, G. (2009). Sexual harassment and the glass ceiling. In M. Barreto, M. K. Ryan, & M. T. Schmitt (Eds.), The glass ceiling in the 21ˢᵗ Century: Understanding barriers to gender equality (pp. 171–199). Washington, DC: American Psychological Association.

Storey, A. E., Walsh, C. J., Quinton, R. L., & Wynne-Edwards, K. E. (2000). Hormonal correlates of paternal responsiveness in new and expectant fathers. *Evolution and human behavior, 21 (2)*, 79–95.

Strasburger, V. C., Wilson, B. J., & Jordan, A. B. (2014). *Children, adolescents, and the media* (3ʳᵈ ed.). Thousand Oaks, CA: Sage.

Strasser, M. (Ed., 2007). *Defending same-sex marriage: "Separate but equal" no more: A guide to the legal status of same-sex marriage, civil unions, and other partnerships*. Westport, CT: Praeger.

Strate, L. (1992). Beer commercials: A manual on masculinity. In S. Craig (Ed.), *Men, masculinity, and the media* (pp. 78–92). Newbury Park, CA: Sage.

Straus, M. A. (1990). *Physical violence in American families: Risk factors and adaptations to violence in 8,145 families*. New Brunswick, NJ: Transaction.

Street, S., Kimmel, E. B., & Kromrey, J. D. (1995). Revisiting university student gender role perceptions. *Sex Roles, 33*, 183–201.

Strong, E. K., Jr. (1943). *Vocational interests of men and women*: Stanford University Press.

Strong, B., DeVault, C., Sayad, B. W., & Yarber, W. L. (2007). *Human sexuality: Diversity in contemporary America* (6th ed.). Boston: McGraw-Hill.

Sue, David, Sue, Derald, Sue, Diane, and Sue, S. (2014). *Essentials of Understanding abnormal behavior* (2nd ed.) Belmont, CA: Cengage.

Sue, D. W., Bernier, J. E., Durran, A., Feinberg, L., Pederson, P., Smith, E., & Vasquez-Nattall, E. (1982). Position paper: Cross-cultural counseling competencies (Education and Training Committee, Division 17, American Psychological Association), *The Counseling Psychologist, 10*, 45–52.

Sugarman, D. B., & Hotaling, G. T. (1989). Violent men in intimate relationships: An analysis of risk markers. *Journal of Applied Social Psychology, 19*, 1034–1048.

Swain, S. O. (1992). Men's friendships with women: Intimacy, sexual boundaries, and the informant role. In P. M. Nardi (Ed.), *Men's friendships* (pp. 153–171). Newbury Park, CA: Sage.

Symons, D. (1987). An evolutionary approach. In J. H. Geer & W. T. O'Donahue (Eds.), *Theories of human sexuality* (pp. 91–125). New York: Plenum.

Szymanski, D. M., Kashubeck-West, S., & Meyer, J. (2008). Internalized heterosexism: A historical and theoretical overview. *The Counseling Psychologist, 36*, 510–524.

Tangri, S., Burt, M. R., & Johnson, L. B. (1982). Sexual harassment at work: Three explanatory models. *Journal of Social Issues, 38*, 33–54.

Tannen, D. (1990). *You just don't understand: Women and men in conversation*. New York: Morrow.

Taris, T. W., van Beek, I., & Schaufeli, W. B. (2012). Demographic and occupational correlates of workaholism. *Psychological Reports, 110*(2), 547–554.

Tavris, C. (1989). *Anger: The misunderstood emotion* (rev. ed.). New York: Touchstone.

Tavris, C. (1992). *The mismeasure of woman.* New York: Simon and Schuster.

Tavris, C. & Aronson, E. (2008). Mistakes were made, but not by me: Why we justify foolish beliefs, bad decisions, and hurtful acts. New York: Houghton Mifflin Harcourt.

Tavris, C. & Wade, C. (2001). Psychology in perspective (3rd ed.). Upper Saddle River, NJ: Prentice-Hall.

Tavris, C., & Wade, C. (2008). Invitation to psychology (4th ed.). Upper Saddle River, NJ: Pearson Prentice-Hall.

Taylor, P. (1995, September 8). His home--the Capitol--was his castle. *The Washington Post*, pp. A1, A17.

Tennenbaum, H. R. & Leaper, C. (2002). Are parents' gender schemas related to their children's gender related cognitions? A meta-analysis. Developmental Psychology, 38 (4), 615–630.

Terman, L. M., & Miles, C. C. (1936). *Sex and personality: Studies in masculinity and femininity.* New York: McGraw-Hill.

Thomas, A., & Chess, S. (1977). *Temperament and Development.* NY, NY, USA: Brunner/Mazel Publishers.

Thompson, Jr., E. H. (Ed.) (1994). *Older men's lives.* Newbury Park, CA: Sage.

Thompson, Jr., E. H., & Pleck, J. H. (1995). Masculinity ideologies: a review of research instrumentation on men and masculinities. In R. F. Levant & W. S. Pollack (Eds.), *A new psychology of men* (pp. 129–163). New York: Basic Books.

Thorne, B. (2009). Girls and boys together… but mostly apart: Gender arrangements in elementary schools. In V. Taylor, N. Whittier, & L. J. Rupp (Eds.), *Feminist frontiers* (8th ed., pp. 176–186). Boston: McGraw-Hill.

Thorne, B. & Luria, Z. (1986). Sexuality and gender in children's daily worlds. *Social Problems, 33*, 176–190).

Thornhill, R. & Palmer, C. T. (2000). *A natural history of rape: Biological bases of sexual coercion.* Cambridge, MA: MIT Press.

Tillich, P. (1952). *The courage to be.* New Haven, CT: Yale University Press.

Tinkler, J. E. (2013). How do sexual harassment policies shape gender beliefs? An exploration of the moderating effects of norm adherence and gender. *Social Science Research, 42*(5), 1269–1283.

Timmers, M., Fischer, A., & Manstead, A. S. R. (1998). Gender differences in motives for regulating closeness. *Personality and Social Psychology Bulletin, 24*, 974–985.

Tjaden, P. & Thonnes, N. (2000). Extent, nature, and consequences of intimate partner violence: Findings from the National Violence Against Women Survey. Retrieved June 22, 2009 from www.ncjrs.gov/pdf-files1/nij/181867.pdf.

Toby, J. (1966). Violence and the masculine mystique: Some qualitative data. *Annals of the American Academy of Political and Social Science, 36*, 19–27.

Toch, H. (1992). *Violent men: An inquiry into the psychology of violence.* Washington, DC: American Psychological Association.

Tooby, J., & Cosmides, L. (2005). Conceptual foundations of evolutionary psychology. In D. M. Buss (Ed.), *Handbook of Evolutionary Psychology* (pp. 5–67). Hoboken, NJ: Wiley.

Trafford, A. (1996, February 20). Boxing's biggest risk. *Washington Post Health*, p. 14.

Tschann, J. (1988). Self-disclosure in adult friendship: Gender and marital status differences. *Journal of Social and Personal Relationships, 5*, 65–81.

Tucker, N. (2003, July 26). Reform plan targets prison rape: Congress unanimously approves study, efforts to stop assaults. *The Washington Post*, A10.

Twenge, J. M. (1997a). Attitudes toward women, 1970–1995: A meta-analysis. *Psychology of Women Quarterly, 21*(1), 35–51.

Twenge, J. M. (1997b). Changes in masculine and feminine traits over time: A meta-analysis. *Sex Roles, 36*, 305–325.

Tyson, P. (1986). Male gender identity: Early developmental roots. *The Psychoanalytic Review, 73*, 405–426.

Unger, R. K. (1979). Toward a redefinition of sex and gender. *American Psychologist, 34*, 1085–1094.

United States Bureau of the Census (USBC) (2009). American Community Survey: Age and sex. Retrieved June 17, 2009 from factfinder.census.gov/servlet/STTable?_bm=y&-geo_id=01000US&-qr_name=ACS_2007_3YR_G00_S0101&-ds_name=ACS_2007_3YR_G00_

United States Bureau of the Census (USBC) (2014). Annual estimates of the resident population by sex, race, and Hispanic origin for the United States, states, and counties: April 1, 2010 to July 1, 2013. Retrieved July 14, 2014 from factfinder2.census.gov/faces/tableservices/jsf/pages/productview.xhtml?src=bkmk.

United States Department of Justice (2008). Criminal victimization in the United States, 2006 statistical tables. Retrieved May 7, 2009, from http://www.ojp.usdoj.gov/bjs.

United States Department of Justice, Office of Justice Programs (OJP) (2008). Most victims and perpetrators of homicides are males. Retrieved July 8, 2009 from ojp.usdoj.gov/bjs/homicide/gender.

United States Department of Labor, Bureau of Labor Statistics (2005). Families with own children: Employment status of parents by age of youngest child and family type, 2003–04 annual averages. www.bls.gov.

United States General Accounting Office (2004). Defense of Marriage Act: Update to prior report [GAO-04-353R]. Retrieved June 10, 2009 from www.gao.gov/new.items/d04353r.pdf.

Uy, P. J., Massoth, N. A., & Gottdiener, W. H. (2014). Rethinking male drinking: Traditional masculine ideologies, gender-role conflict, and drinking motives. *Psychology of Men and Masculinity, 15*, 121–128.

VanderDrift, L. E., Wilson, J. E., & Agnew, C. R. (2013). On the benefits of valuing being friends for nonmarital romantic partners. *Journal of Social and Personal Relationships, 30*(1), 115–131. doi: 10.1177/0265407512453009

Vaillant, G. E. (1977). *Adaptation to life.* Boston: Little, Brown.

Vandello, J. A., Bosson, J. K., Cohen, D., Burnaford, R. M., & Weaver, J. R. (2008). Precarious manhood. *Journal of Personality and Social Psychology, 95*, 1325–1339.

van Hertum, A. (1992, January 17). WHO removes homosexuality from its list of disorders. *The Washington Blade, 23* (3), pp. 1, 12.

Vásquez, D. A., Newman, J. L., Frey, L. L., Caze, T. J., Friedman, A. N., & Meek, W. D. (2014). Relational Health and Masculine Gender Role Conflict in the Friendships and Community Relationships of Bisexual, Gay, and Straight Men. *Journal of LGBT Issues in Counseling, 8*, 124–145.

Vernacchio, A. (2014). *For Goodness Sex: Changing the Way We Talk to Teens About Sexuality, Values, and Health.* NY: HarperCollins.

Vigil, J. M. (2007). Asymmetries in the friendship preferences and social styles of men and women. *Human Nature, 18*, 143–161. doi: 10.1007/s12110–007–9003–3

Vilain, E., Achermann, J. C., Eugster, E. A., Harley, V. R., Morel, Y., Wilson, J. D., & Hiort, O. (2007). We used to call them hermaphrodites. *Genetics in Medicine, 9*, 65–66.

Vobejda, B. (1995, August 17). Survey finds familiar face on sex crime: Four out of five victims report they knew assailant. *The Washington Post*, p. A6.

Voyer, D., & Voyer, S. D. (2014). Gender differences in scholastic achievement: A meta-analysis. *Psychological Bulletin.*

Wade, C. & Tavris, C. (2008). *Invitation to psychology* (4th ed.). Upper Saddle River, NJ: Prentice-Hall.

Wade, J. C. (1998). Male reference group identity dependence: A theory of male identity. *Counseling Psychologist, 26,* 349–383. doi: 10.1177/0011000098263001

Wade, J. C. (2008a). Masculinity ideology, male reference group identity dependence, and African American men's health related attitudes and behaviors. *Psychology of Men and Masculinity, 9,* 5–16.

Wade, J. C. (2008a). Tradtional masculinity and African American men's health related attitudes and behaviors. *American Journal of Men's Health, 3,* 165–172.

Wade, J. C. & Brittan-Powell, C. (2001). Men's attitudes toward race and gender equity: The importance of masculinity ideology, gender-related traits, and reference group identity dependence. *Psychology of Men and Masculinity, 1,* 98–108.

Wade, J. C., & Donis, E. (2007). Masculinity ideology, male identity, and romantic relationship quality among heterosexual and gay men. *Sex Roles, 57*(9–10), 775–786. doi: 10.1007/s11199-007-9303-4

Wagner, E. J. (1992). *Sexual harassment in the workplace: How to prevent, investigate, and resolve problems in your organization.* New York: AMACOM.

Walker, D. F., Tokar, D. M., & Fischer, A. R. (2000). What are eight popular masculinity related instruments measuring? Underlying dimensions and their relations to psychosexuality. *Psychology of Men and Masculinity, 1,* 98–108.

Ward, L. M. & Friedman, K. (2006). Using TV as a guide: Associations between television viewing and adolescents' sexual attitudes and behavior. *Journal of Research on Adolescence, 16,* 133–156.

Wardle, J. Haase, A. M., Steptoe, A., Nillapun, M., Jonwutiwes, K. & Bellisle, F. (2004). Gender differences in food choice: The contribution of healthy beliefs and dieting. *Annals of Behavioral Medicine, 27,* 107–116.

Watkins, S. (1997). *The black O: Racism and redemption in an American corporate empire.* Athens, GA: University of Georgia Press.

Way, N. (2011). *Deep Secrets: Boys' Friendships and the Crisis of Connection.* Cambridge, MA: Harvard University Press.

Way, N., Cressen, J., Bodian, S., Preston, J., Nelson, J., & Hughes, D. (2014). "It might be nice to be a girl... Then you wouldn't have to be emotionless": Boys' resistance to norms of masculinity during adolescence. *Psychology of Men & Masculinity, 15*(3), 241–252.

Webb, J. (2009, March 29). What's wrong with our prisons? *Parade Magazine,* 4–5.

WebMD (2009). Circumcision: A new weapon against AIDS? Retrieved June 19, 2009 from www.webmd.com/hiv-aids/news/20070329/circumcision-new-weapon-against-aids.

Webster, D. W. & Vernick, J. S. (2013). Introduction. In D. W. Webster & J. S. Vernick (Eds.), *Reducing gun violence in America: Informing policy with evidence and analysis.* Baltimore, MD: Johns Hopkins University Press.

Wechsler, H., Kuh, G., & Davenport, A. E. (1996). Fraternities, sororities, and binge drinking: Results from a national study of American colleges. *National Association of Student Personnel Administrators, 33,* 831–847.

Weinstein, M. D., Smith, M. D., & Wiesenthal, D. L. (1995). Masculinity and hockey violence. *Sex Roles, 33,* 831–847.

Weinstock, H., Berman, S., & Cates, Jr. (2004). Sexually transmitted diseases among American youth: Incidence and prevalence estimates, 2000. *Perspectives on Sexual and Reproductive Health, 36,* 6–10.

Weir, D. R., Jackson, J. S., & Sonnega, A. (2009). National football League Player Care Foundation study of retired NFL players. Retrieved October 27, 2009 fromhttp://umich.edu/news/Releases/2009/Sep09/FinalReport.pdf.

Weiss, R. S. (1990). *Staying the course: The emotional and social lives of men who do well at work.* New York: Macmillan.

Wen, P. (2004, November 29). More people are looking for spouses who will share housework, house payments. The Boston Globe, A3.

West, H. C. (2010). Bureau of Justice Statistics Bulletin: Prison inmates at midyear 2009. Retrieved July 14, 2014 from www.bjs.gov/content/pub/pdf/pim09st.pdf.

Wester, S. R., Pionke, D. R., & Vogel, D. L. (2005). Male Gender Role Conflict, Gay Men, and Same-Sex Romantic Relationships. Psychology of Men & Masculinity, 6(3), 195–208.

Wester, S. R., Vogel, D. L., Pressly, P. K., & Heesacker, M. (2002). Sex differences in emotion: A critical review of the literature and implications for counseling psychology. The Counseling Psychologist, 30, 630–652.

Wheeler, L. (1997, October 5). Unofficial estimates point to crowded day on the Mall. The Washington Post, p. A17.

White, H. R., & Huselid, R. F. (1997). Gender differences in alcohol use during adolescence. In R. W. Wilsnack & S. C. Wilsnack (Eds.), Gender and alcohol: Individual and social perspectives (pp. 176–198). New Brunswick, NJ: Rutgers Center of Alcohol Studies.

White, J. (2005, December 23). Air Force Academy shows improvement: Rigorous training credited for decrease in reported cases of sexual misconduct. The Washington Post, A2.

Whiting, B. (1965). Sex identity conflict and physical violence: A comparative study. In L. Nader (Ed.), The ethnography of law (pp.123–140). Menasha, WI: American Anthropological Association.

Whiting, B. B., & Edwards, C. P. (1988). Children of different worlds: The formation of social behavior. Cambridge, MA: Harvard University Press.

Whorley, M. R., & Addis, M. E. (2006). Ten years of psychological research on men and masculinity in the United States: Dominant methodological trends. Sex Roles, 55, 649–658.

Wight, D. (1994). Boys' thoughts and talk about sex in a working class locality of Glasgow. The Sociological Review, 42, 703–737.

Wilkie, J. R. (1991). The decline in men's labor force participation and income and the changing structure of family economic support. Journal of Marriage and the Family, 53, 111–122.

Williams, C. L. (2007). The glass escalator: Hidden advantages for men in the "female" professions. In M. S. Kimmel and M. A. Messner (Eds.), Men's lives (7th ed.). Boston: Pearson/Allyn and Bacon.

Williams, J. E., & Best, D. L. (1990a). Measuring sex stereotypes: A multination study. Newbury Park, CA: Sage.

Williams, J. E., & Best, D. L. (1990b). Sex and psyche: Gender and self viewed cross-culturally. Newbury Park, CA: Sage.

Williams, J. E., Nieto, J., Sanford, C. P., Couper, D. J., & Tyroler, H. A. (2002). The association between trait anger and incident stroke risk: The atherosclerosis risk in communities (ARIC) study. Stroke, 33 (13), 13–20.

Williams, P. (2008, April 17). Ending the guessing game in concussion recovery. The Washington Post Extra, 8.

Williams, R. J. & Ricciardelli, L. A. (1999). Gender congruence in confirmatory and compensatory drinking. Journal of Psychology, 133, 323–331.

Williams, W. L. (1992). The relationship between male-male friendship and male-female marriage. In P. M. Nardi (Ed.), Men's friendships (pp. 186–200). Newbury Park, CA: Sage.

Williams, W. L. (1996). The berdache tradition. In K. E. Rosenblum & T. C. Travis (Eds.), The meaning of difference: American constructions of race, sex and gender, social class, and sexual orientation (pp. 73–81). Boston: McGraw-Hill.

Willness, C. R., Steel, P., & Lee, K. (2007). A meta-analysis of the antecedents and consequences of workplace sexual harassment. Personnel Psychology, 60(1), 127–162.

Wilson, E. O. (1975). Sociobiology: The new synthesis. Cambridge, MA: Harvard University Press.

Wilson, E. O. (1979). *On human nature.* New York: Bantam.

Wilson, G. (2011). Your Brain on Porn Series: Porn Addiction. Retrieved August 12, 2014, from http://yourbrainonporn.com/your-brain-on-porn-series

Wilson, G. (2014). Adolescent brain meets high speed internet porn. Retrieved July 16, 2014 from http://yourbrainonporn.com/adolescent-brain-meets-highspeed-internet-porn.

Wilson, S. (2009, June 18). President wades into gay issues: Order gives some benefits to partners of federal workers. *The Washington Post,* A1.

Wilson, W. J. (1987). *The truly disadvantaged.* Chicago: University of Chicago Press.

Winawer, H., & Wetzel, N. A. (2005). German families. In M. McGoldrick, J. Giordano, & N. Garcia-Preto (Eds.), *Ethnicity and family therapy* (3rd ed). New York: Guilford.

Winstead, B. A., Derlega, V. J., & Wong, P. T. P. (1984). Effects of sex-role orientation on behavioral self-disclosure. *Journal of Research in Personality, 38,* 541–553.

Wise, T. N. (1994). Sertraline as a treatment for premature ejaculation. *Journal of Clinical Psychiatry, 55,* 417.

Wiswell, T. E., & Geschke, D. W. (1989). Risks from circumcision during the first month of life compared with those for un-circumcised boys. *Pediatrics, 83,* 1001–1005.

Wong, Y. J., Pituch, K. A., & Rochlen, A. N. (2006). Men's restrictive emotionality: An investigation of associations with other emotion-related constructs: Anxiety, and underlying dimensions. *Psychology of Men and Masculinity, 7,* 113–126.

Wong, Y. J., & Rochlen, A. N. (2008). Re-envisioning men's emotional lives: Stereotypes, struggles, and strengths. In S. J. Lopez (Ed.), *Positive psychology: Exploring the best in people.* Westport, CT: Greenwood.

Wood, H., Sasaki, S., Bradley, S. J., Singh, D., Fantus, S., Owen-Anderson, A., … Zucker, K. J. (2013). Patterns of referral to a gender identity service for children and adolescents (1976–2011): Age, sex ratio, and sexual orientation. *Journal of Sex & Marital Therapy, 39*(1), 1–6.

World Health Organization (2004). Adolescent Pregnancy: Issues in Adolescent Health and Development. Department of Child and Adolescent Health and Development. Geneva, Switzerland: Self.

Yodanis, C. L. (2004). Gender inequality, violence against women, and fear: A cross-national test of the feminist theory of violence against women. *Journal of Interpersonal Violence, 19,* 655–675.

Name Index

Subject Index